A Theory of Music Analysis

Eastman Studies in Music

Ralph P. Locke, Senior Editor
Eastman School of Music

Additional Titles of Interest

Analyzing Atonal Music: Pitch-Class Set Theory and Its Contexts
Michiel Schuijer

Analyzing Wagner's Operas: Alfred Lorenz and German Nationalist Ideology
Stephen McClatchie

The Art of Musical Phrasing in the Eighteenth Century: Punctuating the Classical "Period"
Stephanie D. Vial

Aspects of Unity in J. S. Bach's Partitas and Suites: An Analytical Study
David W. Beach

Explaining Tonality: Schenkerian Theory and Beyond
Matthew Brown

Music Theory and Mathematics: Chords, Collections, and Transformations
Edited by Jack Douthett, Martha M. Hyde, and Charles J. Smith

Music Theory in Concept and Practice
Edited by James M. Baker, David W. Beach, and Jonathan W. Bernard

The Twelve-Tone Music of Luigi Dallapiccola
Brian Alegant

Unmasking Ravel: New Perspectives on the Music
Edited by Peter Kaminsky

The Whistling Blackbird: Essays and Talks on New Music
Robert Morris

A complete list of titles in the Eastman Studies in Music series may be found on the University of Rochester Press website, www.urpress.com.

A Theory of
Music Analysis

On Segmentation and
Associative Organization

Dora A. Hanninen

UNIVERSITY OF ROCHESTER PRESS

75 PAYS Endowment of the American Musicological Society, funded in part by the National Endowment for the Humanities and the Andrew W. Mellon Foundation.

First published 2012. Transferred to digital printing and reprinted in paperback 2017.

University of Rochester Press, 668 Mt. Hope Avenue, Rochester, NY 14620, USA
www.urpress.com
and Boydell & Brewer Limited, PO Box 9, Woodbridge, Suffolk IP12 3DF, UK
www.boydellandbrewer.com

ISSN: 1071-9989
Hardcover ISBN-13: 978-1-58046-194-8
Paperback ISBN-13: 978-1-58046-589-2

Library of Congress Cataloging-in-Publication Data
Hanninen, Dora A., author.
    A theory of music analysis : on segmentation and associative organization / Dora A. Hanninen.
        pages cm. — (Eastman studies in music, ISSN 1071-9989 ; v. 92)
    Includes bibliographical references and index.
    ISBN 978-1-58046-194-8 (hardcover : alkaline paper) 1. Musical analysis. I. Title. II. Series: Eastman studies in music ; v. 92.
    MT90.H37 2012
    781—dc23   2012023747

A catalogue record for this title is available from the British Library.
This publication is printed on acid-free paper.
Printed in the United States of America

Excerpts from the following pieces are reproduced with permission from European American Music Distributors LLC, US and Canadian agent for Universal Edition Ltd., London; Universal Edition Ltd., Toronto; and Universal Edition A.G., Wien: Morton Feldman, *Patterns in a Chromatic Field* © 1981 by Universal Edition (London) Ltd., London/ UE 17327, all rights reserved; Morton Feldman, *Crippled Symmetry* © 1983 by Universal Edition (London) Ltd., London/UE 17667, all rights reserved; Morton Feldman, *Piano and Orchestra* © 1978 by Universal Edition (Canada) Ltd., Toronto/UE 16076, all rights reserved; Morton Feldman, *Palais de Mari* © 1986 by Universal Edition (London) Ltd., London/UE 30238, all rights reserved; Alban Berg, Violin Concerto © 1936 by Universal Edition A.G., Wien, © renewed, all rights reserved; Webern, Concerto, Op. 24 © 1948 by Universal Edition A.G., Wien, © renewed, all rights reserved; Webern, Symphony, Op. 21 © 1929 by Universal Edition A.G., Wien, © renewed, all rights reserved.

Excerpts from Nancarrow's *Study No. 37* are reproduced with permission from European American Music Distributors LLC, sole US and Canadian agent for Schott Music GmbH & Co. KG.

Excerpts from the following pieces are reproduced with permission from G. Schirmer: Samuel Barber, Concerto for Violin and Orchestra, Op. 14 ©1942 renewed by G. Schirmer, Inc. (ASCAP), international copyright secured, all rights reserved; Colin McPhee, Tabuh Tabuhan © 1960 renewed by Associated Music Publishers, Inc. (BMI), international copyright secured, all rights reserved; Arnold Schoenberg, Concerto for Violin and Orchestra, Op. 36 © 1939 renewed by G. Schirmer, Inc. (ASCAP); Terry Riley, In C © 1964 by Associated Music, Inc. (BMI), international copyright secured, all rights reserved.

Excerpts from Robert Morris's "Between" © 1999 Morris Music, "Kids" © 1999 Morris Music, "Rising Early" © 1999 Morris Music, "Loose Canon" © 1999 Morris Music, and "Glimpse" © 1999 Morris Music are reproduced with permission.

For my parents and grandparents, with gratitude

Contents

Acknowledgments

Over the twenty years since the earliest ideas for this project took shape, spiraled out in new directions, and eventually organized themselves into the book in hand, many people have inspired, accompanied, and inflected their course. Brian Alegant, Benjamin Boretz, Joseph Dubiel, Andrew Mead, and Robert Morris each contributed to the genesis, growth, and fruition of this work in important ways. David Beach provided critical comments and suggested improvements to sketches for chapter 4. Michael Buchler and his spring 2012 graduate seminar were an enthusiastic launch site. Robert Gibson has been a trusted and supportive colleague; as director of the University of Maryland's School of Music and in conjunction with the College of Arts and Humanities, he also secured funding for a research assistant to help with copying the book's many musical examples. Nathan Lincoln-DeCusatis provided this assistance in the book's early stages; Josh Perry-Parrish underwent a magical transformation from a quick study to an expert in Sibelius and Adobe Illustrator, bringing his high standards and persistent good humor to what was often painstaking work. The University of Maryland provided support at a critical stage in the form of a General Research Board Semester Grant. Publication grants from the Society for Music Theory and American Musicological Society helped defray production expenses. The team at the University of Rochester Press expressed its commitment to advanced work in music theory in its professionalism, expertise, and respect for the book's integrity. Thanks to Tim Madigan and Susan Dykstra-Poel, and especially to Suzanne Guiod, Ryan Peterson, Ralph Locke, Carrie Crompton, and Tracey Engel, who put the book in its covers. Boelke-Bomart, Inc.; European American Music Distributors LLC; G. Schirmer, Inc.; Morris Music; Universal Music Publishing Ricordi; Southern Music Publishing Co., Inc.; Sugarmusic S.p.A.–Edizioni Suvini Zerboni, Milano (Italy); and Yale University Press provided kind permission to reproduce musical examples.

I'd also like to thank those who contributed to the book in other ways. My parents, Aarne and Elsie, encouraged my love of music, intellectual bent, and flights of imagination from an early age. Remembering my father's advice to "see what you can observe" and inheriting his sense of humor continue to enrich my life daily. Uncle Urho's youthful spirit and vivid memories, and the experiences we shared in his last years, have become an inspiration to pursue all that is possible. Anneliese, Bob, Laura, Martha, and Yayoi offered everything most of all, themselves. Through a century of friendship we have shared many pots of tea, tough times and crazy ideas, impromptu yoga and arabesques, afternoons in the Rubin and Sackler, miles of walks and hikes, and, of course, a love of music—both making and thinking about it.

Part One

Introduction

A Theory of Music Analysis

"Music theory and analysis." So often, "theory" and "analysis" are paired like that, balanced on either side of a conjunction that suggests a dichotomy of complementary goals and attributes. Music theory takes a broad view: it establishes fundamental concepts and defines terms that generalize across pieces and applications. The theorist's objects and relations are abstract types, exemplified in the body of American music theory developed since the 1950s that uses mathematics as a metalanguage for creating new theories of pitch space, harmony, and voice leading, and formal models of musical structure and syntax. Whereas music theory inscribes a realm of possibilities, music analysis focuses on the particular—on specific moments and qualities, pieces and passages, ways of hearing or thinking about musical experience. To analyze a piece of music is to advance an interpretation of its characteristic, distinctive, and significant features, drawing on and sometimes extending the body of music theory in the process.

Most work in "theory and analysis" emphasizes theory *or* analysis. Replacing the conjunction with a preposition—theory *of* analysis—brings us into another realm. A *theory of music analysis* (in contrast to, say, a theory of musical structure, or of extrinsic or intertextual musical meaning) is a theory explicitly concerned with fundamental issues of analytic practice, relatively independent of any particular theory of musical structure or analytic application. Theory of analysis has two (often intertwined) aspects, one practical, the other philosophical. Practical aspects include criteria and mechanisms for object formation, and interrelations among objects of analytic interest. Important contributions in this area include work on segmentation by James Tenney, Larry Polansky, Christopher Hasty, David Lidov, and Fred Lerdahl and Ray Jackendoff, as well as work on categorization and music analysis by Lawrence Zbikowski and by me.[1] Philosophical aspects include standards for discourse and the purpose or potential of music analysis. Some of the most important and influential writings in this area date from the formative years of contemporary American music theory, the 1960s. A call for responsible—that is, intelligible and falsifiable ("scientific")—language in music discourse is a recurring theme in Milton Babbitt's early writings.[2] While Ben Boretz shares Babbitt's concern with linguistic precision, his theoretic work emphasizes the practical—that is, *musical*—value of theory as a means to locate, expand, and transform the realm of musical experience.[3] David Lewin and Joseph Dubiel have each advanced a similar point of view, repeatedly demonstrating the benefits of a theory of

new perceptions and thereby deepen musical experience.[4]

This book presents a theory of analysis with both practical and philosophical aspects. A theory in the sense of the Greek word *theoria* (an "act of viewing, contemplation, consideration"),[5] the theory provides analysts with a conceptual framework and metalanguage for *looking at* or *thinking about* music.[6] It defines three domains of musical experience and discourse about it: the sonic (psychoacoustic), contextual (or associative, sparked by varying degrees of repetition), and structural (guided by a specific theory of musical structure or syntax chosen or invoked by the analyst). With these three domains as a backdrop, I develop the theory around two practical aspects of music analysis: segmentation (the formation of objects of analytic interest) and what I call associative organization (the formation, internal configuration, and temporal disposition of categories of segments in individual pieces of music). Used in conjunction with criteria for segmentation and perhaps a theory of musical structure or syntax chosen by the analyst (such as Schenkerian theory or twelve-tone theory), this general theory of analysis can illuminate the workings of and interactions among sonic, contextual, and structural aspects of music, at multiple levels of conceptualization and organization. Rather than compete with or seek to replace existing theories of musical structure, it enfolds and works with them, functioning like a lens that increases the grain of resolution of the analyst's own interests and choices.

As for matters of philosophy, the theory is equally committed to precise language and to the interpretive autonomy and imagination of the individual analysts who use it. First and foremost, it is an interpretive tool. The theory is not a methodology, but a multidimensional conceptual space within which one does analysis and thinks about music analytically; its purpose is to *support*, not guide, the analyst's thought process.[7] The theory does not tell the analyst *what* to think or hear, nor does it predict or prescribe particular analytic results (it can, however, be used to frame hypotheses that bear the weight of prediction). What it does do is provide a relatively neutral but precise and highly flexible language and conceptual framework that supports rigorous analysis across a wide range of musical applications. Instead of leading the analyst toward a particular interpretation, the theory offers means to develop and express the analyst's own interpretation; instead of providing easy answers, it helps to raise and frame questions; instead of adjudicating between interpretations, it provides means to mediate or translate between them and clarify their differences. I hope that analysts will find the theory useful in the concerted discovery and investigation of their own musical experiences. But I also hope that they will find the theory *suggestive* and use it strategically to open new lines of inquiry for individual pieces, repertoires, and issues in contemporary music theory. One can use the theory's conceptual framework any number of ways; some of these are illustrated or suggested in the chapters that follow.

overview of the theory that is presented in detail in chapters 2 and 3. The second outlines the organization and topics of the six analysis chapters, chapters 4–9, and the closing chapter, 10. Finally, to set all that follows in proper perspective, at the end of this chapter I return to some aspects of basic philosophy with a little about the theory's relationship to work in perception and cognition, and about its use.

Theory

The theory of analysis unfolds in two dimensions—across three "domains" and through five "levels." Example 1.1 is a schematic representation of the theory that will serve as a point of departure and future reference. The three domains (sonic, structural, and contextual) appear across the top of the diagram. Five levels (orientations, criteria, segments, associative sets, and associative landscapes) proceed, top to bottom, from the purely conceptual (orientations, criteria) to the relatively concrete (the phenomenal world of sounding events and analytic interpretations that collectively constitute "the music"—segments, associative sets, and associative landscapes).[8]

This overview of the theory is organized in two dimensions. Following the layout of example 1.1, I will start with the three domains, then say a little about each of the five levels. This sets the stage for detailed exposition of the first three levels in chapter 2, and the last two levels, associative sets and associative landscapes, in chapter 3. Each theory chapter includes a series of musical illustrations; these are necessarily concentrated at the end of chapter 2, but appear throughout chapter 3. While all of the musical illustrations in chapters 2 and 3, as well as the works chosen for study in chapters 4–9, come from the Western concert tradition from the Baroque to the present, the theory is general and can fruitfully be applied to other bodies of music, including early music in the West and some non-Western musics.

Three Domains: Sonic, Contextual, and Structural

A *domain* is a realm of musical activity, experience, and discourse about it, bounded by the sorts of musical phenomena or ideas under consideration.[9] The theory defines three such domains: the sonic, the contextual, and the structural.[10] Each is affiliated with an orientation to analysis and a basic type of criterion for segmentation.

The sonic domain (S) encompasses the psychoacoustic aspect of music. To ground the theory of segmentation I develop in chapter 2, I will approach sonic organization from the bottom up, starting with individual notes and their attribute values in various sonic dimensions such as pitch, dynamics, duration,

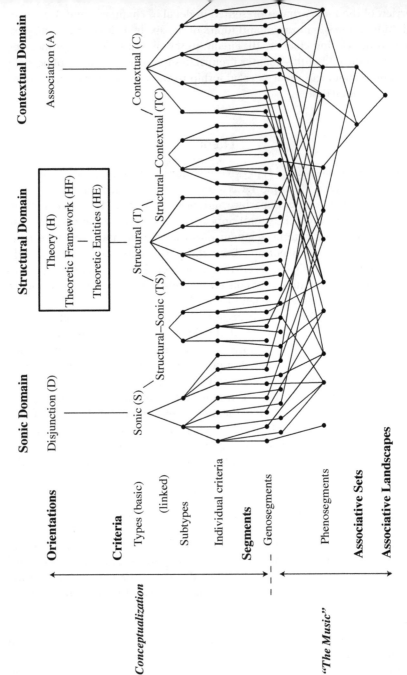

Example 1.1. Schematic representation of the general theory of music analysis

masses). With each note conceived as a bundle of sonic attributes, one can track activity in multiple sonic dimensions independently and concurrently. Sonic organization, from individual musical segments to progressively larger units, is predicated on difference and disjunction: greater differences in attribute values create greater disjunctions and stronger boundaries between units. Sonic organization, along with associative and perhaps structural organization, is one of three basic aspects of musical organization.

The contextual domain (C) recognizes the workings of repetition, association, and categorization in music. The name of the domain affirms the importance of musical context in object formation and identity: it indicates that musical objects (segments) are permeable, suffused by and interacting with their contexts. In the contextual domain, the focus shifts from isolated segments to associations between segments and identification of the many contexts that impinge on musical objects to shape their sound in a particular way.[11] In chapter 2, I develop a theory of contextual segmentation around the idea that repetition is not static, but an active force in object formation: from this point of view, association can itself be a rationale for segmentation. The mechanism invokes sonic attributes of individual notes, but focuses on associations between *groups* of notes related by literal or varied repetition in some respect (such as content or order of pitches or scale degrees, harmonic content, rhythm). Here the properties of interest are group properties (properties a group of notes has as a unit, *not* held by its individual notes) that are also relational properties (they represent an association *between* two or more groups as a property *of* each group so related). The theory of analysis developed in chapters 2 and 3 emphasizes the contextual domain: in fact, all of the theory of associative sets and associative organization in chapter 3 resides squarely in the contextual domain. This is not to suggest that the sonic and structural domains are unimportant (they are *very* important), but to delve into prime territory in music analysis that has remained relatively uncharted in music theory. One of my reasons for writing this book is to recognize and model the role of association and associative organization in music in its own right and as functionally independent of—and therefore capable of significant interactions with—aspects of sonic and structural organization already addressed by existing theories.

The structural domain (T) indicates active reference to a theory of musical structure or syntax (H) chosen (or perhaps developed) by the analyst that recommends segments and guides or confers interpretations for musical events. Such a theory has two components: a theoretic framework (HF) and theoretic entities (HE). In this book, activity in the structural domain generally draws on one of two bodies of theory—Schenkerian theory or twelve-tone theory. These theories have three important advantages for a tutorial: (1) they are well-established and have a large literature in theory and analy-

relatively well defined (this is especially important for the theory of segmentation presented in chapter 2). There are, of course, other possible candidates for H, such as transformational theories (e.g., neo-Riemannian theory, Klumpenhouwer networks), Forte's theory of set complexes, and rotational arrays. Theories differ significantly in the content and relations of HF and HE, and in the extent to which HF defines or simply allows an analyst to describe what is a syntactical or structural HE and what is not.[12] But while they differ in particulars and implementation, these and other theories that accord with the criteria outlined below can all be accommodated and used in conjunction with the general theory's conceptual framework.

Throughout this book I will be using "theory of musical structure" in a restricted sense. Candidates for H must meet a "reference requirement": that is, H must clearly reference sounding aspects of a composition through its HEs. In the most compelling cases, HEs will correlate with groups of notes captured as segments by continuities in the sonic domain or relational properties in the contextual domain. This is not to exclude other approaches in contemporary music theory, but to say that candidates for H as I define it have a specific relationship to the musical surface. The reference requirement ensures that H has the potential to shape the way a listener constitutes a sonic surface as music *from the bottom up*, by recommending particular groupings of notes for consideration as segments. This is in contrast to, for example, theories that provide aggregate snapshots of the musical surface, and critical or cultural theories of music inspired by semiotics, narrative, poststructuralism, feminism, or psychoanalysis that tend to focus their interpretative energies on "music" already constituted.[13] One could certainly connect critical and cultural perspectives on music analysis to example 1.1 through a node "P" that would attach to the arrow embracing all of "the music" this theory represents as constituted by complex activity in the sonic, contextual, and structural domains.[14] The role of various candidates for P in music analysis is an important subject in its own right, but one that is outside the current scope of the theory and this book.

All three domains—the sonic, contextual, and structural—are essential to the theory of analysis I present here, but not all are active in every application. The sonic domain is always active and the contextual domain virtually always so: S and C represent basic and complementary strategies of human cognition (disjunction versus association; edge detection and categorization).[15] In contrast, the structural domain is special: while theoretic orientations often inform, shape, and greatly enrich the process of musical interpretation, they are not essential. The structural domain can be activated or deactivated by the analyst according to his or her interests and the music under consideration, or remain dormant by necessity. The structural domain is necessarily dormant when no systematizing principles obtain for the music at issue, or such principles

rary music. Even when such theoretic principles are available, the structural domain can be rendered effectively dormant by the analyst's decision to focus attention elsewhere.

Before moving on to the theory's five levels (orientations, criteria, segments, associative sets, landscapes), I need to say a little about what I mean—and don't mean—by the term "level" with respect to the theory of analysis and levels of musical organization. First, the theory's five levels are a chain of conceptual prerequisites, *not* a methodology or teleology for analysis. In example 1.1, an associative orientation is a prerequisite for contextual criteria; criteria support segments (genosegments, then phenosegments), segments form associative sets, and sets can create landscapes. But the logical progress of these concepts within the theory does not prescribe how the theory should be used in analysis. The theory does not determine—or even suggest—how analytic processes do or should unfold, nor does it necessarily recommend one analytical focus over another. (For more on analytic process, see chapter 10.) Second, as in ecology, a "level of organization" is a realm of interaction among like sorts of things; I do *not* mean to suggest that the contents of these levels of musical organization—the fruits of music analysis—are necessarily hierarchic.[16] On the contrary, the theory explicitly advocates a *non*hierarchic view as the general case: it allows for segments that do not contribute to any associative set under consideration ("independent phenosegs") and notes that associative sets can, and often do, overlap (both in chapter 3). Nor does the theory make any demand that analysis be comprehensive: segments, sets, and landscapes can be highly selective with respect to the musical surface under consideration. Third, interlevel relations within the theory and among levels of musical organization (that is, among associative landscapes, sets, segments, criteria, and orientations as distinct levels) are *non*reductive. Concepts and musical entities at higher (later) levels do not reduce to sets of concepts or entities at lower (earlier) levels without a loss of essential content. A segment is more than a list of supporting criteria: it has a phenomenal presence. An associative set is more than a list of segments: it has group properties, such as range and distribution of variation and an internal configuration. Each of the theory's five levels, and every level of musical organization, is important, with no one level privileged to carry the weight of the whole.

Five Levels: Orientations, Criteria, Segments, Associative Sets, and Associative Landscapes

An *orientation* is a perceptual or cognitive strategy, a mode of attending to or conceptualizing music. The theory defines three orientations: *disjunction (D)*, *association (A)*, and *theory (H)*; these are affiliated with the sonic, contextual, and structural domains, respectively. A disjunctive orientation attends to differences

orientation focuses on relational properties that connect groupings of notes with one another. A theoretic orientation identifies or interprets groupings of notes with respect to a specific theory of musical structure or syntax (H).

A *criterion* is a rationale for musical segmentation. Every segment invokes at least one, but often several, criteria. The theory defines three *basic types* of criteria—sonic, contextual, and structural; each is affiliated with the domain of the same name. Sonic criteria respond to psychoacoustic attributes of individual notes; they place segment boundaries at local maximum disjunctions in individual dimensions such as pitch, duration, dynamics, and timbre. Contextual criteria respond to repetitions that associate groupings of tones in their entirety. A contextual criterion indicates a property predicable of a grouping that acts as a relational property between groupings within a specific musical context. Contextual criteria model repetition of ordered or unordered sets of elements, such as associations among segments by pitch ordering, rhythm, or set class. Whereas sonic criteria involve acoustic attributes of individual sound events, and contextual criteria involve relational properties of sound events, structural criteria involve concepts supported by a theoretic orientation. To contribute to the audible world of musical segments, structural criteria must gain the support of sounding features—they must be realized by sonic or contextual criteria. I discuss realization below and in chapter 2.

Each of the three basic criterion types divides first into subtypes, then into individual criteria. In this regard the schematic is suggestive, not comprehensive: it represents the *idea* of an expansion from each basic type through a number of subtypes (two for sonic criteria; many for contextual and structural criteria) to many individual criteria, rather than mapping out all the possibilities (which, in any case, depend on the specific analytic application). For the realization of structural criteria, the theory defines two linked types, structural-sonic and structural-contextual; these model systematic linkages from individual criteria in the structural domain to those in the sonic and contextual domains, respectively.

Orientations and criteria are concepts that are integral to our conceptualization of sound as music, but independent of the sound-world that is music. The interface between the conceptual world of orientations and criteria (at the top of the schematic) and the sounding world of segments, associative sets, and associative landscapes—"the music"—(at the bottom), occurs when individual criteria are summoned as support for segments. Criteria support segments through *three mechanisms*: instantiation, coincidence, and realization.

Instantiation is the most basic mechanism, essential for all segments (ex. 1.2a). Instantiation is a one-to-one mapping from a sonic, contextual, or structural criterion x to a specific grouping of notes (or other sound-events) q, recognized by that criterion. The grouping of tones q "instantiates" or "is an instantiation of" its supporting criterion x.

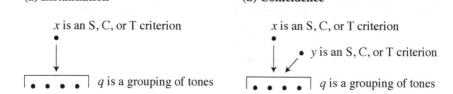

x is an S, C, or T criterion
•
↓
•••• | q is a grouping of tones

x is an S, C, or T criterion
•
• y is an S, C, or T criterion
↓ ↙
•••• | q is a grouping of tones

(c) Realization

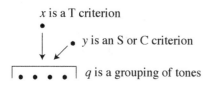

x is a T criterion
•
↓ • y is an S or C criterion
↓ ↙
•••• | q is a grouping of tones

Example 1.2. Three mechanisms

When two or more criteria x and y identify the same grouping q, their instantiations "coincide" or are "coincident"; informally, x and y are "coincident criteria" (ex. 1.2b). *Coincidence* is a many-to-one mapping from the instantiations of at least two criteria x and y to one grouping q; x and y can represent any combination of sonic, contextual, or structural criteria (that is, eligible pairs of criterion types include S–S, S–C, S–T, C–C, C–T, and T–T). Coincidence often (but not necessarily) enhances segment strength; it is also a prerequisite for the realization of structural criteria.

Realization is a special case of coincidence in which x is a structural criterion and y is a sonic or contextual criterion (that is, eligible pairs are limited to types T–S and T–C) (ex. 1.2c). A structural criterion x is *realized* in a grouping q when the instantiation of x coincides fully and exactly with the instantiation of a sonic or contextual criterion y in q. In example 1.2c, the sonic or contextual criterion y *realizes* the structural criterion x; the grouping q is a *realization of x*.

Among music theorists, music analysis is often predicated on matters of segmentation. A *segmentation* is a parsing of the musical surface that includes, at least, a set of segments and their supporting criteria. If segmentation is taken to include higher-level organization of segments, it approaches music analysis *with an emphasis on the segments* thus recognized. Both views of segmentation recognize two aspects of the term in current use: (1) a rationale, strategy, or process of segmentation; and (2) a particular segmentation (or analysis) of a given passage.

A *segment* is a grouping of notes (or other musical events) that constitutes a significant object in an analytic discourse. Segments are the most basic units of musical form; relationships among segments contribute to the construction

kinds of segments, *genosegments* and *phenosegments*; these indicate different levels of segmentation. A genosegment involves *exactly one* sonic or contextual criterion (which can realize a coincident structural criterion); a phenosegment is a readily perceptible musical unit (the usual connotation of "segment") which can involve any number or combination of sonic or contextual criteria, with or without coincident structural criteria. The relationship of genosegments to phenosegments is not one of part to whole but of a prerequisite level of organization. Segments at the same level (that is, genosegments versus phenosegments) vary in size and can be related by succession, superimposition, embedding, or overlap. The benefits of distinguishing genosegments from phenosegments are (1) that it gives analysts a way to recognize and track the individual and cumulative contributions of sonic, contextual, and structural criteria to musical organization at various levels; and (2) that it provides a vantage point for studying interactions among the sonic, contextual, and structural domains.

An *associative set* is a collection of two or more (pheno)segments interrelated and integrated by contextual criteria into a system at a higher level of organization. Every segment in the set is related to one or more of its consociates by contextual criteria; conversely, every contextual criterion that contributes to the set (not just its individual segments) must support two or more of its segments. More general and versatile than the concept of motive, an associative set carries no presumption that all segments share essential features. Associative sets differ widely in their global properties, such as size and range of variation. Sets can be uniform (classical categories in which all segments are supported by the same contextual criteria) or can exhibit a high degree of variation (prototypical categories in which each segment can be supported by a different set of contextual criteria). Sets can also have all sorts of internal configurations. Some sets have clear subsets; others do not. Variation can be distributed evenly or unevenly, and associative configurations (represented in association graphs) can vary in topology from simple linear graphs to binary trees to complex webs with nonplanar graphs. An evolution of an association graph tracks the order in which nodes enter an associative set; evolutions help the analyst assess the degree of fit or misfit between associative configuration and adjacency on one hand, and temporal succession and distance on the other.

Associative sets and configurations are largely atemporal: they represent associations among segments as if these occurred outside the context of time in which a composition unfolds.[17] An *associative landscape* considers associative sets *in* their temporal context, focusing on the temporal distribution of segments within a set and disposition of sets with respect to one another. The associative landscape is the highest level of organization in the bottom-up approach to musical form that we will develop within the contextual domain. A landscape study is a comparative analysis of landscape design across different

tion of the associative landscape.

In the preceding outline that lays some groundwork for the more detailed exposition in chapters 2 and 3, I've presented the sonic, contextual, and structural domains as three separate, functionally independent arenas of musical experience and discourse. This makes didactic sense, but one must remember that while the sonic, contextual, and structural domains are conceptually distinct, in actuality they designate different aspects of a *single piece* of music and that in practice these domains interact. Properties and activity in one domain can affect how a listener perceives activity in the other domains; activity in the sonic, contextual, and structural domains is not phenomenally independent but *interdependent*, integrated through conflict and coincidence in segmentation that has a cumulative effect at higher levels of organization. So rather than think of sonic, associative, and structural organization as discrete perspectives on a piece of music that are then overlaid, combined, or somehow reconciled at a late stage of music analysis, it is best to think of each more holistically, as a conceptual fix on a certain aspect of music that nonetheless admits, and even openly acknowledges, the possibility of subtle interactions among two or even all three domains at multiple levels of organization. Here the metaphor of the general theory as a lens is again apt: whereas music incorporates the full spectrum of activity in the sonic, contextual, and structural domains, theory and analysis are prismatic, separating out sonic, contextual, and structural aspects of music analysis for individual scrutiny.

Overview of the Analyses

Part 3 of this book consists of six analyses, each devoted to a work composed between 1795 and 1999. None of these analyses purports to be comprehensive; rather, each draws upon the repertoire of concepts developed in part 2 and uses it to explore a few issues of special interest.[18] Chapter 4, on the first movement of Beethoven's Piano Sonata No. 2 in A Major, op. 2, no. 2, looks at aspects of associative design and changes in the associative landscape, and considers their relation to aspects of tonal structure from a Schenkerian perspective. Chapter 5, on "Harmonie du soir" from Debussy's *Cinq poèmes de Baudelaire,* is a cross-domain analysis of associative organization in text and music, first in Baudelaire's pantoum, then in Debussy's setting. Chapter 6 explores the variety of associative landscapes in Conlon Nancarrow's *Study No. 37* for player piano and some of the surprising changes in associative organization that emerge in certain sections as a chaotic result of its rigorous twelve-voice tempo canon. Chapter 7 is a comparative analysis of select passages from three performances of Terry Riley's *In C* (1964) in which I show how performers' choices create different sorts of associative landscapes from the same basic

subject of chapter 8, which pursues a comparative analysis of associative sets' global properties and changes in the associative landscape across a series of plots. Finally, chapter 9 begins with a detailed analysis of the associative landscape of "Between," one of Robert Morris's *Nine Piano Pieces* (1999), then looks at the interplay between structural and more improvisatory long-range associations among related passages in several other pieces from the set.

To the reader who wonders why I chose these particular pieces, I can only say that, indeed, I could have chosen any number of others to demonstrate some of things the theory can do and to suggest the analytic potential of its conceptual framework. Each piece is musically interesting in a way that the theory helped me to pursue analytically. The fact that any number of other pieces might have served as well only reaffirms the theory's breadth of application as one of its strengths. There is, however, a reason that I decided to emphasize music written after 1900 in both the illustrations in part 2 and the group of compositions selected for analysis in part 3. The body of work written in the past century is more diverse in its structural principles, associative organization, and use of sonic dimensions such as texture, timbre, and spatial position than that composed within any earlier period of Western music. The greater contextuality of twentieth-century music also means that it is often less well understood than music of the common practice period.[19] By emphasizing recent music in both the theoretic illustrations in chapters 2 and 3, and in four of the six analysis chapters (chapters 6–9), I hope to accomplish two things: first, to illustrate concepts defined by the theory in a wide-ranging and suggestive set of musical examples; and second, to draw attention to some loci of action in music that have received relatively little analytic attention, in hopes of inspiring others to engage with this repertoire more deeply.

The closing chapter rounds out the text and reaches outside the book's covers with a look at relations between transformation and association, and how one can use the theory to support comparative analysis of music analyses, analytical processes, musical styles, and music theories.

Finally, I'd like to say a few words about the reader's process. The detailed exposition of the theory in chapters 2 and 3 introduces many new terms. Each term is italicized when it is defined and all are compiled in a glossary. The influx of terminology is substantial but essential to the theoretic project of constructing a metalanguage that is sufficiently neutral and transparent to support close analysis of a wide range of music, and to work in tandem with the different theoretic orientations, segmentation criteria, and analytical approaches that individual analysts might employ for a given piece or musical situation.[20] While the ten chapters are best read in sequence, I realize that the length of the theoretic exposition in chapters 2 and 3 may try the patience of some readers. For those who prefer to see some of the payoff straightaway, I suggest a thorough read of chapter 1 followed by a look at the glossary, then a perusal

enables one to do. Returning for a careful read of chapters 2 and 3 at that point will then provide or strengthen the conceptual underpinnings for analytic approaches and musical observations the reader is already familiar with, as well as introduce and illustrate additional concepts not covered in detail in chapters 4–9.

Setting the Theory in Perspective

The theory of analysis presented in this book proceeds from the premise that music listening and analysis—from its detail to the accumulation of detail into larger forms—is saturated by musical context. Broadly construed, this context includes a wealth of intraopus detail and interopus knowledge, and perhaps a specific theoretic orientation, along with the analyst's own interests and perceptual habits. This emphasis on musical context and an exploratory bent—the idea that one can use a theory of analysis not only to represent a particular hearing but to imagine alternatives—sets the theory in a complex relationship with research in auditory perception and cognitive psychology. On one hand, the theory assumes a number of basic psychological principles and faculties, such as edge detection; stream segregation; and echoic, working, short-term, and long-term memory. Collectively these constitute a lower bound for music perception. Sonic criteria also assume a mechanism for feature extraction—that is, that the brain can extract and track information from a complex auditory stimulus in individual dimensions such as pitch and duration. Contextual criteria and associative sets exercise the basic human propensity for association and categorization and proceed on the hypothesis that, all else being equal, association tends to enhance perceptual salience.

But as this is a theory of *music analysis*, not of aural perception or cognition, it is not explicitly concerned with these psychological principles per se. The theory does not postulate or propose psychological models, mechanisms, faculties, or processes. Instead, it represents music analysis as an *individual* and *imaginative* account of musical events and their interrelations within a particular piece of music. Whereas psychological studies of aural perception and cognition of music aspire to the general, music analysis—and the theory of analysis I present here—pursue the particular: the distinguishing and characteristic features of individual compositions, musical interpretations, and experiences.[21] Although one can use this theory to support scientific inquiry (say, to identify, suggest, or formulate questions for psychological experiments), the theory itself belongs to the humanities, as a philosophical framework for thought about music.

While the influx of terms renders the theory somewhat technical, ultimately it is not specialized. With its relatively neutral language and ability to accommodate various criteria for segmentation, theoretic orientations, and interests

extend to music of different periods, styles, and structural means, including Western music before 1600 and some non-Western music. The theory can also be read and used in various ways. From one point of view, it offers analysts a general theory of musical form that goes beyond named forms and even formal functions to support the study of forms without names, prevalent in twentieth-century and contemporary music.[22] Here the theory provides valuable conceptual continuity across various levels of organization, from detail below the level of readily audible segments, to segments as the smallest formal units, to associative sets and landscapes. The emphasis on musical context also suggests an active view of musical form not as a noun, but as a verb, as a process of music-formation in which associative sets and even landscapes can be dynamically reconfigured over time.[23] One can also read the theory as a conceptual superstructure that embraces aspects of structure and design, and helps the analyst to probe the relationship between them (as in chapter 4 on Beethoven's Piano Sonata No. 2 in A, op. 2, no. 2, in conjunction with Schenkerian theory; in chapter 6, on Nancarrow's *Study No. 37*, with a rigorous tempo canon; and in chapter 9, on Morris's *Nine Piano Pieces*, with twelve-tone theory and array structure). The theory also provides means to investigate music-text relations (as in chapter 5, on Debussy's "Harmonie du soir"), support comparative analysis of analytic processes, music analyses, musical styles, or music theories (chapter 10), and mediate between competing analytic interpretations. By changing one's theoretic orientation (from one theory to another, one to none, or the reverse), choice of criteria, or the balance among domains in the course of analysis, and plugging these changes into the theory's conceptual framework, analysts can use its relatively neutral language to step outside one way of thinking into another, consider alternative views, and translate or articulate differences between them in a kind of cross-theoretic comparative analysis.

The theory can also support thought about music outside the realm of analysis per se, impinging on aspects of composition, improvisation, pedagogy, perception and cognition, and philosophy and aesthetics of music and of music analysis. A concerted emphasis on criteria for segmentation can be very useful in the pedagogy of music analysis; developing a heightened sensitivity to the effects of conflict and coincidence among various types of criteria in different domains can be useful for young composers. The conceptual framework might also be used to help articulate differences in compositional aesthetics (say, the relative importance or insignificance of a governing syntax and how it is realized; the prevalence and clarity or relative scarcity of associative sets) or summoned to support work in music semiotics or in intertextual analysis where the contextual associations of interest operate not within a piece, but between pieces.

In short, the theory is a tool for thinking about music. And so, to work.

Part Two

Theory

Orientations, Criteria, Segments

Orientations

An orientation is a perceptual or cognitive strategy, a mode of attending or conceptualizing music, a "general or lasting direction of thought, inclination, or interest."[1] The theory defines three orientations: disjunction (D), association (A), and theory (H). Each orientation is affiliated with one of the three domains and is prerequisite to criteria in that domain: sonic criteria (S) assume a disjunctive orientation; contextual criteria (C), an associative one; and structural criteria (T), a theoretic one. Affiliations among domains, orientations, and criteria are illustrated in example 2.1 (an excerpt from ex. 1.1).

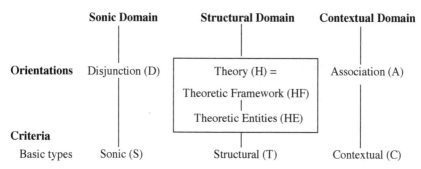

Example 2.1. Domains, orientations, criteria: Affiliations

Disjunction (D)

A disjunctive orientation identifies perceptual salience with difference; edge detection is the means for object recognition. Given a stream of pitches or other musical events, significant disjunctions in sonic dimensions such as pitch, duration, loudness, and timbre (acting individually or in tandem) mark boundaries between sound objects. A disjunctive orientation focuses on individuation: disjunction locates boundaries that imply groupings. Composers adopt a disjunctive orientation when they use sudden changes in register, duration, dynamics, or timbre to lift key moments from their sonic surroundings. Performers do likewise when they shape an interpretation through subtle adjustments in duration, dynamics, and articulation. Composers and analysts with radically different philosophies, aesthetics, interests, and approaches share

sole) means for musical organization, as in some music by John Cage, theoretic work by James Tenney, and analyses by Robert Cogan. Alternately, it can be one aspect of design that articulates musical structure, as in the music of Milton Babbitt and in contributions to Schenkerian theory and analysis by John Rothgeb and Carl Schachter.[2]

Association (A)

An associative orientation focuses on relational properties, such as those supported by repetition, equivalence, or similarity. The potential for association between groupings of notes transforms predicable properties into relational ones and motivates the mutual formation and recognition of specific groupings as analytical objects. Association enacts a disposition toward cognitive chunking at the level of individual segments and at higher levels of organization where it serves as the basis for categorization. Association is the orientation a composer or performer adopts when she asks, "How can I link this moment with that one?"

Like disjunction, association can support different, even seemingly contradictory, philosophies of composition and music analysis. Certainly association is a prerequisite for analysis concerned with unity, whether based on motives, set class language, rhymes in a text, or something else. But an associative orientation is also essential to work in poststructural and intertextual music analysis that challenges unity as an analytical premise.[3] Disunity may look like disjunction in the contextual domain, but if disunity and unity are to be diametrically opposed, it is best understood not as disjunction but as *dissociation*, a byproduct of intra- or intertextual associations that create disconnected networks within the contextual domain.[4]

Disjunction and association are roughly complementary: whereas disjunction is predicated on adjacency in some sonic dimension, association responds to repetition of certain features in a specific context, often over long time spans. Disjunction defines boundaries and implies segments; association defines segments and implies boundaries. Disjunctions locate points of contrast; association, points of correspondence. Disjunction separates sound-events from one another and individuates analytical objects; association groups sound-events into analytical objects and supports categorization. For the listener and analyst, disjunction and association are distinct, functionally independent strategies: disjunction individuates; association groups.

Theory (H)

A theoretic orientation shifts attention from perceptual salience to the interpretation and representation of musical meaning. To adopt a theoretic orientation

system of concepts and rules that guides or governs the recognition, interpretation, and organization of significant musical units. Schenkerian theory, twelve-tone theory, and other candidates for H can influence the course of analytic interpretation in many ways and be evident at multiple levels of musical organization. The concepts and rules of such theories provide means to select segments the theory deems well-formed (that is, intelligible within its orb) and of potential syntactic or structural significance from those it does not. The orienting theory then helps the analyst organize multifarious segments into a coherent musical interpretation. The resulting structure can be hierarchic (as in Schenkerian theory), but it does not have to be (twelve-tone theory admits nested levels of structure in combinatorial arrays, but does not require them). Finally, by giving analysts a vantage point outside a piece at hand, the orienting theory encourages and facilitates the examination of interactions between systemic and particular features of a composition. Analysts can adopt a theoretic orientation and invoke a particular theory of musical structure by conscious choice or subconscious habit (often called "musical intuition"), or they can develop a new theory in the course of analysis.

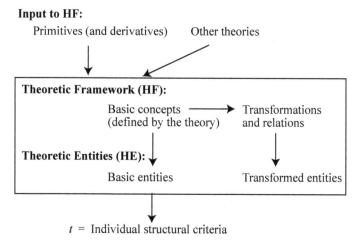

Input to HF:
Primitives (and derivatives)   Other theories

Theoretic Framework (HF):
Basic concepts ⟶ Transformations
(defined by the theory)   and relations

Theoretic Entities (HE):
Basic entities   Transformed entities

t = Individual structural criteria

Example 2.2. Aspects of a theoretic orientation

Candidates for H have two basic parts: a theoretic framework (HF) and a (potentially very large) set of theoretic entities (HE) (ex. 2.2). These comprise the theory and stitch it into a larger context that extends from the primitives assumed as input to HF, through individual structural criteria (t), to the actual musical segments supported by each t and recommended as units by members of HE.[5] Primitives of H are concepts, kinds of elements, transformations, and derived entities (such as pitches, pitch-classes, scale degrees, and diatonic

observation language.[6] HF proper is, or approximates, an axiomatic system: it defines fundamental terms, concepts, transformations, and interrelations among theoretic concepts; it also stipulates means to generate the set of theoretical entities in HE that constitute well-formed formulae and (potential) structural units according to H. Theoretic entities in HE are of two types: basic and transformed. Basic entities in HE (with respect to H) are ordered or unordered sets of primitive elements that correspond with, or represent fundamental concepts defined by, HF. Transformed entities can be derived from basic entities by transformations defined in HF. Basic entities can often be enumerated; transformed entities are indicated by extension.

One can think of the HEs in example 2.2 either "out of context," as purely theoretic constructs, or in relation to a specific musical context. As pure theory, HE is the set of syntactic units potential with H: it includes all basic and transformed entities that can be generated from the concepts, transformations and relations defined by HF. The set of HEs constructed for a specific analytical context is usually much smaller, limited to the basic and transformed entities that the analyst actually posits as occurring in the piece under consideration. The difference between the more general set of HEs identified with H, and the smaller, more specific set of HEs under consideration for a given piece, is one way that the generalizing power of the theory reflects on the individuality of each composition.

In this book, Schenkerian theory and twelve-tone theory figure prominently, both theoretically and analytically, as candidates for H. As a basis for subsequent discussion of structural criteria and their analytical applications, we now identify some primitives, sketch out an HF, and identify some HEs for each theory.[7]

Schenker's "theory of tonal language" is a complex conceptual system that supports the art of interpreting tonal music.[8] Schenkerian analysts tend to assume at least the following as primitives: twelve pitches per octave; octave equivalence; keys; scale degrees; major and minor triads as stable constructs; intervals (including figured bass); and diatonic and chromatic transposition.[9] HF defines fundamental concepts including the *Urlinie, Bassbrechung, Ursatz,* and *Kopfton*; means for prolongation at various structural levels, such as passing motion, neighbor motion, and unfolding; and a hierarchic relationship among levels of tonal structure.[10] Purely theoretic contents of HE include consonant intervals and their prolongations as structural units (and exclude dissonant intervals and their "prolongations"). Reconstructing HE for a specific analytic context reduces the size of HE, which will count among its most prominent members the form of the *Ursatz* that the analyst asserts for the composition, structural motives subject to hidden repetition, and prolongations of these.

Twelve-tone theory has been advanced and formalized by composers including Milton Babbitt, Donald Martino, Robert Morris, Andrew Mead, and others.[11]

pitches per octave (from which twelve pitch-classes are derived by octave and enharmonic equivalence);[12] twelve order positions; mathematical groups and semigroups (as in group theory); and partitions of the twelve-tone aggregate (as in combinatorics). HF then defines fundamental concepts such as the row (e.g., a one-to-one mapping of the twelve pitch-classes onto the twelve order positions that implies a series of eleven intervals); the twelve-tone aggregate (or a trans-formation thereof) as a structural unit; and the array (a combination of two or more rows partitioned into a succession of aggregates). HF also defines the set of transformations that constitute the serial group: transposition, inversion, and retrograde (sometimes also multiplication). Context-free contents of HE include all possible (12!) twelve-tone rows, their row segments, serial transforma-tions of these, and partitions of the aggregate. Conceived in relation to a specific piece, HE includes the row (or rows) of the composition, its row segments, their transformations, and particular partitions of the aggregate that function as struc-turing units within a particular composition. If that composition is based on a twelve-tone array, HE includes that array as a basic entity and its transformations (which can produce weighted aggregates) as transformed entities.

Criteria

A *criterion* is a rationale for cognitive grouping of musical events; criteria sup-port segments through the three mechanisms of instantiation, coincidence, and realization laid out in chapter 1. This detailed exposition of criteria is in three large sections, one for each of the three basic types—sonic (S), contex-tual (C), and structural (T). Each section defines a type, discusses aspects and formal properties of criteria in the type, and identifies some subtypes and indi-vidual criteria. The last section, on structural criteria, also includes a theoretic account of musical realization, defines the two linked criterion types structural-sonic (TS) and structural-contextual (TC), and offers a theory of structural versus pure motive. Interactions among criteria of same and different types are discussed along the way.

Sonic Criteria (S)

A *sonic criterion (S)* is a rationale for segmentation that responds to disjunctions in the attribute-values of individual sounds and silences within a single psy-choacoustic musical dimension. Sonic criteria (S) assume, as primitives, a set of psychoacoustic dimensions that correlate with note-attributes; in Western musical practice (and Western music notation) these note-attributes include pitch, attack-point, duration, dynamics (loudness), timbre, and articulation.[13] Sonic criteria assume a disjunctive orientation. Within each sonic dimension,

sive, and simultaneous, events, respectively. When the analyst thinks in the sonic domain, each note becomes a cluster of attribute-values;[14] disjunctions between attribute-values define boundaries and imply segments.

A brief digression is in order regarding the relationship between sonic disjunction on the one hand, and "similarity" and "proximity" on the other, as these terms have been used in some research on the perception and cognition of music. On the face of it, the idea that sonic criteria respond to and register disjunction rather than continuity may seem at odds with the Gestalt principles of proximity and similarity that underlie work on perception and cognition. But as Tenney and Polansky point out in their computational study of segmentation according to sonic criteria, Gestalt "similarity" derives from difference, or disjunction: "The similarity of two elements is an inverse function of the magnitude of the *interval* by which they differ in some parameter."[15] The primacy of disjunction is reason enough to take it, rather than Gestalt similarity and proximity, as the basis of sonic segmentation. But there is another, better, reason: within the field of music theory, the meanings of "similarity" and "proximity" are ambiguous and various.

Gestalt psychologists developed the principles of similarity and proximity for visual phenomena. In this context, they clearly pertain to different attributes—shape and spatial position, respectively. As Leonard Meyer brought Gestalt principles into music theory and theorists began to apply them to aural phenomena, the distinction between proximity and similarity quickly disintegrated.[16] It may come as no surprise that whether a music scholar collapses similarity into proximity or vice versa has a lot to do with his or her research interests. In work on aural perception or music and cognition, "similarity" is often none other than proximity in a musical dimension other than time, often pitch or loudness.[17] But in music analysis—especially analysis inspired by a transformational perspective—the distinction between proximity and similarity tends to collapse in the other direction. Similarity in the music theorist's sense—that which one might model with similarity relations—becomes a means to assess distance and, thus, relative proximity. Given the ambiguity that surrounds the terms "similarity" and "proximity" in music theory, I will try to avoid them and instead offer "disjunction" and "association" as complementary orientations to music analysis and to segmentation by sonic and contextual criteria, respectively. Whereas disjunction is based on distance and is the inverse of proximity, association is concerned with repetition, equivalence, or similarity between two or more segments within a specific musical context.

Sonic Criteria: Formal Aspects. To think of a note as a set of attribute-values is to locate the note in a multidimensional sonic space: a note-attribute indicates a sonic dimension;[18] an attribute-value identifies an element within a dimension.[19]

certain formal properties: all are linear, ordinal, and (at least potentially) intervallic spaces. These formal properties govern mechanics of sonic segmentation by pitch, duration, attack-point, and dynamics.

In a linear space, each element can be identified with a single numeric value or magnitude. The magnitude of each element is unique within the space; elements are ordered in the space according to their magnitude. Given a pair of elements x and y, one can calculate the size of the unordered interval between x and y by subtraction (or some other arithmetic operation), followed by taking the absolute value ($|y - x|$). Interpreting the resultant interval between x and y (represented as attribute values) as a measure of distance between the corresponding pair of notes is the essence of a sonic-disjunctive strategy. The larger the interval, the greater the disjunction; where disjunctions reach a local maximum—that is, an interval that is larger than those that precede and follow it—sonic criteria recognize a boundary between segments.[20]

Sonic criteria in pitch, duration, attack-point, and dynamics all appropriate a concept of magnitude, ordering of elements, and interval-as-distance from the one-dimensional spaces they inhabit. These linear spaces render the concept of interval formally viable; calculating and comparing distances within the sonic dimensions of pitch, duration, attack-point, and dynamics is fairly straightforward.[21] With appropriate definitions for elements and operations within each space the concepts of interval and distance become perceptually viable as well. In Western music, perception of intervals in pitch, duration, and attack-points tends to be categorical; in dynamics it tends to be ordinal. Intervals in all sonic dimensions are filtered through the perceptual abilities and habits of the observer and limited by just-noticeable differences.

Whereas most sonic dimensions occupy linear spaces, timbre and articulation require more than one mathematical dimension (two or more psychoacoustic subdimensions) for adequate formal description.[22] But music theorists do not yet have a general theory of timbre that indicates even how many timbral subdimensions there are—clearly a prerequisite for devising a metric for timbral distance. Recognizing the importance of timbre and articulation in musical practice, but unable to assign magnitudes to elements or to calculate intervals within these spaces, theorists have tended to treat them as nominal spaces in which any change from one element to another induces disjunction and marks a boundary between segments.[23] This accords with Western music notation, which records changes in timbre and articulation, but does not order or scale timbres and articulations arithmetically or visually as it does with pitch, duration, attack-points, and dynamics.[24]

This contrast between the formal properties of pitch, duration, and dynamics (as psychoacoustic dimensions associated with linear, intervallic spaces) and timbre and articulation (associated with nonlinear, and in practice,

segmentation. Within the linear sonic dimensions of pitch, duration, and dynamics, segmentation is a matter of calculation, not interpretation. The ability to segment by calculation has made segmentation in these spaces an attractive candidate for computer modeling.[25] Sonic criteria are attractive for another reason. Because they appropriate a concept of magnitude and a means to measure distance directly from the sonic dimensions involved (rather than from musical context or subjective judgment), their applications are very broad—essentially, to any music in which the sonic dimension in question is active (meaning that attribute-values in that dimension vary). Of course, the set of relative weights one assigns to various sonic dimensions is always an important consideration and one that is influenced by musical context and individual judgment. Nevertheless, sonic criteria, as the basic type with the broadest applications, generally serve as the substrate for segmentation by the two other basic types, contextual and structural.

Subtypes S_1 and S_2, and Some Individual Sonic Criteria. Because music unfolds in time, temporal succession and temporal adjacency are important factors in object recognition. Sonic criteria in subtype 1, or S_1 *criteria*, assume temporal adjacency as a prerequisite for segmentation. "S" indicates the basic type (sonic); the subscript "1" denotes the sonic subtype that assumes temporal adjacency. Individual criteria within the S_1 subtype identify, within the subscript, the sonic dimension that provides the means for segmentation: $S_{1\text{-pitch}}$, $S_{1\text{-dynamics}}$, $S_{1\text{-timbre}}$, and $S_{1\text{-articulation}}$ are four individual sonic criteria; $S_{1\text{-articulation (slur)}}$ and $S_{1\text{-articulation (staccato)}}$ indicate finer distinctions associated with particular articulations. In each case, an individual sonic criterion segments a temporal succession of events at local maximum disjunctions in the sonic dimension named by the subscript; $S_{1\text{-duration}}$ is an exception: it segments not in duration, but according to distance between attack-points. Some other sonic criteria operate differently, but I consider them S_1 criteria because they segment on the basis of disjunction between temporally adjacent events. $S_{1\text{-attack}}$ segments according to shared attack-point; $S_{1\text{-simultaneity}}$ segments events that sound together, but may have different attack-points. $S_{1\text{-rest}}$ contrasts sound with silence. $S_{1\text{-adjacency}}$ is a (weaker) S_1 criterion that indicates only temporal succession. S_1 criteria support S_1 *segments* and, by extension, S_1 *segmentations*; *s* denotes an individual sonic criterion of unspecified subtype and dimension; s_1 is an unspecified individual criterion within sonic subtype 1.

The fourth movement of Schoenberg's Second String Quartet, op. 10 (1908) opens with a stream of thirty-second notes in which four pitch transpositions of the same idea rise through the quartet in steps of seven semitones from G♯2 to D♯3, B♭3, and F4 (ex. 2.3). The start of each transposition is marked by a downward leap of thirteen semitones—the largest, and only downward, disjunction in pitch between E4 and D♯3, B4 and B♭3, and F♯5 and F4. The first of Babbitt's *Three Compositions for Piano* (1947) opens with what may seem to be an inversion canon between the hands but actually involves pitch-class transposition by T_6 (ex. 2.4a). The low notes in the left hand (stemmed down) come in four packages of 5, 1, 4, and 2 notes, separated by relatively long durations or rests.[26] $S_{1\text{-duration}}$ is the sonic criterion that calculates relative distances between temporally adjacent attack-points within each line of the canon. It places segment boundaries between C2 and D♭2 (in m. 1), D♭2 and G2 (from m. 1 to m. 2), A2 and A♭2 (m. 2), and after E2 (m. 2). In m. 9 (ex. 2.4b), the left hand goes solo, again presenting notes in four packages of 5, 1, 4, and 2, but now grouped by slurs (plus an isolated note). $S_{1\text{-articulation}}$ is the sonic criterion that segments the line in accordance with slurs, between C3 and D♭3, D♭3 and G2, and A2 and A♭2.

Sonic criteria need not be predicated on temporal adjacency. Sonic criteria in subtype 2, or S_2 *criteria*, use relative proximity in a dimension other than time (in practice, usually a linear dimension such as pitch, duration, or dynamics) as both the basis and the means for segmentation. Individual criteria in the S_2 subtype name the sonic dimension in which S_2 segmentation occurs: $S_{2\text{-pitch}}$, $S_{2\text{-duration}}$, $S_{2\text{-dynamics}}$, and $S_{2\text{-timbre}}$ are four individual S_2 criteria; $S_{2\text{-timbre (violin)}}$ and $S_{2\text{-timbre (cello)}}$ are finer distinctions, naming the instruments that distinguish segment contents from their surroundings. Whereas S_1 criteria locate notes first and foremost along a temporal continuum, S_2 criteria use some other continuum (e.g., pitch, dynamics, timbre) for this purpose. The sonic criterion $S_{1\text{-}x}$ assumes that time is continuous and uses discontinuities in dimension x to mark segment boundaries; the sonic criterion $S_{2\text{-}x}$ allows time to become discontinuous, using continuity in dimension x as the basis for segmentation.[27] Most, but not all S_1 criteria, have S_2 correlates; S_1 criteria that segment by rests, attack, and adjacency have no S_2 counterparts.

Example 2.3. Schoenberg, Second String Quartet, op. 10, IV, m. 1

(b) m. 9

Example 2.4. Babbitt, *Three Compositions for Piano*, I. © 1957 by Boelke-Bomart, Inc., Hillsdale, New York. Reproduced with permission.

S_1 and S_2 criteria provide dual perspectives on a passage. The different perspectives of S_1 and S_2 criteria are analogous to edge detection (for events in temporal succession) and stream segregation (for events that are simultaneous), respectively. Informally, one can think of S_1 criteria as segmenting vertically (between notes that are temporally adjacent), while S_2 criteria segment horizontally (between notes that are literally or conceptually simultaneous). More formally, one can think of S_1 criteria as sorting values in a nontemporal dimension—say, pitch—based on temporal adjacency, so that continuous ranges of attribute-values become segments. S_2 criteria do the opposite: they sort events in a temporal succession according to continuity in a nontemporal dimension.[28] The difference between S_1 and S_2 criteria is usually a matter of the distributing, versus distributed, dimension: $S_{1\text{-pitch}}$ distributes pitch over time; $S_{2\text{-pitch}}$, time over pitch. Note that the relationship between $S_{1\text{-duration}}$ and $S_{2\text{-duration}}$ is different: $S_{1\text{-duration}}$ segments according to *distance* between attack-points; $S_{2\text{-duration}}$ segments by note values. Example 2.5 lists some common individual sonic criteria from the S_1 and S_2 subtypes.

After an introductory flourish, the first movement of J. S. Bach's Concerto for Two Harpsichords (BWV 1061) launches into some sixteenth-note figuration that begins in harpsichord I and passes to harpsichord II (ex. 2.6). Segmenting the sixteenth-note activity in the right hand of harpsichord I by $S_{2\text{-pitch}}$ gives two lines in counterpoint: an upper line that descends <G5, F5, E5>,

S criterion	Segments by
S1-pitch	Pitch interval between events that are temporally adjacent
S1-duration	Duration (in beats or seconds) between attack points of events that are temporally adjacent (duration can include sustain and rests)
S1-dynamics	Dynamics, between events that are temporally adjacent
S1-timbre	Timbre between events that are temporally adjacent
S1-articulation	Articulation between events that are temporally adjacent
S1-attack	Simultaneity; events share an attack point (with or without sustain)
S1-simultaneity	Simultaneity; events share some part of sustain (but not an attack)
S1-space	Spatial location; between events that are temporally adjacent
S1-rest	Rest between events that are temporally adjacent
S1-adjacency	Adjacency; events are temporally consecutive, but not otherwise distinguished from surrounding events
S2-pitch	Pitch proximity between events not (necessarily) temporally adjacent
S2-duration	Duration proximity (i.e., lengths of events or rests have proximate values); events not (necessarily) temporally adjacent
S2-dynamics	Dynamics proximity; events not (necessarily) temporally adjacent
S2-timbre	Timbre proximity; events not (necessarily) temporally adjacent
S2-articulation	Articulation proximity; events not (necessarily) temporally adjacent
S2-space	Proximity of spatial location; events not (necessarily) temporally adjacent

Example 2.5. Some individual sonic criteria

Example 2.6. Bach, Concerto for Two Harpsichords in C Major, BWV 1061, mm. 1–3 (excerpts from solos)

terpoint, harpsichord II extends the upper line's descent from E5 to C5, and accelerates the lower line so that it also arrives on C. As this example suggests, segmentation by an S_2 criterion is less easily formalized than segmentation by the corresponding S_1 criterion. The problem lies in the need, first, to formalize the concept of "register" (what determines whether two events are in the same, or different, internally contiguous spans that function as units?) in pitch, duration, dynamics, timbre, or other dimensions one might use in S_2 criteria. As with S_1 criteria, however, so long as we think of S_2 criteria as conceptual tools that support musical interpretation, rather than as the basis for an algorithm that provides a segmentation, there is little problem. The Fuga from the last movement of Beethoven's Piano Sonata No. 31 in A-flat Major, op. 110 begins with a leisurely statement of the subject in dotted quarter-notes in the piano's middle register (ex. 2.7). As the second voice enters in m. 30, $S_{2\text{-duration}}$ (which distinguishes long notes from short ones), supported by $S_{2\text{-pitch}}$, untangles the answer in the upper voice from accompanying material in the lower one. When the third voice enters in m. 36, $S_{2\text{-duration}}$ takes precedence over $S_{2\text{-pitch}}$ as the sonic criterion that separates notes in the soprano subject entry from accompanying material in the alto (some leaps within the soprano and the alto voices are larger than leaps between the voices).

Example 2.7. Beethoven, Piano Sonata No. 31 in A-flat, op. 110, III, mm. 26–40, start of Fuga

or subtype interact through the relative strength of the boundaries they produce. The strength of a sonic boundary depends on two factors: magnitude and weight.

Magnitude, or size, pertains to an interval of sonic disjunction; comparisons of magnitude require two intervals in the same sonic dimension. S_1 criteria affiliated with linear, intervallic spaces (such as pitch, duration, attack point, and dynamics) appropriate the means to assess magnitude from the space they inhabit. The relative strength of two segment boundaries in the same dimension is determined by interval size: larger intervals create stronger boundaries; the greater the difference in interval size, the greater the difference in boundary strength. In practice, boundary strength is also affected by the extent to which the size of the larger interval is typical or unusual in the musical context at hand.

Weight, or multidimensional scaling, involves two or more individual criteria.[29] In the sonic domain, weight applies to the criteria themselves and indicates their relative influence on segmentation.[30] To weight $S_{1\text{-pitch}}$ against $S_{1\text{-duration}}$ is to devise an exchange rate between the sonic dimensions of pitch and duration ("How many semitones is a sixteenth-note worth?"). Once the analyst has a set of weights, he or she can easily calculate the strength of a segment boundary with the equation *weight × magnitude = strength*. To calculate the strength of segment boundaries that involve multiple sonic dimensions, Tenney and Polansky introduce a "composite disjunction measure" that sums the results of *weight × magnitude = strength* across various sonic dimensions.[31] But while the arithmetic is simple, calibrating the set of weights among individual sonic criteria required as input to the equation is a difficult problem. Researchers in perception and segmentation have tackled this problem in various ways.

One approach is to consider weights to be an aspect of human perception, independent of musical context. Taking this view, one might conduct empirical research to develop a normative set of weights, then apply these in analysis. But two problems immediately arise. First, researchers in perception already know that the relative significance of various perceptual cues and processes is context-dependent. Second, whereas research in perception seeks results that generalize, music analysis focuses on particular features of individual compositions and interpretations; this makes the simple appropriation of normative weights for use in music analysis dubious. Although an analyst might want to know how a normative sonic hearing of a passage compares with a more musical one, the normative hearing is only a foil, not the means to a desirable result.

A second approach is to develop a set of weights that produce good musical results for a particular composition.[32] Working by trial, error, and adjustment through successive runs of a segmentation algorithm on a single piece, the analyst calibrates a set of weights that yields a satisfying segmentation, then feeds these back into the algorithm as initial data. This approach ensures fairly good results, but sets the process of devising weights outside the algorithm, suggesting that musical segmentation is ultimately heuristic.

mative approach with a "piece-specific" one by developing an algorithm that can deduce a set of weights from the level of activity in various dimensions within a given passage or piece.[33] The basic idea is a good one: for the excerpt from Schoenberg's op. 10 in example 2.3, say, constant changes in pitch values suggest that $S_{1\text{-pitch}}$ is an important criterion for segmentation (it is), while the constant thirty-second notes produce a stream of equidistant attack-points that disables $S_{1\text{-duration}}$. But there is a catch: the set of weights and segments the algorithm produces depends not on the piece, but on the *part of* the piece under consideration. Not only can two passages from the same composition recommend different sets of weights (in the Schoenberg the roles of pitch and duration in m. 1 nearly reverse in mm. 10–12, where changes in duration segment repetitions of a pitch figure), but the algorithm will segment the *same* passage *differently* depending on the choice of frame: for instance, given just m. 1 of the Schoenberg, then mm. 1–11 (which crosses a boundary marked by a whole note), then the whole movement (where contrast in duration is increasingly important), the algorithm will produce three different segmentations *of m. 1!* Of course the analyst can respond by adjusting the frame to produce the most musical results for a given passage. But then the algorithm reverts to a heuristic.

The fundamental difficulty with all three approaches is the idea that the relative weights of sonic criteria in music analysis are static and somehow normative, either as a feature of human perception or of a given piece, and can be captured by a segmentation algorithm. A reexamination of the premises can solve the problem. Why not just accept that the relative import of different sonic dimensions is, in fact, variable and context-dependent? The specific set of weights among sonic criteria that produce good musical results for a given passage then becomes an analytical statement, not prerequisite data (much less a fact) but an interpretive result. Analysts can identify primary and secondary segmenting criteria in a passage, consider the different effects and functions that individual sonic criteria have, and compare aspects of one passage, piece, or composer's style, with another. A "normative" sonic hearing can be a useful tool in this endeavor: probing the discrepancy between "normative" and musical weightings can shed light on distinctive features of a piece much as Schenkerian theory and norms of tonal syntax reveal significant and characteristic detail.

Contextual Criteria (C)

A *contextual criterion (C)* is a rationale for segmentation based on repetition, equivalence, or similarity between two (or more) groupings of notes within a specific musical context. Contextual criteria assume the availability of basic concepts in music theory such as pitch contour, pitch content, pitch-class set, scale degree, set class, and rhythm, that, in music analysis, are often used *as*

ria assume an associative orientation: they recognize segments not individually but in pairs, such that the potential for association between segments prompts their mutual formation.[35] Associations between groupings define segments and imply boundaries.

The properties that contextual criteria record are not merely predicable but *relational*: a contextual criterion represents an association *between* segments as a property *of* (two or more) segments.[36] Unlike some relational properties such as "mother" or "next to," the properties contextual criteria record are predicable of individual segments: given a segment, one can determine its pitch set, pitch-class set, set class, and so forth, without referring to any other segment. But in music analysis, such predicable properties are usually not significant in their own right. Instead, repetition is often used as a threshold for analytical significance. Predicable properties such as a particular pitch-class set or rhythm *become* significant when they associate two or more segments within a context under consideration—that is, when they function as relational properties. Contextual criteria are the basis for categorization and for aspects of music analysis that depend on categories, such as motivic organization and transformational networks.

Psychologists have established that repetition and the contents of long-term memory have a profound effect on what humans perceive and remember.[37] Repetition figures prominently in a wide range of music analysis as an impetus for object recognition and is the subject of some work in music theory.[38] But if the importance of repetition for perception in general and music analysis in particular is widely understood, it has yet to play a central role in a theory of music analysis.[39]

To use repetition strategically, a theory of music analysis must be able to recognize repetition in various forms, ranging from equivalence to similarity (equivalence plus transformation) in one and in multiple dimensions. "Literal repetition" amounts to repetition in all relevant musical dimensions simultaneously. "Equivalence" deconstructs into repetition plus transformation to within a set of operations that form a mathematical group. "Similarity" can be seen as equivalence in conjunction with some transformation not restricted to the mathematical group in question, operating in either the same or a different musical dimension. Deconstructing equivalence and similarity in this way, we can use the power of repetition embedded in equivalence and similarity to drive a context-sensitive theory of music analysis. Contextual criteria recognize individual musical dimensions in which repetition occurs, and allow analysts to articulate shades of association from literal repetition to vague hunches of similarity with some precision.

Understanding that contextual criteria record *relational* properties, not only predicable ones, may require some mental rearrangement. Rather than fix one's analytical gaze on individual objects within musical contexts, the associative

as constituted not only, or even primarily, in and of themselves, but largely by their contexts.[40] With contextual criteria, the rationale for segment formation and recognition lies *outside* the notes one takes to be the object; much of what a musical object "is"—many of its properties and all of its structural significance—is not to be found in the object proper, but dispersed in and permeable with aspects of musical context.

Contextual Criteria: Formal Aspects. Contextual criteria resemble sonic criteria in an important respect: both types of criteria involve determinate, predicable properties of sound events. For sonic criteria, these properties are attribute-values of individual notes. Assuming reference to an appropriate set of primitives and categorical perception for pitch, duration, and so forth, a note either is, or isn't, of pitch C#4, a half-note duration, *mezzo-piano*, on the alto flute—all elements in psychoacoustic dimensions. For contextual criteria, the determinate, predicable properties usually involve elements in nonacoustic, nonlinear, nonintervallic musical spaces, such as (but not limited to) pitch contour, pitch content, pitch-class set, set class, scale-degree ordering, and rhythm. Whether a grouping of notes forms a member of a particular set class is a matter of fact, not interpretation; set class designation is a determinate, not an analytical, statement.[41] Just as segmentation by S_1 criteria in linear, intervallic spaces is a matter of calculation, so too is the process of naming predicable properties of a designated note-grouping with respect to contour, pitch-class set, set class, and so forth.

Outside this important similarity between sonic and contextual criteria, however, sonic and contextual criteria operate in different formal settings.[42] One important difference is that contextual criteria are concerned with predicable properties not of individual tones, but of sets of tones (a set can have just one element). This reflects the different orientations of sonic and contextual criteria. Sonic criteria segment according to disjunctions in attribute-values of individual notes. Contextual criteria respond to associations between groupings of sound-events within a specific musical context; it is the potential for association between groupings that transforms predicable properties into relational ones. Sonic and contextual criteria also implement different cognitive strategies for object recognition. Sonic criteria recognize objects by their boundaries; contextual criteria recognize objects as holistic entities, by their potential for association with one another.

A second critical difference between sonic and contextual criteria is that contextual criteria usually involve elements from musical spaces that are nonacoustic, multidimensional (nonlinear), and *nonintervallic*.[43] Unlike elements in sonic dimensions, elements in these spaces do not have magnitude—one cannot say that SC 3-1[012] is "more" or "less" than SC 3-4[015], 3-6[024], or 4-17[0347], or that one ordering of scale degrees or one rhythmic motive is

criteria, contextual criteria cannot appropriate a concept of magnitude, interval, or distance from the spaces they invoke.[44]

Individual pitch contours, pitch-class sets, set classes, and so forth, can be conceived as elements in different multidimensional musical spaces in which elements interrelate through content and order. One can think of each element in the space as having a distinct location in a multidimensional lattice of inclusion relations, which suggests that it might be possible to replace magnitude with inclusion relations as the basis for intervals, using the number of inclusion relations that separate two lattice nodes as a measure of the distance between them.[45] But there is a problem. Inclusion lattices contain loops. Loops in the lattice and the type-token nature of equivalence classes make it possible to trace multiple paths between some—even most—pairs of elements, throwing the practical value of the concept of interval-as-distance into doubt. Even if one defines the interval between a pair of elements as the shortest path that will connect them, there is still the converse problem: an element conjoined with a particular interval may not yield a unique result.[46]

For the multidimensional spaces most often used by contextual criteria, then, a reliable distance measure is just not available—a fact that affects interactions among contextual criteria of same and different subtypes, and among sonic and contextual criteria, as discussed below. But this emphasis on intervallic distance as the basis for segmentation is, in a sense, a vestige of disjunctive thinking. Because contextual criteria assume an associative orientation, they do not really require a concept of interval. Contextual criteria use the closest analogy to a concept of interval in the contextual domain—repetition, equivalence, and varying degrees of similarity—differently than sonic criteria do. With an associative orientation, repetition—analogous to interval 0—produces the strongest connection between two groupings and is the strongest impetus for their mutual formation as groupings with certain boundaries. With a disjunctive orientation, interval 0 does not just produce a weak segmentation; it *precludes* segmentation. Rather than use intervals in a musical space to identify and compare segments, as sonic criteria do, contextual criteria appeal to the workings of each individual musical passage. The passage, in conjunction with an analyst's proclivities and interests, provides the means to select, prioritize, and relate elements from each multidimensional musical space essential to form segments by contextual criteria.

Some Contextual Subtypes and Individual Criteria. Whereas sonic criteria have only two subtypes (S_1 and S_2), contextual criteria branch into a number of subtypes and many more individual criteria. A contextual subtype identifies a musical space in which association occurs; individual contextual criteria name elements in the space that produce association in a given musical context, indicating aspects of cardinality, content, and order (whether total, partial, or pitch contour ("cseg"); (ordered or unordered) sets of pitch-classes ("pc"), pitch intervals ("ip"), or pitch-class intervals ("INT"); set class ("SC"); scale-degree ordering ("SD"); and rhythm.[47] Notation for individual contextual criteria is similar to that for sonic criteria: "C" indicates the basic type (contextual); the contextual subtype and individual criterion appear in subscript. For instance, $C_{SC\ 3\text{-}1[012]}$, $C_{SC\ 3\text{-}2[013]}$, $C_{pitch\ <C4,\ D5,\ E5>}$, $C_{pc\ <012>}$, and $C_{pc\ \{012\}}$ are five individual contextual criteria that indicate association between two or more instances of SC 3-1[012], SC 3-2[013], pitch ordering <C4, D5, E5>, pitch-class ordering <012>, and the unordered pitch-class set {012}, respectively. Contextual criteria support contextual segmentations; c, c_1, and c_2 denote individual contextual criteria of unspecified subtypes; c_{SC} is an (unspecified) individual criterion within the contextual subtype "set class."

In the excerpt from Schoenberg's op. 10 given earlier as example 2.3, repetition of the pitch interval ordering <+3, +8, −1, +4, +4, +3, −1> played out among the four pitch transpositions is captured by the contextual criterion $C_{ip\ <+3,\ +8,\ -1,\ +4,\ +4,\ +3,\ -1>}$. In this excerpt, the resulting segments coincide exactly with those produced by $S_{1\text{-pitch}}$ (the three downward leaps of thirteen semitones). Repetition of the pc ordering <A3520> between m. 1 and m. 9 in the first of Babbitt's *Three Compositions for Piano* (ex. 2.4) involves $C_{pc\ <A3520>}$; successive associations between instances of the pc segments <1>, <7B69>, and <84> in mm. 1–2 and m. 9 are rendered by the corresponding contextual criteria, as is repetition of the twelve-note pc ordering as a whole.[48]

Example 2.8 lists a number of contextual subtypes for the analysis of posttonal and twelve-tone music and provides examples of individual criteria. Example 2.9 shows some contextual subtypes for analysis of tonal music and sample individual criteria. Analysts can define other subtypes and individual criteria as they wish. In addition to their present purpose of introducing various contextual subtypes, examples 2.8 and 2.9 will serve as glossaries for contextual criteria that appear in subsequent analyses. Several details of notation warrant explanation. In some musical contexts—especially the analysis of twelve-tone music and of tonal canons and fugues—associations occur by equivalence within the serial group of the twelve transpositions (T_n), inversion (I), retrograde (R), and retrograde inversion (RI). To represent transpositional equivalence one need only replace pitch-class elements with pitch-class intervals, and likewise for pitches, attack-points, and elements in other spaces. So while the pitch-class segment <49B86> in the right hand of m. 1 from Babbitt's *Three Compositions* (ex. 2.4a) is a T_6 transform of that in the left (<A3520>), the *association* between the hands is by the repeated pc interval ordering <529A>, or $C_{INT<529A>}$.[49] To represent transformational equivalence by R, I, or RI within a contextual criterion, I fold the operator into the contextual subtype and render the two elements related by the transformation as individual criteria (ex. 2.8): for instance, $C_{pc\ R<9A10>}$ and

C subtype	Description and comments	Sample individual criterion
C_{seg}	Pitch contour	C_{seg} <0132>
C_{CR}	Contour reduction	C_{CR} <0132>
C_{pitch}	Pitch set (unordered); pitch segment (ordered)	C_{pitch} {C#3, A2}; C_{pitch}<C#3, A2>
C_{pitch} R	Pitch segment retrograde	C_{pitch} R<C#3, A2> pairs with C_{pitch} R<A2, C#3>
C_{ip}	Pitch interval (+/− indicates directed interval)	C_{ip} 8; C_{ip} <81>; C_{ip} <+8, -1>
C_{ip} I	Pitch interval ordering under inversion	C_{ip} I <+9, -8, +7> pairs with C_{ip} I <9, +8, -7>
C_{ip} R	Pitch interval ordering under retrograde	C_{ip} R <+9, -8, +7> pairs with C_{ip} R <+7, -8, +9>
C_{ip} RI	Pitch interval ordering under retrograde inversion	C_{ip} RI <+9, -8, +7> pairs with C_{ip} RI <7, +8, -9>
C_{ipspc}	Pitch interval spacing, read from low to high	C_{ipspc} <81>
C_{pc}	Pcset (unordered); pcsegment (ordered)	C_{pc} {9A10}; C_{pc} <9A10>
C_{pc} R	Pcsegment retrograde	C_{pc} R<9A10>pairs with C_{pc} R<01A9>
C_{int}	Pc interval	C_{int} 5
C_{int} I	Pc interval inversion	C_{int} I<14A> pairs with C_{int} I<B82>
C_{int} R	Pc interval retrograde	C_{int} R<14A> pairs with C_{int} R<A41>
C_{int} RI	Pc interval retrograde inversion	C_{int} RI<14A> pairs with C_{int} RI<28B>
C_{ic}	Interval class	C_{ic} 5
C_{SC}	Set class	C_{SC} 3-4[015]
C_{dseg}	Duration contour	C_{dseg} <0132>
C_{durseg}	Duration segment (commas separate beats)	C_{durseg} <4, 211, 211>
C_{dyseg}	Dynamics contour	C_{dyseg} <0132>
C_{dynseg}	Segment of dynamics	C_{dynseg} <*ff, p*>

Example 2.8. Some contextual (C) subtypes for analysis of post-tonal and twelve-tone music with examples of individual criteria

C subtype[*]	Description and comments	Sample individual criterion
C_{SD}	Ordered set of scale degrees (uninterpreted)	C_{SD} <565>; C_{SD} <543>; C_{SD} <6543>
$C_{SD:\ a:\ <543>}$	Ordered set of scale degrees, key specified (stronger than above)	$C_{SDs:\ a:}$ <543>
C_{SDint}	Scale degree interval (+, – indicate directed intervals)	C_{SDint} <–3, –4, +2, –3> (NB: SDint < D4, C4 > = –2 not –1)
C_{SDintq}	Diatonic interval size and quality (+, – indicate directed intervals)	C_{SDintq} <–M3, –d4, +m2, –M3>
C_{RN}	Roman numerals (uninterpreted)	$C_{RN,\ a:}$ < I, ii6, V, I >
C_{HF}	Harmonic functions (T=tonic; P=predominant; D=dominant) (uninterpreted)	$C_{HF,}$ <T, PD, D T>

[*]Many criterion types defined in ex. 2.8 for post-tonal and twelve-tone music are also useful in tonal contexts, e.g. C_{pitch} and C_{pc}.

Example 2.9. Some contextual (C) subtypes for analysis of tonal music with examples of individual criteria

$C_{pc\ R<01A9>}$ indicate an association under retrograde between two pitch-class segments <9A10> and <01A9> both present in a musical passage under consideration. Similarly, $C_{pc\ T6I\ <9678>}$ and $C_{pc\ T6I\ <90BA>}$ represent equivalence by pitch-class inversion between the opening tetrachords in horn II and horn I of Webern's *Symphony*, op. 21. Admittedly this notational practice is a bit cumbersome and the analyst must seek the best solution for musical situations that involve multiple transformations. For simple cases of two segments associated by R, I, or RI, however, it has the advantage of allowing analysts to identify actual pitch orderings in the music as the basis for association. In example 2.9, scale degree orderings are diatonic within the key given before the colon; upper case indicates a major key; lower case, minor. Chromatic alteration is indicated in the scale degree ordering, as in: "a: <565>" = <E, F, E>; "A: <565>" = <E, F♯, E>; and "a: <5, ♯6, 5>" = <E, F♯, E>. Following tonal conventions, scale degree intervals render a step as a second and a unison as interval one (e.g., the scale degree interval from D4 to C4 is –2, not –1; that from C4 to C4 is 1, not 0). Contextual criteria involving roman numeral and harmonic functions obtain without reference to an orienting theory of tonal syntax: thus in the contextual domain both $C_{RN\ <I,\ IV,\ V,\ I>}$ and $C_{RN\ <I,\ V,\ IV,\ I>}$ are viable, activated only by repetition of a triadic root pattern. Many of the criteria defined in example 2.8 for post-tonal and twelve-tone music are also useful in tonal contexts (e.g., C_{pitch}, C_{pc}). Additional criteria can also be devised, to represent repeated sequences of neo-Riemannian transformations, for example.

in other words, by inclusion. To indicate association by inclusion I attach the prefix "incl" to an individual criterion: thus "incl $C_{pc\ \{013\}}$" indicates repetition of the unordered pcset {013} as the strongest significant association between two or more segments such that at least one of these includes additional pitch-classes. Contextual criteria that obtain only by virtue of formal inclusion among musical spaces or elements are trivial and will not be noted in text or musical examples. However, criteria related by formal inclusion can have independent associative agency; in such cases they are *nontrivial* and should be shown as criteria in their own right. For instance, consider two hypothetical segments, A1 and A2, related by pitch retrograde. Here a retrograde inversion in the less specific space of pitch contour is logically implied but trivial, and so will not be shown. However, if the pitch contour of A1 forges an association with a third segment, A3, based *only* on pitch contour—*not* pitch or pitch intervals—the pitch contour within A1 acquires independent associative agency, becomes nontrivial (with respect to A3), and should be shown. Likewise, contextual associations that obtain solely on the basis of formal inclusion among elements (e.g., $C_{SC\ 4\text{-}3[0134]}$, relative to $C_{SC\ 3\text{-}2[013]}$ and $C_{SC\ 3\text{-}3[014]}$) are trivial and not shown. But if sonic disjunctions within a larger segment articulate a subsegment supported by the logically implied criterion—say, a $C_{SC\ 4\text{-}3[0134]}$ segment includes a clear subsegment that associates by $C_{SC\ 3\text{-}2[013]}$ with a third segment—the association, and included criterion, become nontrivial and should be shown. In general, one should represent all, but only, the *most specific, nontrivial* contextual criteria at work in a passage.

Interactions among Contextual Criteria: Subtypes and Individual Criteria. Contextual criteria interact with one another in two ways: one involves formal relations; the other, boundary strength.

Formal relations determine which criteria can, and cannot, operate simultaneously for the same grouping of notes. Formal relations are governed by the presence, absence, or nature of logical entailment that obtains between predicable properties identified by the criteria. They depend, first, on the primitives and sonic dimensions invoked by the contextual subtype; then, perhaps also on interrelations between the particular elements identified by the criteria. Given any two contextual criteria, three formal relations are possible:

1. Functional independence. Two individual contextual criteria are functionally independent if they are from different subtypes and if elements in these subtypes invoke, as primitives, sonic dimensions that are functionally independent.[50] For example, associations by set class (C_{SC}), pitch-class set, or pitch set are functionally independent from associations by rhythm (C_{rhythm}): a member of a set class can be conjoined with any rhythm. Not only are C_{SC} and C_{rhythm} different contextual subtypes; they are subtypes that assume different sets of sonic primitives (pitch and pc for set class, attack points and durational values for rhythm).

cal entailment: (a) of spaces, if each element in the musical space associated with one contextual subtype logically entails a specific element in the space associated with the other subtype (e.g., a given pitch ordering logically entails a specific pitch contour, pitch-class ordering, and set class); or (b) of elements, if the element identified by one criterion logically includes the element within the same space identified by the other, through content or ordering (e.g., the pitch-class ordering <9A10> includes <9A1> and <9A0>, as well as the unordered pcsets {9A10} and {9A1}).

3. Mutual exclusion. Two individual contextual criteria are mutually exclusive if: (a) they involve different elements from the same contextual dimension; or (b) they involve elements from two different contextual dimensions, but the element in one dimension logically entails an element *other than* the one specified by the criterion in the second dimension.

The second way contextual criteria interact is, like sonic criteria, through the strength of the boundaries they produce. But unlike sonic criteria, contextual criteria cannot derive magnitude, intervals, or distances from the dimensions they invoke. The fact that contextual criteria do *not* involve a concept of magnitude has two consequences for the relative strength of the segments they support. First, all segments supported by the same contextual criterion are equally strong with respect to it. So given two segments supported by $C_{SC\ 4\text{-}9[0167]}$, for instance, neither is stronger or weaker based on that criterion alone. The situation differs sharply from that in the sonic domain, where greater disjunctions produce stronger segments. Second, whereas in the sonic domain *strength = magnitude × weight*, for contextual criteria magnitude factors out and relative strength is reduced to weight. Among contextual criteria the concept of strength applies to the *criteria themselves*, such that the strongest contextual criterion produces the strongest segments.

Two factors contribute to the relative strength of contextual criteria: properties of the criteria in the abstract and aspects of musical context that affect perceived strength.

Abstract properties are of three kinds. Each can be overruled by musical context.

1. *Dimensional specificity.* Contextual criteria associated with more specific musical spaces are stronger than criteria associated with less specific spaces. Given two musical spaces A and B, A is more specific than B if and only if every element in A logically entails a particular element in B but not vice versa. Under these circumstances, given two contextual criteria c_1 and c_2, associated with musical spaces A and B, c_1 is stronger than c_2.[51] For example: pitch space includes pitch-class space, and the set of pitch-class sets is partitioned by the set of set classes; $C_{pitch\ \{B3,\ D\sharp4,\ C5\}}$ is a more specific, and therefore a stronger, criterion than $C_{pc\ \{03B\}}$, which, in turn, is stronger than $C_{SC\ 3\text{-}3[014]}$. More specific criteria are stronger because they imply the action of other criteria: for

{03B} and $C_{SC\,3\text{-}3[014]}$.

2. *Degree of ordering.* Total orderings are stronger than partial orderings; partial orderings are stronger than unordered sets. For example, the criterion $C_{pc\,<9A10>}$ is stronger than $C_{pc\,<\,<9A>\,\{10\}>}$, which is stronger than $C_{pc\,\{9A10\}}$.

3. *Cardinality.* The higher the cardinality of the set identified as an element by the criterion, the stronger the criterion. For example, $C_{SC\,6\text{-}14[013458]}$ is stronger than $C_{SC\,3\text{-}3[014]}$ because it involves a set class of higher cardinality.

Two points warrant further discussion: the relationship between strength and the number of instantiations, and that between strength and formal inclusion.

For dimensional specificity and degree of ordering, relative strength is inversely correlated with the number of instantiations. In both cases, the relation is straightforward: more specific dimensions, and sets with greater degrees of ordering, have fewer possible instantiations and produce stronger criteria. For example, pitch is more specific than pitch-class, the pitch set {B3, D♯4, C5} has fewer instantiations than the pcset {03B}, and so $C_{pitch\,\{B3,\,D\sharp4,\,C5\}}$ is a stronger criterion than $C_{pc\,\{03B\}}$. Similarly, partial orderings have fewer instantiations than unordered sets, so $C_{pc\,<\,<9A>\,\{10\}>}$, is stronger than $C_{pc\,\{9A10\}}$. But the relationship among cardinality, number of instantiations, and relative strength is less clear. Cardinality and number of instantiations correlate *positively*: as cardinality increases, so does the number of possible instantiations. This suggests that higher cardinalities may produce *weaker* contextual criteria (note that larger segments place higher demands on memory and cognition and therefore may also be more difficult to identify and recall). But then again, as cardinality increases, so does the statistical significance of the recurrent (relational) property identified by the contextual criterion. That is, one might argue that $C_{SC\,6\text{-}14[013458]}$ is stronger than $C_{SC\,3\text{-}11[037]}$ because the former notes a repetition of 1 out of 50 hexachordal set classes (and 1 of only 12 of the 924 hexachordal pcsets, a ratio of 1 in 77), while the latter identifies one of only 12 trichords (and 1 of 24 of the 220 trichordal pcsets, roughly a ratio of 1 in 9). If statistical significance, not the number of instantiations, is the critical factor, higher cardinalities may indeed produce stronger criteria.[52]

The second issue with respect to cardinality involves the relationship between criterion strength and formal inclusion. Inclusion relations underlie the strength associated with dimensional specificity and degree of ordering. For dimensional specificity, formal inclusion obtains among musical spaces conceived as finite or infinite sets of elements. Partitioning the set of pitches in pitch-space by octave equivalence and enharmonic equivalence gives the set of twelve pitch-classes; partitioning the 4096 pitch-class sets into disjoint sets of transpositional and inversional equivalents gives the 223 set classes; in each case, formal inclusion structures relations among criteria in different, but

to sets of "order constraints" or "protocol pairs" that model total orderings, partial orderings, and unordered sets.[53] In this case, formal inclusion organizes criteria within a subtype through the addition of order constraints.

In general, however, contextual criteria are not organized within a subtype, and cannot be related by formal inclusion. Consider, for example, the contextual subtype C_{SC} and the four criteria $C_{SC\ 6\text{-}14[013458]}$, $C_{SC\ 6\text{-}30[013679]}$, $C_{SC\ 4\text{-}29[0137]}$, and $C_{SC\ 3\text{-}11[037]}$. Some abstract inclusion relations obtain among the set classes these criteria identify, and literal inclusion may occur among segments that instantiate these criteria in a particular musical passage, but the criteria themselves are unrelated. The criterion $C_{SC\ 4\text{-}29[0137]}$ does *not* include $C_{SC\ 3\text{-}11[037]}$, because the property each criterion records is *relational*, not only predicable. Association by $C_{SC\ 4\text{-}29[0137]}$ may indeed encourage—but it does not ensure—the associative agency of $C_{SC\ 3\text{-}11[037]}$ within a particular musical context; pitch-class ordering within the tetrachord, or intervening sonic disjunctions, may render the trichordal relation untenable. Within the C_{SC} subtype, then, and within other contextual subtypes such as contour and pitch-class content, individual criteria can be mutually exclusive, but they are not formally inclusive.

As noted above, musical context also affects the perceived relative strength of contextual criteria. Two important considerations in this regard are:

4. *Frequency.* The more active a contextual criterion is within a particular musical context (that is, the more frequently its named element occurs as a relational property among segments), the stronger the criterion becomes. For instance, given a musical context in which the criterion $C_{pc\ \{9A10\}}$ associates many more segments than $C_{pc\ <24106>}$ does, it may be perceived as stronger, even though this is contrary to what the elements' degree of ordering and cardinality suggest.

5. *Interactions with sonic, structural, and other contextual criteria.* Contextual criteria with instantiations that are articulated by strong sonic disjunctions, or privileged as structural units by a theoretic orientation in force, tend to be perceived as stronger than they would be otherwise.

In the end, contextual criteria, like different sonic criteria, do not relate to one another through absolute measures of strength, but through multiple factors that affect perception and analytical interpretation. But because contextual criteria record relational properties, their perceived relative strength is far more variable and sensitive to the frequency, sonic prominence, and structural significance of their instantiations within a given musical context than is the case for sonic criteria.

Interactions between Sonic and Contextual Criteria. In analytical practice, criteria of the same and different types interact. While segmentation algorithms have tended to focus on sonic criteria, research concerned with the theory

guished—what amount to both sonic and contextual criteria. Hasty considers both sonic and contextual aspects of musical design in his theory of segmentation, as does Lidov, who goes on to relate these to Gestalt structure and taxonomy, respectively.[54] Lerdahl and Jackendoff recognize "parallelism" (analogous to contextual criteria) as an important force in segmentation, but point out the inherent difficulty of ascertaining relative weights for sonic and contextual criteria.[55]

Interactions between sonic and contextual criteria are complicated by their different formal settings and modes of operation. Sonic criteria segment by disjunctions that define boundaries and imply segments; contextual criteria segment through associations that define segments and imply boundaries. Whereas sonic criteria are often able to appropriate magnitude, interval, and distance from the musical spaces they inhabit, contextual criteria cannot. Interactions among sonic criteria are so complex and variable that one cannot say that sonic criteria determine the set of groupings to consider for significant relational properties, but in practice sonic criteria tend to serve as a substrate for the action of contextual criteria.[56] Sonic disjunctions, or at least minimal sonic support from $S_{1\text{-adjacency}}$, seem necessary to provide potential groupings with perceptual edges that permit or facilitate cognitive processing of the predicable properties subsequently recovered as relational properties. Regarding relations between sonic and contextual criteria, the short story is that whereas sonic criteria tend to constrain segment formation, contextual criteria tend to select and endow segments with analytical significance.

Structural Criteria (T)

A *structural criterion* (T) is a rationale for segmentation that indicates an interpretation supported by a specific orienting theory. Like contextual criteria, structural criteria partake of basic concepts in music theory that are often used nominally and as if observation language, such as pitch-class set, scale degree, and set class. Structural criteria differ from contextual criteria in that they assume a theoretic orientation, not only an associative one, and express interpretations that invoke theoretical terms and concepts defined as part of the orienting theory's theoretic framework (HF) and incorporated in its theoretic entities (HE) (to which individual structural criteria often correspond). As interpretations of musical structure, structural criteria are *concepts* that exist within, and derive meaning from, the orienting theory—not aural percepts located in sound-events. Therefore, while theoretic entities, and structural criteria, can *recommend* segments for analytic consideration, they cannot actually produce convincing musical segments unless they are realized—that is, unless the instantiation of the structural criterion coincides with the instantiation of a sonic or contextual criterion.

music analysis that engage a theoretic orientation that exists outside a piece from those fully constituted by associations within the piece, is suggested by a wide range of music theory and analysis. Schenker's and Schoenberg's concepts of motive, for example, differ as invocations of structural and contextual criteria, as do the "derivation" and "association" views of motive outlined by Richard Cohn.[57] Babbitt draws a comparable distinction between contextual and systemic aspects of musical organization (twelve-tone or otherwise) as those that generalize across differences in syntax versus those that do not.[58] Referencing Saussure, Lidov contrasts the paradigmatic, associational, and contextual with the syntagmatic, theoretical, and structural; McCreless applies Saussure's concepts of the paradigmatic and syntagmatic to the study of chromaticism and motive in tonal music, focusing on the paradigmatic.[59]

Distinguishing contextual from structural criteria, and terms that are relatively observational from those that are theoretical, is a delicate matter. Theoretical and observational terms are not opposed, but points on a continuum; the line that separates them is not fixed or absolute but variable and dependent on analytic context.[60] But although observational and theoretic terms are a continuum, they *can* be distinguished with respect to a specific orienting theory, an idea that derives from Bas van Fraassen's account of theoretic terms as those "introduced or adapted for the purposes of theory construction."[61] What a theory assumes as primitive, it uses as if observation language to support the definition of theoretic terms. The set of terms used but *not* defined by a specific theory provides means to distinguish observational from theoretical terms with respect to that theory. Using the *function* of terms within a specific theoretic and analytical context to divide the continuum into the relatively observational versus the theoretic or interpretive gives analysts a semantic foothold for exploring issues in musical realization, differences in associative and structural organization, and interactions between structure and design.[62]

Structural Criteria: Formal Aspects. Structural criteria differ from sonic criteria, and resemble contextual criteria, in two important respects. Sonic criteria involve attribute-values of individual tones and often appropriate intervals that support distance measures from the linear, intervallic, psychoacoustic spaces they tend to inhabit. But structural criteria, like contextual criteria, typically involve properties predicable of groups of tones and multidimensional musical spaces for which no distance measure is available. On the other hand, structural criteria resemble sonic criteria and differ from contextual criteria in that they recognize segments one at a time, not in pairs. Without a distance measure to determine segment boundaries, or a built-in sensitivity to association within a particular musical context, structural criteria cannot use either of the strategies that sonic and contextual criteria use to identify segments (that is, by boundaries or as groupings). Instead, structural criteria depend on the

ties (HE)—to determine which groupings of tones can be interpreted as structural units according to that theory; which cannot; and, for a given grouping, the range of theoretically cogent interpretations available.

The resemblance between structural and contextual criteria goes beyond the fact that both involve multidimensional spaces. Structural and contextual criteria often partake of the *same* spaces and the *same* elements; for example, both can involve orderings of pitch-classes or scale degrees. But structural and contextual criteria use these spaces and elements in different ways. Understanding this difference is essential, because it underlies the mechanics of musical realization by ("look-alike") contextual criteria (see below) and separates description from interpretation.

Contextual criteria use elements in musical spaces such as pitch contour, pitch-class set, scale degree ordering, set class, and so on, as if they were observational terms.[63] Contextual criteria identify predicable properties that are determinate within each contextual dimension (that is, each grouping maps one-to-one to an element in the space and no interpretation is involved) and that act as relational properties among groupings within a particular musical context. Structural criteria, on the other hand, often use the same elements and predicable properties as contextual criteria do, but conjoin them with theoretical concepts and terms defined by an orienting theory to express musical interpretations shaped or supported by that theory. In contrast to contextual criteria, structural criteria indicate not relational properties but *interpretations* with respect to a specific theoretic orientation.

To underline this difference between structural and contextual criteria that involve the same predicable properties, we consider an example. To say that two musical segments have the same pitch-class ordering involves only a predicable property that serves as a relational property within a specific musical context; a contextual criterion indicates the association. So in the first of Babbitt's *Three Compositions for Piano*, the association between m. 1 and m. 9 by virtue of the repeated pitch-class ordering <A3520> involves the contextual criterion $C_{pc\ <A3520>}$ (recall and compare exx. 2.4a and 2.4b).[64] To say, however, that these two musical segments are instances of the same "row segment" goes further; it appeals not only to pitch-class ordering as a determinate predicable property of two segments, but to the conceptual framework (HF) of twelve-tone theory that defines the concept of a row both formally (as an ordering of eleven pc intervals that defines an ordering of the pc aggregate, or as a mapping of the twelve pitch-classes onto the twelve order positions) and functionally (as a structural basis for a composition). To identify the two segments in m. 1 and m. 9 as instances of the same row segment (the first five order positions of the row $T_A P$ = <A352017B6984>) invokes two specific theoretic entities—the ordering of pitch-class intervals that identifies the row class of the composition, and a subsegment of a particular row in that row class. Whereas the contextual

the structural criterion $T_{\text{row TAP ops 0-4}}$ (which in this case designates the pitch-class ordering <A3520>) identifies a correspondence between a segment in the composition and a member of HE.

Note that the contrast between contextual and structural criteria as criteria concerned with determinate predicable properties versus an interpretation that depends on an orienting theory is but another angle on the difference between observational and theoretical terms. What can be predicated directly is relatively observational and can be captured in contextual criteria; what expresses interpretation with regard to a theory is necessarily theoretical and involves structural criteria.[65]

Some Structural Subtypes and Individual Criteria. Like contextual criteria, structural criteria (T) branch first into a number of subtypes, then into individual criteria. Structural subtypes can nest one within another in hierarchic fashion, with the relative strength and priority of subtypes determined either by differences in dimensional specificity of musical spaces shared by contextual criteria or by concepts defined within the theoretic framework (HF) of the orienting theory. A structural subtype denotes a conceptual space defined by the theory; individual structural criteria indicate interpretations of musical structure and often correspond with individual theoretic entities (elements of HE). Structural subtypes for twelve-tone theory include row ("row"), row segment ("row ops," for row order positions), lyne pair ("lyne pair"), and partition of the aggregate ("partition").[66] Notation of structural criteria specifies the type ("T") followed, in subscript, by the subtype and individual criterion; for instance, $T_{\text{row TAP}}$ (for P = <A352017B6984>) and $T_{\text{row TAP ops 0-4}}$ (= pcsegment <A3520>) are two individual structural criteria that identify the row, and opening row segment, in the left hand of m. 1 from the first of Babbitt's *Three Compositions for Piano* (back in ex. 2.4a). Structural criteria support structural segmentations; t, t_1, and t_2 denote individual structural criteria of unspecified subtypes; t_{row} is an (unspecified) individual criterion within the structural subtype "row." Example 2.10 lists some structural (T) subtypes and individual structural criteria for twelve-tone music, with twelve-tone theory and array structure as the theoretic orientation.[67] Just what one includes in the conceptual framework of "twelve-tone theory" is negotiable, but should include at least order relations, twelve-tone operator groups, partitions, and a general theory of combinatoriality.

Example 2.11 lists some structural (T) subtypes and individual structural criteria for tonal music within a Schenkerian theoretic orientation. Structural subtypes include different kinds of lines and prolongational structures: third- and fifth-progressions (3PRG, 5PRG); upper, lower, and double-neighbor figures (UN, LN, DN); chordal skips (CS); arpeggiation (ARP); and the fundamental line (FL). One can define other structural subtypes that involve

T subtype	Description and comments	Sample individual criterion (abbreviation)
T_{row}	Twelve-tone (pitch-class or timepoint) row	T_{T9P}; T_{tp} row T7P
$T_{row\ ops}$	Row segment, specific order positions of row	T_{T9P} ops 0–4; T_{tp} row T7P ops 0–4
$T_{lyne\ pair}$	Combinatorial or otherwise structural lyne pair	$T_{lyne\ pair}$ (for T_{pc} array lyne pair)
$T_{ag\ bnd}$	Aggregate boundary (in pc)	$T_{pc\ ag\ bnd}$
$T_{partition}$	Partition	$T_{partition}$ 3223

Example 2.10. Some structural (T) subtypes and individual structural criteria for twelve-tone music, with twelve-tone theory and array structure as the theoretic orientation

transformations, such as octave transfers or substitution (e.g., scale degree 7 for scale degree 2). Within each subtype, individual criteria designate syntactic entities and convey an interpretation of the relative structural significance of the tones involved, guided by the theory. The structural subtype T_{3PRG}, for example, includes (among others) the individual structural criteria $T_{3PRG, a:<5(43)>}$, $T_{3PRG, a:<(54)3>}$, and $T_{3PRG, a:<(23)4>}$. Each criterion parses elements of a scale-degree ordering by structural level. The event prolonged occupies a deeper level and is shown without parentheses; elements that prolong are diminutions at a more surface level and are enclosed in (one or more pairs of nested) parentheses to suggest their (successively) subordinate status. Note that different interpretations of the same scale-degree sequence are possible: interpretation is not *determined* by Schenkerian theory (or, for that matter, necessarily by other orienting theories including twelve-tone theory), only guided and elucidated by it. The analyst invokes an orienting theory not to obtain an interpretation so much as to develop and express one.[68]

As in Schenkerian theory, this notational system allows units of same and different structural subtypes to be concatenated (which preserves the number of active structural levels), nested (which increases it), and combined in counterpoint. For structural criteria that involve three or more levels of structure, and for concatenation or combination, notation (especially the proliferation of parentheses and angled brackets) can become cumbersome. As structural interpretations become increasingly complex, one might instead notate criteria as miniature excerpts from a voice-leading graph or just refer to the graphs, which already carry the same interpretive information in a beautifully concise form.

T subtype	Description and comments	Sample individual criterion
T_{UN}	Upper neighbor; e.g., prolongs scale degree 5 in A minor, or scale degree 3 in F# major	T_{UN}, a: <5(65)> T_{UN}, F#: <3(43)>
T_{LN}	Lower neighbor; e.g., prolongs scale degree 1 in A minor	T_{LN}, a: <1(71)>
T_{IUN}	Incomplete upper neighbor; e.g., scale degree 6 prolongs scale degree 5 in A minor	T_{IUN}, a: <(6)5>
T_{DN}	Double neighbor; e.g., scale degrees 2 and 7 prolong scale degree 1 in A minor	T_{DN}, a: <1(27)1>
T_{3CS}	Consonant skip; e.g., by 3rd prolongs scale degree 1 in A minor, upper line or bass.	T_{3CS}, a: <1(31)>
T_{3PRG}	3rd progression; e.g., prolong scale degree 5, 4 in A minor	T_{3PRG}, a: <5(43)>; T_{3PRG}, a: <(23)4>
T_{5PRG}	5th progression; e.g., prolongs scale degree 5 in A minor (PRG: Endpoints delimit 3rd, 4th, 5th, 6th, or 8ve. Upper line or bass.)	T_{5PRG}, a: <5(4321)>
T_{LD}	Linear displacement; e.g., scale degree 3 by scale degree 2 in A minor, upper line only.	T_{LD}, a: <32>
T_{SS}	Scale step progression; e.g., from scale degree 4 to scale degree 5 in A minor, bass line only	T_{SS}, a: <45>
T_{FL}	Fundamental line; e.g., from scale degree 5 in A minor. Linear displacement at deepest level. Upper line only.	T_{FL}, a: <54321>
T_{BB}	Bass background structure; e.g., scale degrees 1, 4, 5, and 1 in A minor; scale degrees 1, 5, and 1 in A major.	T_{BB}, a: <1451> T_{BB}, A: <151>
T_{VE}	Voice exchange; e.g., i^6 prolongs i in A minor. Involves a pair of voices; Roman numerals give the scale degree (and pitch class) succession in each voice.	T_{VE}, a: <i (i^6)>

Example 2.11. Some structural (T) subtypes and individual structural criteria for tonal music, with a Schenkerian theoretic orientation

contextual criteria that involve the same musical spaces, elements, and orderings. Given a structural criterion t_1, its *look-alike contextual criterion* c_1 indicates the same musical space, elements, and ordering, but as a predicable property that functions as a relational property within a given musical context. Whereas t_1 expresses a musical interpretation with respect to a specific theoretic orientation H, c_1 does not involve interpretation in this sense: it does not involve theoretical terms and concepts defined as part of an HF or assumed by individual HEs. Consider the two structural criteria $T_{UN,\ a:\ <5(65)>}$ and $T_{3PRG,\ a:\ <5(43)>}$ and their look-alike contextual criteria $C_{SD\ <565>}$ and $C_{SD\ <543>}$, respectively. The contextual criteria capture associations by scale-degree orderings; set in the key of A minor they also imply associations by $C_{pc\ <EFE>}$ and $C_{pc\ <EDC>}$, respectively. But none of these contextual criteria assert, or assume, any priority or contingency among notes within a segment. Their structural counterparts *do*. $T_{UN,\ a:\ <5(65)>}$ and $T_{3PRG,\ a:\ <5(43)>}$ parse the same scale degree orderings, indicating interpretations of structural priority and transformational generation as an upper-neighbor figure and a third progression, respectively, each prolonging scale degree 5.[69] To recall the opening bars of Babbitt's *Three Compositions for Piano* once more, the relationship between the structural criterion $T_{row\ TAP\ ops\ 0-4}$ that recognizes the first five notes in the left hand as a row segment, and the contextual criterion $C_{pc\ <A3520>}$ that locates the same notes in the score, is one of a structural criterion to its look-alike contextual criterion.

This distinction between structural criteria and look-alike contextual criteria allows us to define two corresponding concepts of motive, structural and pure. Both depend on the idea that a motive can be defined as a set of contextual criteria.[70] Systematic linkage between a structural criterion and a contextual criterion within that set represents one view, the Schenkerian view that a "motive" carries structural interpretation: if two segments do not have the same structural interpretation, they do not instance the same motive. I call this *structural motive*. Contextual criteria represent an alternate, associational, view of motive: two segments associated by repetition in a given passage but with different (or no) structural interpretations can still instance the same motive. I call this *pure motive*.[71] Structural and pure motive, and structural criteria and their look-alike contextual criteria, reframe the question from *whether* or not a segment can be called an instance of a motive to *how* it is one. Analysts who recognize the distinction between structural criteria and their look-alike contextual criteria and admit both views within the same analysis can recognize and retain *all* associations that occur with enough frequency to warrant the designation "motivic," using the interpretive power of an orienting theory where appropriate, without losing contact with associations that fall outside its reach. Rather than a hard line for inclusion or exclusion, the distinction between associations that carry consistent structural interpretations and those that do not becomes an area for analytical exploration.[72]

Sonic and contextual criteria respond to and record sounding features of a musical surface: sonic criteria register disjunctions in attribute-values of individual notes; contextual criteria indicate relational properties for groupings of notes. Both sonic and contextual criteria rely primarily on general perceptual and cognitive faculties such as edge detection, stream segregation, cognitive chunking, and categorization to delimit musical objects of analytic interest. The instantiation of a sonic or contextual criterion is a percept—a grouping of sound-events motivated by a property that is directly predicable of the sound-surface.

Structural criteria differ from sonic and contextual criteria in this respect. As *interpretations* of groupings guided and articulated by a theory of musical structure, structural criteria indicate not percepts but *concepts*—not sounding features, but ways of *interpreting* or *thinking about* such features. In order for structural criteria to acquire aural significance, they must gain the support of sounding features. This occurs through *realization*: a structural criterion t is realized when its instantiation coincides fully and exactly with the instantiation of at least one sonic or contextual criterion s or c. (Note that realization requires the criteria to be *coincident*, not only compatible, as can be the case in segment formation.) Realization of structural criteria does not *ensure* that a particular segment will be perceived as a significant structural unit; instead, it is a necessary, but not sufficient, condition that *enables* the perception of structure. Structural criteria not realized through sonic or contextual criteria are not necessarily insignificant, but their significance is purely conceptual, not aural.

Realization of a structural criterion t can be systematic or nonsystematic. Realization is *systematic* if t functions as part of a linked type in which t is functionally interdependent with, or related by logical entailment to, the action of s or c. Realization is *nonsystematic* if the instantiation of t coincides with the instantiation of a sonic or contextual criterion s or c on a particular occasion, but t is functionally independent of and logically unrelated to s or c.

Systematic Realization: Linked Types (Structural-Sonic, Structural-Contextual). Two linked types supplement the three basic criterion types: structural-sonic (TS) and structural-contextual (TC). The linked types indicate systematic realization of a structural criterion through functional interdependence of a structural and a sonic criterion (TS), or logical entailment between a structural and a contextual criterion (TC). Like the three basic types S, C, and T, the two linked types TS and TC branch into subtypes, then individual criteria; subtypes link to subtypes, and individual criteria to individual criteria. Linked criteria are not proprietary with regard to the individual structural, sonic, or contextual criteria they contain: the individual t, s, and c criteria that contribute to a linked TS or TC criterion remain free agents,

port segments, and contribute to different linked criteria, all within the same analysis.[73]

A *structural-sonic criterion (TS)* links a structural criterion t to a sonic criterion s; the linked TS criterion amounts to a realization rule that ensures consistent projection of structural units through a designated sonic "channel," such as disjunctions between attack points ($S_{1\text{-duration}}$), pitch proximity ($S_{2\text{-pitch}}$), continuity in dynamics ($S_{2\text{-dynamics}}$), or instrumental assignment ($S_{2\text{-timbre}}$).[74] In the opening chorale from J. S. Bach's Cantata No. 140, "Wachet auf," for example, the chorale tune easily projects through and above the choral and instrumental texture by virtue of its systematic realization by sonic criteria that involve long notes in the soprano and horn; the corresponding linked criteria are $T_{\text{tune}}S_{2\text{-duration}}$ and $T_{\text{tune}}S_{2\text{-timbre}}$. In the opening bars of Babbitt's *None but the Lonely Flute* (1991), a composition based on a six-lyne all-partition array, each lyne pair—and each lyne—is realized within one of three octave spans, from C4–B4, C5–B5, and C6–B6 (ex. 2.12).[75] The linked criterion $T_{\text{lyne}}S_{2\text{-pitch}}$ indicates the general case that includes the lyne-to-octave register realization rule. The same basic idea of realizing a pitch structure within a particular octave appears in a Schenkerian context as "obligatory register." In his sketch of J. S. Bach's Prelude in C Major from the *Well-Tempered Clavier* Book I, for example, Schenker shows the descent of the fundamental line within an octave span; the linked criterion $T_{\text{FL} <321>}S_{2\text{-pitch}}$ models this relationship between structure and pitch space.[76]

A *structural-contextual criterion (TC)* links a structural criterion t with a contextual criterion c that ensures its systematic realization; the linked TC criterion recognizes a relational property regulated by structure. Compared to TS criteria, which are relatively straightforward, TC criteria have two significant complications. One derives from the greater complexity of relations among contextual criteria, which often involve logical entailment among musical

Example 2.12. Babbitt, *None but the Lonely Flute*, mm. 1–7 (aggregates 1–2)

cation comes from the fact that structural and contextual criteria can involve not just the same multidimensional musical spaces, but even the same *elements* within these spaces. The relationship between a structural criterion and its look-alike contextual criterion is essential to the workings of TC criteria.

A TC criterion indicates not only that the instantiations of a t and c coincide in a particular case, but that t and c are related by logical entailment. The logical entailment can be (1) *direct*, such that c is the look-alike contextual criterion for t; or (2) *indirect*, such that c (in a more specific musical space) logically entails c' (in a less specific space), which is the look-alike contextual criterion for t.

Whether logical entailment is direct or indirect, the contextual component c of a TC criterion must have its own associative life; that is, as is always the case with contextual criteria, c must identify a relational property shared by *at least two* segments within a specific musical context. Once—and only if—c is thus activated, c has the power to *realize t*, such that the concept t is identified as a structural interpretation of an associative feature of a segment recognized by c.

Within a specific TC criterion t logically entails c, but in general the individual criteria t and c remain free agents. As a result, two or more segments associated by c can have different structural interpretations t_1 and t_2, and some of the segments supported by c may have no (analytically significant) structural interpretation at all. Given two segments A and B such that A is supported by the linked criterion t_1c, and associates with B through the contextual criterion c (which may contribute to a linked criterion t_2c), there are four possible relations between A and B:

1. T_xC–T_xC (*TC xx relation*). The segments are supported by the same TC criterion; c has the same structural interpretation. (A is supported by t_1c; B is supported by t_2c; and $t_1 = t_2$.)
2. T_xC–T_yC (*TC xy relation*). The segments are supported by different TC criteria; c has different structural interpretations. (A is supported by t_1c; B is supported by t_2c; and $t_1 \neq t_2$.)[77]
3. TC–C+T. One segment is supported by a TC criterion; the other is supported by coincident C+T criteria. (A is supported by t_1c; B is supported by functionally independent criteria t_2 and c, and $t_1 \neq t_2$.)
4. TC–C. One segment is supported by a TC criterion; the other is supported by the same contextual criterion, but no structural criterion. (A is supported by t_1c; B is supported by c.)

In practice, these four possibilities for interactions among systematic realization, nonsystematic realization, and pure associations tend to interact and can create complex connections between structural and purely associative

not always, designates a structural unit privileged by the theory (that is, t_1 can correspond to any basic or transformed entity in HE); second, linkage between a structural criterion t and the contextual criterion c that realizes it can be direct or indirect in all four cases.

Nonsystematic Realization: Functionally Independent S+T and C+T Criteria. Realization of structural criteria is not always systematic. Systematic realization occurs when a structural criterion t and the sonic or contextual criterion s or c that realizes it in a particular case are related by functional interdependence (between t and s) or logical implication (direct or indirect, between t and c). Realization is *nonsystematic* when a structural criterion t and the sonic or contextual criterion s or c that realizes it are functionally independent.[78] Nonsystematic realization is represented as coincidence between two functionally independent criteria from different domains: S+T (for sonic and structural) and C+T (for contextual and structural) criteria.

Systematic and nonsystematic realization designate different formal relations between the contributing criteria t, and s or c. This difference does not necessarily connote greater or lesser segment strength, analytical significance, or even frequency of coincidence between the two criteria involved. Nonsystematic realization that involves a particular pair of S+T or C+T criteria can recur, even frequently, and as often, or even more often, than systematic realization by a given TS or TC criterion. What systematic versus nonsystematic realization indicates is a point of choice, and subsequent implications or reiterations of that choice: systematic realization by linked TS and TC criteria involves one choice (to link t with s or c) with a series of implications; nonsystematic realization by recurring coincident S+T or C+T criteria involves a series of choices that replicate the same result.

Systematic and Nonsystematic Realization: Illustrations and Interactions. Several excerpts from the opening of Schoenberg's Violin Concerto, op. 36 will illustrate and suggest the complexity with which systematic and nonsystematic realization, and structural and contextual criteria, can interact in music analysis.[79] Completed in 1936, the concerto is a mature twelve-tone work in which hexachordal combinatoriality plays a prominent role. Thus, in addition to contextual criteria which recognize repetitions of ordered or unordered pitch and pitch-class sets, structural criteria that assume a twelve-tone theoretic orientation are appropriate. The row of the concerto concatenates two members of SC 6-18[012578], a hexachord that can produce I-type combinatoriality. The piece opens with the row T_9P = <9A3B46017825> in mm. 1–4, divided between the violin solo and an orchestral accompaniment of viola and celli, succeeded by its combinatorial partner T_2IP = <218075BA4396> in mm. 5–8, with similar partitioning. The two rows T_9P and T_2IP dominate the

tural and contextual criteria.

After the opening succession of rows T_9P and T_2IP, the violin solo breaks into the next octave with the first hexachord of T_9P in m. 8, accompanied by the first hexachord of T_2IP in winds and lower strings. A second dramatic expansion in register occurs in m. 20, as the violin solo repeats the first hexachord of T_9P, the first three notes an octave higher than before (ex. 2.13a). The resulting repetition of the pitch-class ordering <9A3B46> in the violin solo between m. 8 and m. 20 is a product of the row structure: both hexachordal segments are supported by the linked criterion $T_{\text{row T9P ops 0–5}}C_{\text{pc <9A3B46>}}$; they associate with one another through a TC xx relation. In this case, t indicates a structural unit and corresponds to a member of HE: t indicates a row segment, which is also the row hexachord.

Structural criteria designate theoretic entities for which the orienting theory provides an interpretation, but these HEs are not necessarily *syntactic* units *privileged* by the theory. Rather, the relationship between HEs and syntactic units varies from theory to theory: in some theories all HEs are syntactic units; in others this is not the case.[80] As an example, consider the two segments <A3, B♭3, C4, D♭4> and <D4, C♯4, B3, B♭3> in m. 1 and m. 5 of the violin solo (ex. 2.13b). The two segments realize the same set of order positions (0, 1, 6, 7) of the same row form (T_9P) and therefore stand in a TC xx relation. But order positions 0, 1, 6, 7 are not consecutive: here t designates not a row segment, but one part of a two-partition of the row that is interpreted by the orienting theory but not privileged as a syntactic unit (as rows and row segments are). In the concerto, this particular two-partition inspires numerous contextual associations that suggest it may be considered a structural unit and criterion for segmentation.[81] Locally, the association between m. 1 and m. 5 is articulated by coincidence among three contextual criteria: $C_{\text{INT I<121>}}$ (repeated pitch-class intervals to within inversion, logically entailed by the repetition of order positions), $C_{\text{ip I<+1, +2, +1>}}$ (a stronger association in the more specific dimension of pitch interval, which logically entails the previous association), and $C_{\text{incl rhythm<♩.♪ₒ_♩>}}$ (repeated rhythm for the first three notes). I render the association between m. 1 and m. 5 with the linked criterion $T_{\text{row ops <0167>}}C_{\text{ip I<+1, +2, +1>}}$, in which c is the strongest contextual criterion linked to t by (indirect) logical entailment. Systematic realization by the linked TS criteria $T_{\text{row}}S_{\text{2-pitch}}$ and $T_{\text{row}}S_{\text{2-timbre}}$ also contributes.

Comparing the first two dyads in the violin solo turns up another kind of relationship (ex. 2.13c). The two dyads <A3, B♭3> and <C4, D♭4> derive from different sets of order positions (0, 1 and 6, 7, respectively); the dyads are in a TC xy relation. As in the previous example, pitch-class relationships implied by these order positions are realized as an association in pitch intervals. Thus the dyads <A3, B♭3> and <C4, D♭4> are supported by the linked criteria $T_{\text{row T9P}}$ $_{\text{ops <01>}}C_{\text{ip +1}}$ and $T_{\text{row T9P ops <67>}}C_{\text{ip +1}}$, in which c logically entails the look-alike

T$_9$P ops: 0 1 2 3   4   5   T$_9$P ops: 0 1 2   3 4 5

Example 2.13a. Schoenberg, Concerto for Violin and Orchestra op. 36, violin solo, m. 8 and m. 20

m. 1

T$_9$P ops: 0   1   6   7

m. 5

T$_2$IP ops: 0   1   6   7

Example 2.13b. Schoenberg, Concerto for Violin and Orchestra op. 36, violin solo, mm. 1–4 and mm. 5–8

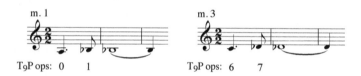

m. 1   m. 3

T$_9$P ops: 0   1   T$_9$P ops: 6   7

Example 2.13c. Schoenberg, Concerto for Violin and Orchestra op. 36, violin solo, m. 1 and m. 3

criterion for t (C$_{\text{int 1}}$). Once again, association by the functionally independent criterion C$_{\text{incl rhythm}}$ also contributes.

After a dramatic break in the orchestral texture, the violin solo returns in m. 52 with a poignant passage based on a repeated rhythm (ex. 2.13d). This rhythm articulates a trichordal partition of the row T$_9$P, followed by a trichordal partition of its retrograde, RT$_9$P. Because rhythmic repetition is functionally independent of the row structure, the realization is nonsystematic. Note, though, that repetition of pitch-class sets given by order positions {345} and {678} *is* systematic; it involves the linked criteria T$_{\text{row (R)T9P ops {345}}}C_{\text{pc {46B}}}$ and T$_{\text{row (R)T9P ops {678}}}C_{\text{pc {017}}}$.

Filtering the ordering of intervals defined by the row through certain partitions can inspire a course of motivic development. In m. 24, the oboe comes

combination of dotted rhythms and sixteenth notes (ex. 2.13e). As the oboe's dyads saturate the chromatic space from G4 to C5 in mm. 24–29, they advance a line of musical reasoning suggested by the partition of the row back in mm. 1–8 into order positions (0, 1, 6, 7) in the violin solo and (2, 3, 4, 5, 8, 9, A, B) in the orchestra that is maintained throughout the intervening bars by details of orchestration (ex. 2.13b). The oboe's dyads have diverse origins in the row structure: some realize adjacent order positions; others involve pitch-classes nonadjacent in the row or order reversals created by repeated notes. Associations among the oboe's semitone dyads derive more from compositional improvisation with a row than from systematic realization of a row; many of the dyads are instances of pure motive supported only by contextual criteria, rather than linkage or coincidence between structural and contextual criteria.

As the oboe line leads up to the return of thematic material in the violin solo in m. 32, instances of pure motive supported only by contextual criteria prepare and give way to instances of structural motive supported by structural and contextual criteria in both oboe (mm. 29–31) and violin solo (mm. 32–35) (ex. 2.13f). Recalling and embellishing the pitch-class orderings <9A01> and <21BA> first stated by the violin solo in m. 1 and m. 5 with the same ordering of pitch intervals (<+1, +2, +1>) in mm. 29–31, the oboe offers two segments in an TC xy relation (supported by criteria $T_{\text{row T9P ops <0167>}}C^{\text{ip}}_{\text{I<+1, +2, +1>}}$ and $T_{\text{row T2IP ops <0167>}}C^{\text{ip}}_{\text{I<-1, -2, -1>}}$). The segments of this pair have TC xx relations with the descending and ascending limbs of the violin line that follow in m. 32 and m. 34 (supported by $T_{\text{row T2IP ops <0167>}}C^{\text{ip}}_{\text{I<-1, -2, -1>}}$ and $T_{\text{row T9P ops <0167>}}C^{\text{ip}}_{\text{I<+1, +2, +1>}}$, respectively).

Reviewing all six illustrations (exx. 2.13a–f) and the course of events from the violin solo's opening semitone dyads, through the oboe line in mm. 24–29, to the prominent return of order positions (0, 1, 6, 7) as a structuring unit in mm. 29–35 prompts a few observations about analysis with structural and contextual criteria, systematic and nonsystematic realization, and structural and pure motive. First, the distinction between systematic and nonsystematic realization is valuable not as taxonomy, but because it allows analysts to venture into the space in which systematic and nonsystematic realization interact. A single t can be realized both ways in close proximity; any change from systematic to nonsystematic realization or vice versa inevitably involves different contextual criteria, meaning that changes in the mode of realization extend the effective associative reach of structural criteria and help to knit structural and associative organization together. Attention to consistency versus change in the means for realization can inform studies of structure and design from Schenkerian analysis of tonal music to the realization of twelve-tone arrays.

Look-alike contextual criteria are the critical link in analysis of structure and realization. Although look-alike criteria are logically entailed by structural criteria, they must have their own associative life and are therefore functionally independent. Rather than duplicate structural criteria, look-alike contextual

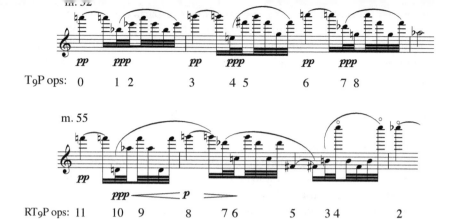

T9P ops: 0   1 2   3   4 5   6   7 8

m. 55

RT9P ops: 11   10 9   8   7 6   5   3 4   2

Example 2.13d. Schoenberg, Concerto for Violin and Orchestra op. 36, violin solo, mm. 52–57 (excerpts)

m. 24

RT9P ops: RT2IP ops:
 9   8   3   1   0   7 6   3

Example 2.13e. Schoenberg, Concerto for Violin and Orchestra op. 36, oboe, mm. 24–28

m. 29

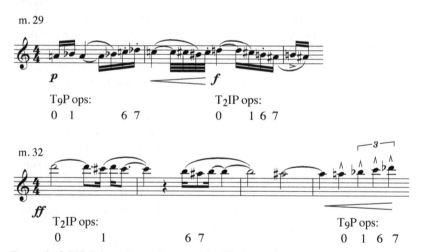

T9P ops: T2IP ops:
 0   1   6 7   0   1 6 7

m. 32

T2IP ops: T9P ops:
 0   1   6 7   0   1 6 7

Example 2.13f. Schoenberg, Concerto for Violin and Orchestra op. 36, oboe, mm. 29–31, violin solo mm. 32–35

over which aspects of music analysis shaped by a particular theoretic orientation leave the abstract realm of theory and flow out into the world of free musical associations.[82] Without look-alike contextual criteria, structure would remain but an idea; through look-alike criteria, structure inspires associative organization and becomes music.

Interactions among Individual Structural Criteria. To the extent that individual structural criteria interact with one another directly—that is, without reference to the sonic or contextual criteria necessary for realization—they do so in the abstract, as determined or suggested by the orienting theory. As with contextual criteria, interactions among structural criteria involve formal relations and relative strength; because structural criteria are concepts, not percepts, however, for them the former essentially determines the latter.

Formal relations among structural criteria are established by an orienting theory and, more specifically, by the theoretic framework (HF) that defines, organizes, and often prioritizes structural subtypes. HF can define a hierarchy of structural subtypes that indicate decreasing criterion strength, as in twelve-tone theory, where a pitch-class array can include, as successive levels of pitch organization, blocks, lyne pairs, lynes, rows, and row segments. Given two individual structural criteria from different subtypes in such a hierarchy, the relative priority of their two subtypes determines their relative strengths: criteria at deeper levels of structure that take in more events are, in an abstract sense, stronger than criteria that operate at more foreground levels and take in fewer events.[83] HF can also suggest that criteria in certain subtypes tend to cut across one another, as is the case for individual row statements and partitions of the aggregate in an all-partition array. In that case, and in the two others where the relative priority of individual structural criteria is not defined by an orienting theory (the criteria belong to the same structural subtype, or to subtypes defined by different theories of musical structure), the relative strength of individual structural criteria is undefined. Plurality of structural organization, as in the clear but often conflicting structural units given by color and talea in an isorhythmic motet, exhibits this kind of nonhierarchic relationship between structural criteria.

The strength of individual structural criteria, then, is essentially a matter of structural weight and implications. For sonic and contextual criteria, strength correlates with perceptual salience; for structural criteria, strength is an abstract property conferred by the orienting theory without reference to sounding features. Just how the abstract strength of a structural criterion relates to the *perceived* strength of its particular instantiations depends on realization—that is, on the strength of coincident sonic disjunctions or contextual associations that realize each instantiation.[84]

In an interesting twist, the strongest structural criteria—those deepest in the hierarchy of structural subtypes defined by an orienting theory—have the

structural criteria such as row segments and foreground diminutions designate short units easily realized by individual sonic or contextual criteria, those
deepest in the hierarchy, such as fundamental lines or entire pitch-class arrays,
often encompass extended passages or complete compositions. As a structural
unit takes in more sound-events and overflows the limits of short-term memory, complications arise with regard to realization.

For sonic criteria, saturation of sonic space—especially pitch (and pitch-class),
but also dynamics, timbre, and articulation—becomes an issue.[85] Over time,
individual sonic dimensions become saturated, not only by elements but also
by *intervals*—including the larger intervals that create disjunctions which could
realize structural criteria at various levels. As passage length and the number of
active structural levels increases, interval size within individual sonic dimensions
becomes less reliable as an indicator of unit strength, and coincidence among
multiple sonic, or sonic and contextual, criteria emerges as the most flexible and
compelling way to identify abstract strength with perceived strength.

For contextual criteria, saturation is usually not an issue. For one thing,
contextual dimensions typically involve many more elements (differentiated
by content and order). Also, because contextual criteria operate on the basis
of association, with frequency being an important factor in perceived strength,
the set of criteria that are active within a given subtype tends to involve a set
of elements that is fairly small relative to that of the space as a whole. What
complicates the realization of high-level structural criteria by contextual criteria is the nature of human memory. Research on memory has established
that the contents of long-term memory are constrained and structured by
the buffer length and chunking capacity of short-term memory.[86] Activated
by repetition, contextual criteria depend on memory and operate subject to
these constraints. In theory, contextual criteria might associate passages of any
length; but in fact, perception of musical association is grounded in, and created from, short units—musical "words"—that are easily stored and retrieved.
Contextual criteria that realize structural criteria deep in the hierarchy do so
not in entirety but by associating shorter units that mark the start and endpoint of the corresponding musical passage (either the start with the end of a
single unit, or the starting points of two consecutive units). Due to the nature
of short-term memory and the workings of contextual criteria, structural criteria strongest in the abstract tend not to be realized as perceptual units so
much as conceptually constructed from perceptual units.[87] Thus, high-level
structural criteria must not only be realized by sonic and contextual criteria,
but realized *differently* than are structural criteria at more foreground levels.

Interactions among Sonic, Contextual, and Structural Criteria. In practice, interactions among sonic, contextual, and structural criteria are complex and idiosyncratic; one must not mistake generalizations for rules. That said, sonic criteria

criteria. In general, one can say that sonic criteria enable segment formation, while contextual criteria select and prioritize segments according to their potential for association. Then, as we have seen, structural criteria depend on sonic and contextual criteria for realization.

This basic model has two significant complications. One involves interactions among contextual criteria, where frequency and logical entailment set up complex feedback loops. Frequency enhances strength, but strength itself often provides the cognitive incentive to use a particular contextual criterion, or those it logically entails or is entailed by, more often. So in practice, interactions among individual sonic and contextual criteria are hardly simple or successive but rather complex and integrated. The second complication lies in the relationship between structural criteria on the one hand, and sonic and contextual criteria on the other. The basic model suggests that sonic, contextual, and structural criteria work in sequence, like a series of perceptual and cognitive filters that respond first to psychoacoustic features, then to the potential for association, then to structural significance, effecting segmentation from the bottom up—from notes to groupings of notes to interpretations of groupings. But in fact, influence also flows in the opposite direction, from structural criteria to contextual and sonic criteria. The decision to adopt one theoretic orientation rather than another, or none at all, can have a profound effect on segmentation, encouraging the analyst to select certain contextual criteria and segments as analytically significant and to reject others as irrelevant or wrong.[88] Because structural criteria and look-alike contextual criteria involve the same musical spaces and elements, an analyst's choice of orienting theory with its accompanying theoretic entities and structural criteria can—even tends to— suggest, select, prioritize, and organize, *as well as interpret*, individual contextual criteria and the segments they support. Structural criteria can mitigate and even override the effect of sonic disjunctions. They can also affect the relative weights of sonic dimensions, promoting dimensions that carry structure (in most Western Classical music, usually pitch and, to a lesser extent, duration) over those that do not. In short, interactions among sonic, contextual, and structural criteria are neither uniformly bottom-up nor top-down but dynamic and interactive, with activity in each of the three domains able to affect the perceptual salience or analytic significance of activity in either of the other two.

One must also recognize that interactions among sonic, contextual, and structural criteria are influenced by the situation in which one does analysis. Music analysis can proceed from the point of view of the listener-as-receiver, where the magnitudes of disjunction in individual sonic dimensions and their coincidence or conflict with the predicable properties that underlie contextual associations are given by the composer and performer. (Note, though, that the relative weights of sonic dimensions and the choice of contextual criteria deemed to be analytically significant are not: these are still shaped by the listener's perceptual tendencies, interests, and shifts in attention.) In this situation,

locating rather than producing coincidences between structural criteria and contextual or sonic criteria.

Composing, performing, rehearsing, and silent audition from a score present different opportunities: in each case, one does not receive an acoustic stimulus but actively creates it, or its aural image. In composition and free improvisation, all interactions among sonic, contextual, and structural criteria are negotiable. In structured improvisation, such as on a North Indian raga or a jazz standard, the performer has structural units to work with, but is free to introduce sonic disjunctions and develop contextual associations that interact with structural units and with one another. In rehearsal, performance, or silent audition of a fully notated score, only sonic disjunctions are negotiable. Inflections in pitch, timing, dynamics, articulation, and tone color within limits prescribed by the notation can enhance or even introduce sonic disjunctions that privilege certain contextual associations over others or that realize particular structural units. And, it is important to remember that composition, performance, and listening are all *activities* that one engages in, not professions or identities: a single analyst can approach a piece of music as a listener or as a performer, or alternate between the two, with each shift effecting a change in how criteria in different domains interact.

Just how music analysis can, or should, inform performance is an interesting question. A directive to "bring out the structure" is simplistic and misguided, in part for reasons that become clear when one compares mechanics of realization with the performer's situation. Structural criteria can be realized by sonic or contextual criteria. But when a piece is fully notated, the performer can make adjustments only in the sonic domain; the predicable properties of groupings that underlie contextual associations are given by the score. So while the performer can enhance or introduce sonic disjunctions that highlight some contextual associations over others, she cannot change the opportunities and basis for association. Within the sonic domain, a performer's license to enhance or introduce sonic disjunctions in order to "bring out the structure" is further constrained by the grain of the notational system. In Western notation, sonic dimensions that carry structure (in much Western classical music, primarily pitch, then duration) tend to have notation that is finer-grained—that is, more specific and that admits only relatively small inflections on the part of the performer—than notation for sonic dimensions that do not carry structure (e.g., dynamics, articulation, and timbre). Thus, the performer who would follow the simple directive to "bring out the structure" risks deforming the texture of sonic disjunctions and contextual associations, and the balance between sonic dimensions that play primary and supporting roles in musical organization, indicated by the composer in the score.

A more sophisticated view of the relations among criteria, performance, and analysis must recognize two things. First, the performer can use sonic disjunctions to bring out both structural units and nonstructural associations. Second, while one's ability to hear musical structure depends on, and can be shaped

ciations that realize structural segments of significance, the nature of musical structure is conceptual and requires that the listener (consciously or subconsciously) adopt a particular theoretic stance. Performers can use disjunctions in various sonic dimensions and their coincidence with contextual associations to encourage a particular structural hearing by creating an acoustic stimulus that is consistent with it, but they cannot provide the listener with the conceptual apparatus necessary to grasp that structure. To "hear structure," a listener must adopt a theoretic orientation, translate perceived sound events into concepts defined by the theory, and organize them accordingly.

Through detailed analysis, a performer can come to use sonic disjunction strategically to articulate contextual associations and structural units that reflect his or her understanding of the piece. Rather than think of performance as an attempt to communicate an analysis, better to think of analysis as an means to refine one's understanding of just what it is that one wishes to perform—not only the notes in the score, but the many details of inflection one uses to project long-range motions, surface patterns, and special moments.

Structure and Design: A Tripartite Division. Dividing criteria into three basic types and then into various subtypes and individual criteria encourages analysts to consider diverse rationales for segmentation and how activity in one domain compares with that in another—that is, aspects of structure and design.[89] The phrase "structure and design" suggests a binary opposition. Our three basic criteria types instead suggest a tripartite division in which design has two aspects: sonic disjunction and contextual association. In addition to recognizing the possibility that structure and design can work against one another, the tripartite model—and especially the idea that structural criteria require realization by sonic or contextual criteria—supports careful study of how structure and design are connected. Once realized, structural criteria can support segments that contribute to structural organization at higher levels. Segments supported by sonic or contextual criteria contribute to sonic or associative organization, which can connect with structural organization through realization and look-alike criteria, or develop independently. The interactive workings of sonic, contextual, and structural criteria support segments, that in turn contribute to relations among sonic, associative, and structural organization at higher levels. In our progress toward those higher levels, we continue with a theoretic account of segments and segment formation.

Segments

An intriguing thing about music is that most of its objects—individual musical segments and the categories of segments we will call associative sets—form and acquire significance only in the context of individual compositions, or even sound-events) one takes to be a significant musical object in an analytic discourse. *Segmentation* refers to the process or product of object formation (not only object recognition).

Segments and segmentation are essential to virtually all music analysis.[90] Rather than a precursor to analysis, segmentation *is* analysis, at least in a preliminary and sometimes in a concerted sense. A comprehensive account of segmentation must embrace not only the groupings identified as segments but also the individual criteria, interactions among criteria, and selection of musical contexts and theoretic entities that encourage the formation of particular segments as significant musical objects.

Individual segments are supported by one or more criteria from the same or different basic types. Segments form through interactions among sonic, contextual, and structural criteria specific to the musical environment and shaped by an analyst's interests, theoretic orientation, and previous interpretive decisions. The theory of segmentation and associative organization set forth in this book proceeds from the premise that segmentation is not normative but highly context-sensitive. With its emphasis on contextual criteria and associative organization, the theory supports a careful examination of the many intratextual contexts that impinge on segmentation, and on musical organization and interpretation at higher levels.

Drawing on some pertinent connotations of the biological terms "genotype" and "phenotype," I define two kinds of segments—genosegments and phenosegments. Whereas *genotype* and *phenotype* distinguish the genetic constitution of an organism from the phenomenal manifestation of character traits (which often involves interactions between the organism and its environment), genosegments and phenosegments indicate different perceptual planes and levels of music analysis. Together with the idea of the genotype (a set of criteria that supports a phenosegment), genosegments and phenosegments help analysts to recognize and track the individual and cumulative contributions of sonic, contextual, and structural criteria in segmentation.

Genosegments

A *genosegment* or *genoseg* is a *potentially perceptible* grouping of notes (or sound-events) supported by *exactly one* sonic or contextual criterion, which can realize a structural criterion. In other words, a genoseg can be supported by one criterion of type S or C, one criterion of the linked types TS or TC, or two criteria representing types S+T or C+T. Put differently, a genoseg corresponds to the *instantiation* of one criterion of types S, C, TS, or TC, or with coincident instantiations of two criteria of types S+T or C+T. Whereas "instantiation" identifies a set of events as a conceptual grouping, "genoseg" indicates that the grouping is (at least) potentially perceptible and has some degree of analytical significance. The

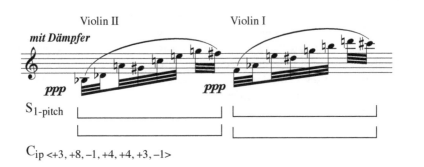

Example 2.14. Schoenberg, Second String Quartet, op. 10, IV, m. 1, sonic and contextual genosegs

strength of a genoseg is determined by, and commensurate with, the strength of the sonic and contextual criteria that define its boundaries.

Sonic criteria support sonic genosegs; contextual criteria create pairs of contextual genosegs. Individual criteria support genosegs in the dimension named by the criterion: for example, the criterion $S_{\text{1-pitch}}$ produces $S_{\text{1-pitch}}$ genosegs. A structural criterion cannot support a genoseg all by itself; it must be realized by coincidence with a sonic or a contextual criterion. (Unrealized structural criteria can be instantiated, but do not produce even the potentially perceptible units called genosegs.) In musical examples, I indicate genosegs with brackets or rings that enclose a set of notes, accompanied by the name of the supporting criterion or dimension.

Example 2.14 revisits the first measure from the fourth movement of Schoenberg's Second String Quartet, op. 10. Sonic disjunctions in $S_{\text{1-pitch}}$ mark off four $S_{\text{1-pitch}}$ genosegs (brackets below the staff); contextual associations by $C_{\text{ip} <+3, +8, -1, +4, +4, +3, -1>}$ produce four more, for a total of eight. The boundaries of the sonic genosegs coincide with those of the contextual ones, enhancing segment strength at the next (phenoseg) level. Example 2.15 returns to the first of Babbitt's *Three Compositions for Piano* for a segmentation of mm. 1–2 and m. 9 at the

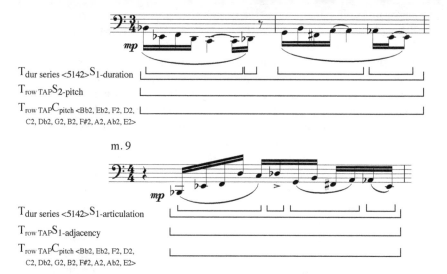

Example 2.15. Babbitt, *Three Compositions for Piano*, I, mm. 1–2, structural genosegs. © 1957 by Boelke-Bomart, Inc., Hillsdale, New York. Reproduced with permission.

genoseg level. Both excerpts yield a sequence of four genosegs that articulate the duration series <5142>; the structural criterion $T_{\text{dur series }<5142>}$ is realized systematically in both cases, but the sonic components of the linked TS criteria differ ($S_{\text{1-duration}}$ in m. 1–2 and $S_{\text{1-articulation}}$ in m. 9). In mm. 1–2 and again in m. 9, two more genosegs indicate systematic realization of the pitch-class row in entirety. Here again, the sonic components of the linked TS criteria differ, but the contextual criterion that indicates the repeated pitch ordering (which logically entails $C_{\text{pc }<A352017B6984>}$, the look-alike criterion for *t*) is the same.

Phenosegments

Interactions among genosegments give rise to phenosegments. A *phenosegment* or *phenoseg* is a *readily perceptible* segment—the usual denotation of the unqualified term "segment" in music analysis and in this book. A phenoseg is supported by *at least one* sonic or contextual criterion; structural criteria may or may not be involved. In other words, a phenoseg can be supported by *one or more* criteria of types S or C, TS or TC, or by two criteria of types S+T or C+T, acting alone or in coincidence with any number of other criteria. Put differently, a phenoseg is a readily perceptible unit identified with a single genoseg or, far more often, with two or more coincident genosegs supported by criteria of types S, C, TS, TC, S+T, or C+T. As noted in chapter 1, the relationship

Every phenoseg has a *genotype*. The genotype of a phenoseg x, written $G(x)$, is the set of sonic, contextual, and perhaps also structural criteria that support its coincident genosegs. Focusing on criteria in one of the three domains, one can also speak of a phenoseg's *sonic genotype* ($SG(x)$), *contextual genotype* ($CG(x)$), or *structural genotype* ($TG(x)$). The contextual genotype is, essentially, the set of properties predicable of a phenoseg that serve as relational properties in a particular musical context. Contextual genotypes are essential to the concepts of the associative set and common set discussed in chapter 3.

Phenosegs can be identified by circling notes in a score. If no criterion is specified, the notes circled must represent a phenoseg. One can also notate phenosegs as score excerpts; however, these can differ from a printed score in two respects. One is the selection of content: a phenoseg can show notes that are not temporally adjacent in the score as if they were adjacent (it can omit intervening notes). The other involves the representation of content: beaming, stem direction, location of dynamics, and other notational details can all be adjusted for ease of reading those events that contribute to the phenoseg as a coherent unit.

Phenosegs form on the basis of strength and (usually also) coincidence among underlying genosegs. When the boundaries of a sonic genoseg are articulated by very strong disjunctions, a single genoseg can produce a readily perceptible unit or phenoseg. (Rarely, however, does a contextual genoseg form a phenoseg without coincident sonic support.) Usually, however, phenosegs involve coincidence among two or more genosegs. Two genosegs are *coincident* if they recognize exactly the same grouping of sound-events but are supported by different criteria; else, they are *noncoincident*.[91] When genosegs coincide, they assert and reinforce the same perceptual boundaries; if these boundaries are strong relative to others in the immediate vicinity, the coincident genosegs tend to form a readily perceptible unit—a phenoseg.

Example 2.16a shows an excerpt from the "Agnus Dei" of J. S. Bach's Mass in B Minor; genosegs in the dimensions $S_{\text{1-duration}}$, $S_{\text{1-pitch}}$, $S_{\text{1-rest}}$, $C_{\text{SD int}}$, C_{rhythm}, and C_{pitch} are bracketed in the violin and alto solo lines of mm. 9–12 and 13–15. Within the contextual subtypes indicated, some individual criteria change at m. 13; some criteria in mm. 9–12 and 13–15 involve inclusion. In mm. 9–12, disjunctions in $S_{\text{1-duration}}$ produce fairly strong genosegs that coincide with those indicated by associations in $C_{\text{SD int}}$ and C_{rhythm}; in mm. 13–15, genosegs in $S_{\text{1-pitch}}$ and $S_{\text{1-rest}}$ or $S_{\text{1-duration}}$ coincide with those in C_{rhythm} and are compatible with four C_{pitch} genosegs. Coincidence among sonic and contextual genosegs in mm. 9–12 and in mm. 13–15 suggests formation of the phenosegs shown in example 2.16b. The result is a segmentation that accounts for every note in the violin and alto lines from m. 9 into m. 15 as part of one and only one phenoseg.[92]

Example 2.16a. J. S. Bach, Mass in B Minor, BWV 232, "Agnus Dei," mm. 9–15: Genosegs in violins and alto solo

Example 2.16b. J. S. Bach, "Agnus Dei," phenosegs in violins and alto solo

or even intersect.[93] Noncoincident genosegs that do intersect (share one or more notes) can do so in two ways: *embedding* and *overlap*. Both embedding and overlap influence phenoseg formation; their interactions with coincidence can affect segmentation various ways.

Two genosegs intersect by embedding when the set of notes recognized by one genoseg is a proper subset of that recognized by the other and the two genosegs share a boundary in time or pitch. Genosegs related by embedding are *compatible*. Compatible genosegs assert and reinforce a shared boundary; like coincidence, compatibility encourages phenoseg formation.

Two genosegs intersect by overlap (but do not embed) if they share one or more notes but no boundary. Overlapping genosegs cut across one another; neither coincident nor compatible, overlapping genosegs *conflict*. Depending on the relative strength of the criteria involved, genoseg conflicts range from mild to intense, in which case the genosegs effectively cancel one another out of perception. Conflict among genosegs discourages phenoseg formation.

Coincidence and conflict are complementary forces that promote and inhibit phenoseg formation and affect the strength of a segmentation overall. Consider the oboe solo that opens the second movement of Stravinsky's *Symphony of Psalms* (1930) (ex. 2.17). Throughout mm. 1–4, $S_{1\text{-duration}}$ conflicts with $S_{1\text{-pitch}}$, while $S_{1\text{-articulation}}$ alternately coincides and conflicts with both criteria. Taking contextual criteria into account clarifies things at the start: the initial repetition of pitch ordering <C5, E♭5, B5, D5> sets up two fairly strong phenosegs in mm. 1–2 (in effect reinforcing sonic disjunctions in duration over those in pitch) and a third following the rest in m. 3. But when the repetition

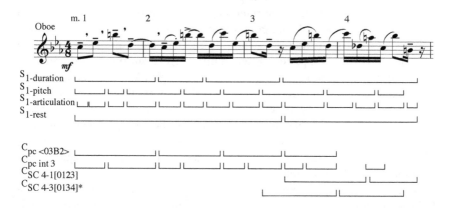

*Repetition of pcsegment <03B2> in mm. 1–3 makes all imbricated tetrachords members of SC 4-3[0134]. Here I show only the stronger pcsegment criterion, but note members of SC 4-3[0134] in mm. 3–4, where a new member of the set-class appears.

Example 2.17. Stravinsky, *Symphony of Psalms*, II, mm. 1–4, conflicting genosegs

$C_{SC\ 4\text{-}1[0123]}$ and $C_{SC\ 4\text{-}3[0134]}$, segmentation disintegrates into ambiguity. Rather than produce one clear segmentation, genoseg conflicts set up a delicate balance among multiple segmentations, putting listeners in the position of having to find their way through the passage each time rather than repeatedly enact a single definitive hearing.[94] This situation contrasts sharply with that at the start of the first movement, where coincidence among strong sonic disjunctions in $S_{1\text{-rest}}$, $S_{1\text{-timbre}}$, and $S_{1\text{-pitch}}$, reinforced by contextual associations among instances of the "Psalms chord" and of octatonic figuration in the oboe, creates clear segments with indisputable boundaries.

So when will a particular genoseg, or set of coincident genosegs, rise above the background noise of competing genosegs as a readily perceptible phenoseg? This is a question without a general answer: phenoseg formation is not a science governed by laws and prediction, but an aspect of music analysis subject to interpretation. But while there are no hard and fast rules, one can make some useful generalizations about phenoseg formation and the strength of a segmentation overall. Individual phenosegs almost always have support in the sonic domain; most also have at least some coincident support in the contextual domain. Whereas coincidence among genosegs enhances phenoseg strength, conflict diminishes it. So there is a positive correlation between the number of coincident genosegs and phenoseg strength.[95] However, there is also an important caveat: phenoseg strength depends not just on the number of supporting criteria, but also on the relative *strengths* of these criteria in the musical context under consideration (subject to the many contingencies among individual criteria and context noted earlier).[96] So phenoseg strength is necessarily subjective to some degree, as is the overall strength and clarity of a segmentation comprised of phenosegs. Two considerations in this regard are the completeness and configuration of phenoseg boundaries. A segmentation is *complete* if it includes every note in the passage under discussion; else it is incomplete. Incomplete segmentations range from those that are virtually complete to those that are more selective, highly selective, and radically incomplete. A *clear* segmentation is comprised solely of disjoint phenosegs; segmentations become progressively ambiguous to the extent that they contain phenosegs with boundaries that overlap. All else being equal, segmentations tend to be stronger to the extent that they are complete and clear: that is, when phenosegs are disjoint, temporally adjacent, registrally contiguous, and account for nearly every note.

As the contrasting passages from *Psalms* I and II suggest, music offers a full spectrum of situations in segmentation, from surfaces that channel perception so strongly that they virtually self-organize (as in *Psalms* I) to those that remain fluid and conflicted even after many hearings (*Psalms* II). Rather than think of clear segmentation as a goal, and ambiguous segmentations as inherently frustrating or flawed, analysts should consider the possibility

sage—an emergent effect of conflict and coincidence at the genoseg level—and thus constitute an important analytical observation. One must resist the temptation to attach value judgments to what may simply be different musical situations.

Some Conceptual Aspects of Genosegments and Phenosegments

Different Perceptual Planes and Analytic Notations. Genosegs and phenosegs occupy different perceptual planes—the "potentially perceptible" and the "readily perceptible." Genosegs are potentially perceptible in the sense that they zero in on a single musical dimension; listening on the genoseg plane requires a sharp mental fix on activity in one dimension and an ability to effectively disregard activity in all other dimensions. Performers exercise this skill when they work out problems with intonation (pitch), articulation, balance (dynamics), or timing (duration). But listening on the genoseg plane requires a concerted effort. To focus on one dimension and disregard others goes against the grain of experience in which multidimensional sound-events continuously interact with one another and with their musical contexts. More often we listen holistically, on the phenoseg plane, assimilating the contributions of multiple dimensions and genosegs and balancing these against one another in real time to produce a set of phenosegs or "readily perceptible" sound-objects.

Representing these different perceptual planes in Western music notation turns out to be trickier than one might think. The problem is that our notational system renders even musical dimensions that are functionally independent, like pitch and time, notationally *inter*dependent: to notate pitch (or attack time) we place a *duration* symbol higher or lower on a staff (or left to right on the page). Standard notation can represent the holistic music perceptions modeled by phenosegs. But to represent perception on the genoseg plane, we must first isolate the dimension in which segmentation occurs. We can do this by naming the dimension as part of a criterion subtype or individual criterion, then enclosing the notes that contribute to the genoseg within brackets or rings.

Levels of Analysis. To represent these different perceptual planes, genosegs and phenosegs appear at different levels of the general theory, where levels indicate logical priority and realms of potential interaction as outlined in chapter 1. Each phenoseg involves at least one genoseg; thus genosegs are logically prior to, and reside at a lower level than, phenosegs.[97] Two segments interact directly only if they reside at the same level: genosegs interact with genosegs (and form phenosegs); interactions among phenosegs contribute to sonic, associative, and structural organization.

phenoseg formation. Empiric studies and computer models of music perception often take this point of view. Activity on the genoseg level relates to that on the phenoseg level as cause and effect; phenosegs become the focal level, with genosegs seen as subordinate, supportive, and explanatory. But the genoseg and phenoseg levels need not be thought of this way.

Unlike empiric studies in music perception or computer modeling, music analysis need not manufacture segments; instead it explores them. Analysts can take the phenosegs they hear *as if* given. But they cannot take them for granted: analytical interpretations—including segmentations—differ from listener to listener. In music analysis, phenoseg formation is *contingent on* the sound-surface, not determined by it. Individual phenosegs are not fixed sound-objects, independent of context or an "observer," but conditioned perceptions that arise at a particular intersection of musical circumstances and analytical attention. When we think of music analysis in this way, activity on the genoseg level becomes important in its own right, not to explain but to *interpret* or *elucidate* activity on the phenoseg level. Analysis on the genoseg level inquires into the constitution of individual phenosegs and the particular conjunction of circumstances that shape each one into a sound-object. When ambiguous or vague phenoseg boundaries, or an inability to identify phenoseg boundaries, confounds analysis, a tactical move from the phenoseg to the genoseg level can bring the analyst behind the scenes where analysis can resume: ambiguity at the phenoseg level is often (but not always) underlain by clear but conflicting segments on the genoseg level. The analyst who works on both the genoseg and phenoseg levels recognizes the value of complementary points of view: coincidence among genosegs that promotes phenoseg formation, and conflict that inhibits it.[98] Much as in Schenkerian analysis, it is the *interactions* among levels, and the interpretation of units at higher levels in terms of activity at lower levels, that is of interest—not the content or activity of any one level in isolation.

Genosegs, Phenosegs, Genotypes: Useful Connotations from the Biological Terms. To bring this theoretical discussion of segments to a close, we review some of the distinctions between phenosegs and genosegs and relate these to connotations of the biological terms "phenotype" and "genotype." Phenotype is defined as "the observable characteristics of an organism as determined by the interaction of its genotype and its environment" and genotype as "the particular alleles at specified locations present in an individual; the genetic constitution."[99] Like phenotypes, phenosegs involve an appearance; like genotypes, genosegs pertain to its underlying constitution. Like phenotypes and genotypes, phenosegs and genosegs reside on different planes of perception. A phenotype indicates an "observable characteristic"; a phenoseg, a "readily perceptible" segment. Through genome mapping, some genes have

traditional Mendelian genetics): a specialist with an electron microscope can locate certain individual genes as particular segments in the DNA sequence of a chromosome. But, as with genosegs, such highly directed perception is not the norm; both individual genes in the genotype and individual genosegs are potentially perceptible, but not readily perceptible.

Phenotypes and genotypes, and phenosegs and genosegs, also correlate with different levels of analysis. Genes interact with genes at the level of the genotype; characters interact with characters and environment at the level of the phenotype. Significantly, interlevel relations between genotype and phenotype, and between genosegs and phenosegs, are complex. Both are predominantly many-to-one, and neither is straightforward cause and effect. In biology, the phenotypic expression (observable effect) of genetic material is influenced by interactions among genes and between genetic material and the environment. Similarly, phenoseg formation involves genoseg interactions that can be complex and context-sensitive, shaped by the activity and relative strengths of individual criteria in a particular musical context—including, most notably, contextual criteria.

The role of environment and context in phenotypes and phenosegs renders interlevel relations between phenotypes and genotypes, and between phenosegs and genosegs, nonreductive and supervenient.[100] Like many interlevel relations among concepts and entities in biology and ecology, phenotype supervenes on, rather than reduces to, genetic material. Similarly, phenosegs cannot be reduced to sets of genosegs or their supporting criteria. A phenoseg is a holistic perception, an emergent—rather than collective—sound-object.

Orientations, Criteria, Segments: Analytical Illustrations

We now move on to a series of analytic illustrations that exercise various aspects of the conceptual framework we have developed thus far. My goals here are more broad than specific: focusing on a few points of interest in each passage, I will show how one can use aspects of the theory to draw analytic attention to distinctive features and, in some cases, to suggest how thinking in terms of orientations, criteria, and segments can fundamentally alter the way one thinks about music and music analysis. These illustrations are organized in two sets: the first four (exx. 2.18–2.21) focus on sonic and contextual criteria; the rest (exx. 2.22–2.28), on interplay between contextual and structural criteria.

In a great deal of music, $S_{1\text{-pitch}}$ and $S_{1\text{-duration}}$ are primary sonic dimensions for segmentation. But, like other individual criteria, their influence depends on musical context—specifically, on the cumulative effect of conflict or coincidence among genosegs in many other sonic and contextual dimensions.

case study and a reminder that analysts need to remain open to questioning assumptions about the roles that particular sonic and contextual criteria play in segmentation and about the nature of music analysis.

Mixed Accents is a short piece (about ninety seconds in performance) that consists of a single roiling run of sixteenth-notes from the piano's lowest register to its highest and back. This large-scale arch contour divides into five "measures," spans demarcated by barlines and rests that vary in length from 53 (m. 5) to 329 (m. 3) sixteenth-notes. Example 2.18 shows m. 1; here uniform sixteenth-notes and smooth transitions in dynamics eliminate disjunctions in $S_{\text{1-duration}}$ and $S_{\text{1-dynamics}}$. Neither pitch nor any other sonic dimension distributes values among discernible "registers" as would be necessary to activate S_2 criteria. With pitch intervals ranging from one to eleven semitones, $S_{\text{1-pitch}}$ is active but weak compared to $S_{\text{1-articulation}}$, the "mixed accents" of the title that create a series of aperiodic groupings reinforced visually by beams. Marking off twelve groupings of two to six sixteenth-notes in m. 1, $S_{\text{1-articulation}}$ immediately assumes the role of a primary sonic criterion. All but one of the largest pitch intervals (eight or more semitones) in m. 1 appear within, rather than between, $S_{\text{1-articulation}}$ genosegs, setting up a conflict between $S_{\text{1-articulation}}$ and $S_{\text{1-pitch}}$ that persists throughout the piece.

Attempts to continue analysis in the contextual domain are immediately thwarted by the near-lack of repetition. In *The Music of Ruth Crawford Seeger*, Joseph Straus identifies some principles of melodic construction in Crawford's music. First on the list is nonrepetition, central to the theories of Charles Seeger, with whom Crawford then studied. Straus gives m. 1 of *Mixed Accents* as an example. A look at activity in the contextual dimensions of set class and contour backs up his claim. As Straus points out, pitch adjacencies include instances of all six interval classes (ics) and eleven of the twelve trichord types. Within the ic gamut there is a definite emphasis on ics 1 and 3 (which together account for 29 of 53 intervals), reflected at the trichord level in the frequencies of SCs 3-2[013] and 3-3[014] (20 of 52 imbricated trichords). The intervallic profiles of the twelve SCs for genosegs captured by $S_{\text{1-articulation}}$ are more diverse. Some set classes are saturated by ic 1 (groupings 1 and 2, members of SCs 6-1[012345] and 5-2[01235], respectively), while others have flat interval class vectors (groupings 7 and 9 are the all-interval tetrachords 4-Z15[0146] and 4-Z29[0137]; grouping 3 is a member of SC 5-18, with the ICV [212221]— maximally flat for a pentachord).[101] Analysis of contour (Seeger's "neumes") using the contour reduction algorithm developed by Robert Morris yields comparable variety but a more even distribution: the twelve groupings include all four contour primes with three elements (with multiplicities of 1, 2, 2, 3) and three of the six primes with four elements.

To the analyst who seeks repetition as the basis for association, contextual segmentation, and analytical significance, the range and distribution of

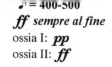

Example 2.18. Crawford, *Piano Study in Mixed Accents*, m. 1

elements in set class and contour space seems to be an analytical dead end. But if we shift analytic attention away from repetition as a desideratum and cultivate our curiosity about segment formation and inhibition, the fact that the piece covers the gamut of ics, trichord types, intervallic profiles, and contour primes in various approximations of an even distribution itself becomes an important discovery. Summarizing his discussion of principles of melodic construction in Crawford's music, Straus refers to a "series of strategies of avoidance."[102] Taking this insight a step further, we might ask *what*, exactly, is avoided, and to what end?

the piece is not just particular elements (set classes, contours) heard most recently, but the segmenting effect of repetition.[103] Repetition activates contextual criteria; by avoiding repetition, she effectively disables contextual criteria as a force in segmentation, much as the homogeneous sixteenth-notes, smooth dynamic transitions within each measure, and inability to invoke stream segregation for pitches, durations, or dynamics disable many sonic criteria. It is in this context that $S_{1\text{-articulation}}$—often a relatively minor aspect of musical organization—emerges as the primary criterion for segmentation in *Mixed Accents*, churning out a stream of clear genosegs that rise above the meager competition to become phenosegs.

The fact that most sonic and contextual criteria in *Mixed Accents* actively resist or inhibit segmentation serves a larger purpose: it promotes large-scale *continuity*. By tightly controlling the segmenting effect of most sonic disjunctions and contextual associations, Crawford focuses attention on the large-scale form, a registral arch that spans the entire piece, animated by unpredictable accents and phenoseg lengths. Placement of pitch leaps within, rather than between, groupings defined by $S_{1\text{-articulation}}$ is interesting in this regard: acting alone, without consistent coincident support from any other sonic or contextual criterion, $S_{1\text{-pitch}}$ energizes phenosegs defined by $S_{1\text{-articulation}}$ but does not fragment them or threaten linear continuity. This energizing role of $S_{1\text{-pitch}}$ has a counterpart in the contextual domain, where distributions of interval classes, trichord types, and contours are fairly even at the large scale, but undergo a series of local perturbations that emphasize one kind of sound-object, then another.[104]

What at first may have seemed to be a failure of the analytic process thus becomes, through the lens of the general theory, a portal to a different way of thinking about the piece and about music analysis in general. Approaching *Mixed Accents* in terms of orientations, criteria, genosegments, and phenosegments shifts attention from local events to the large-scale form and its sinuous path through a realm of possibilities. More generally, the Crawford study demonstrates the role that musical context plays in setting the relative weights of various sonic and contextual criteria. With typically prominent sonic criteria like $S_{1\text{-duration}}$ and $S_{1\text{-pitch}}$ suppressed relative to the usually subordinate $S_{1\text{-articulation}}$, the piece makes clear that identifying and prioritizing criteria as primary or secondary for the recognition of sound-objects is itself an important part of the analytic process.

This idea that identifying the set of criteria most critical to object formation is a task for music analysis, not prerequisite to it, is especially important for analysis of twentieth-century works that explore new musical spaces and approaches to form. In the 1950s Stockhausen composed a number of works concerned with interrelations and continuities among pitch, time, and space. One of these is *Gruppen* (1955–57), composed for three orchestras, each with

orchestra II, with 36 players, is in the center; and orchestra III, with 36 players, to the right. The piece consists of 145 "groups" (essentially, ways of handling musical material). It is serial in conception except for three inserts in which Stockhausen suspends the serial organization to make "allowance for 'sound-concepts' which otherwise could 'not be accommodated by the system.'"[105] One of the most striking sound-concepts is undoubtedly that of the brass choirs in group 119, within the third insert (groups 114–22) (ex. 2.19).[106] Bracketed by texture changes, from points uniformly apportioned among all three orchestras at group 118, to points overlaid with brass chords in orchestra II only at group 120, group 119 stands out from its surroundings.

Example 2.19. Stockhausen, *Gruppen*, start of Group 119, brass only. © 1963 by Universal Edition (London) Ltd., London/UE 13673.

dynamics ($S_{1\text{-space}}$ and $S_{1\text{-dynamics}}$).[107] Although the score may suggest a contextual criterion (the same brass chord appears in each of the three orchestras), in this case visual repetition of an image on the page does not translate to aural repetition of a sound-object in performance. For a listener surrounded by three live orchestras or nestled in stereo headphones, overlapping and masking each *ppp* chord entry with the crescendo to a *ff* cutoff of the previous entry has the effect not of repetition but of *motion*, of a *single* sound-object that *travels* around the listener in space, from one orchestra into another. What makes the passage so unusual is that a sound-object's *location* ($S_{1\text{-space}}$) has become the primary criterion for a perforated segmentation, with coincident support from $S_{1\text{-dynamics}}$. Notice that, as in *Mixed Accents* where $S_{1\text{-articulation}}$ overtakes $S_{1\text{-pitch}}$ and $S_{1\text{-duration}}$ as the primary segmenting criterion, in Stockhausen's group 119 the perceptual prominence of $S_{1\text{-space}}$ depends on tight control of other sonic and contextual dimensions. For three bars, there is no change in pitch content (disabling $S_{1\text{-pitch}}$). Once visually distinct instances of the chords are understood as *persistence* of a *moving* sound-object, $S_{1\text{-duration}}$ and all contextual criteria are disabled as well. This idea that what looks like repetition on the page can sound like motion in musical space applies not only to the literal displacement of a sound-source in three-dimensional space but also more figuratively through cross-domain mapping to "repetition at the octave" that creates "motion" up and down in pitch space, as in Chopin's Étude in C Major, op. 10, no. 1 (ex. 2.20). The idea that repetition and motion are connected also plays out in the theoretic realm, in the complementary relationship between association and transformation (discussed in chapter 10).

Example 2.20. Chopin, Étude in C Major, op. 10, no. 1, mm. 1–2

Qualities such as direction, dissolution, fluidity, and balance are among the most immediate aspects of musical experience—and the most elusive for music analysis. "How does it sound?" and "How does it work?" are, indeed, two different questions: the former is about qualities; the latter, mechanics. Music analysis engages both kinds of questions and usually proceeds on the assumption that their answers are related. To find out more about musical qualities, then, an analyst might focus on the constitution of musical perceptions—that is, on

inhibit segment formation.

Fluidity is a quality one might ascribe to the opening of "Abîme des oiseaux," the third movement from Olivier Messiaen's *Quatour pour le fin du temps* (1941). Example 2.21 (notated at concert pitch) shows the opening melodic phrase and its repetition (mm. 1–5), a fleeting melodic return six bars later (end of m. 11), and the dramatic crescendo on a sustained E5 that brings the section to a close (m. 13). Limited pitch range and the uniform *piano* dynamic in mm. 1–5 give the line a certain continuity, but "fluidity" is more than continuity—it is more like flexibility, or change *with* continuity. The line's fluidity owes more to a subtle ambiguity in the melodic repetition: Does the E4 in m. 3 end the opening melodic segment, or begin its repetition, as the counterpart to the E in m. 1? With *three* long Es (in mm. 1, 3, and 5), the passage admits both interpretations. Coincident boundaries in $S_{1\text{-duration}}$ (also $S_{2\text{-duration}}$), $S_{1\text{-articulation}}$ (the slurs), and $S_{1\text{-pitch}}$ support the first view; a perceptual disposition to hear the first note of a piece, rather than the second, as the start of a melodic unit and local reference point leans toward the second.[108] Two more sonic details contribute to the fluidity of mm. 1–5: occasional sixteenth-notes (marked by arrows) move the line forward (each sixteenth-note groups with the *following* eighth-note), and the sixteenths' placement in the line smoothes over the largest leaps in pitch (from B♭, G♯, or G down to E).

Example 2.21. Messiaen, *Quatour pour le fin du temps*, "Abîme des oiseaux" (III), mm. 1–5 and 11–13 (concert pitch)

events: the melodic repetition smuggled into the end of m. 11, and the isolated E in m. 13. For a "return," the melodic repetition in m. 11 is strangely inconspicuous and remarkably transformed, something one stumbles upon and only recognizes as such just about the time the repetition gives way to change. The unexpected quality of this return can be traced to sonic and contextual features of m. 11 and mm. 1–5. Taking advantage of the melodic ambiguity in mm. 1–5, Messiaen begins the return in m. 11 on G♯—taking the *second* note of the piece as its reference point. Within m. 11, the initial G♯ occurs within a rising contour and sonic genosegs in $S_{1\text{-pitch}}$, $S_{1\text{-articulation (breath mark)}}$, and $S_{1\text{-articulation (slur)}}$, and so it is not marked by disjunction in any sonic dimension.[109] No sooner has a listener heard enough to recognize the melodic repetition as such than it trails off into a half-measure of rest, without the final E4. What comes instead, in m. 13, is the dramatic long E5—which completes the repetition with the right pitch class, but an octave "too high."

The move to E5 in m. 13, and the note's subsequent evolution through a long, dramatic crescendo that suspends musical time, is unprecedented. Prepared in a sense, but nonetheless utterly surprising, E5 is set off from its surroundings by overwhelming coincidence among five sonic criteria: $S_{1\text{-pitch}}$, $S_{1\text{-duration}}$, $S_{1\text{-dynamics}}$, $S_{1\text{-rest}}$, and $S_{2\text{-duration}}$. A phenoseg that consists of a single note, the E5 in m. 13 is a *sonic focus (SF)*, a phenoseg rendered unusually prominent by the remarkable strength of its sonic boundaries. Usually a sonic focus involves coincidence among many sonic criteria; great magnitude in one sonic dimension can also produce a sonic focus, however. The concept of sonic focus can be applied informally; it can also be formalized as the phenoseg with boundaries that yield the highest composite sonic disjunction measure (calculated, say, by Tenney and Polansky's algorithm).

While a sonic focus is highly salient, it need not be especially significant in any other sense.[110] The E5 in m. 13, however, *is*: in a lovely resonance, it has all of the ambiguity of the E4 in m. 3. Following the melodic repetition in mm. 11–12, the distinctive E5 in m. 13 fulfills the expectation for E as a pitch-class, functioning as an end. But when the long crescendo on E and the figures first heard just after it (m. 14) *both* return starting in m. 21, incentive emerges to hear E5 as a beginning. The idea that the searing crescendo on E5 is an end *and a beginning* resonates with the program of the work: with the end of mundane existence comes a glimpse of the eternal and a bridge to the divine.

Throughout the foregoing commentaries on passages by Crawford, Stockhausen, and Messiaen, the structural domain has remained dormant. It is now time to engage it, connect structural with sonic and contextual criteria through the mechanism of realization, and consider the relationship of structure to design, structural to pure motive, and realization to perception, in some musical examples.

of rows realized as a double inversion canon. Rows in one canon unfold as a series of melodic tetrachords; these rows, starting with T_9P and T_9IP in horns II and I, constitute the main canon ("canon I"). Rows in the second canon have an embellishing function; the subsidiary canon ("canon II") begins in the harp and lower strings with T_5IP and T_1P. Within each canon, rows are related by T_6I throughout the first section (mm. 1–23).

Example 2.22 shows the first two quartets of rows, which underlie mm. 1–22 in canon I and mm. 1–16 in canon II. Within each of the four canonic voices, row succession preserves pc content for the three disjoint tetrachords. Within the main canon, the T_6I relation between T_9P and T_9IP also preserves four pc dyads: {78} (in bold type), {AB} (bold italic), {45} (underlined), and {12} (underlined italics). Each of these dyads also occurs as a pc adjacency in one of the two rows that begin the subsidiary canon (T_5IP and T_1P). Because Webern realizes the pc inversion between rows within each canon in mm. 1–23 as strict pitch inversion around the axis A220, pitches within each canon remain frozen in register throughout the opening section and the dyadic invariance composed into the row structure is easily heard as repeated pitch sets in the music.

T_5IP: 5876 A934 0*12*B T_2P: 2B01 9A43 7658 subsidiary canon, voice 1

T_9P: 9678 45***BA*** 2*1*03 T_0IP: 03*21* 54***AB*** 7896 main canon, voice 1
T_9IP: 90***BA*** 2*1*78 45*6*3 T_6P: 63*45* *1*2***87*** ***BA***90 main canon, voice 2

T_1P: 1***AB***0 8932 65*47* T_4IP: 4765 9823 B01A subsidiary canon, voice 2

Example 2.22. Webern, *Symphony*, op. 21, I, rows in main (I) and subsidiary (II) canons, mm. 1–22 and mm. 1–16, respectively, with pc-invariant dyads

For the most part, realization of the row structure is straightforward. In the contextual domain, criteria in three subtypes associate the two rows that form each canon. Strict inversion of pitch intervals effects systematic realization ($T_{row}C_{ip}$) for rows within each canon; repetition of rhythmic and articulation patterns between *dux* and *comes* provides coincident support and realization that is absolutely consistent but nonsystematic ($C_{rhythm}+T_{row}$ and $C_{articulation}+T_{row}$). In the sonic domain, patterns of timbral continuity ($S_{2\text{-timbre}}$) and change ($S_{1\text{-timbre}}$) in the main canon realize the three disjoint tetrachords of each row. In the subsidiary canon, no sonic criterion provides systematic or consistent nonsystematic realization for the corresponding tetrachords, but corresponding row segments (and the rows in entirety) are associated by timbral repetition (C_{timbre}).

Example 2.23 brings together many of the foregoing observations. Example 2.23a is a schematic representation of the row structure for mm. 1–8. The

Main canon (Canon I):

tetrachord 1

Horn I: $T_9IP_{(0-3)}$ = <90**BA**>
Horn II: $T_9P_{(0-3)}$ = <9678>

tetrachord 2
Clarinet: $T_9P_{(4-7)}$ = <45**BA**>

Subsidiary canon (Canon II):

tetrachord 1

Harp, Cello: $T_5IP_{(0-3)}$ = <5876>
Harp, Viola: $T_1P_{(0-3)}$ = <1**AB**0>

Example 2.23a. Webern, *Symphony*, op. 21, I, mm. 1–8, row structure

passage consists of the initial tetrachord from each of four rows arranged
in a double canon, plus the continuation to tetrachord 2 in voice 1 of the
main canon. Example 2.23b shows the corresponding structural segmentation. Notes in the main canon appear on the first two staves; those in
the subsidiary canon, on the third. Within each canon, stem direction distinguishes *dux* from *comes*.[111] For a listener attuned to the row structure
and aware of the significance that pitch inversion, changes of timbre, and
repeated rhythms and articulations have in the *Symphony*, the progress of
tetrachordal segments in the main canon is easy to hear. But there are
many *other* things to hear as well—associations between rows both within
and across canons, and numerous nonstructural segments supported by
various sonic and contextual criteria. Depending on the particular musical
details and their contexts, these cross-row associations and nonstructural
phenosegs can compete with, or reinforce, musical structure. To investigate the complex relation between realization and perception in this passage, then, one must set the structural segments and the criteria that realize
them back in the context of other roughly contemporaneous activity in the
sonic and contextual domains.

Recall that, in general, contextual criteria rarely form phenosegs on their
own but instead tend to select and prioritize sonic genosegs with which they
coincide. Thus even when contextual criteria are strong, the perceptual import
of realization often rests largely on edge detection or stream segregation in
the sonic domain. In mm. 1–23 of the *Symphony*, each of the three disjunct
tetrachords in each row of the main canon is systematically realized by $T_{\text{row tetrachord}}S_{\text{2-timbre}}$.[112] But for a listener unaware of the row structure and in search
of active contextual criteria, attending to continuity or change in timbre is
not quite enough to grasp (much less privilege) the structural tetrachords or

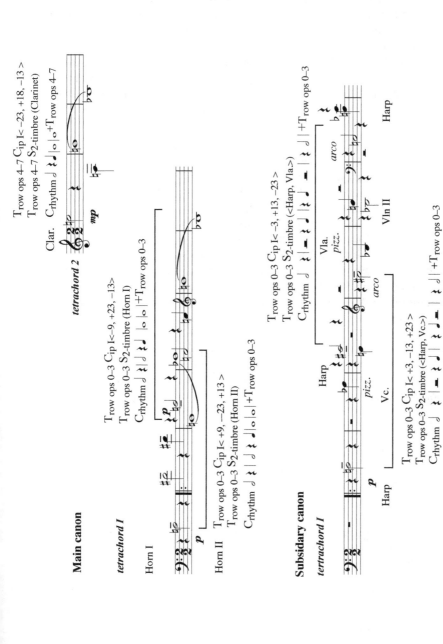

Example 2.23b. Webern, *Symphony*, op. 21, I, mm. 1–8, structural segmentation

(e.g., *both* voices of the main canon begin and end in the horns).[113] Moreover, the row structure and rules for its realization have some implications for the organization and distribution of events in the sonic domain that actually complicate the perception of musical structure. With four rows unfolding simultaneously, notes arranged in strict symmetry on either side of a pitch axis, and the low density of event-attacks per unit time, continuity by temporal adjacency ($S_{\text{1-adjacency}}$) and pitch proximity ($S_{\text{2-pitch}}$) actually cut *across* voices of the texture more often than they connect notes within a row and instrument. As a result, numerous nonstructural segments supported by these and other sonic criteria also emerge.

Example 2.24 shows some nonstructural segments supported by sonic and contextual criteria in mm. 1–6. Attending to attack order ($S_{\text{1-adjacency}}$) and length ($S_{\text{2-duration}}$ ($\downarrow$)) groups the first three notes of the piece, <A3, F♯4, F3>, into a segment that crosses rows, canons, and instruments. Using pitch proximity ($S_{\text{2-pitch}}$) supplemented by duration ($S_{\text{2-duration}}$) as primary criteria for sonic segmentation gives the second segment shown, <A3, F♯4, A3, A♭3>, which stays in the horns but crosses from voice 1 to voice 2 of the main canon. The third segment, which begins on B4 in horn I and continues with E5 in the clarinet across voices and timbres of the main canon, illustrates a situation in which note-attributes that are marked in a particular context can draw the listener's attention and thereby induce a sense of connection and impression of grouping. In this case, two note-attributes of E5—pitch height and timbre—are marked in the

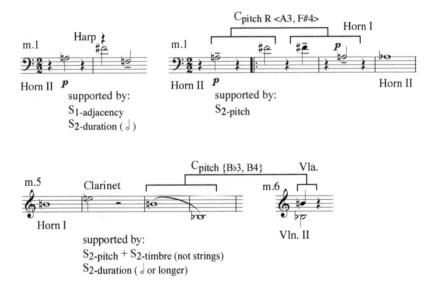

Example 2.24. Webern, *Symphony*, op. 21, I, five nonstructural segments in mm. 1–6

to B4 according to the row, B♭3 in horn I, becomes an inner voice) and introduces a new timbre that, at *mezzo piano*, easily projects over the *piano* horn I and strings. Assessing the relative strength of these or any other nonstructural sonic segments in the passage compared to the structural segments given by tetrachords in canon I is for each individual listener to decide, but suffice it to say that sonic features of the passage do create perceptual competition between structural and nonstructural segments.

Further competition between structural and nonstructural segments and ways of hearing the *Symphony*'s opening section exist in the contextual domain in that motivic associations, often seeded by the row structure, frequently *cross* between rows and canons, or involve nonstructural segments. As in the sonic domain, the resultant complexity with regard to realization and perception is, to an extent, set up by the row structure and the means for its realization: frozen register affiliated with the inversion canon promotes associations by C_{pitch} among structural pc-invariant dyads that belong to different rows, and nonstructural segments that form the same pitch set by drawing individual notes from two or more rows.

In contrast to example 2.22, which showed the first two quartets of rows in the abstract, example 2.25a is a pitch-class map for mm. 1–16 that shows the order of note entry across all four lines of the double canon. Bold type highlights clusters of notes from the pc-invariant dyads {78} and {AB} in mm. 3–10 and the pcset {456} in mm. 11–16.[114] Example 2.25b shows seven corresponding segments associated by repetition of pc (or pitch) dyads {78} and {AB}, along with coincident sonic and, where relevant, structural criteria. Six structural segments include four dyads marked by pitch repetition (<B4, B♭3> and <G2, A♭3>) of slurred whole notes in the main canon. The subsidiary canon contributes two *pizzicato* dyads that involve the same pitches in the reverse order (<B♭3, B> and <A♭3, G2>), along with one nonstructural segment, the simultaneity {B♭3, B4} in m. 6 formed by violin II and viola. Different line weights connect instances of {78} and of {AB} (and foreshadow association graphs, introduced in chapter 3). Layout approximates a cutaway score, showing the embellishing role of the dyads in canon II, each tucked inside the time span of an associate in canon I. These seven segments create a web of associations within which various individual sonic and contextual criteria contribute to the interplay among pc-invariant dyads, cross-row associations, and nonstructural segments.

While the dyadic associations in example 2.25b reinforce select aspects of the row structure, associations among the four trichordal segments in example 2.25c also reach outside the row structure through the workings of look-alike contextual criteria. Referencing instances of the pcset {456} boldfaced in example 2.25a, example 2.25c shows one structural segment and three nonstructural segments, all associated by repetition of the pitch set {F3, F♯4, E5} (C_{pitch} {F3, F♯4, E5}) in mm. 11–16. The first and most prominent of these is the viola's

m.: |1 |2 |3 |4 |5 |6 |7 |8 |9 |10 |11 |12 |13 |14 |15 |16

Main canon (Canon I)
T$_9$P, T$_0$IP   9|6 |7 |8 | |4 5|B |A |2 | |10 | |3 |2 |1 | |5| **4** |
T$_9$IP, T$_6$P | |9 |10 |B |A | |2 1|7 |**8** |**4** | |**5**|**6** | |3 |14 5|

T$_5$IP, T$_2$P | 5| **8**| **7**| 6 | A | {93}| 4 | 0 | 1 | | 2|B 0| 1 | |9 A**4**| 3 | **76**
T$_1$P, T$_4$IP | | | 1| **A**| **B** | 0 | 8 | {93}| 2 | **6** |**5** | **4**| 17 | **6**| 5 |
Subsidiary canon (Canon II)

Example 2.25a. Webern, *Symphony*, op. 21, I, pitch-class map of main and subsidiary canons, mm. 1–16

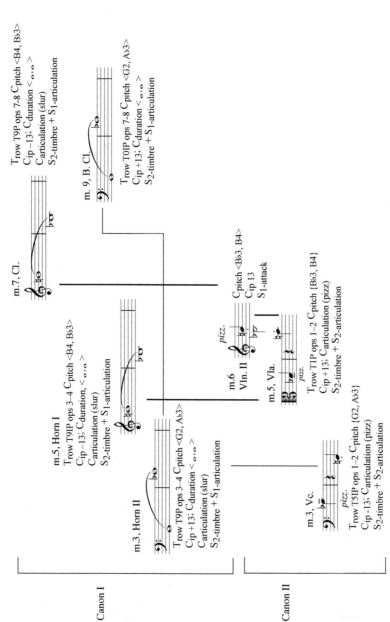

Example 2.25b. Webern, *Symphony*, op. 21, I, structural segments and a nonstructural segment associated by pc-invariant dyads {78} and {BA}, mm. 3–10

Example 2.25c. Webern, *Symphony*, op. 21, I, structural and nonstructural segments associated by pc set {456}, mm. 11–16

melodic line <E5, F3, F♯4> (m. 11), a structural segment terminated by a rest ($S_{1\text{-rest}}$) that lifts three of the four order positions (ops 8–A) from tetrachord 3 of T_9IP in the main canon (also, due to linkage between successive rows, op 0 of T_6P). This structural segment becomes the seed for associations with three nonstructural segments in mm. 11–15. Its strongest tie is to the segment in mm. 15–16, which repeats the pitch ordering <E5, F3, F♯4> as a set of successive attacks in the clarinet, viola, and harp (plus an intervening grace note, G2). The same three pitches occur as an unordered set in mm. 11–12 and in m. 14; the second of these segments also involves three instruments, and both use $S_{1\text{-attack}}$ as the criterion for segmentation. In all three of the nonstructural segments, temporal alignment of notes contributed by different row forms is critical to the association and to segment formation (and perhaps explains why canon II exhibits more variation in note values and in the distribution of rests and articulations than canon I).

To summarize the foregoing observations on row structure, realization, sonic and contextual criteria, and structural and nonstructural segments in mm. 1–16, even though a listener *can* trace entire rows presented as disjunct tetrachords in canon I by focusing on the right criteria, the passage readily admits other hearings. These include: (1) a shift from one set of motivic associations supported by the row structure to another (pitch realizations of the dyads {78} and {AB} in mm. 3–10), and then to a third (focused on the pitch set {F3, F♯4, E5} in mm. 11–16); (2) assorted local connections between structural and nonstructural segments; and (3) even a quasi-statistical hearing of the passage as an evolving texture, in which individual segments are not at issue. What a listener hears as the strongest segmentation may or may not express the underlying structure. The complex relationship between realization and perception can be expressed with an analogy: realization is to perception as genosegs are to phenosegs. Realization is a set of enabling circumstances at the genoseg level. Perception usually takes place at the phenoseg

tors: the relative salience of structural versus nonstructural segments in the music at hand, and the listener's active engagement of the orienting theory that underlies realization.

The Webern *Symphony* illustrates one scenario, where the realization of structure is partially submerged or even engulfed by the workings of competing sonic and contextual criteria. The orchestral exposition that begins the first movement of Beethoven's Piano Concerto No. 1 in C major, op. 15 offers a complementary case study. Example 2.26 provides a score for mm. 1–16. Here the segmentation couldn't be clearer. While the homophonic texture ($S_{1\text{-attack}}$) defines a series of harmonic segments, $S_{1\text{-rest}}$ marks off four four-bar melodic segments in violin I (and across the ensemble); the first two of these subdivide in m. 2 and m. 6. Coincident contextual criteria support this sonic segmentation of the melody: repetition of its pitch and rhythmic material (C_{melody} and C_{rhythm}) associates (and thus demarcates) mm. 1–4 and mm. 5–8, while C_{rhythm} ♩♩♩ also associates mm. 1 and 5 with mm. 9 and 13, setting up a regular four-bar hypermeter. Structural criteria ($T_{\text{RN} <I, V>}$ and $T_{\text{RN} <V, I>}$) join mm. 1–4 and mm. 5–8 in an antecedent-consequent relation to create an eight-bar phrase, while melodic contingency between m. 8 and m. 16 (scale degree 3 vs. 1) binds mm. 1–8 and 9–16 into an even larger phrase.

A durational reduction (ex. 2.27a) underlines the parallelism between the stepwise move from C to D in mm. 1–4 and D to E in mm. 5–8. But the underlying voice leading tells a different story (ex. 2.27b). Whereas design (represented in the durational reduction), parcels out four melodic events among four two-bar hypermeasures in mm. 1–8, voice leading recognizes only three melodic events—an ascent from C through D to E. Reading this third as an initial ascent to the head tone of a fundamental line places emphasis on the final E, which we can represent with the structural criterion $T_{\text{3PRG, C: }<(12)\ 3>}$.[115] Given the clarity of the segmentation, the rationale for hearing this structural segment turns out to be surprisingly complex.[116] First, realization of the structural criterion $T_{\text{3PRG, C: }<(12)\ 3>}$ hinges on the coincidence among $S_{1\text{-rest}}$, C_{melody}, and C_{rhythm} that sets mm. 1–4 and 5–8 off as four-bar units with C, D, D, and E as start- and endpoints. But since these notes are nonadjacent in the music, the listener needs another reason to extract and associate them as part of a single structural segment. Whereas in the Webern linked TS and TC criteria provide systematic realization of the three tetrachordal row segments as musical segments, no linked criterion does the job here. Neither $T_{\text{3PRG, C: }<(12)\ 3>}S_{2\text{-pitch}}$ nor $T_{\text{3PRG, C: }<(12)\ 3>}S_{2\text{-timbre}}$ isolates the notes in question. An attempt to formulate a linked TC criterion fails in an illuminating way: although the stepwise motions from C to D in mm. 1–4 and D to E in mm. 5–8 are associated by $C_{\text{SD int 2}}$, their structural interpretations differ.

Despite the apparent transparency of the structural segment in this simple musical passage, it turns out that realization is actually less straightforward

Example 2.26. Beethoven, Piano Concerto No. 1 in C Major, op. 15, I, mm. 1–16

than in the Webern and that the orienting theory (now Schenkerian theory) is more proactive. First, Schenkerian theory provides a repository of HEs that include the concept of a third progression; its HF lays out a theory of structural levels that justifies the extraction. The theory also provides the means to distill the four start- and endpoints of the antecedent-consequent design to three, conflating the two Ds in m. 4 and m. 5 into a single conceptual event—a passing-tone D. The theory then prioritizes the three tones in a certain kind of HE

(b) Voice leading sketch

Example 2.27. Beethoven, Piano Concerto No. 1 in C Major, op. 15, I, mm. 1–16, durational reduction and voice-leading sketch

(an "initial ascent")—E, then C, then D, contradicting the association by C_{SD} int 2 and parallel design of C–D (in mm. 1–4) and D–E (mm. 5–8).

Interplay between structure and design shifts from competition to cooperation as the larger-scale phrase continues in mm. 9–16. The move to IV in m 9 is marked by a register shift ($S_{1\text{-pitch}}$) and a change in the rhythm of the melody (the sixteenth-note flourish disappears) that separates m. 8 from m. 9, and allies mm. 9–12 with mm. 13–16. Measure 9 begins a parenthetical expansion of the E reached in m. 8 by a neighbor note F, itself embellished by its upper third. Resumption of the lower register in m. 13 announces the end of the parenthesis, drawing attention to the D that connects the E in m. 8 with the C that completes a local descent in m. 16.[117]

Sometimes the workings of sonic, contextual, and structural criteria set up a dramatic conflict between structure and design. Example 2.28a shows the opening of the Sarabande from J. S. Bach's Suite No. 5 in C Minor for Violoncello Solo. In mm. 1–2, coincident segmentations by $S_{1\text{-pitch}}$, $S_{1\text{-dura-tion}}$, and $C_{\text{cseg <43120>}}$, bolstered by the compatible criterion $C_{\text{SDintq <-M3, -d4, +m2>}}$ that recognizes the first four notes of each bar as a genoseg, suggest two phenosegs, each one bar long (ex. 2.28b). Neither segment is a prolongation; each is an instance of pure motive, an aspect of design that is repeated twice more (with slightly different associations) within a melodic descent of a third from G to E♭ over the course of mm. 1–4 (ex. 2.28c). Bach's placement of the A♭ in m. 1 in the low register is noteworthy in two respects.

Example 2.28a. J. S. Bach, Sarabande from Suite No. 5 in C Minor for Violoncello Solo, BWV 1011, mm. 1–8

Each phenoseg is supported by: $S_{1\text{-pitch}}$, $S_{1\text{-duration}}$, $C_{\text{cseg} \langle 43120 \rangle}$, and incl $C_{\text{SDintq}} \langle -M3, -d4, +m2 \rangle$

Example 2.28b. Two phenosegs in mm. 1–2

Example 2.28c. Voice leading in mm. 1–4

First, it secures the association via $C_{\text{cseg} \langle 43120 \rangle}$; second, it suggests a connection between the A♭ in m. 1 and the B♮ in m. 2 (supported by $S_{2\text{-pitch}}$ and $S_{2\text{-duration}}$). But the connection is associative, not structural: the augmented second between A♭ and B♮ violates a fundamental principle of voice leading. The quandary is resolved in m. 3, as A♭ moves up to the tenor range where it gives way to G3 and B♮2 falls to G2 in the bass, providing enough context to untangle the voice leading into normative form. Looking at the use of the diminished fourth in this passage prompts another observation. The diminished fourth occurs once in each of the first four bars, always from the second eighth-note to the third. Contextual associations among these four instances (by $C_{\text{SDintq d4}} = C_{\text{timepoints} \langle 2, 3 \rangle}$) gain just enough sonic support from $S_{1\text{-adjacency}}$ to form weak phenosegments.[118] These segments are nonstructural, unabashed examples of pure motive that cut across voices and structural levels. Still, it is important to recognize them *as* segments, for they are the source of the marked strain between structure and design in mm. 1–4 and the means by which an important

and the diminished fourth normalized to a perfect fourth.[119]

Slippage between structural and nonstructural segments related by look-alike contextual criteria can be an important compositional resource. Brahms's Capriccio in F-sharp Minor, op. 76, no. 1 is saturated by a single motive (e.g., <C♯, D, F♯, E♯> in mm. 14–15) subject to variation and persistent change as it appears in different musical contexts. The motive is transposed and inverted, and later embellished and altered; it also appears in different registers and is reharmonized, with contrasting versions often in close proximity. Example 2.29 shows two instances of the motive in the right, then in the left hand in mm. 26–27 and 28–29, respectively; these are associated by $C_{pc\ <C♯,\ D,\ F♯,\ E♯>}$, realized as the chromatic interval series $C_{ip\ <+1,\ +4,\ -1>}$. The first segment prolongs the dominant; here the contextual criterion has structural support, functioning as part of the linked criterion $T_{SD\ f♯:\ <5,6,1,7>}C_{pc\ <C♯,\ D,\ F♯,\ E♯>}$. The second, modulating, segment is supported only by the look-alike freestanding contextual criterion $C_{pc\ <C♯,\ D,\ F♯,\ E♯>}$. Brahms's Intermezzo op. 117, no. 2 in B-flat Minor indulges in a similar play of associations among structural and nonstructural segmentations.[120]

A chain of such interactions between linked TC criteria and their look-alike C criteria but running in the opposite direction, from nonstructural to structural segments, becomes a poetic device in *Philomel* (1964), with text by John Hollander and music by Milton Babbitt. The "Echo Song" (section II of III) consists of seven exchanges between live voice and tape, each bridged by a homonymic relation between an elision of two words in the voice and a single word emphasized by repetition in the tape (ex. 2.30). Each rhyme can be

Example 2.29. Brahms, Capriccio in F♯ Minor, op. 76, no. 1, mm. 26–29

O Thrush … forest's tongue?	Stung, stung, stung,
O Hawk … unclouded eye?	Die, die, die,
O Owl … forests' light?	Slight, slight, slight;
O sable Raven … robe lack?	Black, black, black;
O bright Gull … breaker's cream	Scream, scream, scream,
The world's despair … hubbub erred!	Bird, bird, bird!
O green leaves! … myth race.	Thrace, Thrace, Thrace!

Example 2.30. Hollander and Babbitt, *Philomel*, homonymic relations in section II

represented by a contextual criterion that uses the international phonetic alphabet (IPA) to show standard pronunciation (e.g., $C_{\text{IPA stung}}$). In the voice, only the look-alike contextual criterion is active; in the tape, the contextual criterion is part of a linked criterion that also gives the part of speech (e.g., $T_{\text{verb (past perfect)}}C_{\text{IPA stung}}$). Repeated slippage between structural and nonstructural segments that share the same contextual criterion serves a programmatic purpose as the tape echoes, reflects on, and articulates what the live Philomel cannot. It also serves a literary purpose, creating a parallel structure among the seven exchanges.

Studies of structure and design, and structural and pure motive, can involve music and text simultaneously. György Ligeti's *Lux aeterna* (1966) is a piece for sixteen *a cappella* voices. The piece has four sections, each a strict microcanon based on a different pitch string and accompanying text.[121] Example 2.31a shows the start of the thirty-one-note string that underlies the eight-voice canon (four sopranos, four altos) for section I (mm. 1–37). The canon is absolutely strict with regard to pitch and syllable ordering, but admits some small adjustments in rhythm. Pitch and syllable orderings defined by the string are structural but belong to different subtypes (T_{pitch} and T_{text}); subsegments of each string generate individual structural criteria (e.g., $T_{\text{pitch <F4, F4, F4, E4, F4, G4>}}$, $T_{\text{text <lux ae-ter-na>}}$).

Example 2.31a. Ligeti, *Lux aeterna*, start of initial pitch string with text

and are rhythmically unpredictable) cooperate to create a seamless texture. Ligeti's notes to the score ("all entries very gentle," "sing totally without accents") also indicate that performers should minimize sonic disjunctions and the aural effect of notated barlines (which have no metric significance). But even in this seamless sonic environment, occasional, tentative segments *do* emerge: repetitions peep out from within individual canonic strands and across strands and voice parts, created by the alignment of parts. Example 2.31b isolates a representative passage from mm. 5–9, where the pitch and text orderings <F♯4, G4, F4, E♭4> ("lux ae-ter-na") and <E♭4, A♭4, D♭4> ("na lux ae-") first introduced by Soprano 1 as subsegments of the underlying string are replicated in approximate diminution across Sopranos 4–3–2–1 in m. 7, and Sopranos 3–2–1 in mm. 8–9. Because each pitch in the underlying string is associated with a specific text syllable, support from at least *two* coincident contextual criteria is assured ($C_{\text{pitch <F♯4, G4, F4, Eb4>}}$ and $C_{\text{text <lux, ae-, ter-, na>}}$ for the first pair of segments; $C_{\text{pitch <Eb4, Ab4, Db4>}}$ and $C_{\text{text <na, lux, ae->}}$ for the second). In each case, the segments formed within a voice are structural, supported by linked TC criteria; segments formed across voices are nonstructural, supported by only the look-alike C criteria. Structural segments in Soprano 1 converge with their nonstructural counterparts on their last pitch, anchoring the aural association.[122] The passage exhibits an interesting mutual dependency between structural and contextual criteria: as always, structural criteria require contextual criteria for realization, but the look-alike contextual criteria also depend on structural criteria for analytic significance.

The emergence of segments from within *Lux*'s exceptionally smooth sonic surface is interesting for two reasons. First, it illustrates a general point about interactions between sonic and contextual criteria. Earlier we noted that contextual criteria rarely form segments alone; they generally require at least minimal coincident support from sonic criteria. The special musical circumstances in *Lux* show how very weak that sonic support can be. In mm. 7–9, the only sonic support for the two structural segments in Soprano 1 is $S_{\text{2-timbre}}$—that is, the subtle difference between the timbre of that particular soprano's voice and those of the others'. In these bars the minimal sonic criterion $S_{\text{1-adjacency}}$ that joins notes from different voices of the canon is often the strongest sonic criterion available. With little competition from other sonic criteria, contextual criteria with minimal sonic support from $S_{\text{1-adjacency}}$ are enough to gently lift segments from their surroundings. But even when these segments form, they remain weak—not distinct units so much as tentative flickers of association in a gradually evolving texture. The near-equilibrium between weak sonic and contextual criteria thus has a *qualitative* effect on the listener's experience: rather than encourage any definitive segmentation, the piece admits only flashes of recognition, luminescent echoes within and between voices in a contemplative sonic space.

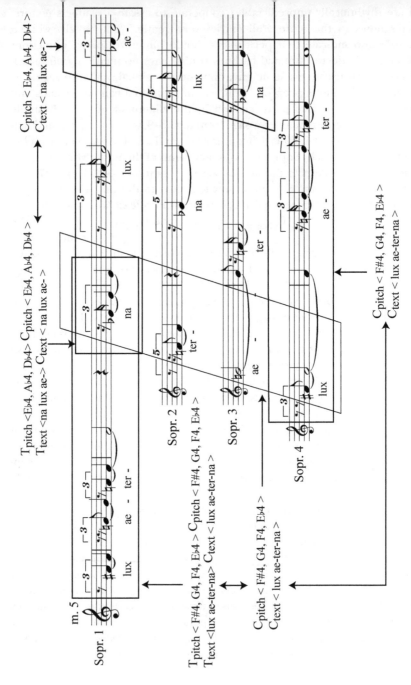

Example 2.31b. Ligeti, *Lux aeterna*, structural and nonstructural segments associated by pitch and syllable orderings

Chapter Three

Associative Sets and Associative Organization

Associative organization, like sonic organization, is a fundamental aspect of musical design. Functionally independent of sonic and structural organization, it interacts with them in complex ways to shape passages, articulate structure, and create musical form. Associative organization has three main components: the associative set, associative configuration, and associative landscape. An associative set is a set of segments bound together by contextual criteria into an integrated system that functions as a unit at a higher level of organization. An associative configuration is a network of relationships among segments of an associative set that reflects an analyst's interpretation of associative adjacency, proximity, and distance. Associative sets and associative configurations are atemporal. An associative landscape places associative sets and configurations *in* the context of time, to see how the associative geography of a piece or passage actually unfolds.

Associative sets, configurations, and landscapes constitute a conceptual framework for a holistic, nonreductive approach to aspects of musical form predicated on association. In contrast to approaches that focus on individual segments or pairs of segments, associative sets and associative landscapes shift the focus to two higher levels of organization—sets of segments with their own global properties, networks of relationships, and temporal dispositions; and the disposition of sets in the musical landscape. When conjoined with analysis of sonic and structural organization, analysis of associative organization gives the analyst a comprehensive approach to musical form.

This chapter has two parts. The first, on associative sets, configurations, and graphs, provides definitions and musical illustrations for associative sets, populations, global properties, associative configurations, and association graphs. The second, on associative landscapes, covers landscapes, association maps, dispositions, distributions, and some features and properties of associative landscapes. As in chapter 2, we will proceed from more abstract and lower levels of musical organization and analysis to more concrete and higher levels. Starting at the place in the schematic (ex. 1.1) where chapter 2 left off, we begin by organizing segments into associative sets, then sets into associative landscapes. From a conceptual standpoint, the theory's five levels form a hierarchy defined by logical precedence and embedding. But in practice the five

of a piece or passage, but to use orientations, criteria, segments, associative sets, and landscapes, to explore associative aspects of musical design and their relationship to sonic and structural ones.

Associative Sets, Configurations, and Graphs

Associative Sets

An *associative set* (*set,* as context permits) is a collection of two or more (pheno-) segments bound by contextual criteria into an integrated system that functions as a unit at a higher level of organization. Every segment in an associative set is related to at least one of its consociates by one or more contextual criteria; conversely, every contextual criterion that contributes to the set (not just to its individual segments) must support two or more of its segments. Segments of an associative set need not be adjacent in time, register, timbre, loudness, or any other sonic dimension; indeed, they can even come from different pieces of music, through quotation or resemblance.

Although the segments of an associative set form a unit, each segment retains its own identity, modeled by its genotype and, especially, its contextual genotype. Thus associative sets can embrace a range of variation: they run the gamut in their internal structure from tight classical categories defined by essential features to diffuse prototypical categories—fuzzy sets based on what Wittgenstein called "family resemblances," with a graded structure from more to less prototypical instances.[1] The greater the degree of intersection among contextual genotypes for segments of an associative set, the more the set approximates a classical category; the less intersection, the more rhizomic the prototypical category. In general, associative sets are best understood as prototypical categories, with classical categories as a special case.

To recognize and use not only the morphological similarities that join segments of a set together but also the full range of *variation* among segments in the set, five access points are required. Spanning three levels of organization and analysis (criteria, segments, associative sets), these are:

1. Contextual criteria (individual relational properties of segments)
2. Segments (basic units of musical organization)
3. Contextual genotypes (sets of contextual criteria that support segments)
4. Associative sets (sets of segments bound together by one or more contextual criteria)
5. Common sets (sets of criteria that represent segments in an associative set or a set overall)

fourth and will soon develop the fifth.

Associative sets are named by italicized capital letters (e.g., associative set *A*); individual segments within a set, by appending arabic numerals to the set name (e.g., *A1*, *A2*) that reflect the segments' chronological order in the score. (In certain circumstances, convenience can suggest other naming practices.)[2] When one segment is embedded in another, the segment that begins first (or, for synchronous beginnings, ends first) receives the lower number. To call a segment *An* means that the analyst recognizes it as a part of set *A*—as an *A*—and thus as having one or more predicable properties that function as relational properties among consociates in *A*.

The associative set is a simple and intuitive concept that, suitably developed, becomes flexible and powerful. Example 3.1 shows the first eight bars of Olivier Messiaen's "L'alouette calandrelle," the eighth piece from the *Catalogue*

Example 3.1. Messiaen, *Catalogue d'oiseaux*, VIII, "L'alouette calandrelle," mm. 1–8: Introducing two associative sets, Provence (*A*) and Lark (*B*)

associative sets: set A takes in three segments ($A1$–$A3$) in mm. 1, 3, and 5; set B, five segments ($B1$–$B5$) in mm. 2, 4, and 6–8. Messiaen's markings indicate that segments of set A portray the static expanse of a landscape in Provence on a hot July afternoon; those in set B, the improvised song of a short-toed lark. Set A is a classical category based on literal repetition; set B, a prototypical one, in which morphological similarities commingle with variation.[3]

A formal definition of associative set proceeds on the basis of intersection among contextual genotypes. Given an associative set A with segments $A1$, $A2$, . . . Az in A, for each An in A (where n varies from 1 to z) and contextual genotype $CG(An)$ there exists a segment Am such that $CG(An) \cap CG(Am) \neq \varnothing$. Note that the criteria in the intersection set need not all be explicit in the contextual genotypes for *both* An and Am, but, as explained in chapter 2, can be implied in one case or the other by (1) literal inclusion (between elements in the same contextual dimension that differ in cardinality, e.g., by $C_{\text{incl pc \{258\}}}$, or between $C_{\text{pc \{258A\}}}$ and $C_{\text{pc \{258\}}}$); (2) logical entailment through dimensional specificity (more specific dimensions imply activity in less specific ones as, say, $C_{\text{pc \{258A\}}}$ is logically implied by $C_{\text{pitch <F5, D5, Bb4, Ab5>}}$); (3) transformation (e.g., under retrograde, inversion, or retrograde inversion); or (4) some combination of these.[4] This formal definition outlines a condition all associative sets must meet. However, it does not dictate when or how associative sets must form: that is not a formal question but an interpretive one, one for each analyst to decide in accordance with his or her own analytical interpretation, interests, and goals.

Associative subsets and *associative supersets* occupy levels of associative organization below and above the associative set, respectively. Like an associative set, an associative subset is a set of two or more (pheno)segments interrelated by contextual criteria. But associative subsets meet two further conditions: (1) every segment in the subset is part of the same larger set; and (2) segments within the subset associate more strongly with one another than they do with other segments in the larger set through stronger contextual criteria, a tendency for specific contextual criteria to coincide, or both. We name associative subsets by appending a slash and italicized lower case letter to the set name: for example, A/a, A/b indicate two associative subsets of a larger set A. Individual segments can be designated by chronological order within a subset ($A/a1$, $A/a2$) or in relation to the larger set, with subset affiliation attached ($A1/a$, $A2/a$). (To avoid confusion I use only the first notation in this book.) An associative set can have any number of associative subsets. A *bifurcated* (trifurcated, etc.) associative set is one that partitions into two (three, etc.) disjoint associative subsets. But associative subsets need not partition a larger set: they can overlap, omit segments, or both. A *variegated* associative set has several subsets, of which two or more can overlap. Associative subsets vary in the strength of connection they have with one another: overlapping subsets can be very closely related; disjoint sets, more distantly so.

they form at the discretion of the analyst in response to a particular musical context and to express a certain analytic interpretation. There are times when more neutral terms are in order, terms one can use to reference individual segments or groups of segments *without* invoking associative sets or perhaps even contextual criteria. The terms "independent segment" and "population" serve this purpose. An *independent segment* is a phenoseg that does not contribute to any associative set in the musical context or analytic interpretation under consideration. Independent segments are named by numerals in square brackets that represent their chronological order: for example, [1], [2], [3]. Independent segments tend to form primarily in the sonic domain, with little or no support in the contextual domain. Although they do have predicable properties (e.g., "the notes of segment [1] form a member of SC 3-4[015]"), these do not necessarily translate into the relational properties modeled by contextual criteria ("segment [1] is an [015], but it is not supported by $C_{SC\ 3\text{-}4[015]}$").

A *population* is a set of segments delimited by temporal adjacency or sonic properties such as register or timbre, with *or without* the integrating action of contextual criteria that is essential to form an associative set.[5] A population can include any number of distinct associative sets or subsets (including none) and any number of segments, independent or otherwise. All associative sets are populations, but not all populations are, or include, associative sets. Populations are named with a letter followed by a numeral (if several are involved), both set in bold italics to distinguish the population from a segment in an associative set. Thus *P1* and *P2* indicate two populations (*P*1, *P*2 indicate two segments of a set *P*).

Properties of Associative Sets. Associative sets have various *global properties*—properties held by an associative set or population in its entirety as a complex entity at a certain level of organization. These properties include size, range of variation, distribution of variation, and strength. Comparative analysis of global properties brings out aspects of organization that contribute to musical form and design.

Global properties are of two kinds: collective and emergent. A *collective* property is an aggregate or demographic property. Collective properties depend only on a set's contents, not the abstract configuration of its segments or their temporal disposition. Size, range of variation, and distribution are collective properties of associative sets and populations. An *emergent* property is a system property that arises at a certain level of organization when parts of the system interact and influence one another, as segments do in an associative set.[6] Strength is an emergent property of associative sets (but not of populations, where segments need not interact in this way). All four global properties depend on the predicable or relational properties of a set's or population's

sider these four properties in turn.

The first global property, size, is straightforward. The *size* of an associative set or population is its cardinality—the number of segments it includes.

The *range of variation* (*range*) of an associative set (or population) is an indication of diversity or richness; rather than judge some properties essential and others insignificant or deviant, it embraces all available variation. Range has two components: element diversity and combinational diversity. *Element diversity* is determined by the relational and predicable properties of contributing segments. ("Common set," to be introduced shortly, formalizes the concept of element diversity.) It notes the various contextual (perhaps also structural) dimensions that occur within the set and tallies the number of elements active as relational properties in each. Element diversity is the basis for distribution. *Combinational diversity* shifts the focus of attention up one level, from criteria to segments. Combinational diversity considers how properties that involve elements from different dimensions (or even domains) combine to create the different genotypes of segments in the set. To contrast element diversity with combinational diversity by way of an analogy from genetics, element diversity is like the diversity of alleles; combinational diversity, the diversity of genotypes among individuals in a population. By comparing element diversity with combinational diversity one can assess the degree of linkage between elements or criteria in different contextual dimensions. The ratio of range (over a specific contextual dimension) to size is also a significant characteristic of an associative set or population.

Distribution of variation (*distribution*) refers to the array of frequencies with which individual elements or contextual criteria occur among the genotypes of a set's segments. Distributions take many forms. Archetypes include flat or "even" distributions, bell curves, and random distributions; however, the full gamut of distributions created by superimposition, intermediate forms, and transformation of archetypes is available. Distribution can be formalized as a multiset of element diversity (perhaps also combinational diversity). In practice, though, informal assessments of the relative frequencies of individual elements or criteria, or of a distribution's overall profile, are often just as useful.

The *strength* of an associative set depends on the strength of its segments in conjunction with their temporal disposition in a musical passage. As noted earlier, a segment's strength is determined by the cumulative strength of its sonic boundaries and supporting contextual criteria. In the sonic domain, boundary strength is synonymous with the magnitude of sonic disjunction (whether in one sonic dimension or as a weighted composite across several dimensions). In the contextual domain, criterion strength involves dimensional specificity, degree of ordering, cardinality, and frequency; it is also influenced by interactions with sonic, structural, and other contextual criteria and by the temporal disposition of the segments it supports. The strength of an associative set also

are clumped together in time are stronger than those in which segments are widely dispersed. Dependent on temporal disposition and musical context, strength is an emergent property of an associative set as a whole: first arising at the level of the set as an integrated system, it cannot be localized or reduced to properties of individual segments at any lower level of organization.

When several associative sets are active, comparative analysis of sets' global properties can yield important information that affects associative aspects of musical design. From the opening bars of Messiaen's "L'alouette calandrelle" (ex. 3.1), clear differences in the sonic attributes and global properties of associative sets A and B easily distinguish the lark from the landscape. Strong sonic disjunctions in register ($S_{1\text{-pitch}}$) and duration ($S_{2\text{-duration}}$) perch the lark high above the landscape sustained by the pedal. Along with striking differences in sonic attributes (low and slow for set A; high and fast for set B), and pitch and rhythmic material, that distinguish the segments of set A from those of set B, the two sets have different global properties: they differ in size, range, and distribution. Over the course of the piece (97 measures), set A remains small and uniform: it acquires only six segments, all related by literal repetition in pitch, rhythm, and loudness. In contrast, set B is large—about ten times the size of set A—with a wide range of variation. Whereas the distribution of set A is flat (necessarily so, since A is a uniform set), that of set B is uneven: many segments are unique, but some exact and near-exact repetitions, as well as clusters of material, suggest ongoing improvisations by different individual birds of the same species.[7] In the opening bars and throughout the piece, this contrast between a uniform associative set and a diverse one serves a pictorial purpose: the different global properties of sets A and B work in tandem with contrasting sonic and contextual properties of individual segments to set the song of the lark in stark profile against a timeless landscape.

The approach to the cadence in Bach's *Chromatic Fantasy* (mm. 75–79) includes another associative set with a similar range and distribution of variation (ex. 3.2). The passage consists of a sequence of eight melodic flourishes that embellish a chromatic descent from D5 to D4 over a tonic pedal. Each flourish is based on the same melodic figure, which begins as a florid upbeat outlining an ascending triad in six-four position followed by a more leisurely appoggiatura (and 7–6 suspension against an inner voice). Apart from scalar transposition, changes in contour and the use of decorative chromaticism make each of the eight segments in set C unique. Here, as in the Messiaen, the distribution of variation is uneven. For instance, only two of the six rhythms present are repeated ($C2$ and $C6$ have four thirty-seconds followed by a sixteenth; $C4$ and $C7$, five); the other four are not. A modest degree of linkage between pitch and rhythm forges stronger connections within the pairs $C1$–$C3$, $C2$–$C4$, and $C6$–$C7$ than those among segments in the set at large. (The pairings $C1$–$C2$ and $C3$–$C4$ gain added support from the larger association between $C1+C2$ and $C3+C4$.)

Example 3.2. J. S. Bach, *Chromatic Fantasy*, BWV 903, mm. 75–79, eight segments of a set *C*

Range and distribution of variation contribute to associative organization, but the form and flow of the musical result depend on a host of other factors including the particular sonic, contextual, and structural criteria involved, interactions among criteria, and temporal disposition of segments. In the Messiaen and the Bach, variation on a motif gives each passage an improvisatory quality, but the associative organization of these improvisations is quite different. The song of the lark in set *B* explores the range of available variation with an air of spontaneity; moving easily from segment to segment, the bird is untutored in the musical teleology of voice leading or systematic changes in pitch or rhythm. In contrast, in the *Chromatic Fantasy* the range of variation is carefully organized with respect to three musical teleologies in rhythm, contour, and pitch. As *C*1 proceeds to *C*8, the density of surface rhythm increases, contours become more diverse and complex, and chromatic voice leading carries the basic motif down a full octave, step by chromatically inflected step. The range of variation in set *C* enlivens an improvisation that is highly structured by

and contour endemic to the passage at hand.

An interest in the formation of associative subsets and relationship between element and combinational diversity proves worthwhile in the opening of Feldman's *Patterns in a Chromatic Field* (1981) for cello and piano (ex. 3.3). The piano begins with eighteen segments (mm. 1–18) of a set *D* that is uniform with respect to pitch content and order but bifurcated with respect to rhythm.[8] The distribution of the two rhythms is uneven, with eleven instances of the short-long pattern, but only seven of the one with equal durations. In m. 19 (start of the third system), the piano introduces a new pair of chords that

Example 3.3. Feldman, *Patterns in a Chromatic Field*, mm. 1–27

trichord previously in the left hand ({D, E♭, F♭}) and two of the three notes previously in the right hand ({E♭, D}), while preserving set class in the right hand (SC 3-1[012]) and expanding that in the left from a chromatic trichord to a tetrachord (SC 3-1[012] to SC 4-1[0123]). The new pair of chords appears in the same two rhythms as before, again with an unequal distribution.

Set D is doubly bifurcated: it partitions into two associative subsets on the basis of pitch and rhythm, but the partitions defined by C_{pitch} and C_{rhythm} are orthogonal to one another. Rather than elevate pitch over rhythm (or vice versa) as a rule, it is best to appeal to other aspects of the specific passage to support an interpretation. Here segments associated by pitch content cluster in mm. 1–18 and in mm. 19–36, but those associated by rhythm are interspersed with their rivals throughout. Temporal disposition thus articulates and strengthens associative subsets defined on the basis of pitch rather than rhythm. Moreover, the two associative subsets in pitch are closely related (they share a pitch pentachord under octave transposition), while the rhythmic subsets are disjoint. Taking pitch as the primary criterion for subset formation, one might consider the first thirty-six measures of the piano part to be one large associative set D with two associative subsets D/a and D/b, each uniform in pitch but bifurcated in rhythm.

Associative organization in the cello line is a different story. From mm. 1–36, the cello presents 32 segments (delineated by slurs) of an associative set E that immerses four pitches (F×4, A♭4, B♭♭4, and A♯4) in a mass of microvariation. Persistent and uncoordinated change in the number of attack points (three to six), distinct pitches per segment (three or four), presence and location of repeated tones, rhythm (number and placement of dotted sixteenths), and pitch order make set E remarkably diverse. It is also highly diffuse. Because pitch content, order, and rhythm vary independently, each of the 32 segments of set E is unique and distribution of variation within the set is entirely flat: no feature or combination of features is emphasized and no associative subsets form.[9] Set E illustrates the difference between element diversity and combinational diversity, and suggests the importance of their relationship. Although set E has limited element diversity, it has great combinational diversity. The inverse relation between element and combinational diversity in set E translates into a superabundance of nuance that is typical of associative sets in Feldman's late music. As the cello continues in m. 38, the core pitch set moves up one octave. At this point set E bifurcates into a "low" subset E/a (mm. 1–36) and a "high" subset E/b (mm. 38–72), which contains another 28 segments. No segment in E/b duplicates or clearly associates with any particular segment in E/a. Instead, the total range of variation in set E continues to expand as a new trend develops: pitch repetition within a segment gradually becomes more frequent until m. 72, where the cello ends the passage with a fivefold repetition of F×5 (ex. 3.4).

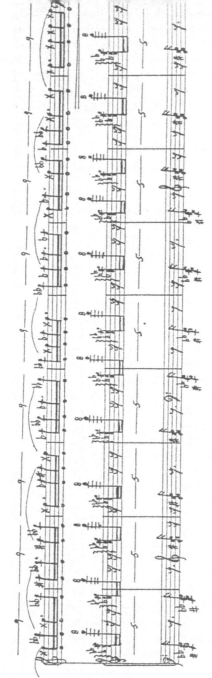

Example 3.4. Feldman, *Patterns in a Chromatic Field*, mm. 64–72

voices, offers the analyst an ideal environment in which to explore relationships among element diversity, combinational diversity, and distributions. Example 3.5a provides a score; successive phrases in the bells and voices are labeled segments B1 through B8, and V1 through V8, respectively, for easy reference. The piece is based on four pitch interval orderings related by P, I, R, and RI, plus six rhythms, two unordered C-type (6-32[024579]) pc hexachords related by T_6 (that produce hexachordal combinatoriality), and two timbres (bells, voices). The text consists of four lines composed by permutation and word play from six monosyllabic words; the text for V5–V8 repeats that of V1–V4. Within each vocal phrase, the permutation of words corresponds exactly with the permutation of pcs within the C-type hexachord; thus the text articulates the P, I, R, and RI relations among pc hexachords in the vocal line. Relations among the four interrelated pitch interval orderings binds all sixteen segments into a single associative set.

Example 3.5b catalogues element diversity in each of the four contextual dimensions C_{ip}, C_{rhythm}, C_{pc}, and C_{timbre} and lists the segments each element associates. The distribution of elements among segments is even for pitch interval orderings (4444), pc hexachords (88), and timbres (88), but uneven for rhythms (442222). Combinational diversity, however, is markedly uneven. Eight of the sixteen segments belong to one of four pairs of segments related by literal repetition (B1–B5, B3–B7, V1–V5, and V3–V7); conjoined element repetition in four dimensions reduces the combinational diversity among phrases from a potential sixteen to just twelve distinct segments. Timbre and rhythm tend to work together throughout the piece such that of the six rhythms, three are found only in the bells, two only in the voices, and one in both. Although the distribution of element diversity for pc hexachords and timbres is even, that for combinational diversity is uneven: {68AB13} appears six times in the bells but only twice in the voices; its T_6 counterpart {024579} does the opposite. The result is a set of segments with varying strengths of connection to one another (Babbitt puts this feature of the associative organization to good use, as we will see).

Variegated associative sets can have numerous subsets, each with its own global properties and function with respect to texture and form. Example 3.6 shows seven figures from the first movement of Beethoven's Piano Sonata No. 17 in D Minor, op. 31, no. 2 ("Tempest"). Each represents a subset of a variegated associative set *F* that develops around the turn figure first heard in m. 6. Subset *F/a* includes the initial turn; it is small and uniform, with just two segments related by literal repetition (in m. 6 and m. 152). Next largest, with four segments, *F/c* is uniform to within pitch transposition by major third (from D minor in m. 22 to F♯ minor in m. 100). *F/e*, *F/f*, and *F/g* each have from nine to twelve segments; *F/d*, twenty-two. *F/g* is uniform to within octave transposition; *F/e*, nearly so (that is, but for transposition by fifth and the extension of two segments). *F/d* is uniform to within transposition by fifth from exposition to recap; *F/f* involves numerous scalar transpositions.

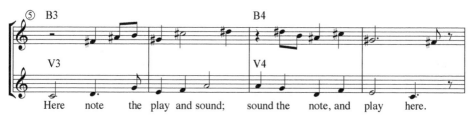

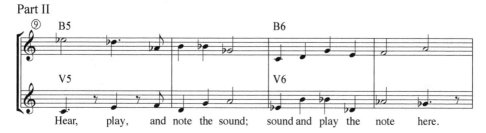

Example 3.5a. Babbitt, *Play on Notes*. From *Exploring Music* Book 6. © 1975 by Holt, Rinehart, and Winston.

Largest and most diverse of the seven subsets is *F/b*, with 33 segments. Tied to set *F* by the truncated turn embedded in its initial segment (<B♭4, G♯4, [G♯4], A4> in m. 9), *F/b* is largely held together by a different pattern in which four notes, slurred in pairs, include a central repeated note. As *F/b* evolves, we learn that this central note can be the high or low point of a segment; it can also be consonant or dissonant. Whereas most other subsets of *F* preserve the outlines of the turn figure but add a characteristic rhythm (e.g., the turn proper for *F/a*, even quarters moving to halves for *F/c*, an iamb that puts an agogic

C dimension	C elements (criterion)	Distribution (segments with criterion in genotype)
C_{ip}	$<-2, -5, +3, -1, -4>$	B1, V4, B5, V8
	$<+2, +5, -3, +1, +4>$	B2, V3, B6, V7
	$<+4, +1, -3, +5, +2>$	V1, B3, V5, B7
	$<-4, -1, +3, -5, -2>$	V2, B4, V6, B8
C_{rhythm}	[rhythmic notation]	B1, V3, B5, V7
	[rhythmic notation]	B2, B6
	[rhythmic notation]	V1, V5
	[rhythmic notation]	V2, V4, V6, V8
	[rhythmic notation]	B3, B7
	[rhythmic notation]	B4, B8
C_{pc}	{68AB13}	B1, B2, B3, B4, B5, V6, B7, V8
	{024579}	V1, V2, V3, V4, V5, B6, V7, B8
C_{timbre}	bells	B1, B2, B3, B4, B5, B6, B7, B8
	voices	V1, V2, V3, V4, V5, V6, V7, V8

Example 3.5b. Babbitt, *Play on Notes*, element diversity in C_{ip}, C_{rhythm}, C_{pc}, and C_{timbre}

accent on a weak part of the bar for *F/e*) or musical quality (e.g., lyrical and plaintive for *F/c*, obsessive for *F/d*), *F/b* largely *replaces* the turn contour with a different figure that becomes the basis for coherence.[10] The range of variation in *F/b* thus extends from segments like those in m. 9 and m. 10, which are well anchored within set *F*, to those in m. 12 and m. 42, which are quite different from those in any other subset of *F* and even on the periphery of *F/b*.

Along with their different properties, subsets *F/a–F/g* serve different purposes in the sonata. Segments of *F/a* are, literally, ornaments (albeit rich and prescient ones); those of *F/d*, part of an accompaniment pattern. *F/f* generates a running bass line; *F/b*, *F/c*, *F/e*, and *F/g* contribute to the main melodic line. Despite their small size, subsets *F/a* and *F/c* are especially prominent, due to their segments' placement at important tonal arrivals and the role these segments play in the form, construed both in the traditional sense of formal sections and functions, and in terms of associative organization (*F/a* and *F/c* are relatively central in set *F*).[11]

As the Feldman and Beethoven examples suggest, the various associative sets and subsets at work in a composition are often differentiated not only by their characteristic contextual criteria but also by their global properties. Example 3.7a shows the first two "systems" from another late work by Feldman, *Crippled Symmetry* (1983). As in Feldman's earlier *Why Patterns?* (1977), the score is

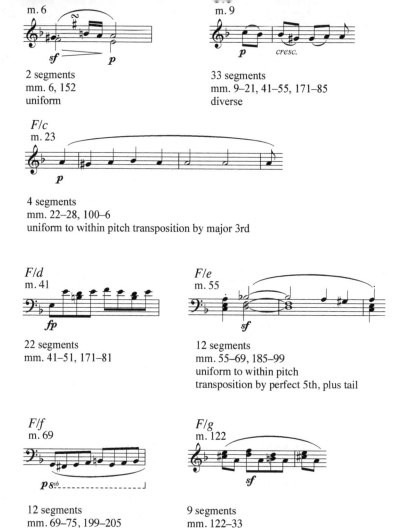

m. 6

2 segments
mm. 6, 152
uniform

m. 9

33 segments
mm. 9–21, 41–55, 171–85
diverse

F/c
m. 23

4 segments
mm. 22–28, 100–6
uniform to within pitch transposition by major 3rd

F/d
m. 41

22 segments
mm. 41–51, 171–81

F/e
m. 55

12 segments
mm. 55–69, 185–99
uniform to within pitch
transposition by perfect 5th, plus tail

F/f
m. 69

12 segments
mm. 69–75, 199–205
numerous scalar transpositions

F/g
m. 122

9 segments
mm. 122–33
uniform to within octave transposition

Example 3.6. Beethoven, Piano Sonata No. 17 in D Minor, op. 31, no. 2, I, representative figures of subsets F/a–F/g

unsynchronized, meaning that vertical alignment indicates temporal simultaneity only within an instrument, not between instruments. With its many internal repeats, the piano's system 1 unfolds in roughly the same time frame as the flute and vibraphone's systems 1 and 2. Taken together, these five systems constitute an opening passage; while its temporal boundaries are blurred in performance, the basic tripartite associative organization remains clear.

Example 3.7a. Feldman, *Crippled Symmetry*, first two systems

   The passage introduces three associative sets, one each in the flute (*F*), vibraphone (*V*), and piano (*P*) with core formative criteria $C_{\text{pitch} \langle \text{Eb4, Db5, C6, D5}\rangle}$, $C_{\text{pitch} \langle \text{Eb4, Db4, D4, Db4, C4}\rangle}$, and $C_{\text{pc \{AB06\}}}$, respectively. (Sets *F* and *V* are subsets of a larger associative set based on $C_{\text{pc \{0123\}}}$, which soon absorbs the piano as well.) Example 3.7b surveys global properties of *F*, *V*, and *P*. A patter of sixteenth-notes punctuated by silences, *V* has 18 segments. Characterized by longer note values and silences, sets *F* and *P* are smaller, roughly half and two-thirds the size of *V*, with 10 and 12 segments. *F*, *V*, and *P* differ in the range and distribution of variation in pitch and rhythm. Sets *F* and *V* are uniform with respect to pitch content and order while set *P*, held together by the more general criterion $C_{\text{pc \{AB06\}}}$, has a range of variation in pitch with five distinct pitch orderings in a minimally uneven distribution (two instances of one ordering and one of each of the others, all multiplied by repeats for

ation obtains with respect to rhythm, but instead aligns set V with P versus F. Whereas even note values throughout all segments of set V, and set P, make each set uniform with respect to duration contour (C_{dseg} criteria), the ten segments of set F have seven different duration contours in an uneven distribution (3211111).[12] Charting actual durations within each segment gives a third perspective, in which set V becomes uniform, sets F and P have considerable variation, and distribution within all three sets is flat.[13]

Set	Size	Range/Distrib. of pitch material	Range/Distrib. of dur. contours	Range/Distrib. of actual durs.
F	10	1* / flat	7 / 3211111	10 / flat
V	18	1* / flat	1 / flat	1 / flat
P	12	5 / 42222	1 / flat	6 / flat

*Pitch content and order preserved.

Example 3.7b. Feldman, *Crippled Symmetry*, global properties of sets F, V, and P

A comparative analysis of sets' global properties can be represented in graphic form. Drawing on the information presented in example 3.7b, example 3.7c represents F, V, and P as figures in a five-dimensional global property space in which size, range of variation, and distribution of criteria are structuring dimensions.[14] In this graph, circle size represents set size. Position along the horizontal and vertical axes represents the range of variation for duration contours, and for pitch content and order, respectively, as listed in example 3.7b. Shadows represent uneven distributions of element diversity within set F (extended in the horizontal dimension for duration contour) and P (extended in the vertical dimension for pitch content and order). Example 3.7c brings out a fairly subtle but significant feature of associative organization in the passage: sets F, V, and P stake out different regions of a space defined in terms of range and variation. Locating sets in such a space focuses attention on the relative proximity or distance of *modes* of associative organization. It can also suggest areas for further investigation, such as how these modes of organization change over time.

Taking roughly the first minute of *Crippled Symmetry* as a passage, we now define a population $P1$ that includes all of the segments in sets F, V, and P within a single unit defined by temporal extent. The different sizes of sets F, V, and P then become the proportions of different kinds of material that unfold in the same time span. Surveying the range and distribution of variation in $P1$ points up an affinity between sets F and V (which can be joined in a single associative superset based on $C_{pc\ \{0123\}}$) versus those of P, which at least emphasize criteria in the same contextual dimension, C_{pc}. Over time, the range and distribution of variation in $P1$ changes. $P1$ begins with three distinct pitch orderings

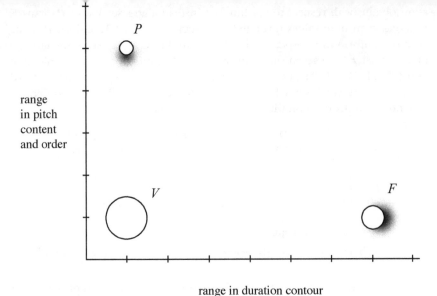

range in duration contour

Example 3.7c. Locating *F*, *V*, and *P* in a five-dimensional global property space

in flute, vibraphone, and piano. With the piano's third notated segment (in performance, its fifth sounding segment), the diversity of associative set *P* and of the larger population **P1** increases. As the passage goes on, intervening rests disappear from the piano part and the increase in variation accelerates. By the end of the piano's first system, *P* contributes twice as many segments to **P1** per unit time as it does at the start, shifting the balance among segments of *F*, *V*, and *P* within **P1**.

Common Sets and Motive. The sound of an associative set is shaped by the contextual criteria that support its segments and their relative frequencies. Different types of common sets formalize and provide a shorthand for the range and distribution of criteria active within a set. One of these—the core contextual common set—is the basis for a formal account of motive.

The *common set (CS)* for an associative set *A* is the set of sonic, contextual, and perhaps also structural criteria that support the segments of *A*. A *weighted common set* is a multiset that not only lists criteria but also shows how many times each occurs. To build the weighted common set for a set *A*, CS(*A*), start with set multiplication among genotypes for segments of *A*: that is, given a set *A* with segments *A1*, *A2*, . . . *An*, the CS(*A*) = {G(*A1*) * G(*A2*), * . . . * G(*An*)} (where '*' indicates set multiplication).[15] CS(*A*) includes sonic criteria, contextual criteria, and any structural criteria realized by systematic (TC, TS) or

of an associative set, each of the contextual criteria in CS(A) must contribute to *two or more* segments of A;[17] therefore, after set multiplication we must prune any contextual criteria that occur only once. For set B from Messiaen's "L'alouette calandrelle" (ex. 3.1) in which segments are set off by sonic disjunctions in pitch, duration between attacks, rests, and changes in duration; and associated by contour and (total or partially ordered) pitch content, one might define the unweighted CS(B) as the set $\{S_{\text{1-pitch}}, S_{\text{1-duration}}, S_{\text{1-rest}}, S_{\text{2-duration}}, \text{incl } C_{\text{pitch <F5, D5, Bb4, Ab5, D5, Bb4>}}, \text{incl } C_{\text{pitch <Ab5, Ab5, Ab5, D5, Bb4>}}, \text{incl } C_{\text{pitch <Ab5, D5, Bb4>}}, C_{\text{CR <1020>}}.\}$.

Sonic common sets and contextual common sets are two more specific types of common set.[18] Like comprehensive common sets, each can be weighted or unweighted. A *sonic common set* (S/CS) is a common set in the sonic domain; it lists the criteria that delineate sonic boundaries for segments of a set.[19] The weighted S/CS of a set A is formed by multiplying the sonic genotypes of segments of A; thus, the S/CS(A) = $\{SG(A1) * SG(A2), * \ldots * SG(An)\}$. For the Provence set A from Messiaen's "L'alouette calandrelle," one might define the S/CS(A) as $\{S_{\text{1-pitch}}, S_{\text{1-duration}}, S_{\text{1-rest}}, S_{\text{2-duration}}\}$. For the cello's set E in Feldman's *Patterns in a Chromatic Field*, S/CS(E) = $\{S_{\text{1-articulation (slur)}}\}$. Both sonic common sets are small and uniform, but the sonic boundaries for segments of E are much weaker in magnitude, dimension, and number of dimensions than those for segments of A.

A *contextual common set* (C/CS) is a common set in the contextual domain. The weighted C/CS of a hypothetical associative set A, C/CS(A), is $\{CG(A1) * CG(A2), * \ldots * CG(An)\}$, again pruned so that every criterion listed has a superscript of *two* or greater.[20] Example 3.8 shows a worked case. Taking the first nine segments of the cello line from Feldman's *Patterns in a Chromatic Field* (ex. 3.3) as the start of an associative set E I'll call E_{START}, we can create the weighted C/CS(E_{START}): $\{C_{\text{pitch \{F×4, Ab4, Bbb4, A♯4\}}}^4, C_{\text{pitch \{Ab4, Bbb4, A♯4\}}}^3, C_{\text{ipspc <111>}}^2, C_{\text{ipspc <11>}}^2, C_{\text{SC[013]}}^2, C_{\text{SC[012]}}^3, C_{\text{SC[01]}}^2\}$. Note that contextual criteria related by logical implication (of dimensional specificity or subset inclusion) have been pruned, except when they form additional pairs of associations. Throughout this book I focus on common sets in the contextual domain, because it is contextual criteria that underlie associative sets and associative organization.

Along with surveys of all criteria that contribute to an associative set in one or more domains, a more selective approach can be advantageous. The *core common set* (CRS) serves this purpose, with a succinct formal representation of (what a particular analyst takes to be) an associative set's central tendency or "sound."[21] The CRS of an associative set A, CRS(A), lists only the contextual, sonic, and perhaps also coincident structural criteria that are *most characteristic of* (not just most frequently represented among) segments of A. Like common sets, core common sets can be weighted or unweighted; they can also be

$$A = \{A1, A2, A3, A4, A5, A6, A7, A8\}$$

$$CG(A1) = \{wx\}$$
$$CG(A2) = \{wxyz\}$$
$$CG(A3) = \{yz\}$$
$$CG(A4) = \{z\}$$
$$CG(A5) = \{xyz\}$$
$$CG(A6) = \{xz\}$$
$$CG(A7) = \{z\}$$
$$CG(A8) = \{wy\}$$

Contextual common set (C/CS(*A*))
$$= \{wx\} * \{wxyz\} * \{yz\} * \{z\} * \{xyz\} * \{xz\} * \{z\} * \{wy\}$$
$$= \{w^3x^4y^4z^6\}$$

Core contextual common set (C/CRS(*A*)) = $\{z\}$

Example 3.8. Contextual common set (C/CS), core contextual common set (C/CRS)

restricted to the sonic or contextual domain. The *core sonic common set* (S/CRS)
of a set *A*, S/CRS(*A*), lists a few select sonic criteria most responsible for forming sonic boundaries for segments of *A*; these are often (but not necessarily)
the criteria that create the strongest sonic boundaries. For Messiaen's Provence
set *A*, one might say that S/CRS(*A*) = $\{S_{1\text{-pitch}}, S_{2\text{-pitch}}, S_{2\text{-duration}}\}$. The *core contextual common set* (C/CRS) of a set represents an analyst's interpretation of its most
characteristic contextual criteria. For set *E* in Feldman's cello line (mm. 1–72),
C/CRS(*E*) = $\{C_{\text{pitch \{F×4, Ab4, Bbb4, A♯4\}}}\}$. Although the criteria in the C/CRS tend
to be those instantiated most often among a set's segments, this is not always
the case. Frequency is not the only consideration, but works in conjunction with
dimensional specificity, degree of ordering, cardinality, and aspects of musical
context to influence the *strength* of each contextual criterion within the specific
musical environment in which the set and its segments appear.

The C/CRS can serve as a formal model of musical motive.[22] In this view, a
motive is a fairly small set of contextual criteria (*relational* properties) that are
highly characteristic of an associative set *A*, in a musical context where segments
of *A* are prominent or numerous and have special analytic significance.[23] Segments that instantiate all or most of the contextual criteria in the C/CRS are
instances of the motive (or "instance the motive"). Instances can be structural
(if they systematically bind particular C and T criteria into TC criteria) or pure
(if the characteristic C criteria remain functionally independent of T criteria,
whether as individual C criteria or in coincident C+T criteria). This concept of
motive entails synergy among three components: a C/CRS (the motive proper),

role that segments that instance the motive play in a passage or piece.

Motive names are mnemonics, set in italicized capital letters (to distinguish them from associative sets, which are named with individual capital letters). Instances are named by appending subscript arabic numerals to the motive name to reflect chronological order.[24] Recalling the turn figure central to set F in the first movement of Beethoven's op. 31, no. 2, we can define the motive $TURN$ and instances $TURN_1$, $TURN_2$, etc. (which correspond to segments $F/a1$ and $F/c1$).

This way of thinking about and representing motive differs from previous formulations in three important respects. First, it considers a motive to be not just a set of features, nor of segments, but a set of *relationships among segments*, represented by contextual criteria in the C/CRS. Second, in accordance with the definition of a C/CRS, contextual criteria in the C/CRS identify *characteristic*—not necessary—features of motive instances.[25] As much as instances of a motive have in common, each remains a distinct segment with its own genotype. Significantly, these genotypes—even the contextual genotypes—can be unique. With the C/CRS model, analysts can focus on an associative set's, or motive's, central tendencies without sacrificing access to the full range of variation among its segments or instances.[26] Analysts can track processes of motivic formation, transformation, and liquidation by monitoring the entry of new segments into a set and corresponding changes in the content of the C/CS or C/CRS. Third and finally, to think of a motive as neither a collection of segments, nor a set of requisite features, but rather as a core set of relational properties that segments acquire in specific musical contexts suggests that "motive" is an *ecological* concept, not an insular or atomistic one. The formally tidy C/CRS is a kind of shorthand for a concept whose workings are actually much more complex and diffuse. The C/CRS abstracts and represents the most important relational properties of a set of segments in a specific musical context; it is suggestive, not comprehensive or reductive.

An important benefit of the C/CRS model of motive is that it enables a kind of motivic analysis that is sensitive to the dialogue between characteristic and distinctive features. Example 3.9 shows the start of four themes drawn from the three movements of Beethoven's Piano Sonata No. 23 in F Minor, op. 57 ("Appassionata"). Bracketed are five additional segments—three instances of the ARP motive and three of $5–6–5$, which derive from two different associative sets A and B.[27] ARP = the C/CRS(A) = $\{C_{\text{pitch, triadic arpeggiation}}\}$; $5–6–5$, the C/CRS(B) = $\{C_{\text{SD} <565>}\}$. ARP_1, ARP_2, and ARP_3 all arpeggiate the tonic triad, but differences between them are just as important to the sonata's overall rhetoric and form as their similarities. Related by a sense of contour inversion around their common head tone (C4), ARP_1 and ARP_2 offer positive and negative contour images of the opening theme. The inversion creates a sense of balance and contrast between the first and second theme groups that is enhanced by the rhythmic identity of ARP_1 and ARP_2. In contrast to both ARP_1 and ARP_2, ARP_3 condenses the arpeggio into a stream of running sixteenth-notes. Still,

contour of ARP_2 onto the pitch material of ARP_1, it makes two long-range associations: one between the openings of the two outer movements (ARP_1 and ARP_3); the other, between theme 2 of the first movement and the start of the third movement (ARP_2 and ARP_3). Individual instances of the 5–6–5 motive also have their own special properties. For example, the upper neighbor D♮ in 5–6–5₁—the peak of the melodic line—sets up a kind of cross-relation with the D♭ in its transposed repetition; also, the actual duration of 5–6–5₃ is nearly three times as long as that of 5–6–5₁ or 5–6–5₂.[28] A concept of motive focused only on essential features would overlook these special properties, as well as pairwise connections such as those between ARP_1 and ARP_2, ARP_1 and ARP_3, and ARP_2 and ARP_3.[29]

Example 3.9. Beethoven, Piano Sonata No. 23 in F Minor, op. 57, *ARP* and 5–6–5 motives

Associative Configurations and Association Graphs

As a collection of two or more segments interrelated and bound by contextual criteria into an integrated system, an associative set is much more than a list of segments: it is a set of *relationships among segments* that form a synergistic whole at a certain level of organization. Shifting the focus from segments and their relational properties (contextual criteria) to relationships among

often lead to differences in the strength of the associative bond from one pair of segments in a set to another. To model these differences we introduce the idea of *associative distance*. Two segments associated by individual or coincident contextual criteria that are especially strong relative to those that associate other pairs of segments in the set form an *associative adjacency*; the segments are *associatively adjacent*. Two segments associated by contextual criteria that are relatively strong in the context of the set are *associatively proximate* or in *associative proximity*. (All associative adjacencies are proximate, but the converse does not hold, because the degree of proximity can vary.) All other pairs of segments in the set are *associatively nonadjacent* and *associatively removed* or *distant* to some degree. Judgments of associative adjacency, proximity, and distance reflect an analyst's holistic assessment of relative distance within a particular musical context. They are qualitative, not quantitative; matters of interpretation, not fact.[30]

Taking a comprehensive view of associative adjacency, proximity, and distance within a set, an analyst can develop and present a *topology of association* in which segments are organized by their degree of connection or remove from one another. With a topology of association as a framework, a *geometry of association* adds an analyst's interpretation of relative (ordinal, not absolute or intervallic) associative proximity and distance. An *associative configuration (configuration)* arranges the segments of an associative set in an associative topology or geometry. An associative configuration is a mental image; an *association graph (AG)* provides a visual representation of an associative configuration. Associative configurations and association graphs are useful tools for the analysis of associative organization, and can draw attention to the degree of fit or misfit between associative and temporal proximity.

Some Useful Concepts and Definitions from Graph Theory. To lay a foundation for the exposition of association graphs, we introduce some basic terms from graph theory.

A *graph (G)* consists of a nonempty, finite set of elements called vertices or *nodes* $N(G) = \{n_1, n_2, n_3, \ldots n_v\}$ and a finite set of *edges* $E(G)$, where each edge is a pair of nodes $\{n_x, n_y\}$ in $N(G)$.[31] In a *simple* graph, each pair of nodes is connected by no more than one edge, and no node is connected to itself by an edge. A *multigraph* is a graph that is not simple; multigraphs can contain *skeins* (two or more edges between a pair of nodes) and *loops* (a loop is an edge from a node to itself). A *subgraph (SG)* of a graph G is a graph in which all nodes belong to $N(G)$ and all edges belong to $E(G)$, but $N(G)$ and $E(G)$ can contain nodes or edges not in *SG*.

Two nodes of a graph are *adjacent* if they are connected by an edge; else they are nonadjacent. Two edges are adjacent if they share a node. Two nodes are *incident* to an edge that connects them; an edge is incident to the two nodes

Two graphs are *isomorphic* if the sets of nodes and edges in one graph can be mapped one-to-one to the sets of nodes and edges in the other. Isomorphism preserves adjacency and degree.[32]

A *digraph* is a graph in which some pairs of nodes in $E(G)$ are ordered pairs, $\langle n_1, n_2 \rangle$. A *walk* is an ordered set of adjacent nodes connected by incident edges: that is, in the walk $\langle n_0, e_1, n_1, e_2, n_2, \ldots e_{x-1}, n_{x-1}, e_x, n_x \rangle$ each edge e_i is incident on n_{i-1} and n_i.[33] A *path* is an ordered set of consecutive nodes drawn from a walk; that is, every pair of nodes adjacent in a path is connected by an incident edge in a graph.[34] A *circuit* is a walk that begins and ends at the same node and in which no other node is repeated.

A graph is *connected* if every node in the graph can be reached from every other node by a walk; else it is *disconnected*. A disconnected graph consists of two or more discrete *components*, each of which is either an isolated node or a connected subgraph.[35] A *disconnecting set* is a set of edges that, when removed from a connected graph G, render G disconnected.[36] A *cutset* is a disconnecting set of which no proper subset is also a disconnecting set.[37] A *bridge* is an edge that itself constitutes a cutset.[38]

The topology of a graph is determined by the number and arrangement of its nodes and edges. There are many kinds of graphs, each defined on the basis of topological properties. Some of those I will reference in subsequent examples and chapters are as follows.

A connected graph is *regular* if all of its nodes are of the same degree. Example 3.10 (compiled from parts of various examples in Read and Wilson's *Atlas of Graphs*) shows connected regular graphs of degrees 2, 3, and 4 with three to eight nodes.

A *circuit graph* is a connected, regular graph of degree two that consists of a single circuit. The circuit graph C_n contains n nodes; the circuit graphs C_3 to C_8 are included in example 3.10 as connected regular graphs of degree 2.

A *tree* is a connected graph that has no circuits. A tree of n nodes has $n–1$ edges. In a tree: (1) every pair of nodes is connected by a unique path; (2) removing any edge disconnects the tree (in other words, every edge is a bridge); (3) adding any edge to an existing pair of nodes creates a circuit. A *spanning tree* for a graph G is a connected subgraph of G that is a tree that includes all the nodes of G, but prunes one or more edges so that it contains no circuits. A *rooted tree* is a tree in which a particular node, the "root," is designated as preceding all others; else, the tree is *unrooted*. Example 3.11 (also adapted from Read and Wilson) shows five of the 23 topologically distinct unrooted trees with eight nodes.[39] Open nodes indicate those that produce distinct rooted trees. A *binary tree* is a tree in which the maximum degree of each node is 3 and in which at each node there can be a left upward branch, a right upward branch, both, or neither.[40]

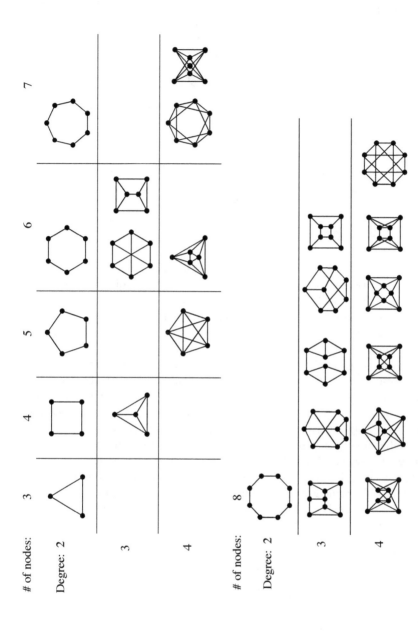

Example 3.10. Connected regular graphs of degrees 2, 3, and 4 with 3–8 nodes

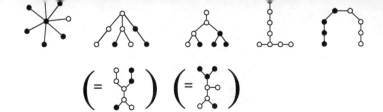

Example 3.11. Five of the 23 distinct unrooted trees with eight nodes

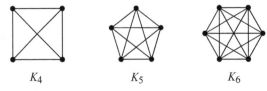

K_4 K_5 K_6

Example 3.12. Complete graphs K_4, K_5, and K_6

A *complete graph* (K_n) is a regular graph of n nodes in which each node is connected to every other node by an edge. The complete graph K_n has $1/2(n(n-1))$ edges.[41] Example 3.12 shows K_4, K_5, and K_6.

A *planar* graph is isomorphic to a graph that can be drawn in a plane without edge crossings; all other graphs are *nonplanar*. All circuit graphs are planar; all complete graphs K_n where $n \geq 5$ are nonplanar.[42]

A *representation* is a diagram of a graph in a plane. A graph can have numerous representations. The *crossing number* of a representation is the number of edges that cross. The *minimum crossing number* of a graph G is the minimum number of crossings in any representation of G. Every planar graph has a minimum crossing number of zero; every nonplanar graph has a minimum crossing number of one or higher.[43] Example 3.13 shows two representations of the complete planar graph K_4. The representation on the left appears to contain an edge crossing between edges 1–4 and 2–3. On the right, a different representation of the same graph that folds node 1 southeast into the center of the graph eliminates this apparent edge crossing and demonstrates that K_4 is, in fact, planar.[44]

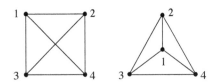

Example 3.13. Two representations of K_4

that includes every edge once and only once.

A *Hamiltonian* graph is a connected graph for which there exists a Hamiltonian circuit that passes through every node once.

The topology of any graph is synonymous with a set of connections between nodes via edges. These relationships can always be represented in the form of a matrix. For a graph G with nodes $n_1, n_2, \ldots n_x$, an *adjacency matrix* is the $n \times n$ matrix whose ijth entry gives the number of edges that join nodes n_i and n_j.[45] For a simple graph (i.e., each pair of nodes is connected by at most one edge), the value of cell M_{ij} is 1 if nodes i and j are connected by an edge, and 0 if they are not.[46] An adjacency matrix provides the same information as a graph, but in a form that is often more manageable, particularly for nonregular, nonplanar graphs with a large number of nodes.

Association Graphs and Digraphs. An association graph *(AG)* depicts an analyst's interpretation of associative adjacency and relative proximity and distance among the segments of an associative set. Association graphs focus on abstract associative organization—that is, on aspects of associative organization identified only with the workings of contextual criteria, rather than with the segments' temporal disposition, distribution, or actual locations in a piece of music (these are all the province of associative landscapes and maps). However, association graphs do retain and reflect some aspects of temporality. Given two segments related by literal repetition and set in different musical contexts, local context can activate one set of relational properties in the first segment but another in the second, giving the two segments different contextual genotypes, sets of connections to other segments, and, as a result, even distinct locations in a graph.[47] Thus an association graph might more explicitly be called a *contextual* association graph: although segments in an *AG look* like isolated snippets of music, each segment is in fact saturated with its original context, its sound being an amalgam of sonic and relational properties activated by the particular nexus of local and long-range musical contexts in which it is embedded.

In formal terms, an *AG* consists of a set of nodes and edges. Nodes represent segments of an associative set; edges, associative adjacencies. Segments can be transcribed in music notation or represented by segment names. Edges are lines (straight, bent, or curved), perhaps labeled with one or more contextual criteria that associate their incident nodes. Line length (short or long) and line weight (thick, thin, or dotted) can be used to convey aspects of associative geometry—differences in the strengths of connection among segments. Some *AGs* include boxes that enclose entire sets or subsets; each box can be labeled with a C/CRS or C/CS for the set inside. Every *AG* has a *basic graph*— an isomorphic graph of empty nodes and unlabeled edges that models topology apart from specific musical segments, criteria, and geometry.[48]

dimensions creates a graph so dense with edges that one can hardly discern the particular relationships of interest in an analytical discussion. To reduce visual clutter and focus on key relationships, I will often modify the graphic representation of connectivity and skeins in an *AG*. Remember that the definition of an associative set ensures that every *AG* is connected: every segment in a set, and every node in its *AG*, can be reached from every other by a walk. However, to focus attention on the strongest connections among segments of a set with strong subsets (say, the bifurcated set *D* in Feldman's *Patterns in a Chromatic Field*), I will often render *AGs* as if they had two or more disjoint component subgraphs (sometimes, but not always, enclosed in boxes).[49] With regard to skeins, the fact that each contextual criterion in an *AG* implies its own edge means that, technically speaking, most *AGs* are multigraphs. But to reduce visual clutter and focus on key relationships, I often bundle all the contextual criteria that relate a pair of segments along a single edge.

The degree of a node in an *AG* is given by the number of its incident edges. *Node degree* (*degree*) is an integer that indicates how many nodes (segments) a given segment references through contextual criteria. *Associative degree* is more specific: it indicates how many *contextual associations* a given segment has with others in the set (i.e., two nodes can be associated by several functionally independent contextual criteria). To find the associative degree of a node, tally the number of contextual criteria attached to each of its incident edges and take the sum. Remember, though, that careful pruning of contextual criteria implied by literal inclusion or logical implication is an essential prerequisite for any meaningful survey of associative degrees for nodes of an *AG*.

Tying the concept of associative degree to contextual genotype, a *relations multiset (RM)* gives a more refined account of the associative affiliations for individual segments in a set. For an associative set *A*, and a segment *Am* in *A*, the *RM*(*Am*) is a set of contextual criteria that is like a weighted version of the CG(*Am*) in that it shows how many segments in *A* are referenced by each contextual criterion. So for an associative set *A* with *k* segments, a segment *Am* in *A*, all other segments *An* in *A* (where $n \neq m$), and corresponding contextual genotypes CG(*Am*) and CG(*An*), we construct the relations multiset RM(*Am*) from CG(*Am*) $\cap$ CG(*An*) where *n* varies from 1 to *k*. Example 3.14 provides a worked example. Given a set *A*, segments *A1*, *A2*, *A3*, *A4*; contextual criteria *w*, *x*, *y*, *z*, and contextual genotypes as shown, we construct the *RM* for each segment by recording the number of element intersections between its contextual genotype and that for every other segment.

The *contextual focus* (*CF*, *focus*) of an associative set is the segment with the relations multiset that combines greatest cardinality with the strongest contextual criteria.[50] In other words, a *CF* is a segment with the most and strongest connections to its consociates, a segment that is most prototypical of

Contextual genotypes for segments of set *A*:

$A = \{A1, A2, A3, A4\}$
w, x, y, z are contextual criteria

$\text{CG}(A1) = \{wx\}$
$\text{CG}(A2) = \{wxyz\}$
$\text{CG}(A3) = \{yz\}$
$\text{CG}(A4) = \{z\}$

Contextual common set C/CS(*A*) $= \{wx\} * \{wxyz\} * \{yz\} * \{z\} = \{w^2x^2y^2z^3\}$

Core contextual common set C/CRS(*A*) $= \{z\}$

Intersections of contextual genotypes:

$\text{CG}(A1) \cap \text{CG}(A2) = \{\text{wx}\}$ $\text{CG(A2)} \cap \text{CG(A3)} = \{yz\}$ $\text{CG}(A3) \cap \text{CG}(A4) = \{z\}$
$\text{CG}(A1) \cap \text{CG}(A3) = \varnothing$ $\text{CG(A2)} \cap \text{CG(A4)} = \{z\}$
$\text{CG}(A1) \cap \text{CG}(A4) = \varnothing$

Relations multisets for segments of set A:
$\text{RM}(A1) = \{wx\}$
$\text{RM}(A2) = \{wxyz^2\}$
$\text{RM}(A3) = \{yz^2\}$
$\text{RM}(A4) = \{z^2\}$

Example 3.14. Relations multiset (RM) for segments of set *A*

an associative set as a whole.[51] A contextual focus references the range and distribution of contextual criteria in a set. Two sets with the same C/CS and C/CRS can differ in focus, and vice versa.

A *directed association graph* or *association digraph* (*DAG*) is an association graph in which at least one edge is replaced by an arrow (single or double-headed) that indicates the order of precedence or *chronology* (if any) for a pair of nodes. The basic graph that underlies an association graph is called an *underlying graph.*[52] Association digraphs can represent one of two types of chronology. *Score chronology* is the order in which segments actually appear in the music. Implicit in most association graphs, where it is encoded in segment names, score chronology can also be represented as a path on a graph. *Associative chronology* indicates an associative precedence that involves analytic interpretation, such as associative derivation, strength of connection, order of recognition or entry into the set, or a listening process. Significantly, score chronology and associative chronology *need not coincide*; the extent to which they synchronize or diverge is an important question for analysis (and one we will revisit).

an association digraph that follows a series of arrows from tail to head.[53] To write paths, we use angled brackets (< >) for ordered sets and braces ({}) for unordered sets; these can be nested as needed to represent all sorts of partial orderings. The nodes and edges visited by a path need not all be distinct: a path can revisit one or more nodes and backtrack over edges. A *node-distinct associative path* (*ND-path*) is a path in which every node is distinct and no node is revisited. An *edge-distinct associative path (ED-path)* is a path in which every edge is distinct—that is, no set of contextual criteria is repeated over the series of edges traces by the path.[54]

An *association matrix* is an adjacency matrix for an association graph.[55] The association matrix AMX(A) for an associative set A compares each segment in A to every other and lists the contextual criteria that associate each pair of segments. Segment names head rows (i) and columns (j); the cell AMX(A)$_{i,j}$ lists the contextual criteria that relate segments A_i and A_j. When A_i and A_j are associated only by criteria common to all segments of A, AMX(A)$_{i,j}$ is left blank; criteria that support the set as a whole are listed outside the matrix.[56] Because an association matrix is symmetrical around its main diagonal, only the upper right half is completed. Threading an association matrix is formally equivalent to tracing a path on an association graph. Given a segment A_i that heads a row, one moves to a segment A_j that heads a column, then through the set of contextual criteria in AMX(A)$_{i,j}$ that associate A_i and A_j to construct the path <A_i, A_j>.[57] One then can repeat the process starting with A_j and moving to A_k, and continue in that fashion, concatenating the results to create longer paths.

Music theory offers some straightforward examples of circuit graphs, complete graphs, and other types or aspects of graphs outlined above. For example, pitch-class intersection among the three octatonic collections forms the circuit graph C_3; pc intersections among the four hexatonic collections, and the twelve major keys distinct to within enharmonic equivalence, form the circuit graphs C_4 and C_{12}, respectively. The three octatonic collections also form the complete graph K_3. In Babbitt's *Partitions* (1957), successive recombination of the four trichord types SCs 3-2[013], 3-3[014], 3-4[015], and 3-7[025] to create trichordal arrays II–VII almost yields the complete graph K_4, but for the edge that represents array VII, which combines SC 3-7[025] with itself (rendering the graph nonsimple), instead of with SC 3-3[014] (ex. 3.15).[58] Douthett and Steinbach's "chicken-wire torus" is a nonplanar, connected, regular graph of 24 nodes of degree 3, in which every major and minor triad is connected to three others by two common tones.[59] Binary trees appear in Lerdahl and Jackendoff's time-span reductions and prolongational reductions and in Lerdahl's reductive analyses.[60]

Circuit graphs, complete graphs, and other regular graphs are more the province of music theory, which tends to focus on associations in one dimension

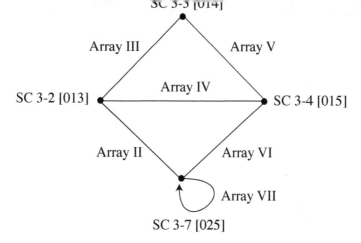

SC 3-3 [014]

Array III

Array V

Array IV

SC 3-2 [013]

SC 3-4 [015]

Array II

Array VI

Array VII

SC 3-7 [025]

Example 3.15. Babbitt, *Partitions*, combinations of trichord types in successive arrays (after Mead, *Introduction to the Music of Milton Babbitt*, ex. 2.58, p. 114)

to the exclusion of all others, than of music analysis, where multidimensional relations among segments prevail. Music does, however, offer plenty of examples of regular graphs with just a few nodes. In J. S. Bach's Toccata and Fugue in D Minor, BWV 565 for organ, two pairs of passes through a move from iv^6 to V create a small associative set of four segments bifurcated in two dimensions, by register (*G1–G2*, versus *G3–G4*), and by texture and rhythm (*G1–G3* and *G2–G4*) (ex. 3.16a). The underlying graph is circuit graph C_4, a regular graph of four nodes, each of degree two. Example 3.16b represents the conformance between associative and score chronology in the Bach excerpt in an association digraph with two distinct paths, each containing three nodes and two arrows (<*G1, G2, G4*> and <*G1, G3, G4*>). The C_4 circuit graph is fairly common in the music literature, easily formed by two types of contextual criteria operating orthogonally to one another.

Examples 3.17a and 3.17b give another example, from mm. 30–31 of Schoenberg's *Klavierstück* op. 23, no. 3 (1923). Here pitch inversion around E4/E♭4 (pitch spacing by $C_{ip\ I\ <2126>}$) associates segments within each measure, while C_{pitch} and C_{pc} criteria bind pairs of segments in the first versus second part of the bar. As in the Bach, the two paths traced on the digraph follow score chronology.

Webern's *Concerto*, op. 24 (1934) provides a third example of a C_4 AG. Eight trichordal segments of an associative set *H* drawn from two successive row forms (T_BIP in mm. 63–64, RT_0IP in mm. 65–67) partition into four two-segment associative subsets in two ways: pitch retrograde within an instrument (*H1–H5, H2–H6, H3–H7, H4–H8*) and rhythmic repetition across instruments

Example 3.16a. Bach, Toccata in D Minor, BWV 565, mm. 16–21

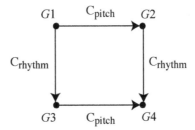

Example 3.16b. Bach, Toccata in D Minor, BWV 565, mm. 16–21, C_4 association digraph

Example 3.17a. Schoenberg, *Klavierstück* op. 23, no. 3, mm. 30–31

Core criteria: $C_{SC\ 5\text{-}10\ [01346]}$, C_{rhythm} ♫♩, $C_{attack\ density\ <41>}$

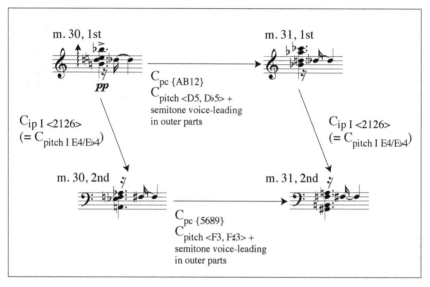

Example 3.17b. Schoenberg, *Klavierstück* op. 23, no. 3, mm. 30–31, C_4 association digraph

(*H*1–*H*8, *H*2–*H*7, *H*3–*H*6, *H*4–*H*5) (ex. 3.18a). Example 3.18b shows the corresponding association digraph, composed of two disjunct underlying C_4 subgraphs, each with four paths of length 1. Segments associated by pitch and timbre align horizontally; segments associated by attack rhythm and articulation, vertically. Each arrow follows score chronology (encoded in segment names), but unlike the digraph for the Bach Toccata, here score chronology does not proceed uniformly left to right or top to bottom in the graph. We will have more to say about this sort of situation later.

Example 3.18a. Webern, *Concerto* op. 24, I, mm. 63–67 (concert pitch)

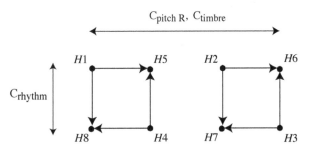

Example 3.18b. Webern, *Concerto* op. 24, I, mm. 63–67, association digraph, two disjunct underlying C_4 subgraphs

Circuit graphs can appear in different guises and in complex relation to the musical surface. Page 14 of Feldman's *Patterns in a Chromatic Field* consists of a series of eighteen events, each a sustained tone in the cello aligned with a chord in the piano of equal duration. Repetition bundles the piano's eighteen chords into seven segments of a variegated associative set *I* (ex. 3.19a). But *I*1–*I*7 involve only four distinct trichordal components in the right hand, and

the left occur only with each other (in *I*4); the remaining three trichords in the right hand are paired, then recombined, with trichords in the left to produce a graph that includes the circuit graph C_6 plus two extra edges, *I*5–*I*6 and *I*6–*I*7 (ex. 3.19c). Cross-referencing this graph against the list of segments and events in examples 3.19a and 3.19b reveals a persistent divergence between associative and score chronology. Of the eighteen events created by repetitions of the seven piano chords *I*1–*I*7 (each a distinct combination of a cello note with a piano chord), there is only one case when an associative adjacency (*I*6–*I*7) is realized as a temporal adjacency (events 16 and 17). Thus the passage is based not so much on repetition as on recycling material as a means to continuous variation (not development).

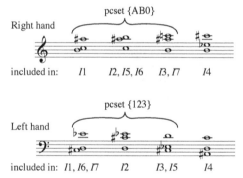

Segment:	*I*1	*I*2	*I*3	*I*4	*I*5	*I*6	*I*7

Event #:	1, 3, 8, 11, 14	2, 6, 10	4, 7, 15	5, 9, 12, 18	13	17	16, 19

Example 3.19a. Feldman, *Patterns in a Chromatic Field*, page 14, seven chords of an associative set *I*

pcset {AB0}

Right hand

included in:	*I*1	*I*2, *I*5, *I*6	*I*3, *I*7	*I*4

pcset {123}

Left hand

included in:	*I*1, *I*6, *I*7	*I*2	*I*3, *I*5	*I*4

Example 3.19b. Feldman, *Patterns in a Chromatic Field*, page 14, trichord components in right and left hands

In *Canonic Variations* (1992) for two pianos by Robert Morris, a circuit graph drives systematic recombination of material between piano I and II and is the basis for large-scale form. The piece is based on a twelve-tone row and combinatorial trichordal array. Its form consists of fourteen "variations" separated by double bars (A, I–XII, and AA in ex. 3.20a).[61] These have strong structural ties

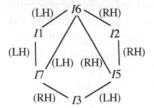

Example 3.19c. Feldman, *Patterns in a Chromatic Field*, page 14, association graph for set *I*

to the opening trichordal array and to one another. First, through transformation and repartitioning, the trichordal array for variation A yields the arrays for variations I–XII.[62] Then, within each piano, the fourteen variations involve only seven distinct pitch realizations: *a–f* plus *x* in piano I, and *g–l* plus *y* in piano II. So each pitch realization appears in two variations, one in the first half of the piece, and one in the second. Realizations *x* and *y* are the only realizations that pair with each other in both halves (variations A and AA). Systematic recombination among the remaining twelve pitch realizations, *a–f* in piano I and *g–l* in piano II, forms the circuit graph C_{12} (ex. 3.20b).

Piano I
Pitch realiz.: *x*   *a*   *b*   *c*   *d*   *e*   *f*
Variations: A, AA   I, VIII   II, VII   III, X   IV, IX   V, XII   VI, XI

Piano II
Pitch realiz.: *y*   *g*   *h*   *i*   *j*   *k*   *l*
Variations: A, AA   I, VI   II, IX   III, VIII   IV, XI   V, X   VII, XII

Example 3.20a. Morris, *Canonic Variations*, locations of material in piano I and II, and variations associated

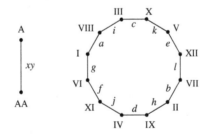

Example 3.20b. Morris, *Canonic Variations*, variations associated by recombination of material trace circuit graph C_{12}

and variation sets, where a cluster of features introduced in the theme's opening bars are selectively retained or transformed in subsequent variations. The theme of Beethoven's Piano Sonata No. 30 in E Major, op. 109 begins with the eight-bar melody shown in example 3.21a. Core features include a sequence of two major thirds aligned with strong-to-weak metric positions (G♯–E, D♯–B in mm. 1–2) and the dotted rhythm in m. 1. Repetition and development of these features, along with harmonic rhythm and phrasing, divides the melody into four two-measure segments that form an associative set held together by C_{pitch}, C_{SDint}, and C_{rhythm} criteria. The opening bars of variations I–VI each retain some of these core features, but reinterpret others and introduce new features that distinguish the individual variations (ex. 3.21b). Thinking of the seven two-bar incipits of the theme and variations I–VI as a higher-level associative set suggests an association graph in the form of a tree, with the theme's incipit as the root and the incipits of variations I–VI as the initial nodes of six branches. One can then adjust the lengths of the six edges from root to branch nodes to reflect differences in associative proximity (e.g., variation VI is most like the theme; variation IV, least).

Example 3.21a. Beethoven, Piano Sonata No. 30 in E Major, op. 109, III, theme, mm. 1–8

Different analytical perspectives on a passage can, and often do, yield contrasting associative topologies. Like many of Steve Reich's compositions, *Eight Lines* (1983) involves canons at the octave and the deconstruction and reconstruction of repeated patterns.[63] Example 3.22a shows two two-measure patterns in the clarinets and pianos, taken from R4 and from just before R9. The latter makes plain the pair of canons between piano I and piano II that structure the entire passage: the right hand of piano II is one beat *ahead* of the right hand of piano I (i.e., a T_{-2} rotation); the left, two beats *behind* the left hand of piano I (a T_{+4} rotation). Throughout the passage, the composite of clarinets I and II doubles notes in the right hand of piano II. Example 3.22b traces the progressive reconstruction of this piano II figure through five composite segments in the clarinets, from R4 to R8. The passage begins with the segment

2), which contains two copies of one idea.[64] Progressive diversification of material in the first, versus second, measures of the segments R5:1+2, R6:1+2, and R7:1+2 eventually reverses in R8:1+2, which brings the material in R8:1 back into closer accord with that of R8:2.

Example 3.21b. Beethoven, Piano Sonata No. 30 in E Major, op. 109, III, theme and variations

Example 3.22a. Reich, *Eight Lines*, clarinets I and II and pianos I and II at R4 and just before R9

Example 3.22b. Reich, *Eight Lines*, composite of clarinets I and II, R4–R8

Interpreting these five two-measure segments as an associative set, example 3.23a represents the associative topology of the reconstruction as a simple tree with five nodes connected in one associative stream. Each of the first four segments serves both as a node and as part of a contextual criterion that associates that same node with its immediate successor. Dividing each two-measure unit in half and thinking of the reconstruction as an associative set of ten one-measure segments (i.e., R4:1, R4:2, R5:1, etc.) changes the associative topology substantially (ex. 3.23b). The repetitions of R4:1 in R4:2 and R5:1, and of R5:2 in R6:2 and R7:2 now appear as associative subsets (in boxes). Starting with R5:2 and continuing through R7:2, first- and second-measure segments diverge, but eventually reconverge in the close association between R8:1 and R8:2 by C_{pitch} and C_{rhythm} criteria (the individual criterion is written out in staff notation). The result is the circuit graph C_6, here shown as a lopsided hexagon in which vertical placement represents temporal order to the extent possible.

Complete graphs are common enough in the music literature if one admits trivial examples: an associative set of n segments in which the contextual genotype for every segment includes the same core contextual criterion can always

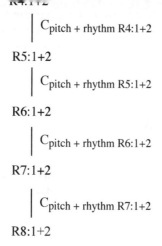

| Cpitch + rhythm R4:1+2

R5:1+2

| Cpitch + rhythm R5:1+2

R6:1+2

| Cpitch + rhythm R6:1+2

R7:1+2

| Cpitch + rhythm R7:1+2

R8:1+2

Example 3.23a. Reich, *Eight Lines*, clarinets I and II, R4–R8, simple tree

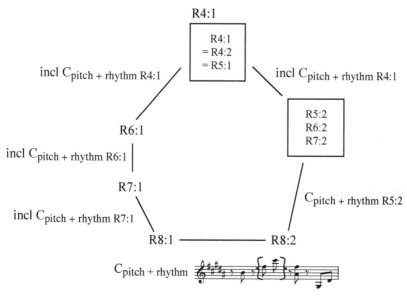

Example 3.23b. Reich, *Eight Lines*, clarinets I and II, circuit graph C_6

be rendered as the complete association graph K_n. More substantial examples are hard to come by but harbor interesting possibilities. Consider the case of an associative A with association graph K_5 shown in example 3.24. Nodes represent five segments $A1$–$A5$; edges are labeled by lowercase letters (b–k) that represent contextual criteria. All segments of A are associated by

tinct contextual genotype; moreover, the contextual criterion that connects each segment to each of the others is also unique in A. The result is a set that is highly variegated, but coherent. Intrigued by this idea, Robert Morris composed *Simple Stars* (2007) for two pianos or other keyboards. The ten-page open score consists of five spreads of one page for each piano; each page has from one to three passages. Every passage within a spread associates with every other through at least one shared salient characteristic, such as an initial set of grace notes or pitch content. The two pianists can play the passages of a spread in any order, both within each piano and between them. Overall, the associative topology of the complete score can be seen as a series of complete graphs K_n, where n varies from 3 to 5 according to the number of passages per spread. Each performance of the piece traces its own path through each graph in the series.[65]

Associative set A

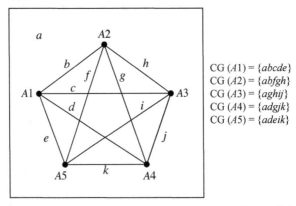

CG (A1) = {abcde}
CG (A2) = {abfgh}
CG (A3) = {aghij}
CG (A4) = {adgjk}
CG (A5) = {adeik}

Example 3.24. Schematic of an association graph isomorphic to K_5 in which the contextual genotype of each segment is unique

Although some association graphs are regular, connected, and planar, most are more idiosyncratic and complex. A brief solo passage from Feldman's *Piano and Orchestra* (1975) provides an opportunity to study a more complex set of associations. Example 3.25 gives a score for the piano solo in mm. 135–40. The passage consists of twelve chords, nine with distinct pitch content. Sixfold repetition of the pitch ordering <A♭5, B♭5> from bar to bar suggests hearing the passage in terms of a set of six segments associated by $C_{pitch\ <Ab5,\ Bb5>}$. But a closer look suggests another interpretation. The nine chords contain only six distinct components in the right hand and eight in the left. I will approach the associative organization of the passage through these smallest functionally independent components.

Example 3.25. Feldman, *Piano and Orchestra*, mm. 135–40, piano solo

Example 3.26a is an association graph for the variegated set that includes the six distinct right-hand components from mm. 135–40. Segment names index score locations by hand, measure, and place in the bar (first or second chord); for example, R135.1 is the first chord in the right hand in m. 135; R135.2 follows in the second part of the bar.[66] Thicker and thinner edges represent stronger and weaker lines of association. Every segment in the set associates with at least one other by some contextual criterion, but differences in the strength of association create a bifurcated set with two associative subsets, rendered as two subgraphs on left and right connected by a bridge. Segments from the first part of a bar, all associated by dyadic and triadic subsets of the

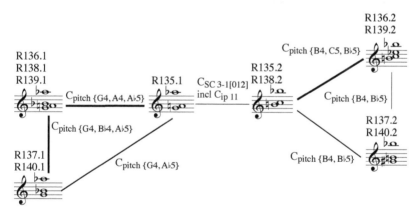

Example 3.26a. Feldman, *Piano and Orchestra*, mm. 135–40, right hand, association graph

to the circuit graph C_3 and complete graph K_3, but the edges differ in strength. Segments from the second part of a bar, associated by $C_{pitch \{B4, Bb5\}}$, cluster on the right in another subgraph that is in a sense isomorphic to C_3 and K_3 but due to the greater associative proximity between R135.2 and R137.2, resembles a tree with a stronger and a weaker branch.[67] The edge that connects the first two chords of the passage (R135.1 and R135.2) by $C_{SC\ 3\text{-}1[012]}$ forms a bridge between the two subgraphs; we will look at this more closely later on.[68]

Associative organization among the left hand's eight component chords is similar in three respects (ex. 3.26b). Once again, chords from the first and second parts of a bar fall in different associative subsets, rendered as subgraphs to the left and right of a central bridge. Once again, the bridge connects the first two segments of the passage, here L135.1 and L135.2, which are associated by the relatively weak criterion incl $C_{ip\ 1}$. This time, however, the two associative subsets are of different sizes. The "first" subset contains five chords; the "second," three. Unlike the "first" subgraph for the right hand, that for the left has a main line of three (distinct) segments (L135.1, L138.1, and L136.1) and includes a trivial C_4 subgraph of four segments associated by $C_{pitch \{B3, C4\}}$ (in the box). But the left hand's "second" subgraph is similar to that in the right: a minimal tree with a head node and two branches, one slightly stronger (to L136.2) and one weaker (to L137.2). Moreover, it is partially *isographic*, in that segments' temporal positions in the right hand's "second" subgraph match those in the left's in every case. A comprehensive survey of the right- and left-hand association graphs suggests a strategy of associative organization in which continued experimentation with the first chord of each bar alternates with relative stability for the second.

Schoenberg's *Klavierstück* op. 23, no. 3 can be seen as a series of explorations of various relational properties of a five-note serial motive.[69] Example 3.27

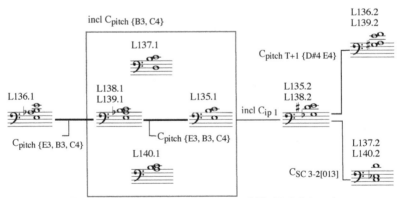

Example 3.26b. Feldman, *Piano and Orchestra*, mm. 135–40, left hand, association graph

Example 3.27. Schoenberg, *Klavierstück* op. 23, no. 3, mm. 1–8, eight segments of an associative set *J*

shows the first eight instances of the motive as segments *J*1–*J*8 from what develops into a much larger set *J* with the core contextual criterion $C_{ip\ I\ <-8,\ +2,\ -5,\ +2>}$.[70] These eight segments are associated in various ways, including by staccato or legato articulation, recto or inverted forms of the motive, total or partially ordered pcsets, and the two partially ordered pc tetrachords <{B♭, D} {B, C♯}> and <{F, A} {F♯, G♯}>.[71]

With multiple contextual criteria at work, the association graph for *J*1–*J*8 is complex and best constructed in stages through several subgraphs. Example 3.28a shows the C_4 subgraph that takes in the four segments *J*1, *J*2, *J*5, and *J*6 associated by staccato articulation and the pitch interval series <–8, +2, –5, +2> that defines the motive, plus other contextual criteria shown attached to individual edges. Thick lines for the edges *J*1–*J*6 and *J*2–*J*5 indicate the strong associations in pitch-class ordering within each pair of segments. Not part of this subgraph per se, the four dotted arrows prefigure the formation of edges from nodes in this subgraph to those in other subgraphs within the fully assembled *AG*. Example 3.28b provides a second subgraph, of associations among the four legato segments *J*3, *J*4, *J*7, and *J*8. The legato subgraph has a different associative topology and a much wider spectrum of associative proximity and distance: whereas *J*3 and *J*7 are in very close proximity, segments in the pairs *J*3 and *J*8, and *J*7 and *J*8, are relatively distant. A third subgraph, for segments associated by the pc partial ordering <{B♭, D} {B, C♯}> is given as example 3.28c. This subgraph is isomorphic to the complete graph K_4, and shows some variation in strength of association. Example 3.29 assembles the three component subgraphs into one connected *AG*. In this representation

3.28b) is pushed to the rear, and the pitch-class partial ordering subgraph K_4 (ex. 3.28c) extends back from the left side of the front face. The resulting graph is nonregular, but all nodes are of degree 3 or 4; differences in edge thickness represent seven strengths of association. While the composite graph is visually complex, it is still planar: by rearranging nodes, and lengthening and bending certain edges, it can be drawn in two dimensions without edge crossings.[72]

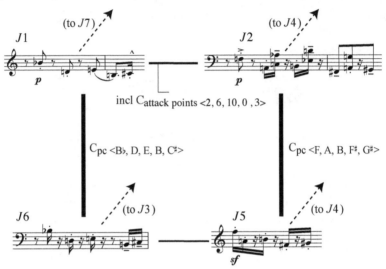

Example 3.28a. Associative topology of $J1$–$J8$, staccato subgraph

For an example of a nonplanar AG, we return to Babbitt's deceptively simple *Play on Notes*. Like the associations among $J1$–$J8$ in Schoenberg's *Klavierstück* op. 23, no. 3, multidimensional associations among the sixteen phrases in bells and voices by pitch interval, rhythm, pc hexachord, and timbre yield a highly complex AG that is best constructed from a series of subgraphs. Example 3.30a shows a subgraph of C_{ip} associations. The four-group of T_n, I, R, and RI transformations divides the sixteen phrases into four equivalence classes; these appear in the corresponding subgraph as four disconnected components, each isomorphic to the complete graph K_4. Example 3.30b shows the subgraph for associations by rhythm. Here the six rhythms form six equivalence classes; the result is a disconnected subgraph with six components, two isomorphic to K_4 and four with two nodes. Subgraphs for associations by pc hexachord and timbre (not shown) are isomorphic to one another: each is a disconnected graph with two components, each isomorphic to K_8 (i.e., the equivalence classes defined by pc hexachords {024579} vs. {68AB13} and bells vs. voices, respectively).

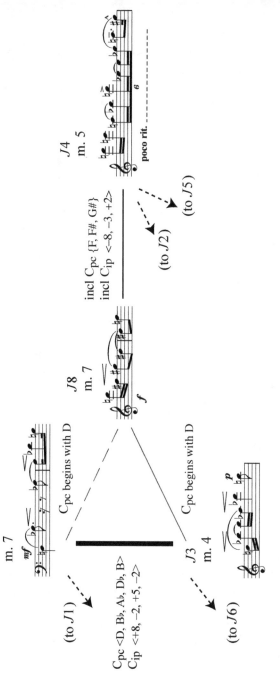

Example 3.28b. Associative topology of J1–J8, legato subgraph

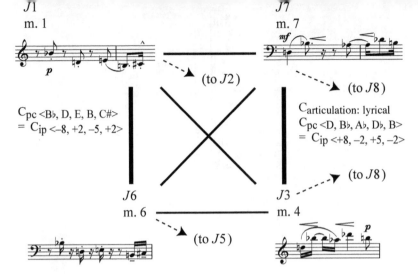

Example 3.28c. Associative topology of $J1$–$J8$, $C_{pc < \{Bb, D\} \{B, C\#\} >}$ subgraph

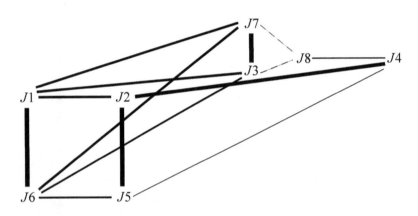

Example 3.29. Association graph, $J1$–$J8$

A comparison of the subgraphs for C_{ip} in example 3.30a and C_{rhythm} in example 3.30b reveals that the two dimensions define different sets of equivalence classes. Other than pairs of segments related by literal repetition (B1–B5, V1–V5, V3–V7, and B3–B7) and four other exceptions (B2–B6, V2–V6, B4–B8, and V4–V8), pairs of segments connected by an edge in the C_{ip} subgraph lie in different components of the C_{rhythm} subgraph and vice versa.

As a result, the two subgraphs can be assembled into a single composite graph of associations by C_{ip} *or* by C_{rhythm}, in which edges *within* components of

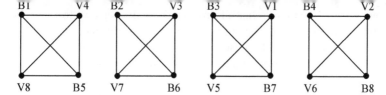

Example 3.30a. Babbitt, *Play on Notes*, subgraph of associations by C_{ip}

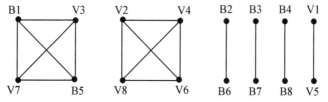

Example 3.30b. Babbitt, *Play on Notes*, subgraph of associations by C_{rhythm}

each subgraph establish links *between* components of the other. The composite graph contains many more, and longer, paths and circuits than either the C_{ip} or C_{rhythm} subgraph does. The degree of most nodes also increases (e.g., V3 changes from degree 3 in the C_{ip} and C_{rhythm} subgraphs to degree 5 in the composite graph, with a corresponding change in associative degree from 3 to 6). Adding edges from the K_8 subgraphs for C_{pc} and C_{timbre} brings an explosion in complexity: the result is a nonplanar multigraph with multiple nodes of degree 11 and some nodes with associative degrees as high as 20, in which every segment is connected to every other by a path if not an edge.[73] The complexity of this *AG* may come as a surprise, given the seeming simplicity of the musical surface and its associations among segments. The graph serves as an important reminder that multidimensional associations among actual musical *segments* generally produce networks of relations that are far more complex than those formed by associations among segments in *a single respect*, as is often the case in work with similarity relations and transformational models.

Association graphs draw attention to overall properties of associative topology, such as connectivity and the presence or absence of circuits. They also depict more specific features of set structure, such as the presence or absence of a contextual focus. Recalling our earlier discussion of motivic connections among themes from the three movements of Beethoven's "Appassionata" sonata, example 3.31 renders the first and second themes of the first movement (mm. 1–4 and mm. 36–37, respectively) together with the themes of the second (II, mm. 1–4) and third movements (III, mm. 20–22) as part of a single associative superset represented by one association graph. The graph recognizes three relational properties—a triadic arpeggiation (motive *ARP*),

Only one of the four themes has all three of these properties—the first theme of the first movement. Consequently, in the graph it appears as the node with the highest degree (3) and highest associative degree (5); thus the topology of the graph represents the opening theme as a contextual focus.[74]

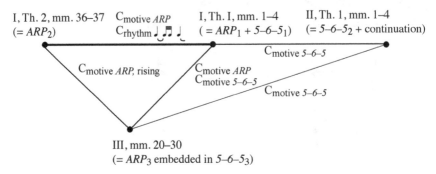

I, Th. 2, mm. 36–37 $C_{motive\ ARP}$ I, Th. I, mm. 1–4   II, Th. 1, mm. 1–4
(= ARP_2) C_{rhythm} ♩ ♫ ♩ (= ARP_1 + 5–6–5_1) (= 5–6–5_2 + continuation)

$C_{motive\ 5–6–5}$

$C_{motive\ ARP,\ rising}$ $C_{motive\ ARP}$
              $C_{motive\ 5–6–5}$
                           $C_{motive\ 5–6–5}$

III, mm. 20–30
(= ARP_3 embedded in 5–6–5_3)

Example 3.31. Beethoven, Piano Sonata No. 23 in F Minor, op. 57, association graph with opening theme as contextual focus

In Schoenberg's *Klavierstück* op. 23, no. 3, a more even distribution of contextual criteria across segments J1–J8 yields a different result. The association graph (refer back to ex. 3.29) shows a four-way tie for the highest degree— J1, J3, J6, and J7 each have four adjacent nodes. Appealing first to associative degree, then to criterion strength, rules out J3 and J7, each connected to J8 by a C_{pc} criterion ("starts with D♮") that is weak compared to the other C_{pc} criteria at work in set J. But resolving the tie between J1 and J6 isn't so easy: to do so would require weighing the contextual criterion $C_{ip\ <-8,\ +2,\ -5,\ +2>}$ (here, pitch transposition by T_{-19}) between J5 and J6 against $C_{pc\ <\{Bb,\ D\}\ \{B,\ C\#\}>}$, which connects J1 and J3. For such close calls, a double focus can be the most accurate representation of associative topology. But sometimes sonic aspects that privilege one segment over the other can decide the question. That is the case here: whereas J1 is an isolated melody, J6 is embedded in a complex polyphonic texture. So J1 emerges as the sole contextual focus.

Issues in Representation. Association graphs raise a number of issues with regard to the planar representation of multidimensional musical space and the fit or misfit between associative adjacency, proximity, and chronology on the one hand, and temporal succession, proximity, and score chronology on the other. The topology of an association graph is determined by node adjacency and degree. Some association graphs are planar—that is, they have at least one planar representation and a minimum crossing number of zero. Others are nonplanar, meaning that edge crossings are inevitable in two dimensions and

always be avoided in three dimensions.) Rendering nonplanar graphs in two dimensions is inherently difficult. Determining the minimum crossing number of a graph (that is, the fewest edge crossings required in a two-dimensional representation) remains an open problem in graph theory.[75] But whether or not one knows the minimum crossing number, developing a representation with the fewest edge crossings is itself a significant task, requiring experimentation with rearranging segments, or extending or repositioning edges inside the graph to the periphery. Like nonplanar graphs, most planar graphs have multiple representations; thus developing visually lucid and analytically accurate representation of planar graphs poses many of the same challenges as for nonplanar graphs.

Using an association graph to represent associative geometry—not just topology—introduces further complications. Rearranging segments or relocating edges to reduce the crossing number of a representation usually changes edge length. When edge length is supposed to convey associative distance (as it does in an associative geometry), these changes become problematic: segments that are associatively adjacent or proximate can end up far apart in a graph, while associatively distant segments can wind up next to one another. Using heavier lines for stronger connections, and lighter for weaker, is only a partial remedy, because the visual impression of spatial proximity and distance remains.

One solution to the problem of representing multidimensional musical associations lies in computer modeling, which transcends the two-dimensional limitation of the print medium. But even in two dimensions, one can convey the complex multidimensionality of association graphs in two ways. First, as we have seen for Schoenberg's *Klavierstück* op. 23, no. 3 and Babbitt's *Play on Notes*, one can gradually assemble a complex planar or nonplanar graph from a series of subgraphs (as in exx. 3.28a, 3.28b, 3.28c, and 3.29 for segments $J1$–$J8$ of Schoenberg's *Klavierstück* op. 23, no. 3), or leave assembly to the imagination (as with ex. 3.30a, ex. 3.30b, and the two K_8 subgraphs for C_{pc} and C_{timbre} in Babbitt's *Play on Notes*). Or, one can use an association matrix (AMX) to represent the strongest association (if any) for every pair of segments in the set in a comprehensive and compact form, regardless of whether the topology of the corresponding *AG* is planar or nonplanar.

Example 3.32 provides an association matrix for the six chords in the right hand of mm. 135–40 from Feldman's *Piano and Orchestra*. The six chords head six rows and six columns; the cell at the intersection of row i and column j gives the strongest contextual criterion that associates segments i and j. In this particular matrix, open noteheads represent C_{pitch} criteria; solid noteheads, C_{ip} criteria that involve a dyad or trichord at the specified pitch or pitch-class transposition. Notice that matrix diagonals alternate between open and solid noteheads (i.e., between C_{pitch} and C_{ip} criteria); this reflects the fact that the set (and the *AG* in ex. 3.26a) is bifurcated, such that chords from different

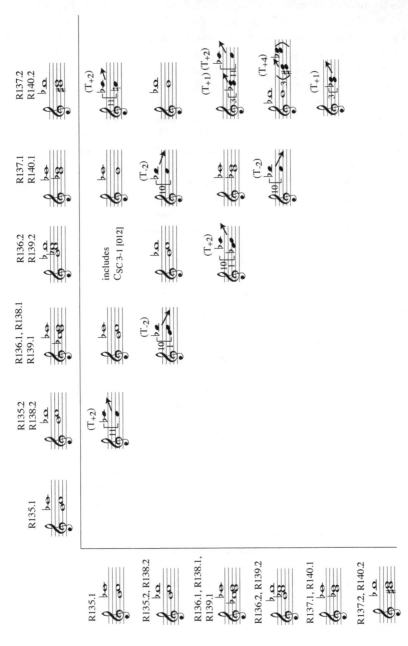

Example 3.32. Feldman, *Piano and Orchestra*, mm. 135–40, right hand, association matrix

associations they represent, the AMX provides a relatively comprehensive view. Global properties focus on the range and distribution of contextual criteria among the segments at graph *nodes*; an association matrix represents the range and distribution of contextual criteria attached to graph *edges*. In this particular matrix, C_{ip} criteria cluster around just four pitch intervals, 1, 3, 10 and 11; the recurrent pitch transpositions T_{+2} and T_{-2} reflect the alternation between A♭5 and B♭5 within each bar.

In this example, every segment is directly associated with every other in some way. This is also the case among segments J1–J8 in Schoenberg's *Klavierstück* op. 23, no. 3 and among the sixteen phrases of Babbitt's *Play on Notes*, where the strong contextual criteria $C_{ip\ <-8,\ +2,\ -5,\ +2>}$ and $C_{ip\ <+4,\ +1,\ -2,\ +5,\ +2>}$ of their respective C/CRSs support nearly every segment and associate nearly every pair of segments under some P, I, R, or RI transformation (i.e., all but J8 in the Schoenberg). Compared to the Feldman, however, both the Schoenberg and the Babbitt sets yield AMXs with greater diversity in the strengths of relation among segments. In the Schoenberg, the strongest associations are in the adjacencies J1–J6, J2–J5, and J3–J7; the weakest, between J8 and two of its four nonadjacencies (J1 and J6), with which it shares only one pc and differs in articulation (legato for J8, staccato for J1 and J6). The sixteen phrases of the Babbitt are even more diverse in their strengths of association. Whereas four adjacencies (B1–B5, B3–B7, V1–V5, V3–V7) are literal repetitions with skeins of four coincident associations in C_{ip}, C_{rhythm}, C_{pc}, and C_{timbre}, four pairs of segments (B1–B6, B1–B8, V1–V6, V1–V8) form adjacencies only by virtue of timbre—never by C_{ip}, C_{rhythm}, or C_{pc}. In sets where no one contextual criterion supports every segment in the set, and where contextual genotypes are diverse and the workings of contextual criteria uncoordinated with respect to one another, the AMX can have holes: these indicate that the segments that head row *i* and column *j* are not associated by any contextual criterion under consideration. Thus the relative completeness or spottiness of an AMX and the uniformity or diversity in the number and strengths of contextual criteria in its cells are ways to gauge the extent to which a set is cohesive or sprawls.

The representation of score chronology, both temporal succession and proximity—is another issue in rendering association graphs. First and foremost, association graphs depict associative topology—that is, configurations of nodes and edges. But individual representations of an *AG* also reflect practical aspects of rendering that topology legibly in two dimensions. Just as associative adjacency need not coincide with temporal adjacency, the layout of segments from left to right or top to bottom in an *AG* need not conform to temporal progress through a score.[76]

Segments in an associative set are usually named by order of appearance. Therefore an *AG*, and any path drawn on an *AG*, often encodes order in two contexts at once. Whereas graph topology indicates associative adjacency, and

names indicate score chronology. Thus *AGs* and paths represent not only associative organization, but also patterns of convergence and divergence between associative and score chronology. For each pair of segments A*n* and A*n*+1 connected directly by an edge, associative adjacency and temporal succession coincide; for each such pair of segments not so connected, they diverge.

Scanning the disposition of segment names in an *AG* or path can prompt observations about the fit, or misfit, between associative and score chronology. Taking associative adjacency as referential, one can see whether a path is also a temporal succession, and whether associative proximity in a subset or subgraph corresponds to temporal clustering in the music. Conversely, taking segment names and temporal succession as referential, one can peruse an *AG* to see whether or not consecutive segments form associative adjacencies, or are connected only by more roundabout paths. Associative graphs and paths thus provide analysts with tools to investigate how pieces of music move through associative space over time, and how score chronology is reflected, refracted, or effectively reconfigured by associative adjacency and proximity.[77]

In some *AGs*, the combined effect of graph topology, the specific assignment of segments to nodes, representation layout, and overlaid associative paths, creates a direct correspondence between associative chronology and score chronology. The association digraph for the four segments *G*1–*G*4 in mm. 16–19 of Bach's Toccata and Fugue in D Minor (ex. 3.16b) is a good example: both of the short paths <*G*1, *G*2, *G*4> and <*G*1, *G*3, *G*4> are also temporal successions.

The *AG* for six distinct right hand chords from mm. 135–40 of Feldman's *Piano and Orchestra* (ex. 3.26a) provides a more complex example. Here the path <R135.1, R136.1, R137.1> traced on the circuit subgraph C_3 on the left side of the graph is a temporal succession, but leapfrogs over every other chord. The longer path through the same subgraph <R135.1, R136.1, R137.1, R138.1, R139.1, R140.1> includes an oscillation between two of the notated segments. On the right side of the graph, the partial ordering <R135.2, {R136.2, R137.2}> is a path; the longer path <R135.2, R136.2, R137.2, R138.2, R139.2, R140.2> completes two circuits through three notationally distinct segments. The bridge that connects the left and right subgraphs can be defined as the path <R135.1, R135.2>, which models the temporal succession from the first chord to the second. Note that on this relatively selective *AG*, which shows only C_{pitch} and C_{pc} criteria, the temporal succession R135.1, R135.2, R136.1, R136.2, R137.1, etc., is *not* a path: nodes alternate between the left and right subgraphs, and between contrasting associative sets. But on the more comprehensive AMX that takes in both C_{pc} and C_{ip} criteria (ex. 3.32) the same ordering of nodes *is* a path. Thus the *AG* and AMX provide different perspectives on the set and its temporal realization: the inability to trace a path by immediate temporal succession on the graph indicates the alternation of two distinct associative subsets; threading

that connect each segment to its immediate successor.

The *AG* for *J*1–*J*8 from Schoenberg's *Klavierstück* op. 23, no. 3 (ex. 3.29) illustrates two general points about *AG*s and paths. First, *AG*s often admit multiple paths between a given pair of nodes. For example, the shortest path from *J*1 to *J*4 has three nodes (<*J*1, *J*2, *J*4>); the longest ND-path, eight (<*J*1, *J*2, *J*5, *J*6, *J*7, *J*3, *J*8, *J*4>). Deleting detours and selecting one node from a pair of nodes that form a partial ordering offers intermediate options, such as the five-node path <*J*1, *J*6, *J*3, *J*8, *J*4>. Second, different pairs of nodes are connected by shortest paths that vary in length. In this *AG*, the shortest path between any pair of nodes is an adjacency; the longest of these shortest paths contains three nodes, as between *J*5 and *J*7—two segments related by inversion in pitch interval ordering, but that differ in pcsets and articulation.

In Babbitt's *Play on Notes*, the composition of subgraphs in examples 3.30a, 3.30b and the two complete graphs K_8 for relations among pc hexachords and timbre add a number of edges not present in any one subgraph. Many of these form new associative adjacencies and enable new paths, while others (e.g., for literal repetitions like B1 and B5) add another edge to an existing edge or skein. *Play on Notes* is characterized by consistent discord between associative adjacency and temporal succession. The four segments within each of the four C_{ip} subgraphs (ex. 3.30a) are evenly distributed across the four pairs of phrases that comprise the score: two of the subgraphs (containing the segments {V1, B3, V5, B7} and {V2, B4, V6, B8}) are maximally even in this respect, with segments only in odd- or even-numbered phrases. Similarly, the six C_{rhythm} subgraphs (ex. 3.30b) are each maximally even with respect to the score: two subgraphs draw segments only from odd, or even, phrases, while four subgraphs each connect two segments four phrases apart (e.g., {B2, B6}, {V1, V5}). Earlier we noted that *Play on Notes* contains four pairs of segments associated by literal repetition (B1–B5, B3–B7, V1–V5, and V3–V7). Distribution of these four associative adjacencies in the time of the composition sets up a two-part form: mm. 1–2 and 5–6 are repeated in mm. 9–10 and 13–14, respectively. Simultaneous segments (e.g., B1 and V1), and successive segments in bells or voices (e.g., B1 and B2, V1 and V2), never form associative adjacencies except, in the latter case, by C_{timbre}. The relationship between associative organization and score chronology is largely orthogonal, reflecting the workings of the piece's pitch-class structure and bipartite form.

Evolutions of Association Graphs and Associative Reconfiguration. Thus far we have approached associative sets and *AG*s as if they came fully formed—as if the composition and configuration of a set, and all the relational properties of its individual segments, were synchronically available and constant over time. But when we listen to music, we hear segments in a particular order, embedded in a series of musical contexts. These contexts, which include

some relational properties while suppressing or failing to activate others (that thus remain, at least temporarily, only predicable). Just when and how individual properties are ignited and transformed from predicable into relational ones is an important question in analysis. Which relational properties and segments that engage those relational properties are available when a segment forms? How might the sound-image of a segment stored in memory change over time as new segments and contexts in which to hear it become available?[78]

To begin to model some of these dynamic aspects of musical experience, we conjoin association graphs with the idea of an evolution. Earlier we defined an association subgraph (SAG) of an association graph AG as an association graph in which all nodes belong to N(AG) and all edges to E(AG). An *evolution* of an association graph, EVOL(AG), is an ordered set of association subgraphs <SAG_m, . . . SAG_n>, where n is the number of nodes in N(AG), m is a number of nodes from 1 to $n–1$, and each SAG in the sequence is a subgraph of its immediate successor, which adds at least one node and some number of edges (perhaps zero). An evolution focuses attention on the order in which nodes enter an AG and edges form—*when* certain associations and relational properties are activated, and the changes in graph topology that these induce. The retroactive transformation of predicable into relational properties continually changes the way we hear, conceptualize, and even organize segments already in the graph.

Example 3.33 shows two evolutions of a graph G with five nodes. Nodes are numbered solely for reference. The graph is a subgraph of K_5; node 1 is of degree 4; all other nodes are degree 3. Evolution A (EVOL$_A$), in example 3.33a, consists of the series of subgraphs <SG_{1A}, SG_{2A}, SG_{3A}, SG_{4A}, SG_{5A}>. Evolution B, in example 3.33b, presents the ordering <SG_{1B}, SG_{2B}, SG_{3B}, SG_{4B}, SG_{5B}>. The two evolutions are similar in three respects: both introduce nodes one by one, the number of edges increases from one subgraph to the next by the same amount in each case, and corresponding subgraphs are isomorphic. But the two evolutions differ in the order in which nodes and edges appear. In EVOL$_A$, nodes 1 and 4 appear before nodes 5 and 2; in EVOL$_B$, nodes 5 and 2 precede 1 and 4. When we consider that each edge in an AG models the workings of one or more contextual criteria that associate its incident nodes—and thus also designate relational properties of those incident nodes—the musical implications of this difference become clear. For instance, if each edge in the final graph (SG_{5A} or SG_{5B}) represents a different contextual criterion, the relational properties and "sound" of node 5 in SG_{3A}, with its ties to nodes 1 and 4, will differ from that of node 5 in SG_{3B}, with ties to nodes 1 and 2. Thus EVOL$_A$ and EVOL$_B$ represent not only different orderings in which nodes and edges appear, but differences in the *sound* of two segments represented by the same bits of music notation.

Example 3.34 illustrates another situation, with two evolutions of a graph with eight nodes. Except for the circuit introduced by an "extra" edge

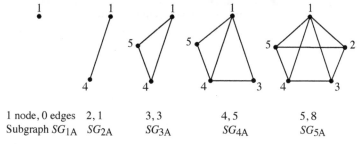

1 node, 0 edges	2, 1	3, 3	4, 5	5, 8
Subgraph SG_{1A}	SG_{2A}	SG_{3A}	SG_{4A}	SG_{5A}

Example 3.33a. A graph with five nodes, evolution A: nodes enter in order 1, 4, 5, 3, 2

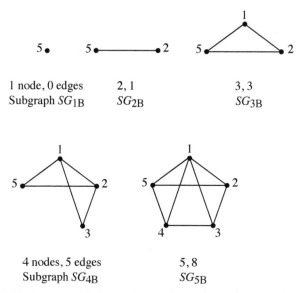

1 node, 0 edges	2, 1	3, 3
Subgraph SG_{1B}	SG_{2B}	SG_{3B}

4 nodes, 5 edges	5, 8
Subgraph SG_{4B}	SG_{5B}

Example 3.33b. A graph with five nodes, evolution B: nodes enter in order 5, 2, 1, 3, 4

between nodes 6 and 7, the finished graph would be a tree with node 1 as a head node. Both $EVOL_A$ (ex. 3.34a) and $EVOL_B$ (ex. 3.34b) consist of eight subgraphs that add nodes one by one. But there the similarities end. Not only do $EVOL_A$ and $EVOL_B$ have different start nodes (nodes 1 and 4, respectively): they also indicate contrasting evolutionary processes. With one exception, edges in $EVOL_A$ form consistently, one by one. Each of the subgraphs SG_{2A}–SG_{8A} is connected. $EVOL_A$ is also fairly systematic: it completes one branch of its near-tree before leafing out the other and adding a circuit on the way. In contrast, $EVOL_B$ is chaotic: no edge appears until SG_{6B}, with an influx of edges in SG_{7B} and SG_{8B}. Only SG_{8B} is connected; SG_{2B}– SG_{7B} are all disconnected.

EVOL$_A$ might model the systematic development of two aspects of a musical idea (represented by its branches), EVOL$_B$ suggests a sudden, radical reconfiguration of apparently unrelated segments into a cohesive unit with the late addition of nodes 3 and 2.

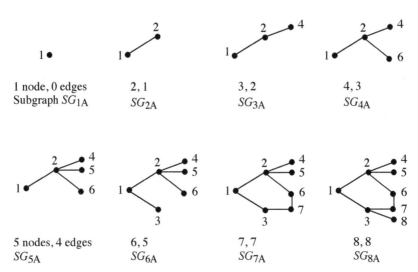

Example 3.34a. A graph with eight nodes, evolution A: nodes enter in order 1, 2, 4, 6, 5, 3, 7, 8

Example 3.34b. A graph with eight nodes, evolution B: nodes enter in order 4, 1, 5, 8, 6, 7, 3, 2

and dramatic changes in associative organization. To recapture a few terms introduced earlier: a disconnecting set is a set of edges that, if removed from a connected graph G, render G disconnected; a cutset is a disconnecting set of which no proper subset is also a disconnecting set (i.e., a minimum disconnecting set); still more specifically, a bridge is a cutset that consists of a single edge. Now consider the situation from the perspective of evolutions—not of deleting edges, but the order in which edges are *added*. Adding a node with incident edges that form a bridge, cutset, or disconnecting set late in an evolution can radically reconfigure the topology of a graph.

Look again at the final graph in example 3.34b. Here the four edges incident to node 2—which connect it to nodes 1, 4, 5, and 6—constitute a disconnecting set. So when node 2 enters late in the evolution, the particular set of edges it creates radically transforms the topology of the entire graph: three disconnected subgraphs in SG_{7B} are suddenly wired together into one connected graph that is nearly a tree. Had node 6 been the last to enter, a different reconfiguration would have occurred, changing a binary tree into a different sort of structure that contains a circuit. Of course, when one is dealing with association graphs that model musical situations, adding *any* segment to an associative set changes the context in which *all* of the set's segments are heard, and perhaps radically. Moreover, this change in context not only surrounds, but *penetrates* individual segments: changing the context in which a segment is heard can change its relational properties—its *sound*—by adding new properties, recalibrating the relative prominence of existing properties, or both.

Example 3.35a shows an evolution of the *AG* from example 3.26a for the six chords in the right hand of mm. 135–40 from Feldman's *Piano and Orchestra*. Here segment names indicate score order; the evolution proceeds in parallel, as a model of score chronology. Each of the six subgraphs is connected; each adds a single node. In sequence, the six subgraphs alternately and evenly expand to the left and right, representing the gradual accretion of diversity in the set and the alternation of events associated with the first part of a bar versus those in the second. For sake of argument, example 3.35b offers a hypothetical evolution in which nodes enter the same graph in the reverse order. Here each subgraph but the last is disconnected. The order of node entry still alternates between left and right, but the graph now evolves from the periphery toward the center; the bridge forms last. This hypothetical evolution focuses attention on the timing of the bridge placement between nodes 1 and 2 in the original *AG*—in actuality (as in ex. 3.35a), it is the first edge to form. Both the topology of association, and the order in which Feldman constructs that topology, are essential to the gently branching form of the passage.

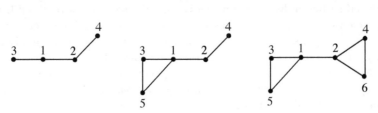

Example 3.35a. Evolution of association graph for Feldman, *Piano and Orchestra,* mm. 135–40, right hand, score chronology

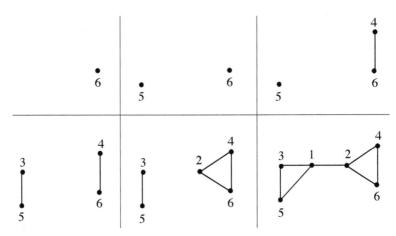

Example 3.35b. Hypothetical evolution in which nodes enter in the reverse order

Example 3.36a provides an evolution for the *AG* in example 3.29 for segments *J*1–*J*8 of Schoenberg's *Klavierstück* op. 23, no. 3. Once again, both the numbering of nodes and sequence of subgraphs model score chronology. Example 3.36b focuses attention on two subgraphs of the final *AG*: the circuit graph C_4 among nodes 1, 2, 5, and 6 that models associations among segments *J*1, *J*2, *J*5, and *J*6 by $C_{artic\ staccato}$ and $C_{ip <-8, +2, -5, +2>}$ (as in ex. 3.28a), and the complete graph K_4 among nodes 1, 3, 6, and 7 that models associations among *J*1, *J*3, *J*6, and *J*7 by $C_{pc <\{Bb, D\} \{B, C\#\}>}$ (as in ex. 3.28c). Both of these critical subgraphs form relatively late in the evolution, with the addition of nodes 6 and 7, respectively. Having established the associative space with the T_7 relation between contrasting pcsets in *J*1 and *J*2, Schoenberg introduces two contrasting elements—first the legato articulation and pitch interval inversion of *J*3, then the more distant relation by pitch-class embedding in *J*4. Only then, in relatively quick succession within m. 6, does he return to complete the circuit graph initiated by *J*1 and *J*2, with their respective pitch-class counterparts *J*6 and *J*5, both staccato. To close out the opening section, he first returns to unfinished business, completing the K_4 subgraph

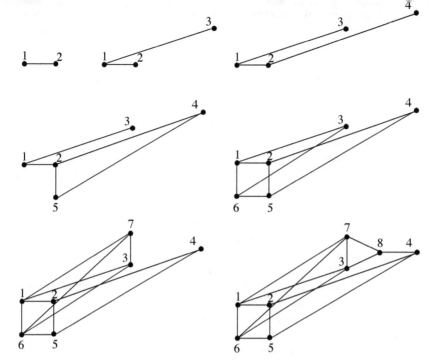

Example 3.36a. Evolution of association graph for Schoenberg, *Klavierstück* op. 23, no. 3, *J*1–*J*8, score chronology

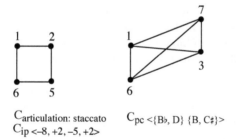

$C_{\text{articulation: staccato}}$ $C_{\text{pc}} <\{B\flat, D\} \ \{B, C\sharp\}>$
$C_{\text{ip}} <-8, +2, -5, +2>$

Example 3.36b. C_4 and K_4 subgraphs

with the addition of *J*7, then adds a new, relatively distant segment—*J*8—that introduces a transposition level explored later in the composition.

Thinking about Associative Sets

Before proceeding to associative landscapes, let's take a quick look back to place associative sets in a broader perspective. An associative set is a set of segments

be fuzzy or crisp; global properties; and an internal configuration that reflects its segments' active influence on one another. To think in terms of associative sets, configurations, and landscapes presumes a concept of categorization, and one of association. But what are these concepts? One can think about categorization and association in different ways, each with its own implications for music analysis.[79]

For psychologists, categorization—the grouping of objects into categories, often based on shared features—is a basic principle of human cognition.[80] Associative sets exemplify this tendency to categorize. But how do we, as music theorists, think about categorization and its purpose in the context of music analysis? Philosopher Ruth Garrett Millikan outlines two views of categorization: classification and reidentification. Whereas "A good classification system aids efficient information storage, retrieval, and transfer of information, or efficient storage and retrieval of the objects classified,"[81] "reidentifying is required not primarily for information storage, retrieval, and transfer, but for information *acquisition* and information *use*."[82] In music theory, categorization is often synonymous with classification: we classify pcsets into set classes, for example. But in music analysis, Millikan's alternate view of categorization as reidentification seems more appropriate, for it speaks to music's temporality, the flash of recognition that transforms predicable properties into relational ones and seeds associative sets. Whereas classification suggests a static end product, reidentification is active, melding segment recognition with the creation and organization of musical relationships.

Association also admits multiple perspectives; these encourage different ways of thinking about the formation, cohesiveness, and internal organization of associative sets, and the roles that associations among "like" segments can play in music analysis. Inspired by the wealth of work on species concepts in philosophy of biology, we consider four perspectives on associative sets: what I call the morphological, populations, lineages, and individuals perspectives.[83]

The *morphological* perspective, based on the idea of similarity, is the mainstream view of association in music theory and analysis. This view casts an associative set as a group of segments with similar features. Within this view I'd like to shift the point of focus from similarity to the full range of variation among a set's segments. Musical segments are multidimensional, holistic perceptual objects. In music analysis, the "ideal" case of similarity as literal repetition construed only as such is dull; what is interesting is how similarity *intermingles with difference* to create varying degrees of associative proximity and distance among the segments of a set.

With a *populations* perspective we transcend pairwise comparisons of segments and shift attention to a higher level of organization—the associative set (or population) as an integrated system.[84] A populations perspective focuses on properties a set has in its entirety: global properties such as size, range and

rations. Thinking in terms of population demographics and processes is useful in many musical contexts but especially when the aural significance of individual segments is dwarfed by their cumulative effect, as in the passage from Feldman's *Patterns in a Chromatic Field* back in example 3.3. Shifting the focus from individual segments to properties of associative sets can help the analyst organize a mass of detail into a comprehensive view of musical processes and form.

A *lineages* perspective also entails a shift from the morphology of individual segments to demographics of populations. But thinking in terms of lineages requires a second shift, from the synchronic to the diachronic, that places individual segments (and perhaps also associative subsets and even associative sets) in a path of associative ancestry and descent.[85] Lineages endow associations with derivational or generational arrows: edges in an association graph are replaced with arrows or paths on an association digraph.[86] Lineages encourage analysts to examine the degree of fit or misfit between associative and score chronology; they can also be used to model complex derivational histories and intermovement connections (as with *ARP* and *5–6–5* in Beethoven's "Appassionata" sonata).

Finally, the *individuals* perspective may be the most, but in another sense also the least, intuitive of the four perspectives.[87] Instead of thinking of an associative set as a collection of segments, it considers the set to be a *single entity, one individual* that persists over time and is revisited (and perhaps transformed) in a series of encounters. An intuitive default in opera and song where the intermittent presence of a character, object, or idea may be expressed by a chain of musical associations among segments, this view is also appropriate for recurring elements in instrumental music (such as the striking $C\sharp/D\flat$ in the first movement of Beethoven's "Eroica" symphony).

Each of these four perspectives on association has its merits; each suggests a different course of analytic inquiry. The morphological perspective privileges associative configurations; the populations perspective, global properties, dynamic interactions among segments, and processes of sets in entirety; the lineages perspective, paths through an evolutionary tree of associations; the individuals perspective, agency and transformation of an individual over time. The point is not to choose among these perspectives—either in general or on a specific occasion—but to consider and explore what each has to offer. Considering alternative formulations for such bedrock concepts as categorization and association can lead to new sorts of questions, spark the development of new analytic tools, and support new observations and adventures in analysis.

Associative Landscapes

Associative sets, global properties, and configurations all model aspects of associative organization shaped by, but conceptualized largely apart from, temporal

associative sets and configurations with the more concrete associative geography of pieces of music. An *associative landscape* is a level of organization and analysis concerned with the actual temporal (possibly registral, timbral) disposition of associative sets and segments in a passage or composition.[88] Dispositions are of two kinds: internal and external. Internal dispositions and distributions model the temporal arrangement of segments within *one* associative set; external dispositions model relations among associative sets with respect to one another. Much as associative sets have collective or emergent global properties and configurations, so can associative landscapes have features and emergent properties of composition. Features of a landscape include the presence or placement of a contextual or sonic focus, contacts between associative sets, and associative discontinuities. Emergent properties of landscape composition include patch-matrix relations between associative sets and the stylistic or structural matrix (e.g., of tonal voice leading or twelve-tone organization) in which they are embedded; high- and low-profile associative organization; and compositional homogeneity or heterogeneity.

The landscape, as a level of organization, is functionally distinct from scale or temporal extent. Landscapes can be small scale (one to several measures) or large scale (encompassing an entire movement or work).[89] A *plot* is a temporal span in a piece of music, often (but not necessarily) delimited by significant sonic disjunctions or changes in associative sets or associative organization. A *landscape study* is a comparative analysis of musical design, or changes in design, across two or more plots.[90]

Our study of associative landscapes and landscape design begins with a look at several kinds of graphic representations of landscapes or "maps." We then proceed to detailed discussion of internal dispositions, patches, and distributions; external dispositions; and finally, landscape features and composition.

Association Maps

An *association map* (*map*) is a visual representation of one or more plots in an associative landscape.[91] A map provides a synoptic view of segments' or sets' temporal disposition or distribution in a passage, as well as general properties of landscape composition. Maps can be small scale or large scale, comprehensive or highly selective. Small-scale maps focus on short passages; large-scale maps, on a few aspects of a substantial passage or complete work.[92] Comprehensive maps account for every (or nearly every) note; highly selective maps, on relatively few events of special interest. Although maps are usually drawn in two dimensions, when implicitly or explicitly conjoined with association graphs they can model associative organization in three or more.

In this book I use three basic kinds of association maps: those in cutaway score format, running text format, and schematics (plus some hybrids).[93] Maps

cal notation, time goes from left to right, and vertical alignment indicates temporal simultaneity.[94] But in place of instrumental parts, horizontal alignment indicates associative set affiliation: segments from the same set (subset, superset) appear in the same row, while segments from different sets (subsets, supersets) occupy different rows.[95] Example 3.37 provides a score for the first five measures of Schoenberg's *Klavierstück* op. 23, no. 3; example 3.38a is a small-scale association map of mm. 1–4 in cutaway score format. This map is comprehensive, in that it includes almost every note in the score as part of one or more segments from four associative sets, *J–M*. A few points on notation. First, a note can contribute to more than one segment (e.g., the pitch A2 in m. 2 contributes to *J*2 and *K*1; the first D5 in m. 4, to *J*3 and *L*3). Also, following notational practices for individual segments outlined in chapter 2, notes shown as adjacent within a segment need not be temporally adjacent in the score. Stems without noteheads (rather than rests) indicate where a segment omits notes within a beam in the score. Depending on the context, one can align notes in a cutaway score map with a swatch of a voice-leading graph, twelve-tone row structure, or other structural matrix, thereby coordinating analysis of associative organization with structural organization.

Example 3.37. Schoenberg, *Klavierstück* op. 23, no. 3, mm. 1–5

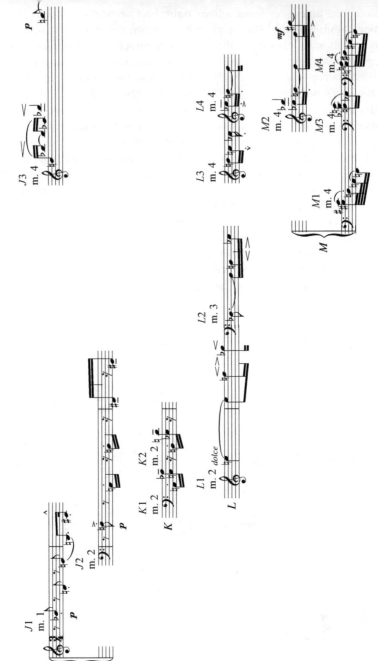

Example 3.38a. Schoenberg, *Klavierstück* op. 23, no. 3, mm. 1–4, association map of sets *J–M*, cutaway score format

from) the distributional taxonomies of Lévi-Strauss, Ruwet, and Nattiez. In running text format, time proceeds from left to right, then top to bottom, as in written English prose.[96] Columns represent associative set affiliation. Because maps in running text format can represent only temporal succession, not simultaneity, they are best suited to passages in which associative organization is strictly monophonic—that is, in which associative sets either succeed each other, or interleave such that only one set is active at a time.

Schematic maps come in different forms. Simple schematics and schematics of associative rhythm represent individual segments and set activity. Simple schematics identify segments by name, while schematics of segment (set) rhythm represent the onset and duration of individual segments (sets) with standard note values. Bar graph schematics represent only set activity, using solid or intermittent horizontal bars aligned with measure numbers to indicate a set's presence or absence. Example 3.38b is a bar graph schematic that corresponds to the cutaway score map of sets *J–M* in example 3.38a. Here, as in most schematics, time goes from left to right; associative sets are represented by horizontal alignment; vertical alignment indicates temporal simultaneity. By eliminating the visual detail of musical notation, schematics focus attention on the dispositions and distributions of segments that contribute to associative organization.

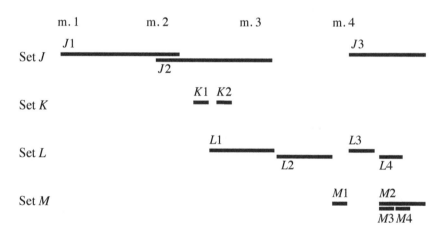

Example 3.38b. Bar graph schematic of sets *J–M* in the same passage

Internal Dispositions and Distributions

An *internal* disposition concerns the distribution of segments within *one* associative set with respect to time (possibly register, or timbre). There are two basic internal dispositions: *clumped* and *dispersed*.[97] An associative set is in *clumped*

imate. The Allegro from Bach's Sonata No. 2 in A Minor for Violin Solo begins with a series of four patterns, each subject to immediate repetition at pitch (in mm. 1, 2, 3–4, and 5–6 of ex. 3.39a). The result is a string of small associative sets, each in clumped disposition.

Allegro

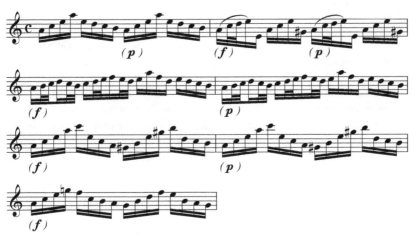

Example 3.39a. Bach, Sonata No. 2 in A Minor for Violin Solo, Allegro, mm. 1–7

Example 3.39b. Associative rhythm of mm. 1–7

A rapid succession of associative sets in clumped disposition tends to set up an *associative rhythm*, a rhythm by which associated segments, or sets of associated segments, form or change on the musical surface. Associative rhythm has two components: segment rhythm and set rhythm. *Segment rhythm* is the rhythm of durational spans defined by individual segments in an associative set or subset. *Set rhythm* is the rhythm of durational spans defined by one associative set or subset versus another. Example 3.39b is a schematic of associative rhythm for mm. 1–7 of the Bach Allegro. Durations above the horizontal line track segment rhythm; durations below the line,

Example 3.40. Stravinsky, *Rite of Spring*, "Glorification of the Chosen One," R110

set rhythm. In mm. 3–4, segments and sets each unfold at two levels by virtue of literal inclusion.

Most associative sets do not come in a single clump, but unfold as a series of patches.[98] A *patch* consists of one or more segments of an associative set that appear in fairly close temporal proximity in a musical landscape. A *minimal patch* consists of a single segment. A *simple patch* is a patch composed entirely of minimal patches that are temporally adjacent. The fourfold repetition of a dramatic sweep in piccolo and flute in "The Glorification of the Chosen One" from part II of Stravinsky's *Rite of Spring* (ex. 3.40) is an example of a simple patch. Patches can be small or large. They can also be dense or porous. A patch is *dense* if its segments are not only temporally adjacent, but also temporally contiguous. (Patches can also be dense with respect to register or timbre.) In very dense patches segments overlap, as in the stretto that concludes Bach's Fugue in B-flat Minor, *Well-Tempered Clavier*, Book I (mm. 67–72). The greater the overlap, the denser the patch. In a *porous* patch, segments are temporally adjacent but not necessarily temporally contiguous. After two grumbly descending lines in the bass, Liszt's Sonata in B Minor for piano begins by silence (ex. 3.41). Some patches are only slightly porous, as in mm. 1–5 of Feldman's *Palais de Mari* (1986), where three segments of an associative set are gently separated by the partial and resonant "silence" of rests over a depressed damper pedal (ex. 3.42). A patch can also change in density over the course of its duration. In the second movement of Bartók's *Sonata for Two Pianos and Percussion* (1937), the patch that forms around the piano quintuplet first heard in m. 31 is porous at first, but quickly becomes more dense as the segment rhythm accelerates (ex. 3.43).

Example 3.41. Liszt, Sonata in B Minor, I, mm. 9–17

Example 3.42. Feldman, *Palais de Mari*, mm. 1–5

Example 3.43. Bartók, *Sonata for Two Pianos and Percussion*, II, mm. 31–36, piano I

A patch can contain other patches. A *compound patch* is a patch composed of two or more *component patches* of the same associative set; each component patch can be minimal, simple, or compound.[99] Like segments in a porous simple patch, components of a compound patch are often separated by brief silences; however, they can also be separated by intervening material. Stravinsky's patch of four flute sweeps in example 3.40 is the last of six component patches (of two, four, one, two, one, and four segments, respectively) in a compound patch that extends from R104 to R111 with repeated interjections of other material. Example 3.44, from the opening of the "Spring Rounds" movement of the *Rite*, shows a small compound patch of folk melody played by the winds that alternates with contrasting material in the strings. The first three segments of the Provence set *A* from Messiaen's "L'alouette calandrelle" (ex. 3.1) are another example of a compound patch.

Example 3.44. Stravinsky, *Rite of Spring*, "Spring Rounds," R49+3–R50

temporal span that greatly exceeds their combined duration. Dispersed sets—especially small dispersed sets—often mark and associate significant points in conventional forms such as binaries, ternaries, rondos, and sonatas. The notated *accelerando* and *rallentando* in the xylophone (ex. 3.45) that opens the third movement of Bartók's *Music for Strings, Percussion, and Celesta* (1936) has just two consociates: one at m. 17, which initiates a move to the B section of an arch form; and one at the very end of the movement (mm. 80–83), which closes A′. Similarly, the grand arpeggio that begins Mozart's Sonata for Piano and Violin K. 296 is the seed of a small dispersed set that creates a formal frame (ex. 3.46). After an early repetition in m 5, the arpeggio returns only twice more—in m. 96, where it announces the recapitulation, and in m. 100, the counterpart to m. 5.

Example 3.45. Bartók, *Music for Strings, Percussion, and Celesta*, III, xylophone mm. 1–4

Example 3.46. Mozart, Violin Sonata in C Major, K. 296, I, mm. 1–2

What begins as a curious trill between a low G♭ and F in the first movement of Schubert's Sonata in B-flat, D. 960 (mm. 8–9) gradually evolves into the center of a larger dispersed associative set with a range of variation. Example 3.47 shows a map of associations and formal functions for thirteen segments of an associative set *N* with four associative subsets *N/a–N/d*. Seven segments are notated on the staff; the other six, represented by segment names, are nearly

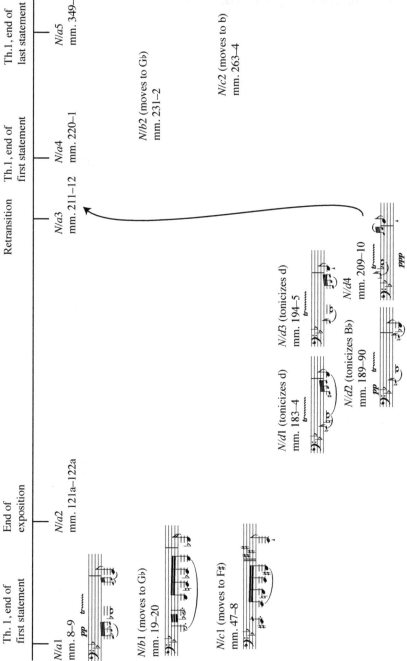

Example 3.47. Schubert, Piano Sonata in B-flat, D. 960, I, map of dispersed set N

and one in case (*N/c*2), transposition. Segments of subset *N/a*, associated by the set's core contextual criterion C$_{\text{pitch trill <Gb1, F1>}}$, outline the form at the largest scale, marking off the end of the first statement of the first theme in the exposition (*N/a*1, mm. 8–9) and recapitulation (*N/a*4, mm. 220–21); the end of the exposition (*N/a*2, mm. 121a–22a); the end of the retransition (*N/a*3, mm. 211–12); and the end of the first theme's last statement in the final codetta (*N/a*5, mm. 349–50). *N/b*1 and *N/b*2 initiate tonicizations of Gb at m. 20 and m. 232 that serve in middleground expansions of the chromatic neighbor motion Gb–F; *N/c*1 and *N/c*2 launch moves to F♯ minor and B minor (in the exposition and recapitulation, respectively) for the second theme. Toward the end of the development *N/d*1 (mm. 183–84), *N/d*2 (mm. 189–90), and *N/d*3 (mm. 194–95) mark off a series of local tonicizations that eventually lead to *N/d*4, which revives the Gb/F trill two octaves "too high" in mm. 209–10, but prepares its return in the original register (in *N/a*3, m. 211).

Dispersed sets need not serve any conventional, or even any idiosyncratic or singular, formal purpose. Example 3.48 shows three segments from "Le merle noir," No. 2 from Messiaen's *Petits esquisses d'oiseaux* (1985). Each segment launches a dispersed associative set found throughout the piece; together the three sets account for most of its material. Although the sets come in a series of four rotations, a conjunction of factors—persistent rhythmic and melodic evolution of the "merle noir" (m. 5) motif; progressive lengthening of the chord sequence in m. 1; the introduction of new material in m. 27 (continued in m. 29); and contrast among the three sets—thwarts any clear sense of formal partitioning or return. The cumulative effect is less that of a rotation among ideas

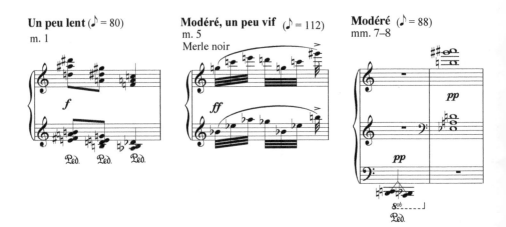

Example 3.48. Messiaen, *Petits esquisses d'oiseaux*, II. "Le merle noir," progenitors of three dispersed associative sets

assumed to persist throughout.

Segments of a dispersed set can come from different movements and even different compositions, serving to relate two or more pieces by quotation, reference, or semblance. Example 3.49 shows two short excerpts that reference the "Dresden Amen," from the first movement of Mendelssohn's Symphony No. 5 ("Reformation") (ex. 3.49a) and the Prelude to Wagner's *Parsifal* (ex. 3.49b). In the symphony, the "Amen" segment is part of a dispersed set that links the move from the introduction into the exposition with that from the development into the recapitulation. In *Parsifal*, with a critical change in its harmonic context, the "Amen" becomes the Grail motive. Pairs of passages from the third movements of Berio's *Sinfonia* and of Mahler's Symphony No. 2 in C Minor, and of segments in the main theme of the fourth movement of Mendelssohn's Octet in E-flat, op. 20 with those that set "And He Shall Reign" in Handel's "Hallelujah" chorus, are two more examples.

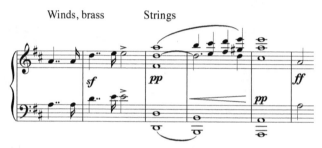

Example 3.49a. Mendelssohn, Symphony No. 5, op. 107, I ("Reformation"), mm. 13–17

Example 3.49b. Wagner, *Parsifal*, Prelude, mm. 39–43 (reduction)

At a given scale of analysis, clumped and dispersed sets define poles of a continuum; a single associative set can be clumped and dispersed at different scales, however. The poignant violin solo accompanied by harp that opens Rimsky-Korsakov's *Scheherazade* forms an associative set in clumped disposition (ex. 3.50). Although the main motif inspires a good deal of material in the first

Example 3.50. Rimsky-Korsakov, *Scheherazade*, I, mm. 14–18

movement, its closest consociates are dispersed among the other three movements, in five additional clumps (in movement II, mm. 1–4; III, mm. 142–45;
and IV, mm. 8, 29, 641–44, and 670–75). The *ARP* and *5–6–5* motives that
form cross-movement associations in Beethoven's "Appassionata" sonata
are two more examples of sets that are clumped and dispersed at different
scales. Within individual movements, instances of *ARP* or *5–6–5* come in
clumps that serve formal functions such as thematic presentation, restatement, sequential repetition, or development. But at the scale of the sonata
as a whole, clumps representing each motive are dispersed among two or
all three movements.

Associative sets can be clumped in time but dispersed in another musical
dimension or vice versa. Performers of the Allegro from Bach's Sonata No. 2 in
A Minor for Violin Solo (ex. 3.39a) often articulate the immediate repetition
of each of the four ideas in mm. 1–6 as a dynamic contrast between *forte* and
piano, and perhaps also legato and détaché.[100] The result is a sequence of four
associative sets, each clumped in time but dispersed in dynamics (and articulation). Bartók's scoring of the first five segments of the primary theme of
the second movement of *Music for Strings, Percussion, and Celesta* (mm. 5–19) as

Example 3.51. Rimsky-Korsakov, *Scheherazade*, II, mm. 229–40: Four instances of the fanfare motive

an exchange between two string orchestras seated at stage left and stage right makes for a subset that is clumped in time but dispersed in the performance space. Example 3.51 shows a brief passage from the second movement of *Scheherazade* in which four segments of a uniform associative set based on a fanfare motive progressively disperse in register and timbre through a series of upward leaps by minor sixth coupled with a series of timbral changes (trumpet, to A clarinet, to octave doublings between flute and oboe, then among piccolo, flute, oboe, and trumpet). The close of the scherzo of Beethoven's Symphony No. 7 (ex. 3.52) is an even more dramatic example of a uniform associative set quickly dispersed over *six* octaves (by four leaps of an octave each), matched by a move in timbre from dark low strings in m. 137 to bright upper winds in m. 141.

Example 3.52. Beethoven, Symphony No. 7 in A Major, op. 92, III, Scherzo, mm. 137–45

nificant range of variation, paths through associative configurations may be coordinated with sonic dispersal in pitch, dynamics, and timbre. Beethoven's Symphony No. 5 opens with a four-note pitch and rhythmic motive that progressively diversifies into a number of associative subsets (mm. 1–58) including those based on a scalar descent (m. 14), upward leap by fourth (cello and bass, m. 28), repeated note (m. 34), rising third (m. 35), cell within an extended arpeggio (m. 44), and others. Progressive variation in the set is coordinated with two waves of expansion in pitch space, dynamics, and timbre (mm. 1–24, mm. 25–58). The second and longer wave breaks in pitch and timbre on roughly the same schedule as the first—in other words, *early* for its larger dimensions. To maintain momentum after this point, continued expansion in dynamics is coupled with an accelerated rate of variation in the set, which only relents when the common-tone diminished seventh arrives in m. 52—just as strong voice leading into the dominant of E♭ takes over. Here the diminished seventh chord serves double duty, signaling a move in the middleground voice leading while enabling construction of a fourfold sequence of the motive *in its original form*—three repeated notes and a fall by third—that plays out in exactly one bar of the four-bar hypermeter.

Distributions. Recognizing that an associative set can be clumped and dispersed in the same dimension at different scales suggests the need for a more comprehensive model of distributions that is sensitive to aspects of frequency, spacing, and density at work on multiple scales.[101] Given an associative set and a scale of analysis (a scale is essential, because distribution patterns are generally affected by a change of scale) one can characterize a distribution in terms of its place along six continua:[102]

1. Scale of activity (relative to the scale of analysis): *widespread* or *localized*?
2. Frequency: *common* or *infrequent*?
3. Patch distribution (in time; perhaps also in register, timbre, or space): *even* or *uneven*?
4. Greatest patch size: *sometimes large* or *always small*?
5. Consistency in patch size: *consistent* or *variable*?
6. Patch density: *dense* or *porous*?[103]

Each of the six continua can be fleshed out with a series of intermediate steps (e.g., for frequency: *ubiquitous, pervasive, common, fairly common, somewhat common, somewhat infrequent, fairly infrequent, infrequent,* and *rare*). Whereas the first three continua reference the full scale of analysis, the last three focus on individual patches and relations among them. Reducing the scale of analysis from large to small (e.g., from the scale of a work or movement to a section

continua brings out successively more detail about a set's distribution. In music analysis as in ecology, "the problem is not to choose the correct scale of description, but rather to recognize that change is taking place on many scales at the same time, and that it is the interaction among phenomena on different scales that must occupy our attention."[104] With the six continua as a framework, we can characterize diverse distributions with some specificity, ranging from "widespread, common and locally abundant, evenly distributed among consistently large patches of high density" through numerous intermediates (e.g., "widespread, fairly common, evenly distributed in usually large patches of low density," "widespread, somewhat infrequent, unevenly distributed, always in small patches of high density," and "localized, somewhat common, unevenly distributed in variable patches of high density") to various cases of rarity (widespread or localized, even or uneven, concentrated or porous) and the vanishing point of "always rare."[105]

Associative sets that are always common, even at the largest scale of analysis, occur in various musical contexts such as figuration patterns in keyboard preludes and études (e.g., the right-hand in the first part of Bach's Prelude in C-sharp from Book II of the *Well-Tempered Clavier* or in Chopin's Étude in F, op. 25, no. 3) and pitch or rhythmic ostinatos (as in the right hand of piano I in mm. 1–2 of Steve Reich's *Eight Lines* or the snare drum of Ravel's *Bolero*). But "always common" does not mean "active at every moment": it includes sets that are "merely" pervasive, like the figures that begin Bach's Prelude in F for Organ, BWV 540 or Debussy's "Des pas sur la neige" from *Preludes*, Book I (1910).[106] Pervasive sets can nonetheless fluctuate in density, as does the pitch interval motive <+3, –1> in Schoenberg's "Nacht" from *Pierrot lunaire* (1912).[107] And, in pervasive sets with a substantial range of variation, different subsets can have different distributions. Taking the first theme and transition in the first movement of Beethoven's Symphony No. 5 (mm. 1–58) as the scale of analysis, example 3.53 designates the main motive as the core of an associative set O and maps out distributions for three subsets O/a, O/b, and O/c, characterized by the falling third, a scalar descent, and a hooked figure that climbs by step, respectively. At the scale of this passage, set O is widespread and always common. But of the three subsets, only O/a is widespread; O/b and O/c are localized. Similarly, segments of O/a are common, while segments of O/c, which clump together in a single patch from mm. 14–19, are relatively infrequent. As one might expect, differences in the distributions of subsets O/a–O/c have a lot to do with harmony and voice leading and, to a lesser extent, conventions of sonata form. Each subset or "form" of the motive is woven into (even inspired by) the structural matrix in its own way—e.g., instances can expand a tertian harmony or embellish ascending or descending stepwise lines that in turn fulfill certain formal conventions.

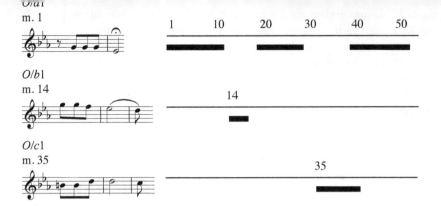

Example 3.53. Beethoven, Symphony No. 5 in C Minor, op. 67, mm. 1–58, distribution of subsets *O/a–O/c*

Thinking in terms of associative sets and distributions draws attention to a certain similarity among these eight pieces that is in the realm of form but cuts across conventional designations such as prelude, ternary, passacaglia, sonata, or, as in the case of the Reich, forms without names. Attending to such similarities in associative organization raises questions about how each set and distribution fits into its particular sonic, associative, structural, and aesthetic musical environment. In just these eight examples, sets that are always common or pervasive appear as harmonic figuration, seeds of melodies, ostinatos, the basis for intricate counterpoint, and accompaniment patterns. Each contributes to or effects form in its own way, in conjunction with other aspects of sonic, associative, and structural organization.

A notch less frequent than sets that are "always common" are those that are widespread and patchy but locally abundant. The jubilant arpeggio that begins Mendelssohn's Octet in E-flat, op. 20 seeds such an associative set. The process of constructing the first theme from successive transpositions and inversions of the arpeggio makes for a long, dense patch in the first group of the exposition and recapitulation. Other dense patches mark formal junctures, including the start of the closing section in the exposition and recapitulation (mm. 113–19, 266–72) and, especially, the start of the development (mm. 127–35), where diminution in the segment rhythm of arpeggio entries (from the measure to the half measure) makes for a passage of high density and drama. Large, dense patches of the motive that opens the second movement of Bartók's *Music for Strings, Percussion, and Celesta* function similarly, outlining its sonata form. The patch in mm. 1–28 establishes the first theme; one in mm. 186–99 launches the development with a point of imitation; another in mm. 310–66 builds a long imitative passage from a chromatically

one more in mm. 373–84 begin the recapitulation. At the scale of the movement, the set is widespread and common, with an uneven distribution among a number of large patches of high density.

Whereas in common-practice tonal music large, dense patches often articulate thematic areas or the boundaries of other sections in conventional forms such as sonatas or rondos, in post-tonal contexts their actual role as *creators*—not just articulators—of form is more clear. The second of Stravinsky's *Three Pieces for String Quartet* (1914) begins with two large patches of a (then-) uniform associative set, separated by an isolated segment from a contrasting, dispersed set (ex. 3.54). After a long absence (mm. 13–47), the set returns near the end of the piece in two dense patches (mm. 48–51 and 57–58) which, despite changes in surrounding material, suffice to shape the movement into a loose ternary. In Feldman's *Patterns in a Chromatic Field*, large patches of high density create a distinctive form outside any rubric. The pair of associative sets *D* and *E* (from exx. 3.3 and 3.4, respectively) and the population $P_{DE}1$ they comprise account for all material in the first two pages of the score (1/1/1–2/4/9)—roughly the first minute in performance.[108] Close relatives of sets *D* and *E* form five related populations $P_{DE}2$ to $P_{DE}6$ in 4/3/1–4/4/9, 6/1/1–6/4/9, 24/1/1–24/4/9, 44/1/7–45/2/2 and 45/2/7–45/4/1. As in the Stravinsky, the distribution of sets *D* and *E* is widespread, in large patches of high density. But *Patterns* also has many other sets distributed in large patches of high density. Over the course of the ninety-minute piece, the prominence of sets *D*, *E*, and every other associative

Example 3.54. Stravinsky, *Three Pieces for String Quartet*, II, m. 1

as a whole, despite the large, high-density patch of sets D and E that begins the piece, the sets are both widespread and somewhat *infrequent*.[109] The end result is a unique musical form synonymous with the formation, dissolution, and distribution of multiple associative sets and populations, in patches of various sizes and densities.

At the opposite end of the spectrum from sets that are widespread, common, and concentrated in large patches of high density are sets that are rare. The dispersed set initiated by the xylophone at the start of the third movement of Bartók's *Music for Strings, Percussion, and Celesta* (ex. 3.45) has three segments (in mm. 1, 17, and 80); these appear in three minimal patches for a distribution that is widespread, rare, uneven, small, and constant. The grand arpeggio that launches the exposition and recapitulation in Mozart's Sonata for Piano and Violin in C, K. 296 (ex. 3.46) has a similar distribution but comes in two small compound patches. The dispersed set N that forms around the low G♭/F trill in mm. 8–9 of Schubert's Piano Sonata in B-flat, D. 960 (ex. 3.47) is also widespread, rare, uneven, fairly small, and constant. Although N is larger than the sets in the Bartók or Mozart, relative to the much larger scale of its movement (354 measures, compared to 83 for the Bartók and 153 for the Mozart) it remains rare. As these three examples suggest, sets that are widespread but rare can articulate boundaries in traditional forms. Like pervasive sets, they can also *create* a sense of form from materials and in contexts outside formal conventions. In Messiaen's "L'alouette calandrelle," the Provence set (A) (ex. 3.1), is widespread, rare, and uneven. Its seven segments (in mm. 1, 3, 5, 70, 72, 74, and 96) are arranged in three patches, of which two are compound. The appearance of the second compound patch in m. 70, after the set's long absence, conjoined with a move back to the center of the Lark set (B) shapes the piece into a ternary form.

Of course, sets that are dispersed and rare need not serve any particular formal purpose, conventional or otherwise; whether or not a given set does is a matter of interpretation. The six rising whimpers in Varèse's *Poème électronique* (three starting at about 1'00", one at 1'35", and two at 7'30") form a set that is widespread, rare, and uneven: six segments are arranged in three small patches of different sizes; one is minimal, two compound. Although the distribution of the whimpers is almost identical to that of set A in the Messiaen, the set has no clear formal function.[110] In Cage's *Williams Mix* (1952), the distribution of associative sets created by different sound sources *cannot* have an intended formal function: Cage's use of chance procedures to ensure a random distribution explicitly rules that out. But even so, listeners and analysts can still reinvest distributions with formal functions in their own hearings or interpretations of the piece.

Inhabiting the vast multidimensional space between sets that are always common and those that are rare are all kinds of distributions that can shape

from music by Stravinsky, Schumann, and Brahms.

The sharp upward sweep in piccolo and flute followed by a brusque descent that opens the "Glorification of the Chosen One" in the *Rite of Spring* (ex. 3.55a) is the first of 24 segments of an associative set *P* distributed throughout the movement. Example 3.55b transcribes the segment rhythm of set *P* to show its overall distribution. Set *P* is widespread. Common in the two outer sections (R104–11, R117–21), it is absent in the middle (R111–16). Where *P* is present, its distribution is uneven. Heightening the effect of changing meters are persistent changes in patch size, which varies from one to four segments (three patches each of one, two, and four segments and one patch of three segments). No patch size is repeated in direct succession and only once is a pair of sizes for adjacent patch sizes repeated (one, then four segments), at the close of the first and last sections. Changes in the length of the silences between patches suggest the formation of two compound patches, *P1–P6*, and *P10–P14*.

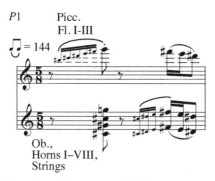

Example 3.55a. Stravinsky, *Rite of Spring*, Part II, "Glorification of the Chosen One," initial segment of an associative set *P*

In Schumann's "Der Nussbaum," no. 3 from *Myrthen*, op. 25, uneven distribution of an associative set *Q* that forms around the piano's introductory figure is integrally related to eccentricities in tonal structure and hypermeter. Example 3.56a shows the two-bar figure that launches set *Q*. As the song continues, the formal function of this figure soon becomes ambiguous, both introductory and cadential. Example 3.56b transcribes the segment rhythm of set *Q* in durational reduction ($\quarternote$ = one bar) to show its distribution. Set *Q* contains numerous literal repetitions at pitch level (in mm. 1, 5, 11, 15, 21, 25, and 45), some transposed repetitions (in mm. 9, 19, 29, and 49), and five intervallic variations partly doubled by the voice in the song's central, contrasting, section (mm. 31–40). The disposition of literal and transposed repetitions largely reflects strophic organization within the A section; the variations, a move to a contrasting B section at m. 31.

Rehearsal #: R104   105   106   107   108

Segment rhythm:

Segments of *P*: *P*1 – 2   3 – 4 – 5 – 6   7   8 – 9

Rehearsal #: 109   110   111   112   113   114   115   116

Segment rhythm: 23

Segments of *P*:   10   11 – 12   13 – 14   3   4   5   4   4   3

Rehearsal #: 117   118   119   120

Segment rhythm:

Segments of *P*: 15   16   17 – 18 – 19   20   21 – 22 – 23 – 24

Example 3.55b. Associative rhythm of set *P*

Piano

p

con Pedale

Example 3.56a. Schumann, *Myrthen*, op. 25, no. 3, "Der Nussbaum," mm. 1–2, initial segment of set Q

<table>
<tr><td>1
11
21</td><td></td><td>5
15
25</td><td></td><td>9
19
29</td><td></td></tr>
</table>

A

G: IV V I   D: IV V I

31   33   35   37   39

B

a: iv ii^7 V$^\#$

41   45   49   59   63

A'

G: II$^\#$ V I   IV V I   I vii^{o7} ii   I ——   I ——

Example 3.56b. Schumann, *Myrthen*, op. 25, no. 3, "Der Nussbaum," segment rhythm and distribution of set Q

Distribution of Q is widespread, common, and uneven in two respects. Taking the entire song as the scale of analysis, segments of Q are most clumped in the B section, where harmony is most fluid, and most dispersed in A' and in the closing section that begins in m. 51, where tonality is most stable. Within the A section, the distribution of Q is even within each strophe (every two bars) but becomes uneven as the ten-bar strophes are joined end to end. The result is a periodic wrinkle in associative rhythm, accompanied by tonal redirection from D major back to G major and a reset of the four-bar hypermeter. In "Der Nussbaum," associative rhythm, tonal rhythm, and hypermeter work together to create a sense of wakeful dreaming in A and A', and sustained reverie in B, all carried along by segments of Q that evoke the sweeping boughs in the text.

In the second movement of Brahms's Piano Concerto No. 2 in B-flat, op. 83, the piano's opening figure seeds an associative set R that is pervasive in the two outer scherzos but absent in the trio. Example 3.57a shows the initial segments

3.57b shows the segment rhythm and distribution of *R/a* and *R/b* in Scherzo I (mm. 1–188) in a durational reduction (♩. = one bar of 3/4; each 12/8 measure represents one four-bar hypermeasure). At the scale of Scherzo I, set *R* is widespread, common, and uneven. Patch size is highly variable, ranging from a minimal patch of *R/a* in m. 1 to a large patch (13 segments) of *R/b* in mm. 103–15. Patch density also varies considerably, from a sparse compound patch of *R/a* in mm. 1–21, through a less sparse compound patch in mm. 141–49, to a fairly dense compound patch of *R/a* (with segments that embed those of *R/b*) in mm. 67–81, and two very dense patches of *R/b* in mm. 103–15 and mm. 178–88. Although set *R* is widespread at the scale of Scherzo I, sometimes it is locally abundant; other times, rare. Moves back and forth from rarity to abundance, and from a focus on *R/a* toward one on *R/b*, conjoin with aspects of tonal structure to create the scherzo's form. At first *R*, available only in the form of *R/a*, is expansive and rare. After a contrasting thematic interlude in mm. 44–67, *R/a* returns in m. 67 in the first of a series of small dense patches; this time, however, sustained D5s in the right hand of the piano solo also introduce *R/b* as a distinct idea. An extensive dense patch of *R/b* (which, being shorter than *R/a*, encourages faster segment rhythm) ends the A section of Scherzo I and forms a bridge into the B section (in mm. 103–15); a second dense patch brings Scherzo I to a close (mm. 178–88). Over the course of Scherzo I, changes in distribution fulfill formal functions: material is created, and used, in different ways at different points in the form.[111]

Example 3.57a. Brahms, Piano Concerto No. 2 in B-flat, op. 83, II, initial segments of two associative subsets *R/a* and *R/b*

The idea that distributions are not incidental to musical material but, along with contextual criteria and global properties such as size and range of variation, can actually characterize and serve to distinguish different kinds of material manifests in various musical contexts. In some South Indian ragas, traditional music theory and the practice of highly accomplished musicians dictate that some phrases characteristic of the raga are common, introduced early, and heard throughout an improvisation or composition, while others are rare and saved for certain places or special moments in a performance.[112] In Western classical music, a similar fusion of form with content effected by characteristic distributions appears in music from the twentieth century and later. Example 3.58 shows a collection of excerpts from Edgard Varèse's *Ionisation*

Measure #:   1   17 19   67   75

Segment rhythm: 12/8

Segments of R/a: R/a1   2 3   4 5 6   7
Segments of R/b: R/b1 2 3   4

Measure #:   103   107   111

Segment rhythm:

Segments of R/a: R/a8 9
Segments of R/b: R/b5 6   7 8 9 10 11 12 13 14 15 16 17 18 19

Measure #:   141   145   149   178 179   182   185

Segment rhythm:

Segments of R/a: R/a10 11 12   13   14
Segments of R/b: R/b20 21   22   23 24 25 26

Example 3.57b. Brahms, Piano Concerto No. 2 in B-flat, op. 83, II, mm. 1–188, associative rhythm and distribution of associative subsets R/a and R/b

Type 1
Military drum
motive
with bongo
accompaniment

Type 2
Siren *gliss.*

Type 3
Pitched
percussion

Type 4
Triplet and
grace figure,
tenor and
bass drums

Type 5
Quintuplets
(Chinese
blocks)

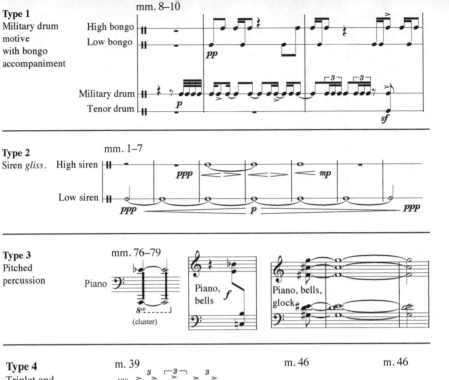
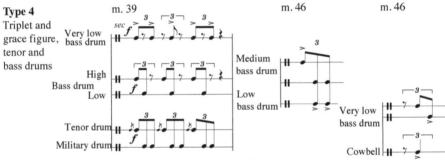
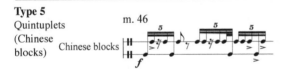

Example 3.58. Varèse, *Ionisation*, five types of material

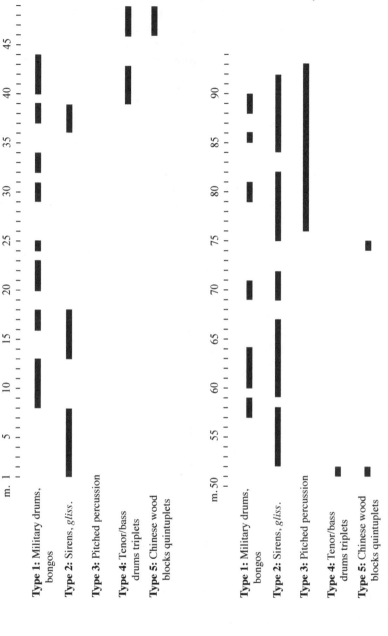

Example 3.59. Varèse, *Ionisation*, schematic map showing general distribution of five kinds of material

associated with the military drum and bongos (mm. 8–10); sirens (mm. 1–7); pitched percussion (piano, bells, and glockenspiel, mm. 76–79); tenor and bass drums (m. 39 and m. 46); and Chinese wood blocks (m. 46). Each excerpt contains one or more segments that initiate an associative set. In each case, the set's C/CRS includes the instrument in which the set originates; but in some cases (e.g., the figures in the military drum and bongos), the core figure eventually migrates to other instruments.

Taking the entire piece as the scale of analysis, the five types of material exhibit different sorts of distributions (ex. 3.59). At this scale, only two types of material—the figure introduced by the military drum and bongos, and the glissando in the sirens—are widespread and common. Chords and clusters in the pitched percussion appear only at the end of the piece (mm. 76–89), where they are locally abundant; however, as segment rhythm decreases, so does set density. Vigorous eighth-note triplets introduced by the tenor and bass drums in mm. 39–42 (also mm. 46–48, and 51), and various quintuplet rhythms introduced by the Chinese wood blocks (in mm. 46–48, 51, and 74) are highly localized. At first the triplets are locally abundant, but the initial density of the first patch tapers off; the second, compound, patch (in mm. 46–48) is highly porous, interspersed with bits of a much denser compound patch of quintuplets in the Chinese wood blocks, drums, maracas, military drum, and high cymbal. Varèse's musical landscapes are often described in terms of the formation and interpenetration of planes and textures. Studying distributions provides another perspective: assigning contrasting musical materials different distributions enables diverse modes of interaction among these materials.

External Dispositions

Whereas internal dispositions and distributions concern the temporal arrangement of segments from a single associative set, external dispositions (and contacts) involve the arrangement of segments from one or more sets in an associative landscape. There are three basic external dispositions: associative monophony, associative polyphony, and associative heterophony. These are reminiscent of, but for the most part functionally independent of, traditional textural distinctions among monophony, polyphony, and heterophony.

In *associative monophony*, a set is unaccompanied for most or all of its duration.[113] The fact that monophonic associative sets, or sets or passages of associative monophony, are temporally disjunct from their surrounds allies monophony with S_1 criteria. In *associative polyphony*, two or more sets unfold within the same temporal span. Segments of associative sets in polyphony are distinguished by contextual criteria and usually also by S_2 criteria that channel segments into relatively distinct perceptual streams defined by register, duration,

ciative polyphony in which an associative set and one of its subsets, or two subsets of the same associative set, unfold in the same time span, presenting two or more versions of the same basic material.

Associative organization within the vocal line of "Todas las tardes," the fourth song from George Crumb's *Ancient Voices of Children* (1970), is a clear example of associative monophony (ex. 3.60). The two lines "Todas las tardes en Granada, todas las tardes se muere un niño" (Each afternoon in Granada, a child dies each afternoon), a fragment from a longer text by Federico García Lorca, constitute the song's entire text. Crumb sets the lines as a monophonic sequence of two associative sets. The first is a lyrical intonation of three closely interrelated diatonic phrases separated by rests; the second, a melismatic lament in which each of four falling segments outlines a tritone. The move from the first set to the second takes place on the critical word "muere" (dies). As the associative organization links "muere" forward to "un niño," it underlines both the extraordinary event of the death of a child and the deeply disturbing paradox of the text—that this extraordinary event is somehow also ordinary, "a child dies each afternoon."

Associative monophony, polyphony, and heterophony are functionally independent of textural monophony, polyphony, and heterophony traditionally defined by register or instrumentation. Associative monophony can be orchestrated as a polyphonic texture; conversely, associative polyphony can be folded into a single musical line. The opening bars of Allegro II from Corelli's ("Christmas") Concerto in G Minor, op. 6, no. 8 (ex. 3.61) illustrate a monophonic associative design realized as canonic imitation; the sense of textural polyphony is enhanced by the exchange between small and large instrumental forces typical of *concerto grosso* style. The complementary situation, of associative polyphony embedded in textural monophony, can be found in the fusion of

Example 3.60. Crumb, *Ancient Voices of Children*, IV, "Todas las tardes," vocal line

Example 3.61. Corelli, Concerto Grosso in G Minor, op. 6, no. 8, Allegro II, mm. 1–8

color and talea within a single voice of a medieval motet or, for a more recent example, in the first movement of Messiaen's *Quatour pour le fin du temps*, where the homorhythmic piano part conjoins cyclic repetitions of a twenty-nine-element pitch series and seventeen-element duration series. Various works for solo instruments by Milton Babbitt, such as *My Ends Are My Beginnings* (1989) for clarinet, offer additional examples in which polyphonic associative organization unfolds within a single instrumental line.

When a passage of associative monophony is composed from a series of small associative sets in clumped disposition, associative rhythm—both segment rhythm and set rhythm—is often a compelling force in the musical landscape. Example 3.62 continues the transcription of associative rhythm from the Allegro from Bach's Sonata No. 2 in A Minor for Violin Solo back in example 3.39b through the end of the first section (mm. 1–24). As before, durations in the top part of the example track segment rhythm; durations below, set rhythm. In mm. 3–4 segments and sets each unfold at two levels; these, along with two sets connected by elision (in m. 15), are shown separately. Rests in m. 18 and 24 represent diversions from the prevailing associative organization of small clumped sets.

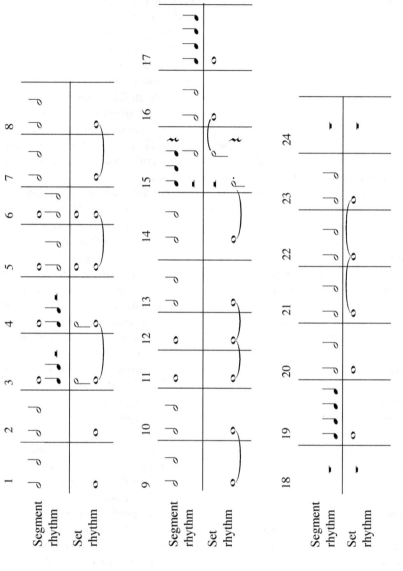

Example 3.62. Bach, Sonata No. 2 in A Minor for Violin Solo, IV, Allegro, mm. 1–24, associative rhythm

strategically placing high or low points of a line on weak beats or parts of a beat. A study of the disposition of associative sets in the first half of the Allegro reveals another source of rhythmic vitality: the associative rhythm is in constant motion, with a change in segment rhythm, set rhythm, or both, about every two bars. Over the course of mm. 1–24, the associative rhythm forms two large arcs (mm. 1–13, mm. 17–24) connected by a transition zone (mm. 14–16) that includes a syncopation in set rhythm (in mm. 15–16).[114] In the first arc, set rhythm begins at the measure, slows to two measures (in m. 3), then three measures (in m. 11). In the second arc, set rhythm takes a similar course, starting at the measure (in m. 17) but moving directly to three measures in m. 21—a move modulated by a change in segment rhythm one measure earlier (from the quarter to the half in m. 20). Over the course of the passage, changes in segment rhythm and set rhythm are sometimes synchronized (m. 3, 5, 11, 17), sometimes staggered (m. 7, 13–15, 20, 21). Along with surface rhythm and tonal rhythm, associative rhythm contributes to the temporal life of the passage.

In chamber music, associative rhythm can conflict with or enrich interactions among instruments. Stefan Wolpe's *Trio in Two Parts for Flute, Cello, and Piano* (1963–64) begins with six associative sets of two segments each, arranged in a monophonic disposition composed of sequential, sometimes overlapping, clumped dispositions (ex. 3.63a). The piano articulates three sets of two inversionally related segments each in mm. 1, 3, and 4–6; these roughly alternate with three sets of two segments formed between the flute and cello in mm. 1–2, 3–4, and 6–7. Example 3.63b transcribes segment and set rhythm for the flute and cello duo versus the piano. Set rhythm is fairly regular in the duo, but variable in the piano. The resultant texture sees a marked shift in interaction among the three instruments: two quick interchanges separated by a brief silence in mm. 1–2 and 3–4, followed by a more leisurely and complete response in mm. 4–7. Quick changes in associative rhythm are common in Wolpe's music, as are other changes in landscape composition.

The opening of the Prelude from Stravinsky's *Agon* (1954–57) is a good example of associative polyphony (ex. 3.64). Three associative sets unfold in the same time span: sixteenth-note runs from C4 to C5 in the flute and solo cello; sixteenth-note leaps by octave or twelfth, usually followed by an isolated note in the bassoon; and figures of repeated notes on different pitches passed between timpani and trumpet. Differences in the three sets' global properties enhance the associative polyphony: whereas the flute-cello set is uniform, the bassoon and timpani-trumpet sets each have a range of variation, with more in the latter. Shaping the passage is a move in all three sets from dispositions that are relatively porous (in mm. 122–25) to those that are much more dense (in mm. 126–27).

Associative polyphony can also be implied rather than literal. "Glorification of the Chosen One" from the *Rite of Spring* begins with three patches of the

Example 3.63a. Wolpe, *Trio in Two Parts for Flute, Cello, and Piano*, I, mm. 1–7.
Reproduced with permission from Southern Music Publishing Co., Inc.

flute sweep (set *P*, ex. 3.40), each interrupted by a patch of chords (in the
bassoons, brass, and strings) from a different associative set (see, e.g., R106–
R109). The perceived effect of repeated intersplicing between the sets is less
that of associative monophony or raw juxtaposition than of an implied associative polyphony in which both sets persist throughout the passage but each is
only intermittently available to the listener.

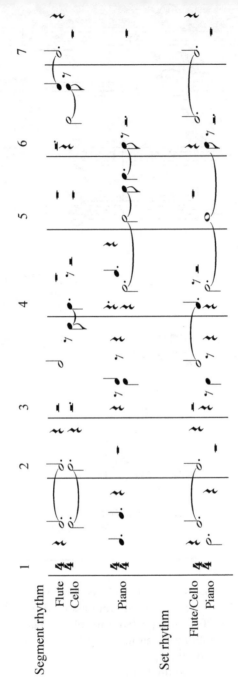

Example 3.63b. Wolpe, *Trio in Two Parts for Flute, Cello, and Piano*, I, mm. 1–7, associative rhythm

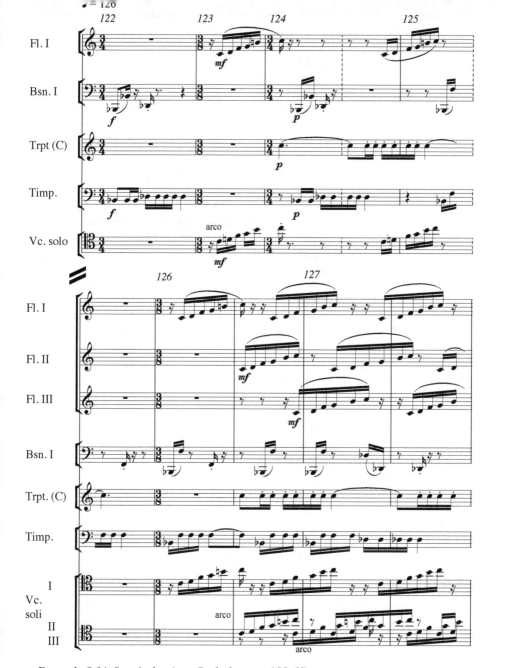

Example 3.64. Stravinsky, *Agon*, Prelude, mm. 122–27

Schoenberg's music throughout his career.[115] The *Klavierstück* op. 23, no. 3 begins with tight counterpoint among four associative sets *J–M* (as in ex. 3.38a). *J*, the main melody and the composition's serial motive (core criterion $C_{\text{ip I} <-8, +2, -5, +2>}$), spans the opening bars, accompanied by three other sets, *K–M*. Set *L*, a chromatic trickle, appears throughout mm. 2–4, while set *K* (core criterion $C_{\text{SC 3-3[014]}}$) in m. 2 gives way to set *M* (core criterion $C_{\text{SC 3-5[016]}}$) in m. 4. Each of the four sets is important in the piece as a whole. Example 3.65 provides a map in cutaway score format of mm. 10–11. The excerpt begins with tight five-part counterpoint among segments of *J* (some statements of the motive are incomplete) in associative polyphony with segments from sets *K* and *L*. The five segments of *J* demonstrate that so long as segments are carried on clear sonic channels (here, $S_{\text{2-pitch}}$, conjoined with rhythmic associations), notes within a segment need not be temporally adjacent and can even be separated by material in other registers and voices. Taken together, segments from *J*, *K*, and *L* account for most of the notes in mm. 10–11. Notice also that the gradual turnover from sets *J* and *K* to set *L* recalls the order in which the three sets were first introduced in mm. 1–4.

We have already seen a preview of the crystallizing moment that comes near the end of the piece, in mm. 30–31 (for the score and an association digraph, return to exx. 3.17a and 3.17b). Example 3.66 provides a cutaway score map of ten segments from sets *J*, *K*, and *M*, named by set, measure number, and location in the bar. Taken together, these include every note; segments are associated by inversion (within sets *J*, *K*, and *M*) and inclusion (segments of *K* are literally included in those of *J*; segments of *M* and *J* are related by abstract inclusion).

The contrast between associative monophony and associative polyphony can be used dramatically and strategically. The second movement of Mozart's Piano Concerto No. 9 in E-flat, K. 271 begins with a melody in violin I based on a five-note figure that conjoins a downward leap with a semitone upper neighbor (ex. 3.67a). Although the figure is clearly defined, segment boundaries are ambiguous—conflicts at the genoseg level permit both a downbeat-to-downbeat interpretation (e.g., <C4, G3, G3, A♭3, G3>, following key melodic events and harmonic rhythm) and an upbeat-to-upbeat one (e.g., <G3, A♭3, G3, C4, G3>, set off by $S_{\text{1-rest}}$). Either way, subsequent transformed repetitions encourage formation of an associative set. Setting the melody in canon at the quarter-note between violin I and II in mm. 1–4 creates a dense textural polyphony from a monophonic associative design. When the piano enters in m. 17, the strings repeat the canon from mm. 1–4 as mm. 17–20. But the piano's *arioso* introduces a new associative set, composed from successive transformations (following changes of harmony) of a one-measure unit characterized by an upward octave leap followed by a scalar descent to a trill (ex. 3.67b). The move from the orchestra's associative set to the piano's, conjoined with the shift from

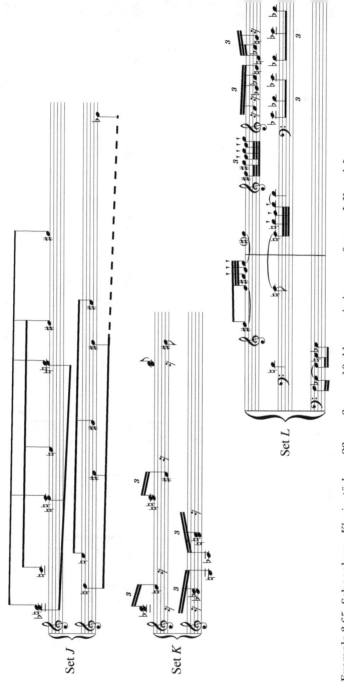

Example 3.65. Schoenberg, *Klavierstück* op. 23, no. 3, mm. 10–11, association map for sets *J*, *K*, and *L*

(mm. 1–4) to associative polyphony for the second (mm. 17–20), puts a spotlight on the piano like a character on stage. The metaphor is underlined by the orchestral material in m. 16 that prepares the solo entry with a cadential formula straight out of eighteenth-century opera.

Example 3.66. Schoenberg, *Klavierstück* op. 23, no. 3, mm. 30–31, association map of sets *J*, *K*, and *M*

Example 3.67a. Mozart, Piano Concerto No. 9 in E-flat, K. 271, II, mm. 1–5

Example 3.67b. Mozart, Piano Concerto No. 9 in E-flat, K. 271, II, mm. 16–21, piano solo

Sonic features and associative sets' global properties can enhance the effect of associative polyphony. Just before the end of the Presto in moto from Barber's Violin Concerto op. 14 (1940), the soloist goes off on a wild run punctuated by eight instances of an orchestral chord (ex. 3.68). As the violin whirls through a string of small associative sets each in clumped disposition, the orchestra becomes intransigent with its own uniform set, which is dispersed unevenly throughout the passage. Associative polyphony and the contrasting dispositions of solo and orchestral material (clumped versus dispersed) are heightened by sharp contrasts in the sonic domain—a fast, steady attack rhythm, tight registral compass (usually less than an octave), and medium dynamic in the violin, versus sporadic attacks, a six-octave span, and the full dynamic power of the orchestra.

Changes in the relationship between textural and associative monophony and polyphony can make for active and diverse musical landscapes. The Minuet from Mozart's String Quartet No. 18 in A Major, K. 464 begins with two segments of an associative set S, followed by two of an associative set T, both in clumped disposition (ex. 3.69). The textural and associative monophony of set S, then T, in mm. 1–8 is replaced by textural and associative polyphony in mm. 9–12, as $S3$ and $S4$ are set in counterpoint with $T3$ and $T4$. In m. 13, associative monophony returns, but now in conjunction with textural polyphony as four segments of set S (in mm. 13–16), then eight of T (in mm. 17–22), appear in two patches of dense imitative counterpoint. In twenty-two bars, Mozart's musical landscape explores all the possibilities for two sets in textural and associative monophony and polyphony.

Moves between associative polyphony and monophony shape the dialogue among instruments in Elliott Carter's String Quartet No. 2 (1959), suggesting

Example 3.68. Barber, Concerto for Violin and Orchestra, op. 14, III, mm. 169–178

varying degrees of cooperation and independence. The Introduction (mm. 1–28) traces two arcs from associative polyphony among four instrumental parts with distinct intervallic vocabularies and characteristic gestures toward associative monophony and instrumental cooperation, where pairs of instruments contribute dyads to form all-interval tetrachords. Progress from associative polyphony toward associative monophony in the Introduction plays out at a larger scale in the quartet as a whole, as each of the four instruments gradually "learns" the languages of the others and the musical landscape becomes more integrated.

Associative polyphony often involves sets that unfold at different scales. The fourth of Webern's *Five Pieces for String Quartet*, op. 5 (1909) traverses a musical landscape populated by six associative sets, *A–F*. Example 3.70 is a comprehensive map of the piece in cutaway score format. Example 3.71 extracts and reproduces the external dispositions of sets *A–F* in a bar graph schematic. At the scale of the piece as a whole, only set *B* is truly widespread, active in all sections. Sets *A* and *C* are more localized, each with two patches (in mm. 1–5

Example 3.69. Mozart, String Quartet No. 18 in A, K. 464, II, Minuet, mm. 1–28

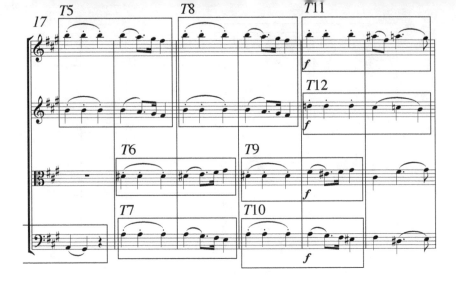

Example 3.69. Mozart, String Quartet No. 18 in A, K. 464, II, Minuet, mm. 1–28—(concluded)

appear in clumped disposition; set B is dispersed at the scale of the movement; set D is dispersed such that its three segments mark the end of A, B, and A'. Except for these intermittent visits from set D, the piece is associatively polyphonic. Canonic imitation among $A/b1$, $A/b3$, and $A/b4$ in mm. 3–4, and between $C1$ and $C2$ in mm. 4–6, unfolds in the same time span as $B3$ and $B4$ of the larger-scaled set B. Similarly, $B5$—a long segment defined by the cello's E4 harmonic—persists throughout sets E and F in the B section. A survey of the map suggests that two sets, B and D, take on special and opposing roles: B contributes to every case of associative polyphony; D, to none. Perhaps not surprisingly, the C/CS(B) contains a somewhat diverse group of fairly weak contextual criteria, while C/CS(D) contains only one, much stronger, contextual criterion ($C_{ip <+4, +2, +5, +2, +6, +3>}$).

Associative heterophony is a special case of associative polyphony in which the relationship between sets is especially close, as with an associative set and one of its subsets or with two subsets of the same set. The formation of clear associative subsets arranged in distinct patches is an essential feature of associative heterophony (and distinguishes it from associative monophony of a single variegated set).

Reflecting its roots in Balinese gamelan music (in which heterophonic textures are common), the opening of Colin McPhee's *Tabuh-Tabuhan* (1936) is a straightforward example of associative heterophony (ex. 3.72). Immediate repetition of pitch and rhythmic material in the flutes, oboes, and clarinets, versus the piano, marimba, and bassoons creates two distinct patterns—two clear associative subsets such that the former is a rhythmic elaboration of (and series of four rotations through) the pitch ordering of the latter. In Steve Reich's *Violin Phase* (1967), each resultant pattern extracted from, then pushed back into the texture (R9–R23) contributes to an associative heterophony, with each successive heterophony exploring a new subset of the same associative set.

In common-practice repertoire, associative heterophonies occur in passages where a melodic idea in basic and more elaborate versions appear simultaneously. Example 3.73 illustrates with a few bars from the violin I and piano solo parts from the first movement of Mozart's Piano Concerto No. 20 in D Minor, K. 466 (mm. 99–104). As violin I outlines a melody composed largely of sequential repetitions of a three-note figure that rises a third, then falls a second, the right hand of the piano solo provides an embellished version in running sixteenths. Associative organization in a short passage from Debussy's *Jeux* (1913) is similar: as the winds (here represented by the flutes) outline a sequence of falling major thirds, the strings (represented by violin I) provide an ornamented version of the same idea (ex. 3.74). The micropolyphony of György Ligeti's *Melodien* (1971) is a virtual library of associative textures and different kinds of associative heterophonies, including some in which associative sets are weak and distinguished only by instrument (mm. 1–10); others

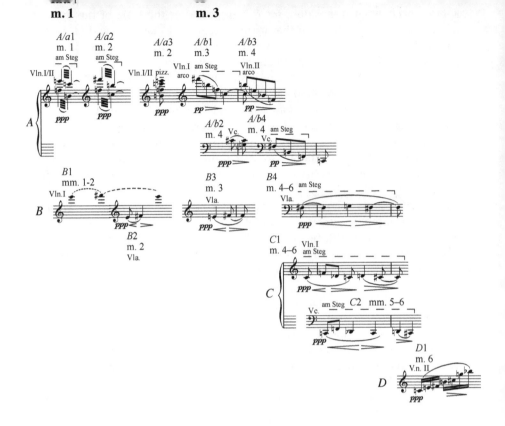

Example 3.70. Webern, *Five Pieces for String Quartet*, op. 5, no. 4, association map in cutaway score format, sets *A–F*

B
m. 7

A′
m. 11

*A/b*5
m. 12

*B*5
m. 7–10

*B*6
mm. 11–12

*C*3
mm. 11–12

*D*2
m. 10

*D*3
mm. 12–13

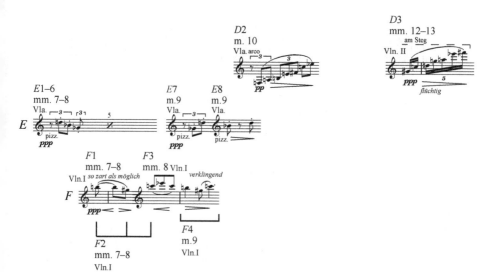

*E*1–6
mm. 7–8

*E*7
m.9

*E*8
m.9

*F*1
mm. 7–8

*F*3
mm. 8

*F*2
mm. 7–8

*F*4
m.9

Example 3.70. Webern, *Five Pieces for String Quartet*, op. 5, no. 4, association map in cutaway score format, sets *A–F*—*(concluded)*

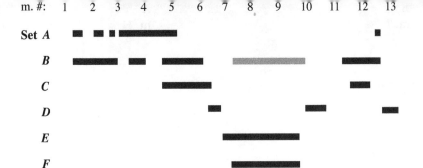

Example 3.71. Webern, *Five Pieces for String Quartet*, op. 5, no. 4, bar graph schematic of sets *A–F*

Example 3.72. McPhee, *Tabuh-Tabuhan*, I, mm. 1–8 (selected instruments)

where associative subsets are very closely related and differ mainly in alignment or by augmentation or diminution (e.g., mm. 14–19); and still others in which associative subsets are more varied (mm. 110–12). There are also passages that combine two or more associative heterophonies in higher-level associative polyphony (mm. 46–57).

As the opening of the Double Pas-de-Quatre from Stravinsky's *Agon* demonstrates, the line between associative heterophony and associative polyphony can be tenuous (ex. 3.75). When the movement begins, shared pitch (or pc) content and the prevalence of neighbor-note contours in both oboe/bassoon

Example 3.73. Mozart, Piano Concerto No. 20 in D Minor K. 466, I, mm. 99–104

Example 3.74. Debussy, *Jeux*, mm. 43–46 (Flutes and Violin I)

Example 3.75. Stravinsky, *Agon*, Double Pas-de-Quatre, mm. 61–64

associative set. But as the movement continues, the wind material develops into a distinct melodic line and the two subsets progressively diverge. By m. 64, the texture has morphed into associative polyphony, which continues through the end of the passage (m. 68).

Features in the Landscape

Along with the disposition of associative sets, the composition of landscapes involves features such as contacts between sets, associative discontinuities, and contextual or sonic foci. The temporal placement of a contact, discontinuity, or focus is an aspect of musical form.

Contacts. Two associative sets easily distinguished by supporting criteria can share notes and even some segments, yet retain distinct identities for the most part. A *contact* is a place in the associative landscape—a specific temporal location—where two associative sets, subsets, or patches of a single set meet. There are three types of contacts: elision, conflux, and flash. All are important features in the landscape, linking sets, subsets, or patches without challenging their integrity.

An *associative elision* is a brief temporal overlap between two associative sets (or subsets) that are otherwise in monophonic succession with respect to one another. An elision can be (but does not have to be) coextensive with the boundaries of a segment that participates in both sets. In such cases, the segment has dual affiliation and forms a bridge between the sets (technically, between their association graphs).

An *associative conflux* is a point of contact between two or more sets (subsets) literally or conceptually in polyphonic disposition at some scale of analysis. When the associative polyphony is literal—the sets literally unfold in the same time span—the conflux is *concrete*; else, it is *conceptual*. Like an elision, a conflux can coincide with the boundaries of one or more segments that form a bridge between the association graphs of two otherwise disjunct associative sets.[116]

An *associative flash* is a psychological link between two temporally distant segments or patches of a *single* associative set embedded in distinct musical contexts. The flash effects a sudden long-range connection that temporarily overwhelms local continuity, opening a seam in the associative landscape.[117] Like an elision or conflux, a flash can often be identified with a particular segment that creates the flash.

A brief temporal overlap between two sets otherwise in monophonic succession, an associative elision can be seen as a kind of modulation between sets through a pivot segment or area. An example occurs in m. 15 of the Allegro from

Example 3.76. Bach, Sonata No. 2 in A Minor for Violin Solo, IV, Allegro, mm. 14–17

Bach's Sonata No. 2 in A Minor for Violin Solo (ex. 3.76). Modified repetition of a figure introduced in m. 14 (*G*1–*G*5) overlaps with the start of a new figure in the second part of m. 15. As sequential repetition in m. 16 launches a new associative set with segments *H*1–*H*3, an associative elision forms around *G*5. Interestingly, *G*5 initiates the syncopation in set rhythm noted earlier (ex. 3.62), as well as a change in segment rhythm from the quarter note to the half note.

In the third movement of Beethoven's Piano Sonata No. 4 in E-flat, op. 7, hypermetric expansion of an eight-bar antecedent into a sixteen-bar modulating consequent is conjoined with two associative elisions (ex. 3.77). The consequent begins in m. 9 with *I*2, a slightly abbreviated repetition of *I*1. After three beats' silence, sequential repetition of the last four notes of *I*2 forms an associative subset *I/a*, with segments *I/a*1 and *I/a*2. Repeating the pitch ordering <E♭5, C5, D5> an octave higher in mm. 15–16 creates an associative elision between *I/a* and the first segment of a new associative subset, *I/b* (in retrospect giving *I/a*2 a second name, *I/b*1). The second associative elision occurs in mm. 18–19, where *I/b* overlaps with *I/c*: here the four notes <E♭6, C6, D6, F6> contribute to both *I/b*5 and *I/c*1. The playfulness and humor of the scherzo's opening section comes in large part from its rather long-winded associative organization, in which two associative elisions link three associative subsets, each in a monophonic, clumped disposition. Although much darker in tone, the solo's opening statement in the first movement of Rachmaninov's Piano Concerto No. 3 in D Minor has a discursive quality with similar roots: four associative subsets (mm. 3–11; mm. 12–16; mm. 16–19; mm. 19–27) join end-to-end through a series of associative elisions (mm. 12–13; m. 16; and the B♭ on the downbeat of m. 19).

Example 3.77. Beethoven, Piano Sonata No. 4 in E-flat, op. 7, III, mm. 1–24, right hand melody

Whereas temporal overlap makes the associative elision a concrete and relatively local phenomenon, an associative conflux can be more abstract. Confluxes also tend to involve longer-range associations. Whereas both sets in an elision are represented locally by significant (nonminimal) patches that surround the point of contact, many, even most, of the associations that support a conflux can be long-range rather than local; local activity of one or both sets can be limited to just one segment at the point of contact. The map in example 3.78a shows a conflux between two associative sets *J* and *K* in mm. 16–17 of Schoenberg's *Klavierstück* op. 11, no. 1. Included are three segments of a set *J*: the opening melody in the right hand (m. 1), and two close relatives from m. 9 (which begins a′ in a small aba′ form, mm. 1–11) and m. 17 (which opens A′ in a larger ABA′ form from mm. 1–24).[118] Below are two segments of a set *K*: *K*1 joins two dyadic wisps (faint recollections of m. 1 and m. 9) into a segment that forms only in retrospect, when their downward octave transposition returns as a clear unit in *K*2. The otherwise separate associative streams of *J* and *K* meet in the pitch succession <F♯4, D4> over the barline of mm. 16–17, which simultaneously ends *K*2 and begins *J*3.

A closer look at the passage suggests an alternate interpretation that preserves the idea of a conflux between relatively distinct associative streams, but renders

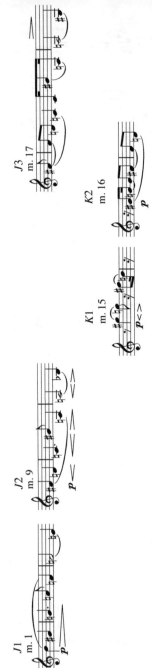

Example 3.78a. Schoenberg, *Klavierstück* op. 11, no. 1, map showing conflux between sets *J* and *K*, mm. 16–17

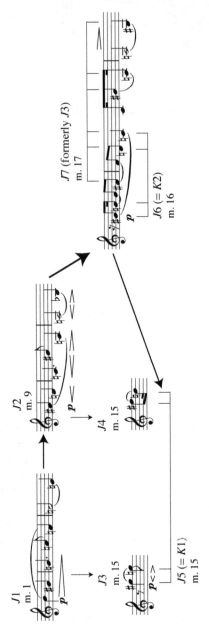

Example 3.78b. Schoenberg, *Klavierstück* op. 11, no. 1, association digraph, set *K* absorbed into set *J*

K. Picking up on the hint of recollection of ordered pc dyads from *J*1 (<G♯, G>) and *J*2 (<F♯, D>) in the two wisps that comprise *K*1, example 3.78b recognizes each dyadic wisp as a distinct segment (articulated by $S_{1\text{-rest}}$) and places it, along with all the segments in example 3.78a, in an association digraph of (select segments from a larger) set *J*. As before, the strongest relations obtain between the pairs of segments in mm. 9 and 17 (now *J*2 and *J*7), and mm. 15 and 16 (now *J*5 and *J*6); these recommend formation of two associative subsets comparable to our previous sets *J* and *K*. But the digraph also shows the more subtle connections between opening segments *J*1 and *J*2, and the dyadic wisps *J*3 and *J*4 in m. 15, that foreshadow the start of A′ in m. 17. The paths <*J*1, *J*3> and <*J*2, *J*4> traced by arrows in the digraph represent temporal precedence and the formative influence of *J*1 and *J*2 upon *J*3 and *J*4. Note that the path <*J*6, *J*5> goes *against* temporal order, modeling the *retrospective* formative influence of *J*6 upon *J*5 (and *K*2 on *K*1 noted earlier). Using the chronology encoded in segment names we can mentally construct an evolution of the underlying graph that represents score chronology. The order in which nodes enter the graph relates to differences in associative proximity and distance (modeled by line weight) in an interesting way. The last two nodes to enter, *J*6 and *J*7, both create the conflux and participate in the strongest associations among pairs of segments anywhere in the graph (*J*5–*J*6 and *J*2–*J*7). Securing the conflux with increased associative proximity gives mm. 16–17 a cumulative effect and draws attention to m. 17 as a significant point in the form.

An especially beautiful associative conflux occurs in the second movement of Berg's Violin Concerto (1935), where the sound worlds of Bach's harmonization of the chorale "Es ist genug" and Berg's twelve-tone row meet (ex. 3.79). After the chorale's final phrase passes from the soloist to the clarinet choir, the soloist repeats it as a series of faltering dyads, an octave higher and harmonized by tetrachordal row segments (mm. 154–57). The last of these tetrachords, a member of the whole-tone subset SC 4-21[0246], participates in a TC *xy* relation between the last four order positions of the row (supported by $T_{\text{row TOP ops 8–B}}$) and, in a scalar ordering, the first phrase of the chorale ($T_{\text{Es ist genug, Phrase 1}}$). The result is an associative conflux that works on multiple levels—between chorale and row, tonality and twelve-tone organization, music of Bach and Berg, sacred and secular. By placing the conflux relatively late in the concerto, and at the very *end* of the chorale harmonization, Berg endows the conflux with a sense of formal function, effecting closure through reconciliation.

Another example of a late conflux appears in Schoenberg's *Klavierstück* op. 23, no. 3. In mm. 30–31, just bars from the end of the piece, the three associative sets *J* (with core criterion $C_{\text{ip I} <-8, +2, -5, +2>}$), *K* ($C_{\text{SC 3-3[014]}}$), and *M* ($C_{\text{SC 3-5[016]}}$) meet in the remarkable moment of inversional symmetry seen back in examples 3.66 and 3.17b. Although every segment of *J* embeds a member of SC 3-3[014] and of SC 3-5[016], and earlier passages have explored associative polyphony between sets *J* and *K* (mm. 26–30), and *J* and *M* (m. 8) (the piece

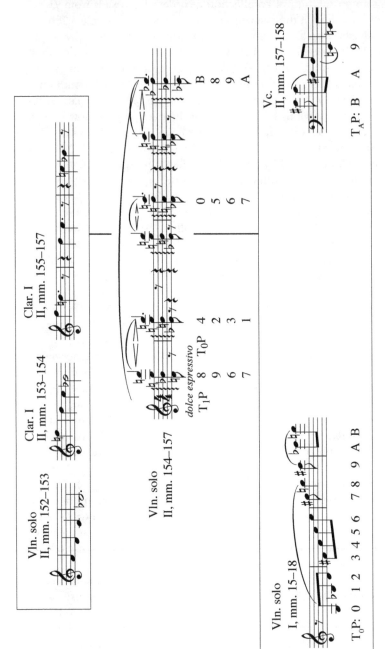

Example 3.79. Alban Berg, Violin Concerto, associative conflux

and harmonic contexts for segments of *J*), no other passage involves segments of all three sets, yet distinguishes them so clearly. Placed at the end of the piece, the conflux among *J*, *K*, and *M* smoothes the harmonic contrast between sets *K* and *M*, and dissolves both in their point of origin—the harmonic content of the serial motive that is the core criterion for set *J*.

Whereas a late conflux can contribute to a sense of closure, an early conflux can set up a process of progressive differentiation or associative fission. The theme that opens the first movement of Beethoven's "Appassionata" sonata works this way. We have already seen (in ex. 3.31) how the opening theme serves as the contextual focus of an associative superset that takes in the primary and secondary themes of the first movement plus the main themes of the second and third movements. The topology of the graph that defines the focus is itself atemporal. But the chronology encoded in segment names and measure numbers also allows us to recognize the opening theme as an early conflux between the two motivic streams *ARP* and *5–6–5*, which then separate to generate the second theme (*ARP*) and the theme of the second movement (*5–6–5*). The early conflux is balanced by a late conflux: the two streams rejoin in the main theme of the third movement. Note that the associative organization of *ARP* and *5–6–5* within this theme is different than before: whereas the two motives appear in succession, in associative monophony, in the primary theme of the first movement, in the main theme of the third movement several instances of *ARP* are embedded in a larger statement of *5–6–5*, forming associative polyphony.

A conflux that comes midway through a composition can be ambiguous in formal function, as associative streams join only to part again and go their separate ways. The oboe melody from the "Air de danse—Orphée" of Stravinsky's *Orpheus* (1947) illustrates such an intermediate conflux, again involving associative sets that span multiple movements.[119] Example 3.80 shows the start of the melody. Orpheus's plaintive song references three of the ballet's central dramatic elements and their corresponding associative sets—the tears of the lyre that open and close the ballet; pitch and rhythmic configurations associated with the Furies (e.g., R5 from the Air de danse, or the start of Scene Two); and angular chromatic lines that represent the anguished souls of Tartarus (e.g., as at R43, where "The Angel and Orpheus reappear in the gloom of Tartarus," or R89 in the Interlude of the Air de danse, where "the tormented souls in Tartarus . . . implore him to continue"). Orpheus's song incorporates all three elements in a musical conflux that encapsulates his dramatic situation—having ventured into Tartarus in search of Eurydice, it is Orpheus who connects the sorrow of the living with the suffering of the dead and the vengeful passion of the Furies.[120]

A flash continues the progression in abstraction from elision to conflux, and from the relatively concrete world of sets' temporal dispositions to the more

Example 3.80. Stravinsky, *Orpheus*, "Air de danse–Orphée," R80–R82, oboes

abstract world of mental events. A flash is *primarily* a mental event, a rupture in the associative landscape where the balance of associative force suddenly shifts from local to long-range. A flash involves three musical contexts: two passages that are temporally and for the most part also associatively distant from one another, plus a long-range association between two segments from a set with a strong presence in the earlier passage, but perhaps only a single segment in the later one, that brings the passages into associative proximity. Whereas both an elision and a conflux form bridges between associative sets, a flash connects two musical *contexts* though a long-range association between patches of the *same* set—usually a larger earlier patch and a later minimal or small one. While all dispersed sets involve long-range associations, a flash is a relatively rare event in which a long-range association meets two special conditions: both of the segments that participate in the flash must be securely embedded in their own local contexts; and these contexts, at least initially, appear relatively indifferent to one another.

A good example of a flash occurs near the start of the development in the first movement of Chopin's Sonata No. 2 in B Minor, op. 35. Example 3.81a shows the opening bars. Example 3.81b identifies the initial upbeat figure as the seed of an associative set *L*, and follows the growth of *L* to the start of the transition (which continues with a dense patch of five segments with segment rhythm at the half note). Example 3.82 shows the start of the development, which is based on a new idea. The passage includes a segment of *L* (*Lm*, on the last beat of m. 93), but it is the segments of *M*, a new associative set, that drive the counterpoint. Conjoined acceleration in surface rhythm and set rhythm propels segments of *M* into a sequence that

downbeat of m. 97. No sooner is the flash back to the start of the movement confirmed by a recollection of m. 2 in m. 97 than the music moves on: segments of *M* reclaim the surface and the glimpse of *L* in mm. 96–97 turns out to be a local anomaly. But the temporal placement of the flash marks the event for perception. Flouting convention and threatening to derail the typical course of events, the flash interjects a feint toward a third repeat of the exposition, or even a premature recapitulation, at the very start of the development section.

Example 3.81a. Chopin, Piano Sonata No. 3 in B Minor, op. 58, I, mm. 1–4

Example 3.81b. Chopin, Piano Sonata No. 3 in B Minor, op. 58, I, segments of an associative set *L*

Example 3.82. Chopin, Piano Sonata No. 3 in B Minor, op. 58, I, mm. 92–97, flash

Another example of a flash occurs in Schoenberg's *Klavierstück* op. 23, no. 3, with the sudden return of a melody from m. 5 in m. 23. Example 3.83 shows mm. 22–23. (Measure 5 appears in the context of mm. 1–5 back in example 3.37; example 3.27 identifies the right hand melody in m. 5 as a segment of set *J*, *J*4.) Here the sudden recall is actually prepared by a recomposition of material from mm. 4–5 in m. 22, but changes in the rhythm, ordering, and registral placement of individual figures conspire to disguise the long-range connection until the *a tempo* marking in m. 23 (specifically, the arpeggiated chord in the left hand, beat 2), where materials from mm. 4–5 resume their original order and registers. Leaping out from its local context in a flash to m. 5, the right hand melody in m. 23 repeats the nine-note pitch ordering of *J*4 (with some minor adjustments in durations), injecting a transient sense of return roughly two-thirds of the way through the piece and subtly preparing the return of *J* as the basis for the extended inversion canon in m. 26–30.

Associative Discontinuities. Roughly the inverse of a contact, an *associative discontinuity* is a place in the landscape where materials with different associative

Example 3.83. Schoenberg, *Klavierstück* op. 23, no. 3, mm. 22–24

affiliations are juxtaposed rather than integrated. Discontinuities are of two kinds: *set dissociations* and *local anticontextualities*. These involve different levels of organization—associative sets and segments, respectively.

A *set dissociation* is a shift from one associative set to another that is largely unmediated by elision or the workings of contextual criteria. Although something like a disjunction in the contextual domain, a set dissociation differs in that its origins lie not in disjunction but in *association*: it is a by-product of differently directed associations, a residual repulsion across the temporal boundary between patches of different associative sets. Crumb's "Todas las tardes," from *Ancient Voices of Children* (ex. 3.60) includes an example of a set dissociation: on the word "muere," the soprano abandons her opening intonation of associated diatonic fragments for a series of falling whole-tone segments. Here, as is often the case, the dissociation is enhanced by a sonic disjunction (in $S_{\text{1-pitch}}$ after the long B♮ that ends the first set).

While most associative discontinuities involve two associative sets, a discontinuity can arise between a segment and its surrounding context. A *local anticontextuality* is a segment that does not contribute to any associative set in the vicinity and has no, few, or only very weak associations with segments nearby. Local anticontextualities can be independent segments not affiliated with any associative set, or minimal patches of a dispersed set. The strongest anticontextualities are further isolated by strong sonic disjunction. Far from mere misfits, local anticontextualities can be important formal and rhetorical devices that articulate formal junctures or facilitate long-range connections.

tions in $S_{1\text{-pitch}}$ and $S_{2\text{-duration}}$) and curiously at odds with the lyrical melody that preceded it, the first appearance of the low G♭/F trill in the first movement of Schubert's Piano Sonata in B-flat, D. 960 (mm. 8–9) is a local anticontextuality. Eleven bars later the G♭/F trill finds a partner in mm. 19–20 and enters the dispersed associative set N, which continues to grow throughout the sonata. Yet on repeated hearings the segment in m. 8–9 remains anomalous within its own local context, its status as a local anticontextuality refreshed each time one hears the sonata.

In sharp contrast to the melodic phraseology within the small aba' that opens Schoenberg's *Klavierstück* op. 11, no. 1 (mm. 1–11), the burst of *ppp* thirty-second notes in m. 12 is another example of a local anticontextuality. Here the associative anomaly is magnified by coincidence with strong sonic disjunctions in $S_{1\text{-pitch}}$, $S_{1\text{-dynamic}}$, and $S_{2\text{-duration}}$ over the barline of mm. 11–12 (ex. 3.84a). Compared to the trill in the Schubert, this anticontextuality is less easily resolved. Two close consociates do eventually appear (in m. 39, almost two-thirds of the way through the piece), but sonic continuities in register, surface rhythm, and dynamics over the barline of mm. 38–39 soften the segmenting effect of the contextual criteria that create the long-range association with m. 12 (ex. 3.84b). Pitch transposition by T_{-1} between the two segments within slurs in m. 39 soon confirms segment formation and the formation of an associative set that takes in all three segments, but one barely has time to register this before the music moves on. Once again, although the local anticontextuality eventually finds its way into an associative set, it is never fully absorbed; the outburst in m. 12 remains a local anomaly even after many hearings.

Contextual Focus, Sonic Focus. Whereas all three types of contact (elision, conflux, flash) identify specific points in a landscape, a contextual focus is defined on the basis of associative topology and a sonic focus according to combined sonic disjunctions. Neither is primarily a temporal phenomenon. Nonetheless, the actual temporal locations of these features in the landscape do matter: each kind of focus can serve different formal functions, depending on its placement and relation to surrounding material.

The first movement of Debussy's *La Mer* (1903–5), "De l'aube à midi sur la mer" (From dawn to noon on the sea), begins with soft, murky repetitions of the rising dyad <F♯, G♯> staggered between a pair of harps and the cellos, where it is coupled with the iambic rhythm ♪♪., over a B pedal in timpani and basses. From this inchoate beginning, a set begins to coalesce: the rising second paired with a dotted rhythm moves into other instruments, where it becomes an incipient melody (e.g., m. 6, oboe; m. 7, clarinet) and gradually acquires new characteristics (e.g., two before R9, cello; R13, trombone). But it is not until the very end of the movement that the seeds planted in the

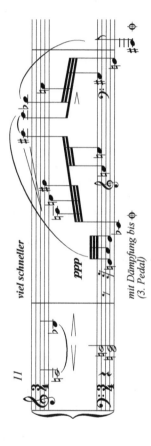

Example 3.84a. Schoenberg, *Klavierstück* op. 11, no. 1, mm. 11–13

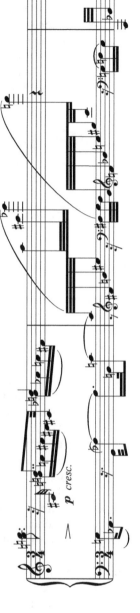

Example 3.84b. Schoenberg, *Klavierstück* op. 11 no. 1, mm. 38–39

with the rising figure shown in example 3.85, the contextual focus of a large set that takes in all instances of the figure in this movement (and many in the third movement as well). The effect of culmination that Debussy achieves by placing the contextual focus so late in the movement is greatly intensified by the coincidence between the contextual focus and sonic focus, marked by the cymbal crash and timpani attack that end rolls (on the downbeat of the bar before R15) and the peak of a steep crescendo from p to f in the brass. The entire trajectory of the piece's associative and sonic organization leads up to this point; once achieved, the movement is over.

Example 3.85. Debussy, *La Mer*, I, R15+1 to end, trumpets 1 and 2

The first of Schubert's three *Gesänge des Harfners* op. 12 (D. 478, 1816) illustrates a different relationship between contextual and sonic focus and shows how the temporal placement of these features in the landscape can support a poetic and musical narrative. The poem by Goethe has sixteen lines in four quatrains. These are tightly interwoven by a complex system of internal and end rhymes in which the "ein" rhyme, representing the Harper's perseveration on the pain of loneliness (in the words "*ein*" "m*ein*," "*ein*sam," "s*ein*," "P*ein*," and "all*ein*"), is especially prominent. Example 3.86 summarizes four aspects of the rhyme scheme: (1) the poem has four end rhymes: a, b, c, and d (a1 and a2, e.g., indicate distinct words that rhyme); (2) six of the eight *words* used as end rhymes in lines 1–8 return in analogous positions in lines 9–16 (shown in bold); (3) four of these six words involve the "ein" rhyme (rhyme "b"); and (4) word repetition or strong internal rhymes join lines 4 and 5, and lines 12 and 13, into couplets that straddle quatrain boundaries and associate with one another through end rhyme. The four quatrains align with sections of Schubert's *ternary* (ABA') form as shown. While A and A' set fewer lines of text than B does (4 and 3 versus 9 lines, respectively), line repetition renders the musical sections of comparable length.

The vocal line builds a complex network of associations around two motifs: (1) a descending upper neighbor motion 6–5 as <F5, E5> in the key of A minor; and (2) a descent from scale degree 5 to 1 in A minor (<E5, D5, C5, B4, A4>).

Form: **Intro** **A**   **B**
Measure: 1   5   15

Lines 4–5: und laßt ihn seiner Pein. / Ja! laßt mich meiner Qual!

Line:	1	2	3	4	5	6	7	8
Quatrain/rhyme:	I: a1	b1	a2	b2	II: c1	c2	b3	b1 — Line 8: dann bin ich nicht allein
Segment:				$N1$				

Form: **A'**   **Postlude**
Measure: (30) 32 (36)   47–52

Lines 12–13: mich Einsamen die Pein, / mich Einsamen die Qual!

Line:	9	10	11	12	13	14	15	16
Quatrain/rhyme:	III: d1	d2	b2	IV: c1	c2	b3	b1 — Line 16: da läßt sie mich allein.
Segment:				$N2$			$N3$	

Example 3.86. Schubert, "Gesang des Harfners," op. 12, no. 1: Goethe's rhyme scheme aligned with Schubert's ternary form

the segments $N1$, $N2$, and $N3$ shown in example 3.87a (also referenced in ex. 3.86). $N1$ and $N2$ secure major cadences at the end of the A and B sections, respectively; $N3$ sets the first statement of line 16. The three segments form the core subset of a larger and more diverse set N that includes a number of other instances of both the 6–5 and scale degree 5-to-1 motifs.

Example 3.87b arranges $N1$–$N3$ into an association graph. $N1$ and $N2$ are associated by the coincident contextual criteria C_{rhythm} ♪♪ and $C_{\text{pitch <F5, E5>}}$; $N1$ and $N3$, by $C_{\text{text "läßt"}}$ in conjunction with the appearance of V_5^6 as the voice moves to E5. The topology of the graph identifies $N1$ as the contextual focus, both of the core subset and by extension also of the larger set N. Placed early in the song (in m. 11, at the end of the first quatrain and the A section), $N1$ sets up a process of associative fission that parallels the protagonist's psychological disintegration. But the song's *sonic* focus comes much later—not until m. 36, near the end of A'. Strong disjunctions in $S_{1\text{-pitch}}$ and $S_{1\text{-dynamic}}$ mark the start of $N3$, while disjunctions in $S_{1\text{-duration}}$ isolate the segment at both ends. Within $N3$, a dramatic crescendo from *ff* followed by a fall back to *p* as the singer cries out the last line, "da läßt sie mich allein" isolates the pitch motif <F5, E5>. The sonic and dramatic highpoint of the song, $N3$ appears about two-thirds of the way through—a typical position for a focal event. While associative proximity helps to bridge the temporal distance between $N1$, the contextual focus in m. 11; and $N3$, the sonic focus in m. 36; their temporal separation awards them complementary formal functions. Whereas the contextual focus $N1$ sets up a process of associative and psychological dissolution, the sonic focus at $N3$ serves as the goal in a dramatic trajectory played out in text and music.

Along with the possibilities that a contextual focus and sonic focus can either coincide (as in the Debussy) or not (as in the Schubert), there is a third possibility: a sonic focus can coincide with the antithesis of a contextual focus—a local anticontextuality. The sudden intrusion of a homophonic passage for brass and wind choir shortly before the end of the fourth movement of Schumann's Symphony No. 3 in E-flat, op. 97 is unprecedented at the scale of the movement, both with regard to orchestral texture and melodic material (ex. 3.88). A striking local anticontextuality, the passage is also a sonic focus, astonishingly bright and loud against the brooding strings. Expanding the scale of analysis to the symphony as a whole allies the brass and wind choir's arpeggio in dotted rhythm with the first theme of the first movement. Coupling the local associative discontinuity (a set dissociation, given the repetition of mm. 52–54 as mm. 56–58) with a sonic focus lifts the passage from its surroundings to secure the long-range connection, across two intervening movements.

Example 3.87a. Schubert, "Gesang des Harfners," op. 12, no. 1, three segments of a set N

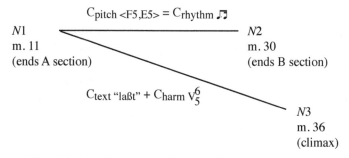

Example 3.87b. Schubert, "Gesang des Harfners," association graph of $N1$–$N3$

Emergent Properties of Associative Landscapes

Just as associative sets have global properties and configurations, associative landscapes have certain properties that arise only at the level of the landscape—properties that depend on, but are not held by, any of its contributing sets. These include patch-matrix relations, high- and low-profile associative organization, and homogeneity or heterogeneity of landscape composition.

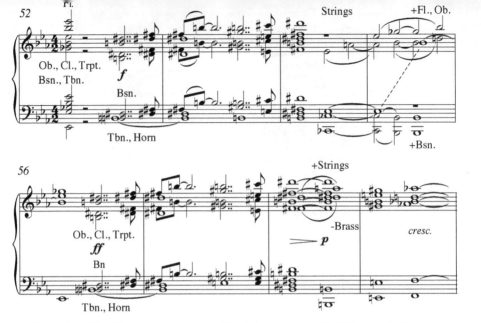

Example 3.88. Schumann, Symphony No. 3 in E-flat, op. 97 ("Rhenish"), IV, mm. 52–59

Patch-Matrix Relations. Within a landscape, patches of associative sets relate both to one another and to an underlying structural, stylistic, or sonic background *matrix.*[121] A *structural matrix* can take the form of voice leading in tonal music; row or array structure in twelve-tone music; or voice-leading norms in sixteenth-century counterpoint. It can also result from the consistent application of any number of other structuring principles, such as process canons in the music of Steve Reich, microcanons in Ligeti, or even the rigorous application of chance procedures in the compositional process of certain works by Cage, such as *Music of Changes* (1951) and *Williams Mix* (1952–3). Patch and structural matrix can be fused and coextensive, as in the third movement of Beethoven's Piano Sonata No. 17 in D Minor, op. 31, no. 2 ("Tempest") or the start of the first movement of Philip Glass's *Violin Concerto* (1987) (ex. 3.89). In the Glass, "repeated figures" are synonymous with pulsed articulation of an underlying voice-leading matrix in which voices in adjacent harmonies generally move by common tone, step, or octave displacement. Here, set rhythm is indistinguishable from harmonic rhythm; segment rhythm is given by the basic pulse in the orchestra, then also the solo (which introduces cross-rhythms in m. 12 (♪. against ♪) and in m. 21 (♩. against ♪)). A *stylistic matrix* relaxes the rigor and consistency of a structural matrix to focus on charac-

generally, on gestures, modes of interaction, and musical behaviors. Stylistic matrix embeds intermittent associative patterning in much contemporary music as in Carter's Cello Sonata (1948), Feldman's *Rothko Chapel* (1971), or Adams's Violin Concerto (1993).

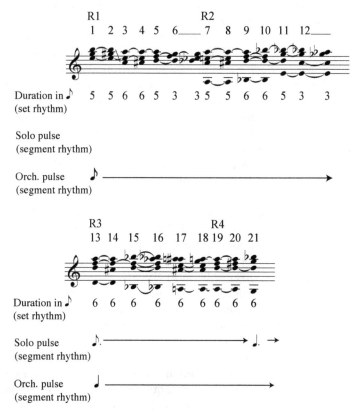

Example 3.89. Glass, *Violin Concerto,* voice leading and surface rhythm, mm. 1–21

Patch-matrix relations vary from passage to passage and piece to piece. Some pieces are composed entirely, or almost entirely, of patches with no, or very little, independent matrix. Feldman's *Patterns in a Chromatic Field* (exx. 3.3 and 3.4) is like this, with patches that range from fairly small (a few measures to a system) to very large (two or more pages). As changes in patch size scroll over the fixed-size window of the perceptual present (a few seconds), landscape composition shifts between passages that are highly continuous (e.g., pages 1–2 and 4–6, two passages based on sets *D* and *E*) and those that are more fragmented (e.g., pp. 8–9, which proceed through seven distinct local landscapes, of which the longest is two systems). Stravinsky's "Glorification of

much shorter average patch size (commensurate with the movement's smaller scale, measured against the fixed window of the perceptual present) and faster set rhythm makes for a highly fragmented landscape. Set rhythm in its A and A' sections (R104–R111 and R117–R121) can be gleaned from the map of segment rhythm for set *P* given in example 3.55b, where rests longer than a dotted quarter indicate a shift from set *P* to a different associative set.

Some pieces are predominantly matrix, with few or no patches other than those comprised of surface or hidden repetitions identical with the weave of the structural matrix. Bach's D-minor harmonization of "O Haupt voll Blut und Wunden" from the *St. Matthew Passion* (Riemenschneider No. 74) is full of motivic thirds, but these are virtually inseparable from essential voice leading. Systematic in conception and implementation but stochastic in result, the structural matrix of Xenakis's *Pithoprakta* is a world away from that of Bach's chorale in compositional aesthetics and technique. Yet patch-matrix relations in parts of *Pithoprakta* are comparable to those in the chorale, in that surface repetitions that form audible patches are synonymous with the workings of matrix.

Between the two extremes of all patches and no distinct matrix, and all matrix with no distinct patches, are all kinds of possibilities. For example, Bach's Fugue in C-sharp Minor from the *Well-Tempered Clavier*, Book I begins with a porous patch of subject entries deeply embedded in a voice-leading matrix. Babbitt's *Emblems (Ars Emblematica)* (1989) is dominated by a pc array matrix, interwoven with numerous small patches and long-range associations between segments. Patch-matrix relations can be fluid, changing many times over the course of a composition as patches emerge from or recede back into matrix. Renaissance counterpoint is full of give and take between patch and matrix, as points of imitation form a series of patches and dissolve back into the contrapuntal flow. Jazz solos are often dynamic in this respect, as is Coltrane's solo from the 1960 recording of "Equinox," where a series of patches from associative sets that vary in profile and extent twice dissolve back into Tyner and Davis's cycles through the harmonic matrix. Illustrating a common pattern in tonal music, the Bourrée from Bach's Suite No. 4 for Violoncello Solo begins with a large patch (dominated by a sixteenth-note run upward by fifth, mm. 1–10) that dissolves back into the voice-leading matrix at the cadence (mm. 11–12) (ex. 3.90). Reich's *Violin Phase* (1967) for four violins elevates changes in patch-matrix relations to a compositional technique. The piece is composed from a single pattern, progressively phased against itself to create a matrix of canons at the unison. Starting at R9, a series of gradual *crescendi* and *diminuendi* in Violin 2 (the live solo) alternately extract individual resultant patterns from, and submerge them back into, the canonic matrix. Superimposing a series of small-scale oscillations in patch-matrix relations on a large-scale phasing process, Reich advances the compositional technique and

Come Out (1966) and *Piano Phase* (1967) to create the sort of multiscaled processes characteristic of his later music.

Example 3.90. Bach, Suite No. 4 in E-flat for Violoncello Solo, Bourrée, mm. 1–12

High-Profile and Low-Profile Associative Landscapes. Along with patch-matrix relations, associative landscapes can be conceived in terms of a continuum from high-profile to low-profile associative organization. Both high- and low-profile organization engage aspects of segmentation, set formation, and set disposition. A paradigmatic case of *high-profile associative organization* involves clear segments organized into one or more associative sets characterized by strong contextual criteria, strong core contextual common sets, and crisp boundaries, with the sets disposed in a passage or composition so that temporal or sonic adjacency support set unity, while sonic disjunctions articulate associative discontinuities. At the other end of the spectrum, paradigmatic cases of *low-profile associative organization* involve segments supported by weak or uncertain contextual criteria, landscapes in which associative set boundaries are fuzzy or obscured by aspects of sonic organization, or associative sets with weak internal organization.

"Spring Rounds" from Stravinsky's *Rite of Spring* begins with a paradigmatic case of high-profile associative organization (return to ex. 3.44 for a short score of R49–R50). The landscape alternates between simple patches of two associative sets—three dragging chords in the strings combined with a rising line in the low strings and bass clarinets, and a much higher melody with grace notes in the double reeds. At least at first, both sets are uniform and sonic disjunctions in timbre and register articulate the associative discontinuities between them. In "Glorification of the Chosen One," high-profile organization occurs at the scale of a short movement (ex. 3.40 gives the opening patch of four measures). Each of the associative sets in this highly fragmented landscape is near-uniform; once again, sonic disjunctions underline the associative discontinuities

ciative organization opens Wolpe's *Trio in Two Parts for Flute, Cello, and Piano* (1963–64) (for a score of mm. 1–7, refer back to ex. 3.63a). Although each in the series of small associative sets in monophonic disposition harbors some variation (mostly through pitch inversion), set boundaries remain clear, articulated by temporal and sonic disjunctions in dynamics, timbre, articulation, and surface rhythm. A sharp contrast with the Wolpe in style and tonal structure, the opening of Bach's *Chromatic Fantasy* (mm. 1–7) is nonetheless similar with regard to some basic aspects of associative organization: a series of small, clear sets in associative monophony, each with internal variation, shape a high-profile surface that, in this case, rides along on a matrix of predominantly stepwise voice leading. Domenico Scarlatti's Sonata in D Major, K. 492 (mm. 1–8) (ex. 3.91) also, characteristically, begins with high-profile organization: three associative sets with four, two, and one segment (in mm. 1–2, 3, and 4, respectively) create a monophonic sequence in mm. 1–4. Repeating this sequence of sets as mm. 5–8 binds the three sets together into one large-scale unit and softens the effect of its internal dissociations. Bartók's "Harvest Song," no. 33 from the *44 Duos* for two violins (1931), has high-profile associative organization throughout. Measures 1–10 (ex. 3.92) set up the landscape: working in the context of textural polyphony, two sets alternate in associative monophony with associative discontinuities articulated by disjunctions in $S_{1\text{-rest}}$, $S_{1\text{-dynamics}}$, $S_{2\text{-duration}}$, and, twice, in $S_{1\text{-pitch}}$. Within each monophonic disposition is a polyphonic disposition of two associative subsets distinguished by pitch-class content (e.g., $C_{pc\ \{9B02\}}$ versus $C_{pc\ \{3568\}}$ in mm. 1–5) and scoring (violin I versus violin II, $S_{2\text{-instrumentation}}$). The result is a two-part form with internal binary divisions, within which material in each violin is diatonic but the composite is octatonic.

Low-profile associative organization is typical of Feldman's late music; the opening of *Patterns in a Chromatic Field* (refer back to exs. 3.3 and 3.4) is a paradigmatic example. Although instrumentation clearly distinguishes the large patch of set *D* in the cello from set *E* in the piano, flat distribution across an extensive range of minute variations within set *D* discourages the formation of associative subsets, creating a low-profile surface. Low-profile organization is also fairly common in Messiaen's birdsong music, where it mimics natural improvisation. In mm. 28–43 of "L'alouette calandrelle" (*Catalogue d'oiseaux*, Book VIII, No. 1) an extended duet between a short-toed lark (*l'alouette calandrelle*) and a crested lark (*le cochevis huppé*) exhibits low-profile organization within two sets of a polyphonic disposition, the two birds distinguished by register and characteristic figures.

High-profile and low-profile associative organization are, for the most part, functionally independent of scale.[122] High-profile organization can be small scale, as in the opening of Wolpe's Trio or Bach's *Chromatic Fantasy*. Or, it can unfold at a much larger scale, as in the Introduction to Act I, Scene 1 (mm. 1–78) from John Adams's *Nixon in China* (1987), where pitch-class

Example 3.91. Scarlatti, Sonata in D Major K. 492, mm. 1–11

Example 3.92. Bartók, *44 Duos for Two Violins* No. 33, "Harvest Song," mm. 1–10

content defines a series of associative subsets in associative monophony relative to one another. (Here the overlay of a second series of associative subsets
defined by diminution creates associative heterophony within each time span).
Similarly, low-profile organization can be either large scale, as in the opening
of Feldman's *Patterns in a Chromatic Field* (exs. 3.3 and 3.4) or small scale, as
in the opening of the fourth movement of Schoenberg's Second String Quartet, op. 10 (ex. 2.3), where segments from the three associative sets initiated
by the rising figure in m. 1, the falling fifth motif in mm. 3 and 6, and the

oritized. Moves from high- to low-profile organization can align with formal functions, as in Schoenberg's liquidation within a phrase, or in moves from thematic statements to transitional or developmental material in a sonata. The introduction to the first movement of Schumann's Symphony No. 2 in C, op. 61, traces the opposite path, from the diffuse beginnings of low-profile organization in a polyphonic disposition (mm. 1–14) to higher-profile organization as new material enters in m. 25. Moves between high- and low-profile organization are common in Wolpe's music: the *Piece for Two Instrumental Units* (1962) begins with a move from high-profile organization in mm. 1–4 to low-profile in mm. 13–19.

Homogeneity and Heterogeneity, Material and Compositional. While we have considered internal and external dispositions, patch-matrix relations, and high- and low-profile organization within time spans at different scales, we have not yet compared time spans with one another to see whether associative organization is relatively constant or if it changes over the course of a passage or composition. To do this, we invoke the idea of a plot and compare plots with one another for homogeneity or heterogeneity in two respects: material and compositional.

Earlier we defined the plot as a temporally continuous musical span, often delimited by a significant sonic disjunction or a change in associative sets or organization. Homogeneity and heterogeneity are poles of a continuum in plot (landscape) design. Each obtains in two respects: material and compositional. *Material homogeneity* (or *heterogeneity*) refers to the associative sets or subsets involved. *Compositional homogeneity (heterogeneity)* refers to the way these sets are arranged in the landscape—whether the mode of arrangement, apart from the materials, is relatively constant, or changes. Material and compositional homogeneity and heterogeneity are functionally independent; they define two orthogonal continua in a three-dimensional space. However, they are usually scale-*dependent*: except for landscapes with a fractal design, a change in the scale of analysis usually effects a change in landscape structure.[123] There is no *a priori* "right" scale for music analysis. Instead, analysts need to think about the scale of analysis they use and its apparent effect on associative organization.

Pattern preludes for solo keyboard, such as Bach's Prelude in C from the *Well-Tempered Clavier*, Book I and Chopin's Prelude in C, op. 28, no. 1, are good examples of associative landscapes that are materially and compositionally homogeneous at or near the scale of an entire piece.[124] Comprised mostly of large patches of a single set, often in dense canons, the associative landscape of the two outer sections of Schumann's *Kreisleriana* No. 5 (ex. 3.93) is relatively homogeneous both materially and compositionally. Composed of just two

combines large-scale material and compositional homogeneity with relentless, directed change in the sonic dimensions of loudness and timbre to create an effect of musical inevitability.

(Sehr lebhaft)

Example 3.93. Schumann, *Kreisleriana* No. 5, mm. 5–9

The first reprise of the Minuet from Mozart's String Quartet No. 18 in A Major, K. 464 (mm. 1–28, ex. 3.69) is an example of an associative landscape that is materially homogeneous but compositionally heterogeneous. Once associative sets *S* and *T* are established (by the end of m. 8), the materials in play remain constant; only their compositional arrangement changes, from associative monophony (for set *S* in mm. 1–4, and set *T* in mm. 5–8, each in textural homophony), to associative polyphony (in mm. 9–12), and back to associative monophony (for set *S* in mm. 13–17, and set *T* in mm. 17–22, this time each in canon, for textural polyphony). Variation V from movement II of Webern's *Symphony*, op. 21 (ex. 3.94) is another example of a materially homogeneous but compositionally heterogeneous landscape. While three associative sets in the harp, violins I/II, and viola/cello account for all of the variation's material, each of the three possible pairs of sets appears twice in the variation (as dictated by its retrograde symmetry) as do two of the three possible solos (the harp has none).

In contrast, variation II of the same movement is materially heterogeneous but compositionally homogeneous (ex. 3.95). Toggling back and forth between corresponding order positions of two row forms, horn I reels off a series of dyads. Immediate repetition of each dyad creates a string of small associative sets that stand out (by virtue of timbre and temporal adjacency) from the dyads of an accompanying pair of rows in the rest of the ensemble that complete the structural matrix. Despite the quick set turnover in the horn, landscape composition is constant throughout. Except for some differences in patch-matrix relations, the monophonic sequences of small associative sets that begin Wolpe's Trio (mm. 1–7, exx. 3.63a and 3.63b) and the final Allegro from Bach's Sonata no. 2 in A Minor for Violin Solo (mm. 1–7, ex. 3.39a) are comparable: each creates a materially heterogeneous and compositionally homogeneous associative landscape.

Example 3.94. Webern, *Symphony* op. 21, II, mm. 55–57 (Variation V)

In the first movement of the *Concerto*, op. 24, Webern balances tight pitch-class organization with a materially and compositionally heterogeneous associative landscape. The row partitions the aggregate into four members of SC 3-3[014]. Webern tends to realize the row as a series of trichordal segments of a single associative set H with C/CRS = $\{C_{SC\ 3\text{-}3[014]}\}$ (e.g., as in ex. 3.18a). Variation among segments of H with regard to rhythm, articulation, dynamics, timbre, contour, pitch and pc content, and interval orderings suggests a number of associative subsets. To study the disposition of subsets and emergent properties of the landscape, we form a series of plots, each delineated by changes in tempo and surface figuration. Plots 1–5 are in mm. 1–5, 6–8, 9–10, 11–12, and 13–27; plot 5 has six subplots, in mm. 13–16, 17–18, 19–22, 22–23, 24–25, and 25–27.

Example 3.96a is an association graph of the eight segments in plot 1 (mm. 1–5). The graph consists of two component C_4 digraphs; segment names represent four associative subsets H/a–H/d defined by rhythm and articulation. Arrows within each digraph model temporal succession. Note that each digraph represents *two* orthogonal sets of associations, by $C_{pitch\ R}$ (read horizontally) and C_{rhythm} (vertically). So each component digraph actually represents *four* associative subsets and the full graph, *eight*; these are disposed in mm. 1–5 as eight-part associative polyphony. Example 3.96b maps out the eight segments of plot 2 (mm. 6–8), which involves three associative subsets—H/a, H/b, and a new

Example 3.95. Webern, *Symphony* op. 21, II, mm. 23–26 (Variation II)

subset, *H/e*. Plot 2 begins with two-part associative polyphony between *H/a* and *H/e* in m. 6, then changes to associative monophony as subset *H/a* moves to *H/b* in mm. 7–8. Example 3.96c is a map of the four segments in plot 3 (mm. 9–10). Plot 3 introduces two new subsets, *H/f* and *H/g*, with C/CRS of an ip 4 dyad plus a note, versus an SC 3-3[014] trichordal simultaneity, respectively. Associative organization in plot 3 is strictly monophonic—*H/f*, then *H/g*. Over the course of plots 1 through 3, new material (associative subsets *H/e*, then *H/f* and *H/g*) and new arrangements of material (eight-part polyphony, two-part polyphony followed by monophony, then monophony) are continually introduced. As the movement goes on, this process continues. For instance, each but the first of the six subplots of plot 5 (mm. 13–27) consists of two-part associative polyphony that brings in at least one new associative subset (defined by a distinctive rhythm, articulation, pitch content, aspects of ordering such as dyads versus single notes, etc.). Thus the machine-tight weave of the underlying twelve-tone structural matrix is continuously rewoven by changes in landscape composition.

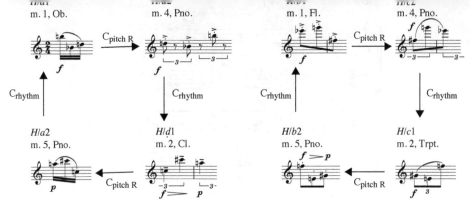

Example 3.96a. Webern, *Concerto* op. 24, I, graph of plot 1, mm. 1–5

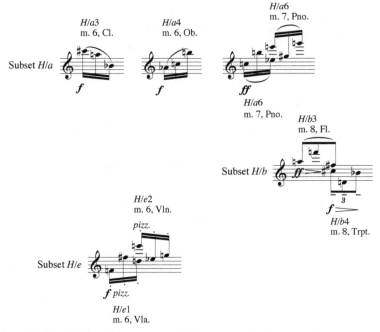

Example 3.96b. Webern, *Concerto* op. 24, I, map of plot 2, mm. 6–8

Stockhausen's *Gruppen für drei Orchester* (1955–57) exemplifies material and compositional heterogeneity in a large-scale work. Its 174 "Groups," identified by the composer and articulated by changes in material, arrangement of materials, and orchestration, invite interpretation as 174 plots. Overall, associative organization within these plots tends toward low profile, but among plots it

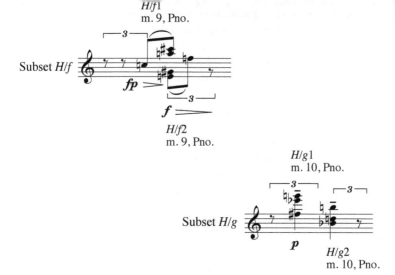

Example 3.96c. Webern, *Concerto* op. 24, I, map of plot 3, mm. 9–10

is highly heterogeneous with respect to materials, the disposition of materials within or among the three orchestras, and scale in three dimensions—time (group length and aspects of surface rhythm, both governed by Stockhausen's compositional plan); timbre (the swatch of the timbral spectrum active at once); and physical location (created by the horseshoe arrangement of the three orchestras around the audience). A quick survey of even a few plots suffices to suggest the remarkable compositional heterogeneity of associative organization in the whole. Group 1 (plot 1) is a short dense patch of associative monophony confined to orchestra I, small-scale in time and space but fairly large-scale in terms of timbre (with flute, alto flute, trumpet, drums, marimba, piano, and strings). Based on different material, group 121 is also associatively monophonic, but large-scale in time and space (with orchestra I, II, and III) and small-scale in timbre (drums, plus tuba in orchestra I, piano in orchestra II, and contrabass trombone in orchestra III). Groups 49 and 77 are associatively polyphonic, each pitting material shared by the flanking orchestras I and III against that in the central orchestra II.

Associative Sets, Landscapes, and Levels

With associative sets, configurations, and landscapes, we have gradually assembled a conceptual framework that supports a holistic and nonreductive approach to the analysis of associative design as an aspect of form in music.

not reduce to, a set of supporting criteria or genosegs, an associative set is not just a collection of segments but a *system of relationships among segments* that itself functions as a unit at a higher level of organization. Instead of privileging certain shared features as necessary and sufficient criteria for membership, an associative set recognizes the complexity of relationships among its individual segments and embraces the full spectrum of similarity and difference. Variation is not incidental but essential, represented in global properties of range and distribution; emergent properties of configurations and graphs such as connectivity, regularity, and planarity; and functions that individual segments can assume in the context of a set, such as a contextual focus or bridge. Each of these arises at the level of the set, a cumulative result of each segment's relations with its consociates; none is held by the contributing segments individually. Thus associative sets strenuously resist reduction: the set is a higher-level unit that supervenes on, but cannot be reduced to, the individual segments or criteria it includes.

A similar relationship obtains at the next-higher level, between associative landscapes and associative sets. An associative landscape is more than a collection of associative sets: it is an *arrangement* of sets in time with respect to one another and perhaps also a background matrix. Features and properties that first arise at the level of the landscape include internal dispositions (clumped, dispersed), external dispositions (associative monophony, polyphony, and heterophony), associative discontinuities, patch-matrix relations, high- and low-profile associative organization, and material and compositional homogeneity and heterogeneity. Like sets, landscapes strenuously resist reduction to lower levels of organization and analysis, whether sets, segments, or criteria.

The reader will no doubt have noticed that while I have said a great deal about associative sets and associative landscapes, I have said very little about how associative sets form. There are two reasons for this. One is that associative sets are *interpretative* categories: they represent the interpretations, interests, and goals of individual analysts, not the normative result of cognitive or computational processes. Studies in music cognition and computer modeling can reveal important constraints on the interpretive process, but proceed by tenets (including prediction) and pursue goals that are fundamentally different from those of music analysis as a humanistic endeavor.

The second reason is more complex. Associative set formation is an ecological process, characterized by a complex and dynamic interdependence among actions and entities at various levels including: (1) the activation of contextual criteria; (2) segment formation, or *mutual formation* whenever contextual criteria are involved; (3) associative set formation; and (4) the disposition of sets in an associative landscape.[125] Although in theory criteria, segments, sets, and landscapes occupy successive levels, in practice these levels intertwine and often develop simultaneously. In music analysis causality flows in both

nosegs, sets, landscapes) involve *but can also influence* those at lower levels (criteria, genosegs, phenosegs, sets) in a kind of downward causation.[126] Instead of a kind of executive selection from segments already formed by sonic and contextual criteria, the process of associative set formation is an interactive one. Once, or even as, an associative set becomes established, segments can form directly *within* the set: the set becomes an active presence in the analytic process, promoting the contextual criteria at work among its segments by triggering the transformation of predicable to relational properties in additional potential segments.[127] Similarly, the disposition of sets in an associative landscape can influence content and organization at lower levels. Whereas clumped dispositions, large patches, and associative monophony facilitate the formation of associative sets and segments, dispersed dispositions, very small patches, complex associative polyphony, and other perceptual challenges tend to inhibit it. Thus the interdependence among criteria, segments, sets, and landscapes creates a dynamic web of relationships that defies any purely linear account of set formation. As biologist Richard Lewontin says of part-whole relationships in dialectic ecology: "It is not [only] that a whole is more than the sum of its parts, but that the parts themselves are *redefined and recreated* in the process of their interaction."[128]

Within the general theory, interactions obtain not only "vertically," among the five levels of orientations, criteria, segments, associative sets, and landscapes, but also "horizontally," across its three domains and sonic, associative, and structural aspects of musical organization. This may be clearest with respect to segment formation, where structural criteria depend on sonic or contextual criteria for realization and contextual criteria usually require at least some coincident support from sonic criteria to support convincing phenosegs. While sonic criteria can act alone to form phenosegs, coincidence with contextual or structural criteria often proves critical in the process of sifting and prioritizing segments. But interaction and interdependence among the three domains also obtains at higher levels of organization. Associative sets belong to the contextual domain, but set formation is shaped by aspects of sonic and structural organization. For example, clumped sets and large patches are often set off or strengthened by S_1 or S_2 criteria (especially $S_{1\text{-rest}}$ and $S_{1\text{-duration}}$); sets in associative polyphony are often distinguished by one or more S_2 criteria (usually $S_{2\text{-pitch}}$ or $S_{2\text{-timbre}}$). Associative sets in dispersed disposition often rely on strong sonic disjunctions to mark the first segment in the set for memory (as with the G♭/F trill in the first movement of Schubert's Piano Sonata in B-flat). Whether sonic and associative organization reinforce one another (as at the start of Stravinsky's "Spring Rounds," or in the coincident placement of sonic and contextual focus in Debussy's *La Mer*, ex. 3.85) or shape the musical landscape in complementary ways (as in Ravel's *Bolero*, which imposes a clear sonic trajectory on a static associative landscape, or in the distant placement of the

relationship between sonic and associative aspects of musical organization is a potent force in the landscape at the largest scale.

When the structural domain is active, structural criteria and an orienting theory can have a profound effect on all levels of organization and analysis, from the choice of contextual criteria, to segments, sets, and the shape of the associative landscape. Theoretic orientations tend to privilege contextual criteria that correspond to structural units in the orienting theory and organize contextual criteria and the segments they support according to its conceptual framework. A change in theoretic orientation can redefine the set of segments recognized, their configuration with respect to one another, and the disposition of associative sets in the landscape.

So sonic, associative, and structural organization can interact in all kinds of ways: they can cooperate, reinforce, shape, or complement one another. Such interdomain relationships are aspects of compositional structure and style on the one hand (areas for analytical investigation) and analytical perspective and interpretation on the other (open to introspection and self-knowledge). The real value of the theory as a conceptual framework that encompasses orientations, criteria, segments, sets, and landscapes and attends to activity in the sonic, contextual, and structural domains lies not in its ability to define or prescribe, but in its capacity to stimulate imagination, frame questions, elicit observations, and articulate ideas about pieces of music—all with a vigorous new focus on associative organization as an aspect of musical form and design.

Part Three

Six Analyses

Beethoven, Piano Sonata No. 2 in A Major, Op. 2, No. 2, I

Associative Organization and Tonal Structure

Beethoven's Piano Sonata No. 2 in A Major, op. 2, no. 2, dates from the composer's early years in Vienna.[1] The first movement is a bright, mercurial sonata form, full of sharp sonic contrasts in register, surface rhythm, and dynamics, and characteristic juxtapositions of associative sets, themes, and textures. Together these make the movement a veritable study of landscape design that is unique among the thirty-two piano sonatas. The conceptual framework we have developed in chapters 2 and 3 will help us navigate this complex associative landscape and support a comparative analysis of sonic, associative, and structural organization. We begin with a chronological first pass through the movement, mapping the associative landscape section by section and studying the global properties, configurations, distributions, and dispositions of individual sets, as well as landscape composition. On the second pass we shift attention to changes in the relative priority of, and interactions among, associative organization, sonic organization, and structural voice leading as primary and subsidiary agents of musical form.

First Pass: The Associative Landscape

The associative organization of the first tonal area (FTA) is an unusual patchwork design[2] with two thematic components: an inaugural theme (mm. 1–8), followed by the primary theme proper (mm. 9–20)[3] (ex. 4.1). Each theme introduces the seeds of two or three associative sets. The inaugural theme begins with a brief alternation of an upbeat figure and a scalar descent that seed two associative sets A and B ($A1$ and $B1$ in ex. 4.1). This is followed by an arpeggiated V^7 that extends the basic idea of A (mm. 5–8); together these comprise an eight-measure sentence structure. The primary theme begins with a triplet upbeat followed by a staccato scalar ascent of an octave (mm. 9–10); subsequent occurrences suggest interpreting these as two distinct elements of

point that follows, two figures, a descending third from E to C♯ that establishes scale degree 3 as *Kopfton* (set *D*) and a rising scalar fourth (set *E*), play hide and seek in the texture (mm. 11–16).

Example 4.1. Beethoven, Piano Sonata No. 2 in A, op. 2, no. 2, I, mm. 1–25

The centrifugal force of the FTA's diverse design elements is counterbalanced by the simplicity of its harmonic language, which is firmly centered on tonic and dominant. The inaugural theme (mm. 1–8) moves from I through ii to V⁷, setting up the tonic that begins the primary theme in m. 9. The

D♯ appears at the end of m. 16, diverting the phrase toward a tonicized half cadence. After an abbreviated recall of the inaugural theme in mm. 21–22, the primary theme begins its second statement in m. 23. This time, however, it reaches a perfect authentic cadence in A in m. 32, completing what is essentially an antecedent-consequent structure (the primary theme in mm. 9–20 and mm. 23–32) with two prefixes (the inaugural theme in mm. 1–8 and its recall in mm. 21–22).

Example 4.2 organizes the segments of sets A–E from the first statements of the inaugural and primary themes (mm. 1–16) into an association map that shows the patchwork design of the FTA. The inaugural theme begins with intercutting and implied associative polyphony between sets A and B; it closes with a longer segment of A. The primary theme begins with a single longish segment of set C, followed by associative and textural polyphony between set D in the primary melodic voice and set E, which provides accompanying and connective material.

Even this early in the piece, each of the sets A–E is set off as a distinct design element not only by its core contextual criteria, but also by its global properties. Whereas set A quickly establishes a range of variation from short upbeat figures in m. 1 and m. 3 to the longer descending arpeggiation in mm. 5–8, set B is uniform except for tonal transposition. The internal organization of set D is even tighter. All six segments of set D in the FTA (arranged in two patches, mm. 11–16 and mm. 25–30) are associated by C_{rhythm} ⟨♩.♪|♩⟩ and the coincident linked criterion $T_{3PRG,\ A:\ <(54)\ 3>}C_{pc\ <E,\ D,\ C♯>}$ that represents the pitch motive's consistent structural interpretation as a descending third progression from scale degree 5 to 3 in A major. Sonic criteria are more important to some sets than to others. In the implied polyphony of mm. 1–8, $S_{2\text{-pitch}}$, $S_{2\text{-duration}}$ and $S_{2\text{-articulation}}$ project the segments of sets A and B on distinct sonic channels. But in the associative and textural polyphony of mm. 11–16, the legato segments of sets D and E easily flow into and around one another, exchanging places in a shared set of registers.

Example 4.3 represents the associative organization of sets A–E in the FTA in a large-scale cutaway score map of the entire exposition that shows associative rhythm and dispositions for seven sets A–G. Reflecting the movement's prevailing 4/4 hypermeter, durations represent diminutions by half (i.e., ♩ = one 2/4 measure; each 4/4 measure represents one four-bar hypermeasure). Measure numbers and major sections of the sonata form appear across the top of the map. Within sets, stem direction or vertical position approximates the registral disposition of voices within contrapuntal passages (e.g., for sets D and E in mm. 11–16, and set C in mm. 32–41). By focusing on associative rhythm, the map brings out some aspects of segment rhythm that are quite audible but nonetheless easy to miss in the bustle of surface pitch activity. For example, whereas intercutting between sets A and B in mm. 1–4 is mediated by a common

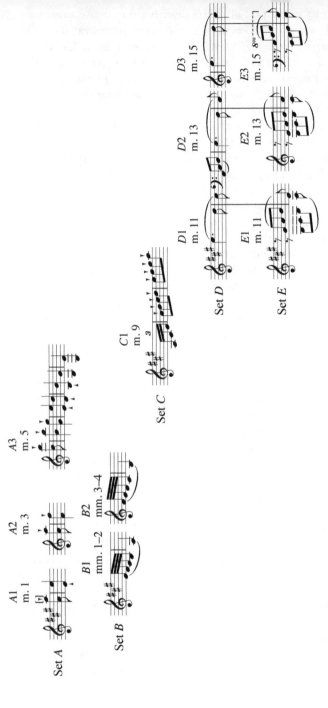

Example 4.2. Beethoven, Piano Sonata No. 2 in A, op. 2, no. 2, I, mm. 1–16, association map

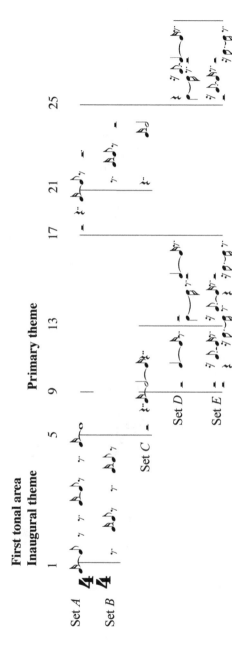

Example 4.3. Beethoven, Piano Sonata No. 2 in A, op. 2, no. 2, I, association map, exposition (mm. 1–117)

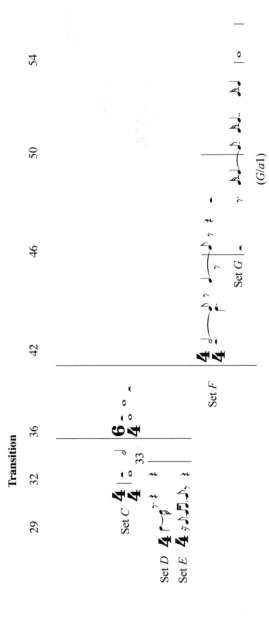

Example 4.3. Beethoven, Piano Sonata No. 2 in A, op. 2, no. 2, I, association map, exposition (mm. 1–117)—*(continued)*

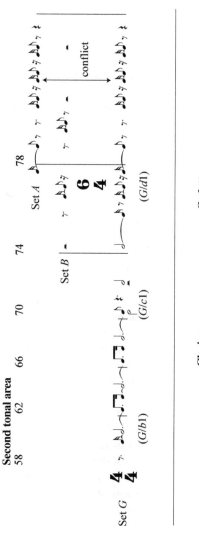

Example 4.3. Beethoven, Piano Sonata No. 2 in A, op. 2, no. 2, I, association map, exposition (mm. 1–117)—(concluded)

9–16, segments of sets D and E are distinguished by unique attack points. Surveying the associative organization of the FTA in this larger-scaled map also brings out a parallel between the interspliced design of the inaugural theme and that of the FTA as a whole: both can be interpreted as implied polyphonies, with the FTA formed from a polyphony of two associative polyphonies, one implied (sets A/B), the other actual (D/E), connected by a thread of set C.

An elision between the FTA's cadential tonic (the last "beat" in the last hypermeasure of sets D and E, mm. 29–32) and the tonic that begins the transition on the downbeat of m. 32 (and first beat of a new 4/4 hypermeasure with two segments of set C) creates the first wrinkle in the 4/4 hypermeter (ex. 4.4). Coming after a series of simple tonic-dominant exchanges in the FTA, even the conventional move to V/V that sets the keystone in the harmonic arch of the transition (mm. 38–48)—but especially the retreat into E minor at m. 49—creates a sense of instability and greater harmonic complexity. But as the harmonic language becomes richer, the composition of the associative landscape is simplified: associative polyphony in the FTA gives way to associative monophony at the start of the transition, which proceeds through successive patches of sets C (mm. 32–41), F (mm. 42–46), and the first inklings of G (mm. 49–57).

The change in design at m. 32 from associative polyphony to associative monophony is mediated by a more gradual move from textural polyphony to monophony over the course of the transition. The transition begins with a lively but dense patch of set C in which the triplet arpeggio upbeat from $C1$ (m. 8) is extended and transformed into a two-octave scale that omits a note in each octave to accommodate the triplet rhythm (m. 32). This arpeggio-become-scale appears in invertible counterpoint with a descending staccato eighth-note scale, an inversion of the arpeggio's original companion figure in $C1$ (mm. 9–10). After the figures exchange places in register three times, the counterpoint dissolves and the voices join in descending staccato parallel sixths. Extending the scalar portion of the patch's final segment through a second octave forces a hypermetric extension from 4/4 to 6/4 in mm. 40–41. Just as the root of V/V arrives in m. 42, set F appears, in a small patch and minimal stretto in which each segment shares its first note, last note, or both, with a consociate (e.g., $F1$ is <D♯4, D♯4, E4, A♯3, B3>). With the C♮ in m. 49 that reorients the harmony toward E minor and the start of the second tonal area (STA), the seventh and last important set in the movement, set G, enters with a patch of three temporally adjacent but discrete segments (in mm. 49–50, 51–52, and 53–54) that presage features of the second theme.

Heard in the context of the exposition as a whole, changes in associative organization during the transition effect a sort of design modulation between the contrasting associative landscapes of the first and second tonal areas. The second tonal area (STA) begins with a lazy quasi-turn figure followed by two chromatic steps (mm. 58–61); this figure seeds the main subset of G that generates

Example 4.4. Beethoven, Piano Sonata No. 2 in A, op. 2, no. 2, I, mm. 29–37, hypermetric overlap at start of the transition

the thematic content of the STA (ex. 4.5).[4] After being sequenced twice at the minor third (starting on G in m. 62 and B♭ in m. 66), the turn figure is condensed and sequenced twice more at the second (mm. 70–75), then liquidated into a semitone descent with an upbeat rhythm that recalls *A1* (m. 78). Whereas the associative landscape of the FTA is materially and compositionally heterogeneous with two themes, five sets (*A–E*), and plots that alternate between implied and literal associative polyphony, that of the STA is homogeneous, dominated by a single associative set (*G*) in associative monophony with a melody and accompaniment texture.

Example 4.5. Beethoven, Piano Sonata No. 2 in A, op. 2, no. 2, I, mm. 55–61

transition (m. 48), connects it to figures from mm. 58, 70, and 78 as initial segments of four associative subsets G/a–G/d, and organizes these into an association graph. Differences in line weight represent relative associative proximity for the three associative adjacencies G/a–G/b, G/b–G/c, and G/c–G/d. The strongest connection is between G/b and G/c, the two figures at the heart of the STA. The graph inspires some observations about associative organization within the STA. First, linear topology plays out as musical chronology: a walk on the graph from G/a to G/d traces the course of motivic development from mm. 48–78. In a refinement to this basic plan, greater associative distance between each of the central subsets G/b and G/c and the corresponding peripheral subsets G/a and G/d correlates with moves into and out of the STA. On the way in, the edge G/a–G/b bridges the tonal and textural divide from the end of the transition to the start of the STA. On the way out, increased associative distance between the compressed turn G/c and its liquidation in G/d prepares for the departure of set G, just after the hypermetric extension in mm. 78–83.

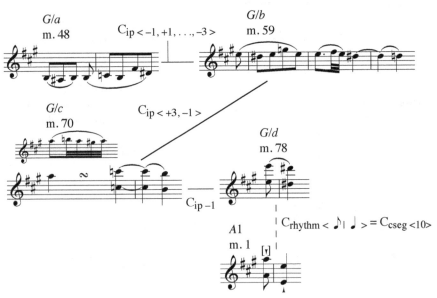

Example 4.6. Beethoven, Piano Sonata No. 2 in A, op. 2, no. 2, I, representative segments of four associative subsets G/a–G/d with a conflux to set A

Toward the bottom of the graph, a dotted line between the G/d segment and $A1$ represents a conflux between sets G and A in mm. 77–82. Lest the association between these two segments by the coincident criteria $C_{rhythm} \langle \flat | \flat \rangle = C_{cseg \langle 10 \rangle}$ seem weak or insignificant, in context it is underlined by the sudden return of set B in m. 76 that, interspliced with segments of G/d and A, recreates

association between these two small plots in turn encourages a listener to hear the triplet arpeggio that bursts out of the high register in mm. 84–85 as part of set *A*—that is, as a florid consociate and local counterpart to *A*3 that completes an altered copy of the design of the inaugural theme (mm. 1–8) in a plot that extends from mm. 76–88. What makes the parallel in associative organization so striking is the fact that the tonal structure and formal contexts of the two passages are so different. Whereas the inaugural plot in mm. 1–8 moves easily from I through ii to V^7, the recomposed version in mm. 76–88 hangs on vii$^{o6}_5$ in E minor for eight bars, then blasts into E major with a I^6 in m. 84 that moves to a provisional cadence in m. 88. The two small plots also play near-complementary roles in the sonata form. Whereas the original plot opens the FTA and presents a distinct theme, its correlate not only ends the STA but does so in a most unusual way, trailing off the edge of set *G* in a cross between a transition and a dead-end (mm. 76–83), only to reappear triumphant with a segment of

Example 4.7. Beethoven, Piano Sonata No. 2 in A, op. 2, no. 2, I, mm. 74–88.

on, the music proceeds efficiently toward essential expositional closure in m. 92, with patches dissolving back into the voice-leading matrix just before the preliminary cadence in m. 88 and again before m. 92.

The long-range association between these two plots of similar design but different tonal structures and formal functions is one of two in the exposition. The closing section that begins forthwith in m. 92 finds its design correlate in the first part of the transition, in mm. 32–41.[5] Both passages begin with a dense patch of set *C* in associative monophony and imitative polyphony, but the later passage is recomposed harmonically and in register to confirm the newly attained goal of E major. Here too the design parallel supports an ironic role reversal: whereas the task of the transition is to leave its starting point of A major, the closing must reconfirm its opening tonic of E (originally E minor, now E major) as a provisional goal. Once the design parallel has run its course (the closing plot is two bars longer, with IV and V added in mm. 102 and 103 to secure the cadence), a codetta begins in m. 104. At this point there is a slight adjustment in associative organization as set *C* continues, but associative monophony gives way to associative heterophony with scalar segments in eighth-notes and half-notes moving against one another in contrary motion.

The development section continues the pattern of polarizing and juxtaposing thematic materials, but rather than apply this strategy to material drawn from the FTA versus STA, as in the exposition, here Beethoven exploits the availability of existing contrast between and within the inaugural and primary themes. The development has two large parts, defined by tonal structure aligned with changes in associative set activity and landscape composition, followed by a retransition. Part I (mm. 123–61)[6] centers around a C tonic; part II, around F major, then D minor (162–203) en route to V$^{8-7}$ at the start of the retransition (203–25).[7] Part I of the development begins like the exposition, with a statement of the inaugural theme, now in C major (♮III) (ex. 4.8). This time the inaugural theme sticks around: its associative sets *A* and *B* provide all of the thematic material for part I, with a vigorous sixteenth-note accompaniment derived from the STA. As in the FTA, intercutting between sets *A* and *B* creates a landscape of implied polyphony (mm. 123–48). After three exchanges, this gives way to associative monophony with set *A* (mm. 149–58).

Example 4.9 models the associative rhythm and associative landscape of part I in a large-scale map of the entire development in the same cutaway score format as example 4.3. The map brings out two features of part I's landscape design. One is a change in the relative distributions of sets *A* and *B*. At the start of the development, the two sets are equally common, with two exchanges in the first four bars of the inaugural theme (mm. 123–26). After m. 131, set *B* becomes more rare as the move to a single exchange between sets *A* and *B* in mm. 131–48 shifts the balance in favor of set *A* and puts a wrinkle in the

Example 4.8. Beethoven, Piano Sonata No. 2 in A, op. 2, no. 2, I, mm. 123–37

hypermeter, now 6/4 (actually 2+4/4). As implied polyphony gives way to associative monophony at m. 149, the exchanges cease, set *B* disappears, and 4/4
hypermeter is restored. Within part I, then, sets *A* and *B* develop different distributions and functions. Whereas set *A* is widespread, common, and fairly
evenly distributed in the landscape, set *B* is more localized and gradually
phased out. Balancing the persistence of set *A*, which guarantees continuity
through a tonally unstable passage, the phase-out of set *B* effects a change in
landscape composition by removing, rather than adding or otherwise reconfiguring, material. The second aspect of the landscape brought out by the
map is a design parallel between the inaugural theme, which appears transposed to C as the first eight bars of the development (mm. 123–30), and the
main body of part I (131–61). Both passages begin with intercutting between
sets *A* and *B*, followed by set *A* alone. Thus the associative organization of the
main body of part I replicates, at a larger scale, that of the inaugural theme
that provides its motivic materials.

Part I

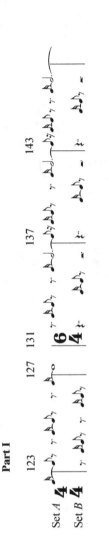

Part II

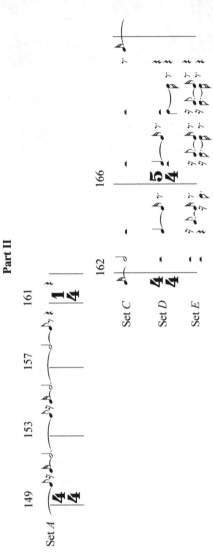

Example 4.9. Beethoven, Piano Sonata No. 2 in A, op. 2, no. 2, I, association map, development (mm. 123–225)

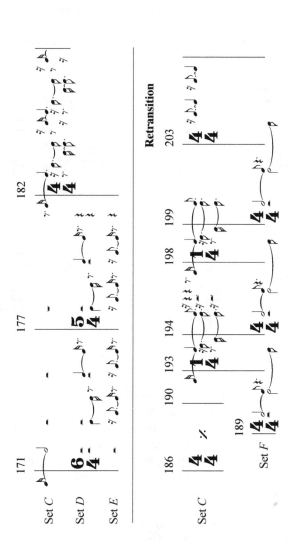

Example 4.9. Beethoven, Piano Sonata No. 2 in A, op. 2, no. 2, I, association map, development (mm. 123–225)—*(concluded)*

longation of the chromatic third divider ♮III), part II of the development begins in m. 162 (ex. 4.10). While part I plays with sets *A* and *B* of the inaugural theme, part II draws its material from sets *C*, *D*, and *E* of the primary theme and set *F* from the transition. Although on average the surface rhythm in part I is faster than in part II, changes in design tend in the opposite direction, such that the associative landscape of part II is more active—more dense and much more variable in composition—than in part I.

Example 4.10. Beethoven, Piano Sonata No. 2 in A, op. 2, no. 2, I, mm. 162–71

Part II begins with a statement of the primary theme in F major. (Throughout this discussion, please refer back to example 4.9 in parallel with the score excerpts given as examples 4.10–4.14.) As before, an introductory segment of set *C* leads to a dense patch of sets *D* and *E* in imitative counterpoint. This dissolves back into the voice-leading matrix in an appended cadence that forces a hypermetric extension from 4/4 to 5/4 (mm. 169–70). A restatement in F omits the cadential matrix (mm. 171–76), proceeding instead to a third iteration in D minor which restores the matrix, only to be truncated by the sudden appearance of a large and dense patch of set *C* in m. 182.

In this first section of part II (mm. 162–82), landscape design essentially recreates that of the primary theme of the FTA at a larger scale, much as part I does for the inaugural theme. The second section brings some striking changes in landscape design. Starting in mm. 182–90, a patch of dense imitative counterpoint among twelve segments of set *C* in a revolving three-voice stretto establishes a new kind of landscape, in which associative monophony overlaps the start of a patch of set *F* by one full measure (m. 189), creating an associative conflux between sets *C* and *F*, and a hypermetric elision between the last beat of the second 4/4 hypermeasure defined by set *C* (mm. 186–89) and the first of that defined by set *F* (mm. 189–92) (ex. 4.12). In an added twist, the motifs in the right and left hand in m. 189 each participate in their own weaker associative conflux between set *F* (in the right hand) or *C* (in the left) and set *D* (ex. 4.13). Pitch contour parses the melody in the right hand as two segments of set *F*, but the attack rhythm (now with an eighth-rest) recalls that of set *D* (mm. 189–92). In the left hand, coming as the tail end of set *C*'s stretto, the rising third <F, G, A> represents a truncated fifth. But forward-directed affinities with the rising and falling thirds in mm. 189–92 also support hearing the third *as a third*, recalling the pitch contour of set *D*.

Example 4.11. Beethoven, Piano Sonata No. 2 in A, op. 2, no. 2, I, mm. 182–85

Example 4.12. Beethoven, Piano Sonata No. 2 in A, op. 2, no. 2, I, mm. 189–94

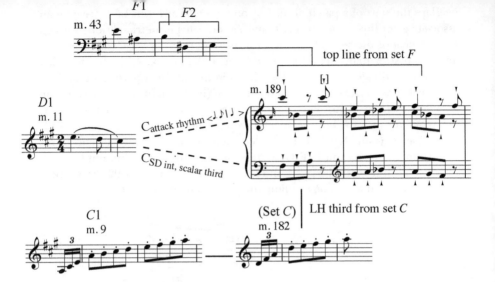

Example 4.13. Beethoven, Piano Sonata No. 2 in A, op. 2, no. 2, I, m. 189, as associative conflux

While both sets *C* and *F* persist through the rest of part II, the hypermetric elision at m. 189 is a unique event. The next two encounters between sets *C* and *F* are more confrontational, as two individual 1/4 hypermeasures of set *C* (mm. 193 and 198) are thrust between successive 4/4 hypermeasures of set *F* (mm. 189–92, 194–97, and 199–202) (refer back to ex. 4.9).[8] While the intersplicing of sets *C* and *F* in this passage recalls the implied polyphony of sets *A* and *B* in the inaugural theme, there is an important difference: in the inaugural theme, sets *A* and *B* articulate a common hypermeter; here, patches of set *C* interrupt the 4/4 hypermeter of set *F*, creating distinct layers in an irregular landscape unlike any other in the movement.

Once V arrives and the retransition begins in m. 203, the associative landscape flattens out. Set *C*, first represented only by its lead-in arpeggio, takes over in a passage of associative and textural monophony that picks up and maintains the 4/4 hypermeter established by set *F* in preparation for the recapitulation. As set *C* dissolves back into the voice-leading matrix five bars before the recap (mm. 221–24), the melody traces a bare outline of *G/b*, recalling the contour of the main figure in the STA and, more generally, set *G*, the only associative set from the exposition *not* explored in the development (ex. 4.14).

Having traversed the associative landscape from the start of the exposition to the end of the development on foot, as it were, we now briefly circle back for

Example 4.14. Beethoven, Piano Sonata No. 2 in A, op. 2, no. 2, I, mm. 221–24

a more commanding and synoptic view. Example 4.15 summarizes the activity of sets *A–G*, their external dispositions, and participation in associative and textural monophony or polyphony (separated by slashes), from m. 1 to m. 225. Vertical alignment between sections of the exposition and development underlines parallels in the course of set activity and landscape composition. Both sections introduce sets *A/B*, *C/D/E*, and *C/F* in the same order as representatives of the inaugural and primary themes of the FTA and the transition, often in landscapes of similar composition. The closest ties are in the "developmental" passage based on sets *D* and *E* (mm. 162–81), which is essentially a series of transposed repetitions of the primary theme. There are, however, important differences. One is a reprioritization and move toward greater equality among sets *A–E*. For sets *A* and *B* of the inaugural theme, this manifests as a change in scale: sets *A* and *B* control, in measure count and as a proportion, far more of the development than they do of the exposition. For set *C*, reprioritization entails a shift in formal function. Although set *C* controls substantial parts of the exposition, it often has an ancillary formal function—transition, closing, or codetta.[9] In the development, set *C* becomes a center of attention, the stuff that generates two novel landscapes: the dense patch of canonic imitation in mm. 182–90, and the interjection of small patches into the hypermeter of set *F* (mm. 189–203). These changes in sets' proportions of activity, formal functions, and other aspects of landscape design, are important mechanisms for "development" in a movement where themes and motifs generally remain intact but for transposition and fragmentation.

Perhaps the most notable difference in landscape design between the exposition and development involves set *G*. Although set *G* is prominent in the exposition, controlling about 35 measures centered in the STA, it is absent from the development, which completes, in Hepokoski and Darcy's terms, a "half rotation" through material from the FTA and transition. This omission may well be explained by a longer-range connection. The main theme of the *second* movement begins with a melody that recreates the contour of *G/b* (a turn figure followed by step descent), thus applying the pattern of sequential

Exposition

FTA		Transition	STA	Closing	Codetta
inaugural theme	primary theme				
m. # 1	9	32	58	92	104
Sets active: Sets A/B intercut	one segment C, then D/E	Set C, then F	Set G	Set C	Set C
External disposition/ Texture* implied assoc P/M	P/P	M/P, then M/M	M/M	M/P	H/P

Development

(Part I)	(Part II) (II, Section 1)	(II, Section 2)		Retransition	
m. # 123	162	182		203	
Sets active: Sets A/B intercut; phase out B	one segment C, then D/E (2x)	Set C; then C thrust between 4/4 hypermeasures of F		Set C	
External disposition/ Texture* implied assoc P/M	P/P	M/dense P; then implied assoc P/ textural M		M/M	

* M = monophony; P = polyphony; H = heterophony.

Example 4.15. Beethoven, Piano Sonata No. 2 in A, op. 2, no. 2, I, summary map of set activity in exposition and development

of relations between successive movements.

Second Pass: Cross-Domain Comparative Analysis

So far we have focused on the workings of associative sets and composition of the associative landscape. But associative organization does not occur in isolation: it is engaged in an ongoing dialogue with aspects of sonic and structural organization. Just as S, C, and T criteria recommend units that coincide or conflict at the genoseg level, changes in the sonic or associative landscape, and significant structural events, can reinforce one another or conflict at higher levels of organization. Even when the boundaries of such higher-level units do coincide, the relative priority of the sonic, associative, and structural domains as the locus of activity can shift, such that a distinctive or changeable associative landscape dominates one passage, sonic peaks and troughs shape another, and sequential foreground voice leading or resumed progress of the fundamental line are the main action in a third. We now review some of our observations on the associative landscape of this movement in conjunction with aspects of sonic and structural organization. Considering activity in the sonic, contextual, and structural domains first individually, then collectively and cumulatively, can help analysts develop an increasingly comprehensive and holistic view of form that recognizes the relative and variable importance of activity in all three domains.

With its patchwork organization, the FTA is a good place to begin comparative analysis. Associative organization—more specifically, changes in landscape materials and composition—define two thematic areas, the inaugural and primary themes. From an associative standpoint, the inaugural theme is more active; the primary theme, more stable. Sonic organization effects a comparable division between the inaugural and primary themes and a corresponding trend from more to less active surface design. In the inaugural theme, sets A and B occupy different sonic (S_2) channels: high versus low register, moderate or fast surface rhythm, and staccato or legato articulation. Intercutting between sets A and B corresponds to quick moves between local extremes in register, duration, and articulation, making for a highly active sonic surface. In contrast, the primary theme is more unified in its sonic organization. In mm. 9–10, $C1$ opens up the registral space that houses the associative and textural polyphony of sets D and E. Although the segments of D and E repeatedly exchange registers in the imitative counterpoint, the total active pitch range is fairly constant, shaped by a gentle expansion to local high and low points in m. 15 (E5 and E2, respectively) and contraction toward the cadence in m. 20 (to E4). Durations and articulation are constant throughout.

thematic areas with more, versus less, active surface designs, they do not prioritize these areas as "inaugural" and "primary" themes. It is structural organization that adds this critical dimension.[10] Example 4.16 provides a voice-leading sketch for mm. 1–20.[11] From a structural perspective, the inaugural theme (mm. 1–8) is clearly preliminary, an auxiliary move: the C♯ that initiates the fundamental line is withheld until the primary theme (m. 12), as the endpoint of the local third progression <E, D, C♯> outlined by $D1$. But the contrapuntal content of the inaugural theme is itself significant. Hidden in the structural voice leading that underlies the patchwork design of sets A and B (mm. 1–8) are structural segments that subtly introduce core criteria of sets D and E, the figures at play in invertible counterpoint in the primary theme (mm. 9–20). Starting from the opening E, one line descends by third from E5 (m. 1) through D5 (m. 6) to C♯5 (m. 9), forming an enlarged member of set D supported by the linked criteria $T_{3PRG, \text{A:} <(54)3>}C_{\text{pitch} <E5, D5, C♯5>}$ and $T_{3PRG, \text{A:} <(54)3>}S_{2\text{-pitch}}$. Meanwhile, doubled between the highest voice and the alto register another line rises in counterpoint from E (m. 1) through F♯ and G♯ to A (mm. 9–10), forming two enlarged members of set E supported by the linked criteria $T_{4PRG, \text{A:} <5(678)>}C_{pc <E, F♯, G♯, A>}$ and $T_{4PRG, \text{A:} <5(678)>}S_{2\text{-pitch}}$. Even as sonic and associative organization on the surface create sharp contrast between the inaugural and primary themes, structural organization (and a more nuanced reading of associative organization) so beautifully integrates the two themes that when the figures <E, D, C♯> and <E, F♯, G♯, A> appear on the surface as segments $D1$ and $E1$ at the start of the invertible counterpoint in mm. 11–12, the motifs sound new, but also like a logical outgrowth and summary of preceding events.[12] A structural reading of registral play within the invertible counterpoint of the primary theme between segments of sets D and E suggests a pair of voice exchanges in mm. 12–16.[13] As sets D and E dissolve back into matrix in m. 16, the fundamental line proceeds from scale degree 3 to scale degree 2 in the first limb of a local interruption that is reinitiated and completes a foreground descent to scale degree 1 at the end of the FTA (m. 32).

Now that we have surveyed of the locus of activity across the three domains, the patchwork associative organization of the FTA starts to look more strategic. The focus on sonic and associative aspects of design in the inaugural theme (mm. 1–8) is counterbalanced by the emergence of the fundamental line in the primary theme (m. 12). As deeper levels of voice leading become activated and begin to move, sonic and associative organization stabilize, prompting a shift in attention from aspects of surface design to underlying counterpoint.

Throughout the transition, associative organization is fairly straightforward and stable. The three associative sets C, F, and G each appear in successive passages of associative monophony; together these trace out a move from textural

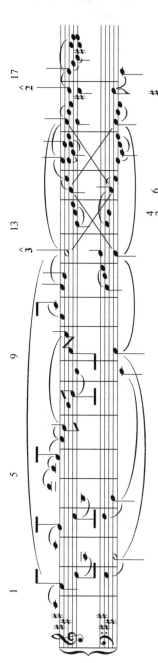

Example 4.16. Beethoven, Piano Sonata No. 2 in A, op. 2, no. 2, I, sketch of mm. 1–20

endpoints in set *F*, mm. 42–46; then discrete segments in set *G*, mm. 49–58). As expected in a sonata form, structural organization of the transition reaches one milestone: the fundamental line makes an initial descent from scale degree 3, prolonged throughout the FTA, to scale degree 2 for the start of the STA. Otherwise business in the structural domain is slow, with V/V, or its surrogate (vii^{o7} in e minor) prolonged through the sixteen-measure passage that directly precedes the STA (mm. 42–58). With only moderate activity in the contextual domain and only one deep-level event in the structural domain, it is sonic organization that gives the transition its sense of shape and energy. Broad sonic curves in register (high points in mm. 35 and 39, a low point in m. 46, and gradual return to mid-range for the start of STA), surface rhythm (faster to slower note values), articulation (staccato to legato) and dynamics (*f* in mm. 32–39 to *ff* in mm. 40–41, followed by a sudden shift to a prevailing *p* in mm. 42–57) all contribute, but the critical changes in each dimension are staggered to maintain continuity (while register peaks in m. 39, dynamics peak in m. 40, and the change to legato occurs in m. 42).

We have already seen that changes in associative organization divide the STA into three parts: mm. 58–76 (the second theme proper), mm. 76–84 (dead-end/transition), and mm. 84–92 (arrival and close in E major). The associative landscape of the second theme proper is the most homogeneous in the movement, a monophonic succession of melodic figures from subsets *G/b* and *G/c* that move from the center toward the periphery of set *G* over a steady accompaniment figure. The sonic landscape of this passage is also fairly homogeneous, as constant surface rhythms and articulation support a stepwise ascent of an ninth in the bass from E3 in m. 58 to F♯4 in mm. 76–80. Here a more lively associative and sonic landscape begins as the patchwork organization of sets *A* and *B* affiliated with the inaugural theme returns. Heightened activity in the sonic and contextual domains continues through the final bars of the STA, where the blunt juxtaposition of florid arpeggios (counterparts to *A3*) and cadential matrix in the associative landscape is underlined by abrupt sonic changes in duration and register (mm. 84–87 and 88–92).

Correlating a study of structural organization in the STA with changes in associative and sonic design turns up shifting allegiances and varying emphases among domains and levels of structure. Example 4.17 provides a voice-leading sketch for mm. 48–92, prefixed with two key events—the start of the fundamental line in the FTA and its move to scale degree 2 in the transition. A change in surface design and a turn to the minor mode at m. 48 initiate a local fifth descent from B to E that is embellished by premonitions of the second theme (segments of subset *G/a*). The line closes, trailed by a covering B–A–G♮ in the tenor, on E3 at the start of the STA in m. 58. From a structural perspective, the first part of the STA—the homogeneous associative landscape of the second theme proper (mm. 58–76)—is characterized by active sequential voice

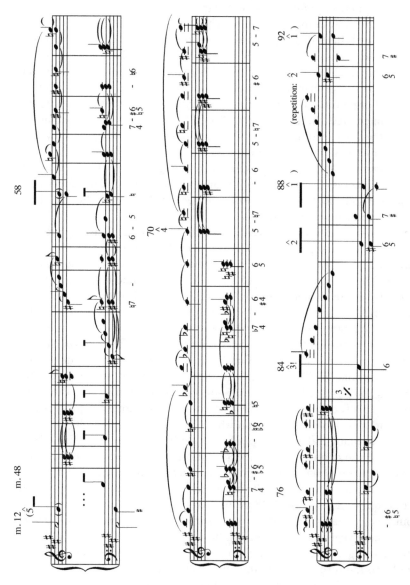

Example 4.17. Beethoven, Piano Sonata No. 2 in A, op. 2, no. 2, I, sketch of mm. 48-92

consists of two voice-leading patterns: the first, which rises by minor thirds with overreaching (mm. 58–70), is coextensive with segments of G/b; the second, a more straightforward ascending 5–6 chain, corresponds to G/c (mm. 70–76). The two sequences point up two middleground events, the B that initiates the local fifth descent within the dominant (implied, rather than literally present, in m. 58) and the A that represents its continuation (in m. 70, an octave "too high").[14] Set against the relatively stable associative and sonic landscape, the strong sequential voice leading in mm. 58–76 focuses attention on foreground structure as the primary domain of activity. But the balance among levels of structural organization, and structural relative to sonic or associative organization, soon changes. In the next part of the STA, the dead-end/transition (mm. 76–83), the voice leading stalls on D♯6 (an inner voice covering A5) over F♯4, just shy of its goal. It is at this point that the busy patchwork associative design of the inaugural theme returns, enhanced by registral play between F♯4 and F♯2 (in segments of B), and abrupt changes in duration and dynamics (*ff* to *p* or *pp*) that shift the focus of attention and activity back from the structural to the sonic and contextual domains.

From the perspective of cross-domain comparative analysis, the move into E major in the final part of the STA is especially interesting. Having climbed more than an octave in E minor, then spent ten bars on F♯4 as the bass tone for a vii^{o6}_{5} in the first two parts of the STA, the bass line is strongly directed toward G♮4 and a first inversion tonic. So the arrival on a first-inversion E-*major* triad in m. 84 with G♯3 stands out for two reasons: first, G♯ finally replaces G♮, bringing the STA into the major mode; second, the strong downdraft resolution from F♯4 to G♯3 in the bass throws the expected scale degree 3 into a new register, halfway between the two registers touched on by the bass in mm. 76–82. Meanwhile in the sonic domain, strong disjunctions in $S_{1\text{-pitch}}$, $S_{1\text{-dynamics}}$, $S_{2\text{-duration}}$ over the barline of mm. 83–84 threaten to sever the first two parts of the STA from the third, creating a conflict between sonic and associative organization which has yet to complete its recomposition of the inaugural theme's patchwork design. It is at this point of greatest sonic disjunction—the downbeat of m. 84—that sonic features shift their allegiance from articulating segments and sets in the contextual domain to highlighting deeper-level events in the structural domain. Marked in a way that no one can miss, this G♯3 in m. 84 represents the point where middleground voice leading erupts onto the surface to complete its local descent. The striking registral placement of the G♯ is explained by its double function: this single note represents two structural tones, scale degree 3 in the middleground fifth descent in the upper voice (an octave "too low") and bass support for I^6 on the way up to V (an octave "too high").[15] Progress to the cadence proceeds apace in both voices (mm. 84–88), with immediate confirmation two octaves higher (mm. 88–92).

give and take between voice-leading structure and sonic and associative organization. Earlier I said that associative organization divides the development into three sections. The landscape of part I, derived from that of inaugural theme, is an associative polyphony of sets A and B, in which B is gradually phased out (mm. 123–61). Part II has two subsections: the first of these, based on the primary theme, is an associative polyphony of sets D and E (mm. 162–81); the second, based on the transition, is an active landscape in which very dense patches of set C are interspliced with less dense patches of F (mm. 182–203). The retransition consists of associative monophony on set C (mm. 204–25). For the most part, sonic organization reinforces these patterns of change and continuity. The strongest sonic disjunction in the development marks the boundary between parts I and II at m. 162 with coincidence among $S_{1\text{-duration}}$, $S_{1\text{-pitch}}$, and $S_{1\text{-dynamics}}$. Part I inherits the active sonic surface of the inaugural theme; part II, section 1, the more unified sonic environment of the primary theme. The sonic surface is most active in part II, section 2, where the stretto among segments of set C effects a number of quick register changes, by octave at the quarter note.

Harmony and voice leading define the same three large sections, as tonicizations of C major, the chromatic third divider ♮III (part I, mm. 123–61); F major (as a voice-leading corrective that offsets parallel octaves) moving to D minor as a passing iv (part II, mm. 162–203); and $V^{8–7}$ (retransition, mm. 203–25). From a structural perspective, part I composes out a single harmony, ♮III, through the arpeggiation C–A♭–F–C.[16] Transient tonicizations of A♭ major and F minor, the two intermediate steps in this arpeggiation (which represent mixture in C major, as C♮ does in A major), make for active voice leading until C major is regained at the end of part I (mm. 157–61). Although activity is fairly evenly balanced among the sonic, contextual, and structural domains at the start of part I, the reduction in sonic and contextual activity after set B departs in m. 145 gradually tips the balance toward the structural domain.

In the first section of part II (mm. 162–81), foreground voice leading replicates the paired voice exchanges and tonic-dominant alternations found in the primary theme, first in F major, then D minor. Compared to part I, however, most of the voice-leading activity remains near the surface, a trend that continues through the second section of part II. From a structural point of view, part II, section 2 does little more than introduce F major as a voice-leading corrective between C and D minor, extend the bass passing tone D♮ (harmonized as iv), then make a brief transit through A minor in order to replace B♭ with B♮, G♮ with G♯, and inflect D♮ to D♯, in preparation for V in the retransition. It is in the second section of part II—where deeper-level voice-leading activity has effectively ceased—that the movement's most active and unusual associative landscape appears, in which patches of set C are thrust between those of set F. With the arrival on V at the start of the retransition in m. 203, the associative

in preparation for the recapitulation.

Not surprisingly, landmarks in the development's middleground voice leading are consistently articulated by changes in design. The noteworthy point is that these changes involve not only the *material* that populates the landscape (a change in associative sets) but also the *composition* of the associative landscape. Whereas part I (prolonging C as ♮III) has a monophonic patchwork design with sets *A* and *B* taken from the inaugural theme, the move to F major at the start of part II is marked by a change to the associative polyphony of sets *C* and *D* from the primary theme, which repeatedly dissolves back into the structural matrix. The move to D minor at m. 182 introduces a new landscape that represents a peak in sonic and associative activity within the development and the movement. Intercutting (implied associative polyphony) between sets *C* and *F* combined with variable set rhythm destabilizes the surface, applying the developmental principle to the very composition of the landscape itself. With the arrival on V at m. 203 the landscape changes again, to become as static as the harmonic goal it extends.

Thinking in terms of associative organization, landscape design, and changes in the interactions and relative priority of the sonic, contextual, and structural domains can give analysts a new, highly flexible and potentially comprehensive approach to musical form. Instead of thinking of form as a set of conventions, a study of associative organization—the nature and disposition of musical material in pitch and time—brings the analyst into the intrinsic form of each individual composition. In this movement, detailed analysis of associative organization reveals parallels in the progress of associative landscapes between exposition and development, directed change in the course of landscape composition, and shifting balance and allegiances among the three domains. Used in conjunction with Schenkerian analysis, such close study of associative organization can serve to advance the study of structure and design in tonal music.

Debussy, "Harmonie du soir," Cinq poèmes de Baudelaire, No. 2

Associative Organization and Form in Text and Music

Associative organization is not only the province of music. In poetry and prose, literal repetition as well as the phonemic and semantic properties of words—aspects of rhyme, character portrayal, and imagery—create layers of associations.[1] When a poem is set to music, layers of associative organization in the text can be enhanced by layers of association in the music to create a composite landscape and highly individual form.

In the 1880s, Debussy set texts by a number of nineteenth-century French poets, including Banville, Bouchor, Bourget, Gautier, Musset, and Mallarmé. Toward the end of the decade he turned first to Verlaine (for the set later published as *Ariettes oubliées*), then to Baudelaire, selecting five poems from *Les fleurs du mal* (1857) for his *Cinq poèmes de Baudelaire* (1887–89). "Harmonie du soir," the second of the *Cinq poèmes*, is based on a pantoum, a spiraling poetic form in which the second and fourth lines of each successive quatrain return as the first and third lines of the next.[2] The programmed repetition and recontextualization of lines creates a fractured continuity in which shifts in attention enact the workings of memory. The dense, continuously evolving web of internal references that results approaches the condition of music in words.

Paradoxically, for a song composer in Debussy's day, the very "musicality" of Baudelaire's text poses a compositional problem.[3] The pattern of line repetition, in which two lines *non*adjacent within a quatrain are repositioned from one quatrain to the next (even lines become odd), conflicts with conventions of strophic song, where melodic repetition and tonal syntax usually connect pairs of adjacent lines that retain their relative positions from strophe to strophe. To create a musical setting that incorporates the structure of Baudelaire's

melodic continuity, and motivic organization. His solution is to develop a highly original musical form that responds to the structural demands of both text and music with a new degree of freedom.

Our analysis of associative organization and form in text and music begins with a look at structural and free associative organization in Baudelaire's poem, then proceeds to a parallel analysis of layers of associative organization in Debussy's setting. Toward the end of the chapter we consider how these two layers of associative organization come together in the rich and idiosyncratic artistic form of the song "Harmonie du soir."

Baudelaire's "Harmonie du soir"

Baudelaire's poem "Harmonie du soir" melds a strict form and systematic rhyme scheme with fluid and atmospheric Symbolist imagery. Just as we can speak of structural (TC) and pure (C) motive in music, certain poetic forms— including the pantoum—support a comparable distinction in poetry, between associations regulated by poetic structure and freer uses of rhyme and imagery. We begin with a look at the structure of Baudelaire's pantoum, then consider other aspects of the poem's associative organization.

Example 5.1 reproduces the poem and an English translation by M. Cecile Stratta. The poem has sixteen lines, each a twelve-syllable alexandrine. Most lines have a slight caesura after the sixth syllable and stresses on the third, sixth, ninth, and twelfth syllables.[4] The sixteen lines group into four quatrains, such that lines 2 and 4 of quatrains I, II, and III return as lines 1 and 3 of quatrains II, III, and IV, respectively. The ten distinct lines of text are identified by lowercase roman numerals; primes track structural repetitions supported by TC criteria. The poem has two end rhymes, the masculine "oir" and the feminine "ige."[5] Instead of adopting the alternating rhyme scheme *abab* typical of the pantoum, Baudelaire arranges his two rhymes in a nested fashion, with *abba* in quatrains 1 and 3; *baab* in quatrains 2 and 4. This pantoum is irregular in another respect: the last line, rather than repeating the first line as pantoums generally do, is new.

Overlaid on this pattern of line repetition and end rhyme are two freer layers of associative organization. One of these involves rhymes *not* governed by the poem's structure—that is, associations by C rather than TC criteria. These include alliteration, assonance, and internal rhyme.[6] Internal rhymes can balance and unify parts of a line, as in line 1 where the sequence of phonemes $<v,$ $\triangleright$ in the first half is repeated in the second ("voici venir les temps où vibrant sur sa tige"). This association by $C_{phoneme <v, \triangleright}$ is enriched by cross-play between the nasal vowels in "temps" and "vibrant." Similarly, a retrograde of the phonemes $<v, la>$ (association by $C_{phoneme R <v, la>}$) connects the first part of line 4

Harmonie du soir

1 Voici venir les temps où vibrant sur sa tige   [i*a*]
2 Chaque fleur s'évapore ainsi qu'un encensoir;   [ii*b*]
3 Les sons et les parfums tournent dans l'air du soir;   [iii*b*]
4 Valse mélancholique et langoureux vertige!   [iv*a*]

5 Chaque fleur s'évapore ainsi qu'un encensoir;   [ii'*b*]
6 Le violon frémit comme un coeur qu'on afflige;   [v*a*]
7 Valse mélancholique et langoureux vertige!   [iv'*a*]
8 Le ciel est triste et beau comme un grand reposoir.   [vi*b*]

9 Le violon frémit comme un coeur qu'on afflige;   [v'*a*]
10 Un coeur tendre, qui haït le néant vaste et noir!   [vii*b*]
11 Le ciel est triste et beau comme un grand reposoir;   [vi'*b*]
12 Le soleil s'est noyé dans son sang qui se fige.   [viii*a*]

13 Un coeur tendre, qui haït le néant vaste et noir!   [vii'*b*]
14 Du passé lumineux recueille tout vestige!   [ix*a*]
15 Le soleil s'est noyé dans son sang qui se fige.   [viii'*a*]
16 Ton souvenir en moi luit comme un ostensoir!   [x*b*]

Evening Harmony

The time draws near when, trembling on its stem,
Every flower releases its vapor like a censer;
The sounds and the scents whirl in the evening air,
A melancholy waltz and dizzying languor!

Every flower releases its vapor like a censer;
The violin sighs like a grieving heart,
A melancholy waltz and dizzying languor!
The sky is sad and beautiful like a great altar.

The violin sighs like a grieving heart,
A tender heart, which hates the vast and gloomy void!
The sky is sad and beautiful like a great altar.
The sun has drowned in its own congealing blood.

A tender heart, which hates the vast and gloomy void!
It gathers every trace of its bright past!
The sun has drowned in its own congealing blood.
My memory of you shines like a monstrance.

Translation by M. Cecile Stratta, from liner notes to *Forgotten Songs: Dawn Upshaw Sings Debussy*, James Levine, piano, Sony Classical 67190.

Example 5.1. "Harmonie du soir," Baudelaire, from *Les fleurs du mal* (1857)

line	Scent	Sound	Catholic Symbolism	Human
2	Chaque fleur encensoir;		(encensoir;)	
3	parfums	Les sons		
4		Valse mélancholique		
5	*Chaque fleur encensoir;*		*encensoir;*	
6		Le violon		frémit coeur qu'on afflige;
7		*Valse mélancholique*		
8			reposoir.	
9		*Le violon*		*frémit coeur qu'on afflige;*
10				Un coeur tendre
11			*reposoir.*	
12			sang	(sang)
13				*Un coeur tendre*
15			*sang*	*sang* Ton souvenir
16			ostensoir!	

Example 5.2. Four realms of imagery of "Harmonie du soir," association map in running text format

to the second ("Valse mélancholique et langoureux vertige!"). Baudelaire also uses internal rhymes to highlight or associate words essential to the poem's imagery. In line 2, for example, the seemingly innocuous word "ainsi" sonically foreshadows and thus adds a slight emphasis to the first instance of "encensoir." In line 9, successive associations by $C_{\text{phoneme} <m>}$ and $C_{\text{phoneme} <c>}$ draw attention to the word "coeur" ("frémit comme," "comme un coeur"), which is then reinforced by immediate repetition at the start of line 10 ("Un coeur tendre . . ."). Line 12 ("Le soleil s'est noyé dans son sang qui se fige") is rife with resonances created by two internal rhymes, between sol*eil* and no*yé*, and alliteration among *s*oleil, *s*'est, *s*on, *s*ang, and *s*e.

Baudelaire balances the poem's strict form with a supple play of imagery among four realms: scent, sound, Catholic symbolism, and human experience. Example 5.2 groups words and images from each realm into an associative set, then organizes these into an association map in running text format. As in the poem, text in the map reads right to left, then top to bottom. Vertical alignment

pantoum's structure. Arabic numerals indicate lines of origin. A capital letter marks the start of a line; trailing punctuation, line endings. Two words, "encensoir" (censer) and "sang" (blood), each inhabit two realms. For each of these, set affiliations that are latent rather than active when the word first appears are enclosed in parentheses.

The columnar organization of the map brings out the temporal disposition of imagery. The poem opens with the delicate fragrance of flowers grasped by a faint breeze (lines 1–2). *Sounds* soon join the *Scents*, intermingling in the evening air (line 3). In line 4, the sounds coalesce into a melancholy waltz, which gains focus when the violin enters (in line 6). Of these two sets, *Scent* forms earlier and is quite condensed: two *Scent* images appear in line 2; these in conjunction with their structural repetition in line 5 enclose the remaining *Scent* image, "parfums," in line 3. The *Sound* set is more dispersed: its three images and two repetitions spread over six lines (lines 3–9) in a path of increasing specificity—"sons," "Valse mélancholique," "violon."

While *Scent* and *Sound* imagery pervades the poem's first half, except for a brief return by the violin at the start of line 9 (mandated by the pantoum's structure), it is absent from the second, which moves into the *Human* realm. *Human* imagery and *Catholic Symbolism* intertwine on several occasions, most notably in the word "sang" (blood) and in the closing simile, "Ton souvenir en moi luit comme un ostensoir!" where temporal proximity and salient word placement (the *Human* "souvenir" and the *Catholic* "ostensoir" are the first and last words in the line) underline the connection between the two realms.

The *Catholic Symbolism* set is the most dispersed of the four. The only set active at the scale of the entire poem (lines 2–16), it is also the only one strongly articulated by structural end rhyme. Associations by the linked criterion $T_{\text{end rhyme}} {}_b C_{\text{rhyme "oir"}}$ are enhanced by free associations between final syllables that begin with an unvoiced "s" ("encensoir"; [censer], "ostensoir" [monstrance]) or voiced "s" (in "reposoir" [altar]). A double rhyme between "ostensoir" (the last word of the poem) and "encensoir" (end of the first line) softens the structural irregularity introduced by not repeating the first line as the last, as most pantoums do.

An important aspect of the poem's texture implicit, if not explicit, in the map is the play of associations brought about by recontextualization.[7] When the pantoum repeats a line, the words are the same, but the change in context sets the words in a different light, sometimes igniting new meanings. For instance, when "Chaque fleur s'évapore ainsi qu'un encensoir;" first appears as line 2, it completes a thought initiated by line 1 ("Voici venir les temps où vibrant sur sa tige"). Repeated as line 5, the same words become an independent statement that initiates a quatrain and announces the pantoum's

phoric—the flower releases scent *as* a censer does; the Catholic symbolism is largely held in abeyance. It is only later, when the "grand reposoir" appears at the end of line 8, that the association between "reposoir" and "encensoir"— underlined by coincident structural end rhyme—activates the Catholic imagery latent in the earlier instances."[8] Other words also accrue new layers of meaning. Whereas in line 3 "tournent" refers only to the invisible motion of sounds and scents in the evening air, in line 4 references to the "Valse mélancholique" and "langoureux vertige" add a physical sensation of whirling through space. At the start of line 8 the "ciel" [sky] image is fairly literal, referencing only "l'air du soir" [evening air] back in line 3; with the appearance of the "grand reposoir" at the end of line 8, it acquires a second, more metaphoric meaning.

A survey of the map suggests a broad sweep from the intangible, ephemeral world of scents and sounds toward the emotional and corporeal realm of human experience. This trajectory is deftly interwoven with a longer, slower stream of Catholic symbolism in which two words do double duty—"encensoir" in the *Scent* realm and "sang" in the *Human*. As intimations of human mortality accumulate ("soir" [evening], "coeur qu'on afflige" [grieving heart], "le néant vaste et noir" [the vast and gloomy void], "le soleil s'est noyé" [the sun has drowned]), they are overlaid with Catholic symbols of the death and the resurrection ("reposoir" [altar], "ostensoir" [monstrance]), suggesting a view of the poem as one about death and redemption. But the last line ("Ton souvenir en moi luit comme un ostensoir!" [My memory of you shines like a monstrance]) hints at another meaning: Baudelaire scholar Barbara Wright suggests that the poem can also be read as a spiritually imbued love poem that, through a process of cyclic recollection and progressive self-reflection, reconciles the sensory and sensual with the spiritual.[9]

Debussy's Setting of "Harmonie du soir"

Debussy's setting respects and conveys many aspects of the associative organization of the text, both structural and free. Example 5.3 provides a score for mm. 1–33 which takes in the first two quatrains and the start of the third. Uppercase roman numerals followed by arabic numerals at the start of each line indicate quatrains and line numbers, respectively (e.g., I/1, II/5). As in example 5.1, lowercase roman numerals at the *end* of each line identify the ten distinct lines of text, primes indicate repeated lines, and italicized letters track structural end rhymes (e.g., i*a*, ii′*b*). Horizontal brackets highlight two motives in mm. 1–6: an appoggiatura figure (in A1, mm. 1–3) seeds an associative set *A*; a triplet motive inside a fourth (*B*1, mm. 1–2) begins an associative set *B*.

Example 5.3. Debussy, "Harmonie du soir," *Cinq poèmes de Baudelaire*, mm. 1–33

Example 5.3. Debussy, "Harmonie du soir," *Cinq poèmes de Baudelaire,* mm. 1–33—*(continued)*

Example 5.3. Debussy, "Harmonie du soir," *Cinq poèmes de Baudelaire,*
mm. 1–33—*(continued)*

Example 5.3. Debussy, "Harmonie du soir," *Cinq poèmes de Baudelaire*, mm. 1–33—*(concluded)*

structural line repetition in the text with literal, transposed, or modified melodic repetition in the voice. Two rhythms carry the poem's structural end rhymes *a* and *b*: six of the eight occurrences of the feminine *a* rhyme "ige" (all but line 4 and its repetition) are set as appoggiaturas, while the masculine "oir" rhyme (rhyme *b*) always appears as one long note, also on a downbeat.

The modular approach to composition Debussy inherits from the text is evident in the song's harmonic language and fragmented tonal design. Although the song begins and ends solidly in B major, the harmony is fluid and often highly chromatic, especially in passages where the tonal moorings are less secure. Striking harmonic changes, often bridged by proximate pitch-class voice leading, mark off lines of text. Example 5.4a sketches out the pitch-class voice leading for the piano introduction and line 1 (mm. 1–6), where a descending fifth in an auxiliary motion from ii (c♯) to V (F♯ ♮$^9_7$) makes a chromatic pass through an extended A^7 (mm. 3–5). Changes of harmony in m. 3 and m. 6 mark the entry of the voice and the first structural end rhyme ("ti-ge"). By withholding the tonic until the start of line 2, Debussy expresses the grammatical contingency of line 1 upon line 2 and marks line 2 for memory, setting up its return as the poem's first structural repetition. Example 5.4b traces proximate pitch-class voice leading through the setting of lines 5–7 in mm. 17–26 (= lines ii′, v, and iv′). Once again, significant changes of harmony mark the start and end of each line. Two especially striking harmonic maneuvers that accompany the enharmonic transformation of D♯ (m. 17) into E♭ (at m. 19) and back (m. 20) set off the final syllable of "encensoir" in line 5 (= line ii′), helping to secure the long-range association with "reposoir" in line 8 (mm. 30–31) that establishes the *Catholic Symbolism* set as central to the poem's imagery.

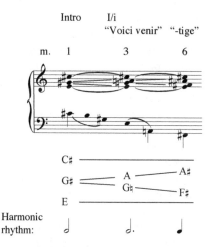

Example 5.4a. Harmony and pitch-class proximate voice leading, mm. 1–6

Example 5.4b. Harmony and pitch-class proximate voice leading, mm. 17–26

In addition to marking the endpoints of lines, Debussy gives each line a distinct harmonic signature. Whereas the harmonization of lines 4 and 7 ("Valse . . ." = lines iv and iv') is an outgrowth of simultaneous upper- and lower-neighbor motions (e.g., A–G♯–A and A–B–B♭–A in m. 14); that of lines 6 and 9 ("Le violon . . ." = lines v and v') includes a two-measure expansion of a diminished seventh chord. Lines 8 and 11 ("Le ciel . . ." = lines vi and vi') are based on two root-position major triads a fifth apart (G and C in mm. 28–31) each enhanced by chromaticism; lines 12 and 15 ("Le soleil . . ." = lines viii and viii') explore whole-tone sonorities. Reaching across the harmonic gulf between the relatively diatonic universe of line 11 ("Le ciel . . . reposoir," = line vi', mm. 39–43) and the whole-tone world of line 12 ("Le soleil . . . fige." = line viii, mm. 44–48) is a bold assertion of enharmonic equivalence between B♭ and A♯. Example 5.5a provides a score for the passage (mm. 39–48); example 5.5b sketches the proximate pitch-class voice leading from the B♭ harmony in mm. 42–43 to the F♯ harmony that controls mm. 44–48. Retaining the pc B♭/A♯ across the phrase boundary, all other voices move by semitone in proximate voice leading that forges a tenuous connection between two harmonically and poetically distant phrases.

Aspects of free rhyme in Baudelaire's poem also find their way into Debussy's setting. In line 1 ("Voici venir les temps où vibrant sur sa tige"), repetitions of the appoggiatura figure <D♯5, C♯5> (the formative criterion for set A) amplify the vowel echo between "temps" and "vibrant." The song's many instances of text painting include the setting of line 3 ("parfums tournent dans l'air du soir," mm. 11–13), in which contrary motion between piano and voice depicts the wafting scents; that of the "valse mélancholique" in line 4 (mm. 14–16)

Example 5.5a. Debussy, "Harmonie du soir," *Cinq poèmes de Baudelaire*, mm. 39–48

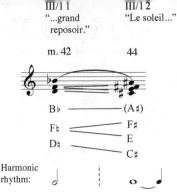

m. 42   44

Bb ————— (A♯)
F♮ ————— F♯
D♮   E
            C♯

Harmonic
rhythm:

Example 5.5b. Harmony and pitch-class proximate voice leading, mm. 42–44.

with its flamboyant arabesques in the piano accompaniment; and of "le violon frémit" in line 5 (mm. 20–23), where a brief hesitation on the downbeat leads to a fifth descent in the voice from D♯5 to G♯4. At the end of the song, the repetition of "Le soleil s'est noyé dans son sang qui se fige" in line 15 (mm. 59–62) is set at the very bottom of the singer's range, setting up a dramatic climb through a minor tenth to F5 for "luit" (shines) in the last line. The brilliance of the "shine" and the transformation from "souvenir" to "ostensoir" by way of simile are encapsulated in the enharmonic reinterpretation of F5, which enters as a minor seventh over the bass G, but then rises, resolving upward as an augmented sixth (E♯) to the singer's last note, F♯5.

Although Debussy effectively translates the pantoum's structure and much of its free rhyme and imagery into music, from a musical point of view, the associative landscape he inherits from the pantoum is somewhat problematic. Whereas poetry can rely on the semantics of natural language, music creates its own vocabulary through a process of statement, repetition, and internal reference—a process facilitated by clumped dispositions but complicated by dispersed ones. Example 5.6 provides an association map of structural line repetition in the pantoum. Each line of text is a segment, represented by a horizontal bar. Each of the six lines subject to structural repetition (lines ii and iv–viii) serves as the core criterion (C/CRS) for a small but strong associative set with two segments in dispersed disposition. From line 4 (= line iv) to line 13 (= line vii') these six sets are continuously interwoven in evolving three-part associative polyphony. Except for the start-up and phase-out periods, the landscape is compositionally homogeneous. Given the strength of the contextual criteria at work in the text and their melodic expression in the voice, these six small sets easily survive the perceptual challenges posed by their dispersed dispositions and associative polyphony.

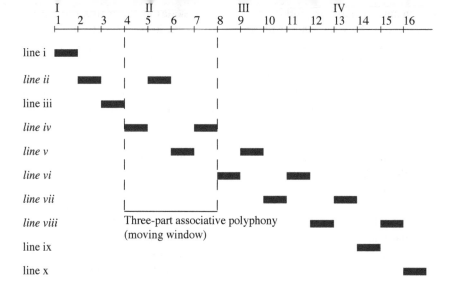

Example 5.6. Baudelaire's "Harmonie du soir," association map of structural repetition in the pantoum

But even as Debussy expresses the associative polyphony of lines of text with an associative polyphony of melodic phrases in the voice, he softens the effect of the poem's modular construction on the form of its musical setting by adding two layers of purely musical associative organization. One of these involves melodic connections between *adjacent* phrases of the vocal line; the other involves local and long-range motivic connections.

Debussy expresses each of the pantoum's six structural line repetitions with melodic repetition in the voice, but in five of six cases the repetition is *transposed,* by intervals ranging from a minor second up (lines 10 and 13 = vii and vii′) to a perfect fifth down (lines 12 and 15 = viii and viii′).[10] The use of transposition and choice of specific transposition levels is significant: by making the pitch level of each melodic repetition a variable, Debussy can associate bits of melodic material in adjacent phrases and thereby counteract the tendency toward modular composition he inherits from the poem. One chain of melodic associations extends from lines 2 through 5. The auxiliary harmonic motion that reaches tonic at the start of line 2 (m. 7) fixes the pitch levels of the descending sixth E5–G♮4 that ends the first phrase ("ti-ge," m. 6, over V♮9) and its resolution in the rising sixth F♯4–D♯5 that begins the second ("Chaque fleur . . . ," m. 7). The move from I to ii at the start of line 3 ("Les sons . . . ," mm. 10–11) adds a third sixth (from G♯4 to E5), creating a small associative set of three segments.

the change of harmony and entry of the arabesques in the piano, the last two measures of the vocal line in phrase 3 (from C♯5 in m. 12 to G♮4 in m. 13) return note-for-note but for two chromatic alterations (D♯ and G♯ are replaced by D♮ and G♮). Finally, line 5—the structural repetition of line ii ("Chaque fleur . . .")—adds a fifth link, as the pitch ordering <C♯5, B4, F♯4> from phrases 3 and 4 returns for a third time (with E♯4 and G♯4 inserted between B4 and F♯4), before closing with a stepwise ascent through a third en route to the last pitch (<B, C♯, D♯, (F♯), D♯>).

The possibility of forging melodic connections between adjacent phrases of the vocal line may well have inspired Debussy's choice of transposition levels in two other cases. Setting the first tone in line 9 ("Le violon . . ." = line v′) in mm. 32–35 at C5—three semitones below the corresponding pitch in mm. 20–23 (line 6 = line v)—reactivates the peak of the previous vocal phrase (line 8, "Le ciel . . ." = line vi, mm. 28–31). Here the echo of <C4, G4> over the phrase boundary helps soften the radical shift from predominantly diatonic harmony ("soir," m. 31) to a whole-tone environment ("le violon," m. 32). Toward the end of the song, downward transposition by perfect fifth from F♯4 to B3 from the first occurrence of line viii ("Le soleil . . . ," line 12, mm. 44–48) to the second (line 15, mm. 59–62) sets up a convincing close in B major essential to the song's tonal plan. But if the desire for tonal closure fixes the start of the first instance of line viii on F♯, the possibility of drawing a local melodic connection between its highest stable tone (A♯) and the peak of the preceding line (B♭) may well have inspired the transposition level for its immediate predecessor, the repetition of line vi ("Le ciel . . . ," line 11, mm. 39–43) on B♭, a major second below its first occurrence in mm. 28–31.

While these and other connections between adjacent vocal phrases soften the effect of structural line repetition in the song, two problems remain: how to create local continuity *within* musical phrases and how to create longer-range continuity in the song as a whole. Debussy's solution is to superimpose yet another layer of associative organization, a purely musical layer of motivic associations among segments of the two associative sets *A* and *B*.

As noted earlier, the seeds of both sets are sown in the opening bars. (Refer back to exx. 5.3 and 5.5a for scores of mm. 1–33 and 39–48). Segment *A*1 begins on the opening C♯ and extends through the appoggiatura in the right hand of the piano in m. 3 (<D♯, C♯>); *A*2, in the voice, immediately prefixes the appoggiatura with a stepwise ascent (voice and piano, mm. 3–4), a feature retained by most segments of *A*. *B*1 is the triplet figure in the left hand of the piano in m. 2; the only moving line, it catches the listener's attention but remains an anomaly until m. 9 when *B*2 appears.

Over the course of the song, sets *A* and *B* each acquire a small set of core contextual criteria and develop several associative subsets. Set *A* has the form of an accented upper neighbor (when approached by step from below) or an appoggiatura (approached by leap). The accented dissonance forms an augmented fourth against the bass that resolves to a major third (as in mm. 4–5, mm. 12–13, mm. 44–48, and m. 68) or a major ninth that falls to an octave (as in mm. 11–12, mm. 37, 50, 55, and 65). Supplementary criteria for set A include two prefixes—a repeated note (as in mm. 2–3, 4–5, 12–13, 36–37, 46–47, 49–50, and 60–61) and a stepwise ascent by fourth (e.g., in mm. 3–6, 9–13) or third (mm. 12–13)—and one suffix of a descending perfect fourth that forms a bridge to set B (e.g., mm. 26–27, faintly recalled in mm. 61–64).

Set B has two core contextual criteria: an upper-neighbor figure embedded in a descending fourth or fifth that varies in quality (i.e., C_{cseg} <21210>, where cps 1 and 2 are always a second apart, but the interval between cps 0 and 1 varies from a diminished fourth to a perfect fifth), fused with a sixteenth-note triplet. Variation in the size of the spanning interval suggests several subsets. Segments that span a perfect fourth (e.g., $B1$, m. 2; also in mm. 21 and 33) and augmented fourth (e.g., $B2$, m. 9; also in mm. 44–48, and 59–62) are most common. Truncating the figure creates the murmuring triplets in mm. 28–29, 39–41, and 47–48. Echoing and embellishing the appoggiatura <F♯, E> heard just before in the voice (m. 47, "fi-ge"), these play on the close relationship between sets A and B: the triplet upper neighbor within the core contextual criterion of set B can be seen as an embellishment of the stepwise descent that is the core criterion for set A. Additional variation in set B includes an ascending version in m. 55 and passing tone figure in m. 60.[11]

Example 5.7 organizes segments from sets A, B, and a third associative set, the *Valse arabesque* (formed by presentations of the waltz material first heard in m. 14) into an association map for mm. 1–49. (Once again, exx. 5.3 and 5.5a provide the corresponding scores.) Measure numbers, line numbers, and the first word in each line of text track across the top; italics indicate structural repetitions. Down the left margin, subsets of A have the following core criteria: A/a, a repeated note; A/b, prefix of a stepwise ascent; A/c, a move from an augmented fourth to a third against the bass. Here the unqualified "set A" at the top of the map represents the remaining segments of A. Below, subsets B/b, B/a, and B/c are listed according to the size of the spanning interval, largest to smallest. Some segments (those with more than one supplementary criterion) belong to more than one subset (e.g., the segment in m. 4 belongs to A/b and A/c; that in m. 5, to A/a and A/b). Short horizontal bars represent individual segments; longer bars represent timespans in which a set or subset is active, accompanied by an arabic numeral that shows how many segments appear in that timespan. Segment rhythm in the individual subsets is usually one segment per bar, except for clusters of segments in mm. 28–29 and 40–42.

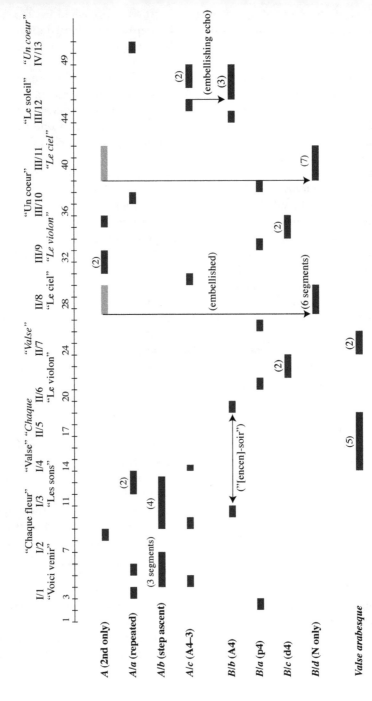

Example 5.7. Debussy's "Harmonie du soir," mm. 1–49, association map of sets *A*, *B*, and *Valse arabesque*

formed by sets A, B, and the *Valse arabesque* complements the landscape inherited from the pantoum in two ways. First, while the pantoum defines six small dispersed associative sets of two segments each, sets A, B, and the *Valse* are all larger and occur in patches of two to seven segments. Second, whereas structural line repetition in the pantoum and hence phrases in the vocal line create a landscape of three-part associative polyphony, the landscape created by sets A, B, and the *Valse* is predominately monophonic, both at the level of the associative set and, within the timespan of set B, often also the associative subset. At the largest scale, set A, the *Valse*, and set B control successive spans (mm. 1–14, 14–18, and 21–49, respectively). Within the span dominated by set B, Debussy often marks the move from line to line with a change of associative subset: "Le violon" engages subsets B/a and B/c; "Le ciel," primarily subset B/d; and "Le soleil," B/b. The temporal disposition of these subsets parallels and reinforces Debussy's use of different harmonic environments to distinguish vocal phrases, even as the continued presence of set B, and the higher-level connection between sets A and B, contributes to large-scale continuity.

Toward the end of the song, set A recedes and the liquidation of set A and B's distinguishing features facilitates their rapprochement (ex. 5.8, mm. 59–73). The stepwise descent that contributes to the core contextual criteria for both sets becomes a focal point which is echoed and embedded in several descents through a fourth in the right hand of the piano in mm. 61–64 that clearly recall set B but lack its characteristic sixteenth-note triplet. Two lazy triplets in the piano postlude (mm. 70–71) recall set B just before the close, but more as a reminiscence than a reinstatement of difference between sets A and B.

The multiple layers of associative organization in text and music created by structural repetitions, freer aspects of rhyme, and the disposition of imagery and segments from sets A, B, and the *Valse arabesque* induce a parallel layering in the realm of form. One layer is prescribed by the form of the pantoum. But changes of harmony and texture add a second layer that complicates the form of the musical setting.

The poem's form is largely determined by its structure: four quatrains continuously interwoven by structural repetition of alternate lines move from *Scent* and *Sound* imagery in quatrains I and II toward *Catholic Symbolism* and *Human* experience in quatrains III and IV. Debussy marks the boundary between quatrains II and III at m. 32 with an abrupt shift from diatonic to whole-tone harmony, which he underlines with a change in tempo and character. But he also introduces an interesting tension *within* the first two quatrains, between poetic and musical form. In the poem, line 5 ("Chaque fleur . . . ," = line ii′) is marked by the onset of structural repetition. But in

Example 5.8. Debussy, "Harmonie du soir," *Cinq poèmes de Baudelaire*, mm. 59–73

of emphasis back a line, to line 4. Retaining the *Valse* across the quatrain break then softens the emphasis on line 5 inherited from the poem: although the vocal line from line 2 returns at pitch level, the piano retains only its end rhyme ("encensoir" in m. 19 is set as it was in m. 9, with a triplet from the *B/b* subset). As a result, m. 14—not m. 17—emerges as a local reference point. Measure 14 finds its counterpart in m. 24 when the *Valse* returns followed by a progressive descent in register and deceleration in surface rhythm over the next two lines (mm. 24–31) that suggest it, too, serves as a local point of reference and the start of a significant unit.

The net result is a reorganization of lines within the first two quatrains that contradicts the form of the poem—in the music, lines within the first two quatrains group 3 + 3 + 2, rather than 4 + 4 as in the poem (ex. 5.9).[12] This alternate organization finds a parallel in quatrains III and IV, where it is realized by an abrupt shift from primarily diatonic to whole-tone harmony that strengthens the boundary between lines 11 and 12 ("Le ciel . . ." and "Le soleil . . ."). Coincident changes of key and character then support hearing the first and second occurrences of "le soleil" (lines 11 and 15) at mm. 44 and 58 as parallel points of initiation.

Whereas the form of Baudelaire's poem is unequivocal and symmetrical, that of Debussy's setting is more fluid, asymmetrical, and ambiguous as structural line repetition and textural and harmonic features alternately coincide (at m. 32) and conflict (in m. 17 as opposed to mm. 14 and 24 in quatrains

	Harmonie du soir		Alternate groupings	
1	Voici venir ... tige	[i*a*]		3
2	Chaque fleur ... encensoir;	[ii*b*]		
3	Les sons ... soir;	[iii*b*]		+
4	Valse mélancholique ... vertige!	[iv*a*]		
				3
5	Chaque fleur ... encensoir;	[ii′*b*]		
6	Le violon ... afflige;	[v*a*]		+
7	Valse mélancholique ... vertige!	[iv′*a*]		
8	Le ciel ... reposoir.	[vi*b*]		2
9	Le violon ... afflige;	[v′*a*]		3
10	Un coeur ... noir!	[vii*b*]		
11	Le ciel ... reposoir;	[vi′*b*]		+
12	Le soleil ... se fige.	[viii*a*]		
				3
13	Un coeur ... noir!	[vii′*b*]		
14	Du passé ... vestige!	[ix*a*]		+
15	Le soleil ... se fige.	[viii′*a*]		
16	Ton souvenir ... ostensoir!	[x*b*]		2

Example 5.9. Poetic and musical form in Debussy's "Harmonie du soir"

ing the challenge that the modular composition and interlocking quatrains of Baudelaire's "Harmonie du soir" posed to strophic song conventions of his day, Debussy creates an original musical form in which multiple layers of associative organization in text and music, and of poetic and musical form, collaborate to extend the prismatic quality of the text to new dimensions.

Nancarrow, Study No. 37

Calibrated Canons, Changeable Landscapes

Nancarrow's fifty *Studies* for player piano are a dazzling repertoire of wild and weird musical landscapes, a fortuitous outgrowth of an eccentric coupling of rigorous tempo structures and strict counterpoint with a more informal approach to the basic pitch and rhythmic material. To date, most Nancarrow scholarship has focused on tempo and rhythm, systematic aspects of this music that invite formalization. Pitch organization has received much less attention and form less still: but for occasional references and a few tantalizing comments by Nancarrow, James Tenney, Kyle Gann, and Margaret Thomas, form in this music remains uncharted territory.[1] But this is an intriguing subject. Form in the *Studies* is non-traditional and idiosyncratic, concerned not with themes and returns but with growth, transformation, and collapse of holistic processes—less intentional than an emergent effect of Nancarrow's systematic realization of a structural plan at work on specific pitch and rhythmic materials. In a 1975 interview, the composer asserts this view of form in his music as an emergent property: "I never really think of form as such. I work in a certain way, but I don't think of any specific form. It comes out for me more or less as a result of other things."[2]

The complex origins and idiosyncratic nature of form in the *Studies* elude traditional approaches to musical form, but can be explored using the conceptual framework we have developed. This chapter investigates some aspects of form in *Study No. 37*, a strict twelve-voice canon that unfolds as a procession of twelve contrasting associative landscapes. After a look at the structure of the canon and the disposition of tempi among its twelve lines, I'll focus on particular features of segmentation, associative organization, and their interactions with sonic and structural features, as these contribute to the composition's diverse musical landscapes.

Structure of the Tempo Canon

The twelve sections of *Study No. 37* are marked off by strong sonic disjunctions in dynamics, articulation, and note values and by changes in pitch material. Within each section, twelve tempi set the quarter note across the range of

160 5/7, 168¾, 180, 187½, 200, 210, 225, 240, 250, 262½, 281¼. As James Tenney points out:

> A little manipulation of these numbers uncovers the fact that they relate to each other as in the following series of simple ratios . . . : 1/1, 15/14, 9/8, 6/5, 5/4, 4/3, 7/5, 3/2, 8/5, 5/3, 7/4, 15/8. . . . one of several possible versions of a 12-tone-per-octave 'just' scale . . . identical, in fact, to one proposed by Henry Cowell in his book, *New Musical Resources*, [ ] a scale of tempos analogous to our 12-tone scale of pitches.[3]

Horizontal lines in the example (at the start of sections I, II, IV, and VII) mark what Gann calls *convergence points* (CPs)—"the infinitesimal moment at which all lines have reached identical points in the material they are playing."[4]

	Pages	Start*	↑/↓	**Tempo**–Register Map**	Pitch T_n
I	1–4	0:00	↓	< BB, AA, 99, 88, 77, 66, 55, 44, 33, 22, 11, 00 >	−7
II	4–8	0:23	↓	< B0, A1, 92, 83, 74, 65, 56, 47, 38, 29, 1A, 0B >	+5
III	8–11	0:46	↑	< 00, 11, 22, 33, 44, 55, 66, 77, 88, 99, AA, BB >	+5
IV	11–19	1:07	↑	< 0B, 1A, 29, 38, 47, 56, 65, 74, 83, 92, A1, B0 >	−2
V	19–32	2:02	↑	< 00, 11, 22, 33, 44, 55, 66, 77, 88, 99, AA, BB >	various
VI	32–40	3:23	↑	< 00, 13, 26, 39, 41, 54, 67, 7A, 82, 95, A8, BB >	+15 [+5]
VII	40–48	4:16	↓	< BB, AA, 99, 88, 77, 66, 55, 44, 33, 22, 11, 00 >	−3
VIII	48–62	5:05	↓	< B4, 81, 57, 23, A9, 7B, 46, 18, 92, 6A, 36, 00 >	various
IX	62–70	6:19	↑	< 00, 33, 66, 11, 99, 44, 77, AA, 22, 55, 88, BB>	+15 [+5]
X	70–75	7:02	↓	< BB, 8A, 57, 24, A9, 75, 41, 10, 96, 62, 33, 08 >	various
XI	75–82	7:36	↓	< BB, 88, 44, AA, 77, 33, 99, 66, 22, 11, 55, 00 >	+2
XII	82–107	8:10	↑	< 00, 12, 25, 37, 41, 54, 68, 79, 83, 96, AA, BB >	various

*Start time on CD Wergo 6907 2
**Tempo scale: slowest = lowest:

0	150	3	180	6	210	9	250
1	160 5/7	4	187 ½	7	225	A	262 ½
2	168 ¾	5	200	8	240	B	281 ¼

Pitch: lowest = 0; highest = B

Example 6.1. Nancarrow, *Study No. 37*, overview of realization

Throughout *No. 37*, Nancarrow consistently realizes the tempo canon through a line-to-register rule that channels each of the twelve voices into its own pitch range (for segmentation by the linked criterion $TS_{2\text{-pitch}}$).[5] But the

from section to section, as shown in the example. Roman numerals indicate sections, followed by page numbers and start times on the 1999 Wergo CD (and Open Minds reissue). Arrows indicate whether the sequence of tempi in the canon goes from fast to slow ($\downarrow$) or slow to fast ($\uparrow$). "Tempo-register map" pairs each of the twelve tempi with one of twelve registers, or *lines*. Here I borrow a convention from atonal music theory, using the twelve integers from 0 to 9, plus A for 10, and B for 11 to represent both tempi (in boldface) and pitch registers (in roman type). For tempi, **0** represents the slowest tempo; **B**, the fastest. For registers, 0 represents the lowest line in a section; B, the highest. So the tempo-register mapping "**B**B" means that the fastest tempo is in the highest register; "**B**0," that the fastest tempo is in the lowest one. The twelve tempo-register mappings for each section are then ordered and enclosed in angled brackets to reflect the order in which the twelve canonic voices enter. Thus the ordering <**B**B, **A**A, **9**9, . . .> for section I means that the twelve tempi enter fast-to-slow and high-to-low in register; <**B**0, **A**1, **9**2, . . .> for section II inverts the relationship between tempo and register so that fast-to-slow now goes from low to high. The sequence of tempo-register mappings in section III is the retrograde of that in section I (slow to fast and low to high), while that for section IV completes the four-group of transformations, with slow to fast moving high to low.[6] Tempo-register mappings in other sections include "chromatic" tempi mapped to interval 3-cycles among the registers (section VI), interval-9 cycles in tempo mapped to noncyclic series in register (sections VIII and X), and identical noncyclic series in both domains (sections IX and XI).[7] The last column of the table, "Pitch T_n," gives the index of transposition between successive voice entries in those sections where voices are separated by a constant interval. Where successive voices enter at different intervals, transpositions in square brackets give the distance between lines that are registrally adjacent. Finally, "various" indicates that transposition levels between successive entries are irregular.

A look through example 6.1 indicates that relations among tempo, register, and voice entry order change at every section boundary. Over the course of the piece only one tempo-register mapping is repeated (from section I to VII), but with a change in the interval of transposition (from –7 to –3 semitones between successive voices). The piece begins with two canons that trend from fast to slow, followed by four that trend slow to fast—types of canons that Thomas calls *diverging* and *converging*, respectively.[8] Each of the canons in sections I–IV has a uniform pitch transposition, but the interval of transposition varies from section to section (–7, +5, +5, and –2, respectively). Differences in the transposition levels between adjacent lines lead to differences in the total pitch range covered by individual sections: whereas the twelve lines in section I (with lines and voices at T_{-7}) cover more than six octaves, those in section IV (with lines and voices at T_{-2}) reach less than two. Changing the transposition

in which registers enter), also affects segmentation and the resultant texture. When successive voices appear in registrally adjacent lines separated by a small pitch interval, the basic pitch material may overlap (as in section VII), effectively disabling segmentation by register ($TS_{2\text{-pitch}}$), or even by articulation (as in section IV, with its saturated pitch space). When adjacent voices are separated by larger intervals and enter nonsuccessively—as they do in section VI, which has an interval-3 cycle in register and a uniform pitch interval of +15 (but for the necessary wraparound from low to high) and in section VIII, which charts an irregular, spiraling pattern through pitch space—segmentation by register is more active and the canonic imitation among voices is more apparent. Spiraling through tempi in an interval-9 cycle, or in an irregular pattern, also affects segmentation and texture. Whereas "chromatic" moves up or down the tempo scale lead to straightforward converging or diverging canons, applying an interval-9 cycle (as in section X) or irregular series in tempo (section XI) to a fairly long subject creates a texture of varying density, as the number of voices active at once rises and falls.[9]

Form and Process in the *Study No. 37*: Changeable Landscapes

While Nancarrow strictly observes a twelve-voice tempo canon throughout the *Study No. 37*, form in the piece turns out to be a surprising and changeable thing, the cumulative result of a complex set of interactions among four factors: (1) a set of tempo ratios; (2) mappings among tempi, pitch registers, and voice entry order within each section; (3) the pitch and rhythmic material that constitutes the canonic subject for each section; and (4) the tendencies and limits of human perception.[10] Regarding *No. 37* Nancarrow says this: "There are all kinds of sections with completely different types of atmospheres—melodic and rhythmic relationships. The rhythmic proportions between lines stay the same except that they appear to change because of the way I realize them, because of the varying entrance patterns of voices."[11] We'll touch on most of the twelve sections in *No. 37*, but our analysis will focus on four of these—sections II, IV, VI, and VIII. Each raises different issues; together they illustrate a variety of associative landscapes.

In the first three sections, melodic material is minimal: section I is based on a five-note diatonic fragment in long note values; section II, a chromatic one of eight staccato eighth-notes, one per 4/4 measure; and section III, a string of fourteen triads, each a staccato eighth-note in a 2/4 measure, grafted onto a line that wanders chromatically through a span of a minor sixth. In all three sections, consecutive attack points stream across voices rather than tracking within individual voices. Interactions between the regular spacing of attacks

the tempo canon makes for dynamic flow through each section.

Section I begins with a fortissimo cascade of perfect fifths from E7 to B0, one note in each of the twelve lines from high to low in register, and fast to slow in tempo. Just after the lowest voice enters, a second cascade begins, starting a fourth higher on A7 but otherwise analogous to the first. Repetition of the descending fifth pattern favors a segmentation that cuts across all voices in the texture (rather than by $TS_{2\text{-pitch}}$, which here is only relatively weak), forming an associative set of two segments, each a fragment of a fifths cycle. As the tempo canon progressively accelerates the top voice relative to the bottom, a third cascade interrupts the second at the two-thirds mark. Temporal overlap between distinct segments of the descending fifths cycle (supported by $C_{\text{ip} <-7, -7 \ldots -7>}$) spews out a series of chromatic clashes between G7 and A♭3 (lines B and 4), D7 and D♭3, and so on down to E♭5 and E♮1 (in voices 7 and 0). Two progressively elongated cascades of fifths conclude section I, each eventually dissolving in the resultant texture. Strict progress of the tempo canon makes quick work of the orderly landscape of descending fifths cycles that stream across voices, transforming it into a turbulent pool of pitch chroma and attack points. This progressive dissolution in clarity of segmentation over the course of section I is essential to the form of the passage.

Section II starts in the low bass where section I left off. It resembles section I in several respects: both sections begin just after a convergence point marked by a rest, maintain a slow attack rhythm within each line (a whole note or longer), and trace segments of the circle of fifths across lines of the tempo canon. But there are also sharp contrasts between the two sections. First, section II reverses the tempo-register mapping so that fast-to-slow now goes low-to-high. Pitch material within each line changes from diatonic to chromatic. And strong sonic disjunctions by four criteria in three dimensions ($S_{1\text{-dynamics}}$ and $S_{2\text{-dynamics}}$; $S_{2\text{-duration}}$; and $S_{2\text{-articulation}}$.) mark the boundary between the sections: whereas section I is *ff*, with long, sustained notes; section II is *pp*, with short, staccato ones.

As in section I, uniform progress of the tempo canon in section II has a dynamic result. But this time, rather than having segments and segmentation dissolve, a new associative set emerges. Example 6.2 is an association map in cutaway score format for two sets, A and B. According to the map, section II begins with two circle-of-fifths segments (now rendered as rising perfect fourths and shown as segments of set A, associated by $C_{\text{ip}<+5, +5, \ldots +5>}$). Note that the segments of A arise only in the *combination* of lines; the generating material within each canonic voice is *distributed across* successive segments of A (for instance, the pitches <C2, C♯2, D2>, originally adjacent within the lowest voice of the canon, now appear as successive low points, twelve notes apart).

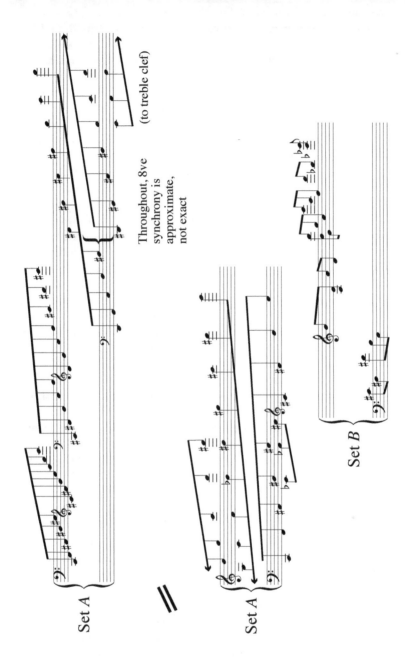

Example 6.2. Nancarrow, *Study No. 37*, section II, association map, sets *A* and *B*

roughly three-octave gap between near-synchronous notes, both cycles can still easily be heard as phenosegs. (Priming of, and associations with, circle-of-fifths segments in section I facilitates perception of the second segment as a complete cycle despite the interruption.) Temporal overlap between the third and fourth interval +5 cycles turns out a series of slightly asynchronous octave doublings that jump out of the texture much as octaves do in a twelve-tone context. By the time the sixth cycle of fourths begins back on C2, three cycles are active at once. But by then the perceptual viability of the +5 cycles as segments has begun to dissolve and soon a new set of associations among shorter figures of one or two descending fifths starts to pop out of the texture—segments of a second set, B, associated by $C_{ip<-7>}$ or $C_{ip<-7, -7, \ldots -7>}$, form as the tempo canon's lower, faster lines overtake its higher and slower ones, working in tandem with a change in the intervallic makeup of the line. Here again, the segments of B are an emergent effect of the tempo canon: they form across, not within, lines. Overall, then, the landscape of section II takes form in three stages: it begins with a series of long ascending fourths cycles and segments of set A, moves through some effective octave doublings, and ends with the much shorter, descending fifths fragments of set B.

In section III, the tempo-register mapping inverts again, so that slowest becomes lowest and first; the fastest, highest and last. Once again, strong sonic disjunctions in three dimensions (now $S_{1\text{-dynamics}}$, $S_{1\text{-pitch}}$, and $S_{2\text{-density}}$) mark the section boundary (ex. 6.3). But even as the punchy fortissimo triads of section III replace the pianissimo individual tones of section II, the idea of descending fifths fragments introduced in set B continues. Once again, the fact that attack point distances are shorter between voices than within voices, and that tempos accelerate from low to high, has an emergent effect: temporal proximity (segmentation by $S_{1\text{-duration}}$) brings out overlapping fragments of descending-fifths cycles (associated by $C_{ip<-7, \ldots >}$) that, in turn, forge an associative continuity across the boundary between sections II and III, mitigating its effect. Very quickly, however, the cyclic fragments at the start of section III dissolve into a chaotic surface of triads that bounce all over the keyboard, then gradually build to a convergence point just before the start of section IV. Thus the process of dissolution found in section I recurs with a different set of particulars; the associative landscapes of both sections I and III contrast with that of section II, which more clearly moves from one associative set to another.

After the triadic frenzy of section III, a pianissimo tottering between B6 and C7 at the start of section IV makes for a strange sort of peace (ex. 6.4a). With just enough cohesion to define a voice, the notes don't quite form a melody. Things start out securely enough, with immediate repetition of the pitch ordering <B6, C7, B6> and a short-long-short attack point rhythm setting off the

Example 6.3. Nancarrow, *Study No. 37*, section III, p. 8

neighbor-like fragment as a fairly clear segment (by coincidence among $S_{1\text{-duration}}$, $C_{\text{pitch <B6, C7, B6>}}$, and $C_{\text{rhythm attack points <010>}}$). But after that, segmentation becomes more tenuous. The pitch sequence is unpredictable, as are mappings from pitches to durations (a quarter-note or a sixteenth) and articulations (slurred or detached). Coincident genosegs in $C_{\text{pitch <B6, C7, B6>}}$ and $C_{\text{rhythm attack points <010>}}$ take in the next three notes, but a conflicting genoseg in C_{rhythm} groups the fifth through seventh notes. Sonic criteria fail to resolve the conflict: $S_{1\text{-duration}}$ is inactive until after the ninth note. If the first three notes, and next three, form a pair of phenosegs associated by contextual criteria, the second phenoseg is noticeably weaker than the first, and is nested inside another, almost as weak, six-note phenoseg.[12] When the second and third voices enter, each at T_{-2}, the prospects for hearing either one as a distinct voice fade (ex. 6.4b). Each voice introduces two new pitches, but the shaky and changeable distribution of pitches and durations complicates segmentation within a voice, while coincidence between $S_{1\text{-adjacency}}$ and various contextual criteria (e.g., $C_{\text{pitch <B6, A6, C7>}}$, and later $C_{\text{incl pitch <A6, G6, B6, B♭6>}}$,

voices. As the tempo canon works its way through the twelve registers (now squeezed into less than two octaves) over the course of section IV, the texture grows more dense and the integrity of individual lines dissolves in an evolving mass of micropolyphony. But still there is differentiation and intermittent segmentation: a motif composed of a quarter note connected to a sixteenth note by a slur intermittently pokes out of a more pointillist background of isolated sixteenths to form a fairly large and very low-profile associative set. Form in section IV, then, involves a different kind of process than in any previous section. Whereas sections I, II, and III all began with segments formed across voices, section IV clearly begins within a single canonic voice and moves from a linear to a distributed mode of listening in which figures from one large associative set in low relief peep out from a diffuse ground.

Example 6.4a. Nancarrow, *Study No. 37*, section IV, pp. 11–12, top line

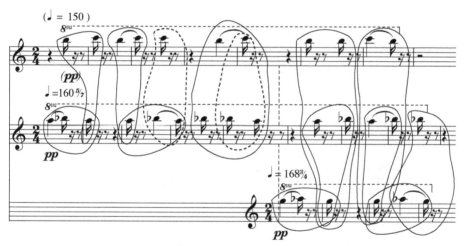

Example 6.4b. Nancarrow, *Study No. 37*, section IV, pp. 12–13, top three lines

Like the tempo canon in section III, that in section VI runs forward to a convergence point at the start of the next section. But section VI also tries out some new strategies. The first section to map a "chromatic" tempo scale

voices and spiraling back around twice from high to low), it is also the first to work through several subjects within each voice. With adjacent lines at T_{+5} and temporally adjacent voice entries at T_{+15} (wraparounds at T_{-28}), $TS_{2\text{-pitch}}$ effectively distinguishes individual voices within the texture.[13] Each canonic voice goes through a series of four subjects separated by rests (ex. 6.5). Each subject begins a new subsection; subsections begin with entries in the lowest line on pages 32, 36, 37, and 38. Subject 1 is long and wiry, and ends with a process of liquidation. Successive voice entries are relatively far apart (seven measures). Subject 2 is shorter and more contained. Subject 3 binds together two new

Section VI, Subject 1, p. 32

Section VI, Subject 2, p. 36

Section VI, Subject 3, p. 37

Section VI, Subject 4, p. 38

Example 6.5. Nancarrow, *Study No. 37*, section VI, four ideas

fold repetition of the arpeggio forms a clear associative set within the subject itself, which then expands with imitation among voices. Subject 4 seeds three more associative sets, based on a chromatic pseudo-trill in sixteenths, followed by a longer arpeggio through two octaves and a chromatic run up a minor sixth, both in thirty-seconds. Although subjects 3 and 4 each contain distinct segments—subject 4 even establishes several distinct associative sets—to keep the focus on the landscape as a whole, I have rendered each subject as a single associative set.

Running each voice of the tempo canon through these four subjects at its own pace effects changes in the landscape that are apparent to the listener, but hard to predict. Subject 1—the longest of the four subjects, and the one with the longest time lag between successive entries—takes a while to accumulate in the texture. Progressive acceleration in the rate of voice entry produced by the tempo canon is moderated but not matched by the intermittent departure of the earliest voices as they run their course. The net result is a gradual increase in the number of voices playing subject 1 from two or three (pp. 33–34), to three or four (pp. 35–36, exit of line 1), followed by a rapid climb to eight (p. 36, with entries in lines 2, 5, 8, and B) just about the time subject 2 enters (p. 36, line 0). But the dense textural polyphony that accompanies the move to associative polyphony is short-lived, collapsing precipitously as the last and fastest voices complete subject 1 to just one or two voices (over the page break of pp. 37–38). Yet two-part associative polyphony is maintained through the entry of subject 3 (p. 37, line 0) as set rhythm and segment rhythm accelerate (subjects 2 and 3 are shorter than subject 1). Example 6.6 provides a score for pages 38–39; entries within each subject are numbered consecutively across all voices. This passage is one of remarkable change in the associative landscape. Associative polyphony expands from two to three sets with the first entrance of subject 4 in line 0; the textural polyphony also becomes more dense, rapidly reaching a second peak of eight active voices (p. 39).[14] But this time it is the associative polyphony that is short-lived, dissolving as the faster voices complete their runs of subject 2 and subject 3. At the end of the passage eight voices remain, but the associative polyphony has given way to associative monophony, with all active voices on subject 4 in the lead-in to the convergence point at the start of section VII.

Section VIII replays two of the strategies from section VI, each with a new twist. Once again, successive voice entries spiral through the twelve registers from low to high by "minor thirds" (with one exception) and pitch transposition by T_{+15}, but this time voices also move through tempo space in the same way rather than "chromatically." Like section VI, section VIII is dominated by associative polyphony, but here the polyphony has different origins and results. Whereas each voice in section VI runs through a series of four discrete subjects, creating associative polyphony among them, section VIII crafts a single

Line:

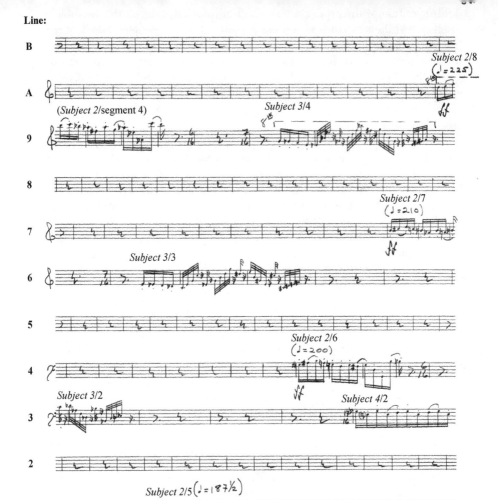

Example 6.6. Nancarrow, *Study No. 37*, section VI, changing textural and associative polyphony among subjects 2, 3, and 4, pp. 38–39

Example 6.6. Nancarrow, *Study No. 37*, section VI, changing textural and associative polyphony among subjects 2, 3, and 4, pp. 38–39—*(concluded)*

sists of a brusque alternation between semitone neighbor figures in staccato eighth-notes (set D) and longer, isolated major triads (set C) that creates associative polyphony from textural monophony within each canonic voice (ex. 6.7).[15] (The reason for the apparent reversal of letter names C and D will become clear in a moment.) The subject closes with a chromatic descent in staccato eighths (not shown, set E). Common sets for the two alternating sets D and C include sonic and contextual criteria. The neighbor figures of set D are short (♪) individual notes at *mp*; the triads of C, longer (♩. or ♩) bunches of notes at *ff*. Sharp disjunctions in $S_{2\text{-duration}}$, density (S_1 and S_2), and dynamics (S_1 and S_2) broadcast the segments of sets C and D on distinct sonic channels. Sets C and D also differ in distribution. Both sets are widespread in section VIII, but whereas D is pervasive, its segments arranged in large patches that dominate the landscape, set C is relatively infrequent, with many minimal patches of just one segment. Over the course of section VIII, the progress of the tempo canon induces local perturbations in patch sizes and relative densities of sets C, D, and E. Here and there sets C or E come to the fore, only to recede into the background as an intermittent presence.

Both associative sets C and D have consociates in other parts of the piece that place section VIII in a nexus of relationships among sections. The triads of set C recall section III; the semitone neighbor motions of D recall section V (hence the reversal of letter names within section VIII). Example 6.8 represents these associations among sections III, V, and VIII in the form of an association map that takes in three more sections—IX, XI, and part of XII (from pp. 101–4). Early in the piece the triads and semitone neighbor figures of sets C and D are introduced one at a time, as basic material for two contrasting and nonadjacent sections, III and V. Section VIII brings sets C and D into close temporal proximity, juxtaposing them within each voice of the tempo canon and creating a landscape of contrasting patches with subtle shifts in relative densities. Section IX takes the synthesis a step further, grafting the triads of C onto the melodic idea of D in a conflux that erases the sonic distinctions between them. The result is a vigorous but much more homogeneous landscape, in which both sets are continually present in equal proportions. Section XI reverses the process, continuing with an associative fission that reinstates the sonic contrast between sets C and D by $S_{2\text{-duration}}$, while distilling the core criterion of D to just two repeated notes without the characteristic neighbor. Like section VIII, section XI has a form that is subtly dynamic, shaped by gentle flexing in the relative densities of C and D that arise in the contrapuntal composite of canonic voices. Finally, a relatively brief subsection of section XII (pp. 101–4) reasserts the triad of set C as an isolated figure, recalling its initial state in section III.

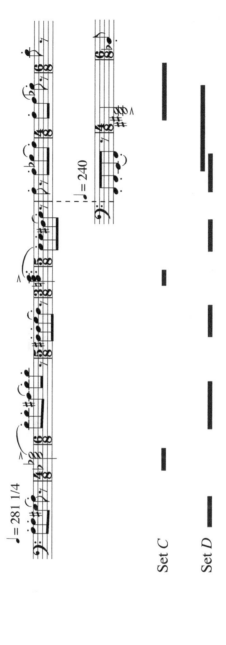

Example 6.7. Nancarrow, *Study No. 37*, section VIII, pp. 48–49, sets *C* and *D* in lines 4 and 1

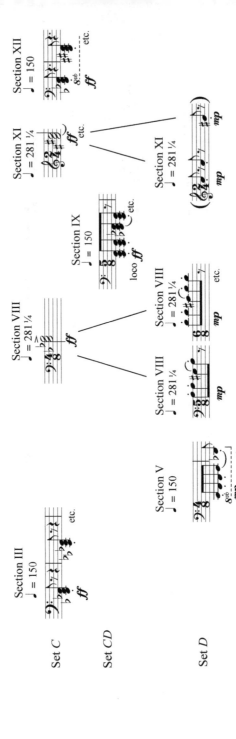

Example 6.8. Nancarrow, *Study No. 37*, cutaway score map of sets *C* and *D* over sections III–XII

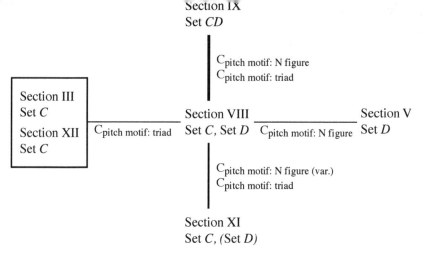

Example 6.9. Nancarrow, *Study No. 37*, association graph centered on section VIII

The association graph in example 6.9 provides an alternate representation of the nexus of associations among sections III, V, VIII, IX, XI, and XII created by the core criteria of sets C ($C_{\text{pitch motif: triad}}$) and D ($C_{\text{pitch motif: N figure}}$). The layout of nodes from left to right and top to bottom corresponds with temporal order to the extent possible (evident in the roman numerals used for section names). The graph encourages some observations about form in *Study No. 37*, conceived in terms of the relationship between associative and temporal proximity and distance. Among these six sections, section VIII is central, the only node of degree 4 in a graph in which most nodes are of degree 1 (sections V, IX, XI). Located on opposite sides of the graph, sections III and V are associatively distant but temporally proximate; conversely, section III and part of section XII (pp. 101–4) are associatively proximate but temporally distant. Both associative and score chronology trace the same partial ordering for sections V, VIII, IX, XI, and XII, pp. 101–4 (that is, the chronological partial ordering of roman numerals proceeds from right to left on the graph). Heavier line weights for the edges VIII–IX and VIII–XI reflect my view that associations among these three temporally proximate sections are stronger than those along other edges in the graph, where associative and temporal proximity tend to conflict. They also suggest that section VIII might be seen as a contextual focus for the piece as a whole, the nexus of a dynamic process of confluence and separation for sets C and D.

A remarkable feature of the associative landscape of *Study No. 37* is the material and compositional heterogeneity of the associative landscape that results from strict adherence to a compositional plan through its interactions

gent effects appear at multiple levels of organization, from segments to sets to landscapes. In a tantalizing paradox, it is exactly Nancarrow's rigorous development and application of structural constraints that creates his wild and wondrously imaginative musical surfaces.

Riley, In C

Configurations and Landscape Studies of Select Plots in Four Performances

Terry Riley's *In C* (1964) is a landmark in American minimalism.[1] Riley conceived the piece one night on a bus en route to a gig; it was premiered on November 4, 1964, at the San Francisco Tape Music Center by a group that included Riley, Pauline Oliveros, Morton Subotnick, Steve Reich, and others.[2] Composed for any number and ensemble of performers,[3] the score consists of an ordered set of 53 "figures,"[4] each fully notated with respect to pitch and rhythm, along with a set of performance instructions added later by the composer.[5] Each player traverses the 53 figures in order, repeating each as many times as he or she chooses while attending to the communal progress of the ensemble. Players can omit patterns that "are too difficult or unsuitable for their instrument"; all entries and exits should be "as inconspicuous as possible," and performers should try to remain within 2–5 figures of one another, merging into a unison at least once during a performance.[6] Riley's instructions admit three more variables: individual figures can be transposed up at the octave (downward transposition is discouraged, as is transposition of patterns in running sixteenth-notes) or realigned with respect to one another and the notated bar, and players can intersperse parcels of repetitions with rests (to give wind players and singers time to breathe). The notes also suggest the appropriate time scale for a performance: "Performances normally average between 45 minutes and an hour and a half" and performers should not be in a hurry to move from figure to figure. Riley's original conception did not include the pulse, which Reich suggested in rehearsal in order to keep the ensemble together.[7]

In performance, Riley's 53 figures develop into what composer David Behrman has aptly (and with respect to the theory of associative organization and associative landscapes we have developed, very suggestively) described as "a teeming world of groups and subgroups forming, dissolving, and reforming within a modal panorama which shifts, over a period of about forty-five to fifty minutes, from C to E to C to G."[8] The musical complexity of the piece is substantially increased by the range of instrumental forces and philosophies of its performance, evident in recordings by mixed ensembles of various sizes (Bang on a Can, Ictus, and Riley and friends at

cus), voices and marimbas (Ars Nova Copenhagen/Percurama Percussion Ensemble under Paul Hillier), and traditional Chinese instruments (Shanghai Film Orchestra).[9]

For a piece of its stature, *In C* remained remarkably inconspicuous in the analytic literature for over forty years. In part, this silence reflected a gulf between East Coast philosophies and aesthetics of music and approaches to music analysis that emerged from Princeton and Yale in the 1960s and 1970s, and Riley's West Coast compositional aesthetics. It also belies a fundamental question over the very subject of analysis—is it the score of *In C*, or individual performances?[10] In his important 2009 book on *In C*, Robert Carl outlines the evolution of Riley's compositional practices up to 1964 and the history of the piece's composition, première, and reception. His analysis of the piece takes both the score and its performances into account, with many insightful observations, a careful accounting of the distribution of pitch-classes and durations among the 53 figures, consideration of their implications for performance, descriptive accounts of all fourteen recorded performances, and more.

But surely one reason that *In C* resisted analysis for so long is a distinctive feature of the piece itself: while music theorists tend to focus on musical structure, *In C* is really about associative organization—about the fit or misfit of associative and temporal proximity among figures notated in the score and the realignment of figures in individual performances that effectively constructs and reconstructs the musical landscape in different ways. Our conceptual framework provides a new way into these aspects of the piece. I begin by defining and translating some key terms. Analysis begins with a look at associative sets and associative configurations of figures in the score, followed by comparative analysis across five recordings. The chapter concludes with three short landscape studies of comparable plots in three performances that illustrate contrasting approaches to the formation and evolution of the musical landscape.

Definitions and Translations of Terms

To facilitate analysis, example 7.1 provides a glossary of select terms introduced in chapter 3, interpreted for use with *In C* (terms not listed retain their original definitions). Four terms will figure prominently in our analysis. The associative set, subset, and superset correspond to one of Riley's 53 figures, versions of a single figure, and sets of associated figures, respectively. The fourth key term is the plot, here interpreted as a passage of a performance with a designated start and end time defined by the entrance and exit times of one or more figures. A caveat is in order. Given the high degree of similarity among certain pairs of temporally adjacent or proximate figures, the complexity of the texture in some recordings, Riley's directive to "make all exits and entries as inconspicuous

timbral doublings, and microphone placement, it can be very difficult if not impossible to determine start and exit times for every figure in certain passages and performances. In general, it is easier to hear entrances than exits[11] (especially if the entry introduces a new pitch, pc, or duration, or if it reintroduces an element that hasn't been around for a while),[12] and easiest to hear the entrances of figures that cross boundaries between associative supersets.

While I will discuss some aspects of individual performances and plots without the support of visual representations, the landscape studies at the end of the chapter are greatly facilitated by maps which serve as surrogates for scores of individual performances. Maps support the analysis of plots for range of variation, the relative prominence of figures (is the distribution of segments among figures even or skewed?), rate of change (do figures enter and exit gradually, or in surges and population crashes?), and other aspects of plot design such as material and compositional homogeneity or

element: Attribute of a note in a figure; a specific pitch or duration.

segment: Instance of one of Riley's 53 figures (or resultant pattern) in a performance, with a specific timbre, register, start and end time, etc.

associative set: One of Riley's 53 figures.

associative subset: A set of instances of a figure associated by instrument, part, register, or timbre; rhythmic alignment; or transformation by augmentation, diminution, retrograde, or inversion; in a particular performance.

associative superset: A set of two or more figures related by contextual criteria.

range of variation: For an associative superset, the number of sets (figures) it includes. For an associative set: the subsets active *in a particular performance* with respect to timbre, register, loudness, articulation; rhythmic alignment; or transformation by augmentation, diminution, retrograde or inversion.

plot: A passage of a performance, with a designated start and end time. For *In C,* a plot usually involves several figures.

map/bar graph schematic: A visual representation of one or more plots in a landscape in which time flows left to right and shaded horizontal bars indicate the extent of a set's activity. The shading from light to dark, and its gradient, represent changes in the relative prominence of figures and, to the extent possible, the speed of transition.

landscape study: A comparative analysis of musical design, or changes in design, in two or more plots from one or more performances.

Example 7.1. Glossary of terms as interpreted for *In C*

of the plot is that of a *figural window*—the number and span of figures, earliest to latest, that appear in a plot defined by the entry and exit times of a single figure.[13] The figural window has two parts, forward and backward. The *forward window* is the number of figures active between the entry and exit times of a given figure; *backward window*, the number of figures already in the texture when that figure enters.

Finally, I need to say a little about the term "figure," which I adopt from Riley and use to refer to one of the 53 fragments notated in the score. Certainly, the term applies in the sense that each fragment is a configuration of tones with distinct pitch and rhythmic content.[14] But perceiving each figure *as* a figure is complicated by the act of performance. Boundaries of white space on the page don't translate into frames of silence; in performance, associative sets overlap and shade into one another. Entrances and exits can be hard to hear; even when they are clear, they, and even the individual figures, may be less important than the emergent effect of their massed repetition within a complex texture.

In performance, a number of Riley's figures sound less like "figures" than stages in a process of pitch, rhythmic, or textural recalibration. For example, settling into a tentative and transient E minor, figures 22–26 effect a process of pitch recalibration: as the players of an ensemble travel through these figures, E gradually gives way to F♯, F♯ to G, G to A, and A to B. Figures 36–41 similarly prescribe a series of recalibrations among the pcs F, G, B, and C, as do figures 49–53 among F, G, and B♭. Figures 1–5 combine pitch calibration within the ordered set <C, E, F, G> with rhythmic recalibration: grace notes and quarter notes give way to a steady eighth-note pulse. Extending this idea to a third sonic dimension, figures 45–47 combine pitch recalibration (a move from D and G to D and E) with rhythmic and textural recalibration. Figure 45 begins with surface rhythm at the quarter, within a slower dotted half pulse set by figure length. Figure 46 maintains only the quarter-note pulse as the basis for a new faster surface rhythm of eighths and sixteenths. The move to figure 47 replaces the rests in figure 46 with constant repetition of a shorter figure that includes an attack on every eighth or sixteenth. The result is a gradual shift in the resultant texture of the ensemble. The move through figures 9–13 provides another example of textural and rhythmic recalibration. From figure 9 to figure 10, textural density increases as the rests that dominate instances of figure 9 are gradually replaced by continuous repetition of two sixteenth-notes in figure 10. Figure 11 maintains the sixteenth-note surface rhythm, but also introduces a slower dotted quarter pulse, defined by figure length. Figures 12 and 13 continue to recalibrate the relative densities of sound-events, initiation points, and rests, integrating long notes into figures with shorter values.

At times, coordinated changes in surface rhythm and figure length effect something like metric modulation. This happens, for example, in the move from the effective compound meter of figure 26 (present since fig. 22) to simple meter (2/4) in figure 28, a move mediated by the metrically ambiguous figure 27, which

ulation plain.) In all of these cases, Riley's "figures" are indistinguishable from "ground"; both are part of one continuous and evolving musical process.

Associative Sets and Associative Configurations

As a collection of segments, *In C*'s 53 figures (and 53 associative sets) suggest a range of associative proximities and distances. Although associative and temporal proximity are, in theory, functionally independent, some of the clearest associative supersets in *In C* do in fact form among consecutive figures. Example 7.2 reproduces Riley's 53 figures from the score. Associated by pitch content, figures 1–5 gradually unfold the C major triad from C4 to G4, with F first as an upper neighbor to E, then as a passing tone from E to G. As features are introduced, then dropped, one by one (first the grace note, then the neighbor note, even durations, and rise to G), the strongest associations form between figures that are temporally adjacent; the associative topology is linear and corresponds with temporal order (ex. 7.3). Associative organization in the superset formed by figures 22–26 is comparable: linear associative topology plays out in temporal order, but the superset has a smaller range of variation. In this case there is also a recursive aspect, as the series of pitch recalibrations given by the linear topology traces the same pitch sequence as the superset's core criterion $C_{\text{pitch} <E4, F\sharp4, G4, A4, B4>}$. Figures 45–47 are a third example of a superset in which linear associative topology and temporal order coincide.

In some parts of the piece, contiguous figures form associative supersets in which associative topology is nonlinear or conflicts with temporal order. Figures 49–53 form a superset in which associative adjacency approximates, but does not quite follow, chronological order (ex. 7.4a). Here figure 51, the node with the highest degree in the graph (degree 3), also occupies the middle position in the temporal sequence. But for an extra node and edge, and two dotted edges, the basic graph for figures 36–41 is the same, but there is a different mapping of associative adjacencies to temporal order (ex. 7.4b). This superset can be expanded to include figures 31–34, which all involve the same three pitches and, in some cases, stronger associations between segments in the earlier, versus later, patch (e.g., figs. 31 and 36 are related by rotation; figs. 34 and 37 by retrograde). Compared to figures 31–34 and 36–41, figure 35 is an anomaly: although it begins with the same pitches and surface rhythm as figure 36, its distinctive continuation as a long melodic line in a high register and inclusion of both F♯ and B♭ place it in a different superset at a higher level of organization.

Thinking in terms of associative supersets suggests that one might hear the piece as a series of overlapping passages, each with fuzzy boundaries. The gradual unfolding of the C major triad from figure 1 to figure 5 is the first passage, which can be extended to include the rise to C5 in figure 6 and the introduction of a new rhythmic figure on C4 in figure 7. Figure 8 begins a new passage;

in C.

Example 7.2. Riley, *In C*

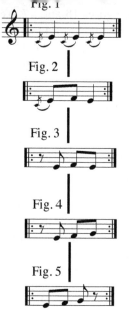

Example 7.3. Association graph for figures 1–5: linear topology

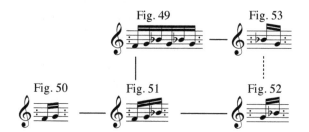

Example 7.4a. Association graph for figures 49–53

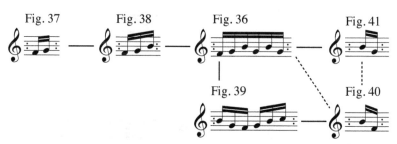

Example 7.4b. Association graph for figures 36–41

the focus to G4, B4, and C5; figures 16 and 17 are also absorbed into this superset. The process of pitch recalibration in figures 22–26 outlines another superset; it combines with a second superset that includes six figures presented in two patches (figures 18–21 and 27–28) to form a long passage in E (natural) minor. Aspects of pitch content, surface rhythm, and contour recommend merging the supersets of figures 31–41 and figures 49–53 around the intervening figures 42, 48, and two smaller subsets (figures 43–44 and 45–47) to round out the piece.

Cutting across this prevailing organization of fairly large associative supersets made of temporally proximate figures are several small supersets made of figures that are associatively proximate but temporally distant. One of these joins the two long C5s in figures 6 and 30, anchoring a larger association between figures 1–6 and 29–30 (each passage spells out the ascending first-inversion triad <E4, G4, C5>). Repetition of the pitch ordering <G4, F4> in long note values associates figures 8 and 48, two figures with relatively loose ties to other figures in their immediate vicinity. Riley's 53 figures also include three pairs of figures that are identical except for temporal placement. One of these pairs, containing figures 18 and 28, delimits the central E minor passage; another (figs. 37 and 50), the start of two patches of a large, merged associative superset. The third (figs. 11 and 36) makes a long-range association between two even more distantly related passages. Pitch interval content also suggests a long-range association between two pairs of figures in the first and last parts of the piece. The associative topology of the superset that connects figures 16–17 with figures 43–44 is the circuit graph C_4 (ex. 7.5), with temporal order within the second pair of segments (as traced by a path on the graph) reversed relative to the first. The twelve figures that include F♯ (figures 14, 18, 20–28, and 35) can also be seen as a large and diffuse superset. As an additional complication in the abstract associative organization of the 53 figures, there are a few small supersets that balance strong associations with sharp contrast. The

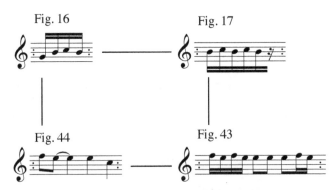

Fig. 16   Fig. 17

Fig. 44   Fig. 43

Example 7.5. Association graph for figures 16, 17, 43, and 44

frame, but create a striking opposition in octave placement, duration, and the ratio of sound to silence. The relationship between figures 19 and 21 is similar: both set long notes in a context dominated by short ones, but juxtapose high and low registers, and the pcs G and F♯.

Comparative Analysis of Performances

The indeterminacy of *In C* poses a significant challenge for analysis. With so much of the music taking shape only in performance, analysis that recognizes individual performances, and comparative analysis across performances, is essential. The following discussion references, with varying degrees of emphasis, five recordings: by Terry Riley and players from the Center of the Creative and Performing Arts at SUNY Buffalo (1968), the Twenty-Fifth Anniversary Concert in San Francisco (1990), Ictus (2000), Bang on a Can (2001), and Ars Nova Copenhagen/Percurama Percussion Ensemble under the direction of Paul Hillier (2006). Example 7.6 surveys these recordings with respect to year, instrumentation, length, and some distinctive features.

Length and instrumentation are some of the most obvious differences. The original 1968 Columbia recording involves 11 players (mostly winds), expanded by two overdubs to 27 parts plus the pulse.[15] At 42 minutes, it is the shortest of the four recordings, timed to fit on two sides of an LP.[16] Slightly longer is Bang on a Can's 2001 recording, which runs for 45′32″ and has 11 players. Combining a wider range of timbres, which are fairly evenly distributed among a pair of winds (clarinet, soprano sax), three bowed strings (violin, cello, contrabass), three plucked strings (mandolin, pipa, electric guitar), piano, and two percussionists (glockenspiel/vibraphone and marimba/chimes) with a smaller effective ensemble (no overdubs) makes for a more soloistic (or less communal) performance. Next in length is Hillier, at 55′19″. With 22 performers—twelve voices (three each on S/A/T/B), eight marimbas, one bass marimba, and a conductor (Hillier)—it has both the smallest range of timbres and the sharpest timbral bifurcation (voices versus mallets).[17] As conductor, Hillier brings out the timbral contrast between voices and mallets on several occasions, and shapes dynamics, surges of entries, and exits, throughout. Ictus times in at 64′58″, with a smaller ensemble of 16 players nicely spread across a spectrum of timbres from winds (oboe, clarinet, sax quartet), through accordion, to piano, harp, guitar, strings (violin, cello, and two contrabass), and percussion. Finally, at 76′20″, the Twenty-Fifth Anniversary Concert is the longest of the five, with the most performers (31) and slowest tempo.[18] The instrumentation resembles that of the 1968 recording, but with the addition of voices, more strings (including guitar), percussion, and a conductor (Loren Rush), whose influence is felt in the many dynamic swells and tapers, and occasional merges into a unison.[19]

Performers (label)	Year	Instrumentation	Time	Notes
Terry Riley/Center of the Creative and Performing Arts, SUNY Buffalo (CBS Records)	1968	[28] 11 performers, 2 overdubs of 9, 8 performers 3 fl., 3 ob., 2 cl., 2 bsn., 3 sax, 3 tpt., 3 trbn, 3 vib., 2 mar., pf. (pulse), 3 vla.	42′01″	Usually 4–5 figures active at once Some figures: octave transposition
25th Anniversary Concert (Loren Rush, Conductor) (New Albion)	1990	31 performers fl., cl., b. cl., 5 sax (2S, ATBar), 2 trbn., 2 syn., pf., glock., 2 xyl., acc., mar., drums, 2 gui., 2 vln., vla., vc., 4 vv., asst. instruments, pulse	76′20″	Dynamics coordinated by conductor; some unisons; texture "breathes" Some figures: octave transposition, augmentation
Ictus (Cypres)	2000	16 performers ob., cl., 4 sax (SATBar), 2 perc., hp., pf., acc., gui., vln., vc., 2 cb. (+ perc.)	64′58″	On average, largest figural window (reaches 13 for figs. 22–35). Some figures intermittent within their plots, disposed in patches. Downward transposition, some multiphonics

Example 7.6. Five performances of *In C*

Ensemble	Year	Performers	Instruments	Duration	Notes
Bang on a Can (Cantaloupe)	2001	11 performers	cl., S sax, glock./vib, chimes, mar., pf., mand., pipa, el gui., vln, vc., cb.	45'32"	Figural window is relatively large: often 5–7, up to 10. Also, size of figural window varies considerably, from 2–3 at the start to 10 (for #35). Includes downward octave transposition
Ars Nova Copenhagen/Percurama Percussion Ensemble (Paul Hillier, Conductor) (Da Capo)	2006	21 performers	12 voices (SATB), 7 mar., 1 bass mar., vib./Bali gong	55'19"	Usually 2–3 figures active; some unisons. Dynamics, surges, coordinated by conductor. Some figures: octave transposition (up, down), augmentation, diminution, inversion, retrograde. "Sacred syllables" for voices provided by Riley

Example 7.6. Five performances of *In C*—(*concluded*)

important difference is in the size of the typical, and maximum, figural window. Hillier's performance has the smallest figural window (2–4); usually only two or three figures are active at once. In a few spots (e.g., within the plots for figures 6 and 30), the texture dissolves into repetitions of a single figure (consistent with Riley's note that players can occasionally try "to merge together into a unison"), or even just the pulse. Although the number of figures present at a time is always small, the Hillier performance explores the full range of textures available within those limits. The figural window in the 1968 performance is slightly larger (3–5 figures); here three or four figures are usually present. The number of figures in play moment to moment is much more constant than in the Hillier—never two or one except at the very start and end of the piece, and rarely five.

A comparison of the size and evolution of the figural window in Bang on a Can's performance with that in the 1968 performance is instructive. Although the two performances are about the same length (Bang on a Can's is 3½ minutes, or 8.3 percent, longer), they distribute the entries and exits of figures across this timespan quite differently. Both begin the piece with a figural window of 3 or 4, but Bang on a Can's pacing is much faster: whereas figures 1–7 enter at 0'08", 1'05", 1'28", 1'45", 2'30", 3'27", and 4'05" in the 1968 performance, in the Bang on a Can performance they enter at 0'05", 0'40", 0'50", 1'24", 1'35", 2'02", and 2'44"—on average, about 33 percent earlier. This faster pacing continues through most of the piece: although Bang on a Can's recording is more than three minutes longer than the 1968 recording, all but the last few figures enter earlier—some as much as five minutes earlier (e.g., figs. 22 and 35).[20] Starting with figure 8, the Bang on a Can players begin to spread out, with some instruments (electric guitar, contrabass, cello) assuming the role of leaders; others (mandolin, sax, violin), trailers; and the rest somewhere in between.[21] As a result, the average forward window gradually increases, first to 4–5 figures (figs. 8–14), then to 5–6 figures (figs. 15–21), until it reaches a maximum of 10 for figures 35–36, then collapses to 6 or so for the rest of the piece. As the array of players nears the end of the piece, the process reverses and the size of the *backward* window gradually increases. Once the vanguard has reached figure 53, the trailers' entries are progressively accelerated and telescoped in order to catch up and maintain a sense of proportion between the G minor closing passage and the rest of the piece.

The Ictus performance has a similar trajectory, in that a fairly standard window of 3–4 figures in the early part of the piece is gradually expanded as the piece goes on. Here, however, the forward window reaches a maximum of 13 (the largest in any of the five recordings) thirteen figures earlier, at figure 22, which places the first entry of figure 35, the distinctive long melody, in the tail end of the central E minor passage. Like Bang on a Can, Ictus reaches its maximum figural window at figure 35, but the relative sizes of the forward and backward window are reversed (6:13 for Ictus versus 10:7 for Bang on a Can). The result is a more even distribution of figures across the

Relating differences in the size of the figural window to ensemble size and instrumentation sheds light on other differences in associative organization across the performances, including the degree of material heterogeneity among associative subsets and differences in landscape composition. Small figural windows translate into low plot diversity at the level of the associative set. In the Hillier performance—the one with the smallest average figural window—the range of timbres is also the most limited. Perhaps to compensate for the relatively narrow range of possibilities in these two respects, it is the Hillier performance that takes the lead in transforming the figures themselves. Figures are freely transposed by octave up and down to accommodate vocal ranges and, occasionally, for effect (e.g., one soprano rises to C6 in figure 29); augmentation and diminution are fairly common, and even retrograde and inversion occur.[22] The result is a shift in the locus of material heterogeneity within a plot from the level of the figure or associative set to that of *versions* of a figure or associative subsets.

In Bang on a Can's performance, the much larger figural windows keep material heterogeneity within a plot focused at the level of the associative set. But here the relatively small size of the ensemble interacts with the relatively large sizes of the figural windows such that, in contrast to the 1968 recording where there are usually several players on a figure at any given time, Bang on a Can often has just one or two players. As the eleven players get spread out among five, six, eight, and eventually ten figures, figures tend to come and go in the texture with the individual players, rather than remaining in the texture from initial entry to final exit, as they do in the 1968 recording. The result is a much patchier landscape in which some figures come in a series of fairly discrete associative subsets defined by timbre (e.g., electric guitar; a pairing between pipa and mandolin) or octave placement (e.g., especially in the contrabass, which often takes figures down *two* octaves).[23]

Overlaying figural windows of different sizes on the abstract associative organization of Riley's 53 figures into supersets of contiguous or nonadjacent figures ultimately leads to differences in large-scale form. In performances with a small figural window, associative supersets of contiguous figures engender a series of relatively long and internally unified passages connected by transitions that cross junctures between associative supersets. When the figural window is small, two figures placed midway in the temporal sequence of successive passages never come into contact with one another, nor do figures positioned first or last in the temporal sequence of a large superset. In the Hillier performance, for example, figures 31–34 and 36–41—the two flanks of the very large superset from figures 31–41—barely touch. Figure 34 leaves just 13 seconds after figure 36 enters and even then it is subordinate to figure 35. Patches of the two identical figures 18 and 28 are discrete, as are the passages based on figures 18–21 and 27–28 that embed them. The much larger figural windows in the Bang on a Can and Ictus recordings effectively merge figures 31–34 and 36–41 into a single extended

sage, with figure 21 present all the way through the entries of figures 27 and 28. An important consequence of a large figural window is that most plots, even those only a second or two long, splay across junctures between supersets. Superimposing a large figural window on the underlying associative organization of temporally continuous supersets in effect compounds the material heterogeneity of the average plot: not only are more figures present at a time, but, because they represent more than one superset, the plots are also more diverse.

Three Short Landscape Studies

We now move on to three short landscape studies that each involve comparative analysis of comparable plots from different performances. For *In C*, we can define "comparable plots" two ways: by clock time or by the temporal extent of one or more figures. Defining plots of equal size in minutes and seconds with comparable starting points (e.g., the initial entry of a certain figure) brings out differences in content and scale. Sampling the opening of the 1968, Twenty-Fifth Anniversary, Bang on a Can, and Hillier performances with a standard plot size of 50 seconds quickly brings out some representative differences. The plot of the 1968 performance is the most uniform with respect to timbre (mostly winds), spatial position (roughly equal activity at left, right, and center), and figure alignment (instruments in unison). Figure 2 doesn't enter until 1'05", well outside the bounds of the plot. The Bang on a Can recording begins differently: its figure 1 is much more diverse in timbre, alignment, and register, with octave transpositions both up (in mandolin and pipa) and down (in the contrabass).[24] Here a 50-second plot takes in two associative sets: figure 2 enters at 40 seconds and spreads to three instruments (vibraphone, bass, and electric guitar) by 50 seconds. In range of variation, the first 50-second plot of the Twenty-Fifth Anniversary Concert is somewhere in between the two. Different alignments appear by 20 seconds, the flute enters an octave higher at 48 seconds, and graduated entry of left and right channels makes spatial position a new area of diversity. Still, the plot has only one set: figure 2 is relatively far off, with an entrance in the clarinet at 1'10". The Hillier plot introduces a few more parameters. Starting with a solo marimba pulse for 14 seconds, it has the largest truly uniform set. Once the voices enter, figure 1 is fairly uniform in terms of alignments, but bifurcated in timbre (voices versus mallets) and register (women's versus men's voices). Superimposed on this basic texture are cyclic changes in loudness and the number of instances present per unit time.

Although landscape studies of plots defined by equal time-slices are revealing, they in effect impose a fixed temporal yardstick on the temporal unfolding of each individual performance. To get around this problem, we might instead define plots by the initial entry and final exit of one or more figures. By absorbing differences in scale among performances, this approach allows us to focus more exclusively on differences in plot content and composition.

graph schematics that indicate the entrance and exit times of individual figures in a particular performance.[25] In the schematics, time flows left to right; shaded horizontal bars indicate the extent of each set's activity. Shading from light to dark, and the gradient of shading, represent changes in a figure's prominence within the texture and, to the extent possible at the scale of the schematic, its speed of transition into or out of the texture. The bar graph schematics represent my best approximation of start and exit times, as well as a figure's peak activity, gradient, and relative prominence within the texture. My sense of a figure's peak, gradient, and prominence is influenced by the figure's associative proximity or distance from other figures active at the same time; length or attack-point density; and various properties defined only in the act of performance, such as timbre, number of players on a figure, dynamics, register (octave transposition up or down), and augmentation or diminution. It is also reckoned relative to *a particular scale* of activity, averaged and rendered in 30-second increments (thus *not* a comprehensive, second-by-second transcription). Activity more fine-scaled than the scale of the schematic (such as successive entrances of individual instruments, surges of activity within short time spans, or dynamic swells) is either not represented or represented only in a cumulative sense, inasmuch as it contributes to the plot's overall design.

After the neat linear topology and chronological sequence of figures 1–5, figures 6 and 7 stand out as new, albeit related, events. Figure 6 reaches a fourth above the previous high note, introducing a much longer duration in the longest segment so far. Figure 7 accelerates the surface rhythm, but cycles at roughly the same pace as figure 6. Examples 7.7a, 7.7b, and 7.7c provide maps for the three plots defined by figures 6–7 in the 1968 Columbia, Bang on a Can, and Hillier recordings. Although the complete Hillier performance is about 30 percent longer than the 1968 recording, the plots for figures 6–7 almost align on the clock: both begin at about 3½ minutes and run for about 4½ minutes. (The Hillier is 20 seconds shorter). In contrast, the corresponding plot in the Bang on a Can recording is significantly earlier and shorter, starting at 2'00" and clocking in at just about 3 minutes.

The three maps represent a number of differences among the landscapes with respect to content, continuity, and overall design. In terms of the number of figures present, the 1968 plot is the most diverse: it has seven figures (versus six in the Bang on a Can recording and five or six in the Hillier), with three to four usually active at once. Only three figures are active at once through most of the Bang on a Can plot. The Hillier plot is more sparse: most of the time, only two figures are active.[26] The 1968 plot is absolutely continuous: there are no breaks in the texture; the ensemble gradually and seamlessly shifts its point of focus from one figure to the next, and the pace of figure turnover is fairly regular.[27] The Bang on a Can plot is gently segmented at around 3'30": figures 4 and 5 leave just about the time figure 7 enters. Also, as I've tried to show in the shading, whereas the transition from figure 6 to 7 is very smooth in the 1968 plot,

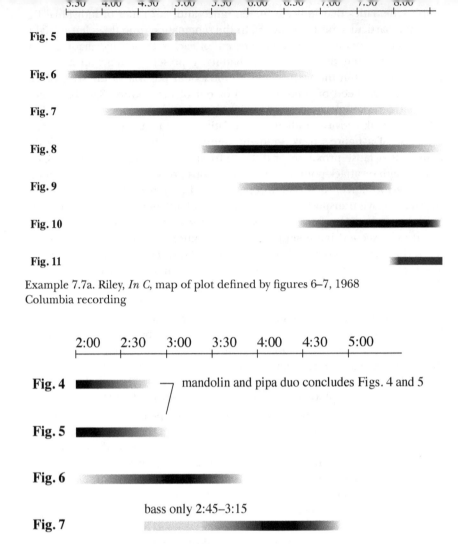

Example 7.7a. Riley, *In C*, map of plot defined by figures 6–7, 1968
Columbia recording

Example 7.7b. Riley, *In C*, map of plot defined by figures 6–7, Bang on a Can

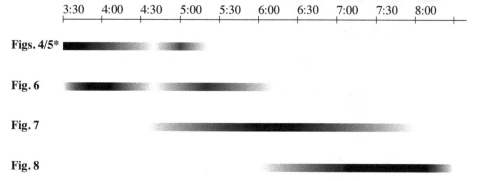

| 3:30 | 4:00 | 4:30 | 5:00 | 5:30 | 6:00 | 6:30 | 7:00 | 7:30 | 8:00 |

Figs. 4/5*

Fig. 6

Fig. 7

Fig. 8

Fig. 9

*In that Figs. 4 and 5 differ only by alignment, they cannot reliably be distinguished in performance (realignment of a figure is permitted).

Example 7.7c. Riley, *In C*, map of plot defined by figures 6–7, Hillier/Ars Nova/Percurama

it is more pronounced in the Bang on a Can plot, with a fairly clear shift in emphasis from figure 6 to figure 7 between 3′30″ and 3′45″.

The Hillier plot differs from the other two in that it has a clear break across the entire texture at 4′35″ where figures 5 and 6 temporarily disappear, leaving only the pulse when figure 7 enters (figures 5 and 6 soon return and remain equal partners with figure 7 until about 5′40″, when figure 7 supersedes). Like the Bang on a Can plot, the Hillier also has sharper contrast between foreground and background figures; whereas the surface of the 1968 plot is relatively low profile, the Bang on a Can and Hillier are progressively more high-profile. Overall, although the 1968 plot is the most heterogeneous of the three in terms of materials, it is also the most homogeneous in design—about the same number of figures are active throughout, and the flow from figure to figure is smooth and even. The Hillier plot is less heterogeneous in materials, but the most heterogeneous and, arguably, assertive in its design, actively sculpting its materials in the act of performance.

Differences in landscape composition among these three plots—more materials, lower profile, and homogeneous design in the 1968 recording; fewer materials, higher profile, and a more crisp, varied design in the Hillier; somewhere in between in both respects for the Bang on a Can—are not only local. Earlier, I noted that figure 6 and figure 30 (both long C5s) form a small superset that cuts across a substantial temporal distance. Thus the relative prominence or submergence of figure 6 has long-range consequences: only when both figures 6 and 30 are prominent in a particular performance is this long-range connection

which five or six figures are always active at once. As a result, no long-range connection develops between the passages that surround figure 6 and figure 30. Examples 7.8a and 7.8b provide maps for the plots defined by the first entry and last exit times of figures 29–30 in the Bang on a Can and Hillier performances. Whereas Bang on a Can has a clear shift in emphasis from figure 6 to figure 7 early in the piece, and a series of such shifts from figure 25 to figures 26, 27, and 28 later on (that close out the E minor passage), figures 29 and 30 are coequal for most of their duration (ex. 7.8a). With figures 29 and 30 equally prominent for about two minutes, the long-range connection between figures 6 and 30 is available, but clouded. In the Hillier performance, however, figure 30 is the center of attention in a passage with just two figures (ex. 7.8b). So whereas in the 1968 recording the connection between figures 6 and 30 remains on the page, and in Bang on a Can's it is available but not especially prominent, in the Hillier performance it is very audible, connecting passages 25 minutes apart and in effect reshaping the landscape of the entire piece. But this isn't a question of loss and gain so much as one of difference. The 1968 recording flirts with a *different* long-range connection that involves the pitches C5, F4, G4, and B4 spread among figures 6 and 8–13 early in the piece, and figures 30–34 later on. In the 1968 recording, figures 6 and 8 overlap for about 30 seconds, intermingling C with F and G and grounding a long-range connection with figures 30–31. Figures 6 and 9 (which adds the B) are a very near miss, only about two seconds apart. But in the Hillier, figures 6 and 8 are a near miss and figures 6 and 9, out of reach (about 90 seconds apart); the potential long-range connection between the passages described by figures 6–8 and figures 30–31 never materializes.

Example 7.8b supports a few more points about the passage that surrounds figure 30 in the Hillier. Like the plot for figures 6 and 7, this plot has a break in the texture at about 30′00″, where the voices collapse to a unison, then a bare pulse, before restarting figure 29, then 30. As with the plots for figures 6 and 7, the Hillier plot for figures 29–30 has fewer figures, and is more disjunct, higher profile, and more heterogeneous in design than its 1968 counterpart. Sometimes three figures are present, sometimes two, one, or none; sometimes two or three figures are equally strong (at the start, and just after the break); other times, one clearly dominates (e.g., figure 29 over figure 28 at 27′30″, and figure 30 over 29 around 29′00″).

The third and last of our landscape studies comes from earlier in the piece, and a set of plots defined by figures 19–21. Earlier I said that these figures can be taken to form an associative superset: each stands out as a single long note (G5 in figure 19, F♯4 in figure 21) in an environment dominated by short ones. But pitch content can easily dissolve this affinity in the much larger superset from figure 18 through figure 28. What does each performance do with this potential?

Example 7.9a maps a six-minute plot defined by figures 19–21 in the 1968 recording. Although timbre changes create occasional bright spots where one figure juts above the others (these being more fine-scaled than the map can show),

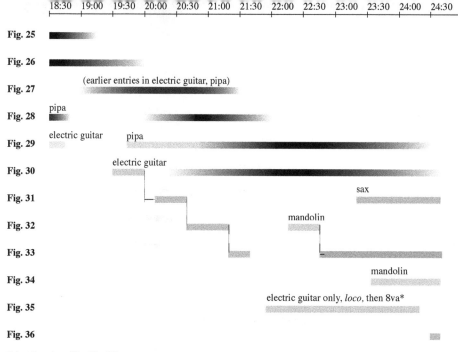

| | 18:30 | 19:00 | 19:30 | 20:00 | 20:30 | 21:00 | 21:30 | 22:00 | 22:30 | 23:00 | 23:30 | 24:00 | 24:30 |

Fig. 25

Fig. 26

(earlier entries in electric guitar, pipa)
Fig. 27

pipa
Fig. 28

electric guitar   pipa
Fig. 29

electric guitar
Fig. 30

sax
Fig. 31

mandolin
Fig. 32

Fig. 33

mandolin
Fig. 34

electric guitar only, *loco*, then 8va*
Fig. 35

Fig. 36

*electric guitar skips Fig. 34

Example 7.8a. Riley, *In C*, map of plot defined by figures 29–30, Bang on a Can

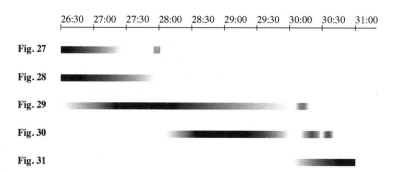

| | 26:30 | 27:00 | 27:30 | 28:00 | 28:30 | 29:00 | 29:30 | 30:00 | 30:30 | 31:00 |

Fig. 27

Fig. 28

Fig. 29

Fig. 30

Fig. 31

Example 7.8b. Riley, *In C*, map of plot defined by figures 29–30, Hillier/Ars Nova/Percurama

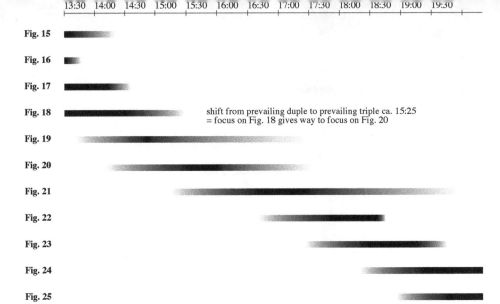

Example 7.9a. Riley, *In C*, map of plot defined by figures 19–21, 1968 Columbia recording

for the most part simultaneous figures are equally strong, and successive figures blend one into another in a series of almost imperceptible shifts of emphasis. (One of the most perceptible shifts is around 15′25″, about halfway through the passage, where the rhythm shifts from duple to triple groupings as figure 18 (a bar of 2/4) surrenders to figure 20 (a bar of 3/4), around the fulcrum of figure 19.) Although at any given point the landscape is materially diverse (four or five figures are usually present), overall it is beautifully homogeneous in design.

Example 7.9b shows the corresponding plot from the Bang on a Can performance. Here five or even six figures are active at any given time; the plot runs for 5½ minutes. But now the three figures 18, 19, and 21 are more prominent (represented by darker shading), at least for part of their duration, than any of the others. Also, the landscape is not so continuous as in the 1968 plot. Here figure 18 comes in two distinct patches, in electric guitar (before the plot begins) and double bass followed by the other instruments (10′45″). More importantly, the timing of successive figures' initial entries, and last exits, is much less regular than in the 1968 performance. Instead of the sinuous curve in the map of the 1968 plot, here the progress of entries and exits is uneven, creating jagged edges on the map.

Once again, Hillier does something else with the score. Example 7.9c maps out the corresponding plot, which covers only four minutes. Instead of the

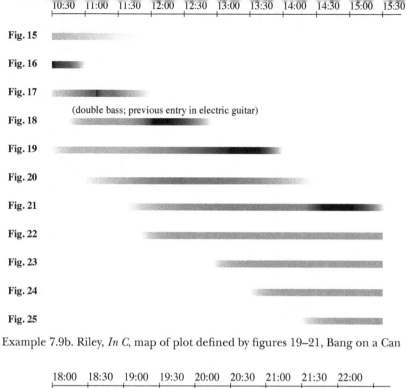

Example 7.9b. Riley, *In C*, map of plot defined by figures 19–21, Bang on a Can

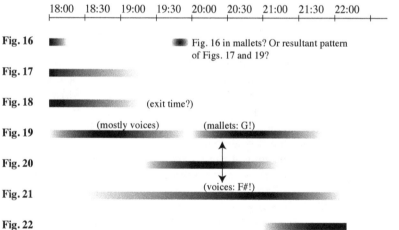

Example 7.9c. Riley, *In C*, map of plot defined by figures 19–21, Hillier/Ars Nova/ Percurama

mances, and the relatively homogeneous design of the earlier recording, the Hillier landscape sets fewer figures and sharper contrasts in a more fragmented and heterogeneous design. Here figures 17 and 18 fade out at about the same time, and just before figure 20 enters. Figure 19 has two discrete patches, associated with voices, then mallets. A particularly remarkable spot occurs shortly after 20′30″, where the durational affinity between figures 19 and 21 becomes the basis for a strident opposition between G and F♯, high and low registers, and mallets and voices. This conflict between G and F♯ is a focal point in the plot, unlike anything in the 1968, or even the Bang on a Can, plots. Instead of steady progress through a low-profile landscape, jagged start and end times and marked shifts from one figure to another make for a landscape of faults and folds. Whereas the landscape of the 1968 plot, and even to some extent Bang on a Can's, emerges quite directly from the characteristics of the figures themselves, Hillier shapes the plot from above, arranging the figures *into* a landscape that takes advantage of, rather than arises from, the individual figures and their associative organization.

Our three landscape studies have brought out some remarkable differences among individual performances of *In C* that serve to shape, and reshape, the piece at the largest scale. Whereas the 1968 recording is characterized by material heterogeneity and compositional homogeneity, the Hillier is more materially homogeneous and compositionally heterogeneous. Bang on a Can's performance falls somewhere in between, combining material heterogeneity with progressive change in landscape design. The three studies are also highly suggestive, as an approach to other compositions in which notated patterns are subject to indeterminacy in performance, as well as to music composed or organized by more traditional means. A distinguishing feature of our analysis has been the level, or levels, of organization of interest: above the segment, at the level of the associative set or superset as a unit (where the focus is on configuration and diversity), or even higher, at the level of the landscape, with a focus on the *interaction* and *arrangement* of materials, rather than the materials proper. This sort of higher-level analysis can be especially useful for minimalist music, where action is often slow and large-scale.

As I suggest toward the end of the chapter, for *In C* this kind of higher-level thinking can be used to support a critical assessment of individual performances with respect to a philosophy of the piece and score-performance relations. Is, or should, the higher-level landscape be but an emergent effect of a group's collective progress through the 53 figures in an engaged but interpretively neutral performance? Or is, or can, it be shaped from the top down by a more active interpretation of the score? As landscape studies help analysts identify just how performances of *In C* differ from one another at various scales of organization, they can provide a basis for new critical and philosophical discussion of the piece as musical form and culture.

Chapter Eight

Feldman, Palais de Mari

Pattern and Design in a Changing Landscape

Palais de Mari (1986) is Morton Feldman's last composition for piano solo and, at about twenty-five minutes, among the shortest of his late works.[1] Revoicings and changes of register, temporal flexing, and tones added and withdrawn create a music of glancing repetition and constant change in which individual figures, chords, and pairs of dyads embellished by grace notes intermingle and seep into resonant silences. With segmentation clearly defined by rests and near-repetition, attention naturally rises to higher levels of musical organization—to associative sets and populations, along with their global properties, internal configurations, and disposition in the landscape.[2] A focus on associative organization allows us to engage this music at the level and scale where activity unfolds, thereby incorporating and integrating its meticulous detail in a large-scale study of changes in pattern and design.

This chapter focuses on two contrasting landscapes: an opening passage from mm. 1–73 and an extended closing passage from mm. 287–437.[3] The former introduces six of the composition's seven primary associative sets in a heterogeneous associative landscape; the latter is an extended monologue on a single associative set in a more homogenous landscape. The two landscapes frame a course of change that encompasses the entire composition. Within each we will proceed roughly chronologically, pausing to examine the internal configuration, properties, or evolution of particular sets and aspects of landscape composition.

A theme of this chapter is the idea that our interpretations of individual segments and of associative organization at the level of the set and the landscape are dynamic and continuously renegotiable in response to changes in musical context. Two segments with the same notational image—what look on the page like literal repetitions—can sound quite different as changes in their musical contexts activate different relational properties.[4] Even the sound of a single segment—a notational image coupled with a specific temporal location in a score—can be transformed over time as the segment acquires new relational properties. At the next-higher level of organization, the associative set, every segment and contextual criterion that enters a set subtly (sometimes dramatically) alters the total web of relational properties in play, with effects that

boundaries between associative sets or subsets are themselves permeable and renegotiable. A progressive strengthening in the boundaries of two associative subsets can lead to associative fission, where one set becomes two. Conversely, formation of a bridge between two associative sets can radically reconfigure the associative landscape at the largest scale.

The Opening Passage: Measures 1–73

Comprising about one-sixth of the piece and bracketed by instances of the opening figure, the music from m. 1 to m. 73 introduces six associative sets *A–F*, each with different global properties and a characteristic distribution. We'll look first at the formation of sets *A–D* in mm. 1–34, then gradually expand the context under consideration to m. 51 and m. 73, noting changes in associative organization within and among sets along the way.

Example 8.1 provides a score for mm. 1–34. The piece begins with a porous patch of three segments related by literal or near-literal repetition, gently separated by bars of rest. With the damper pedal depressed virtually throughout *Palais*, each segment bleeds into the notated "rest" that follows; here, as throughout the piece, rests indicate not silence but the absence of new input as the preceding figure is absorbed into the resonant ground.[5] The opening figure has an unsettled quality, poised just off balance. A move up ten semitones from F4 to D♯5 is answered by one down eleven semitones from D♯5 to E4; this near-symmetry is skewed by its asymmetry with respect to the opening dyad <A♭4, F4>. Interval class content reinforces the sense of imbalance: with an interval-class vector of [211110], the figure's 4-4[0125] tetrachord is just shy of an all-interval set. Feldman's pitch realization <A♭4, F4, D♯5, E4> brings out five pitch intervals: pitch succession gives intervals 3, 10, and 11; the dyad <A♭4, D♯5> in the right hand gives interval 7; <F4, E4> in the left, interval 1. Pitch-class order suggests a contrast between two trichordal subsets: the first three notes (<A♭, F, D♯>) form a member of SC 3-7[025]; the last three, of SC 3-1[012]. The contrast between harmonies rich in ics 2 and 5, versus those rich in ic 1, resonates throughout the piece.

The segments in mm. 1, 3, and 5 are the seeds of an associative set *A* that appears sporadically through the first third of the composition. Set *A* is modest in size, with six distinct notational images (twelve actual segments) that exhibit a relatively small range of variation in pitch and rhythm. Example 8.2 organizes the six notational images of set *A* into an association graph; individual segments are named by set and measure number as in the 1995 typeset score.[6] Literal repetition forms two very strong associative subsets represented by the clusters of segment names attached to two notational images

Example 8.1. Feldman, *Palais de Mari*, mm. 1–34

in the second row (*A*1, *A*5, *A*76, *A*172, *A*174; and *A*74, *A*176, *A*178). Boxes indicate five somewhat weaker associative subsets, which recognize partial orderings in pitch (horizontal boxes) and total orderings in pitch-class, pitch interval, or attack rhythm (vertical boxes).

The perpendicular orientation of subsets in the graph represents an important aspect of set *A*'s internal organization: the six notational images in set *A* can be partitioned either by pitch content *or* by pc ordering and attack rhythm, but these partitions (and their perceptual counterparts) cut across rather than reinforce one another.[7] As usual, the measure numbers encoded in segment

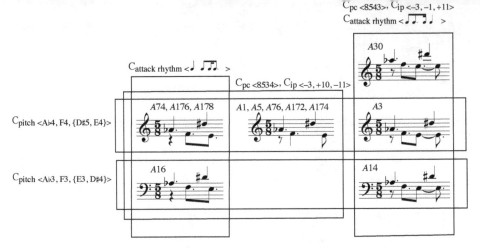

Example 8.2. Six notational images and twelve segments of an associative set A

names also convey information about set disposition. They indicate that set A unfolds in five porous patches (mm. 1–5, 14–16, 30, 74–76, and 172–78) dispersed across the first half of the composition at increasing distances; each of these five patches is comprised of segments from a single subset of A.

Example 8.3 reconstructs the configuration of segments depicted in example 8.2 as a series of five subgraphs that trace the evolution of set A through its five patches.[8] Each node in the graph represents one of the six distinct notational images in set A, laid out as before; names of individual segments are abbreviated to measure numbers given as arabic numerals; arrows on each successive subgraph trace a path (or set of paths) that represent score chronology. The graph indicates that set A begins with a circuit between two notational images with the same pitch content ($A1$–$A5$ and $A3$). The second patch begins in m. 14; it too introduces two new notational images associated by pitch content. The evolution of the entire graph shows that each of the first four patches begins by introducing a new node (a new notational image) and contains one to three new nodes. Having exhausted the six nodes, the fifth patch returns to the node of origin ($A1 = A172$) and closes with the last node introduced ($A178$). The horizontal alignment of components within each subgraph shows that temporal proximity privileges associative subsets based on pitch repetition over those based on repeated attack rhythm.[9] Clustering of arabic numerals in the second row of the fifth and final subgraph also identifies the C4–B4 octave as the primary register for set A, taking in its opening, central, and closing patches.

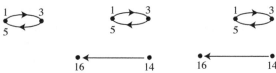

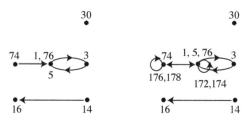

Example 8.3. Evolution of set *A* in five patches

After the porous patch of set *A* in mm. 1–5, a new figure enters in m. 7 (refer back to ex. 8.1). This figure has four consociates in mm. 8, 10, 11, and 12. Partitioning pitches between the hands gives {D5} plus {D♯5, E5}; temporal order gives {D5, E5}, {D5, D♯5}. Three threads of association connect m. 7 to set *A* in mm. 1–5. Partitioning *A*1 and *A*3 (mm. 1 and 3, respectively) as the dyads <A♭4, D♯5> and <F4, E4> in right and left hands prompts the observation that the right hand in m. 7 also ends on D♯5. Repartitioning m. 1 as the dyads <A♭4, F4>, <D♯5, E4> defined by temporal order and adjacency leads one to notice that the second dyad, pcs {D♯, E}, returns in the right hand in m. 7, its pcs reversed, <E, D♯>. Rehearing m. 1 a third way, as an isolated note (A♭) followed by the SC 3-1[012] pcset {D♯, E, F} that converges on E, brings out a related feature of m. 7, where D5 initiates a different pcset from SC 3-1[012], {D, D♯, E}, that converges on D♯. With only mm. 1–12 as context, all three observations support the view that the material in mm. 7–12 is a peripheral extension of set *A*.

In m. 14, a sudden register shift marks the return of set *A* an octave lower than before. This sets mm. 7–12 in relief as contrasting material and prompts reconsideration of the relation between mm. 1–5 and mm. 7–12. Whereas set *A* will return three more times in the piece, the material in mm. 7–12 never does; it is purely local. Even locally, the two sets have different properties: whereas set *A* comes in porous patches and has a range of variation, set *B* has dense patches and is uniform (Feldman's autograph has repeat signs for mm. 7–8

ferences suggest a revised interpretation in which the five segments in mm. 7–12 form a set B that is tangential to, but distinct from, set A.

Following the second patch of set A in mm. 14–16, an expansion into the high and low registers accompanies the entry of two new figures in m. 18 and m. 20 (see ex. 8.1). Each is a pair of dyadic simultaneities with an emphasis on interval classes 2 and 5. Partitioning m. 18 by right and left hand, and high and low register, gives the ics $\frac{4}{1}$; partitioning into the two successive simultaneities gives ics 2|5. Partitioning m. 20 by hand and simultaneity gives $\frac{2}{2}$ and 5|5, respectively. The two pcsets {G, A♭, B♭, D} (a member of SC 4-29[0137]) and {B♭, C, F, G} (SC 4-23[0257]) share two tones, G and B♭, which appear here for the first time. Associated with one another and dissociated from sets A and B by C_{ic} and C_{pc} criteria as well as by texture, the two figures in m. 18 and m. 20 launch an associative set C. Over the course of the piece, set C becomes more widespread than A (its segments are dispersed from m. 18 to m. 285) but, like set A, its segments are also relatively infrequent (24 segments altogether) and come in minimal-to-small patches of 1–3 segments that are unevenly distributed in the landscape.[10] Additional segments in mm. 22, 25–26, 28–29, and 32 retroactively cast the figures in m. 18 and m. 20 as the seeds of two subsets C/a and C/b, each with a range of variation in pitch register and pc order. C/a forms first, with the downward octave transposition of C/a18 in C/a22. But C/b ultimately proves the larger, more widespread, and more varied subset that includes distillations (C/b25–6) and suffixes (C/b28–9), as well as changes in register and order.

A look at Feldman's autograph reveals an interesting feature of the associative landscape to this point. Like many of Feldman's late manuscripts, the autograph for *Palais* has some visual symmetries and patterns that suggest a graphic approach to temporal disposition: page layout seems to have exerted at least an occasional influence on the disposition and progress of musical material.[11] So in addition to associative sets and landscape composition, page and system boundaries in Feldman's autograph can suggest a series of plots to consider in a landscape study.

Page layout in the autograph is uniform: there are eight pages, five systems per page and nine bars per system, for a total of 360 notated measures. The prominent placement of new material at the top of a few pages and start of systems suggests at least an intermittent concern with layout in the compositional process. Unfortunately, the visual rhythm and layout of the autograph is largely lost in the typeset edition, with its nine pages, seven systems per page (six on page one), and five to nine bars per system (usually six to eight). Whereas Feldman indicates repetitions with repeat signs, the typeset edition writes out all repeats, increasing the number of notated measures from 360 to 437. Example 8.4 cross-references pages of the autograph with measures in the typeset score.

Replicating the layout of Feldman's autograph, example 8.5 provides an association map for sets A, B, and C in plots I/1 and I/2, the first two system

Plot (= page in autograph)	Measures (in typeset edition)
I	1–48
II	49–96
III	97–141
IV	142–90
V	191–239
VI	240–86
VII	287–351
VIII	352–437

Example 8.4. Feldman, *Palais de Mari*, plots I–VIII

plots of *Palais* (roman numerals indicate pages in Feldman's original; arabic numerals, his systems). Like the autograph, the map is laid out on a uniform grid in which every measure is the same width and odd-versus-even bars of successive systems spread down the page in a checkerboard pattern. Five segments occupy the odd-numbered bars of plot I/1. The move from an initial patch of set *A* followed by set *B* is a straightforward example of associative monophony. Plot I/2 has the same basic structure as plot I/1 but this time four segments fill the system's even-numbered bars, with *A*14 and *A*16 nestling in the white spaces below and between *A*1, *A*3, and *A*5. Once again, a patch of set *A* is followed by a patch of a contrasting set, here the seeds of subsets *C/a* and *C/b*. Interestingly, sets *B* and *C* explore different harmonic subsets of *A*1: set *B* zeros in on the SC 3-1[012] embedded as the last three tones of *A*1; set *C* brings out the ics 2 and 5 embedded in the SC 3-7[025] formed by *A*1's first three tones. Associative organization in both plots is high profile.

The new spaciousness of set *C* mysteriously evaporates in m. 24 as the tetrachord {G♮4, A♮4, D♯5, A♭5} settles into what is roughly the opening register. With the lull in surface rhythm, the listener has plenty of time to contemplate this curious sonority. Although the harmony (SC 4-5[0126]) and texture (tetrachordal simultaneity in whole notes) are new, the chord has subtle ties to all three associative sets in play: the pcs A♭ and D♯, and pitch D♯5, recall set *A*; the embedded SC 3-1[012] trichord forms a weaker link to set *B*; and partitioning of ics by hand ($\frac{5}{2}$), ties to set *C*. Suspended somewhere between sets *A*, *B*, and *C*, the segment in m. 24 is an unusual example of a local anticontextuality in which three lines of association are available, but none is decisive; all are tempered by sonic disjunctions in register and duration. Located inside a larger patch of set *C*, this tetrachord remains an anomaly until m. 34, where the same four pcs return but with three of the four notes in new registers and ics 5 and 2 exchanged between the hands ($\frac{2}{5}$). As m. 34 activates the strong criterion $C_{\text{pc }\{G♮, A♮, A♭, D♯\}}$ that binds m. 24 to m. 34 to form a new set *D*, the weaker ties

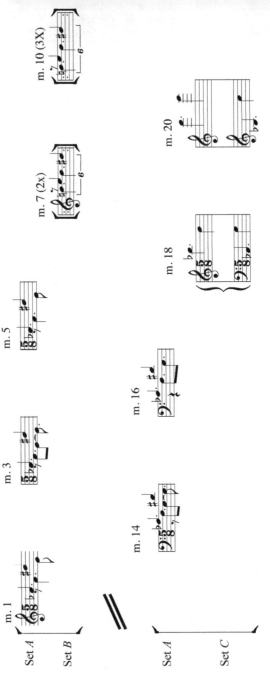

Example 8.5. Feldman, *Palais de Mari*, map of plots I/1 and I/2 (mm. 1–10 and 11–21)

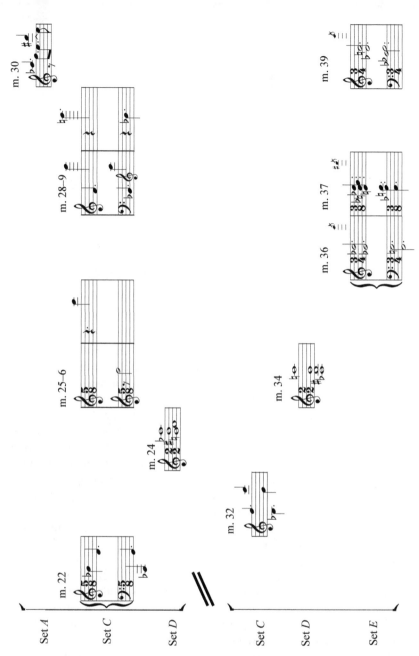

Example 8.6. Feldman, *Palais de Mari*, map of plots I/3 and I/4 (mm. 22–30 and 31–39)

Example 8.7. Feldman, *Palais de Mari*, mm. 36–51

between m. 24 and sets *A, B,* and *C* effectively dissolve. Over the course of the piece, set *D* acquires three distinct notated segments (in mm. 24, 34, and 97) and eleven actual segments (from m. 24 to m. 256). All but two of its segments are in minimal patches, with these unevenly distributed in the landscape.

Example 8.6 continues our study of the opening landscape through plots I/3 and I/4, which each involve three associative sets. Sets are now unevenly distributed within each plot, and successive plots are no longer parallel in construction. Still, one aspect of the associative organization remains constant: all four plots exhibit high profile associative organization. That is about to change.

A shift in register and move to denser sonorities mark the start of a new passage in m. 36, in which a mobile series of interrelated harmonies is overlaid with a thread of grace notes. Example 8.7 provides a score for mm. 36–51. The passage is based on five chords defined by pitch content, loosely bound together by pitch and pc repetition into an associative set *E*. The chords are introduced in mm. 36–43, then reordered and subject to temporal flexing in mm. 44–51 to make a larger patch of eleven actual segments. Repetition of pitch content establishes each of the five chords as the seed of an associative subset *E/a–E/e*.[12] Each subset acquires additional segments in the patches of set *E* found in mm. 55–61, 68–71, and beyond.

Set *E* has a wider range of variation than any of the sets *A–D*. Four of the five chords represent different set classes (although each embeds a member of SC

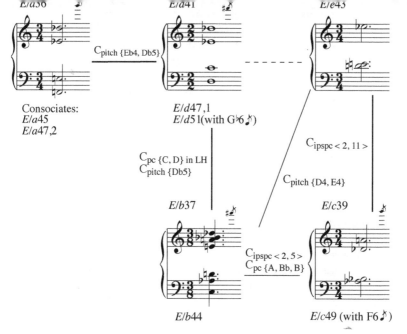

Example 8.8. Association graph of seed segments for E/a–E/e, mm. 36–43

3-1[012]) and pc distribution across the aggregate is uneven (pcs 1–4 and 8–A occur three or more times each; pcs 6, 7, and B are excluded from the chords, but 6 and 7 do appear as grace notes). Over time, set E adds five more subsets, E/f–E/j, that form around seed segments in mm. 71, 88, and 94 (again emphasizing pcs 1–4 and 8–A, and recalling the chords in mm. 36–43 in other ways) and, at greater associative remove, the two chords in mm. 230–31 that are a persistent, if intermittent, presence in last part of the composition. The ten resulting subsets E/a–E/j exhibit varying degrees of associative proximity and distance from one another.

Example 8.8 represents an associative configuration of segments E/a36–E/e43 based only on C_{pitch} and C_{pc} criteria, not the segments' actual temporal order in the music (which we will look at in a moment). As usual, heavier lines represent stronger associations; lighter or dotted lines, weaker ones. Consociate segments with the same (or nearly identical) notational image are listed below four of the five segments. The strongest associations follow the edges E/a36–E/d41 (two common tones in the right hand, E♭4 and D♭5), E/b37–E/d41 (pcs C and D exchange registers in the left hand; D♭5 remains in the right), and E/c39–E/e43 (the pitch interval spacing <2, 11> is preserved as the trichord {A♭3, B♭3, A♮4} in E/c39 moves to {D♮4, E♮4, E♭5} in E/e43 by T_{+6}).

adjacent in the music. The weaker connection between $E/b37$ and $E/e43$ by $C_{\text{pitch }\{D\natural 4,\,E\natural 4\}}$ is also subverted by temporal distance.

When the five chords are reordered in the second part of the patch and in the next patch of E (mm. 55–61), associative and temporal proximity come into closer alignment. Measure numbers encoded in the names of consociate segments allow us to trace this process on the same graph. Temporal adjacency between $E/e43$ and $E/b44$ articulates the association by $C_{\text{pitch }\{D\natural 4,\,E\natural 4\}}$ previously suppressed by temporal distance between $E/b37$ and $E/e43$. Associative proximity between the subsets E/a and E/d by virtue of the repeated pitches $E\flat 4$ and $D\flat 5$ also becomes easily audible through the temporal adjacency $E/d47,1{\sim}E/a47,2$. (Here and throughout this chapter I use "~" to represent a temporal adjacency in the score, as opposed to "–" which indicates associative proximity represented by an edge in a graph.) Most interesting is the progressive foregrounding of associative proximity between subsets E/b and E/d created by register exchange of C and D in the left hand. At first, segments $E/b37$ and $E/d41$ are separated by a contrasting chord (in m. 39). Next, the two subsets are associated by their analogous placement as the penultimate chord in a repeated cadential gesture ($E/b44$ and $E/d47,1$). When this cadential gesture returns in mm. 55–59, the associative adjacency by register exchange of C and D is expressed in the temporal adjacency of $E/b55{\sim}E/d57,1$.

Associations among the five chords that seed subsets E/a–E/e are only part of the picture. Voice leading, octave transfers, and pitch transformations provide a complementary perspective on local coherence and process in mm. 36–51. The temporal adjacency $E/e43{\sim}E/b44$, for example, melds an association by $C_{\text{pitch }\{D\natural 4,\,E\natural 4\}}$ with a stepwise descent from $E\flat 5$ to $D\flat 5$ in the top voice and an influx of four new tones with no proximate voice-leading counterparts. As $E/b44$ moves to $E/a45$, the top voice retains $D\flat 5$ as a common tone, while an inner voice slips a semitone from $E\natural 4$ to $E\flat 4$. The other five tones in $E/b44$ have no proximate counterparts in $E/a45$: they simply vanish.

Along with association, voice leading, and transformation, subtle but persistent recontextualization is an important feature of the passage from mm. 36–51. When the five chords introduced as $E/a36$–$E/e43$ are reordered in mm. 44–51, the musical context for each chord changes: the segments that directly precede and follow a particular segment activate some relational properties more than others, drawing attention to certain tones in the notational image the segment shares with other segments. Thus within each of the subsets E/a–E/e, individual segments are *not* identical but only synonymous; each segment has its own characteristic tint. Example 8.9 illustrates the recontextualization of notational images that effects these subtle changes in chord color with four segments from subset E/b, in mm. 37, 44, 102, and 168. Each is preceded by a segment from a different subset of E—E/a, E/e, E/d, and E/c, respectively. Approaching $E/b37$ from $E/a36$ draws attention to the two tones $D\flat 5$ and $E\natural 4$ that participate in common tone or semitone (T_{+1}) voice leading. These focal

line arrows labeled with transformations, voice-leading motions. Coming from $E/e43$ also brings out D♭5 and E♮4 (E♮4 is now a common tone) in $E/b44$, but adds a third pitch, D♮4. Going from $E/d102,1$ to $E/b102,2$ once again brings out D♭5 and E♮4, but the latter recedes in comparison to two new focal tones, the C and D reached by register exchange in the left hand. Finally, the move from $E/c166$ to $E/b168$ primes and highlights two pitches not emphasized in any of the other contexts: A♭3 and A♮4. Rendered phenomenally distinct by these subtle differences in color, each of the four consociate segments $E/b37$, $E/b44$, $E/b102,2$, and $E/b168$ that shares the same notational image occupies a slightly different place in the piece's associative organization.

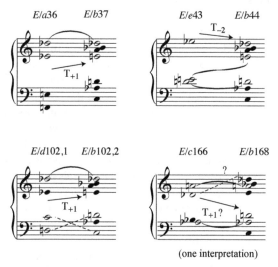

(one interpretation)

Example 8.9. Recontextualization of the notes of $E/b37$ in three consociates

Along with changes in set material, the passage in mm. 36–51 brings an important shift in associative organization. Whereas the landscape in mm. 1–34 is high profile, with four sets in associative monophony or polyphony at various scales, that in mm. 36–51 is low profile, based on one set (E) with five distinct subsets ($E/a–E/e$), each with a range of internal variation brought about by recontextualization. Continuing to m. 73, the landscape regains some of its earlier diversity and clarity. Segments from sets C and D are reintroduced and interspersed with those of set E and with what turn out to be two peripheral segments of a new set F (in m. 66 and mm. 72–73), characterized by a short attack in the left hand and one or more sustained tones in the right over a change of pedal.[13]

Surveying mm. 1–73 as a single plot encourages a review of the global properties and distributions of sets E and F and comparison with those described above for sets $A–D$. Once set E appears, its segments are fairly common,

porous. In contrast, the segments of set F are rare, distributed in dispersed minimal patches. The distribution of set F resembles that of set D, but its segments come much later in the plot. As always, observations about distribution depend on the plot chosen, but it turns out that distribution patterns established for sets A–F in these bars do hold up over the piece as a whole.

The Closing Passage: Measures 287–437

By m. 73, six of the seven primary associative sets in *Palais* have entered the landscape. Segments of the final set, G, first appear in mm. 123–31, but these turn out to be peripheral rather than central segments of G (like set F, set G evolves from periphery to center). For the heart of set G, we must go all the way to m. 287, the start of the extended closing passage that accounts for more than a third of the composition. It is here that the associative organization of set G becomes clearer, then more complex, and that set G becomes a dominant, rather than only an intermittent, presence in the landscape.

Literal and varied repetition within the extended closing passage (mm. 287–437) suggests grouping the segments of G into three associative subsets, G/a, G/b, and G/c. Example 8.10 shows a central segment of each, $G/a287$–88, $G/b332$–34, and $G/c384$–86, respectively. Each segment is two or three measures long, with two or three one-bar subsegments. As before, pairs of numerals separated by a horizontal line above the staff represent the ics of melodic intervals between long notes within the right and left hands; numerals separated by a vertical line below the staff represent harmonic intervals between the hands. The trichord type for each bar is also shown. Segments of all three subsets begin with an ascent of a minor third between two long notes in the right hand; each note is prefixed by a grace note ten or eleven semitones below. In contradistinction to the core criteria for sets A–F, these attributes suffice to join the various segments of subsets G/a, G/b, and G/c into a single higher-level set G. Segments of the three subsets differ in length, pc content in the right hand, tones supplied by the left hand, and harmonic content. The first segment of G/b (in mm. 332–34) starts out as a pitch transposition of $G/a326$–27 by T_{+1}, but with a different left hand component (and harmonic content), plus a third subsegment. Excepting the first long note in the left hand, the first segment of G/c, in mm. 384–86, is a pitch-class transposition of $G/b332$–34 by T_B.[14] This transposition restores the melodic pcs C and E♭ found in segments of G/a, but retains the set-class of the second and third subsegments of G/b.

Whereas associations among these three representatives of subsets G/a, G/b, and G/c suggest that segments of G/a are relatively central within set G, the associative configuration for the range of variation within subset G/a places segment $G/a287$–88 at the center of G/a. Its closest consociates are $G/a315$–16 and $G/a326$–27 (and their immediate repetitions $G/a317$–18 and $G/a328$–29), as well

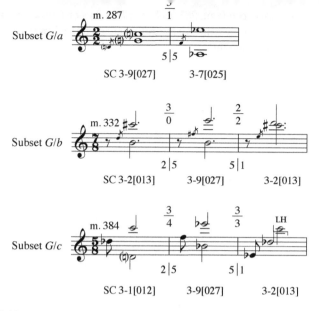

Example 8.10. Representative segments of three associative subsets *G/a*, *G/b*, and *G/c*

as the four segments in mm. 430–37 that bring *Palais* to a close. Other close consociates are *G/a*299–300 (transposed by T_{+1}), *G/a*376–77 (at pitch-class T_1, with the right hand moved an octave higher), and *G/a*354–55 (also at pc T_1, but with one note displaced by octave and the order of the two subsegments reversed).

However, as noted earlier, *G/a*287–88 is not the first segment of *G/a* that appears. Example 8.11 shows four peripheral segments of *G/a* from mm. 123–31. Their nine constituent one-measure subsegments form population **G1**. Example 8.12a brackets three features of *G/a*287–88 subject to literal and varied repetition among the three segments and nine subsegments of **G1**: two grace note leaps from D to C, and F to E♭, and the falling seventh from G to A♭. Example 8.12b is a (disconnected) association graph of the right-hand components of **G1**'s nine subsegments. Example 8.12c adds the left hand. In this composite graph, right- and left-hand components, here shown as nodes, in effect function as contextual criteria; dotted lines with measure numbers represent the nine segments in population **G1**.[15] Scattering of consecutive measure numbers around the graph reflects the free and relatively unpredictable associative organization of **G1** that results from variation, recombination, and reordering of a few functionally independent right and left hand components. Associative adjacencies inevitably involve *left*-hand components (e.g., mm. 123 and 124; mm. 130 and 131), while affiliations in the right hand operate at greater associative or temporal remove (e.g., mm. 127 and 128; mm. 129 and 131). The improvisatory associative organization of **G1** recurs in two

profile patches of *G/a* precede m. 287. In fact, *all* patches of *G/a* before m. 287 are low profile; afterward, they are only high profile, characterized by strong segments with clear ties to other segments.

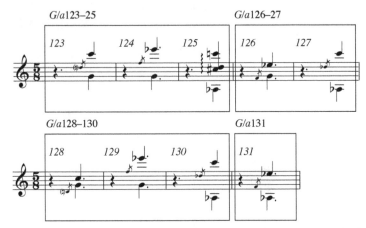

Example 8.11. Nine subsegments of population **G1** and four segments of subset *G/a*, mm. 123–31

Example 8.12a. Right and left hand components of *G/a*, mm. 287–88. Feldman, *Palais de Mari.*

Example 8.12b. Graph of right hand components in population **G1**, mm. 123–31

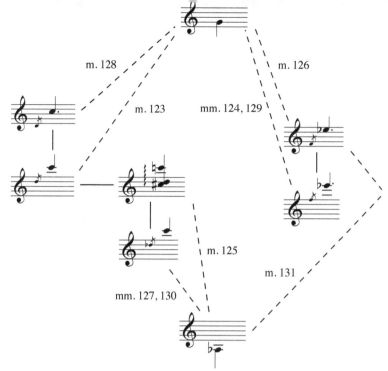

Example 8.12c. Composite graph of right and left hand associations in *G1*, mm. 123–31

This shift from low- to high-profile organization for patches of *G/a* at m. 287 is part of a bigger picture. Coincident with the appearance of *G/a*287–88, the central segment of *G/a* (and arguably also of set *G*), this shift signals an important change in associative organization at the largest scale—over the piece as a whole. From m. 74 through the end of plot VI in m. 286, the associative landscape is fairly diverse. Segments of set *E* prevail, with a sprinkling of minimal patches of sets *C* and *D*, small patches of sets *A* and *F*, and several simple or compound low-profile patches of set *G*. Example 8.13 maps out plots VI/3–5. As in much of the piece to this point, both set rhythm and segment rhythm (given by changes in meter and duration) are irregular. Set turnover is rapid through plot VI/3, but slows in plots VI/4 and VI/5. At the start of plot VII/1 in m. 287, Feldman restructures the associative landscape. Example 8.14 maps out plots VII/1 and VII/2. Plot VII/1 begins with *G/a*287–88 and its literal repetition as the first of three four-bar groupings or "limbs" in mm. 287–90, mm. 291–94, and mm. 295–98 (bracketed and labeled with roman numerals I, II, and III, respectively),

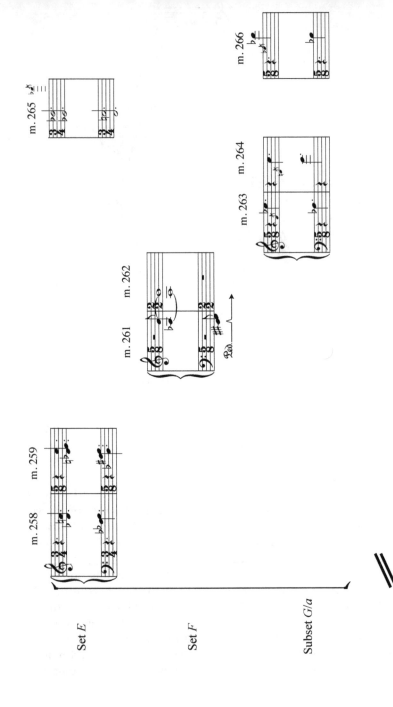

Example 8.13. Feldman, *Palais de Mari*, map of plots VI/3, VI/4, and VI/5 (mm. 258–66, 267–77, and 278–86)

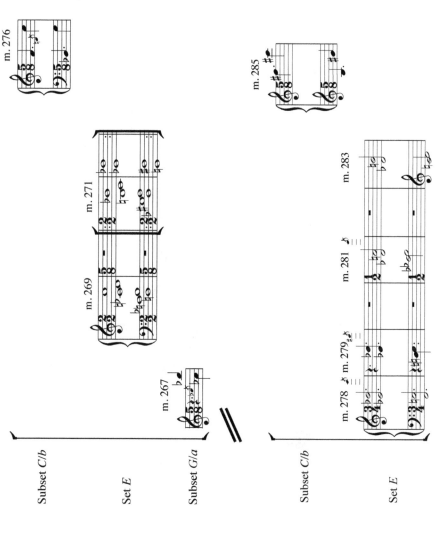

Example 8.13. Feldman, *Palais de Mari*, map of plots VI/3, VI/4, and VI/5 (mm. 258–66, 267–77, and 278–86)—*(concluded)*

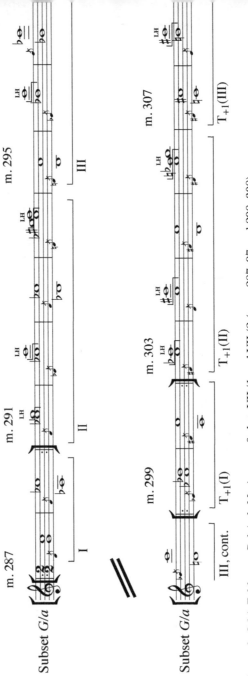

Example 8.14. Feldman, *Palais de Mari*, map of plots VII/1 and VII/2 (mm. 287–97 and 298–308)

ity of plots VI/3–5, where sets *C*, *E*, *F*, and *G* were all active, is replaced by a much more homogeneous landscape based only on segments of subset *G/a*. The six four-bar limbs that make up plots VII/1–2 suddenly render set rhythm absolutely regular, with a change every four bars. Fixed by the 2/2 meter and a stream of whole notes, segment rhythm also becomes regular for the first time in the entire composition. Another textural change occurs over the plot boundary at m. 287: the alternation of sounding segments and notated rests heard at the end of plot VI (which recalls a pattern found throughout plot I and much of plot II) ends when plot VII begins; now every bar brings a new sounding segment.

The synchronization of these changes in the associative landscape marks the start of plot VII—and the appearance of the segment *G/a*287–88— as an important event in the large-scale form. We have already considered *G/a*287–88's centrality in the associative configuration of *G/a* and the larger set *G*. The formal emphasis on m. 287 suggests there may be more at stake. It turns out that we can trace the origins of *G/a*287–88 to material at a greater associative remove.

Example 8.15 shows two interpretations of segment *A*1: a "voice-leading" partition of interval classes $\frac{5}{1}$ defined by the hands, and a "temporal succession" partition into two dyads of ics 3|1. Segment *G/a*287–88 reconfigures the basic intervallic material in *A*1, turning its successive pitch intervals (ics 3 and 1, pitch intervals 3 and 11) into voice leading within each hand while rearranging the pcs A♭ and D♯/E♭ from the right hand of *A*1 to form the second harmonic dyad of *G/a*287–88. Example 8.16 shows the reconfiguration of ics 3 and 1, which form a member of SC 4-4[0125] in segment *A*1, to create one of SC 4-20[0158] (whole notes) in *G/a*287–88. But *G/a*287–88 has a second stream of precursors—segments of subset *C/b*. Like *G/a*287–88, *C/b*20 partitions into two successive dyads of ic 5|5. Whereas in *C/b*20 these join to form a member of SC 4-23[0257], in *G/a*287–88 they form one of SC 4-20[0158]. Two critical changes in segment *C/b*54 lay the foundation for a bridge from subset

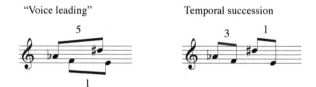

"Voice leading"	Temporal succession

Reconfiguring ics . . . can produce SCs:

ics 5+1 = 4-4[0125], 4-6[0127],   ics 3+1 = 4-1[0123], 4-4[0125],
4-10[0235], 4-14[0237],   4-13[0136], 4-18[0147],
4-17[0347]   4-20[0158]

Example 8.15. Two dyadic interpretations of the figure in m. 1

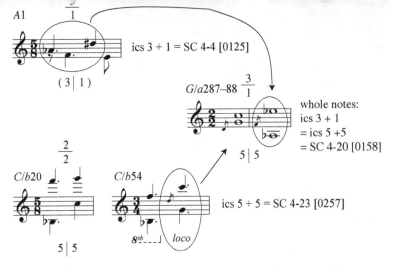

Example 8.16. Dyadic reconfiguration in associative conflux at m. 287, sets *A* and *C*

C/b to *G/a*: first, a grace note D is added; second, realization of the second ic 5 changes from a fifth (actually a twelfth) to a fourth (eleventh). Both features are typical of subsequent segments of *C/b*, and reappear shortly before m. 287, at the end of plot VI/4 in *C/b*276.

The arrival of *G/a*287–88, then, is the keystone in a remarkable conflu-ence of events. First, it defines the center of subset *G/a*, and also of set *G*. Sec-ond, it forms a bridge to set *A*, recalling and rearranging intervals and key pcs of *A*1. Third, it forms a second, stronger bridge to set *C*, through segment *C/b*276 with which it shares the grace note D♮4 moving to C♮5 in the right hand over a G♮ in the left. The end result is a large-scale associative conflux via set *G* between sets *A* and *C*—two sets that clearly represent *contrasting* mate-rial at the start of *Palais*. The critical node, *G/a*287–88, comes quite late in the composite evolution of sets *A*, *C*, and *G*—long after the last segment with sole allegiance to set *A* appears in m. 178 and first segments of *G* in mm. 123–31, and even after the last segment tied only to subset *C/b* in m. 285. The result is a radical reconfiguration of associative organization for the entire composition at mm. 287–88. As *G/a*287–88 claims the center of subset *G/a*, it suddenly con-nects what had been three separate association graphs for sets *A*, *C*, and *G* into a single large graph with three well-defined subgraphs. Thus the synchronized and unprecedented changes in set materials and landscape design at the start of plot VII take on an articulative role, drawing attention to *G/a*287–88 as a critical segment in the piece's large-scale form, as conceived in terms of asso-ciative organization.

sity. Example 8.17 maps out plots VII/3–5. Subset G/a prevails in plots VII/3–4, with a varied repetition and partial retrograde of material from limbs I–III flanked by brief visits from set E in mm. 311–12 and set F in mm. 330–31. Moving into plot VII/5, subset G/b appears and begins to develop its own range of variation, interspersed with segments of G/a and E. From here on, the landscape materials and composition become progressively more heterogeneous, reaching a point of maximum diversity and fragmentation in plot VIII/4 (ex. 8.18). The final plot, VIII/5, reverses this trend, recreating the relatively uniform landscape of plot VII/1–2 to round out the extended closing section.

Whereas score chronology is an essential part of our landscape study, a quick survey of the sets' global properties and distribution from a quasi-temporal perspective (temporal but nonchronological) is also illuminating. Example 8.19 uses a combination of image attributes and two spatial dimensions to place each of the seven sets A–G in a four-dimensional global property space that represents their relative size, range of variation, patch size, and scale of activity. Circle diameter indicates set size, counting actual segments rather than notational images.[16] The shading gradient represents the range of variation in a set. No gradient (the crisp, black edge for set B) indicates a uniform set; the fuzzier the edges and wider the gray scale (sets E and especially G), the wider the range of variation. Placement along the horizontal axis represents scale of activity: highly localized, set B appears far to the left, while the three widespread sets E, F, and G cluster at the right. Although scale of activity is distinct from chronology, the graph suggests a fairly strong correlation between them: for example, the local set B comes very early in the composition, while those sets that are active at the largest scale (sets E, F, and G) enter last. Placement along the vertical axis represents average patch size: sets D and F, which come in minimal patches, hug the bottom of the graph, while set G, which has the largest patches, rises to the top.

Although this graphic representation is approximate, it is precise enough to bring out some aspects of associative organization that shape the landscape overall. First, the seven sets A–G cover a spectrum of ranges of variation, from the uniform set B, to fairly uniform set F, to significant variation in sets A, C, and D, and substantial variation in sets E and G. Sets with the widest range of variation—E and G—are also the largest sets and form the largest patches. (This correlation is not inviolable: set A has smaller patches than B, but it is active over a larger scale.) Even on a first hearing of the piece, it is clear that set G dominates the landscape after m. 287. But the fact that sets G and E are similar in size, range of variation, patch size, and scale is masked by differences in the two sets' temporal realization. Where set G predominates (after m. 287), the landscape is high profile; where set E prevails (e.g., mm. 36–51), it is low profile. Temporal adjacency reinforces segment associations within the subsets G/a, G/b, and G/c, but temporal distance and changes in musical context tend to dilute associations

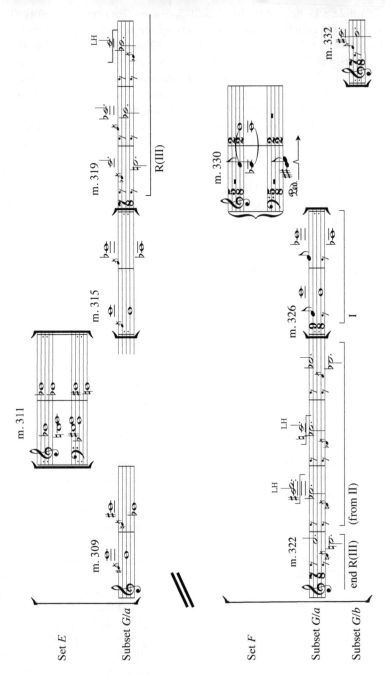

Example 8.17. Feldman, *Palais de Mari*, map of plots VII/3, VII/4, and VII/5 (mm. 309–21, 322–32, and 333–51)

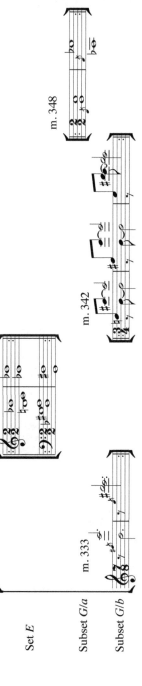

Example 8.17. Feldman, *Palais de Mari*, map of plots VII/3, VII/4, and VII/5 (mm. 309–21, 322–32, and 333–51)—*(concluded)*

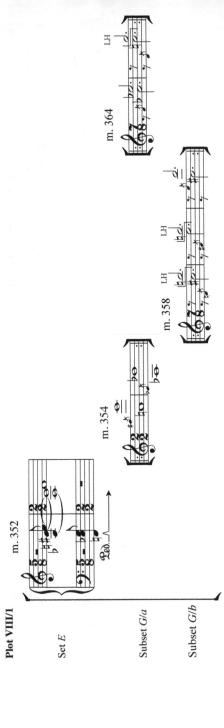

Example 8.18. Feldman, *Palais de Mari*, map of plots VIII/1–5 (mm. 352–437)

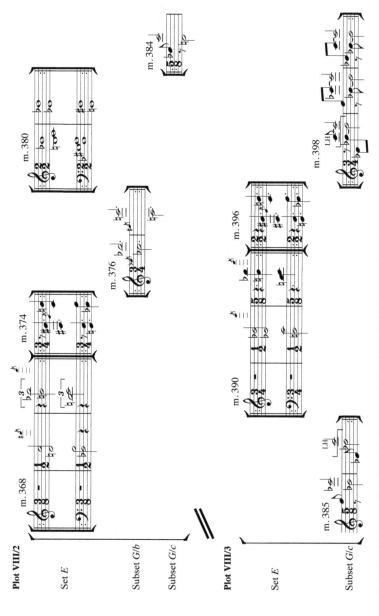

Example 8.18. Feldman, *Palais de Mari*, map of plots VIII/1–5 (mm. 352–437)—*(continued)*

Example 8.18. Feldman, *Palais de Mari*, map of plots VIII/1–5 (mm. 352–437)—*(concluded)*

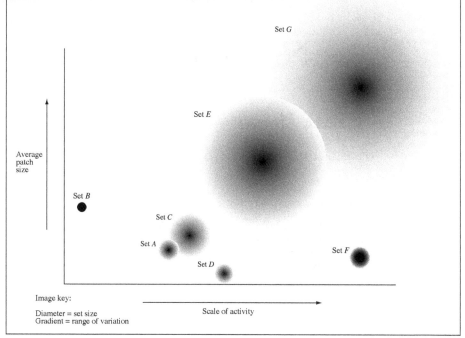

Set G

Set E

Average
patch
size

Set B

Set C

Set A

Set D

Set F

Image key:

Diameter = set size
Gradient = range of variation

Scale of activity

Example 8.19. Global properties of sets *A–G*

among segments of the subsets *E/a–E/e*. Temporal placement also has a critical effect for set *A*: its privileged placement in m. 1 and as the first set to return (m. 14) makes it far more important for the form overall than a look at only its global properties and aggregate distribution would suggest.

As a large composition that is through-composed, *Palais* resists traditional approaches to musical form. And yet aspects of form and formation are easily heard, from its clear segments, to their organization into a fairly small number of associative sets, to the sets' different habits of presentation, evolution, change, recollection, and disposition in the landscape. With a bottom-up approach to musical form focused on segments and associative organization, analysts can venture into the unique form of *Palais*—its structured plots, contrasts between low- and high-profile associative organization, and the radical reconfiguration of the associative landscape that occurs at m. 287 with the confluence of sets *A* and *C*. Approaching the piece with a flexible language and few assumptions allows us to explore form as the intermingling of diverse musical materials and change rather than as sectionalization, as particularity rather than convention.

Chapter Nine

Morris, Nine Piano Pieces

Between Moment and Memory— Reflections on and among the Nine

Robert Morris's *Nine Piano Pieces* (1999) is an album of moods and characters that develops a rich harmonic language from a single melodic structure—a thirty-five-note string of thirty-four pc intervals subject to transformation by transposition, inversion, or retrograde.[1] The *Nine Piano Pieces* date from August to early November 1999. The longest piece, "Rising Early," came first; Morris then extracted and reworked the central part of its structure to create the array for a second piece, "Between."[2] Over the next two months, seven more pieces followed, roughly one a week. Notes to the score indicate that the *Nine* can be played selectively and in any order. Changing the order brings out new connections and contrasts, with the emergence of new resonances essential to the composer's conception of the set and to the listener's experience.[3]

Like most of Morris's music since about 1980, each of the *Nine Piano Pieces* is based on a *compositional design*—an "abstract, uninterpreted array of pitch-classes"—that functions in his compositional process essentially as a basis for improvisation.[4] Each of the *Nine* pieces is based on a different compositional design with distinct structural premises. But the fact that all nine pieces share the same melodic string—and often specific transformations of the string—inspires numerous associations among passages within and between pieces. Special to the *Nine* is the way each piece takes form not only in and of itself, but refracted through fleeting recollections of moments from other pieces.

The agenda for this analytical sketch is twofold: to examine the relationship between structural origins and realization in shaping some of the *Nine*'s diverse associative landscapes; and to investigate the compositional underpinnings of a few of the characteristic resonances among pieces. Some detailed discussion of the pitch-class array structure for individual passages and pieces will be essential to our musical purposes, as will a pinpoint focus on individual notes, their origins in the array, and features of the musical surface, all as prerequisites to the discussion of higher levels of musical organization. The conceptual framework for segmentation and associative organization developed in chapters 2 and 3 will prove useful in this analytical endeavor, especially the distinctions

motive; and the concepts of the flash, recontextualization (referenced in chapters 5 and 8), and differences in the material content and composition of associative landscapes.

Preliminaries

Terminology

We begin with some terminology. The *string* that underlies the *Nine Piano Pieces* is an ordered set of thirty-five pcs, much like a row but with more order positions and just eleven (not twelve) distinct pcs. I write transformations of the string as in twelve-tone theory: $T_A P$ and $T_A IP$ indicate the prime, and inverted, forms of the string that begin with pc A (A = 10; B = 11), respectively; $RT_A P$ and $RT_A IP$ are the retrograde, and retrograde-inverted, forms that *end* with pc A. *Order positions* (*ops*) within a string are numbered from 1 to 35 for P and I-forms but *in reverse*, from 35 to 1, for R and RI-forms.

A *string segment* (comparable to a row segment) indicates a run of consecutive order positions within a string. Whereas string segments are structural units, pcsegments and pitch segments make no such commitment with regard to structural origins. Like rows, strings and string segments can contribute to structural or linked criteria. For instance, the linked criterion $T_{string}S_{2\text{-pitch}}$ indicates systematic realization by a lyne-to-register realization rule; $T_{string\ ops\ 1\text{--}5}C_{int}$ $_{<9119>}$ indicates a contextual association grounded in the first five order positions of the string; $T_{string\ TAP\ ops\ 1\text{--}5}C_{int}\ _{<A7896>}$ indicates an association between pcsegments that involve the same five order positions of the string $T_A P$.

Each of the *Nine Piano Pieces* is based on a different compositional design, or pitch-class array (like Morris, I will use the two terms interchangeably).[5] *Lynes* slice each array horizontally; a lyne contains one or more successive forms of the string.[6] Lynes of an *n*-lyne array are numbered from top to bottom, with "lyne 1" in the first row and "lyne *n*" in the last. Columns slice the arrays vertically; each column contains a partially ordered pcset that represents the union of string segments contributed by its individual lynes. Although the number of pcs in an array column is consistent in most of the *Nine* pieces, array columns rarely produce twelve-tone aggregates: usually one or more pcs is duplicated, while others are omitted. A *partition* is a set of pcsets within a column. Following Morris's own terminology, I will occasionally refer to "thin" partitions and "long" partitions. A *thin partition* is made of many short string segments; a *long partition* is dominated by one or two long ones. A *block* is part of an array defined by the coordinated initiation and conclusion of strings in different lynes. All but one of the nine pc arrays used in the *Nine* have more than one block. Within this chapter I use the word "section" in a special sense: a *section* is a passage of music that realizes a single block of an array.

others reflect choices made in realization. *Horizontal weighting* refers to the repetition of a pitch-class within a lyne between adjacent columns of the array in which that lyne participates. (Because a lyne can go dormant for a while, columns that are adjacent with respect to a lyne may not literally be adjacent in the array.)[7] *Pitch-class duplication* refers to repetition of one or more pitch-classes between string segments in different lynes within the same column. I reserve the more specific term *vertical weighting* for cases of pitch-class duplication in arrays where the columnar pcsets are of uniform size. A *free repetition* is a repetition of a pitch-class (in the *Nine*, almost always of a pitch) within the same lyne and column. Whereas horizontal and vertical pc weighting are evident in a pc array, free repetitions are introduced only in realization.

Structural Properties of the String

The string for the *Nine* has three important properties. First, its successively overlapped pc hexachords (i.e., those at order positions 1–6, 2–7, and so on to ops 30–35) yield one each of the thirty set classes from the fifteen hexachordal Z-pairs. Thus the string is harmonically diverse, but avoids hexachords saturated by a particular interval class (that is, it excludes five of the six all-combinatorial hexachords—SCs 6-1[012345] (ic 1), 6-35[02468A] (ic 2), 6-20[014589] (ic 4), 6-32[024579] (ic 5), and 6-7[012678] (ic 6)—plus the self-complementary SC 6-27[013469] (ic 3)).[8] This emphasis on Z-related hexachords and harmonic diversity is fairly typical of Morris's recent music (and a point of contrast between his compositional designs and Babbitt's).

Second, string segments in the first five, and last five, order positions (i.e., at ops 1–5, and 35–31, respectively, with SC 5-1[01234] and INT <9119>) are related by RT_2.[9] This close relationship spawns the many patches of close imitative counterpoint that help create a sense of cadence around block boundaries and audibly relate array blocks to sections of music. String segments in ops 1–5 and 35–31 also have a weaker association with those in ops 10–13 (with INT <3B9> in P-forms of the string), which emphasize ics 1 and 3 in a member of SC 4-3[0134], an abstract subset of SC 5-1[01234].

A third distinctive feature of the string is that each form omits one of the twelve pcs. For example, T_AP, the string that opens "Between" in lyne 1, omits pc 3; T_9IP, the string in lyne 2, omits pc 4. In general, strings T_nP and RT_nP omit pc $n+5$; strings T_nIP and RT_nIP omit pc $n+7$.

Arrays and Aspects of Realization

Taking the string as a basic compositional structure, Morris creates nine pc arrays that differ in the number of lynes, blocks, degree or basis of harmonic consistency, partitioning, and aspects of realization.[10] None of the arrays completes unweighted

izontal weighting, as well as pc duplication or vertical weighting. In six arrays, columns are of uniform size, but diverse in set class.[11]

Details of realization vary from piece to piece, but some general principles obtain. Typical of Morris's work is a lyne-to-register realization rule ($T_{string}S_{2\text{-pitch}}$) that sends each string within a block into its own pitch range for the duration of the corresponding section. The width and location of these pitch ranges varies from piece to piece and often changes from section to section. Although systematic realization by $T_{string}S_{2\text{-pitch}}$ is always in force, its terms are stricter in some pieces than in others. On the strict side of the spectrum, "Between" and the two outer blocks of "Loose Canon" realize each form of the string in its minimal pitch span of ten semitones (i.e., the string has eleven, not twelve, distinct pcs). Here the four registers adjoin without touching, so that their concatenation saturates the total pitch span from the lowest note in a section to the highest with no gaps. Pitch realization in "Kids" is a bit more flexible: most of its strings occupy a pitch span of ten semitones, but some spans are as large as eighteen. Edge pitches of adjoining registers can be as far as an octave apart and registers tend to move from section to section. In "Rising Early," pitch ranges are even more flexible and mobile. Not only do they vary in width from ten semitones to over two octaves, but adjacent voices sometimes overlap and often migrate upward within a section. Over the course of the piece the total pitch range gradually rises from section to section, hence the title.

Another fairly strict realization rule involves the temporal domain. As in much of Morris's music, aspects of rhythm, from the pacing of array columns to the shaping of surface details, are relatively free in the *Nine*; however, each array column is generally realized as a measure of music.[12] This column-to-measure rule affects musical form over longer spans. Although array lynes often go their own way in the middle of a section, corresponding order positions tend to align at the start of a section and come back into alignment at the end, in a musical manifestation of block boundaries.

"Between"

First in the score and on the Open Space recording, "Between" is a good point of entry to the set. Example 9.1 provides a score for the entire piece, with thirty-eight segments from four associative sets A–D marked. The opening bars are delicate and translucent, taking and changing form as slowly and gently as wisps of cloud. An initial gesture that tumbles from high B♭ into the low register contains two smaller segments, <B♭5, G5> and <B2, G♯2>, set off by $S_{1\text{-pitch}}$ with coincident support from $S_{2\text{-pitch}}$ and $C_{ip\,-3}$. The two segments seed an associative set A and establish the polyphonic texture that continues in mm. 2–3, where a relatively active high register contrasts with a slow chromatic ascent in the bass.

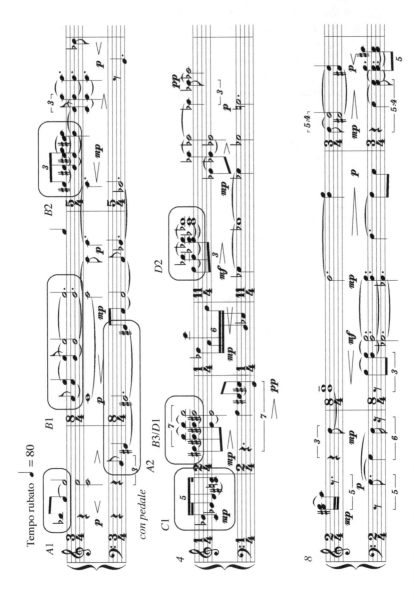

Example 9.1. Morris, "Between"

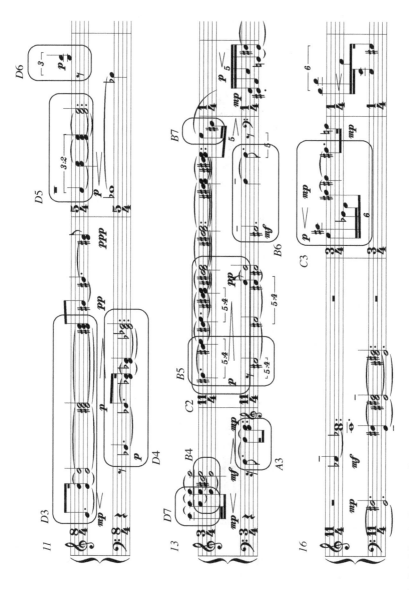

Example 9.1. Morris, "Between" —(continued)

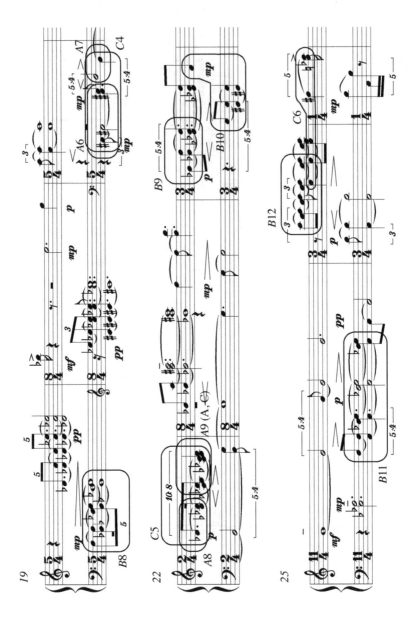

Example 9.1. Morris, "Between"—(continued)

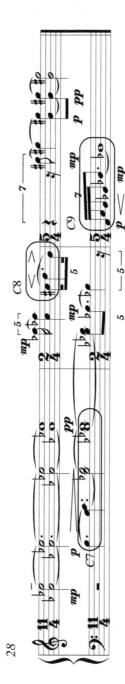

Example 9.1. Morris, "Between"—(concluded)

tone motion with a much larger interval in a bent contour (C, G, B in m. 2, and G♯, B, A in m. 3). Recognizing the recurrence of similar figures throughout "Between," I hear these as the start of a second associative set, B, and call them $B1$ and $B2$. Each is embellished by a soft leap to a repeated note (G5 in m. 2 and A5 in m. 3). These embellishments also associate with one another, as instances of a "touching gesture" that reappears in m. 7 and beyond. Associations among these form the C_4 circuit graph shown in example 9.2. The tidiness of the circuit is nicely smudged by the tenuous boundary between the second and third segments: G5 at the end of the second segment in m. 2 is only a semitone below, and one quarter-note before, the G♯5 that begins the third segment in m. 3. So while contextual criteria suggest four segments, the sonic criteria $S_{1\text{-pitch}}$ and $S_{1\text{-duration}}$ recognize only three: $B1$, an expanded second segment that prefixes <C4, G5> in m. 2 to $B2$ in m. 3, and <C4, A5> in m. 3. The result of these conflicting genoseg boundaries is a wrinkle in the associative landscape—an elision between the two subsets of B located within mm. 2 and 3 (represented by vertical edges on the graph).

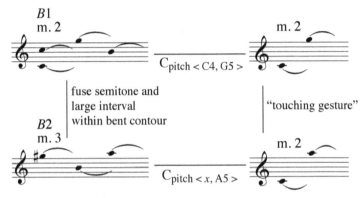

Example 9.2. Morris, "Between," C_4 graph of segments in mm. 2–3

Example 9.3 provides the complete pitch-class array for "Between." The array has one block of four lynes and thirty columns, all hexachords. Four set classes account for twenty-four of these: these are the chromatic and near-chromatic SCs 6-1[012345] and 6-2[012346] (which occur six times each), plus SC 6-9[012357] and SC 6-27[013469] (seven and five times, respectively).[13] Each lyne is realized within its minimal pitch span of ten semitones; the four spans adjoin, but do not touch. The realization of lyne 4, RT_1P, occurs in the range G2–F3; lyne 3, RT_AIP, F♯3–E4; lyne 2, T_9IP, F4–E♭5; and lyne 1, T_AP, E5–D6. Together, these span three-and-a-half octaves centered on the midpoint of the piano keyboard, E4/F4. Conjoining the lyne-to-register realization rule with a minimal pitch span determines the contour and series of pitch intervals for each string, and thus also the distribution of notes over the pitch spectrum within each measure.[14]

	1	2	3	4	5	6	7	8	9	10	11	12	13	14	15
1 T_AP	A7-	-7	89	-A	62	0	518-	-8BA[1]	7-	26	B8	-72	04-	-4-	
2 T_9IP	9	0B-	-BA-			157	637-	2-	-2-	-B1	4	905	73-	-36128	6-
3 RT_AIP	0-	-0-	-0-	-03214-	-498	23		-7	B-	-40	A71	A	52-		-2894
4 RT_1P	B8-	-89A-	-A7-		-7			5-	-584-						
SC	6-1 012345	6-1	6-1	6-2 012346	6-9 012357	6-9	6-9	6-27 013469	6-27	6-9	6-9	6-32 024579	6-8 023457	6-9	6-9

	16	17	18	19	20	21	22	23	24	25	26	27	28	29	30
1 T_AP		-4165	B2		A47	9-		-9152			0B47	658-		-8-	-8
2 T_9IP	85-		-5	93-	-30-	-0		A	625	7	2-	-2B-	83	012B-	-B
3 RT_AIP	-69		748	61-	-1-		-1A907-		3	86			-B01A-	-A-	
4 RT_1P	-73	32		5A-	-A12B-		-B	-7	48	359-	-9-	-9-	-B		-90BA[1]
SC:	6-2	6-1	6-27	6-Z24 013468	6-27	6-1	6-2	6-31 014579	6-2	6-2	6-32	6-27	6-8	6-2	6-1

[1] Pc A in lyne 1, op 12, is realized as pc 9, creating SC 6-Z45[023469] in m. 8 of the score instead of SC 6-27[013469] as in the array.

Example 9.3. Morris, "Between," array

opening bars is a direct result of the array, which holds a single pcset, the chromatic set from G to C, over its first three columns. But the associative organization of mm. 1–3 develops largely in realization. $A1$ and $A2$ in m. 1 realize string segments; they are supported and associated by the linked criteria $T_{string}S_{2\text{-pitch}}$, $T_{string\ ops\ 1\text{-}2}C_{ip\ -3}$, and $T_{string\ ops\ 35\text{-}34}C_{ip\ -3}$ (i.e., the string segments in ops 1–5 and 35–31 are related by retrograde). But neither $B1$ nor $B2$, nor either of the "touching" segments in mm. 2 and 3, is a string segment. $B1$ and $B2$ each draw pcs from lynes 1 and 2; the two touching gestures take pcs from lynes 1 and 3. Whereas the array clearly implies four-part counterpoint, the effective musical counterpoint has just two parts, lynes 1 and 2, versus lyne 4. (With its repeated C4, lyne 3 doesn't sound like a voice until m. 4, when it finally moves.)

Note that here strict adherence to the $T_{string}S_{2\text{-pitch}}$ realization rule actually facilitates the formation of *non*structural segments: the fact that the first four pcs in the strings in lynes 1 and 2 (<A789> and <90BA>, respectively) form a loose cluster around the register break between lynes 1 and 2 (E5/E♭5), rather than being more evenly distributed across the full pitch span for each lyne, supports formation of the cross-lyne segments $B1$ and $B2$. This observation leads to another point about the workings of register and effective counterpoint in the *Nine*: even when the pitch span used to realize each lyne of the array is fixed, the musical tessitura and effective texture change continuously with the fit between the particular pcs available in each string at a given moment and the boundary pcs that define pitch spans. For instance, compare the effective fusion of lynes 1 and 2 in mm. 1–3 into a single perceptual stream with the clear two-voice counterpoint that comes from the same two lines in mm. 23–24 (see ex. 9.1). Here the most prominent pcs in lyne 1 are at the top of its pitch span (C♯6, D6 in m. 23), while two of the three pcs in lyne 2 are at the bottom of its span (G♭4, F4 in m. 24); the association and echo between the pcs D and F that occur in both registers reinforces the registral contrast between lynes.

Continuing our study of associative organization beyond m. 3, the interjection of faster surface rhythms in mm. 4 and 6 helps to bring out the T_{+1} relationship between <F♯5, D6> in m. 5 and the first two notes of the triadic segment <F5, D♭6, A♭5> in m. 7. While each of these rising sixths shares an interval with $B1$ or $B2$, and the second one is again echoed by a touching gesture, these two segments can also be seen as the start of an associative set D that gains prominence when coincidence among $C_{cseg\ RI\ <021>}$, $C_{SC\ 3\text{-}11\ [037]}$, and $S_{2\text{-pitch}}$ forms the pair of segments <E4, B4, G♯4> in m. 11 and <A4, C5, F4> in m. 12 (ex. 9.4).[15] A third segment, <B♭2, G2, D♭3> in m. 11, gets in the mix with its bent contour and opening minor third (the outer interval is adjusted, from seven to six semitones). Taking the rising sixths in m. 5 as a doubly affiliated segment $B3/D1$, and in m. 7 as $D2$, the two segments in the right hand

imposed on this patch of set *D* are three segments with a competing set of associations: coincidence between $C_{SC\ 3\text{-}5[016]}$ and $S_{1\text{-adjacency}}$ recommends the segments <E4, B4, B♭2> and <G♯4, G2, D♭3> in m. 11, and <E4, {A4, B♭3}> over the barline of mm. 11–12. The cumulative result is a shift from a surface full of semitones and tritones gleaned from the octatonic SC 6-27[013469] in m. 11 to the diatonic hexachord in m. 12.

Example 9.4. Morris, "Between," mm. 11–12, three segments of set *D*

Returning to example 9.3 for a look at columns 11 and 12 of the array, we see that the relationship between structure and associative landscape in these bars is more straightforward than in mm. 2–3, but still involves some creative work with the array. *D*4 and *D*5 correspond to string segments, but at different sets of order positions (25–23 and 12–14, respectively); *D*3 affixes a note from lyne 3 to a string segment from lyne 2. Thus the strongest association, between *D*3 and *D*5, once again arises only in realization, as do all three of the weaker segments associated by $C_{SC\ 3\text{-}5[016]}$, created by Morris's total orderings for the partially ordered array columns 11 and 12. The darker sound of m. 11 compared to mm. 1–10 reflects the absence of lyne 1 (and thus the high register) from m. 10 to the end of m. 12; the fact that the pcs in lyne 2 in mm. 11–12 tend to gravitate toward the bottom of its pitch range (F4); and the prevalence of SC 3-5[016]—a harmony previously absent from the surface—as a local harmonic seasoning.

Set *B* returns in mm. 13–14 with the segments <E5, G4, D♯5> in m. 13 (*B*4) and <D♯5, F♯4, D5> in m. 14 (*B*5). Like *B*1 and *B*2, both *B*4 and *B*5 fuse pcs from lynes 1 and 2 into an instance of a familiar figure. The first clear patch of a fourth set, *C*, finally comes in mm. 21–22, where string segments at ops 13–10 in lynes 4 and 2 inspire a pitch inversion around F♮3/F♯3 between the segments shown as *C*4 and *C*5 in example 9.5a. A second patch of set *C* appears at the end of the piece, where the three structural segments *C*7 (<B3, C4, D♭4, B♭3> in m. 28, representing ops 4–1 of RT$_A$IP in lyne 3), *C*8 (<C5, C♯5, D5, B4> in m. 28–29, ops 32–35 of T$_9$IP in lyne 2) and *C*9 (<A2, C3, B2, B♭2, D♭3> in m. 30, ops 5–1 of RT$_1$P in lyne 4) shown on example 9.5b associate with

with *C*1 back in m. 4. As in mm. 1–3, the relatively static pc content in mm. 29–30 comes right out of the array, which retains five of the six pcs from column 29 in column 30.

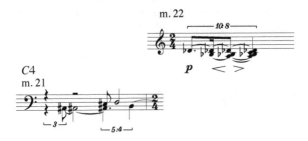

Example 9.5a. Morris, "Between," mm. 21–22, two segments of set *C*

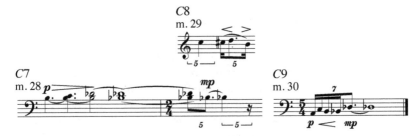

Example 9.5b. Morris, "Between," mm. 28–30, segments of set *C*

Having studied the musical surface and structural origins of segments in the main patches of sets *A*, *B*, *C*, and *D*, we now step back for a synoptic view of the associative landscape. Example 9.6 is a map of all the segments discussed so far, plus a number of consociates,[17] in a shorthand notation that represents pitch exactly but distills rhythmic information for longer notes to attack order and the presence or absence of a sustain.[18] From the map it is easy to see that sets *A*, *B*, *C*, and *D* have different distributions. Active at the scale of the entire piece, set *B* is the largest and most widespread of the four, with fourteen segments from m. 2 to m. 30. Sets *A* and *C* are more regional in their distribution. The nine segments of set *A* congregate in the first two-thirds of the piece, mm. 1–22. Set *C* develops later and dominates the end of the piece; six of its ten segments come in two patches, in mm. 21–22 and mm. 26–30. Set *D* is the most localized and smallest of the four sets; its seven segments come in two patches in mm. 5–7 and 11–13. The size and spacing of patches varies in all four sets.

Example 9.6. Morris, "Between," association map of sets A, B, C, and D

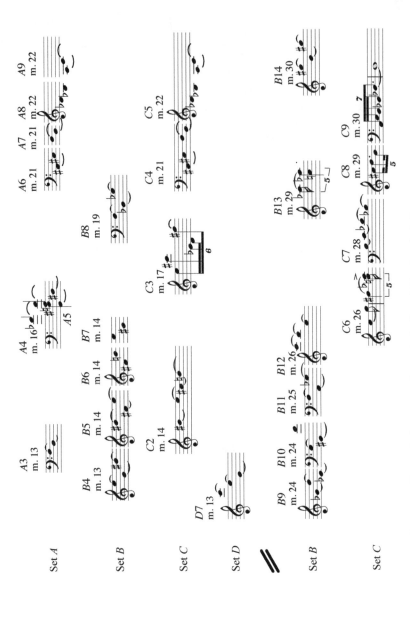

Example 9.6. Morris, "Between," association map of sets *A*, *B*, *C*, and *D*—(concluded)

reflect differences in their segments' origins with respect to the array as these are filtered through the ten-semitone pitch spans of the lyne-to-register realization rule. The most dispersed sets, A and B, have core contextual criteria that occur or can be crafted from many places in the array. Associated by $C_{ip\,3}$, segments of set A can appear anywhere that one of the ten ic 3s between adjacent order positions of the string projects through one of the ten-semitone pitch spans to reach the surface as a segment with coincident support from $T_{string}S_{2\text{-pitch}}$ and $C_{ip\,3}$. With boundary pitches of adjoining registers just a semitone apart, segments of set A can also form across adjacent lynes, without structural support. In fact, segments of set B usually form this way.[19] This lack of structural support explains the set's relatively wide distribution and substantial range of variation in interval content. In contrast, the strong structural support for segments of set C, which realize string segments at ops 1–5, 10–13, or 31–35 by $T_{string}S_{2\text{-pitch}}$, constrains that set's distribution to a few dispersed patches, which tend to flank section boundaries. Segments of C can form whenever string segments in ops 1–5 or 31–35 coincide with long partitions in the array (as in mm. 28–30), but are filtered out when these same string segments cross a series of thin partitions (as they do at the start of the piece except for C1 in m. 4). Because the core contextual criteria of set C represent the intervallic ordering of the string, the set's range of variation must explore other dimensions, such as pc content and rhythm.

The composite disposition of sets A–D in "Between" makes for an associative landscape that is materially and compositionally heterogeneous. At the start of the piece (mm. 1–13) associative monophony prevails: small patches of sets A, B, and D unfold in succession, largely without temporal overlap. In the middle of the piece (mm. 13–22), associative polyphony is the norm as a passage that involves segments of all four sets (mm. 13–16) proceeds through a transitional area to two-part associative polyphony between sets A and C (mm. 16–22). The end of the piece is dominated by two successive patches of set B (in mm. 24–26) and set C (mm. 26–30). Throughout "Between," changes in the rate of pc turnover, harmonic rhythm (defined by columnar hexachords and changes in bar length), and segment and set rhythm, further complicate the musical surface. The flexible relationship between the array and the associative organization of its musical realization also creates an opportunity for varying degrees of associative proximity and distance from moments in other pieces of the set, some of which we will soon explore.

"Kids"

Second on the Open Space recording and fourth in compositional order, "Kids" is based on a three-lyne pc array in four blocks. Each string in block I

IV. The twelve string forms chosen from the group of 48 tend to promote pc duplication at the start and end of blocks and some pc invariance across block boundaries. Block I (ex. 9.7) consists of the strings T_9IP, RT_AIP, and RT_1P—the same three strings found in lynes 2–4 of the "Between" array. Two of these (RT_AIP and RT_1P, in lynes 2 and 3) occupy the same pitch spans in both pieces; the third (T_9IP in lyne 1) sits two semitones higher in "Kids" (F♯4–F♮5, versus E4–E♭5 in "Between"). As a result, mm. 1–10 of "Kids" traverse what is essentially the same partial ordering of *pitches* as the three lower lynes of all of "Between": within each string, the same notes appear in the same registers in the same order.

	m. #	1	2	3	4	5
1	T_9IP	90BA1572	6	B89057	3	61
2	RT_AIP	032	419863	7B1	4	A693
3	RT_1P	B89A7235	58	40A	7	152894

	m. #	6	7	8	9	10
1	T_9IP	2	85930A6257-	-7	8	3012B
2	RT_AIP	274	861A	9073	862B	01A
3	RT_1P	7	35A12B	4	83590BA	1

Example 9.7. Morris, "Kids," block I of array (mm. 1–10)

Example 9.8 provides a score for mm. 1–14 of "Kids," which realize block I of the array (mm. 1–10) and the start of block II (which extends from m. 11 to m. 18). While the strong structural connection between this passage and "Between" is quite audible, the relationship is one of active recomposition and recontextualization, not repetition, even with regard to structural segments. "Kids" begins with a cluster of three segments from set *C* that take advantage of the RT_2 relationship between the string segments at ops 1–5 and 35–31 (circled in ex. 9.8). Although the three lower lynes of "Between" trace the same partial ordering of pitches, in that passage slower progress through the array, longer durations, and repeated notes conspire to dissolve each five-pc string segment in the overall texture in which two other associative sets with segments less tied to the array, sets *A* and *B*, prevail.

Counterbalancing the structural affinities between the two pieces are some important differences in the harmonic structure of their arrays that effectively reshape the associative landscape. Recall that in the "Between" array each column is a hexachord, with most of these of just four types (SCs 6-1[012345],

Example 9.8. Morris, "Kids," mm. 1–14

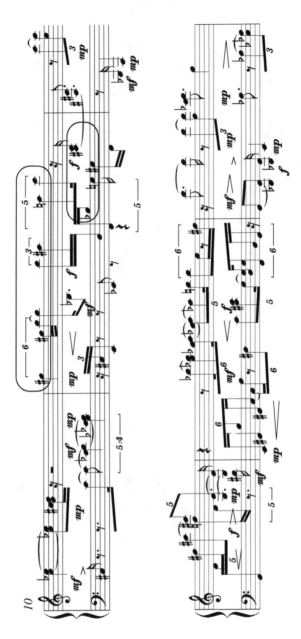

Example 9.8. Morris, "Kids," mm. 1–14—(concluded)

tions the strings in the top three lynes to make a new array in which columns have from three to twenty pcs and form sets from trichords to twelve-tone-aggregates with pcs duplicated at various multiplicities. Morris reintroduces harmonic consistency in the process of realization by aligning pitches from different strings within a column to create a bouncy surface that repeatedly forms sets from a small number of trichordal set classes. In section I these trichords are SCs 3-2[013], 3-3[014], and 3-7[025]—three SCs that occur frequently among the string's 33 trichordal segments. SC 3-2[013] occurs six times in the string; SC 3-7[025] is next, with five string segments. SC 3-3[014] appears only three times in the string, but it, too, has a synecdochic quality: along with set class 3-2[013] it is twice embedded in the RT_2-invariant string segment at ops 1–5 and 35–31, taking in its ends pitches plus an adjacent order position.

Example 9.9 maps out segments from the three associative sets *3-2[013]*, *3-3[014]*, and *3-7[025]* in mm. 1–6 of "Kids." Most of these trichordal segments have coincident support from one or more of the sonic criteria $S_{1\text{-adjacency}}$, $S_{1\text{-rest}}$, $S_{1\text{-simultaneity}}$, or $S_{1\text{-dynamics}}$, but pervasive conflicts with $S_{1\text{-pitch}}$ and the fact that the C_{SC} segments involve *un*ordered trichords (rather than ordered trichords and stronger C_{ip} criteria) make the resulting segmentation fairly weak. The two strongest segments in the passage— the long, *mp* chords in m. 4 and m. 6—highlight members of SCs 3-3[014] and 3-7[025], respectively.

Differences in the associative landscapes of section I of "Kids" and "Between" go beyond harmonic vocabulary and the types of core criteria that form associative sets to landscape composition. Compared to the variable patch sizes and associative polyphony found in the first half of "Between," the trichordal landscape of "Kids" tends to have smaller patches, often in monophonic disposition, and more frequent intercutting between sets. Example 9.10 maps out the trichordal surface of mm. 9–10, from the end of section I. Once again a continual flow of weak segments supported by the same three C_{SC} criteria accounts for every note. Associative polyphony between sets *3-3[014]* and *3-7[025]* in m. 9 gives way to associative monophony of set *3-2[013]* over the barline of mm. 9–10. Example 9.11 continues the trichordal map over the block boundary into mm. 11–12, where the start of block II brings a change in trichords. While set *3-3[014]* remains active, sets *3-2[013]* and *3-7[025]* are replaced by sets *3-4[015]* and *3-11[037]*, two more trichords that are relatively common in the string (3-11[037] occurs four times; 3-4[015], three). These three trichords are also interrelated by interval content: each shares two of its three interval classes with each of its companions.

Like the opening bars of "Kids," the end of section I admits two contrasting hearings. In addition to the cross-lyne, harmonic hearing dominated by contextual criteria (the unordered trichords), the music encourages a linear,

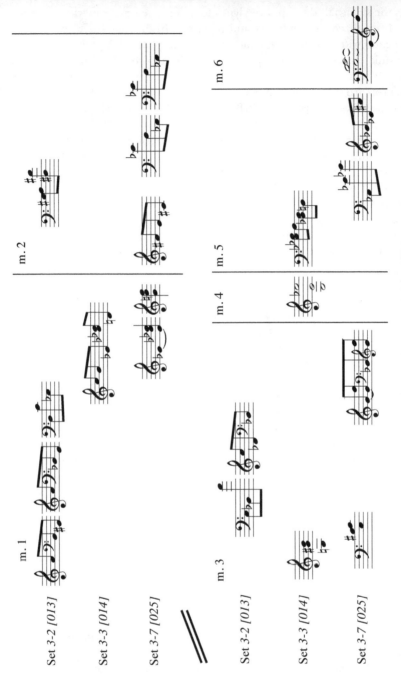

Example 9.9. Morris, "Kids," mm. 1–6, map of sets *3-2[013]*, *3-3[014]*, and *3-7[025]*

Example 9.10. Morris, "Kids," mm. 9–10, map of sets *3-2[013]*, *3-3[014]*, and *3-7[025]*

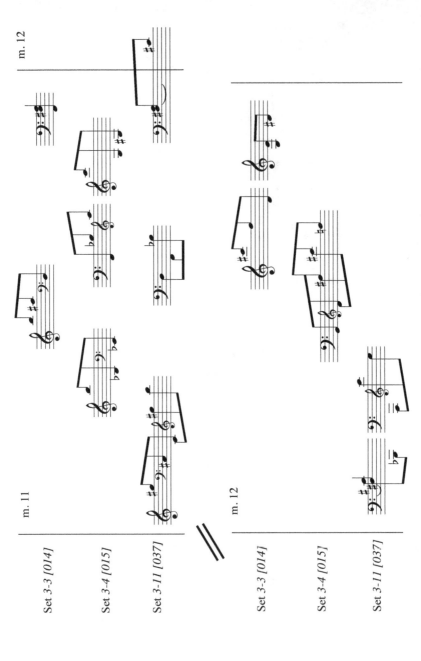

Example 9.11. Morris, "Kids," mm. 11–12, map of sets *3-3[014]*, *3-4[015]*, and *3-11[037]*

structurally motivated hearing of mm. 9–11, where synergy between two string segments in m. 10 grounds a patch of set *C*. This time the associations among string segments are not only local: we have heard (or will hear) the very same notes in the music that comes from the corresponding swatch of the array at the end of "Between" (mm. 28–29, in ex. 9.5b). The result is a strong flash between the two passages that adds a new layer to the associative organization of both passages.

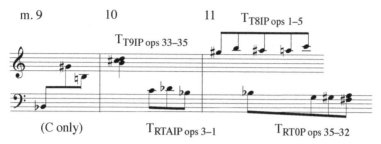

Example 9.12. Morris, "Kids," structural hearing of mm. 10–11; five segments of set *C*

While a change in the pitch spans used to realize individual lynes of the array at the start of section II (m. 11) may seem like little more than a bit of engineering, here and in many spots throughout the *Nine* such changes have a direct, audible effect on the musical landscape. Obviously, they affect sonic organization: changes in pitch range can create a sense of registral process (this is a premise of "Rising Early," discussed below). But they can also have a profound effect on associative organization, as they rebalance the specific sonic and contextual criteria that underlie segment formation. Where pitch spans are contiguous, as in section I (mm. 1–10), $S_{2\text{-pitch}}$ is a relatively weak criterion. Here the most active criteria are $S_{1\text{-adjacency}}$ and the three trichordal C_{SC} criteria that tile the surface with segments of the sets *3-2[013]*, *3-3[014]* and *3-7[025]*, bracketed by two patches of the more melodic set *C* (mm. 1–2, mm. 9–10). But as an octave gap opens between the spans that realize lynes 1 and 2 in section II (mm. 11–18), $S_{2\text{-pitch}}$ and coincident structural and contextual criteria gain strength. As a result, two more segments of set *C* (ex. 9.12, m. 11; also circled in ex. 9.8) pop out of the texture, extending the patch in m. 10 another bar. The result is a shift in the composition of the associative landscape such that purely contextual criteria (the trichordal associations) and structural ones (string segments) are more in balance.

Comparing the associative landscapes of "Between" and "Kids" in broad terms is instructive. In "Between," compositional heterogeneity of the

four sets, *A–D*. In "Kids" the landscape involves not only multiple associative sets, but multiple layers of associative organization: first, locally, the trichordal tiling (supported almost exclusively by purely C criteria); second, structural string segments (set *C*); and last, long-range associations or flashes with moments in other pieces in the set, secured through realization of the underlying structure.

"Rising Early"

Composed first but taking a central position in the score and on the Open Space recording, "Rising Early" is the longest, slowest, and weightiest piece of the *Nine*. Its array has four lynes and five blocks that represent three different structures. Blocks I and IV are related by RT_AI, as are blocks II and V by RT_8I, with lyne exchange from high to low in both cases (lynes 1 and 4 exchange, as do lynes 2 and 3). Array columns produce hexachords throughout. We'll focus on block III, which inspired the pc array for "Between": both use the same four forms of the string, but have different harmonic plans (ex. 9.13). Whereas "Between" balances the harmonic diversity of the string's thirty imbricated Z-sets with a fairly small repertoire of self-complementary columnar hexachords, block III of the "Rising Early" array nearly replicates the string's harmonic diversity in its twenty-five columns, which include all but five of the thirty Z-related hexachords once each.[20] (The other four blocks explore intermediate degrees of harmonic diversity: blocks I and IV each include fourteen of the thirty Z-related hexachords, over thirty columns; blocks II and V have twelve, in twenty-eight columns.)[21]

Like "Between" and "Kids," "Rising Early" observes a lyne-to-register rule, but here the pitch spans for adjacent lynes often overlap. Over the course of the piece, the pitch spans for each lyne rise from block to block so that the music gradually moves from the piano's lowest register (A0–E4 in section I) to its highest (F3 to C8 in section V). By section III, lynes 3 and 4 have moved into the pitch range originally occupied by lynes 1 and 2 in section I, underlining the long-range structural connection with "Between." As in section I of "Kids," the very forms of the string found in lynes 1–3 of "Between" reappear in exactly the same ten-semitone pitch spans, thus again retracing the partial ordering of pitches for lynes 1–3 in all of "Between."[22]

Overlaid on this slow rise in pitch are some gentle undulations in harmonic rhythm. These reflect the workings of a temporal plan. While every array column is realized as a measure of music, the number of beats in a measure changes from bar to bar, as does the average length of a measure from section to section. Example 9.14 shows the temporal plan for bar lengths in section I (mm. 1–30). The music begins low and slow, with the longest bar in the section

Block 1 — mm. 59–71:

m. #	59	60	61	62	63	64	65	66	67	68	69	70	71
1 T_AP	A	789	6205	1	8	BA72-	-20	6		4	165	B2	A47
2 T_9IP	9	0	9-	B	A157	8	637	B1-	B89	05	327	48	61
3 RT_AIP	032	14	8	9A72	-9	3	5	840	-14A	69		71	5
4 RT_1P	B-									A			
SC	6-Z3	6-Z44	6-Z49	6-Z10	6-Z39	6-Z19	6-Z11	6-Z48	6-Z40	6-Z43	6-Z4	6-Z50	6-Z42
	012356	012569	013479	013457	023458	013478	012457	012579	012358	012568	012456	014679	012369

Block 2 — mm. 72–83:

m. #	72	73	74	75	76	77	78	79	80	81	82	83
1 T_AP	9	15	2	28593	0A625		0-	0		B47	6-	-658
2 T_9IP	73	6	1	-7	3		7-	-783		01-	-12-	-2B
3 RT_AIP	A	907-	9473			862B		01A-	-A			
4 RT_1P	28					5A-	-A12B		48359-	-9	0BA	1
SC:	6-Z38	6-Z17	6-Z41	6-Z12	6-Z24	6-Z28	6-Z36	6-Z25	6-Z6	6-Z46	6-Z37	6-Z29
	012378	012478	012368	012467	013468	013569	012347	013568	012567	012469	012348	023679

Example 9.13. Morris, "Rising Early," block III of array (mm. 59–83)

m. #	1	2	3	4	5	6	7	8	9	10	11	12	13	14	15
# beats/measure (in ♩)	14	12	9	5	8	10	11	9	6	2	5	7	8	10	7
change in bar length (from previous bar)		−2	−3	−4	+3	+2	+1	−2	−3	−4	+3	+2	+1	+2	−3

m. #	16	17	18	19	20	21	22	23	24	25	26	27	28	29	30
# beats/measure (in ♩)	3	6	8	7	5	2	6	3	5	6	4	7	11	8	10
change in bar length (from previous bar)	−4	+3	+2	−1	−2	−3	+4	−3	+2	+1	−2	+3	+4	+2	−3

Example 9.14. Morris, "Rising Early," temporal plan for section I (mm. 1–30)

and in the piece. From mm. 1–4 bar lengths progressively contract by 2, 3, and 4 beats, respectively. Measures 4–7 reverse this trend in two respects: bar lengths increase, and by progressively smaller amounts (3, 2, and 1 beat). The result is a wave in the harmonic rhythm with a crest in m. 4 (i.e., the shortest bar and fastest hexachord turnover). Measures 7–10 and 10–14 repeat the pattern, forming another crest at m. 10 and a trough at m. 14. Measure 16, the next crest, initiates a retrograde in the series of *differences* in bar lengths (not actual bar lengths) that continues to the end of section I (with some sign changes due to the retrograde symmetry). Although the resulting sequence of differences in bar length is not governed by a single arithmetic series, it does conform to a rule: $| f(n+1) - f(n) | = | f(n) - f(n-1) | \pm 1$, where $f(n)$ is a function that indicates the number of quarter-note beats in measure n and $| f(n+1) - f(n) | \leq 4$. The temporal plans for sections II–V have the same premises but different particulars.[23] As with section I, the temporal plans for sections II and IV have axes of retrograde symmetry that involve both size and direction; the retrograde patterns in sections III and V involve only size, leaving the direction of change free.

Conjoined with the long-range pitch ascent in "Rising Early," the gentle but persistent waves in harmonic rhythm help shape the moment-to-moment flow of the piece and the large-scale proportions of its five sections. Section length decreases by about 28 percent from section I (214 beats over 30 columns) to section II (154 beats over 28 columns), and again from section II to III (110

I.[24] But the rest of the piece reverses this trend, with section length increasing about 15 percent from section III to IV (127 beats over 30 columns) and 20 percent from section IV to V (153 beats over 28 columns). Sections II and V are almost exactly the same length.

Our account of the structural underpinnings of "Rising Early" sufficiently complete, we now turn to a detailed analysis of the music. Compared to "Between" and "Kids," the opening bars of "Rising Early" sound dark indeed. Set in the low register with long durations, pedal, and a prevailing dynamic of *mf*, notes enter one or two at a time, barely enough to sustain a sense of motion from bar to bar. Columnar hexachords are fairly discrete in the realization, as sustained notes or large leaps mark many of the barlines. Yet the music is remarkably continuous, for reasons gleaned from a close look at mechanics of segmentation and the associative landscape. Example 9.15 provides a score for mm. 1–4. With successive notes in the realization separated in time or register, $S_{1\text{-duration}}$ and $S_{1\text{-pitch}}$ might seem to be the main segmentation criteria. But the audible import of each is mitigated by a persistent tension between them, and by a delicate balance between $S_{1\text{-duration}}$ and $S_{2\text{-pitch}}$, which supports string realization through the linked criterion $T_{\text{string}}S_{2\text{-pitch}}$. Pitch repetitions motivated by horizontal weighting in the pc array (e.g., the repetitions of E♭4 and D♭1 from m. 1 in m. 2) and moves by semitone or other small intervals within rather than across strings (e.g., D4 to C♯4, and E1 to E♭1, from m. 2 to 3) articulate and reactivate lynes from measure to measure, reaching across lulls in surface rhythm and boundaries of $S_{1\text{-duration}}$ genosegs to move the music forward.

Although contextual criteria tend to be somewhat weak (or at least subtle) in mm. 1–4, as in much of "Rising Early," they do contribute to the associative landscape nonetheless. Example 9.16 is a map of mm. 1–4, again in shorthand notation. The map shows eleven segments from five sets; taken together, these account for all but one note in the score (the B♭2 in m. 4).[25] (I have not named the first three sets, which are very small and essentially local.)[26] Each connects two segments by C_{pitch}; the third also involves C_{ip} and C_{cseg} criteria. Horizontal weighting motivates the pitch repetition in all three sets, complementing the disjunctive role it plays in string realization (by $T_{\text{string}}S_{2\text{-pitch}}$) with an associative one in segmentation and set formation. The remaining two sets, each tied to pc intervals in the string, are our associative sets *A* and *C* from "Between" and "Kids." Here set *A* has two patches, a minimal patch in m. 1 and a clump of three segments in mm. 2–3. Although the segment of set *C* realized by the linked criterion $T_{\text{string ops 1–4}}S_{2\text{-pitch}}$ in m. 4 is locally isolated, it has many consociates in the intermittent patches of set *C* that arise around block boundaries (in mm. 28–33, 55–61, 79–86, 110–17, 137–41), as they do in "Between," "Kids," and other pieces from the *Nine*.

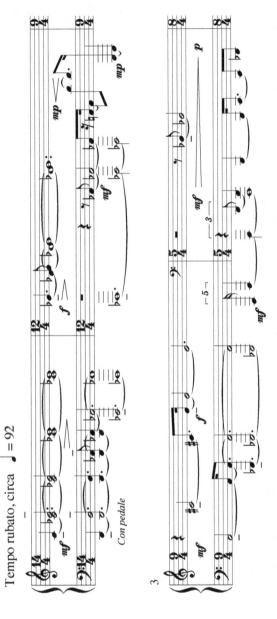

Example 9.15. Morris, "Rising Early," section I, mm. 1–4

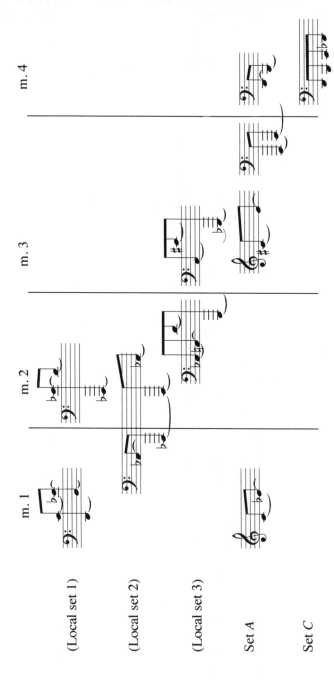

Example 9.16. Morris, "Rising Early," association map of mm. 1–4

that parallels and reinforces that achieved in the sonic domain by calibrated conflict among $S_{1\text{-pitch}}$, $S_{1\text{-duration}}$, $S_{1\text{-dynamics}}$, and $S_{2\text{-pitch}}$. Three of the four set junctures are associative elisions, each arising from the dual affiliation of one or two notes in the score (i.e., D♭1 in m. 2 contributes to segments in the first and second sets; C♯4 in m. 3, to segments in the third and set A; and the dyad <D2, B1> in m. 4 to segments in sets A and C). From m. 1 to m. 4, the music moves from purely contextual associations formed across lynes (the first three sets, in mm. 1–3) to associations with a structural basis, among string segments within lynes (segments of sets A and C, mm. 3–4). Listeners who follow the progress of individual lynes in register can hear the lone segment of set C in lyne 3, m. 4, as a synopsis of the preceding bars. While the same ordering of pitch intervals actually occurs to within inversion in all four lynes, each of these potential consociates in lynes 1, 2, and 4 is dissolved by the array's thin partitions in columns (and measures) 1–3. In a performance that places "Rising Early" after "Between," as in the score and on the Open Space recording, one can also hear this segment in m. 4 as a flash to mm. 1–3 of "Between," where the first four pitches of lyne 4 trace out the same three pitch intervals nine semitones higher, or to a moment from some other piece in the set. In any case, perceiving the string segment in m. 4 *as* a segment depends in part on the harmonic rhythm: as the first wave in harmonic rhythm crests in measure 4, the four notes in lyne 3 come together in a relatively small timeframe. This temporal proximity itself helps to encourage segment formation.

The tight and virtually comprehensive associative landscape in mm. 1–4 is neither unique in "Rising Early," nor representative of the piece as a whole. Perhaps more than any other piece in the set, "Rising Early" roams the range of landscape composition. Sometimes the associative landscape is sparse, with just a few faint segments forming occasional patches of small, transient sets embedded in a differentiated but irreducible matrix of array realization. This is the case in mm. 15–26, where only two small local sets seem to emerge (ex. 9.17). One is in mm. 20–22, where $C_{\text{pc }\{6A1\}}$ associates three segments (even these are partially submerged by conflicting genoseg boundaries, say, with the segment <{A♯2, C♯3} D3, B2> in m. 21, which has a long-range TC xx association with $C4$ in m. 21 of "Between," also supported by $T_{\text{string RT1P ops}}$ $_{12\text{-}9}C_{\text{ip <+3, +1, −3>}}$ and $T_{\text{string}}S_{2\text{-pitch}}$);[27] the other set flanks the barline of mm. 22–23, with core criterion $C_{\text{SC 3-3[014]}}$. In the next five bars, mm. 27–31, landscape composition swings to the other extreme as the first of the five patches of set C that form around block boundaries reshapes the landscape into one that is dense, uniform, and comprehensive (ex. 9.18). These intermittent patches of set C do more than recall a particular type of material: they periodically and predictably recreate a distinctive landscape design. Shifts from long to thin array partitions, and crests and troughs in the harmonic rhythm

another (encouraging segment formation) only to force them apart again (and discourage it), also contribute to the compositional heterogeneity of the associative landscape.

Example 9.17. Morris, "Rising Early," section I, mm. 20–23

Like other pieces in the *Nine*, "Rising Early" is dotted with longer-range associations that operate within and across sections, and among pieces. In section I, for example, the recollection and recomposition of an ordered set of three gestures from mm. 11–12 (four relatively fast notes, two falling, two rising; an isolated semitone ascent in the low register; and an isolated descending dyad in a very low register) in mm. 16–17 is a bit cumbersome to describe, but easy to hear as a shadow of a reminiscence (exx. 9.19a and 9.19b). Flickers of recollection of moments from "Between" add another dimension to the local landscape.[28] Even as the pitch succession <B4, G♯4, A4> in m. 31, lyne 1 (in ex. 9.18), fits into the patch of set *C* that surrounds the first block boundary, temporal placement of the left hand's B♭3 from lyne 2 forms a cross-lyne segment that recalls the pitch sequence <B4, G♯4, {B♭3, A4}> in mm. 11–12 of "Between." Note that this association is purely contextual: the two segments come from different strings, different array columns, and passages shaped by different associative sets (set *D* in the case of "Between," mm. 11–12, versus set *C* for m. 31 of "Rising Early").

(Segment of set *C* recalls "Between," mm. 11–12, at pitch level)

Example 9.18. Morris, "Rising Early," section I, mm. 27–31

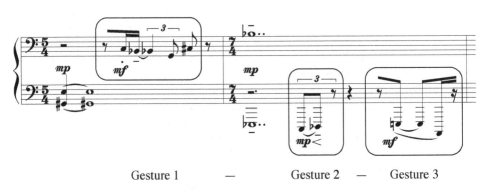

Gesture 1   —   Gesture 2   —   Gesture 3

Example 9.19a. Morris, "Rising Early," section I, mm. 11–12

Gesture 1   —   Gesture 2 — Gesture 3

Example 9.19b. Morris, "Rising Early," section I, mm. 15–17

The nexus of associations grows as we move into section III, where another instance of the pitch sequence <B4, G♯4, A4> appears in m. 67 (ex. 9.20). Like its consociate in m. 31 this too is a string segment, but it comes from a different string and set of order positions (that is, the segments in mm. 31 and 67–68 are in a TC xy relation, not TC xx). The plot thickens when we realize that Morris is also using the structural connection between section III of "Rising Early" and "Between" to create flashes between the two pieces. Measures 67–68 of "Rising Early" are based on the same bits of strings as mm. 11–12 of "Between." The structural affinity enables a faint flash between the two passages, in which the three segments shown collectively recall the triadic segments of set *D* that appear at the corresponding point in "Between."[29] Measure 69 continues the long-range association between the two pieces, but the flash is discrete and discontinuous: rather than summon m. 13 of "Between," the segment <C♯6, G♭5, F5> in lyne 1, m. 69 recalls <C♯6, F♯5, F5> in lyne 1 from *m. 17 (not m. 14)* of "Between." (The discontinuity in associative referents reflects the repartitioning of the array from block III to create the array for "Between.") This important wrinkle in the structural connection between the two pieces manifests audibly as the expansion or contraction of time (depending on which piece one takes as the referent), and as a distinct sense of recollection that is nonetheless hard to place.

Example 9.20. Morris, "Rising Early," section III, mm. 67–69

I hope by now to have conveyed a sense both of the interconnective detail at work among the *Nine* pieces and the diversity of their associative landscapes. Both aspects of the set are shaped by the structure of the pc array and guidelines for realization in conjunction with some improvisation in realization. Before closing, I'd like to pay a quick visit to two more pieces that represent extremes of landscape composition in the *Nine*, "Loose Canon" and "Glimpse." While the associative organization in "Canon" is unusually clear, dense, and comprehensive, that of "Glimpse" is unusually sparse.

The pc array for "Loose Canon" has three blocks. Block I, and its transformation by T_9I in block III (plus lyne exchange from top to bottom) has three lynes and 14 columns; block II, four lynes and 19 columns. The columns in all three blocks are usually octachords.[30] Each of the columnar SCs in block I (and block III) is unique; a few repetitions occur within block II. Strings appear to have been chosen to maximize audible relations among strings within and between blocks. The strings in block I (and block III) are related by transposition (ex. 9.21). Those in block II form two transpositional pairs; each replicates two strings from block I or III.

Block I	Block II	Block III
T_9IP	T_AP	T_AP
T_AIP	T_BP	T_BP
T_BIP	T_AIP	T_0P
	T_BIP	

Example 9.21. Morris, "Loose Canon," string forms

True to its title, "Loose Canon" is a strict canon with respect to pitch intervals and gestures, but one beset by rhythmic stutters and falters. The stutters are slight expansions or contractions in the durations of notes or rests from *dux* to *comes*; falters reflect differences in the pacing of lynes from column to column. The canon of gestures makes for a dense associative landscape unlike any other in the *Nine*. Example 9.22a is a score for mm. 1–9; boxes enclose eighteen segments of seven local associative sets *E–K*. Example 9.22b provides the corresponding swatch of the array. Example 9.22c represents the segmentation shown on the score in a schematic association map that indicates the extent of each segment in *E–K*.

The landscape unfurls as a series of associative elisions: $S_{1\text{-duration}}$ marks off a set of gestures in the *dux*; each becomes the seed of an associative set that acquires segments as it spills from voice to voice. Just as in Nancarrow's *Study*

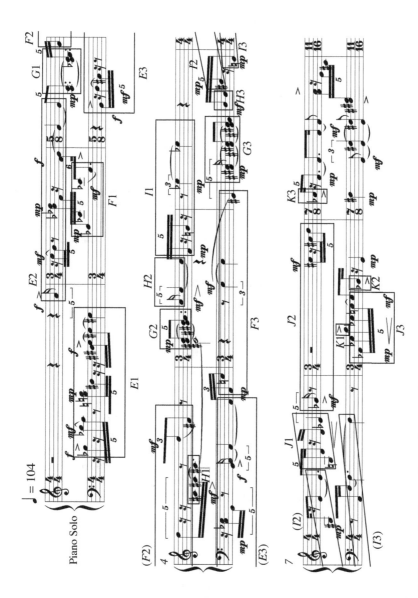

Example 9.22a. Morris, "Loose Canon," mm. 1–9, with eighteen segments of local sets E–J

m. #		1	2	3	4	5	6	7	8
1	T_9IP	9	0BA157-	-7-	26	B89057	3	6	12
2	T_AIP	A10B268-	-837	09A	1-	-1	6	84723	9
3	T_BIP			B21	03794-	-4	81AB27	95	834A7-
	SC:	8-2	8-22	7-2	8-13	8-19	8-20	8-1	8-9

Example 9.22b. Morris, "Loose Canon," block I, columns 1–8

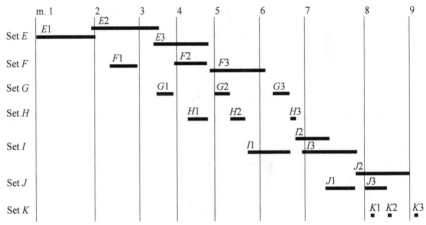

Example 9.22c. Morris," Loose Canon," mm. 1–8, schematic map of sets *E–J*

No. 37, although the pitch canon is absolutely strict, the associative landscape is surprisingly dynamic, ever changing in its material and compositional heterogeneity. This play in the landscape reflects the partition scheme of the array: partitioning the strings of each block into a set of columns of uniform size requires lynes to repeatedly exchange the roles of *dux* and *comes*. The first such exchange occurs in m. 5, where lyne 2 overtakes lyne 1; the next is in m. 8, where lyne 3 overtakes lyne 2. These exchanges, conjoined with differences in the lengths of string segments that form gestures, fluctuations in harmonic rhythm (number of beats in a bar), and a sprinkling of rhythmic "stutters," continuously reinvent the associative landscape and help Morris to create some remarkable moments, such as the bold unison between lynes 1 and 4 in m. 15 that announces the start of section II.

"Glimpse"

The compositional design for "Glimpse" is unique in the *Nine* in that it consists of a single lyne that concatenates four forms of the string (T_AP, T_BP, T_0IP, and RT_3IP), each realized over the piano's full range. The first string, T_AP, is the string from lyne 1 of "Between." The strings T_AP and T_BP occur many times throughout the *Nine* pieces (in "Rising Early," "Had," Figurine," and "Loose

formation of the string, T_9IP, is embedded in the concatenation of the other four. Example 9.23 shows the start of this string, tucked inside the faster-moving T_AP. The embedded string T_9IP is realized a note at a time, always set on the first beat of a measure within the same ten-semitone span it occupied as lyne 2 of "Between." Its notes are made to stand out in various ways: they are often longer, and isolated by attack points or gaps in register.

I. (mm. 1–9)

```
                                             1
Ops:      1  2  3  4  5  6  7  8  9  0  1  2  3  4  5  6  7  8

               9  1  1  9  8  A  5  8  7  3  B  9  7  A  4  9  5  B
1: T_A P   A   7  8  9  6  2  0  5  1  8  B  A  7  2  0  4  1  6
2: T_9 IP               9        0              B  A                 1

Ops:           1        2              3  4                 5
```

```
          2                          3
Ops:      9  0  1  2  3  4  5  6  7  8  9  0  1  2  3  4  5

               6  3  8  6  3  2  4  4  9  A  B  5  3  B  B  3
1: T_A P   5   B  2  A  4  7  9  1  5  2  0  B  4  7  6  5  8
2: T_9 IP  5                    7              2              6

Ops:       6                    7              8              9
```

Example 9.23. Morris, "Glimpse," block I of array

Composed from a single lyne, the musical surface of "Glimpse" inherits and reflects the harmonic diversity of the underlying string. Local associations by contextual criteria that involve pitch (i.e., by C_{SC}, C_{int}, C_{pc}, C_{ip}, and C_{pitch}) are rare; the cluster of three members of SC 3-2[013] in mm. 9–12 (among {F♯4, F6, A♭6} in m. 9, <B4, G♯4, A4> in mm. 10–12, and {G3, B♭3, A4} in m. 12) that falls out of the retrograde relation between ops 1–3 and 35–33, and RI relation between ops 1–3 and 3–5, is a notable exception. Nor does rhythm support the formation of associative sets. Instead, segmentation proceeds largely by sonic criteria: sustained notes, often coupled with sudden changes in register, encourage segmentation by $S_{1\text{-duration}}$ and $S_{1\text{-pitch}}$; $S_{1\text{-attack}}$ and $S_{1\text{-rest}}$ also contribute. But contextual criteria still play a very important role. In "Glimpse," associative proximity and temporal proximity are diametrically opposed. Rather than operate locally, the strongest associations are long-range, between moments that coalesce around fragments of the embedded string T_9IP and fragments of the same string—*realized with the same pitches*—in lyne 2 of "Between."[31] Thus the "Glimpse" of the title is of "Between" itself, as what appears to serve as the final piece in the set.[32]

Connections between the two pieces drift in and out of focus, but they can be easy to hear when coincidence between sonic and contextual criteria in the realization of lyne 2 of "Between" creates strong segments that can then be recalled in "Glimpse." Example 9.24 shows mm. 10–15 of "Glimpse," which realize ops 10–15 of T_9IP; these correspond to mm. 11–12 of "Between," shown back in examples 9.1 and 9.4. In "Between," registral proximity supported an association between segments $D3$ and $D5$ by $C_{SC\ 3\text{-}11[037]}$ and $C_{cseg\ <021>}$. Although both segments are major triads with a bent contour, they have different origins with respect to the array: $D5$ realizes three consecutive order positions of T_9IP in lyne 2; $D3$ connects a note from lyne 3 to two notes from lyne 2. A third segment, $C4$ ($<B\flat 2, G2, D\flat 3>$), a diminished triad in an inverted twist contour, appears within the same time frame in the low register. Synergy among $D3$, $D4$, and $D5$ helps secure a place in memory for all three. In the corresponding passage of "Glimpse," isolating $<B4, G\sharp 4>$ (ops 10 and 11 of T_9IP) with a slur triggers a flash back to $D3$ in m. 11 of "Between." Although the next three notes that participate in the flash ($<A4, C5, F4>$) are much farther apart in "Glimpse" than in $D5$ of "Between," the TS_2 realization rule, bolstered by the longer durations of C5 and F4 relative to other notes in the bar and by the availability of the long-range association, encourages the listener to connect and to hear them as a segment.

Another strong flash appears toward the end of "Glimpse." "Between" closes with three segments ($C7$, $C8$, and $C9$ in mm. 28–30) that form a patch of set C (refer back to ex. 9.5b). The end of "Glimpse" recalls the pitches of $C8$,

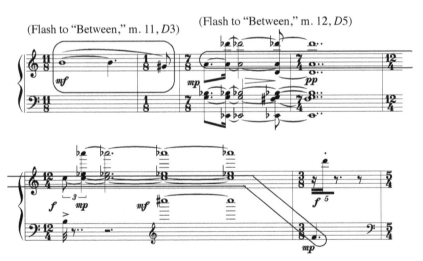

Example 9.24. Morris, "Glimpse," mm. 10–15

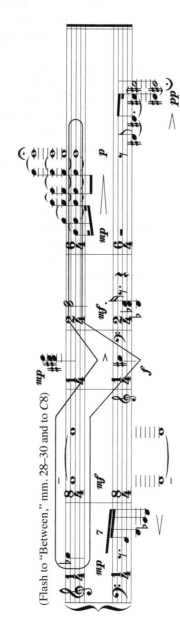

Example 9.25. Morris, "Glimpse," mm. 32–36

D5, B4> (ops 31–35) shaped by a rise and fall in dynamics (<*mp, mf, f, mf, mp*>) (ex. 9.25). In "Glimpse," a local pitch invariance ({B4, B♭4, C5, C♯5}) shared by the pitch realizations of the T_0I-related ops 1–5 and ops 31–35, reinforces recognition of the latter *as* a segment, that then participates in a long-range relationship with the end of "Between."

An important thread throughout this chapter is the relationship between musical structure and surface—both the musical implications of structure conjoined with principles of realization, and the range of choice that remains available until late in the compositional process. This thread is easily sewn into analyses of other works by Morris, music by Babbitt and other composers (such as Andrew Mead and Richard Swift) that raises similar issues, and more generally to music in which relations between structure and surface are a persistent concern. But other aspects of our analysis are quite specific to the *Nine*, most notably the degree of communication among pieces in the set, mutual permeability of pieces, and range of musical landscapes and situations that results. Over the course of the *Nine*, the listener visits a variety of musical landscapes connected by a web of associative paths that have a curious tendency to turn in on themselves and run into one another. Only through multiple hearings, and performances of the set in various orderings, are the common structural forces and distinct ecologies of each of its *Nine* landscapes gradually revealed.

Part Four

Outward and Onward

Chapter Ten

Further Considerations and Extended Applications

Writing the last chapter of a book that opens up a way of thinking is a paradoxical endeavor. Rather than open or close, I will attempt to do both by exploring two ideas that set the theoretic exposition of chapters 2 and 3 and the six analyses of chapters 4–9 in a larger context while opening up new areas for pursuit. The first idea is the relationship between association and associative sets on the one hand, and musical transformations and transformation networks on the other. The second is how the conceptual space defined by our theoretic framework and its schema might be used to support comparative analysis of musical styles, of analytic approaches and individual analyses, and studies of musical processes.

Association and Transformation

At a certain remove, association and transformation, and association digraphs and transformation networks, can look a lot alike. Both association and transformation are predicated on equivalence in a certain respect; this is explicitly recorded by individual contextual criteria for associations among segments, but usually just a tacit prerequisite for transformations. The visual representations of associative and transformational topology and precedence, which both involve graphs in which the node contents are specified, edges are labeled, and arrows indicate precedence between nodes, also suggest a certain affinity. But association and transformation represent distinct analytical "attitudes" focused on space and action, respectively; association and transformation graphs represent compatible but complementary approaches to music analysis.[1] We will begin by exploring some important differences between associative and transformational approaches to analysis. We then consider how one might use associative sets, association digraphs, and associative landscapes in conjunction with transformation networks as complementary analytical perspectives.

First, a review of some basic concepts. Back in chapter 3, we defined an associative set as a collection of segments bound by contextual criteria into an integrated system, an associative configuration as a topology of segments in an associative set, and an association graph (*AG*) as the visual representation

nodes are populated by segments, and edges indicate associative adjacency. An association digraph (*DAG*) is an association graph in which one or more edges is replaced by an arrow that indicates the order of precedence for a pair of nodes. In an association digraph, either all arrows represent associative chronology, or all represent score chronology.

The association digraph is the associative counterpart of a transformation network.[2] In *Generalized Musical Intervals and Transformations*, David Lewin defines a transformation network as the ordered sextuple (S, NODES, ARROW, SGP, TRANSIT, CONTENTS),[3] which includes the formal definition of a transformation graph in the ordered quadruple (NODES, ARROW, SGP, TRANSIT).[4] NODES is a "set in the mathematical sense";[5] ordered pairs of nodes in the ARROW relation map into members of the semigroup SGP; and TRANSIT is a function that maps ARROW into SGP. In a transformation network, "S is a family of objects (that are to be transformed in various ways)" and "CONTENTS is a function mapping NODES into S."[6] Within any particular network, the contents of NODES are restricted to members of a single set S comprised of objects that are formally equivalent and related to one another by transformations in the semigroup SGP.

Association digraphs and transformation networks are closely related. In simple cases, one can map an association digraph onto a transformation network just by changing the contents of nodes from segments to elements that represent predicable properties of segments within a single dimension, and changing the labels for edges from contextual criteria that identify grounds for equivalence to transformations predicated on equivalence.[7] But association digraphs differ from transformation networks in some important respects. For one thing, while the nodes of an association digraph are filled with *actual musical segments*—multidimensional entities that engage any number of musical dimensions and individual contextual criteria—the nodes of a transformation network are filled with *abstract* musical objects—pcsets, *Klangs*, tones of a fundamental bass, or other elements from a *single* musical (contextual) dimension that can be interrelated by transformations within a semigroup. This critical difference in the dimensionality of the objects that occupy nodes also applies to edges. In an association digraph, the contextual criteria that label an edge can be as numerous and diverse as the relational properties that associate its incident segments (recall, though, that for clearer visual presentation two or more contextual criteria can be bundled along an edge). In a transformation network, each ARROW that accompanies an edge between NODES carries a *single* transformation and all transformations in the network derive from a *single* semigroup, SGP.[8] So whereas the nodes and arrows of a transformation network involve *one* musical dimension and *one* set S whose members are interrelated by *individual* transformations drawn from *one* semigroup SGP, the nodes of an association digraph typically involve *many* musical dimensions, and

contextual criteria, and the set of elements defined by contextual criteria evident in the graph need not form—in fact, it very rarely forms—a mathematical semigroup, group, or direct product group.

These differences in node content account for the relative complexity, or inherent "messiness," of working with associations among segments, association graphs, and association digraphs as opposed to transformations and transformation networks. Transformation networks owe much of their formal power and elegance to restrictions on the contents of S and ARROW. If formalization is the goal, removing these restrictions is a huge concession: in general, *association graphs and digraphs have no (requisite) (semi)group structure*. But the very freedom from restrictions on S and ARROW that undermines semigroup structure has its advantages. The multidimensional segments that occupy the nodes of an association graph preserve musical detail that is lost in a transformation network. Association graphs are also more flexible than transformation networks, with greater breadth of application. So even when it is relatively easy to make an association digraph into a transformation network by changing segments to elements and contextual criteria to transformations (or vice versa), the choice of model enables or precludes certain analytic opportunities. Whereas transformation networks harness the power of mathematical structures and generalization, association graphs and digraphs provide means to explore the complex geometry of musical detail and variation.

As graphs, association digraphs and transformation networks raise many of the same issues in visual representation, such as how to represent a complex topology in two dimensions; the degree of fit or misfit among score chronology, node precedence, and node layout; and visual emphasis as a means to express analytical interpretation. Recall that a graph, as a collection of nodes and edges, defines a topology but no particular spatial representation of that topology. A single graph can have many representations. The arrangement of nodes on the page from left to right and top to bottom—which causes arrows in a transformation network to point right or left, up or down—can itself be used as a means to express aspects of musical chronology.[9] The different sorts of objects that occupy the nodes of association digraphs and transformation networks, and the different origins and significance of the arrows attached to these nodes, affect the relationship among node precedence, spatial placement, and musical chronology in each type of graph. There are two basic issues to discuss; the first is relatively superficial, the other more fundamental.

The first issue is the naming of nodes. When Lewin discusses transformation networks, he takes pains to distinguish the chronology of transformations represented by arrow chains from "musical" chronology, which he often (but not always) represents by left-right or top-bottom placement on a page to the extent possible for a given network.[10] When the nodes of a transformation network are named by the elements they contain (as is often the case), it can be difficult, if

tional counterpart of our associative chronology) and musical chronology (score chronology) simultaneously in a two-dimensional representation, and thus also to ascertain the degree of fit or misfit between these two types of chronology.[11] In contrast, on an association graph where segment names usually encode score chronology, it is much easier to assess fit or misfit between score and associative chronology. Of course, one can simply recast transformation networks along these lines, naming nodes to reflect score chronology and thereby releasing the spatial dimension for interpretive purposes. Lewin does this in his analysis of Dallapiccola's "Simbolo" (which we will discuss shortly).

The second, more substantial issue concerns the origins of arrows and node precedence in transformation networks and association graphs. In transformation networks arrows are intrinsic: the pair of objects housed in an arrow's incident nodes determine the kind of transformation and the arrow's direction of travel (for instance, most pitch-class transpositions imply single-headed arrows that point in a specific direction; T_0, T_6, retrograde, inversions, and other involutions imply double-headed arrows). But in an association graph arrows are optional: the contextual criteria that attach to edges indicate equivalence, which is neutral with regard to node precedence. To make an association graph into an association diagraph one adds arrowheads to one or more edges *only as desired*. Thus what is a formal requirement for transformation networks is optional for association graphs, giving analysts an "extra" graphic channel to highlight aspects of score chronology (embedded in segment names), indicate flows of associative chronology, or track the order with which segments were recognized or added to the set during the analytic process.

Comparative Analysis with Association Graphs and Transformation Networks: A Case Study

Whenever the elements that occupy the nodes of a transformation network can be mapped one-to-one and onto the set of segments that occupy the nodes of an association graph, the two conceptualizations and representations can be conjoined in comparative analysis as complementary perspectives on musical organization. Transformation networks, and network isography in particular, model structural regularities. Association graphs, evolutions of graphs, digraphs, and associative landscapes model range of variation and its temporal disposition and unfolding. Using both transformation networks and association graphs, analysts can uncover parallels and conflicts in topology and among different sorts of chronology—the chronology of transformations, of associations, of events in the score, and perhaps also of events in the analytic process.

For a sketch of what comparative analysis with transformation networks and association graphs might look like, we turn to Dallapiccola's "Simbolo," the

transformational relations among the pitch-class configurations that realize its individual row statements.[12] Lewin identifies three tetrachordal melodies, subject to registral permutation. These are the "BACH" motive (the series of pitch intervals <–1, +3, –1> or its inversion), the "conjunct line" (chromatic descent through a minor third), and the "2e2" line (which traces the pitch interval ordering <+2, –1, +2> or its inversion).[13] He also points out a large-scale shift from an "odd-dyad-out" pc configuration in mm. 1–16 to a purely trichordal one in mm. 17–36. Having organized his observations about each half of the piece into a pc network, Lewin places the two networks side by side in his example 1.5, reproduced here as example 10.1.[14] In accompanying text he emphasizes a structural correspondence between the left and right networks that represents the transformational chronology of mm. 21–36 as a "variation on a substructure" of that in mm. 1–16.[15]

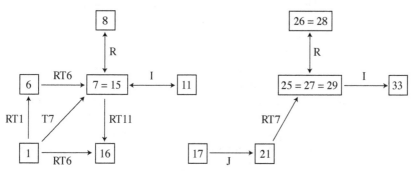

Example 10.1. Lewin, *Musical Form and Transformation: Four Analytic Essays*, example 1.5. © 1993 Yale University Press. Reproduced with permission.

Before we can create an association graph and engage in comparative analysis, we must first ask whether the measure numbers that occupy nodes in Lewin's network correspond to musical segments and, if so, whether all these segments and pc configurations can be considered part of the same associative set. The answer to both questions is yes. Every measure number that occupies a node in Lewin's network indicates the start of a row form realized by sonic and contextual criteria as a musical segment; every one of the resulting segments is supported by a TC criterion that involves the row and one of Lewin's "odd-dyad-out" configurations (mm. 1–16) or trichordal configurations (mm. 17–36).[16] Individual row statements explore a range of variation in texture, duration, articulation, and register. The relative prominence of Lewin's three melodic lines changes, as do specific pc partitions of the aggregate. Although one certainly can group these variations into two relatively distinct associative subsets, to facilitate dialogue with Lewin's network analysis I will consider all variation to be internal to a single large associative set *A*.

that account for all of mm. 1–16. To facilitate comparison with the network on the left side of Lewin's example 1.5, I name segments by set and measure number. As in Lewin's network, score chronology proceeds from left to right and bottom to top on the graph to the extent possible. Differences in line weight indicate relative associate proximity: thicker edges indicate stronger associations; thinner edges, weaker ones. Arrows indicate which associative adjacencies are articulated as temporal adjacencies; edges without arrows indicate associative adjacency only. To focus attention on the topology and geometry of the underlying graph, example 10.2b extracts segment names from example 10.2a, labels the edges with contextual criteria, and adds two boxes that enclose associative subsets in mm. 1–10 and 11–16.

Topologically, the underlying graph can be seen as almost a simple tree (a linear sequence of eight nodes) but with an extra edge ($A1$–5—$A11$–14) that introduces a loop. This "extra" edge connects two associative sets with isomorphic subgraphs that represent associative organization in mm. 1–10 and mm. 11–16. Along with the twelve-tone row and pitch-class configuration that associate all segments of A in mm. 1–16, segments in the left subgraph are associated by $C_{ip\ I\ <-1,\ +3,\ -1>}$ (the "BACH" motive), an association that is strengthened by repetition of a pitch spacing plus some individual pitches and dyadic subsets from a trichordal pc partition. Segments in the right subgraph belong to a different associative subset based on the pitch dyad {F3, G♭4} (also found in $A8$–10 in a transitional capacity) with a melodic focus on the pcs B♭, A♮, A♭, and G. Within each subgraph and subset, two ninety-degree turns indicate three smaller overlapping subsets of two segments each. The resulting design parallel between mm. 1–10 and mm. 11–16 is underlined by the associative adjacency of $A1$–5 and $A11$–14: both segments are slow tetrachordal melodies (of the "BACH" and "2e2" types, respectively) that span a series of four verticalities, accompanied by a "walking" minor ninth and followed by three shorter segments with faster surface rhythm.

Comparing the association digraph in example 10.2b to Lewin's left network turns up an important similarity. The left subgraph of the digraph is isomorphic to a subgraph of Lewin's left network: both trace a path from m. 1 to mm. 6, 7, and 8–10. But there are also important differences. Lewin's network represents the pitch-class configuration in m. 7 as the T7 of that in mm. 1–5. But when we change the musical objects under consideration from pitch-class configurations to actual musical segments, aspects of surface rhythm and gesture suggest that $A7$ has closer ties to $A8$–10 or $A6$, than to $A1$–5. As a result, there is no edge between $A1$–5 and $A7$ in the association digraph comparable to the T7 arrow in the network. Another difference involves mm. 7 and 15. Because these two bars present the same pitch-class configuration, the network conflates them to a single node (7=15).[17] But mm. 7 and 15 contain distinct musical segments that differ in register, contour, and their top-line melodies (the BACH figure in

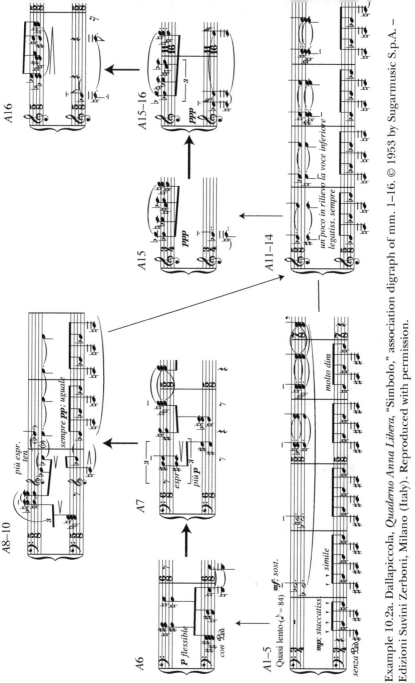

Example 10.2a. Dallapiccola, *Quaderno Anna Libera*, "Simbolo," association digraph of mm. 1–16. © 1953 by Sugarmusic S.p.A. – Edizioni Suvini Zerboni, Milano (Italy). Reproduced with permission.

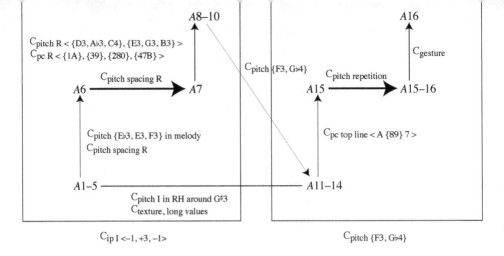

Example 10.2b. Dallapiccola, "Simbolo," digraph of mm. 1–16 in schematic format

m. 7, the conjunct line in m. 15). The association digraph represents both segments, but places them in different subgraphs. It also recognizes another segment not explicitly represented by any node in Lewin's network, A15–16. A slight rhythmic variation on A15, A15–16 completes the design parallel between mm. 1–10 and 11–16. Whereas the network represents all eight segments in mm. 1–16 as part of a single structure, the left and right subgraphs of the association digraph indicate a formal division at m. 11.[18] The association graph focuses on the local design parallel between mm. 1–10 and mm. 11–16; the arrangement of nodes in Lewin's left network instead supports a larger isography between the network representations of mm. 1–16 and mm. 17–36.

With regard to mm. 1–16, the transformation network and association graph do agree on an important point: with one exception (the arrow from m. 1 to m. 7 in the network), nodes temporally adjacent in the music are connected by an edge that represents a single transformation or an associative adjacency. So if we detach m. 7 from m. 15 in the network and rearrange nodes on the page, we can bring the two representations into relative harmony.[19] In the second half of the piece, however, topological differences between an approach focused on pitch-class configurations and transformational networks and one that is more explicitly concerned with associative organization become more substantial.

Example 10.3a is an association digraph for mm. 17–46; once again, score chronology proceeds left to right and bottom to top to the extent possible (and as in Lewin's right network). Example 10.3b extracts nodes and edges from

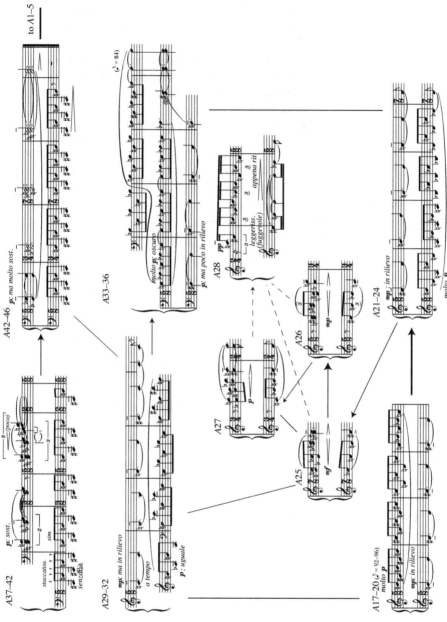

Example 10.3a. Dallapiccola, "Simbolo," association digraph of mm. 17–46. © 1953 by Sugarmusic S.p.A. – Edizioni Suvini Zerboni Milano (Italy). Reproduced with permission.

structed from two C_4 subgraphs (containing nodes A17–20, A21–24, A29–32 and A33–36; and nodes A25, A26, A27, and A28) connected by a path through node A25 (<A21–24, A25, A29–32>). A third subgraph of two nodes (A37–42 and A42–46, top left) represents the coda. Notice that temporal adjacency (encoded in segment names) is not always expressed as associative adjacency. Nodes along the top edge of the C_4 subgraph held together by the BACH line ($C_{\text{ip I}\,<-1,\,+3,\,-1>}$, lower left in ex. 10.3b) are *associatively* adjacent to those in the bottom edge, but not *temporally* adjacent: the quasi-developmental material in the second C_4 graph (upper right in ex. 10.3b) intervenes. But with regard to associative chronology, it is A29–32 that intervenes: recalling the BACH melody of A17–20 (under T_{-4}), it retains the pitch-class configuration introduced in A25 and maintained through A28. Also note that the full graph has no ND- (node-distinct) or ED-path (edge-distinct) path: because no edges represent the temporal adjacencies of A28 and A29–32, or A33–36 and A37–42, we must trace three paths to visit every node on the graph. These three paths correspond to three formal sections in the music: A17–20 through A28 (melodic statement followed by developmental activity); A29–32 through A33–36 (parallel to mm. 17–24), and A37–42 to A42–46 (coda).

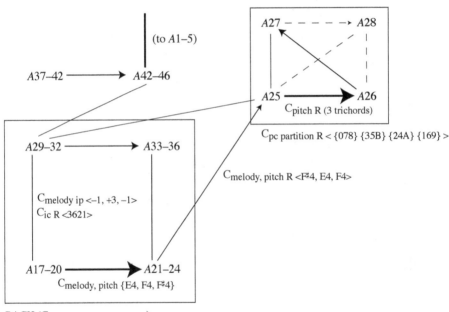

Example 10.3b. Dallapiccola, "Simbolo," digraph of mm. 17–46 in schematic format

digraph for the same passage turns up a number of differences in interpretation. Once again, whereas the network conflates multiple instances of a pitch-class configuration into a single node, the graph recognizes distinct segments. As a result, two nodes in Lewin's network (25=27=29 and 26=28) become five segments in the graph; the involution between these two network nodes unfolds into the "developmental" C_4 subgraph plus a fifth node, A29–32 (the return of the BACH melody that creates a design parallel with m. 17). This time the overall topologies of the network and the graph have little in common. The network is a tree (with 25=27=29 as its root); the graph contains multiple loops. And whereas Lewin's left and right networks and his text discussion emphasize transformational isographies between mm. 1–16 and 17–36, the association graphs in examples 10.2b and 10.3b show a design parallel within the first part of the piece but not within the second, nor between the two parts.

But the case for or against a design parallel between mm. 1–16 and 17–36 depends not only on the topology of a graph—the configuration of nodes and edges—but on the particular *representation of a graph* one uses. Example 10.4

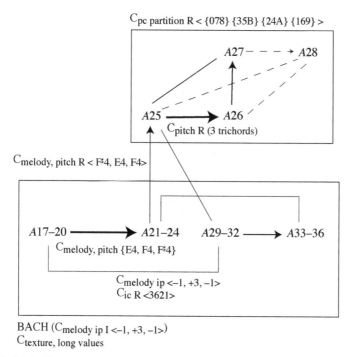

Example 10.4. Alternate representation of a subgraph from 10.3b

10.3b (without the coda), but rearranges nodes to bring out a design parallel with mm. 1–16. The two C_4 subgraphs in the lower left and upper right of example 10.3b now appear in the lower and upper half of the graph in example 10.4, respectively. Nodes along the path <A21–24, A25, A26, A27> are rearranged to show an isography with nodes in the left subgraph of mm. 1–10 in example 10.2b. Both the overlapping subset organization and relative strength of association (relative line weights) among segments in mm. 1–10 is preserved in mm. 21–27. The two nodes at the lower right of example 10.4 add a companion segment to the melodic statement A33–36 (analogous to A11–14 in ex. 10.2b) but there is no discursive material comparable to that in mm. 15–16. By rearranging nodes on the page, we have added a facet to our musical interpretation: isographies between the two *representations* of graphs for mm. 1–16 and 17–36 now suggest a parallel in associative design at two levels: within mm. 1–16, and between mm. 1–16 and mm. 17–36.

The foregoing analysis of "Simbolo" shows how one can use transformation networks and association graphs to bring out complementary aspects of musical organization. Transformation networks can focus on pitch-class organization and association graphs on form, for example. "Simbolo" is a fine, controlled environment for such a study: all of the segments in a single large associative set involve pitch-class configurations related to one another by serial transformations. But what if transformational relations are not so crisp or tight? Perhaps nested Klumpenhouwer networks or other sorts of transformational voice leading will support the formation of networks for comparative analysis with association graphs. But perhaps more often the inherent disparity between the relatively low dimensionality of elements conducive to a transformational approach and higher dimensionality of musical segments, associations, and association graphs will inspire different, even complementary, ways of thinking about a piece or passage.

Using the Schematic of the General Theory:
Spaces and Traversals

Just as we can use an association graph to represent the topology of associations among segments, and paths on an association digraph to show temporal or associative precedence, we can think of the schematic in example 1.1 as depicting a topology of ideas defined by the general theory upon which we sketch traversals that represent various musical processes. The rest of this chapter explores these possibilities. It has three parts. The first part provides the theoretic basis for this endeavor, beginning with the schematic as a map of a conceptual space that includes sonic, associative, and structural aspects of musical organization, then moving on to traversals that represent motions within this space. The second

tive Analysis of Musical Spaces" shows how one might use the schematic to bring out differences in intra- and interopus musical style, or between music analyses. "Applications 2: Traversals and Processes" shows how one might use traversals to model chronology and motivation in music analysis, or in other musical processes such as composition, improvisation, and pedagogy of analysis.

Theory

To minimize opportunities for confusion between the relatively concrete world of association graphs and paths in chapter 3 and the more abstract world that we will now inhabit, I will use the term *schematic* specifically to denote a graph that represents the topology of concepts defined by the general theory. A *traversal* is a path on such a schematic.[20] A traversal can visit any of the schematic's nodes in any order.[21] It can visit the same node more than once (a traversal need not be an ND-path) and define a total or partial ordering of nodes.

Spaces. The schematic embraces the sonic, contextual, and structural domains. But we can also think of it as a composition of three domain-specific *subschematics* that intersect at the phenoseg level. Each of these subschematics offers a distinct perspective on, and approach to, music analysis; conversely, both individual segments and higher-level aspects of sonic, associative, and structural organization can be seen as projections from the sonic, contextual, and structural domains.

The sonic subschematic begins with a disjunctive orientation, then proceeds through sonic criteria, subtypes, and individual criteria to sonic genosegs that coincide or conflict to produce phenosegs. Although sonic subschematics can include higher levels of sonic organization, I do not develop a theory of higher-level sonic organization in this book: to do so would be a substantial project in its own right and one that would take us quite far from my intended focus on associative organization. Work by James Tenney and Larry Polansky and by Robert Cogan provides two contrasting examples of what a theory of higher-level sonic organization might look like.

As noted earlier, Tenney and Polansky have developed a recursive algorithm for hierarchic segmentation of a monophonic line that provides a consistent approach to sonic organization from individual segments through progressively larger spans.[22] They begin by representing each note as a set of psychoacoustic attributes—a value for pitch, duration, loudness, and timbre. This information becomes input data for the algorithm, together with a set of values for multidimensional scaling across sonic dimensions. Scrolling note by note through the input data, the algorithm calculates the magnitude of disjunction from each event to its immediate successor and locates segment boundaries at points of maximum disjunction before proceeding recursively to the next

of psychoacoustic attributes of individual notes recedes in relation to that of aggregate properties of groups of notes and to sonic disjunctions and segments defined over progressively larger spans. Tenney's concepts of "state" and "shape" represent these higher-level aspects of sonic organization identified with averages and the locus of change, respectively.[23]

Whereas Tenney and Polansky start with psychoacoustic attributes of individual notes in a single melodic line, Cogan starts with the acoustic trace of sonic spectra in a complex musical texture as recorded in a spectrograph.[24] Focusing on higher levels of sonic organization, he emphasizes aggregate features of the sonic surface, often pointing out correspondences with (what amount to) events in the contextual and structural domains. Like Tenney and Polansky, Cogan bases his work on something much like sonic disjunctions— his theory of "oppositions."[25] But the fundamental philosophy and purview of his work is very different—more holistic and heuristic than hierarchic or algorithmic, it focuses on acoustic rather than psychoacoustic features.

Compared to the sonic subschematic, the contextual and structural subschematics are well worked out. The contextual subschematic is the theoretic and analytic focus of this book. Starting with an associative orientation, it includes contextual criteria, subtypes, and individual criteria; contextual genosegs and phenosegs; and associative sets and associative landscapes. All of chapter 3 and much of the analysis in chapters 4–9 takes place within a contextual subschematic or focuses on relationships between aspects of contextual segmentation or associative organization and sonic or structural organization. The structural subschematic begins with a theoretic orientation and proceeds through structural criteria, subtypes, and individual criteria, to structural genosegs subject to realization by coincidence with sonic or contextual genosegs. Realization effectively joins the structural subschematic to the sonic and contextual sub-schematics at the phenoseg level. Higher levels of structural organization proceed according to the choice of orienting theory, its HF, and HEs. So structural organization above the segment level need not be defined by the general theory: it is shaped by the theory or theories one summons as H, whether Schenkerian theory, twelve-tone theory, or something else.

So far we have seen the schematic only in its abstract form, as a map of a conceptual space defined by the theory apart from any specific musical application. One can also interpret the schematic to represent relations among criteria, segments, sets, and so forth in a particular piece or passage. A maximum of eight nodes are fixed by the theory proper: these *fixed nodes* include the three orientations (disjunction, association, and theory), the three basic criterion-types (sonic, contextual, and structural) and the two linked criterion types (TS and TC).[26] All other nodes in the schematic are *variable*—nodes can

as specific individual criteria, segment and set names, and swatches of the associative landscape appear in a particular application. An *interpreted schematic* is a schematic in which the content of at least some variable nodes is specified. Example 10.5 shows the start of an interpreted schematic created for the inaugural theme of Beethoven's Sonata No. 2 in A, op. 2, no. 2. In addition to the fixed nodes, this interpreted schematic shows which sonic and contextual criteria are active in the passage (e.g., $S_{1\text{-pitch}}$, C_{rhythm} ♩| ♪), the five segments they support (*A1–A3*, *B1*, and *B2*), and how these group into associative sets *A* and *B*. In theory one builds an interpreted schematic with each analysis of a composition. But in practice these schematics usually remain purely mental constructs; literal graphic representations and even traversals are best limited to the few nodes essential to develop or make a specific analytic point, such as about chronological precedence or analytical motivation.

Thinking of the schematic as a composite of three sonic, contextual, and structural subschematics helps us untangle aspects of sonic, associative, and structural organization and focus on their attendant differences in analytic approach. But while the sonic, contextual, and structural domains are conceptually distinct, it is important to remember that they refer not to different things, but to different *aspects* of a single multidimensional musical object. Activity in the sonic domain can influence one's impression of associative or structural organization. Associative organization springs most directly from the workings of contextual criteria, but it also depends, to a remarkable extent, on the workings of sonic and even structural criteria that influence segment formation and categorization.[27] Although sonic organization is relatively self-sufficient, even it can be influenced by associations or aspects of musical structure that affect the relative weights of sonic dimensions and perceived significance of sonic disjunctions. With sonic support virtually essential for phenoseg formation, the prevalence of coincidence between sonic genosegs, and contextual or structural genosegs, effectively binds the three subschematics together through nodes at the phenoseg level. Whether considered from a perceptual, interpretive, or even a formal standpoint, sonic, associative, and structural organization are *not* entirely independent, but integrated and interactive. We can represent cross-domain interactions, and the domains' shifting priority in perception or as motivation for analytic observations, with schematic traversals.

Traversals. A traversal is a path that represents an order of precedence, usually conceived as chronology or the motivation to recognize or include two or more nodes in a generic or interpreted schematic. For sake of clarity or convenience in different sorts of analytic situations, I offer two systems for notating traversals: standard order notation and arrow notation. Both name schematic

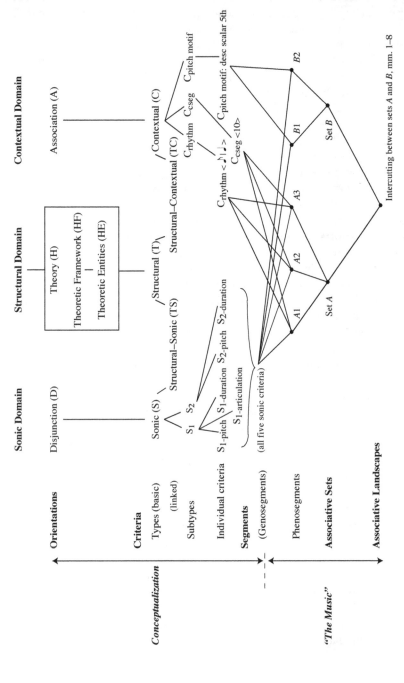

Example 10.5. Interpreted schematic for the inaugural theme of Beethoven's Piano Sonata No. 2 in A, op. 2, no. 2, I

the three basic criterion types sonic, structural, and contextual; $C_{cseg\ <2301>}$, an individual criterion; $A1$ and $A2$, segments of a set A. In standard order notation, nodes are enclosed in angled or curly brackets, nested as needed to indicate partial orderings. For example, $<D, S>$, $<D, S, S_1, S_{1\text{-pitch}}>$, $<T, \{S, C\}>$, and $\{<S, T> <C, T>\}$ represent traversals in standard order notation. In arrow notation, nodes are connected by arrows that indicate ordering. Arrows can point right, left, or in both directions as needed for the most succinct notation; these are supplemented by parentheses or curly brackets to model partial orderings or other nested orderings. For example, $D \rightarrow S$; $D \rightarrow S \rightarrow S_1 \rightarrow S_{1\text{-pitch}}$; $C \leftarrow T \rightarrow S$ (or $\{(T \rightarrow S), (T \rightarrow C)\}$); and $\{(S \rightarrow T) (C \rightarrow T)\}$ (or $C \rightarrow T \leftarrow S$) translate each of the four traversals above into arrow notation. Tracing a traversal directly on a schematic enacts arrow notation. Standard order notation and arrow notation have different strengths. Depending on the traversal, one notation can be clearer or more concise than the other. For example, order notation is more concise for the traversal $<D, S, S_1, S_{1\text{-pitch}}>$, but arrow notation is clearer and more concise for $S \rightarrow T \leftarrow C$, where the conventions of left-to-right orthography built into standard order notation would force a counterintuitive repetition of the T node.

The idea of a traversal is simple—one defines an ordering of nodes that represent orientations, criteria, phenosegs, or other things on a schematic. But understanding just what such orderings of nodes may *mean* with respect to a generic or interpreted schematic is not so easy. Consider a path between two nodes on an association graph, transferred to a schematic. By definition the path connects two phenosegs. But phenosegs never occupy adjacent nodes in a schematic; they can only be connected by visiting a node at a higher (associative set) or lower (criterion) level of organization or analysis. To make sense of such orderings in light of the theory, we must find a way to represent them in terms of concatenated adjacencies.

To do this, we distinguish between two types of adjacencies on a schematic: literal and represented.[28] Two nodes on a schematic are *literally adjacent* if they share an edge. The definition of literal adjacency implies two things: (1) the nodes reside at different levels; and (2) they can be connected without visiting any other nodes. A pair of nodes that is adjacent under these conditions is a *literal adjacency*. But a traversal can also define an ordering of nodes that represents a pair of nodes *as if they were adjacent* even though the nodes are not literally adjacent in the schematic. Such a pair of nodes is a *represented adjacency*.[29]

Armed with this distinction, we define two kinds of traversals, explicit and implicit. For greater clarity as we define terms, I will notate explicit and implicit traversals differently for the time being: explicit traversals will appear in standard order notation; implicit traversals, in arrow notation. This notational distinction is not essential to the concepts and will be lifted shortly (beginning with our first schematic illustration).

that do not correspond to literal adjacencies. Using standard order notation, <D, S>, <D, S, S_1, $S_{1\text{-pitch}}$>, <D, $S_{1\text{-pitch}}$>, <S, T, H>, and <T, {S, C}> denote explicit traversals. Of these five traversals, only the first two define orderings in which each pair of nodes represented as an adjacency corresponds to a literal adjacency on the schematic. Each of the other three contains one or more pairs of nodes that are nonadjacent in the schematic and can only be connected by concatenating schematic edges and visiting intermediate nodes.

In contrast, an *implicit traversal* defines an ordering of nodes in which *every* represented adjacency corresponds to a literal adjacency. For now, we write implicit traversals in arrow notation: $D \rightarrow S$, $D \rightarrow S \rightarrow S_1 \rightarrow S_{1\text{-pitch}}$ and $D \rightarrow S \rightarrow \{(S_1 \rightarrow S_{1\text{-pitch}}) (S_2 \rightarrow S_{2\text{-pitch}})\}$ are two implicit traversals. Arrow notation is appropriate for implicit traversals because it allows us to trace them directly on a schematic. Doing this helps us remember and visualize the arrangement of nodes and edges defined as schematic adjacencies by the theory, which will be useful as we go on to interpret explicit traversals.

Any ordering of nodes can be designated an explicit traversal; an implicit traversal unfolds the implications of an explicit traversal relative to a schematic. Every explicit traversal can be embedded in one or more implicit traversals with the same or a greater number of nodes; conversely, every implicit traversal embeds one or more explicit traversals. To make the distinction plain, I will reserve the term "implicit traversal" for an ordering of nodes that embeds a designated explicit traversal as a proper ordered subset.

To formalize this relationship between explicit and implicit traversals under embedding, we define a process of *interpretation*. To *interpret* an explicit traversal is to identify a specific implicit traversal that embeds it and for which it is a symbolic, abbreviated form. Most explicit traversals can be interpreted in more than one way—that is, they can be identified with more than one implicit traversal that includes the ordering of nodes they define as an ordered proper subset. Hence a few ground rules are in order.

The process of interpretation begins by identifying each represented adjacency with an arrangement of nodes on the schematic. Three arrangements are possible: the nodes of the represented adjacency are (1) *literally adjacent* and therefore belong to different levels or sublevels of the theory; (2) *nonadjacent and nonrevisiting*, meaning that they occupy different levels but can be connected through a series of edges and nodes that does not revisit any level or sublevel; or (3) *nonadjacent and revisiting*, meaning that the nodes occupy the same or different levels but can only be connected through a series of edges and nodes that revisits at least one level or sublevel.

Interpretation proceeds by unfolding each represented adjacency in an explicit traversal into a concatenation of literal adjacencies suggested by the nodes' arrangement as a shortest path. The mechanics of interpretation are as follows: if the represented adjacency corresponds to an arrangement of nonrevisiting, unfold it into the shortest concatenated series of literal adjacencies that does not revisit any level or sublevel; (3) nonadjacent and revisiting, unfold it into the shortest concatenated series of literal adjacencies that revisits levels or sublevels as infrequently as possible.

Example 10.6 interprets the explicit traversal $<D, S, S_{1\text{-pitch}}, T>$, which contains three represented adjacencies, $<D, S>$, $<S, S_{1\text{-pitch}}>$, and $<S_{1\text{-pitch}}, T>$. Each represented adjacency corresponds to a different kind of arrangement of nodes on the schematic: $<D, S>$ is a literal adjacency; $<S, S_{1\text{-pitch}}>$ is nonadjacent and nonrevisiting; $<S_{1\text{-pitch}}, T>$ is nonadjacent and revisiting. The left side of the example shows the explicit traversal in arrow notation. The right side interprets each represented adjacency as a series of literal adjacencies, then concatenates these interpretations into a single implicit traversal as the interpretation of $<D, S, S_{1\text{-pitch}}, T>$.

$$< D, S, S_{1\text{-pitch}}, T >$$
$$= < D, S, S_1, S_{1\text{-pitch}}, \text{genoseg}, T \text{ criterion}, T \text{ subtype}, T >$$

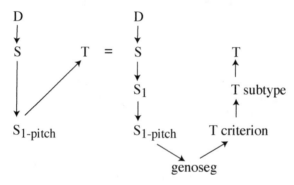

Example 10.6. Interpreting an explicit traversal as an implicit traversal

The idea of revisiting requires some elaboration. Revisiting involves transit through a *branch node*, a node that forms a literal adjacency with two or more nodes that are at the same level as one another but itself resides at an adjacent level. A traversal that connects two nodes at the same level via a branch node is a *branching*. While branchings occur many places in the schematic, those at the genoseg level are privileged in two ways. First, from a formal perspective, the schematic can be seen as two (or more) inverted trees of inclusion relations focused on concepts (orientations, criterion types, subtypes, individual criteria, genosegs) and percepts (genosegs, phenosegs, associative subsets, sets, and landscapes) that meet at the genoseg level. So every pair of nodes that are nonadjacent and require revisiting can be joined via a branching that passes through a

perceptible units, in order to ensure that the conceptual process a traversal represents has a perceptual correlate the traversal must pass (explicitly or implicitly) through one or more genosegs. Thus branchings that include the genoseg sublevel are the default whenever it is necessary to interpolate a branching in order to interpret a lateral or semilateral motion in an explicit traversal.[30]

Our theoretic account of explicit and implicit traversals concludes with two guidelines for expressing explicit traversals and two guidelines for interpreting them.

An explicit traversal is most succinctly notated as an ordering of nodes in which (1) each represented adjacency corresponds to an arrangement of nodes that are either literally adjacent, or nonadjacent but can be connected in the schematic without revisiting; and (2) every node but the first and last is a branch node. These two guidelines ensure that branch nodes are articulated rather than inferred. This constrains, and therein facilitates, the process of interpretation.

There are two guidelines for interpreting an explicit traversal as an implicit traversal: (1) when possible, unfold a represented adjacency into an arrangement of nodes that are adjacent, or nonadjacent and nonrevisiting; (2) when a represented adjacency cannot be unfolded into an arrangement of nodes without revisiting, first postulate a branching that involves the genoseg level (the branch node can occur at the individual criterion, genoseg, or phenoseg level as need be), then unfold the represented adjacency into a concatenation of two literal adjacencies that revisits a level. If the explicit traversal conforms to both of the guidelines for expression given earlier, its interpretation will require reference only to the first guideline for interpretation; else, it will require both interpretation guidelines (1) and (2).

With a theoretic account of the schematic as a conceptual space and of explicit and implicit schematic traversals in place, we can now leave the details in the background and focus on using the schematic and its traversals to support discussion of characteristic features of musical styles and analyses, and to model analytical and other musical processes.

Applications 1: Comparative Analysis of Musical Spaces

Every musical composition, and analysis of a musical composition, has certain characteristics or distinctive features that can be grouped together as elements of style. The neutral metalanguage we have developed and schematic representations of the theory can support comparative analysis of musical style, as well as a kind of meta-music analysis—analysis of music analysis—in terms of (1) the relative import of activity in the sonic, contextual, and structural domains; (2) characteristic criteria and interactions among criteria; (3) global properties, configuration, and disposition of associative sets; and (4) stability or variability

more suggestive than conclusive. I hope that the reader will nonetheless find it stimulating and that it will serve to inspire future work in this area.

Musical Styles. When musicians refer to "early" or "late" Beethoven, the chronological descriptor serves as shorthand for a host of interopus traits and stylistic tendencies in the composer's use of dynamics, register, and other aspects of sonic organization; habits of phraseology and thematic development; and landscape composition. We can use our metalanguage and a schematic of the theory to get at some of these aspects of musical organization in two first movements, one early, one late, from the sonatas No. 2 in A major, op. 2, no. 2 and No. 30 in E Major, op. 109.

As we saw in chapter 4, the first movement of the A-major sonata op. 2, no. 2 has a highly active sonic surface. Within the inaugural theme, sonic disjunctions channel associative sets *A* and *B* into distinct sonic streams. They also separate the inaugural theme from the primary theme, the transition from the second theme, and create the striking intercutting of sets *C* and *F* in the development. But while sharp sonic disjunctions are common in this movement, they don't go particularly deep. All of the sonic disjunctions just mentioned are relatively local, serving to enliven a single associative landscape or separate two sections of modest length.

Although equally striking, sonic organization in the first movement of the late E-major sonata is quite different. The sonic surface moves in large waves and the few strong sonic disjunctions that do occur cut much deeper into the sonic organization. Coordinated activity in multiple sonic dimensions, often synchronized with abrupt changes in the associative landscape, articulate section boundaries at the largest scale. Sonic and contextual dimensions work together to slice the exposition and recapitulation into two sections (the FTA and transition versus the STA), separate the end of the STA from the start of the development, and announce the start of the coda. Compared to the A-major sonata, where the inaugural theme of the FTA is full of sonic disjunctions and the most stable associative landscape occurs in the STA, in the E-major sonata the relative stability of the landscape in the first and second theme groups is reversed. Here the FTA and transition fuse into eight measures that trace one sonic arc based on a single associative set; the *least* stable associative landscape in the movement, composed of a series of short or interlocking associative sets, is in the STA.

Abrupt changes are often supposed to be a hallmark of Beethoven's late style. But in this case it turns out that despite the extraordinary concision of the first movement of op. 109, its associative landscape is actually *more* stable than that for op. 2, no. 2, not only proportionally but in *absolute* terms. In the A-major movement (337 measures), the most stable associative landscapes cover just 18 and 30 measures (mm. 58–76 in the STA, and mm. 131–61 in part I of the development, respectively). The strongest sonic disjunction separates

the first movement of the E-major sonata is less than a third as long (99 measures), a single associative landscape takes in not only the entire development (32 measures, from mm. 16–48) but, propelled by a long-range voice-leading trajectory, spills over and almost effaces the section boundary at the start of the recapitulation, taking in 41 measures (mm. 16–57). In absolute terms, this landscape is about a third longer than the most stable landscape in the A-major sonata; proportional to the length of each movement, the difference is much greater—about *five times as long* in the late sonata as in the early one—in a clear counterexample to prevailing norms.

The two movements also differ in the way they prioritize or integrate activity across the sonic, contextual, and structural domains. In the A-major movement, frequent trade-offs among the three domains as centers of activity help to delineate sections. In the E-major sonata, the sequential and motivic repetition that underlies the stable associative landscapes of the FTA and development is synonymous with progress through the voice-leading matrix. Thus associative and structural organization is tightly integrated in the late sonata, with both nested inside the same broad sonic curve.

The conceptual framework and metalanguage we have developed can inspire and support various sorts of style analysis, limited in scope only by the analyst's imagination. One might enlist the theory, say, in a comparative study of the associative landscapes of notated improvisations (such as the fantasias of C. P. E. Bach, or cadenzas from Schoenberg's Piano Concerto, op. 42 or first movement of Rachmaninov's Piano Concerto No. 3) compared to other compositions by the same composer to see whether "improvisatory" pieces or passages tend to exhibit larger patches and monophonic dispositions, more heterogeneous landscapes, or shifts from the structural toward the sonic and contextual as the primary domains of activity. Or, hypothesizing that patterns of relation among structure, realization, and sonic and contextual aspects of surface design are an aspect of a composer's style, one might use the theory to investigate these patterns, say, in comparative analysis of depth of structure and tendencies toward landscape uniformity or change in the music of Beethoven versus that of Schubert, clarity of segmentation and habits of landscape composition in Schoenberg versus Webern, or use of TS and TC criteria in serial music by Babbitt versus Boulez. One can use the metalanguage to get at stylistic differences between the music of Steve Reich and Philip Glass (Glass's music tends toward more uniform associative sets, tighter patch-matrix relations, and greater coordination between sonic disjunctions and the turnover of associative sets). Or, one could use the theory to trace a course of style change in the music of Morton Feldman from early works such as *Extensions I* (1951), where strong sonic disjunctions prevail and associative set formation is weak, through late pieces such as *Patterns in a Chromatic Field*, in which sonic disjunctions are relatively rare, and clear but

and contextual criteria often conflict.

Responsive to repetition in the realms of music and text, the theory can support comparative analysis of associative organization in different settings of the same poem. In chapter 5 we studied Debussy's setting of Baudelaire's poem "Harmonie du soir." American composer Bernard Rands recalls this setting in a section of his *Canti del sole* (1991) dedicated to the memory of Cathy Berberian. Recalling and recomposing Debussy's vocal line phrase by phrase, Rands preserves the rhythm and much of the original pitch contour but with critical adjustments that dissolve Debussy's whole-tone-flavored B major into the whole-tone-tinged harmonic environment of his own song cycle. Rands even preserves most of Debussy's transposition levels between pairs of vocal phrases. He also preserves an essential feature of Debussy's associative organization—the six small but strong associative sets, each in dispersed disposition and continuously interwoven in an evolving three-part associative polyphony, inherited from Baudelaire's pantoum. But Rands expands the musical space in which these operate from within a song to between two songs. Still, the total associative landscape of his setting is very different from Debussy's. Shedding Debussy's overlay of a second, associative landscape created by instances of the appoggiatura figure (set *A*) and triplet motive (set *B*), Rands adds his own overlay of harmonic associations in the orchestra that have no clear ties to Debussy's piano accompaniment. Continuous cycling through the pitches E♭4, F4, and G4 in the piano, vibraphone, and bells forms a harmonic cloud that persists through much of Rands's song. These forge entirely new associations between vocal phrases with different lines of text (for instance, variants of the chord first heard in the winds as accompaniment to lines 3 and 4 of the first quatrain return for lines 3 and 4 in the second quatrain to new, or rearranged, text) and organize the landscape into a few fairly large sections. Sometimes Rands's harmonic overlay gently counters associations in the text and vocal line: for example, the string tremolo on B♭, C, and E♭ that accompanies the first occurrence of "sang qui se fi-ge" disappears the second time around. The waxing and waning of associations between vocal phrases in Rands's setting, and between his setting and Debussy's, adds an important dimension to the song's overall organization. The cumulative effect is one of transformation: Debussy's relatively heterogeneous associative landscape gives way to Rands's more homogeneous one, which recalls its inspiration like a faded fragrance.

Theories and Analyses. Whereas Schenkerian theory, twelve-tone theory, and other theories of musical structure provide concepts and language that analysts can use to develop and advance a specific interpretation, the general theory provides a broad and relatively neutral metalanguage that accommodates, absorbs, and mediates between different theoretic orientations and analytic interpretations. We can use this metalanguage to pry into areas that fall "between the cracks" of

starting point on its head, we can use the theory of analysis to engage in comparative *analysis of theory* with regard to the domain and level of focus, criteria for segmentation and association, characteristic interactions among the three domains, or temporal progress of the analytic process.[31]

Analysis of theory, and meta-music analysis, is a large area. As just a peek in this direction, we might reflect on each of the analyses in chapters 4–9 with regard to the domain or level of organization of primary interest. The analysis of the first movement of Beethoven's op. 2, no. 2 (chapter 4) engaged all three domains and a Schenkerian theoretic orientation but focused on associative organization at the landscape level and on trade-offs among the sonic, contextual, and structural domains as centers of activity. For Debussy's "Harmonie du soir" (chapter 5) we focused almost exclusively on associative organization, but extended the realm under discussion to sonic, contextual, and structural features of Baudelaire's poem. Gradually we built up a view of higher-level associative organization in which three layers of associative organization in the text (structural repetition, repetition of phonemes, and repetition of imagery) are overlaid with three layers in the music (melodic repetitions conjoined with the text, adjacent melodic repetitions, and two motive-families represented by associative sets A and B). Chapter 6, on Nancarrow's *Study No. 37*, reactivated the structural domain and turned new attention to the criterion and segment levels, specifically to the role that linked TS and TC criteria play in segmentation and their interactions with S and C criteria. From there, we proceeded to the landscape level and to changes in landscape composition that arise as an emergent effect of segment interactions in the underlying pitch and tempo canon. Although Riley's *In C* (chapter 7) is also canonic, here we essentially disconnected the structural domain. With segmentation and even associative sets largely given by the score and the indeterminate alignment of parts in performance as a new variable, we set our sights on comparative analysis of higher-level associative organization—the associative landscapes of comparable plots across several performances. The structural domain remained dormant through our study of Feldman's *Palais de Mari* (chapter 8) where, with segmentation again pretty well defined by the score, we focused on two levels of associative organization—the associative set (with its global properties, associative configurations, and the evolution of sets A, C, and E) and the associative landscape. Finally, the analysis of Morris's *Nine Piano Pieces* in chapter 9 reengaged the structural domain, now with a twelve-tone theoretic orientation, to involve all three domains and all five levels of the theory. Segmentation, set formation, and landscape composition all were live issues, as were the flashes between pieces that are a distinguishing feature of the set.

Applications 2: Traversals and Processes

Like music itself, music analysis unfolds in time. We can use schematic traversals to model analytic processes, with the ordering of nodes representing both

organized around two ideas. First is the direction of flow across the interface between the purely conceptual world of orientations and criteria in the upper part of the schematic and the relatively concrete world of musical segments, associative sets, and landscapes in the lower part. The question is, given two nodes located on opposite sides of the interface, does the conceptual node precede and motivate formation of the musical object, or does the analytical process run in the opposite direction, from the object to its conceptualization? Although this question can involve criteria in any of the three domains, I will focus on the relationship between structural criteria and the segments they support. The second idea, restricted to the lower part of the schematic ("the music" in example 1.1), is the contrast between a bottom-up approach to musical organization and a top-down one. Do segments precede the formation of associative sets and landscapes, or does analysis begin at the highest level, with the associative landscape, and proceed to its constituent associative sets and segments?[32] Of course, a music analysis of any length or subtlety will probably cross the concept-object interface many times, proceeding bottom-up and top-down at different times. I also address this possibility.

Crossing the Concept-Object Interface. Although theoretic orientations are not essential to music perception in general, they *are* often essential to the rich perceptions of interest in music analysis. The direction of flow between an orienting theory and the musical objects it recognizes as structural units is potentially bidirectional: traversals can proceed "downward" on the schematic, from concept to musical object (HE → T criterion → segment), or "upward," from object to concept (segment → T criterion → HE).

In a cognitive process akin to realization, "theory-driven" listening begins with a theoretic framework, a repertoire of HEs, and affiliated structural criteria that recommend particular groupings of tones as segments of potential analytical significance. Recall the structural segmentation of the opening bars of Webern's *Symphony* op. 21 given back in example 2.23b. The example includes four segments that realize the opening tetrachords of two pairs of inversionally-related rows (in the main canon and subsidiary canon), plus their supporting TS, TC, and C+T criteria. Although a listener *can* extract these segments from the texture solely on the basis of coincidence among $S_{2\text{-timbre}}$, C_{ip}, and C_{rhythm} criteria, the tetrachordal segmentation is far from obvious given conflicts with $S_{2\text{-pitch}}$, $S_{1\text{-duration}}$, $S_{2\text{-duration}}$, $S_{2\text{-articulation}}$, and other criteria. What privileges this tetrachordal segmentation over competing segmentations is the listener's active engagement of the structural domain in the process of hearing: in other words, by listening *for* the row structure, one *can hear* the row structure. When this happens, the primary motivation for the tetrachordal segmentation is structural, with the process of realization played out quite literally in cognition as the structural criterion $T_{\text{row T9P ops 0-3}}$ is realized in the segment <A3, F♯4, G2, A♭3> I'll call A1. Subsequent scrutiny of the passage yields the realization. We can represent this snippet from an analytic process by extracting the appropriate nodes from an interpreted schematic and connecting them as in example 10.7.

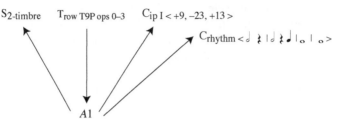

Example 10.7. Explicit traversal modeling the opening tetrachord of Webern's *Symphony*, op. 21, I

An orienting theory can be highly persuasive with regard to music perception. For instance, consider William Rothstein's comments on the closing bars of Schubert's "Mein" from *Die schöne Müllerin*.[33] At issue are what Rothstein calls "implied tones"—tones with "syntactic presence and phenomenological absence."[34] Here the implied tone E, supported by a Schenkerian theoretic orientation, the concept of substitution, and linear descent of the fundamental line from F♯ through E to D as an HE, binds the first attempt at descent into a segment—despite the acoustic absence of E as the "glue." Schenkerian theory also recognizes each of the three vocal phrases in mm. 87–88, 91–92, and 93–95 as an instance of the same HE despite their apparent, or actual, differences. It then elevates this HE, and thus also the three vocal segments that represent its successive realizations, to a position of great importance in the song and in its analysis.

Listening or analysis that is more "surface-driven" tends to move in the opposite direction, from sonic disjunctions and contextual associations apparent in the music to structural interpretations supported by a theoretic orientation (that is, C → T ← S). As an example of an analysis that proceeds, at least initially, in this direction, consider Benjamin Boretz's analysis of the *Tristan* Prelude in part IV of *MetaVariations*.[35] Rather than approach the Prelude with an "off-the-shelf" theoretic orientation, Boretz sets out to develop his own theory of its structure from the piece itself by identifying those pitch configurations that are most characteristic and their various resonances. Supported by a metalanguage that recognizes pitch-class equivalence, transformations, and set classes, he begins with careful observation and incipient theorizing focused on the contrapuntal complexes in mm. 2–3 and mm. 6–7, then gradually develops a theory of pitch structure unique to the musical universe that is *Tristan*. Boretz's analysis and the theory of pitch structure he offers for *Tristan* strike at

harmonic relations based on perfect fifths as privileged constructs, he zeroes in on inversional symmetries between the two T_n-types [0258] (the "Tristan chord") and [0358], and on pitch-class constellations parsed in terms of the three distinct [0369] cycles and the disposition of tritones. Although Boretz's analysis is a radical departure from previous motivic and tonal approaches to the Prelude, it is much less radical with regard to the pitch phenomena of the Prelude itself: his analysis and its supporting theory of pitch structure is the only one to recognize the Tristan chord and the pitch-class constellations parsed in terms of [0369] cycles found throughout the Prelude as structural entities, rather than as anomalies seen through the lens of Schenkerian theory or some other theory of common practice tonality.

Early in his analysis Boretz repeatedly traverses the concept-object interface "upward," from objects (segments) to contextual criteria. As analysis proceeds and redundancy increases among segments and criteria, contextual criteria begin to recommend look-alike structural criteria, which in turn suggest theoretic entities and structuring principles. When the weight of theory reaches a critical mass, it begins to exert its own "downward" force on the course of analysis, recommending or selecting certain groups of tones as structural segments and traversing the interface in the opposite direction, from concepts to objects. From this point on traversals can cross the interface in either direction: segments acquire structural interpretations; structural entities recommend segments.

Our analysis of the first movement of Beethoven's A-major sonata op. 2, no. 2 in chapter 4 also touched on this issue of bidirectional traffic across the concept-object interface, but with an established theory. Analysis began in the contextual domain, focusing on associative sets and changes in the associative landscape.[36] After working through the entire movement, we circled back to consider the relationship between associative organization and voice leading. Activating Schenkerian theory motivated recognition of two incipient members of sets D and E, segments $D0$ and $E0$, hidden in the counterpoint and surface intercutting of sets A and B in the inaugural theme (mm. 1–8) (T → C). The belated recognition of these segments was an exception to our prevailing chronology of analysis (which emphasized the contextual domain) and to score chronology: although $D0$ and $E0$ occur in mm. 1–8, it was their consociates in the primary theme (mm. 9–16) and subsequent repetitions that inspired us to recognize them as segments of analytic significance.

Even after we engaged Schenkerian theory in the Beethoven analysis we still found occasions to cross the concept-object interface in the opposite direction (C → T). In mm. 12–16, for example, I read two voice exchanges aligned with individual segments of sets D and E, reflecting the influence of associative organization (namely, the role that segments of these two sets play in the movement). A structural reading without reference to contextual criteria would likely recognize

dialogue between a theoretic orientation and sonic or contextual aspects of the music is part and parcel of Schenkerian analysis, a point Carl Schachter explores in his essay "Either/Or." Whereas an orienting theory recommends alternative structures, aspects of sonic and associative design can provide the rationale for selecting one interpretation over another. So even when a theoretic orientation is active, as long as the theory admits some play in interpretation, traffic across the concept-object interface remains bidirectional, sometimes even at deep levels of structure.

"Top-Down" and "Bottom-Up" Analysis. With respect to the musical objects represented in the lower part of the schematic, analysis can proceed primarily "bottom-up," from lower to higher levels of organization, or "top-down," from higher to lower levels.

Bottom-up analysis begins with individual segments, then forms associative sets and landscapes from these. This was the prevailing approach in the analysis of Nancarrow's *Study No. 37* (chapter 6). Having established the structure of the tempo canon as a frame, we proceeded section by section, starting with the nature of the melodic material and the balance of sonic, contextual, and TS and TC criteria at work within and across canonic lines as rationales for segmentation. We then shifted our focus of analytic attention to successively higher levels of organization, first to the formation (or dissolution) of associative sets, then to the changes in landscape composition that come about as emergent effects of lower-level interactions between specific melodic materials and the alignment of voices given by the tempo canon. This bottom-up strategy grounded our study of the changing higher-level landscape firmly in underlying musical detail.

Top-down analysis proceeds in the opposite direction, from an associative landscape to its lower-level constituents, associative sets and individual segments. Our landscape studies of passages from several performances of Riley's *In C* (chapter 7) worked this way. With segments and associative sets pretty much given by the score and performance instructions, swatches of the landscape became the primary objects of interest. To study the material and compositional homogeneity or heterogeneity of individual plots, we shifted attention to the next lower level of organization—the associative sets (Riley's "figures") active in each plot, their associative proximity or distance from one another, and the range of variation within sets with regard to timbre, register, augmentation, and so on. Given the degree of indeterminacy in Riley's score, our top-down strategy was almost inevitable: each performance of *In C* can be seen as an act of recomposition for which the scores or transcriptions needed to support atemporal bottom-up analysis do not exist.

Like traversals that cross the concept-object interface, traversals within the lower part of the schematic can, and often do, proceed in opposite directions

de Mari in chapter 8 is a case in point. With segments delimited by barlines in the score, analysis focused on associative sets and associative landscapes, with the prevailing direction of flow gradually shifting from bottom-up to top-down over the course of the chapter. We began by gathering twelve segments dispersed over the first half of the composition into an associative set A that we then studied for its global properties and internal configuration. Returning to m. 1 for a second pass, we continued bottom-up, expanding the context under consideration from mm. 1–5 through mm. 12, 16, 22, 24, and 34, looking at the formation of associative sets B, C, and D and expansion of existing sets A and C. Circling back to the start of the piece once more but shifting attention to a higher level of organization, we considered the landscape composition of plots I/1 (mm. 1–12) and I/2 (mm. 13–22) from Feldman's autograph. As we continued past m. 34, analysis often reverted to bottom-up as new sets were introduced (for instance, as with the formation and internal configuration of set E in mm. 36–51 and later of set G), but the prevailing direction of flow shifted toward top-down analysis, culminating in the study of plots VI, VII, and VIII at the end of the chapter. Such shifts from a bottom-up to top-down approach are not unusual: as the analyst develops a body of musical detail to work with, she can summon that detail in the analysis of larger-scale patterns.

Traversals across the concept-object interface usually involve different sets of nodes than those that proceed bottom-up or top-down in the lower part of the schematic. But these can overlap at the segment level, and flows in either direction between concepts and objects can interweave various ways with those among segments, associative sets, and landscapes. Our study of Morris's *Nine Piano Pieces* (chapter 9) hints at the possibilities. Assuming a twelve-tone theoretic orientation, we focused on the changing relationship between the pc array and details of its realization as means to shape the associative landscapes of individual pieces and to create flashes and more subtle resonances between pieces. The short section on "Loose Canon" took the most direct path from string segments (HEs) through structural criteria (T) to segments, associative sets, and a landscape of successive associative elisions. The opening section on "Between" took a more circuitous route. After an initial look at the pc array, we began with associations among individual segments in the musical realization, then worked both bottom-up (forming sets, then landscapes) and top-down, from objects back to their supporting criteria (segments → {S, C, T}). For "Kids," we began with correspondences between its pc array and that for "Between"; saw how these are realized in the music (T → C → segment); then overlaid a second layer of "pure motive" associative organization endemic to "Kids" based on trichordal segments admitted, but not suggested, by the array.

Note that Morris's actual compositional process, which certainly proceeded from the pitch-class array to its realization, did not constrain the trajectory of analysis. Nor, for that matter, did the written presentation in chapter 9 reflect

came to the *Nine* as a listener. I knew that all of the pieces were based on the same thirty-five-note string and that this string included each of the Z-hexachords once as a string segment, but little else about the pieces' structure. Once I had decided that I wanted to study the *Nine* more carefully, I wrote out the string, identified each note in "Between" with a lyne and order position in a string, and wrote out the entire pc array in tabular format. Shifting my attention to aspects of associative organization, I then started over with a second, blank score of "Between," on which I circled segments, identified supporting sonic and contextual criteria, and tracked the formation and disposition of the four sets A–D. Finally, I returned to the array to see how the pitch material in various segments I had identified was crafted from the underlying pc array. For each of the *Nine* pieces I studied, I more or less repeated this process, thereby laying the groundwork for comparative study of the structural underpinnings of aural correspondences between passages. It was only much later, when writing up the analysis, that for pragmatic reasons I decided to reconstruct the prevailing trajectory as T → C: by laying out the entire pc structure first, I could weave structural origins into the discussion of individual segments and associative organization much more efficiently than I would have been able to had I replicated the actual course of analysis.

Schematic traversals can be used to model flows across the concept-object interface and bottom-up versus top-down modes of organization in musical processes other than analysis, including composition, improvisation, listening, and pedagogy of analysis. In composing the *Nine*, Morris's knowledge of the associative potential inherent in the pc array exerted formative influence on the composition of sonic and contextual features of the music that in turn affected segmentation, and the formation of associative sets and landscapes.[38] A jazz musician might trace a similar path when choosing a tune and a series of chord changes as the basis for improvisation. On the receiving end, a listener who recognizes the head of the tune can mentally organize the sonic and associative flow of the improvisation through varying degrees of associative proximity and distance to it. Just as with analysis, even when the structure is known in advance, the trajectory and locus of composition, improvisation, and listening can change repeatedly. During array realization, a composer may settle on a sonic or contextual "hook" and then find ways to configure other passages accordingly—perhaps despite differences in underlying structure. Performers of a graphic work by Morton Feldman may begin to play with certain sonorities or gestures, developing something akin to structure that then begins to exert "downward" force on subsequent events in the improvisation. A listener versed in North Indian classical music can infer the essential features of an unfamiliar raga from a concert-length performance, then apply these through the remainder of the performance as informed music appreciation.

what amount to flow reversals on the schematic. Insightful music analysis is not sequential or algorithmic but holistic and heuristic: it combines technical skill with rich music perception, pattern recognition, an ability to sort through and organize musical detail, a knack for asking interesting questions, and the humanistic quest to develop an original viewpoint. One of the real benefits of analytical experience and one of the most difficult aspects of music analysis to teach may well be the ability to sustain pointed but open attention balanced by a willingness to "go with the flow," change direction, and reconfigure one's musical world, both within a piece and beyond. If the theory and analytic excursions presented in this book prove good companions in this endeavor, they will have served their purpose.

Notes

Chapter One

1. See Tenney, *Meta+Hodos*; Hasty, "Theory of Segmentation" and "Segmentation and Process"; Lidov, "Musical Structure"; Tenney and Polansky, "Temporal Gestalt Perception"; and Lerdahl and Jackendoff, *Generative Theory*. On categorization and music analysis, see Zbikowski, "Musical Coherence" and *Conceptualizing Music*; and Hanninen, "Associative Sets, Categories." For foundational work on categorization in psychology, see Rosch," On the Internal Structure" and "Principles of Categorization"; and Rosch and Mervis, "Family Resemblances."

2. "Our concern is not whether music has been, is, can be, will be, or should be a 'science,' . . . but simply that statements about music must conform to those verbal and methodological requirements which attend the possibility of meaningful discourse in any domain" (Babbitt, "Past and Present," 78). See also Babbitt, "Structure and Function," "Contemporary Music Composition," and *Words About Music*.

3. For Boretz, the quest to uncover the content of uncritical assumptions, and thereby recover or recognize what one already in another sense "knows" is important precisely because it has experiential consequences: "The *externalization* of his theory of musical structure is a significant *experiential* matter for anyone seriously interested in perceiving, reflecting on, or inventing music" (Boretz, *MetaVariations*, 106). Whereas Babbitt (particularly in his early writings) repeatedly argues for a discourse about music that meets "scientific" standards of explanation, prediction, and reduction, Boretz (particularly in his later writings), is at least as interested in the suggestive potential of thinking and writing about music, and in the idea that one can use language to locate, expand, and transform musical experience. In the 1991 essay "Experiences with No Names," he writes: "For me, the whole purpose of thinking . . . is precisely to deepen and intensify the particularity of fully organically involved expressive experience. And I have been convinced that the same faculty for imagining and abstracting that can lead us to psychic anesthesia . . . can equally be mobilized in the opposite direction, of self-directed sensitization and strength in the service not only of creating our own experience, but of making it more real, making it more substantial, and more particular and specific for ourselves" (Boretz, "Experiences with No Names," 339).

4. Lewin says: "My own meta-methodology includes these rules for analysis: mistrust anything that tells you not to explore an aural impression you have once formed" ("Music Theory, Phenomenology," 359). And Dubiel: "Analyses of music are more likely to be valuable as consciousness-raising exercises—or as the tools for such exercises—than as renderings of the content of musical experiences. . . . The value of theories will be in their facilitation of such analyses, and in their making explicit the range of possibilities for what might be heard and the openness of hearing to change" ("Composer, Theorist," 274). This idea that theory might be used not prescriptively but *suggestively*, to excavate, interrogate, and expand musical experience, is central to my own work.

5. *Webster's Third International Dictionary*, unabridged.

native. The definite article refers to the particular theory that is the subject of this book (note the use of the indefinite article in the book's title); it should not be read to suggest that this theory excludes or necessarily supersedes any other.

7. The theory can, however, be used to develop and articulate a methodology. See "Using the Schematic of the General Theory: Spaces and Traversals" in chapter 10, especially the part devoted to traversals of the schematic in example 1.1.

8. Quotation marks around "the music" indicate the dubious ontological status of the definite article. Because music is a cognitive construct, the precise denotation of "the" music varies from listener to listener according to his or her background, interests, abilities, and theoretic persuasions, even for what is, according to the score, the same piece or passage.

9. In "Segmentation and Process," Hasty uses the term "domain" with a different, more specific, meaning (57–58). There, a "domain" is a space or dimension in which segmentation occurs, such as register, duration, set class, or pitch-class ordering. Hasty's domains are analogous to my dimensions.

10. As in Hanninen, "General Theory" and "Orientations, Criteria, Segments." David Lidov draws a similar threefold distinction among Gestalt structure, taxonomy or paradigms, and grammar or syntagms in "Musical Structure" (43–74), but I was unaware of this work until later. More recently, Lartillot, in "Automating Motivic Analysis," recognizes a comparable distinction. So do Meudic and St.-James: "Often the notion of pattern can be linked with the notion of repetition: patterns emerge from repetition [i.e., in the contextual domain]. But a pattern could also be defined by its salient boundaries, and then patterns would emerge from discontinuities in the music [in the sonic domain]. Last, patterns can also be characterized as independent and coherent entities. . . . can we consider as 'patterns' the structural (one would say mathematical) regularities of a musical sequence [in the structural domain], even if these regularities are not perceived?" ("Automatic Extraction," 1–2; bracketed insertions mine, to articulate the correspondence).

11. In "Music Theory, Phenomenology," Lewin introduces a formal model of musical perceptions that situates and defines each perception with respect to a particular musical context, a list of relations with other perceptions, and enabling theoretic constructs. His rigorous and imaginative demonstration that musical context does not surround or contain perceptions, but *creates* (allows a listener to create) them, has had a profound influence on my work.

12. Schenkerian theory and twelve-tone theory are similar in that their HFs define the syntactic units admitted as HEs. In contrast, neo-Riemannian theory has an HF that distinguishes syntactic from nonsyntactic sequences of transformations, but does not, in general, promote or prioritize certain sequences over others as HEs. An analyst working with Klumpenhouwer networks might devise a preference rule for isographic networks, however.

13. Examples of the former include Justin London's "thick" and "thin" meters and Richard Cohn's ski-hill graphs in the realm of rhythm, and Cogan's spectrographic analyses. See London, *Hearing in Time*; Cohn, "Complex Hemiolas"; and Cogan, *New Images*. Regarding the latter, there is a sense in which poststructural rhetoric that dismisses structural accounts of music as abstract and presumptuous is ironic: structural analyses tend to assume less and be more articulate about the considerable cognitive and conceptual input required to constitute "the music" than poststructural analyses, which often assume "the music" already constituted as a starting point.

ments in HF and, especially, HE). This point of view may be particularly appealing for semiotic theories of music. At least for now, however, I would place H and P at different locations in the schematic, in order to contrast the sorts of theories of musical structure and syntax that meet the reference requirement and that I actively engage, with "post-structural" theories of music analysis that emphasize cultural and critical perspectives. "Poststructural" music analyses rarely delve into the multiplicity of interpretation available in segment formation and organization; instead, they tend to assume "the music" as a preconstituted sound object and focus on cultural references and interpretation. What distinguishes "structural" from "poststructural" music analysis (and H from P) is not whether the conceptual organization of sound-objects by sonic, contextual, and structural criteria that constitutes "music" (what nontheorists often mean by "musical structure") is *relevant*, but whether the analysis *investigates and elucidates*, or whether it *assumes*, the means or process by which "music" is constituted from sound.

15. Music analysis can take place exclusively, or almost exclusively, in the sonic domain: see, for example, Tenney and Polansky, "Temporal Gestalt Perception" and Cogan, *New Images*. Strictly speaking, this is not possible for the contextual domain—not only because associations between segments must invoke sonic attributes of the notes they contain, but because the segments one recognizes according to contextual criteria usually require at least some support from sonic criteria. For a detailed discussion of interactions between sonic and contextual criteria as influences on segmentation, see chapter 2.

16. The situation is similar to that in ecology, where individual organisms, species, communities, and ecosystems constitute successive levels. Individual organisms interact with one another, not with species; species interact with one another, not with communities. Yet individuals, species, communities, and ecosystems do not form a strict hierarchy: a species can belong to more than one ecological community, for example.

17. "As if," because the activation of contextual criteria in memory and the formation of coincident sonic boundaries actually do depend on how notes packaged together as a single segment relate to others in the vicinity.

18. Again I must emphasize that each analysis represents my own interests on a given occasion; these are *interpretations*, not products of "applying" the theory. Another analyst might select a different cluster of concepts from the theory and use them to pursue a different line of inquiry, or use the same set of concepts to support a contrasting, even conflicting, interpretation. I consider this flexibility in application and interpretation to be one of the theory's strengths.

19. In the first of his six Madison lectures, Babbitt discusses relational activity or "contextuality" in music, indicating both its pervasiveness in music and talk about it, and its role in musical intelligibility: "Contextuality has to be relative. When you talk about a piece and talk about the relation between a theme here and a theme there or how something is transformed or how something relates, you're talking about contextual characteristics. This is a matter of degree—and matters of degree can be crucial where musical intelligibility is concerned" (*Words About Music*, 9).

20. Boretz explains the need to define terms at an appropriate level of generality as he develops his own versatile conceptual system for musical interpretation: "Thus is discriminated a class of terms with greater generality than their traditional 'counterparts,' terms that require significantly fewer theoretical constructs for their interpretation, to the extent that they may be considered virtually 'observational' relative to most music-theoretical discourse. In this respect, they may be considered to designate properties

interpreted and semantically biased theoretical terms, depend" (*MetaVariations*, 19).

21. A number of writers contrast the interests and goals of music psychology with those of music analysis. David Temperley contrasts the "descriptive" (psychological theory) with the "suggestive" (music analysis) ("Question of Purpose," 68–71). Ian Cross distinguishes music psychology, concerned with the "involuntary" and "reflexive," from music analysis, which concerns the "conscious" and "volitional" ("Music Analysis and Music Perception," 4). Eric Clarke focuses on the role of the individual: "It is a characteristic of the psychology of music that it is primarily *not* concerned with individual pieces of music" ("Mind the Gap," 3). Lewin locates an important difference between "musical" and "auditory" perception in the role of context: "Failing such a CXT [context], you cannot have a musical perception, although you have a perfectly clear auditory perception" ("Music Theory, Phenomenology," 338). Summarizing the contrast between music psychology and music analysis, Clarke says: "Broadly speaking, the aim of musicologists and composers in tackling issues of musical structure can be characterized as the attempt to formulate theories of the structural relations within and between musical works, and their origins, development, and effectiveness as formal devices. A correspondingly brief summary of the aim of psychologists of music is the development of theories of the mental processing of musical events, or the relationship between the listener, performer, or composer and the musical environment. In a number of respects these aims are quite complementary" ("Mind the Gap," 1–2).

22. Regarding formal functions, see Caplin, *Classical Form*, and Hepokoski and Darcy, *Elements of Sonata Theory*.

23. I credit Marion Guck with the succinct and suggestive idea that in music "form" is properly not a noun, but a verb. Personal communication, 1996–97.

Chapter Two

The theoretic content of this chapter and some of the musical examples appeared previously in Hanninen, "Orientations, Criteria, Segments."

1. Webster's *New Collegiate Dictionary*, s.v. "orientation."

2. See, for example, Tenney, *Meta+Hodos*; Cogan, *New Images*; and Rothgeb, "Design as a Key."

3. Regarding unity, disunity, and intertextuality in music analysis, see Street, "Superior Myths"; Maus, "Concepts of Musical Unity"; Korsyn, "Beyond Privileged Contexts" and *Decentering Music*; and Kramer, "Beyond Unity" and "Concept of Disunity."

4. This idea of disunity as dissociation is implicit in work ranging from computational studies to theories of intertextuality. Rens Bod, "Memory-Based Models," develops a segmentation algorithm that uses a memory store of segments outside a piece as the basis for segmentation of a piece. Writing on intertextuality, Kevin Korsyn invokes repetition as the basis for the *déjà lu*: "The potential for repetition—the iterability—of a motive, which allows it to function as a source of internal coherence in, say, the Hallelujah Chorus, also allows it to wander, to summon up other contexts, to evoke what Roland Barthes calls the *déjà lu*, the already read, or, in this case, the *déjà entendu*, the already heard" (*Decentering Music*, 97–98).

5. In other words, the individual structural criteria represented by *t* correspond to members of HE, perhaps under some transformation defined by HF.

into the system without defining it" (*MetaVariations*, 97). Quoting Goodman, he continues: "It is because a term has been chosen as primitive for a system that it is indefinable in that system," and "There is no absolute primitive" (Goodman, *Structure of Appearance*, 64, quoted in Boretz, *MetaVariations*, 98. The set of primitives H assumes, rather than defines, makes it possible to distinguish, first, terms that are (relatively) observational with respect to H from those that are theoretical in H; and thus also to distinguish contextual from structural criteria relative to H. See also the discussion of observational and theoretical terms in "structural criteria," below.

7. My intent here is simply to illustrate what I mean by HF and HE, using familiar primitives, fundamental concepts, and basic and theoretic entities that support individual structural criteria. My goal is neither to advance theory in either area, nor to formalize it. For work of that kind, see, for example, Kassler, "Sketch" and "Trinity of Essays"; Brown, "Rational Reconstruction"; and Brown and Dempster, "Scientific Image" for Schenkerian theory; or Babbitt, "Some Aspects," "Twelve-Tone Invariants," "Set Structure," and "Since Schoenberg"; Morris, *Composition with Pitch-Classes*; and Mead, "Some Implications" for twelve-tone theory.

8. In Ernst Oster's translation: "My concepts present, for the first time, a genuine *theory of tonal language*" (Schenker, *Free Composition*, 9).

9. In Schenkerian analysis, roman numerals are generally interpretive, not nominal, and therefore do not function as primitives. This idea that roman numerals can convey musical interpretation is evident in undergraduate textbooks with a Schenkerian theoretic orientation (as in Aldwell and Schachter, *Harmony and Voice Leading* and Laitz, *Complete Musician*) and distinguishes these texts from those in which roman numerals are essentially labels for "roots" of tertian sonorities.

10. The presentation of Schenkerian theory in *Free Composition* from background through middleground to foreground suggests that it may be represented as a formal system. This idea has been pursued by Kassler ("Sketch of the Use of Formalized Languages," "Trinity of Essays") and more recently by Brown ("Rational Reconstruction," *Explaining Tonality*), as well as by Brown and Dempster ("Scientific Image"). Kassler uses the term "formalized language" ("Trinity of Essays," 85). Brown provides a "rational reconstruction" of Schenkerian theory. The "Six Laws of Tonality" offered by Brown, and by Brown and Dempster, are a concise statement of an important part of HF.

11. See, for example, Babbitt, "Some Aspects," "Twelve-Tone Invariants," and "Set Structure"; Martino, "Source Set"; Morris, *Composition with Pitch-Classes* and *Advanced Class Notes*; and Mead, "Some Implications."

12. Throughout, I notate pitch-classes using the ten integers 0–9, plus A for 10 (or t) and B for 11 (or e), as in Morris, *Composition with Pitch-Classes*.

13. Babbitt lists pitch-class as one of five such dimensions: "Each such 'atomic' event is located in a five-dimensional musical space determined by pitch class, register, dynamic, duration, and timbre" ("Composer as Specialist," 49). While timbre (sound spectrum and envelope) is multidimensional, in many analytic contexts it can be usefully represented nominally by a single dimension (e.g., "flute" versus "oboe"). Note that sonic criteria operate on the basis of *psychoacoustic* musical dimensions—not physical properties of sound. Dimensions rendered separate by a notational system and compositional practice do not always have clear and fully separable physical correlates. For example, although Western music notation and compositional practice tend to render pitch, timbre, and articulation as if they were three separate dimensions, the physical correlates are not fully distinct: if we construe "pitch" as "fundamental frequency," "timbre"

time" and "articulation" as "attack envelope," we see that timbre includes both pitch and articulation. Nor are psychoacoustic musical dimensions universals; they operate within a musical context. The analyst who ventures outside the context for which a particular set of psychoacoustic dimensions can safely be assumed as primitives—say, from Western musical notation and common practice repertoire to electronic music or *Qin* music—soon discovers the extent to which the definition, and separation or merging, of psychoacoustic dimensions depend on musical context.

14. Deconstructing a "note" into a cluster of attribute-values approximates the perceptual process of feature extraction from an auditory stimulus and reverses the process of perceptual binding by which a listener reconstructs individual notes or other sound-events as distinct objects within a complex auditory stimulus.

15. Tenney and Polansky, "Temporal Gestalt Perception," 207.

16. Meyer, *Emotion and Meaning*.

17. The tendency for music research in perception and cognition to collapse similarity and proximity into a single working concept of proximity (usually called "similarity"!) is evident in Deliège's account of the principles that motivate groupings in her figure 2: "Grouping formation (V) in the sequences result from the following principles: *Proximity* for [groupings] a1, a2, and a3: a grouping boundary is perceived at the end of the slur, silence, or prolonged duration, respectively. *Similarity* (called *change* in Lerdahl and Jackendoff's theory) for b1, b2, b3, and b4, where changes in register, intensity, articulation, and length, respectively, are perceived" ("Introduction: Similarity Perception," 235). For more on similarity and proximity in the context of work on perception and music cognition, see Hanninen, "Orientations, Criteria, Segments," note 15, 419–20.

18. In the sonic domain, I use "dimension" for a psychoacoustic attribute of a sound-event. As noted above, sonic dimensions are often articulated by notational practice and roughly correspond to Hasty's "domains" (in Hasty, "Segmentation and Process").

19. Composers often run the correspondence between attribute-values and dimension-elements in reverse: thinking of elements within a dimension as potential attribute-values for notes is essential to compositional strategies that structure sound-events by organizing their dimension-elements, as in twelve-tone music, Babbitt's serialization of timepoints, and Xenakis's pitch sieves.

20. In other words, within a sonic dimension, segmentation proceeds along the lines of Tenney and Polansky's algorithm in "Temporal Gestalt Perception." Starting with the first note of a monophonic note string, consider each pair of adjacent notes in turn. For the magnitudes of any four consecutive notes w, x, y, and z with respect to the sonic dimension in question, find the (nondirected) intervals $|x - w|$, $|y - x|$ and $|z - y|$. If $(|y - x| > |x - w|)$ and $(|y - x| > |z - y|)$, the interval $|y - x|$ is a local maximum; place a segment boundary between x and y. Notice that the algorithm proceeds to the *following* interval before placing any boundary: that is, boundaries are located not when the algorithm first encounters a large interval, but when it discovers an interval that is larger than the intervals that precede *and follow* it. For an extension of the Tenney and Polansky algorithm and its use in music analysis, see Uno and Hübscher, "*Temporal-Gestalt* Segmentation."

21. Fairly, but not completely, straightforward, because pitch, duration, attack-point, and dynamics are psychoacoustic musical dimensions, not mathematical ones. Variations in listeners' sensitivity and cognitive discrimination over the range of values within each dimension play a role.

22. I use "subdimension" to indicate a mathematical dimension that functions as a component of a psychoacoustic musical dimension that is nonlinear.

and Process"), Uno and Hübscher ("*Temporal-Gestalt* Segmentation") and Lefkowitz and Taavola ("Segmentation in Music") have all used such binary representations of timbre with some success. Cogan's theory of oppositions also approaches timbre in binary terms, but within a thirteen-dimensional space (*New Images*).

24. Wayne Slawson, *Sound Color*, points the way to a more general solution. Focusing on a subset of timbre, Slawson's theory of vowel color defines a two-dimensional space (openness and acuteness) and a cycle of twelve (hypothetically equidistant) vowel-color elements in that space. This allows him to determine vowel-color intervals, which in turn could be used as the basis for a sonic-disjunctive segmentation strategy. For an update on this approach, see Slawson, "Sound Structure."

25. See, for example, Tenney and Polansky ("Temporal Gestalt Perception"), Lerdahl and Jackendoff (*Generative Theory*), Uno and Hübscher ("*Temporal-Gestalt* Segmentation"), Lefkowitz and Taavola ("Segmentation in Music"), and Temperley (*Cognition of Basic Musical Structures*). Isaacson ("Neural Network Models") also focuses on linear sonic spaces, but takes a different approach using neural nets.

26. The size of these packages is significant: <5142> is the duration series for the composition, a structural criterion that is realized in these passages through coincidence with sonic criteria.

27. Recognizing S_1 and S_2 criteria as distinct sonic subtypes that share a disjunctive orientation clears up some conceptual problems associated with the terms "proximity" and "similarity." Earlier I noted a tendency for research in perception to use the word "similarity" for what amounts to proximity in a nontemporal dimension. With S_1 and S_2 criteria, researchers can distinguish pitch segmentation based on large leaps between notes that are temporally adjacent ($S_{1\text{-pitch}}$) from pitch segmentation based on pitch proximity of temporally distant events ($S_{2\text{-pitch}}$), thereby avoiding the awkward suggestion that pitches a semitone distant from one another are necessarily "similar."

28. From an S_2 point of view, one can think of a set of notes—and their attendant attribute-values in attack-point, dynamics, or other dimensions—to be distributed not in time but in *pitch* space—a point made by Morris, *Composition with Pitch-Classes*, 281–84. This idea that attribute-values in one dimension can be ordered and distributed by attribute-values in another dimension underlies the pitch and order-number isomorphism introduced by Babbitt ("Twelve-Tone Rhythmic Structure") and later explored by Mead ("Some Implications").

29. Research in auditory perception indicates that individual sonic criteria differ in the effect they have on segmentation. According to Albert Bregman, "not all acoustic differences are equally important in determining grouping" ("Auditory Scene Analysis in Complex Environments," 23).

30. Weights pertain to individual sonic *criteria*, not to segments or sonic dimensions. If one is dealing only with S_1 criteria (as in Tenney and Polansky, "Temporal Gestalt Perception"; and Uno and Hübscher, *Temporal-Gestalt* Segmentation"), sonic criteria correspond one-to-one with sonic dimensions, so the difference between them is moot. But when one includes S_2 criteria, the distinction becomes apparent. Research in perception suggests that, all else being equal, subjects tend to segment a single stream by temporal succession (S_1 criteria) rather than engage stream segregation (S_2 criteria). Thus S_2 criteria tend to be weaker than their S_1 counterparts in the same dimension and so have different weights.

31. Tenney and Polansky, "Temporal Gestalt Perception," 211.

tion") and by Uno and Hübscher ("*Temporal Gestalt* Segmentation").

33. Lefkowitz and Taavola, "Segmentation in Music."

34. Many of these terms appeared in an earlier list of primitives typically assumed by theories of musical structure. The connection is significant, as I will explain in the section on structural criteria that compares structural with their look-alike contextual criteria.

35. The perceptual mechanism by which a listener first recognizes that repetition (whether literal or varied) has occurred—especially when the original is not marked as a unit by sonic or structural criteria—is not clear. Rather than hypothesize a mechanism, I leave the question open for empirical research. I suspect, however, that the ability to recognize repetition of an unmarked original hinges on an ability to identify one or more of its predicable properties as an instance of a previously held concept—in effect displacing the relational property that supports segmentation from within the piece to between the piece and a preexisting body of knowledge.

36. The distinction between predicable and relational properties is important in a great deal of music analysis. Roman numerals, for example, symbolize not predicable properties (chords labeled in isolation) but relational properties (functions of tones and chords relative to a governing tonic). Much of the confused roman numeral "analysis" that beginning students produce results from a misreading of roman numerals as symbols for predicable rather than relational properties.

37. "The contents of long-term memory are a factor in the control of what enters conscious awareness, which in turn controls what enters long-term memory. . . . What we already know literally determines what we see and hear, which means that we see and hear what we look *for* more than what we look *at*" (Snyder, *Music and Meaning*, 11).

38. For example, Ruwet (1966) uses repetition as the means to determine unit status and paradigmatic associations (Monelle, *Linguistics and Semiotics*, 81–83). Lidov writes: "If music is labeled to show all of its repeating parts, this in itself yields a segmentation" ("Musical Structure," 50). Monelle notes that "the formative role of repetition is so obvious and universal that it is seldom discussed. It even appears in contemporary music; innovations which lack the support of an established musical language can appeal to repetition to clarify their vocabulary and procedures" (*Linguistics and Semiotics*, 66–67). Rahn develops a theory of repetition in music ("Repetition"). In the course of developing his theory of meter as rhythm, Hasty writes: "units are not given—they are created under the pressure of antecedent events and are creative for present and future events" (*Meter as Rhythm*, 106). Elsewhere I have used repetition and contextual criteria as the basis for a theory of recontextualization in music ("Theory of Recontextualization").

39. In the introduction to *Tonal Pitch Space* (2001), which builds on and in some respects greatly develops ideas originally presented in *A Generative Theory of Tonal Music* (1983), Fred Lerdahl offers three reasons why, although "GTTM's rule system depends in part on associations (in the form of 'parallelisms') for the assignment of hierarchical structure, it does not have a component for representing associational structure." The third of these reasons is that "on a practical level, it is difficult to make a substantive theory of associations. Within music theory this remains relatively uncharted territory" (*Tonal Pitch Space*, 6).

40. Thinking along these lines, Catherine Hirata identifies the marvelous "sound" of individual notes and dyads in Feldman's early music with their saturation by context. Elucidating the phrase "the sounds themselves" in relation to a single note, F, in Feldman's *Last Pieces*, she writes that it is "an issue, just . . . of being able to focus on the F—in

jected onto the F, is experienced as *part of* the sound of the F" ("Sounds of the Sounds Themselves," 11).

41. Whether one is *interested* in set class in general, in locating instances of a particular set class, or in the set class membership of a certain grouping of notes, however, *is* a matter of analytical interpretation.

42. These differences account for the difficulty of developing an algorithm, or mechanism, for segmentation by contextual criteria. Whereas S_1 segmentation in linear, intervallic spaces invites a computational approach, segmentation by contextual criteria is a complex problem in pattern recognition which, despite real progress in recent years by Emilios Cambouropoulos, Olivier Lartillot, and others, remains, from a musical point of view, at a basic level.

43. Usually, because contextual criteria can associate on the basis of a repeated sonic attribute-value, as in Messiaen's *Quatour pour le fin du temps*, III ("Abîme des oiseaux"), where two instances of the whole-note E5 set with a *crescendo* from ***ppp*** to ***ffff*** occur in m. 13 and m. 21. The relationship between these bars, by repetition of sonic attributes, involves contextual criteria. Each instance of E5 is also set off from the material that immediately precedes and follows it by sonic criteria.

44. David Lidov also alludes to this problem of gauging distance for (what amount to) contextual criteria: "As soon as factors such as harmony enter into grouping, the union of acoustic and formal measurements becomes more dubious. It is difficult to establish clear relationships of similarity and proximity among abstract formal categories like chords" ("Musical Structure," 46).

45. Assessing distance through inclusion relations is closely allied with the idea of similarity relations, as is evident in Forte's R_p and R_1 relations (*Structure of Atonal Music*, 46–60). This raises the more general question of whether similarity relations might solve the problem. The answer is no, for while similarity relations have been developed for many of the musical spaces in question, the space does not tell us *which* similarity relation to use.

46. This violates transitivity, an essential condition for a Generalized Interval System (GIS) as defined by Lewin (*Generalized Musical Intervals*, 26).

47. A "cseg," for "contour segment," is an ordered set of "contour pitches" that indicate relative pitch height but not actual pitch intervals. For instance, the pitch segment <G♯2, B2, G3, F♯3, A♯3, D4, F4, E4> that opens the fourth movement of Schoenberg's op. 10 (ex. 2.3) yields the cseg <01324576>. The term "cseg" comes from Marvin and Laprade ("Relating Musical Contours," 228), who develop a theory of contour-segment classes based on concepts and nomenclature introduced by Robert Morris in *Composition with Pitch-Classes*.

48. Note that the concept of a row does not figure into these observations: the associations among pc orderings involve only contextual criteria. The idea that the resultant ordering of twelve pitch classes realizes a row that serves as a structuring principle for the composition adds an appeal to a theoretic orientation and to structural criteria. For more on this point, consult the sections of chapter 2 on look-alike criteria.

49. For a discussion of the complementary relationship between association and transformation see chapter 10.

50. Note that the sonic dimensions invoked by the contextual subtypes need be *only* functionally independent (as represented in Western music notation and much musical practice), not fully separable. For example, pitch is not fully separable from loudness or timbre; but in Western music notation and practice, pitch and loudness,

that invoke pitch and loudness (and pitch and timbre) are, for the most part, also functionally independent.

51. I call the musical spaces A and B, rather than 1 and 2, because the element specified by c_1 in A need not logically entail the particular element specified by c_2 in B, only *some* element in B. Judgments of dimensional specificity pertain to the contextual subtype, not the individual elements identified by criteria within those subtypes.

52. For dimensional specificity and degree of ordering, statistical significance necessarily correlates with fewer realizations and so the question does not arise.

53. Daniel Starr, "Derivation and Polyphony," formalizes pitch-class ordering with the "pitch-class relation" (PCR), a set of "order constraints" each consisting of an ordered pair of two pitch classes x and y in their order of precedence (if the ordering modeled specifies one). Using the set operations of union and intersection on PCRs, Starr models complex relations among totally, partially, and unordered sets. Lewin develops a similar formalization in "PROT," a set of pitch-class "protocol pairs" (equivalent to order constraints) subject to certain conditions. See Lewin, "On Partial Ordering" and *Generalized Musical Intervals*, 134.

54. Hasty, "Segmentation and Process." Lidov says: "*Gestalt structure* refers to a division of the musical continuum on the basis of similarity and proximity relations between adjacent parts. *Taxonomy* refers to the stratified segmentation induced when like units of music are considered as a group whether they are adjacent or separated" ("Musical Structure," 43).

55. "Although it is not hard to imagine numerically balancing the length of a rest against the size of an adjacent change in pitch, it is much more difficult to balance the strength of parallelism against a break in a slur. Part of the difficulty lies in the present obscurity of the notion of parallelism, but part also lies in a lack of clarity about how to compare parallelism with anything else" (Lerdahl and Jackendoff, *Generative Theory*, 54).

56. Speaking as a composer, Lidov goes a bit further, suggesting that conflicts between what amount to sonic and contextual criteria may be unusual: "In general it is difficult when composing to construct formal arrangements . . . which project strong lines of articulation directly in contradiction to the shortest groups suggested by similarity and proximity" ("Musical Structure," 47).

57. Cohn, "Autonomy of Motives," 151. Cohn explains what distinguishes "derivation" (and motivic instances consistently supported by a structural criterion) from "association" (and motivic instances consistently supported only by a contextual criterion): "The implication is that an ordered list of an entity's components (whether these be pitch classes, pitches, or intervals) is not sufficient to establish its identity. Maintaining contact would seem to require that identity depends at least on a partial account of origins, which in practical terms requires a structural description indicating the status of the components in relation to each other. For example, most theorists would agree that it is not adequate to describe an upper-neighbor figure by its pitch sequence . . . or its intervallic sequence. . . . Its identity depends additionally on the structural description. . . . [The] formal description would require all of the information given by the slurs and stems, which convey the stages of derivation necessary to establish the relative structural status of the components" (159).

58. As primitives that do generalize, Babbitt singles out elements in what amount to the contextual dimensions C_{pc}, C_{INT}, and C_{cseg}: "The inferable primitives of 'contextual' music suggest the analytical primitives applicable to other musical works, without the a priori assumption that such works are instances of a given musical system. These primitives

classes, interval classes, and contours" ("Past and Present," 83).

59. "By repetition the text exhibits internally the opposition of paradigm (association) and syntagm which is characteristic of language" (Lidov, "Musical Structure," 53). "For while Schenker's theory, a number of theories of harmonic progression, and even Ernst Kurth's notion of 'leading-tone tension' focus on how chromaticism works syntagmatically, few theories show how it works paradigmatically" (McCreless, "Syntagmatics and Paradigmatics," 160).

60. Boretz explains that terms are not observational or theoretical in and of themselves, but function one way or the other depending on the domain of application and assumptions of the analyst: "Both terms in such pairs as 'chord' and 'simultaneity'; 'major second' and '2'; 'triad' and '(0 4 7) trichord' will all have *identical extensions* within particular domains—which is obviously why the 'traditional terms' did serve as virtually 'observational' without evident strain as long as those domains were regarded as universal for music" (*MetaVariations*, 19; see also 18–22). The need to examine and externalize the assumptions embedded in language is also a theme of postmodern thought, as in this statement by Kevin Korsyn: "*Ursatz, Urlinie, Kopfton, Übergreifen,* and so on. . . . One is never more alienated from one's language than one is when these terms become second nature, when one loses any outside perspective on them so that they seem self-evident" (*Decentering Music,* 64).

61. Van Fraassen, *Scientific Image,* 14. Relations between observational and theoretical terms (and between observation and theory) have received a great deal of attention in philosophy of science. Writers as diverse as Paul Feyerabend, Ian Hacking, Thomas Kuhn, W. V. Quine, and Bas van Fraassen, however, agree that the distinction between observational and theoretical terms is relative rather than absolute and often depends upon an epistemic community or context.

62. Regarding the function of a set of terms that are relatively observational within music theory, Boretz writes: "Thus is discriminated a class of terms with greater generality than their traditional 'counterparts,' terms that require significantly fewer theoretical constructs for their interpretation, to the extent that they may be considered virtually 'observational' relative to most music-theoretical discourse. In this respect they may be considered to designate properties at a level of thought that forms a conceptual substructure on which the other, partially interpreted and semantically biased theoretical terms, depend" (*MetaVariations*, 19).

63. Thinking of set class as an observational, rather than a theoretical, term may seem counterintuitive (perhaps due, at least in part, to a semantic collision with the locution "set theory" so widely used in music theory). But the properties that can be predicated of an object directly, without interpretation, are relatively observational. Set class is such a property. Whichever formal definition of set class one uses—whether "set class" designates a configuration of pitch-class intervals that corresponds to a prime form, interval-class content (Forte, "Theory of Set-Complexes"), or a configuration of pitch-class intervals to within a set of operators other than the T_nI group (e.g., Rahn's T_n-types or Morris's set groups)—for each set of tones, there is only one answer; no interpretation is involved.

64. Similarly for the associations between mm. 1–2 and m. 9, via <A352017B6984> and <<A3520> 1 <7B69> <84>> by the contextual criteria $C_{pc\ <A352017B6984>}$ and $C_{pc\ <}$ <A3520> 1 <7B69> <84>>.

65. Boretz also relates the question of observation versus theoretical language to predicable properties when he suggests that to mistake the latter for the former is to

rather than being, as they most often are, theoretical terms invoking particular interpretive conceptualizations on particular groupings of observation-data" (*MetaVariations*, 13–14).

66. A lyne is a succession of rows in one "voice" of an uninterpreted pitch-class array; the term originates with Michael Kassler. Two lynes that together yield one or more successive two-row combinatorial subarrays is called a "lyne pair." I use "partition" as defined by Morris and Alegant: "A *partition of the aggregate* is any unordered and disjoint set of pcsets which in union comprise the aggregate," for example, partition "A: {{0532} {4AB} {1} {678} {9}}" ("Even Partitions," 75).

67. A row can be realized with pitches, timepoints, or other musical elements, as suggested by the individual criteria $T_{\text{pc row T2P}}$ and $T_{\text{tp row T2P}}$ and indicated by Babbitt: "The collection is strict simply ordered [*sic*] with regard to this relation; that is, the relation is asymmetric, transitive, and connected (and, of course, irreflexive) in the collection, and—therefore—is indeed a relation which induces a 'serial' ordering. (It should be emphasized that this is the total meaning of the term 'serial': it implies nothing with regard to the operations upon such an ordering, or the nature of the elements ordered)" ("Twelve-Tone Rhythmic Structure," 112).

68. This is true even in twelve-tone music. When the row has multiple symmetries (as in Webern's *Symphony*, op. 21 and *Variations for Orchestra*, op. 30) or pitch-class ordering is relaxed within row segments (as in Schoenberg's twelve-tone music), the orienting theory may not name the row form realized but only constrain it to a few choices.

69. For "upper neighbor," the distinctions between observational and theoretical terms, predicable properties and interpretations, and contextual and structural criteria, are complicated by the fact that music theorists use this term both observationally and theoretically, depending on context. Sometimes, as in the analysis of atonal music (but also for tonal music), "upper neighbor" is used as an observational term that designates an <010> pitch contour in which the notes are a semitone or whole step apart. In a Schenkerian context, however, "upper neighbor" indicates prolongation and becomes a theoretical term.

70. See Hanninen, "General Theory," 409–10.

71. Structural and pure motive correspond to Cohn's derivation and association views, respectively, and to Alegant and McLean's "match, same fit" and "match, different fit," respectively. See Cohn, "Autonomy of Motives"; and Alegant and McLean, "Nature of Enlargement."

72. Kevin Korsyn points out a difficulty that Schenker's privileging of structural ("hidden") repetitions over pure motives poses for intertextual analysis from a Schenkerian perspective: "Because these organic repetitions are attached to the fundamental structure, 'even repetitions which do not fall within the concept of a motive' are organic, while those not connected to the *Ursatz* are not related to each other, even if they are externally identical, like counterfeit coins. To maintain this distinction, however, Schenker must guard the borders of pieces, declaring war on what he calls 'wandering melodies,' melodic or motivic resemblances among different works. . . . he is trying to construct a theory of musical coherence that will not open pieces to the infinite intertextuality of the *déjà entendu*" (*Decentering Music*, 99).

73. The third prospective candidate for a linked type, contextual-sonic (CS), is not formally analogous. While the instantiations of structural criteria are not percepts but concepts that must be realized by coincidence with the instantiation of a sonic or contextual criterion, the instantiations of contextual criteria are already percepts. So unlike

a hypothetical CS type would indicate only consistency, without the contingency of *c* upon *s* by functional interdependence or logical entailment essential to a linked type. Certainly music literature and performance practice offer many examples of consistent and even intentional pairing between specific *c* and *s* criteria, such as when a composer uses articulation, dynamics, or timbre to bring out a stream of associations, or a performer makes slight adjustments in timing or another sonic dimension to achieve the same result. But from a formal standpoint the contextual and sonic criteria involved remain functionally independent and so constitute pairings (modeled as C+S criteria) rather than a third linked type, CS, which is undefined.

74. For a detailed discussion of realization rules in the context of music based on pitch-class arrays, see Morris, *Composition with Pitch-Classes*, especially chapter 5; and Mead, *Music of Milton Babbitt*, chapter 3, 136–44 on "Lyne Projection." In an early paper ("Contour as a Medium"), I consider aspects of contour implied by realization rules for pitch versus those not so governed.

75. This passage from Babbitt's *None but the Lonely Flute* composes out the first two aggregates of a six-lyne all-partition array based on the row P = <01682743B9A5>. The basic array is the same as that for Babbitt's *Joy of More Sextets*, published in Mead, *Music of Milton Babbitt*, 278–79. Lyne-to-octave and other realization rules are common in Babbitt's music. Dubiel notes that "in all cases Babbitt's fundamental interpretive policy is still clearly to make each of the so numerous and so stretched-out set forms a succession of in some respect uniform sounds," but also that "nearly always the rules of interpretation change during a piece" ("Three Essays: Part I," 230).

76. Schenker, *Five Graphic Analyses*, 36–37. On obligatory register, he writes: "No matter how far the composing-out may depart from its basic register in ascending or descending linear progressions, arpeggiations, or couplings it nevertheless retains an urge to return to that register. Such departure and return creates content, displays the instrument, and lends coherence to the whole" (*Free Composition*, 107). See also Cadwallader and Gagné, *Analysis of Tonal Music*, 206–7. Although one can argue that obligatory register is an analytical concept, not a compositional one, as realization would seem to require, Schenker suggests its compositional significance when he refers to "obligatory register as a prime element of the art of orchestration. In keeping with the principle of obligatory register, the instruments should be brought in or retracted according to their distance from the obligatory register" (*Free Composition*, 107).

77. $T_xC–T_xC$ (TC xx) relations correspond to and formalize Alegant and McLean's "match, same fit" (Alegant and McLean, "Nature of Enlargement"). $T_xC–T_yC$ (TC xy) relations are one case of their "match, different fit"; TC and C, and $C_x–C_y$ distinguish the two other cases.

78. In Hanninen, "Orientations, Criteria, Segments," I used the terms "singular" and "ad hoc" for nonsystematic realization. I now use the more neutral term "nonsystematic realization" for the same idea, to avoid the misleading connotation that nonsystematic realization is either unique or arbitrary, as "singular" and "ad hoc" might suggest.

79. Some of these observations come from Mead, "Large-Scale Strategy." Mead identifies a number of local and long-range associations among movements of the Violin Concerto with both structural and purely associative origins. Modeling these differences in origins in terms of TC xx or TC xy relations, and C+T or C criteria, for purposes of illustration is my contribution.

80. In Schenkerian theory, all theoretic entities are syntactic units (derivable as prolongations); in this context, to assert anything other than a syntactic unit as a structural

HEs are well-formed networks, but HF does not define any syntax that privileges one network, or network interpretation, over another. So *no* HE is necessarily syntactic. A twelve-tone theory that includes not only rows and row segments but also partitions of the aggregate is an example of the intermediate case: theoretic entities include rows, row segments, and partitions, but only rows and row segments are privileged by the theory as syntactic units.

81. This idea that, for some orienting theories and structural subtypes, individual structural criteria do not necessarily correspond to privileged syntactic units raises an important question: What, then, limits or guides assertions of structural significance? Here pragmatic value in the context at hand is an important consideration: in the Schoenberg Violin Concerto, for example, the frequency with which the two-partition of order numbers (0, 1, 6, 7) and (2, 3, 4, 5, 8, 9, A, B) recurs, and its intimate connection with a network of other associations, make it both reasonable and useful to assert the partition as a structuring unit that reflects common origins with respect to the row.

82. For a tonal example of such a bridge from the structural to the contextual domains, consider the structural criterion $T_{SD,\ a:\ <5(65)>}$ and its look-alike contextual criterion $C_{SD\ a:\ <565>}$. The structural criterion interprets an ordering of three scale degrees as an upper neighbor figure that prolongs scale degree 5 in A minor. The look-alike contextual criterion $C_{SD\ a:\ <565>}$ logically entails another association, by $C_{pc\ <EFE>}$, which may have its own web of associations (say, with scale degrees <343> in C major or an alternation between E and F) and bring some segments otherwise unrelated to those originally recognized via $T_{SD,\ a:\ <5(65)>}$ or $C_{SD\ a:\ <565>}$ into their relational orb.

83. Some theoretic orientations allow the same structural criterion to operate at many structural levels. This is the case in Schenkerian theory, where third- or fifth-progressions that prolong scale degrees 3 or 5 can occur at any structural level from the *Ursatz* to the surface, and in twelve-tone contexts where transformations of a row with multiple order properties can unfold at different structural levels.

84. In other words, what is most structurally significant from a certain theoretic perspective may not sound that way based solely on surface features. Reconfiguring the idea of "sound" to include structural weight (conferred by structural criteria and a particular theoretic orientation) as well as perceptual salience (conferred by sonic and contextual criteria), and recognizing that the two can diverge or converge to varying extents, can clear up much of the confusion. Structural weight is not entirely, or even necessarily, articulated by perceptual salience; to hear something *as* structurally significant involves not only the sonic and contextual criteria that confer realization, but the *concept* captured by a structural criterion and the significance of that concept within an orienting theory. To hear a musical event *as* structural is to place its sounding features in a specific theoretic context.

85. Especially pitch, because in the context of Western musical notation and practice pitch perception is categorical and pitch organization is often primary. In sonic dimensions where perception is not categorical, as with dynamics, timbre, and articulation, saturation may be more difficult to ascertain or to achieve.

86. Robert Snyder defines short-term memory as "a type of temporary memory that persists for a short time (3–5 sec on average; 10–12 sec maximum) and whose capacity is limited to around 5–9 elements, or one 'chunk'" (*Music and Memory*, 264). Snyder's definition invokes George Miller's work on cognitive capacity and "the magical number seven, plus or minus two" (Miller, "Magical Number Seven").

that the elementary principles of *Gestalt* grouping are most prominently realized in units at the lower end of the segmental hierarchy, that is by short segments. The longer and more complex a section of music is, the more abstract will be the representation of its totality in the mind" ("Musical Structure," 46).

88. McAdams and Bigand indicate that higher-level conceptual processes often influence lower-level perceptual processes: "One of the important implications of event structure perception is that these structures serve as a framework having implications for the structure of acoustic information that has not yet arrived. By way of the interpretive framework evoked from abstract knowledge structures, anticipations and expectations may be set up that orient the listener's attention to forthcoming events of a particular kind or at particular times" ("Introduction to Auditory Cognition," 8).

89. Felix Salzer identifies structure with an underlying contrapuntal framework or voice leading. He describes form as "a principle of architectonic organization of the structure" and design as "the organization of the composition's motivic, thematic, and rhythmic material through which the functions of form and structure are made clear" (*Structural Hearing*, 224). Salzer's distinction among outer form, inner form, and design inspired subsequent work in Schenkerian theory and analysis by those with an interest in structure and design, such as John Rothgeb, David Beach, and William Rothstein. See Rothgeb, "Design as a Key"; Beach, "Schubert's Experiments," and Rothstein, *Phrase Rhythm*. Andrew Mead studies aspects of structure and design in a twelve-tone context in his work on Babbitt's music. See Mead, "Detail and the Array" and *Music of Milton Babbitt*.

90. The concept of the musical segment is metatheoretic to an extent. In electroacoustic music where additive synthesis foregrounds the intimate relation between pitch and timbre and the composer controls the evolution of the sound envelope, the concepts of "segment," "note," "pitch," "timbre," and "texture" are not easily distinguished. Some statistical approaches to music analysis can also proceed without a concept of segment; see, for example, Cogan, *New Images*; and Beran, *Statistics in Musicology*.

91. Distinct phenosegs must be noncoincident by definition: else, they could not be "readily perceived" as distinct units.

92. In terms defined below, the segmentation of the violin and alto lines is "complete" (it includes every note) and partitions the musical surface (all phenosegs are disjoint).

93. Nonintersecting genosegs cannot interact directly unless they instantiate the same contextual criterion, in which case they engage in mutual formation. Nonintersecting genosegs supported by different contextual criteria, by same or different sonic criteria, or by sonic and contextual criteria, interact only indirectly, through the phenosegs they support or, by extension, through the phenosegs' contributions to sonic, associative, or structural organization at higher levels.

94. The amenability of this passage to different ways of hearing finds resonance in the pitch organization of the movement, which draws on tonal models in its double fugue design and profile of the second subject but is also populated by octatonic subsets (including SC 4-3[0134] in mm. 1–4).

95. Lerdahl and Jackendoff make a similar point: "a number of different factors within the music affect perceived grouping, and . . . these factors may either reinforce each other or conflict. When they reinforce each other, strong grouping intuitions result; when they conflict, the listener has ambiguous or vague intuitions" (*Generative*

reinforcement and conflict among criteria as factors in segmentation.

96. Hasty identifies segment strength with the number of supporting criteria. Identifying the strengths of a phenoseg not only with the number of criteria but also their relative strength in a particular musical context avoids the problem implicit in his statement that "stronger segmentations are *usually more apparent to the ear* and are usually borne out in the progress of the composition" [emphasis mine] ("Segmentation and Process," 59).

97. However, phenosegs (products of holistic attention) are usually *perceptually* prior to genosegs (products of directed attention). So far as psychological mechanisms for perception are concerned, genosegs (detection of individual features) may again precede phenosegs (bundling of features into a perceptual object).

98. Focusing an analysis of segmentation on factors that *inhibit* phenoseg formation—that keep a piece of music's options open, as it were—is an intriguing idea that the theory allows one to pursue through comparative analysis on the genoseg and phenoseg levels.

99. Walker, *Chambers Biology Dictionary*, 123.

100. Michael Tooley provides this definition of supervenience: "Properties belonging to a set S supervene upon properties belonging to a set B only if it is necessarily the case that two entities x and y differ with regard to properties belonging to S only if they differ with regard to properties belonging to B" (*Laws of Nature*, 1). Jaegwon Kim identifies these "three putative components, or desiderata, of supervenience: *Covariance*: Supervenient properties covary with their subvenient, or base, properties. In particular, indiscernibility in respect of the base properties entails indiscernibility in respect of the supervenient properties. *Dependency*: Supervenient properties are dependent on, or are determined by, their base properties. *Nonreducibility*: Supervenience is to be consistent with the irreducibility of the supervenient to their base properties" ("Supervenience," 33).

101. Morris, "New Directions."

102. Straus, *Music of Ruth Crawford Seeger*, 20.

103. Some exceptions are highlighted by temporal proximity: for example, groupings 1 and 2 are saturated by ic 1, and both reduce to contour prime <021>.

104. For example, groupings 1 and 2 emphasize SC 3-2[013], and secondarily SC 3-3[014], and three instances of SC 3-10[036] occur between groupings 10 and 11. Straus refers to the tendency for Crawford's melodic lines to open a space, then proceed to chromatic saturation, as a kind of gap-fill technique (*Music of Ruth Crawford Seeger*, 8–9; see also Meyer, *Explaining Music*). The move to establish variety in spaces such as set class or contour, then explore different regions of the space in turn, can be seen as a generalized gap-fill technique.

105. Misch, "Serial Shaping," 145.

106. For ease in reading the brass parts discussed in the text, four events are omitted from ex. 2.19. These are: (1) in orchestra I, a short roll (one eighth-note) on the snare drum on the downbeat of the measure after group 119 begins; (2) in orchestra II, on the same downbeat, an eighth-note chord in the piano that duplicates all pitches sounded at that moment by the brass in orchestra I; (3) in orchestra II, resonance of the same piano chord through the following three measures with a half pedal; (4) also in orchestra II, simultaneous with the last attack shown in the brass, a second chord in the piano that duplicates its pitches and a short roll on the snare drum. Orchestra III is complete as shown.

sonic dimension.

108. Another preference rule avoids "groupings" with only one event, as in Tenney and Polansky, "Temporal Gestalt Perception"; Lerdahl and Jackendoff, *Generative Theory*; and Temperley, *Cognition of Basic Musical Structures*.

109. For another example of a return softened by continuity in the sonic domain, see Varèse's *Density 21.5*, m. 41. In "Temporal Gestalt Segmentation," Tenney and Polansky segment the piece with their computer-implemented algorithm. As they point out, the program misses the return because the sonic disjunctions at that point are too weak to promote the boundary to the next hierarchic level and recursive pass through the program.

110. In this respect, sonic foci are very different from high-level sonic boundaries in the Tenney and Polansky algorithm, in which the cumulative effects of segment boundaries and composite disjunction measures at each successive level confer high-level structural significance.

111. The "tetrachordal" segmentation of rows in the subsidiary canon is incidental and indicates only that both voices complete tetrachords by the end of m. 7. The tetrachords are supported by contextual criteria but, unlike in canon I, they lack coincident support from sonic criteria.

112. For the three disjunct tetrachords of T_9P, the *dux* in the main canon, the individual linked criteria would be $T_{row\ T9P\ ops\ 0-3}S_{2\text{-timbre (horn II)}}$, $T_{row\ T9P\ ops\ 4-7}S_{2\text{-timbre (clarinet)}}$, and $T_{row\ T9P\ ops\ 8-B}S_{2\text{-timbre (viola)}}$.

113. The situation in the subsidiary canon is even more complicated: both voices begin in the harp, but it is ultimately not changes in timbre (a sonic criterion) but the *order* of timbres (a contextual criterion) that realizes row segments. *No* sonic criterion consistently realizes the disjoint tetrachords of rows in the subsidiary canon as structural units and significant segments.

114. Additional instances of these pcsets (especially {78} and {AB} in mm. 3–8) occur across row forms. The example includes only those I find most compelling as phenosegs, shown in exx. 2.25b and 2.25c. The mechanics of these cross-row associations are interesting. Recall that in mm. 1–23 rows within each canon are related by T_6I and those in the corresponding voices (i.e., *dux*, *comes*) but between canons starting with T_2I (for voice 1 of canons I and II) and T_AI (for voice 2 of canons I and II). Had Webern realized rows note-for-note, order position for order position, rather than as a pair of canons, only *even* intervals would have been available and no resonance between the four pc-invariant dyads within the rows of canon I ({78}, {AB}, {45}, and {12}) and pitch sets formed across rows would have been possible. The initial offset of three order positions between the voices of canon I, and of one order position between canons I and II, is essential to the complex interplay between instances of structural and pure motive in mm. 1–23.

115. Subsequent events admit readings from scale degrees 5 or 3, but within the context of mm. 1–8 the ascent to scale degree 3 in mm. 1–8 obtains regardless.

116. "Realization" indicates coincidence between a structural criterion and one or more sonic or contextual criteria; it does not necessarily imply any *intent* to realize on the part of the composer. (However, in some cases the intent to realize a structural segment through sonic or contextual means is clear, as in Webern's *Symphony*, op. 21.)

117. The register shift that sets off this parenthetical expansion illustrates a principle of structure and design identified by John Rothgeb: "changes in surface design usually coincide with crucial structural points" ("Design as a Key," 231).

my point is to draw attention to the diminished fourths, rather than how it might be absorbed or accommodated within a consonant framework.

119. Another set of relationships along these lines emerges as the Sarabande continues, in the hints of cross-relation between D♭ and D in mm. 5–6 and m. 9; E and E♭ in mm. 12–13; and A and A♭ in mm. 17–18. None, of course, is an actual cross-relation between a pitch and its chromatic alteration at the same level of structure, but the potential for association among these nonstructural near-juxtapositions tends to enhance their prominence, again gently tugging at tonal coherence.

120. See Cadwallader, "Foreground Motivic Ambiguity."

121. On the canonic structure of *Lux*, see Bernard, "Voice Leading" and Clendinning, "Structural Factors."

122. Two other features prompt recognition of the first three segments associated by $C_{\text{pitch} <F\sharp4, G4, F4, E\flat4>}$ and $C_{\text{text} <\text{lux ae-ter-na}>}$. First, "lux ae-ter-na" forms a complete grammatical unit and is the title of work, two extramusical reasons that can predispose a listener to segment accordingly. Second, the F♯4 that starts the segment is gently marked by the fact that it revives the syllable "Lux," which saturates all eight voices from m. 1 through the first half of m. 4 but then disappears. The prospect that a new statement of the text unit "Lux ae-ter-na" may be underway draws attention to the F♯4, which then unfolds the structural segment <F♯4, G4, F4, E♭4>.

Chapter Three

1. The terms "classical category" and "prototypical category" derive from psychology, as in Rosch, "Principles of Categorization"; Margolis and Laurence, "Concepts and Cognitive Science"; and Smith and Medin, *Categories and Concepts.* Zbikowski's *Conceptualizing Music* brings these terms into the field of music theory. In "Associative Sets, Categories" I look at issues that arise with associative sets and categories in the context of music analysis.

2. For example, for Babbitt's *Play on Notes* (ex. 3.5, below), I name segments by instrumentation (bells or voices) and phrase number. In mm. 135–40 of Feldman's *Piano and Orchestra* (exx. 3.25 and 3.26), I identify right- and left-hand segments within twelve piano chords by measure number, hand, and position in the bar (first or second event).

3. For segments related by literal repetition (like *A*1, *A*2, and *A*3), it can be tempting to name just one segment and designate individual recurrences by measure number. But even segments that are morphologically identical can sound different when placed in different musical contexts. Therefore, it is best to identify the concept of "segment" with a particular *sound*, not a notational image, and to recognize every segment as a distinct entity in the earliest stages of analysis. One can then assess the perceptual equivalence or independence of literal repetitions on a case-by-case basis. See Hanninen, "Theory of Recontextualization" and "Feldman, Analysis, Experience," as well as the section on association graphs, below.

4. As noted in chapter 2, I omit transposition because it can be represented as repetition of an ordered set of intervals. Those who prefer to show particular transpositions as transformations can do so. Other transformations, once clearly defined, are also possible.

5. I developed the idea of the population while working on some of Morton Feldman's late music (in "Feldman, Analysis, Experience") and engage populations in a

spective on association in music analysis in "Species Concepts in Biology."

6. Philosopher William Wimsatt defines an emergent property as "roughly—a system property which is dependent upon the mode of organization of the system's parts" ("Aggregativity," S373). For additional philosophical accounts of emergence, see, e.g., Stephan, "Varieties of Emergentism" and "Emergentism"; and Wimsatt, "Emergence as Non-Aggregativity." For critiques of the concept of emergence, see, e.g., Kim, "Making Sense of Emergence" and Nagel, "Teleology Revisited." Emergent properties have received a fair amount of attention in ecology, where they have been identified with numerous phenomena including growth rates of populations, predator-prey cycles, species diversity, and ecosystem stability. See, e.g., Loehle and Pechmann, "Evolution: The Missing Ingredient"; and Bergandi, "Reductionist Holism." I consider emergent properties of associative sets and populations of musical segments in "Feldman, Analysis, Experience" and "Species Concepts in Biology." Mailman, "Temporal Dynamic Form," explores emergent properties of dynamic musical processes.

7. For example, compare the material in mm. 2, 4, 6–8, 22–23, 27, 51, 75–77; and 97 with that in mm. 28–46.

8. Changing the metric placement of notes within the bar gives the passage a floating quality, but these changes are not readily perceptible to listeners *as* changes in metric placement per se. For performers, however, they are, with visual, psychological, and kinesthetic aspects.

9. A long pitch retrograde in the cello between mm. 11–18 and mm. 20–27 is submerged by changes in bowing that reassign notes between adjacent segments, so although the pitch series is a strict retrograde, the segments that realize it are not.

10. The exception to "most other subsets" is *F/f*, which retrogrades and reinterprets the turn contour as the seed of an ascending line.

11. "Centrality" alludes to prototypicality within set *F*. I explore this idea further in the next major section, on associative configurations.

12. Following up on Robert Morris's work on contour, Elizabeth West Marvin defines the terms "duration space" and "duration segment" (dseg): "Duration space (or d-space) is defined here as a type of temporal space consisting of elements arranged from short to long. Elements in d-space are numbered in order from short to long, beginning with 0 up to (n–1), where n equals the number of elements in the segment and where the precise, calibrated duration of each dur is ignored and left undefined. A d-segment (dseg) is defined as an ordered set of durations in d-space" ("Perception of Rhythm," 66). See also Morris, *Composition with Pitch-Classes* and Marvin, "Generalization of Contour Theory."

13. Gauging actual durations is greatly complicated by interactions among changing meters, tuplets, and note values, especially in the piano, where their combined effect is less a change of note values than a change in *tempo*—a gradual deceleration in the piano relative to the other instruments. For this reason, I eschew actual durations in subsequent discussion of this passage.

14. For another example that locates associative sets in a multidimensional global property space, see my "Words, Musical Organization," 40, where example 7 compares eight sets ("wordspaces" from Boretz's music-text "Thesis") for size, strength, temporal disposition, and thematic centrality and locates each in a different region of organizational space.

15. Set multiplication differs from set union. Given a set *A*; segments *A*1 and *A*2; three contextual criteria *a*, *b*, and *c*; and genotypes for *A*1 and *A*2 $G(A1) = \{ab\}$ and

$G(A2)$ yields the multiset $\{a^2b^2c\}$, in which superscripts indicate the number of segments supported by each criterion.

16. Again, because structural criteria do not themselves yield sounding percepts, the coincidence with sonic or contextual criteria that constitutes realization is required.

17. Recall that the contextual genotypes for segments in A can include criteria not replicated within A but that form associations with segments outside A. Segments of A can also have properties that are solely predicable, not relational.

18. Structural common set is not defined, because structural criteria can only form phenosegs (the basis for associative sets) when realized by coincident sonic or contextual criteria.

19. But for the fact that the segments of an associative set can be dispersed in time, a sonic common set roughly approximates Tenney's concept of "state" (Tenney, *Meta+Hodos*, 107).

20. When constructing contextual genotypes for individual segments, it is important to prune criteria implied by literal inclusion but not independently realized. The failure to do so can substantially skew subsequent analytic findings.

21. "Core common set" replaces "reduced common set" in Hanninen, "General Theory," 93–94.

22. As in Hanninen, "General Theory," 409–10.

23. The *idea* as defined in Hanninen, "Theory of Recontextualization," 70, is a related but more general concept. Like a motive, an idea is a set of one or more contextual criteria; like motives, ideas have instances. However, an idea does not imply the degree of repetition assumed of a motive and instances of ideas need not be segments.

24. In "Theory of Recontextualization" I use mnemonics in roman type (not italics) for ideas and append subscript numerals for instances of ideas.

25. This is an important difference from Zbikowski's model in *Conceptualizing Music*. Zbikowski identifies a motive with a cognitive category (16) "structured around a conceptual model" (155). "The model for the category consists of . . . correlated conceptual elements, characterized as the things *necessary* for a melodic fragment to count as an instance of the motive" (155, emphasis mine).

26. That is, the C/CRS model of motive allows analysts not just to think of, but to formally represent, sets of motive instances as prototypical categories rather than classical ones. Zbikowski makes the important conceptual distinction between prototypical and classical categories with respect to musical motives, but his definition of a conceptual model for a motive as containing "things necessary to count as instances of a motive" (*Conceptualizing Music*, 155) in effect transforms "prototypical categories" of motive instances back into classical categories. See, for example, his analyses of Mozart's K. 465, I and Beethoven's op. 18 no. 1, I and op. 18 no. 6, I (chapter 4). Recognizing "forms" of a motive (as Zbikowski does) doesn't solve the problem; it simply transfers it to a lower level of organization (comparable to associative subsets).

27. Of course the sonata includes many other instances and forms of *ARP* and *5–6–5*. In the first movement, for example, the *5–6–5* motive dominates the transitions from theme 1 to theme 2 in the exposition and recapitulation.

28. In *5–6–5*$_1$, notes are paced at the half-bar in 12/8 *Allegro assai*, or about MM 54; the quarter-note pacing of *5–6–5*$_2$ in 2/4 *Andante con moto* is about the same. Placing the notes of *5–6–5*$_3$ on successive downbeats in a four-bar hypermeter slows the pace considerably, to about MM 15. The faster surface rhythm heightens the sense of durational extension from *5–6–5*$_2$ to *5–6–5*$_3$.

lished in theme 1 of the first movement, where ARP_1 (mm. 1–2) precedes 5–6–5_1 (mm. 3–4 or mm. 1–4). In the opening theme of the last movement, ARP_3 (m. 20) again precedes 5–6–5_3 (mm. 29–30). At a larger scale, ARP opens movement I while 5–6–5 opens movement II. This pattern, which involves the temporal disposition of segments in associative sets, is part of the sonata's associative landscape.

30. Buteau and Mazzola, "Motivic Analysis," introduces a formal model of what amounts to associative distance among instances of a motive or segments of an associative set. But even with such a formalization, the relative weights of different contextual dimensions, and thus the strengths of individual contextual criteria that support the formalization, require some degree of interpretation.

31. Basic terminology for graphs and matrices is adopted or adapted from Wilson, *Introduction to Graph Theory*; Wallis, *Beginner's Guide*; and Lipshutz, *Discrete Mathematics*, in conjunction with Lewin, *Generalized Musical Intervals*.

32. Lewin's *isography* also preserves labeling of edges. See, e.g., *Generalized Musical Intervals*, 199–200.

33. As in Lipschutz, *Discrete Mathematics*, 83. Wilson identifies the term "walk," and attendant concepts such as "circuit" or "cycle," as "another instance of widely differing terminology by various authors. A walk appears in the literature as an edge-sequence, route, path or edge-progression; a trail appears as a path, semi-simple path, or chain; a path as a chain, arc, simple path, or simple chain; a closed trail as a cyclic path, re-entrant path or circuit; and a circuit as a cycle, elementary cycle, circular path, or simple circuit!" (Wilson, *Introduction to Graph Theory*, 26). Wilson defines a "walk" as a "finite series of edges." Lipshutz's definition provides a better basis for my definition of an associative path as a sequence of nodes—that is, of segments, not edges (which correspond to contextual criteria).

34. For Lipschutz, "path" has a more specific meaning—a walk in which all vertices (nodes) are distinct (*Discrete Mathematics*, 83).

35. There are various ways to assess the degree of connection among nodes in a graph. One is *connectivity*, or the ratio between the number of edges present among the nodes of a graph and the maximum number possible for a graph with the same number of nodes. Another is *circuitry*, the ratio between the number of circuits present in the graph to those possible in a graph with the same number of nodes.

36. Wilson, *Introduction to Graph Theory*, 28.

37. Ibid.

38. Ibid.

39. Designating a root increases the number of possibilities considerably, from 23 to 115.

40. Read and Wilson, *Atlas of Graphs*, 63.

41. Wilson, *Introduction to Graph Theory*, 16.

42. There is no easy way to be sure a graph G is planar, but there are ways to tell at a glance if it is nonplanar. For instance, by Kuratowski's theorem, if G is isomorphic to a graph that includes the bipartite graph $G_{3,3}$ (also knows as the "utility graph") or K_5 as a subgraph, G is nonplanar (Wilson, *Introduction to Graph Theory*, 61); and no graph without a node of degree 5 or less is planar (67). Every graph can be drawn without edge crossings in three-dimensional space (21).

43. Definitions of representation, crossing number, and minimum crossing number are taken or adapted from Wallis, *Beginner's Guide*, 105–6.

44. Figure 3.13 is adapted from figure 8.1 in Wallis, *Beginner's Guide*, 105.

46. As in Lipschutz, *Discrete Mathematics*, 87–88.

47. I explore this idea with four measures (mm. 5, 14, 27, and 34) from Feldman's *Piano, Violin, Viola, Cello* (1987) in "Feldman, Analysis, Experience."

48. A basic graph is to an association graph as an abstract compositional space is to a literal one in Morris, "Compositional Spaces." Multiple *AG*s can have the same underlying graph.

49. Connectivity at the level of the set can always be made explicit by placing a box around the perimeter of the graph, labeled with the set's C/CS or C/CRS.

50. I introduce contextual focus in Hanninen, "General Theory," 92–93. A contextual focus is roughly analogous to a sonic focus, in that each identifies an event of special significance in its domain. But because a sonic focus presumes a disjunctive orientation and a contextual focus an associative one, sonic and contextual focus differ in function and effect: whereas a sonic focus identifies a segment that is most *isolated* from surrounding segments, a contextual focus locates one most *connected* to other segments.

51. The contextual focus is a prototypical instance in the sense outlined by psychologist Eleanor Rosch: "Prototypical instances . . . contain the attributes most representative of items inside and least representative of items outside the category" ("Principles of Categorization," 30) and "appear to be just those members of a category that most reflect the redundancy structure of the category as a whole" (37). Note, though, that Rosch's prototypicality and prototypical instances do not reify: "To speak of a *prototype* at all is simply a convenient grammatical fiction; what is really referred to are judgments of degree of prototypicality" (40), which are then projected onto individual segments.

52. "If *D* is a digraph, the graph obtained from *D* by 'removing the arrows' . . . is called the underlying graph" (Wilson, *Introduction to Graph Theory*, 101).

53. An associative path is the association graph counterpart of Lewin's "arrow chain": "An *arrow chain from node N to node N'* in a node/arrow system is a finite series of nodes $N_0, N_1, \ldots, N_J$ satisfying criteria (A), (B), and (C) below. (A): $N_0 + N$. (B): For each j between 1 and J inclusive, (N_{J-1}, N_J) is in the ARROW relation. (C): $N_J = N'$ " (Lewin, *Generalized Musical Intervals*, 194–95).

54. My "ND-path" and "ED-path" correspond to "path" and "trail," respectively, in Lipschutz's *Discrete Mathematics*. Finding the connotations of "path" better suited than those of "walk" to the flow of associations I want to model, I will use "path" for the general case and add the modifiers "node-distinct" and "edge-distinct" to distinguish the two special cases.

55. I introduce the association matrix in an analytic context in "Association and the Emergence of Form."

56. Analysts who wish to devise a set of relative weights among contextual criteria active in set *A* might produce a *weighted association matrix* WAMX(*A*) that replaces the list of criteria in each cell AMX(*A*)$_{i,j}$ with a single number in WAMX(*A*)$_{i,j}$ that indicates (the analyst's interpretation of) the total strength of connection between segments A_i and A_j, calculated as the sum of the products of the individual criteria in AMX(*A*)$_{i,j}$ and their relative weights. Given the many problems that attend the weighting of contextual criteria, however, I do not pursue this route.

57. Threading a weighted association matrix according to the greatest values of WAMX(*A*)$_{i,j}$ would be formally comparable to traversing an association graph through a path of greatest proclivity (or least resistance).

chords A, B, C, or E can be partitioned into a pair of trichords from SCs 3-3[014] and 3-7[025]. For more on Babbitt's *Partitions* see Mead, *Music of Milton Babbitt*, 113–18.

59. Douthett and Steinbach, "Parsimonious Graphs," 248.

60. See Lerdahl and Jackendoff, *Generative Theory*, and Lerdahl, *Tonal Pitch Space*, respectively.

61. In the score, "variations" are neither named nor numbered. I introduce names for analytic convenience: A and AA distinguish the outer sections, which share a particular pairing of material in pianos I and II, from the twelve inner variations, which are bound together by cyclic recombination.

62. The number of lynes active within individual variations ranges from two to eight. The array for variation AA is obtained by superimposition and repartitioning. Repeated pitch realizations are subject to rhythmic change, often motivated by repartitioning. For more on the arrays, as well as analysis and commentary on *Canonic Variations*, see Hanninen, "General Theory," chapters 6 and 7.

63. In performance notes to the score, Reich writes: "*Eight Lines* (1983) is exactly the same piece as my *Octet* (1979) with the addition of a second string quartet." Reich indicates that he made the change to strengthen and improve the intonation of what had been double stops in violin I and II, and to break up what was originally continuous figuration in the viola and cello. With the publication of *Eight Lines*, Reich has withdrawn the *Octet*.

64. Here again, particular musical circumstances recommend an alternate means for naming segments as the clearest and most convenient.

65. Elliott Carter's music abounds with more relaxed versions of the idea that every segment in a set (or, every player in an ensemble) is characterized by a unique set of criteria and a unique set of relations to every other segment in the set (player in the ensemble). See, for example, relations among the first six long chords of *90+* (1994) (mm. 1–7) or the play of interval content and personae among the four players of the String Quartet No. 2 (1959). Andrew Mead explores this idea systematically and strategically in a number of recent works, including his *Sextet* (2005).

66. Some nodes in the graph represent two or more distinct segments in the score— e.g., the pitch content of R136.1 is repeated in R138.1 and R139.1. Once again, as a general practice, and particularly in Feldman's music, I urge analysts not to collapse what look like literal repetitions into a single segment but to maintain contact with each one as a distinct musical event. Changes in musical context can activate different relational properties, and thus individuate the sound of "literal repetitions," placing them at distinct locations in an association graph.

67. The criterion $C_{\text{pitch }\{B4,\ Bb5\}}$ is represented as creating a stronger association between R135.2 and R137.2 than between R136.2 and R137.2, where its effect is diluted by the addition of contrasting elements in R136.2.

68. Gauging the distance between segments by proximate voice leading—that is, in terms of *transformational* rather than associative distance—gives different results throughout the graph. For more on the relationship between association and transformation, and association graphs and transformational networks, see chapter 10.

69. Regarding Schoenberg's opus 23, no. 3, see especially Babbitt, "Since Schoenberg"; and Lewin, "Transformational Considerations."

70. For the moment I exclude the retrograde inversion that grabs the left hand's first F3 to produce <D4, E4, B3, F3, C♯4> and spells out an important common tone rela-

Lewin ("Transformational Considerations," 203).

71. *J*4 embeds the pitch ordering <F6, A5, G♭5, G♯5>, which extracts a four-note ordered pitch segment related by transposition to those supported by the conjoined contextual criteria $C_{pc\ <F,\ A,\ B,\ F♯,\ G♯>} = C_{ip\ <-8,\ +2,\ -5,\ +2>}$ at work between *J*2 and *J*5.

72. Readers who wish to verify this can start with the staccato subgraph; place *J*7 and *J*3 to the left of *J*1 and *J*6, respectively; place *J*8 below *J*3, and *J*4 to the right of *J*5; and use curved lines for edges as needed. The resulting representation preserves every node adjacency in the original but eliminates all apparent edge crossings.

73. Conjoining the three compositional premises of hexachordal combinatoriality, rhythmic differentiation, and RI-related pitch-interval orderings in the bells and voices guarantees that no pair of segments presented simultaneously in bells and voices is connected by an edge.

74. Extending the set-up to the theme of the third movement from m. 20 through m. 30 adds two 5–6–5 edges to the multigraph (connecting it with movement I, theme 1 and with movement II) but does not affect the contextual focus.

75. In graph theory, this is known as "Turán's brick factory problem" (Wallis, *Beginner's Guide*, 106).

76. David Lewin raises the issue of fit or misfit between node precedence in a graph and score chronology in a discussion of node/arrow systems. He first defines a node/arrow system as "*precedence-ordered* if there is no pair of nodes (N, N') such that N both precedes and follows N'" (Lewin, *Generalized Musical Intervals*, 210, Definition 9.7.3. See also Theorem 9.7.4, which stipulates the conditions for PRECEDENCE, a strict partial ordering on the nodes of a node/arrow system). He then notes that "A precedence-ordered system is at least potentially compatible with our naïve sense of chronology" (210). But, as Lewin goes on to point out, "We must be very careful to recognize that the words 'precedence' and 'precede' . . . refer to formal aspects of the node/arrow configuration, and *not* necessarily to the musical chronology of any passage upon which a network using that node/arrow system may be commenting. Even when the node/arrow system is precedence-ordered, it is perfectly possible for a node N to precede a node N' in a network, while the contents of N are heard after the contents of N' in the pertinent music" (212–13). In ensuing discussion, Lewin raises a number of questions about the relationships among precedence in a piece of music, graphic layout of a node/arrow system, and arrow chains traced on such a system (see especially 209–15)—that is, translated into our terms, among score chronology, layout in a particular representation of an *AG*, and associative paths. Lewin notes the rhythmic implications of node/arrow systems as these correspond to or diverge from temporal succession in the music: "the arrows of any node/arrow system have a formal rhythmic structure of their own, a structure which can engage musical rhythm in varied and sometimes complicated ways. Our practice of laying out graphs visually so that most arrows go from left to right on the page has made it easy for us to put off investigating the issues that arise when we try to match the internal arrow-flows of a network with the temporal flow of the music upon which the network comments. Here, now, we shall attempt to explore some of those issues, though we can hardly do them justice in one section of one chapter" (209).

77. This idea of ordering values in one dimension by those in another, and of reversing the role of ordering versus ordered dimensions, is rooted in Babbitt's pitch-class/order number representation of twelve-tone rows, its extensive exploration by Mead, and generalization to the realm of contour by Morris. See Babbitt, "Twelve-Tone Invariants"; Mead, "Some Implications"; and Morris, *Composition with Pitch-Classes*.

Quartet in "Associative Sets, Categories," 177–81; and the analysis of Feldman's *Palais de Mari* in chapter 8 of this book.

79. Points in the following discussion are excerpted from Hanninen, "Associative Sets, Categories," 188–93.

80. "It is possible to account for almost any aspect of cognition in terms of categorization. Much perception can be viewed as classifying sensory input" (Hahn and Ramscar, *Similarity and Categorization*, 5). For music psychologist Irene Deliège, "a categorization process is always operational during attentive music listening" ("Introduction: Similarity Perception," 239). Zbikowski advances a similar view: "my proposal, then, is that categories are where conceptualization of music starts" (*Conceptualizing Music*, 59).

81. Millikan, *Clear and Confused Ideas*, 35.

82. Ibid., 38.

83. For background on phenetic, biological, phylogenetic, and individuals species concepts in biology, followed by theoretic accounts and analytic illustrations of their approximate analogues as perspectives on association in music analysis (morphological, populations, lineages, and individuals, respectively), see Hanninen, "Species Concepts in Biology."

84. Biologist Ernst Mayr introduced and often used the term "population thinking," which philosopher of biology Elliott Sober describes this way: "The population is an entity, subject to its own forces, and obeying its own laws. The details concerning the individuals who are parts of this whole are pretty much irrelevant. Describing a single individual is as theoretically peripheral to a populationist as describing the motion of a single molecule is to the kinetic theory of gases. In this important sense, population thinking involves *ignoring individuals*: it is holistic, not atomistic" ("Evolution, Population Thinking, and Essentialism," 175).

85. Associative lineages, like associative paths, need not correspond to temporal precedence and succession.

86. The difference between an associative configuration (or association graph) and an associative lineage (or association digraph) is comparable to that between a transformation graph and a transformation network.

87. The individuals perspective is a musical interpretation of biologist Michael Ghiselin's idea that instead of sets or classes of organisms, species might better be seen as individuals: "Individuals are single things, including compound objects made up of parts, [which] need not be physically connected" ("Species Concepts," 128). Millikan's view of categorization as the reidentification of persistent substances also reflects an individuals view.

88. The term "associative landscape" is inspired by work in landscape ecology, a field concerned with the composition and spatial arrangement of elements in the landscape. Beeby and Brennan describe landscape ecology as the "study of the spatial arrangement of ecosystems and the processes that unite them" (*First Ecology*, 219). For Pickett and Rogers, "A critical insight of landscape ecology is that not only is spatial heterogeneity, per se, significant to the structure and function of the natural world, but the exact way that the components of natural systems are arranged is important" ("Patch Dynamics," 116).

89. Similarly, associative sets and their associative subsets—two nested levels of associative oganization—have a variable relationship to scale. Whereas an associative set and one of its subsets can unfold at the same scale, two or more sets (entities at the same

ject for analytic inquiry.

90. The idea of a landscape study derives from landscape ecology, in which the homogeneity or heterogeneity of landscape structure is an experimental variable. "A landscape ecological study asks how landscape structure affects (the processes that determine) the abundance and/or distribution of organisms. To answer this, the response variable (process/abundance/distribution) must be compared across different landscapes having different structures. . . . The entire study is comprised of several nonoverlapping landscapes having different structures" (Fahrig, "Landscape Perspective," 5).

91. "Association map" replaces the term "configuration plot" in Hanninen, "General Theory." Like contextual association graphs, maps might more accurately be called "contextual association maps," as a reminder that each segment in the map carries with it all and only those relational properties activated by aspects of its musical context.

92. The concept of scale implies a comparison between two measures, small and large, or *grain* and *extent*. For association maps, segment size determines the coarsest useful grain; small-scale and large-scale maps are distinguished by the extent of the passage under consideration (the "scale of analysis"). Small-scale association maps cover short passages; large-scale maps, long ones, entire movements, or works. Note that this musically intuitive usage is the *reverse* of that in cartography, where small- (e.g., 1:250,000) versus large-scale (e.g., 1:24,000) maps parallel the ratio between grain size and extent such that small-scale maps cover larger areas, while large-scale maps cover smaller ones.

93. For earlier work that employs maps in cutaway score format, see my "Understanding Stefan Wolpe's Musical *Forms*" and "Association and the Emergence of Form"; in running text format, "Words, Musical Organization"; and for schematic maps with segment names, "General Theory" and "On Association, Realization, and Form" (there called "plots").

94. Edward T. Cone uses this kind of representation in "Stravinsky: Progress of a Method" in his analysis of the first movement of Stravinsky's *Symphony of Psalms*.

95. Association maps in cutaway score format are a little like the distributional taxonomies of Lévi-Strauss, Ruwet ("Methods of Analysis in Musicology") and Nattiez ("Varèse's *Density 21.5*"), and paradigmatic analysis of Agawu (*Music as Discourse*, chapter 5), but with horizontal and vertical axes exchanged so that sets ("categories" in Ruwet and Nattiez) unfold horizontally rather than vertically. There are, however, three important differences. First, in a distributional taxonomy time flows first left to right, *and then* top to bottom, as in English text and in my "running text format," which is a much closer analogue. Because distributional taxonomies use both horizontal and vertical dimensions to represent temporal succession, they cannot model temporal simultaneity or, therefore, textural or associative polyphony (Ruwet and Nattiez are aware of this limitation); cutaway score maps can handle both. Second, in a distributional taxonomy, segmentation *partitions*—each note in the score contributes to one, and only one, segment. In cutaway score format, one note can contribute to two or more segments that overlap or embed one another. Third, whereas the organizational components of Ruwet's and Nattiez's distributional taxonomies are "categories," the components of an associative landscape, and thus also of its graphic representation in a map, are associative formations—that is, not only associative sets (categories), but *configurations* of segments in a specific temporal disposition or distribution that relates associative to temporal proximity and distance.

resent associative organization in a passage from Benjamin Boretz's "Thesis," part I of *Language ,as a Music*. Words and phrases in the text are segments; groups of words or phrases associated by sound, semantics, or imagery form associative sets. I also use running text maps in chapter 5 in the analysis of Debussy's "Harmonie du soir."

97. The "clumped" disposition replaces "condensed" in Hanninen, "General Theory."

98. Thinking in terms of patches and patchy distributions relative to a background matrix derives from landscape ecology. Referencing influential work by Richard Forman and Michel Godron (1981), Beebe and Brennan write: "Landscape ecologists recognize three basic spatial elements—the patch (say, an area of woodland), the matrix (the background ecosystem which dominates the landscape—the fields or vineyards), and the corridors that traverse the matrix, connecting the patches (such as hedgerows or streambanks" (*First Ecology*, 221). Natural landscapes are "patchy," meaning that the distribution of species populations and ecological communities is neither uniform nor random, but forms a number of patches within a dominant landscape type. Patches can be isolated from one another, surrounded by matrix or patches of other types, or connected by corridors (as hedgerows connect small patches of woods in a farmland matrix).

99. The compound patch is something like the original meaning of the term "metapopulation" in ecology: "In 1970 Richard Levins coined the term *metapopulation* to describe a 'population' consisting of many *local populations*, in the same sense in which a local population is a population consisting of individuals" (Hanski, *Metapopulation Ecology*, 1–2). More recently, the term often has a more specific meaning that doesn't translate as well to music analysis: "A *metapopulation* consists of a number of populations that exchange individuals through immigration and emigration" (Mackenzie, Ball, and Virdee, *Ecology*, 199).

100. As in Nathan Milstein's 1975 performance on Deutsche Grammophon CD 289 457 701–2 or Rachel Podger's 2002 performance on Channel Classics (CCS SEL 2498).

101. This more general model of distributions and scale was inspired by a study of geographical distributions of plants of the British Isles by Rabinowitz, Cairns, and Dillon ("Seven Types of Rarity"). The authors consider "seven kinds of rarity," defined by the product of three variables: wide or narrow geographic distribution, broad or restricted habitat requirements, and populations that are somewhere large or everywhere small. The eighth theoretic possibility—plants with a wide range, restricted habitat, and populations that are everywhere small—did not occur in their study, perhaps because this kind of distribution cannot support the level of reproduction necessary to sustain plant populations. While not subject to these biological constraints, associative sets that are widespread, infrequent, and distributed in minimal patches do pose perceptual challenges.

102. Distributions can also be formalized using statistical methods, but for our purposes a less formal approach is more useful and can be nearly as informative.

103. Keep in mind that patches can also be simple or compound, and at multiple levels.

104. Levin, "Problem of Pattern," 1947.

105. Naturalists often use the terms "common," "locally abundant," "infrequent," and "rare" to convey information about the geographic range and distribution of plants and animals at different scales. Paying careful attention to the birds and plants one sees on a day-long hike over varied terrain is a good way to get a feel for distributions at work

ing to music are temporal and linear activities punctuated by moments of recognition.

106. Although these figures do sometimes leave the surface, they exert a constant presence over a wide range of scales from the largest to fairly short time spans of, say, ten seconds or so (just a few times longer than the typical two-to-three-second window of working memory).

107. The motive saturates the surface not only in pitch transformations, but in stretto (mm. 1–3, 24), diminution (e.g., mm. 9, 11, and 19), 1:1 counterpoint between recto and inversion (e.g., mm. 19–23), and as the basis for harmony set against itself in diminution (e.g., m. 12, mm. 13–14).

108. Here, due to Feldman's frequent use of repeat signs starting on page 3 but especially after page 10, score references are by page, system, and measure. Score layout is uniform throughout: 47 pages of four systems per page, nine measures per system. Page 13 is intentionally left blank.

109. Whether the distribution is even or uneven is a matter of interpretation: bundling the first three patches, and last two, into two compound patches at either end of the composition gives a fairly even distribution of three patches at beginning, middle, and end; else, the distribution is decidedly uneven, with more, and larger, patches located at the beginning than anywhere else.

110. Cogan takes the return of the opening gong sound shortly after 2′30″ as the end of part I in a two-part form plus coda, an interpretation supported by the change in sound material immediately afterward (*Music Seen, Music Heard*, 9–44).

111. Contrasting his concept of "formal functions" with traditional formal labels such as A, B, etc., William Caplin defines formal function as "the more definite role that the group plays in the formal organization of the work" (*Classical Form*, 9).

112. Robert Morris offers Natai and Saranga as particularly good examples of ragas in which key phrases are distinguished in part by different characteristic distributions (personal communication, August 6, 2007).

113. The qualifier "most or all" allows monophonic sets to be connected by overlap or elision, defined in the section on "Contacts," below.

114. If one hears mm. 1–2 as an introduction rather than as part of the first wave, the start of the second wave (m. 17) recalls the melodic figure that begins the first (in m. 3).

115. Alban Berg commented on the polyphony of themes and complex associative rhythm at the start of Schoenberg's First String Quartet, op. 7: "In counterpoint with the first five-bar phrase of the first violin, there is an eloquent melody in the middle voice, built up—as an exception—of one- and two-bar phrases. . . . It requires the hearing faculty at least of an external ear capable of keeping track of all the voices that are so pregnant in their different characters, and of recognizing as such the beginnings and endings (which are all at different points) of all these parts of melodies of different lengths, and of dwelling (with understanding) on their sounding together" ("Why?," 194–95).

116. Although a single segment can function as both a contextual focus and a point of conflux, the two concepts are distinct. A CF is a segment, ascertained with respect to *one* associative set (subset) on the basis of *atemporal* associative topology among its segments. A conflux designates a temporal location in an associative landscape; it involves two associative sets (subsets) and identifies a point of confluence between them.

117. "Flash" connotes both a flashback and a flash of recognition. The term replaces "jump" in Hanninen, "General Theory," 107–8, and "Association, Realization, and Form," 87–93.

Forte, "The Magical Kaleidoscope," 131.

119. To speak of a passage, rather than one or two segments, as a contextual focus is extended usage, but nonetheless clear.

120. Given Stravinsky's documented concern with proportions and timings in the composition of *Orpheus*, the fact that the Air that achieves this dramatic conflux spans the midpoint of the ballet may be significant. For a reproduction of Stravinsky's working notes for the ballet, see Joseph, *Stravinsky and Balanchine*, 194; for an English translation of these notes, see Carr, *Multiple Masks*, 238–41.

121. Like the patch, the idea of a background matrix is inspired by landscape ecology, where patches reside in a matrix defined as the "dominant element of the landscape" (Burel and Baudry, *Landscape Ecology*, 355) or "the background ecosystem which dominates the landscape" (Beeby and Brennan, *First Ecology*, 221). In music analysis as in landscape ecology, matrix surrounds and embeds patches; it must be at least as large in scale as the largest patches under consideration. Patch and matrix are like figure and ground, but whereas ground is a negative concept (the absence of figures), matrix is a positive concept—a compositional element with its own integrity. In landscape ecology, matrix is itself a highly structured ecological system that interacts with patches to shape the overall landscape. In music analysis, matrix is characterized by internal consistency with respect to structural or stylistic principles.

122. The hedge "for the most part" acknowledges the effect that scale can have on music perception: a large-scale, high-profile landscape may seem low-profile on a smaller scale.

123. Cf.: "It is the bane of the empiricist to discover that the degree to which a population is clumped in space depends on the scale that is used for analysis" (Vandermeer and Goldberg, *Population Ecology*, 163). Simon Levin goes further, to identify scale as "the fundamental conceptual problem in ecology, if not in all of science" ("Problem of Pattern," 1944).

124. Whether one considers the repeated pattern in either prelude to be an associative set, or just a figurated realization of a structural voice-leading matrix, the landscape remains materially and compositionally homogeneous.

125. For more on the complex relations between object formation (segments) and category formation (associative sets) in music analysis, see Hanninen, "Associative Sets, Categories" 172–88.

126. Donald Campbell introduced the term "downward causation" in the 1970s to describe the interplay between levels of biological organization in natural selection. Among philosophers the concept of downward causation remains controversial. Campbell and Bickhard write: "That downward causation occurs is a fact; how to understand the phenomenon is the contentious issue" ("Physicalism, Emergence, and Downward Causation," 25). But Jaegwon Kim finds downward causation either "circular and incoherent" ("Making Sense of Emergence," 28) or "causally, and hence explanatorily, inert" (33). Kim admits that downward causation may be significant under a "*conceptual* interpretation. That is, we interpret the hierarchical levels as levels of concepts and descriptions, or levels within our representational apparatus, rather than levels of properties and phenomena in the world" (33). It is this sort of interpretation I have in mind with regard to downward causation and levels of musical organization and analysis.

127. This process of selection and promotion underlies recontextualization by contextual criteria. For a general account of recontextualization that includes sonic, contextual, and structural criteria, see Hanninen, "Theory of Recontextualization." For an

man's *Piano, Violin, Viola, Cello* (1987) see Hanninen, "Feldman, Analysis, Experience," 238–50.

128. Lewontin, "Corpse in the Elevator," 37. Emphasis mine.

Chapter Four

1. Composed in 1794–95, the A-major sonata was published in 1796 with the sonatas commonly referred to as No. 1 in F Minor (op. 2, no. 1) and No. 3 in C Major (op. 2, no. 3). But these are not Beethoven's first works in the genre. The 2007 Cooper edition of *The 35 Piano Sonatas* includes three earlier sonatas from the Bonn years: WoO47 No. 1 in E♭ Major, WoO47 No. 2 in F Minor, and WoO47 No. 3 in D Major, published as a set in 1783.

2. In a section on "nonconventional formal organization," William Caplin cites the first tonal area of Beethoven's op. 2, no. 2, I, as an example of "loose-knit organization" (*Classical Form*, 201), probably because of the "diversity of [its] melodic-motivic material" (17) but perhaps also because of some "inefficiency or ambiguity of functional expression, and asymmetrical phrase groupings (arising through extensions, expansions, compressions, and interpolations)" (17). Although this composite design is unusual for the FTA of a sonata form, there are other examples in the literature. The first movement of Mozart's Piano Sonata in C, K. 309 begins with a two-bar fanfare followed by a more lyrical theme proper; both prove (by virtue of the fanfare's repetition before the second statement, its role in the retransition, and its return at the start of the recapitulation) to be essential thematic material for the movement as a whole. The first movement of Beethoven's Piano Sonata No. 6 in F, op. 10, no. 2 also begins with a first group comprised of an introductory thematic figure (two chords) followed by a more lyrical and characteristic theme. Beethoven underlines the introductory quality of the opening chords with a striking off-tonic recapitulation in D major, but withholds the return to F major until the second statement of the lyrical theme.

3. Caplin hears the formal functions of the two constituent themes in the opening bars of op. 2, no. 2 differently. For him, mm. 1–8 are the "primary initiating unit of the theme," while mm. 9–20 have "a definite continuational quality" (*Classical Form*, 201).

4. Caplin attributes a "continuation function" to the second theme that enters in m. 58, citing the prevalence of sequences and tonal mobility throughout the STA (*Classical Form*, 113).

5. Caplin considers the material in m. 92 to be the second of two subordinate themes (that is, a second idea within the STA) and therefore places the start of the closing later, at m. 104 (*Classical Form*, 113). Hepokoski and Darcy also note the parallelism between the closing in m. 92 and the start of the transition in m. 32 (*Elements of Sonata Theory*, 186).

6. Notes to the Cooper edition indicate that three available sources for op. 2, no. 2 all have two measures of rest at the end of the exposition (mm. 117–18), as in the modern Cooper and Henle editions. Readers using the Peters, Dover, or other editions that show only one measure of rest at the end of the exposition (m. 117) will need to compensate to resolve discrepancies in measure numbers from there on.

7. The proportions of these three sections suggest an architectonic conception. Parts I and II are nearly equal in length (38 and 40 measures, respectively); the retransition is just about half as long (22 measures). Within part II, the move from F major to D minor

(mm. 162–81, mm. 182–203). The fact that each of these is about the same length as the retransition suggests an underlying proportional scheme based on fifths.

8. One can also hear the composite texture in mm. 188–202 as a threefold alternation of hypermetric 2/4 (mm. 188–89, 193–94, and 198–99) and 3/4 (mm. 190–92, 195–97, and 200–2). To me, the hypermetric conflicts between 4/4 in two different phases, and intrusions of 1/4 shown in ex. 4.9 are more persuasive, as they are closely tied to the associative organization of the passage—specifically, to the segment rhythm within sets *C* and *F*.

9. Set *C* launches the primary theme, but the theme proper is based on sets *D* and *E*.

10. Beethoven's dynamic markings (*p* for mm. 1–8, but *fp* at m. 9) also suggest that the later theme takes priority.

11. I thank David Beach for sharing his sketch and insights about the movement with me and for his comments on my earlier attempts to deal with some of its thornier passages. The sketches in exx. 4.16 and 4.17 reflect some of his ideas and are much improved as a result of his suggestions.

12. Having discovered these segments of sets *D* and *E* embedded in the voice leading of mm. 1–8, one could renumber segments of the sets *D* and *E*. I've not done this, for three reasons. A practical reason is that it's clearer to stay with a single naming system. The theoretical reason is that I want to bracket the issue of temporal order in the analytic process until I have the proper occasion to discuss it (see chapter 10). Finally, there is an analytical reason: sonic support for these preliminary structural segments of sets *D* and *E* is very weak compared to that for nearby segments of sets *A–E*. By not numbering these preliminary structural segments (or perhaps calling them *D*0 and *E*0), I mean to convey a qualitative difference between them and their consociates that are the focus of this chapter.

13. In this reading, associative organization influences the interpretation of voice-leading structure. David Beach has suggested an alternate, more strictly structural, reading that places more emphasis on the structural outer voice tones C♯5 and A2 maintained throughout mm. 12–16 (personal correspondence, March 2009). This reading also recognizes the contrapuntal dance of sets *D* and *E*, but assigns it less structural weight. I consider such differences in analytical approach and motivation in the section on traversals in chapter 10.

14. I thank David Beach for pointing out the structural connection between B and A (personal correspondence, March 2009).

15. Given the registral placement of G♯3 in m. 84, one can also draw a long-range connection (albeit one that is nonstructural from a Schenkerian point of view) between the thirds <B3, A3, G♮3> in the lead-in to m. 58 and <G♯3, F♯3, E3> in mm. 84–88. As a trailing voice nestled inside the preliminary fifth descent from B to E in mm. 48–58 and set against a foreground summary descent from B–E in the treble in mm. 57–58, the first "third" sounds like a truncated fifth that gives out on the third of the "wrong" mode (G♮). Although the second "third" in mm. 84–88 represents the continuation of a middleground descent in a different register, it can also be heard as reactivating and finally completing the line abandoned in m. 58 at the start of the STA.

16. As per Schenker's sketch of the development section (*Free Composition*, Volume II, Fig. 100/5). Unfortunately, the sketch contains a misprint—D♯, instead of D♮—to represent the move to D minor at m. 182. Also, because the purpose of Schenker's sketch is to illustrate arpeggiation, it is quite incomplete regarding other aspects of voice leading in the development.

1. For an analysis of associative organization in a passage of music-text by Benjamin Boretz, see Hanninen, "Words, Musical Organization."

2. The pantoum form is an adaptation of the Malay *pantun*, which usually has four lines (sometimes six to twelve) and two rhymes, disposed *abab*. "The form enjoyed a vogue in France and England in the later 19th-century revival of French fixed forms. . . . As altered and adapted into these languages, the pantun became a poem of indeterminate length composed of quatrains in which the second and fourth lines of each stanza serve as the first and third lines of the next, through the last stanza, where the first line of the poem reappears as the last and, in some English pantoums, the third line of the poem as the second" (Preminger and Brogan, *New Princeton Encyclopedia*, s.v. "Pantun," 875–76).

3. Arthur Wenk suggests that the high degree of repetition in "Harmonie du soir" may have inspired Debussy to set the poem: "*Le jet d'eau*, like the two preceding poems ["Le balcon," "Harmonie du soir"], displays more repetition than most of Baudelaire's poetry. It may have been this repetition—more typical of music than of poetry—which attracted Debussy to these particular poems" (*Debussy and the Poets*, 88).

4. For conventions governing the syllabification of mute *e* in French poetry, see Broome and Chesters, *Modern French Poetry*, 8–9.

5. In French, "Rhymes are either masculine or feminine (masculine describes a rhyme that does not end in a mute *e*, feminine a rhyme that does)" (Chesters, *Baudelaire*, 97).

6. Chesters draws a comparable distinction, referring to these aspects of rhyme as Baudelaire's "handling of the inessential" (*Baudelaire*, 14).

7. Recontextualization in music is a "phenomenal transformation of repetition . . . induced by a change in musical context. It is a strange kind of repetition—better, an *estranged* repetition, in which repetition doesn't sound (primarily) like repetition" (Hanninen, "Theory of Recontextualization," 61). Of course, words can also be recontextualized: here, "encensoir," "tournent," and "ciel" all amount to cases of recontextualization by a change in active contextual criteria (cf., 71–72).

8. Eithne O'Sharkey offers three interpretations of the word "reposoir." One is "a temporary altar, or Altar of Repose, erected at certain points on the route of an outdoor procession of the Blessed Sacrament" ("A Note on Baudelaire's 'Harmonie du soir,'" 155). Second, "reposoir" can denote "the table in a sickroom, covered with a white linen cloth, on which the consecrated Host is placed between lighted candles by the priest before he administers the Last Sacrament, as the Viaticum, to a dying person" (155). But it is the third and most common meaning of "reposoir," connected with Holy Thursday liturgical ceremonies of the Catholic Church, that O'Sharkey attaches to the "grand reposoir" in "Harmonie du soir," as the best explanation for the local reference to sadness ("Le ciel est triste et beau comme un grand reposoir"): "The symbolism of the removal of the Host from the high altar and the stripping of the high altar of all its decorations—the tabernacle door is left open and the tabernacle empty—recall the sufferings and death of Christ which will be commemorated solemnly on Good Friday. The Altar of Repose on Holy Thursday is a reminder to the faithful of the coming day of mourning, and, despite its beauty, it creates an atmosphere of sadness" (156).

9. "There are three traditionally established love cycles in *Les fleurs du mal*, which include most, but not all, of the love poems of Baudelaire: the Jeanne Duval cycle

cycle (XL–XLVIII), inspired by spiritual love; and the Marie Daubrun cycle (XLIX–LVII), inspired by the love that comes in later years" ("Baudelaire's Poetic Journey," 35). "'Harmonie du soir,' in the Madame Sabatier cycle, is like 'Le Balcon,' in the earlier cycle, in that it is a moment of peace and reconciliation. Here, however, night is not a memory: it is a gradual unfolding in the present, echoed in the prosody, where the second line of each stanza becomes the first of the following one" (38).

10. The exception is line ii', "Chaque fleur . . . ." One line (line v, "Le violon . . .") also has a modified continuation.

11. One could define additional associative sets, such as a set C that grasps whole-tone sonorities expressed melodically (e.g., mm. 3–4, 45–46, and 59–61, voice) or harmonically (e.g., m. 32, downbeat).

12. Raymond Monelle offers a different interpretation of the song's form: 5 + 3 + 3 + 5 ("Semantic Approach," 201).

Chapter Six

1. Philip Carlsen, the only analyst of Nancarrow's music to make pitch his primary focus, writes: "Surprisingly, the existing literature has virtually ignored such pitch aspects in Nancarrow's studies. One reason for this neglect may be that Nancarrow himself has diverted attention away from his treatment of melody and harmony: 'I don't think of a line, but of a collection of temporal relationships and, in fact, the melodic line is simply a crutch in order to realize certain temporal ideas'" (*Player-Piano Music*, 19). In his indispensable and comprehensive book on Nancarrow's oeuvre, Gann says that whereas "Tempo structure in Nancarrow's music is systematically developed from study to study, and forms the primary interest; pitch manipulation is largely intuitive and ad hoc, and would require more space to examine work by work" (*Music of Conlon Nancarrow*, xi). He does, however, provide a series of diagrams that survey canon-based aspects of form in a section titled "Tempo canon and its formal results" (ibid., 19–28). Thomas makes a number of observations that indicate a real sensitivity to the complex interactions among tempo structures, rhythm, and pitch material that create form in the studies (see, e.g., "Nancarrow's Canons," 121, 128; and "Nancarrow's 'Temporal Dissonance,'" 144); however, she does not take up the subject of form per se. Tenney identifies form as one of two major innovations in Nancarrow's music: "The two most distinctive characteristics of Nancarrow's work as a whole are his rhythmic procedures and his exploration of manifold types of polyphonic texture—and thereby, polyphonic perception" (Liner notes to *Conlon Nancarrow*, 7). While Tenney's analytical comments on each of the fifty *Studies*, included as liner notes for the Wergo and Open Minds CDs, are perhaps the most balanced and holistic approach to pitch, rhythm, and form in Nancarrow's music, the format precludes any extensive discussion of form in a particular study or passage.

2. Reynolds, "Conlon Nancarrow: Interviews," 10.

3. Tenney, liner notes to *Conlon Nancarrow*, 21. Nancarrow confirms that he got the idea of a twelve-voice tempo canon from Cowell: "That's something that Cowell suggested as a 'tempered scale,' *suggested* also as a time relationship. So I just took it. It's in [his book] *New Musical Resources*; I'm almost sure that's where I got it from" (Reynolds, "Conlon Nancarrow: Interviews," 22). Implementing the idea in a composition became possible when Nancarrow acquired a punching machine with the requisite flexibility:

evenly spaced notches anymore. You could adjust it to punch in any place" (20).

4. Gann, *Music of Conlon Nancarrow*, 21.

5. Within each section of *No. 37*, a line is roughly analogous to a lyne in a twelve-tone array in that many of the same considerations for realization apply, including the lyne-to-register realization rule captured by the linked criterion $T_{lyne}S_{2\text{-pitch}}$.

6. The formal diagram in Gann's example 8.20 gives CD timings for sections I–XII, indicates convergence points, and shows the tempo structure from slow to fast (*Music of Conlon Nancarrow*, 195). But, as Gann points out, it does not show either the mapping from tempi to registers or the order in which voices enter. In accompanying text, Gann does mention the four-group aspect of tempo-register mappings in sections I–IV, and the interval-3 and -9 cycles (his "minor thirds") in tempo later on (197, 199).

7. The series in section IX approximates an interval-3 cycle, while that for section XI includes two statements of the interval ordering 9–8–6.

8. Thomas defines four types of tempo canons: *converging* (the slowest voice starts first); *diverging* (all voices start simultaneously); *converging-diverging* (a concatenation of the two, in that order); and *diverging-converging* (another concatenation, but one that requires faster and slower tempi to exchange voices in the texture where the second canon begins) ("Nancarrow's Canons," 108–10).

9. Textural contrasts produced by changes in the mapping of tempi to registers and voice entry order from section to section argue against Gann's characterization of all of *Study No. 37* as a "sound mass canon." Although some sections, in which both tempi and register proceed "chromatically" and in accordance with voice order (as in section III, composed of wildly scattered triads; or IV, of micropolyphony), or material within individual voices is fairly uniform (section V) fit that description; others in which tempi move through interval-3 or -9 cycles in register (e.g., sections VI and IX), or registers are otherwise decoupled from consecutive voice order (e.g., sections VIII and XI), sound more like straightforward polyphony, not "masses."

10. Gann and Thomas both address the issue of perception in Nancarrow's tempo canons by focusing on their formal implications. Gann writes, "In the [late] sound-mass canons, the very point was that no one could *possibly* hear a discrete difference; here Nancarrow is not illustrating tempo differences, he is using subtleties of tempo to create forms and textures that had never been heard before, and which could have been created no other way" (*Music of Conlon Nancarrow*, 175). Similarly, Thomas concludes that while complex tempo relations may or may not be perceptible as such, their emergent effects, as forms, *are* easily perceptible: "[Each] of Nancarrow's four basic canon types (converging, diverging, converging-diverging, diverging-converging) creates a unique formal shape. The points of synchrony . . . operate as significant structural moments and thus help to articulate the design of the studies. As a result, the works achieve a directed flow toward and from these focal points" ("Nancarrow's Canons," 111).

11. Reynolds, "Conlon Nancarrow: Interviews," 6.

12. "Almost as weak," because the entrance of a new note, A6, suggests a boundary of some kind.

13. These wide register gaps between simultaneous voices coupled with changes in the nature of the pitch material within individual voices over the course of the section make section VI more of a traditional canon than a sound-mass canon.

14. By the time the last, fastest, and highest voice of the tempo canon reaches subject 2 in the dramatic run-up to the start of section VII (pp. 39–40), interactions among

lengths of rest between different subjects, have the combined emergent effect of shuffling the order of voice entries compared to that established at the start of section VI. For example, the last and fastest line of the tempo canon in the top register (MM = 281¼ in line B) reaches its statements of subjects 2, 3, and 4 a bit earlier than either of the next two fastest lines (MM = 262½ in line 8 and MM = 250 in line 5) do. Although the end result of the complex interactions among lines and tempi in this and other cases is calculable by hand (Nancarrow had to do this to create scores for punching) in practice, the effects are otherwise unpredictable, introducing subtle instabilities in the form that, here, contribute to the dynamic build-up to section VII.

15. Tenney calls this kind of situation "compound polyphony," which he identifies as an important feature of Nancarrow's style: "The presence of such aggregates and/or resultants in the *Studies* often creates a type of texture that I have elsewhere [Tenney, *Meta+Hodos*, 1988] called *compound polyphony*, to distinguish it from both *simple polyphony* (in which each of several voices is made up simply of single tones) and *compound monophony* (consisting of a single perceptual stratum—either a resultant or a succession of aggregates heard one at a time). All three of these textural types are to be found among the *Studies*, but Nancarrow is a great master of compound polyphony" (Liner notes to *Conlon Nancarrow*, 8).

Chapter Seven

An abridged version of this chapter was presented at the sixth annual meeting of the Music Theory Society of the Mid-Atlantic on March 28, 2008, at the Library of Congress in Washington, DC.

1. Among the many writers to award *In C* this status are Robert Carl, who proclaims that "*In C* is a shining landmark within a remarkable period in American Music" (Carl, *Terry Riley's "In C,"* vii); Robert Palmer, "*In C* has proved to be the single most influential post-1960 composition by an American" (Palmer, "Doctor of Improvised Surgery," 17); William Duckworth, "[*In C*] gave voice to the minimalist movement in America" (Duckworth, *Talking Music*, 266); and Cecelia Sun, "Recent reception places *In C* not just at the center of minimal music, but also at its very genesis" (Sun, "Experiments in Musical Performance," 147).

2. In Riley's words: "At that time I was playing piano every night in San Francisco at the Gold Street Saloon. So one night I was riding in to work on the bus, and *In C* just popped into my mind. The whole idea. I heard it. It was one of those things. I didn't want to work that night. And as soon as I got off work I came home and wrote it all down" (Duckworth, *Talking Music*, 277).

3. In performance notes to the 2005 edition of the score Riley says: "A group of about 35 creates a rich, full overlay but interesting performances have been created with many more or many less."

4. Riley uses the terms "figures" and "patterns" in different incarnations of the performance instructions; Carl, Potter, and Strickland, among others, use "modules."

5. According to Keith Potter, the first performances in San Francisco evolved "'by consensus, almost,' without any written instructions, and the composer has himself done much over the ensuing years to encourage performances of *In C* to be conceived more as contributions to an ongoing exploration of its potential than as merely a faithful reproduction of the score" (*Four Musical Minimalists*, 109). Potter also notes that

describes the "fairly copious instructions" that accompany the 2005 edition of the score as "a sort of afterthought . . . the results of decades of performances during which Riley determined what decisions and approaches, to his taste, seem to work best" (Carl, *Terry Riley's "In C,"* 59–60).

6. While the performance instructions to the 2005 edition also say that "performers should stay within 2 or 3 patterns of each other" and that the "ensemble should aim to merge into a unison at least once, but preferably often during the course of a performance," an earlier edition indicates "performers should remain within a compass of 4 or 5 figures of each other, occasionally trying to merge together in a unison."

7. Steve Reich, 2007 interview with Robert Carl (Carl, *Terry Riley's "In C,"* 44). According to Potter, "Reich is correct, Riley thinks, in claiming that the pulse was his idea, but he has no clear memory of when this was introduced. The original intention had been to perform the work without a time-keeper of any kind, but this proved impossible" (*Four Musical Minimalists*, 109). Sun describes "Steve Reich's suggestion of the pulse [as] motivated by the pragmatic need to keep all the players together" ("Experiments in Musical Performance," 170).

8. Liner notes to the 1968 Columbia recording by Terry Riley and members of the Center of the Creative and Performing Arts at the State University of New York at Buffalo. At the time, Behrman was a producer at Columbia records, and Riley, a Creative Associate at SUNY Buffalo. The 1968 Columbia LP has been reissued on CD as CBS MK 7178.

9. Sun lists the thirteen commercial recordings available in September 2004 along with their dates of performance and release, performers, tempo, timing, CD catalog number, and other titles on the same disc in "Experiments in Musical Performance," appendix 5, 216–19. Robert Carl adds the 2006 recording by Percurama/Hillier and provides a "capsule analysis of the most distinctive moments and choices made by the performers" in all fourteen recordings (Carl, *Terry Riley's "In C,"* 105–6).

10. In *Four Musical Minimalists*, Potter focuses on the score. Sun's "Experiments in Musical Performance" traces performance history over four decades.

11. This reflects the psychological principle that the ability to detect positive change in the environment—the introduction of something new (say, a predator)—usually has greater survival value than the ability to detect negative change or absence (the predator leaves) as elements depart. Although our senses regularly scan the environment for changes, with habituation, awareness and attention erode. In addition, specifically with regard to *In C*, individual performances and performers can, and often do, bring out the entrance of a new figure into the texture by the choice of timbre or register in which it occurs, or by a change in articulation or loudness.

12. Instrumentation is a factor, for it can affect the pitch or rhythmic content of individual figures through octave transposition or forced subdivision of long tones by plucked or mallet instruments that have no true sustain. Both of these affect the perception of figure entries and exits on Bang on a Can's 2001 recording, which includes cello and double bass (downward transposition), as well as mandolin and pipa (which perform sustained tones as tremolos).

13. Because figural window extends on *both* sides of a given figure, it depends somewhat on a figure's location in the series. For instance, if figure 1 persists for four minutes, until figure 6 enters, its figural window is 6. But if figure 6 persists for four minutes, entering just as figure 1 leaves and remaining in the texture until just after figure 8 enters, its figural window is 8, not 6.

identity of rhythm and contour, often used repetitively or in conjunction with other such ideas to build a larger melodic idea or theme. It thus belongs to the category of musical ideas commonly called motifs." ("Figure (ii)," *Grove Music Online*, accessed 14 December 2007, <http://www.grovemusic.com>).

15. A piano string snapped during the performance, explaining the deterioration in sound quality of the pulse (Sun, "Experiments in Musical Performance," 170). Sun points up a disparity between the apparent freedom of the performance and the rigor of its production: "Instead of capturing a spontaneous happening, Riley meticulously assembled the recording by overdubbing his group of nine musicians twice. In what represents perhaps the most methodical traversal of *In C* ever recorded, each additional layer moves systematically through the melodic cells to produce canons at ever decreasing intervals. The predictability of the resultant acceleration is most easily discernible with Fig. 15 where, as each additional sixteenth-note G enters to fill in the sonic spaces, the cumulative effect of the layers of over-dubbing is startlingly similar to Steve Reich's best substitution technique, arguably one of the most determined processes of the New Determinacy. The fact that Columbia Records had allotted Riley and his players only three hours of studio time could well explain the formulaic way they put the three layers together" (169–70).

16. As are Columbia's paired 1969 releases of Riley's *Rainbow in Curved Air* (1968, 18'39") and *Poppy Nogood and the Phantom Band* (1965, 21'38"), the latter a suggestive microcosm of one of Riley's all-night concerts.

17. Hillier's recording also includes "sacred syllables" provided by the composer: "[Riley] sent me a copy of the score in which the notes were underlaid with 'sacred syllables' for the singers to use. He also suggested that a certain amount of vocal scoring would be a good idea, thus planning some groupings of the singers rather than leaving that entirely to chance" (Hillier, liner notes to Ars Nova CD 8226049).

18. The Twenty-Fifth Anniversary Concert and Bang on a Can performances illustrate Potter's observation that there is a rough correlation between performance length and ensemble size: larger ensembles usually take longer to work their way through the 53 figures (Potter, *Four Musical Minimalists*, 113).

19. Sun laments the use of a conductor: "One of the basic tenets of the piece—that the group's collective choices determine the progress of the work—was violated by the presence of a conductor, Loren Rush, who controlled the ensemble's dynamic levels and cued in the various groups of instrumentalists. The CD release of the event acknowledges Rush's contribution to the anniversary concert in the most inconspicuous way" ("Experiments in Musical Performance," 189). Joshua Kosman confirms Rush's contributions as conductor in his review (cited by Sun), "Concert Does Justice to Landmark Riley Work," *San Francisco Chronicle* (January 16, 1990), E3.

20. Some representative mileposts include figures 10, 22, and 35, which enter at about 6'40", 16'40", and 27'25" in the 1968 recording, but 5'02", 11'50", and 22'10" in Bang on a Can's.

21. The Twenty-Fifth Anniversary Concert recording also has this kind of organization, where certain instruments tend to assume the role of leaders, followers, or trailers.

22. Transformation by augmentation and diminution is apparently sanctioned by the composer, as it also occurs on the Twenty-Fifth Anniversary Concert recording in which Riley performs. In liner notes for the 2006 recording, Hillier says, "Encouraged by the composer's own performance notes, we have taken to heart his notion of treating the motifs to various polyphonic processes: octave transposition, proportional augmentation

of gamelan as well as medieval music, such as those playing and singing here." Potter also mentions the possibility of transforming the figures ("modules") themselves and suggests that such transformations are sanctioned by the composer: "Even the modules themselves have developed variants which have Riley's own approval. For example, any module may be subject to any augmentation or diminution, though in practice few performances, even those under the composer's direction, take much advantage of this. (The interpretation of modules 22–26 at double speed on the commercial recording of a performance in celebration of *In C*'s twenty-fifth anniversary is thus not, as some might think, a mistake)" (*Four Musical Minimalists*, 111).

23. At times, a single player creates two subsets an octave apart, as when the sax begins figure 28 in the lower register, then begins a second patch an octave higher.

24. Placing E in the bass transforms and destabilizes the sonority.

25. Robert Carl provides a similar graph for all 53 figures in the 1968 Columbia recording (*Terry Riley's "In C,"* figure 5.4, 90–92). Not knowing of Carl's work, I gathered my own data from the recordings and created my own graphs in summer and fall of 2007 for the paper presented at a regional conference of the Music Theory Society of the Mid-Atlantic in March 2008.

26. The range of variation within individual figures (not shown) complicates but does not change this basic assessment of relative diversity: for example, in the 1968 plot, figure 7 is stippled by timbre changes; in the Hillier, it is more polarized by register changes.

27. In the 1968 plot, figure 5 nearly fades out before returning in the flute (at about 4′40″), then remains in the background for most of the rest of its time.

Chapter Eight

1. Feldman composed *Palais* on commission for a work of modest scope from the composer and pianist Bunita Marcus, a close friend and former student of his at the University at Buffalo. Universal Edition first published *Palais* in autograph, then in a typeset edition in 1995 (UE 30 238). The piece is dedicated to the painter Francesco Clemente. The pianists Sabine Liebner, Markus Hinterhäuser, Aki Takahashi, Marianne Schroeder, and Jeffrey Burns have all recorded it. In liner notes to her CD, Schroeder says that the title derives from that of a painting by Degas in the Metropolitan Museum of Art in New York; a different source traces the title to a photograph in the Louvre ("Palais de Mari," Art of the States, accessed February 23, 2009, http://artofthestates. org/cgi-bin/piece.pl?pid=92).

2. Equating analysis with categorization, Mörchen ("Music as a Musical Process") and Sani ("Morton Feldman's *Palais de Mari*") provide exhaustive hierarchic classifications of the pitch and rhythmic material in every bar of *Palais*. My work intersects with theirs in a way, but differs fundamentally. Associative sets are not classes of things (as the categories in Mörchen's and Sani's classifications are), but evolving sets of musical relationships; not ends in themselves, but means to study various aspects of associative organization, such as the fit or misfit between associative configurations and temporal proximity, and large-scale changes in landscape design. For more on issues surrounding the use of associative sets as categories for music analysis, see Hanninen, "Associative Sets, Categories," which also includes a critique of Mörchen's analysis (150–53).

sures that corresponds with a significant element or change in associative organization. Neither mm. 1–73 nor mm. 287–437 is clearly set off from its surroundings by strong sonic disjunctions or the kind of obvious change in design often signaled by the word "passage."

4. A *notational image* "is part of a score, a visual trace that prescribes sound production" (Hanninen, "Feldman, Analysis, Experience," 247). A notational image differs from what, after Catherine Hirata ("Sounds of the Sounds Themselves"), I call a "sound"—"an *experience* of notes saturated by some context, that is, notes with a particular potential for disjunction and association, notes with a place in associative organization" ("Feldman, Analysis, Experience," 247). These are two of the four contact points I have defined for musical phenomena in Feldman's music. The other two are the *note*, "an aural event; it involves physical vibration and aural reception, but not musical context" and the *sound concept*, which "is a mental representation of the determinate and relational properties of a sound; it does not involve physical vibration" (247). On recontextualization, see my "Theory of Recontextualization."

5. Feldman marks thirteen pedal changes in the score (each identified with a segment of set *F*); otherwise, the damper pedal remains depressed throughout.

6. The fact that segment boundaries coincide with barlines throughout *Palais* suggests this slightly idiosyncratic naming practice. So *A*1, *A*3, and *A*5 indicate the first three segments of set *A* in mm. 1, 3, and 5; *A*178 happens to be the twelfth segment; *B*7 designates the first segment of a new set *B* in m. 7. This convention has the advantage of clarity in a musical context rife with the potential for confusion: some notational images have numerous literal repetitions and material enclosed in repeat signs in Feldman's autograph is written out in the typeset edition, meaning that many measures in the typeset score have *no* distinct visual counterpart in the autograph. For reasons that will soon be apparent, I need to be able to refer to both Feldman's autograph and the typeset score. Thus, a naming practice that is explicit about its point of reference is essential.

7. Raoul Mörchen ("Music as a Musical Process") confronts this feature of set *A* (his pattern alpha) in the course of developing a comprehensive hierarchic classification of pitch and rhythmic patterns in *Palais*. But because Mörchen assumes that patterns form crisp categories organized in a strict hierarchy, he is forced to prioritize associations in different dimensions. In our set *A*, he takes rhythm as the higher-level criterion for association ("variations") and relegates pitch associations to a lower level ("versions"). Back in chapter 3, I emphasized that associative sets and subsets need *not* be crisp classical categories: sets can overlap and their boundaries can be fuzzy. Elsewhere I have argued that the assumption that sets form crisp classical categories can be problematic, because it forces the analyst to make false choices ("Associative Sets, Categories," 151–53, 158–59). In the case of our set *A*, it turns out that—contrary to Mörchen's view—associations in pitch are actually much easier to hear than those in rhythm, for reasons discussed below.

8. Remember that the disconnected subgraphs represent associative *sub*sets: all six segments represented by notated images in ex. 8.2, and nodes in ex. 8.3, are associated by virtue of their membership in set *A*.

9. Indeed, pitch takes priority over rhythm as the primary means for association throughout *Palais*, for all of its sets: changes in duration essentially amount to temporal flexing in a structure defined by pitch. For some particularly clear examples of duration as temporal flexing, compare mm. 287–88, 326–27, 430–31, and 432–33.

10. Counting the pairs of dyads within the right hand, and within the left hand, of m. 82 as two separate segments.

late scores. For a look at a symmetrical passage from *Coptic Light* (1986) see Hanninen, "Feldman, Analysis, Experience."

12. Although the segment in m. 43 shares D♯/E♭5 and all three pcs with segment *B*7, the facts that it is a simultaneity, relatively long in duration, embedded in a large patch of set *E*, and that its later consociates also tend to appear inside patches of *E*, suggest that it is best seen not as part of set *B* but a distinct subset of *E*, *E/e*. However, recognizing the associative proximity of *E/e*43 to *B*7, and set *B*'s connection to set *A* noted above, one can also think of set *B* as a bridge between sets *A* and *E*.

13. The segments in mm. 66 and 72–73 are also associated by $C_{\text{pitch \{D♭3, G♭4\}}}$.

14. One can also trace the origins of *G/c*384–86 to mm. 296–98, which present the same three subsegments but in the reverse order. Because musical context privileges $C_{\text{ip}+3}$ as a core criterion of set *G*, however, this association is at best secondary and much harder to hear.

15. In formal terms, this reversal of the conventional roles of nodes and edges as representing segments and contextual criteria, respectively, creates a "dual" graph.

16. To fit the largest sets on the page without losing size and gradient differentiation among the smaller sets, and to minimize overlap between sets *E* and *G*, some compromise was necessary: sets *E* and *G* are about 10 percent smaller than they should be.

Chapter Nine

1. The score is available from Morris Music in Rochester, New York. The *Nine Piano Pieces* are recorded by pianist Margaret Kampmeier on "Robert Morris: *Nine Piano Pieces, Tête-à-Tête, Wabi*," Open Space CD 14, 2001. For more on Morris's compositional work, development, and philosophy, see especially Morris's *Composition with Pitch-Classes*; "Compositional Spaces," "Some Things I Learned," "Musical Form, Expectation," and other essays in *The Whistling Blackbird*; and Brody, "'Down to Earth.'"

2. In liner notes to the 2001 Open Space CD, Morris says that "Rising Early" preceded "Between" and explains the structural relationship between them.

3. The order of pieces in the score corresponds to the order of fair copy dates, not necessarily the order of composition (telephone conversation with the composer, August 18, 2008). Two performances by pianist Margaret Kampmeier order the pieces differently. Mutual agreement between Morris and Kampmeier led to the arrangement on Open Space CD 14—"Between," "Kids," "Had," "To Wit," "Loose Canon," "Rising Early," "Figurine," "Fever," "Glimpse" (telephone conversation, August 18, 2008). In this ordering, "Rising Early," the earliest and by far the longest of the *Nine* pieces, occupies a central position, creating a nice registral connection with its successor, "Figurine." Surface rhythm also develops nicely through the set in this ordering, with the active surfaces of "Kids" and "Loose Canon" contrasting with the slower pacing of "Between," "Had," and "Rising Early." Performing in Kilbourn Hall at the Eastman School of Music on February 7, 2007, Kampmeier played seven of the pieces (all but "Between" and "Rising Early," the two with the strongest structural relationship) in this order: "Had," "Kids," "Figurine," "To Wit," "Loose Canon," "Fever," "Glimpse."

4. Morris, *Composition with Pitch-Classes*, 3. Morris has likened compositional designs to figured bass in a Baroque continuo or a lead sheet in jazz, "in that such notations guide both composition and improvisation but, once mastered, do not, directly or indirectly, influence stylistic and personal choice" (4). Close study of the music reveals that

tion, usually to enhance harmonic consistency or forge local or long-range associations that otherwise could not be obtained. In a telephone conversation in which the author confirmed with the composer that these deviations were intentional, not errors, Morris reasserted the role of the array as an inspiration for improvisation (telephone conversation, August 18, 2008).

5. Morris defines an array as "a two-dimensional arrangement of rows and columns which intersect in positions. . . . Arrays are compositional designs that can be readily interpreted as music" (*Composition with Pitch-Classes*, 339).

6. As in chapter 2, after Michael Kassler.

7. Weighted aggregates appear in a number of Babbitt's compositions from the 1970s on. Babbitt discusses the practice in "Since Schoenberg"; see also Mead, *Music of Milton Babbitt*, 133–35 and Morris, "Some Things I Learned," 89–92. The terms "horizontal weighting" and "vertical weighting" originate with Morris, "Why Weight," which gives a thorough account of weighting in twelve-tone pc arrays.

8. After Howard Hanson, Ian Quinn identifies these set-classes as tentative prototypes for six qualitative genera (Quinn, "General Equal-Tempered Harmony, Part I," 130); then, in a second pass, SCs 6-1, 6-35, 6-27, and 6-32 become "super maxpoints" for cardinality 6 (132). See also Eriksson, "The IC Max Point Structure."

9. In a lecture on the *Nine Piano Pieces* presented to the Composition Colloquium at Harvard University on February 26, 2007, Morris related this incipit and cadential melody to the opening melodic material of Schoenberg's *Klavierstück* op. 23, no. 1 and of Bartók's *Music for Strings, Percussion, and Celesta* (personal communication). For analyses of these pieces see Morris, "Modes of Coherence" and "Conflict and Anomaly."

10. The number of lynes and blocks in each of the *Nine* arrays is as follows: "Between," 4 lynes, 1 block; "Rising Early," 4, 5; "Had," 4, 4; "Kids," 3, 4; "Figurine," 2, 6; "Loose Canon," 3 or 4 (depending on the block), 3; "To Wit," 5, 2; "Fever," 2, 6; "Glimpse," 1, 4.

11. Array columns in "Between," "Rising Early," and "Figurine" always have six distinct pcs; those in "Loose Canon," eight; in "To Wit," eleven. Columns in "Had" have 11 pcs, but with considerable vertical weighting. Morris's *Cold Mountain Songs* (1993) for soprano and piano is based on a series of pc arrays in which columns are uniform in both cardinality and set class, but do not form twelve-tone aggregates.

12. More specifically, the pacing of array columns usually conforms to a temporal plan Morris works out in advance of realization, but with different (or no particular) structural principles than the pc array.

13. The remaining columns produce members of SCs 6-32[024579] and 6-8[023457] twice each, and 6-Z24[013468] and 6-31[014579] once each.

14. For a related discussion of the influence of pitch ranges on contour and associations among segments in Babbitt's *Tableaux* (1973), see Hanninen, "General Theory," chapter 3.

15. The apparent gap in the order of set names—skipping from set B over set C to D—arises because $C1$, in m. 4, is a local anomaly. The first consociates appear in m. 14 ($C2$) and m. 17 ($C3$); the larger patches that motivate formation of set C come even later, in mm. 21–22 and 28–30, drawing segment $C1$ into set C only in retrospect.

16. Although the rising sixth <F♯5, D6> in m. 5 doesn't instantiate the core criterion for set D ($C_{SC\ 3\text{-}11[037]}$), its strong association with the opening interval of what I call $D2$ in m. 7 (<F5, D♭6, A♭5>, under T_{-1}) leads me to call it $D1$.

17. As usual, the selection or exclusion of particular segments represents my sense of their relative importance in shaping the associative landscape. One could certainly add

3, and 7 could be accommodated as an associative subset of B; the three segments associated by $C_{SC\ 3\text{-}5[016]}$ in mm. 11–12 could be added as part of a new set E.

18. Although rhythmic detail is critical to segment formation, it does not figure into the core criteria for sets A, B, C, or D.

19. An exception is $B12$ in m. 26, which comes only from lyne 1.

20. The five omitted hexachords are SC 6-Z13[013467] plus the two Z-pairs 6-Z23[023568]/6-Z45[023469] and 6-Z26[013578]/6-Z47[012479].

21. Blocks I and IV, and II and V, emphasize different set classes. In blocks I and IV, SCs 6-Z24[013468] and 6-Z36[012347] are most common, with five and four instances, respectively. In blocks II and V, SC 6-Z43[012568] occurs six times, and 6-Z17 [012478] and 6-Z40[012358], four times each.

22. There are a few differences in lyne 4, which has a wider span in "Rising Early" (19 semitones, B♭1–F3) than in "Between" (10 semitones, G2–F3).

23. Sections II and III each reduce the maximum difference in the length of adjacent bars: in section II, $|f(n+1) - f(n)| \leq 3$; in section III, $|f(n+1) - f(n)| \leq 2$. Sections IV and V successively restore it, first to 3 beats (section IV), then 4 beats (section V).

24. The length of section III may also relate to that of "Between." With 157 beats at 80 bpm, "Between" has an estimated performance time of just under 2 minutes (1.963 min.). With 110 beats at 92 bpm, that for section III is a little over one minute (1.196), for a ratio of the latter to the former of about .609—not far from the Golden Section ratio of approximately .613. The *tempo rubato* indication for both pieces can easily make up (or increase) the difference.

25. The B♭2 in m. 4 fits into a small associative set that straddles the barline of mm. 4–5: {B1, B♭2} in m. 4 and {B♭2, B0} in m. 5, share a pitch ($C_{pitch\ B♭2}$), both pcs ($C_{pc\ \{AB\}}$), and a pc interval above the lowest sounding note ($C_{pc\ FB\ 11}$).

26. "Essentially" local, in that one might hear a recollection of the first set in m. 15.

27. The associative reach of this relation extends further, to take in a cross-lyne four-note segment that embeds $C8$ from m. 29 of "Between," associated with $C4$ by $C_{pc\ <A12B>}$ and incl $C_{int\ <+1,\ -3>}$.

28. Here I reference the order of our analytical discussion, which corresponds to the order of pieces in the score and on the Open Space recording. Recall, though, that "Rising Early" actually predates "Between" and that a performer or listener can reorder the pieces at will.

29. The flash is faint, due to conflicts from $S_{1\text{-adjacency}}$, $S_{1\text{-simultaneity}}$, and $C_{pitch\ <B4,\ G\sharp 4,\ A4>}$.

30. Three are not: column 3 has seven pcs, as does column 25; column 26 has nine.

31. Although one can identify the entire thirty-five-note pitch realization of T_9IP originally heard as lyne 2 of "Between," then embedded in "Glimpse," with a pair of segments related by $C_{pitch\ <A4,\ C5,\ B4,\ ...\ C\sharp 5,\ D5,\ B4>}$, there are complications to perceiving either one of these *as* a segment. First is the length. Is it possible to perceive the string in its entirety as *a* segment in either piece (rather than as a concatenation of shorter segments)? Second, whereas notes of the embedded string in "Glimpse" are all realized as perceptual "edges"—not only the first, but also the highest, lowest, or longest note, in the measure they control—in "Between," the progress of consecutive order positions is often obscured by play among lines and contextual associations formed across lines. Not until m. 6 (ops 5 and 6) are two notes of lyne 2 realized as temporally adjacent attack points, and not until m. 12 (ops 12–14) are three notes of the string not only temporally adjacent but reinforced as a segment by contextual association.

comes last in the score, in both of Kampmeier's performances, and in the sequence of fair copy-dates.

Chapter Ten

1. Lewin presents intervals (Cartesian) and transformations (actions) as complementary perspectives or "attitudes" in music analysis; the phrase "transformational attitude" is his (*Generalized Musical Intervals*, 158–59). Lewin points out that the complementary perspectives of space and action apply to the interval itself (xi, figure 0.1). Association graphs also admit both possibilities—a static perspective, concerned with topology or geometry (in an association graph), and a kinetic one (in an association digraph).

2. Association graphs are not comparable to transformation graphs because their nodes contain segments while the nodes of a transformation graph are (ostensibly) empty. Nor are they comparable to transformation networks, because the nodes of an association graph are connected by edges, not arrows (no precedence is defined).

3. Lewin, *Generalized Musical Intervals*, 196.

4. Ibid., 195.

5. Ibid., 193.

6. Ibid., 196.

7. A transformation network and its companion association digraph are not isographic by Lewin's definition that "the same transformations are combined in the same structure of nodes and arrows, even though the contents of the nodes are different" (*Generalized Musical Intervals*, 183), because only the network, not the digraph, involves transformations.

8. Bundling transformations along an edge of a transformation graph is often problematic because it can lead to contradictions when transformations along different edges compose with one another. But transformation graphs don't often need such bundling for visual clarity: transformations usually derive from a single musical dimension (e.g., pc content), so most pairs of nodes are related by only one or two transformations.

9. "The graph, as a configuration of nodes and labeled arrows, knows no 'right' and 'left.' We are using those visual distinctions here to indicate musical chronology, not graph-structure as such. Musical chronology is naturally crucial" (Lewin, *Generalized Musical Intervals*, 173).

10. Lewin provides a formal account of node precedence and discusses a host of issues by way of musical example. See Lewin, *Generalized Musical Intervals*, 174–75 and 209–19, especially page 209 and the discussion of examples 9.14 and 9.15 (on the second movement of Beethoven's "Appassionata" sonata) on pages 212–16. For an excerpt from Lewin's discussion, refer back to chapter 3, note 76, of the present text.

11. In some cases, Lewin designates input and output nodes that clarify the relationship between spatial placement (score chronology) and musical priority. See, for example, in *Generalized Musical Intervals*, 207 and 212–14.

12. Lewin, *Musical Form and Transformation*, 1–15. Lewin's term "pitch-class configuration" corresponds to "partition" as defined by Morris and Alegant: "A *partition of the aggregate* is any unordered and disjoint set of pcsets which in union comprise the aggregate" ("Even Partitions," 75); "A *mosaic* is a set of partitions that are equivalent under transposition and/or inversion (T_n or T_nI)" (76). As in Lewin, I will also occasionally

and Alegant, to denote a particular set of pc sets that in union comprise the aggregate.

13. Lewin, *Musical Form and Transformation*, 1.

14. Ibid., 13. The operation "I" on the example refers to "I-inversion," a context-sensitive inversion around Lewin's "odd-dyad-out" (i.e., ops 0 and 1 for P- and I-forms of the Dallapiccola row, and ops B and A for R- and RI-forms).

15. "One sees from the visual motifs of the example how clearly the transformational picture of mm. 21–36 can be regarded as a variation on a substructure from the picture of mm. 1–16. . . . After some preliminary maneuvering, an early configuration is transposed by T7 (and possibly retrograded). The result is then elaborated by its retrograde; it is also elaborated by its I-inversion" (Lewin, *Musical Form and Transformation*, 13–14). For a critique of Lewin's analysis and a different approach that emphasizes transformations and inclusion relations among the partial orderings they induce on the row, see Morris, review of *Musical Form and Transformation*.

16. That the nodes of Lewin's network contain measure numbers, rather than pitch-class sets or letters that designate pitch-class sets, is unusual in Lewin's practice. But while the measure numbers may suggest musical segments, the transformations indicated and topology of the network confirm that pitch-class configurations, not segments, are the objects under consideration.

17. "The configuration of m. 15 applies the operation I to the configuration of m. 11. This restores the configuration of m. 7, so far as pitch classes are concerned. Indeed, the pitches of the homophony are the same, except that the 'C' and the 'H' of the BACH voice are an octave 'too low' in m. 15" (Lewin, *Musical Form and Transformation*, 7–8).

18. In accompanying text, Lewin recognizes m. 11 as a significant formal juncture. My point is simply that the network representation focuses attention on certain kinds of relationships, while association graphs tend to focus on others.

19. That is, relative to our starting point, but by no means complete harmony: neither of the critical edges that connect the left and right sides of the association graph (A1–5—A11–14 and A8–10—A11–14) has a counterpart in the network (the latter, also a temporal adjacency, is the exception noted in the text).

20. The indefinite article—"a" schematic, not "the" schematic—is required because although the structure of concepts illustrated in example 1.1 is fixed by the theory, the particular criterion types, subtypes, individual criteria, segments, associative sets, and landscapes involved change with the analytic application, as discussed below.

21. Nodes represented as adjacent within a traversal need not be adjacent on the schematic. Such "implicit" traversals can always be unfolded into "explicit" traversals, as explained below.

22. Tenney lays the conceptual foundation for this work in *Meta+Hodos*. Tenney and Polansky, "Temporal Gestalt Perception in Music," presents the algorithm, three analytic applications, and critical discussion of the results. For a description of the algorithm, see chapter 2, note 20.

23. Tenney, *Meta+Hodos*; Tenney and Polansky, "Temporal Gestalt Perception in Music," 214.

24. Cogan and Escot, *Sonic Design*; Cogan, *New Images* and *Music Seen, Music Heard*.

25. Inspired in part by Jakobsen and Waugh's work in linguistic phonology, Cogan's theory of oppositions represents thirteen "sonic features" or polarities, such as grave/acute, centered/extreme, narrow/wide, and compact/diffuse (*New Images*, 133–40).

26. A *maximum* of eight nodes, because the four nodes H, T, TS, and TC are present only when the structural domain is active.

tual domains, see Hanninen, "Associative Sets, Categories," 182–85.

28. The distinction between literal and represented adjacencies applies only to the schematic, not to association graphs. The fact that, by definition, an association graph consists of a set of segments (nodes) interrelated by contextual criteria (edges) prevents such a distinction.

29. This distinction between a literal adjacency and a represented adjacency with respect to a schematic is comparable to that between a full lattice and a pruned lattice of order constraints used in Starr, "Derivation and Polyphony," to define a partial ordering.

30. Explicit traversals, however, can specify branchings that do not involve the genoseg level: as long as each pair of nodes represented as an adjacency unfolds into a succession, there is no need to postulate further. For instance, the explicit traversals and branch at the associative set and landscape levels, respectively.

31. Each theory of structure is compartmentalized within the T domain, and the HFs and HEs defined by different theories are often incommensurate. So, strictly speaking, one can compare *analyses* supported by different theories, but not the theories themselves.

32. Note that "bottom-up" and "top-down" here refer to inclusion relations among musical objects, *not* the direction of travel down or up on the page (which would suggest the opposite assignment of terms).

33. Rothstein, "On Implied Tones," 290–93.

34. Ibid., 290.

35. Boretz, *MetaVariations*, 253–313. At the start of part IV of *MetaVariations*—just before the *Tristan* analysis—Boretz discusses relations between general systematic models and individual pieces of music, underlining his concern with the trajectory of the analytic process in this section.

36. Of course, a substantial body of theory of tonal harmony and counterpoint tacitly underlies and informs virtually all scholarly analysis of tonal music.

37. I thank David Beach for pointing out the viability of both interpretations.

38. Personal communication with the composer.

Glossary

Domains

contextual domain: The domain concerned with repetition, association, and categorization.

domain: a realm of musical activity, experience, and discourse about it, bounded by the sorts of musical phenomena or ideas under consideration.

sonic domain: The psychoacoustic aspect of music.

structural domain: The realm of interpretation shaped by active reference to a theory of musical structure or syntax (H) chosen (or developed) by the analyst.

Orientations

association (A): The orientation concerned with relational properties conferred by repetition, equivalence, or similarity. Association supports cognitive chunking through categorization.

disjunction (D): The orientation concerned with difference and the magnitude of change. Disjunctions separate musical events from one another and lift segments from their surroundings.

orientation: A perceptual or cognitive strategy; a mode of attending or conceptualization.

theory (H): The orientation that identifies or interprets musical events in terms of a specific theory of musical structure (H), its theoretic framework (HF), and theoretic entities (HE). A theoretic orientation involves conceptual input beyond that stimulated by psychoacoustic attributes or by aspects of repetition, equivalence, or similarity at work in a particular passage.

Three Mechanisms

coincidence: A many-to-one mapping from the instantiations of at least two criteria x and y to a single grouping of notes q; x and y can represent any combination of sonic, contextual, and structural criteria.

instantiation: 1. A one-to-one mapping from a single sonic, contextual, or structural criterion x to a specific grouping of notes q; x is instantiated in q. 2. A grouping of notes recognized by such a mapping.

realization: A special case of coincidence in which x is a structural criterion and y is a sonic or contextual criterion. Realization can be *systematic* (through one of the *linked types* TS or TC) or *nonsystematic*.

basic type (of criterion): A large class of criteria affiliated with one of the three domains (*sonic, contextual,* or *structural*).

contextual criterion (C): A *basic type* of criterion that responds to repetition in a certain respect (e.g., contour, scale degree ordering, or set-class) between two or more groupings of notes within a specific musical context. Contextual criteria assume an associative orientation; they represent associations *between* segments as relational properties *of* segments. Contextual criteria are essential to categorization and to the formation of associative sets and motives.

contextual subtype: A subtype of contextual criteria that names the musical space in which association occurs, e.g., contour; ordered or unordered sets of pitches, pcs, scale-degrees, roman numerals, durations, dynamics or timbres; and set-class. For more on individual contextual criteria within a subtype, see examples 2.8 and 2.9.

criterion: A rationale for the cognitive grouping of musical events or segmentation.

linked type: A criterion type that binds a structural criterion to a sonic or contextual one and ensures systematic realization. There are two linked types: *structural-sonic (TS)* and *structural-contextual (TC)*.

nonsystematic realization: Realization of a structural criterion through coincidence with a functionally independent sonic or contextual criterion (S+T, C+T).

S_1 *subtype*: A subtype of sonic criteria predicated on temporal adjacency. Individual S_1 criteria include $S_{1\text{-pitch}}$ and $S_{1\text{-attack point}}$. For more on individual S_1 criteria, see example 2.5.

S_2 *subtype*: A subtype of sonic criteria predicated on proximity *in the named dimension*, with respect to time. Individual S_2 criteria include $S_{2\text{-pitch}}$ and $S_{2\text{-duration}}$. For more on individual S_2 criteria, see example 2.5.

sonic criterion (S): A *basic type* of criterion that responds to disjunctions in the attribute-values of individual sounds and silences within a single psychoacoustic musical dimension such as pitch, attack-point, duration, dynamics (loudness), timbre, or articulation. For descriptions of some individual sonic criteria see example 2.5.

structural criterion (T): A *basic type* of criterion that assumes a theoretic orientation and indicates an interpretation supported by a specific orienting theory (H). Structural criteria invoke theoretic entities (HE) defined or formulated with respect to a theoretic framework (HF); these are often syntactic (or other abstract) units governed by grammatical or compositional constraints. To produce *musical* (not only conceptual) segments, structural criteria must be realized. For descriptions of some individual structural criteria, see examples 2.10 and 2.11.

structural-contextual criterion (TC): A *linked type* of criterion that indicates logical entailment (direct or indirect) between a structural criterion and a contextual one. Structural-contextual criteria recognize relational properties regulated by structure.

structural-sonic criterion (TS): A *linked type* of criterion that indicates functional interdependence between a structural criterion and a sonic one. Structural-sonic criteria amount to realization rules: criteria within the structural subtype are

dynamics. The "lyne-to-register" realization rule $(T_{lyne}S_{2\text{-pitch}})$ is a common TS criterion in some twelve-tone contexts.

systematic realization: Consistent realization of a structural criterion through one of the two linked types, TS or TC.

Segments

genosegment (genoseg): A *potentially perceptible* grouping of notes (or other sound-events) supported by *exactly one* sonic or contextual criterion, which can realize a structural criterion. In other words, a genoseg corresponds to the instantiation of one criterion of type S or C, or of the linked types TS or TC, or two criteria of types S+T or C+T.

genotype: A set of criteria that supports a *phenosegment*. The genotype of a segment *x*, written $G(x)$, is the set of sonic, contextual, and perhaps also structural criteria that support its coincident genosegs. $SG(x)$, $CG(x)$, and $TG(x)$ indicate a segment's sonic, contextual, and structural genotype, respectively.

phenosegment (phenoseg): A *readily perceptible* musical segment supported by *at least one* sonic or contextual criterion (and perhaps also structural criteria). That is, a phenoseg can be supported by *one or more* criteria of types S or C, TS or TC, or by two criteria of types S+T or C+T, acting alone or in coincidence with any number of other criteria. A phenoseg is the usual denotation of the unqualified term "segment" in most music analysis and in this book.

segment: A grouping of notes (or other sound-events) that constitutes a significant musical object in analytic discourse.

sonic focus (SF): A *phenoseg* rendered unusually prominent by the strength of its sonic boundaries. Although these often involve coincidence among many sonic criteria, great magnitude in a single sonic dimension can also produce a sonic focus.

Associative Sets

associative set (set): A collection of two or more (pheno)segments interrelated and integrated by contextual criteria into a system at a higher level of organization. Within a set, every segment is related to at least one of its consociates by one or more contextual criteria; conversely, every contextual criterion that contributes to the set (not just its individual segments) must support two or more of its segments. Sets are usually named by capital letters in italics (e.g., "set *A*"); individual segments in the set, by appending an arabic numeral that reflects chronological order (*A*1).

associative subset (superset): A level of associative organization below (above) the *associative set*. An associative subset is essentially an associative set, that (1) is part of a larger set under consideration; in which (2) its segments associate more strongly with one another than with others in the larger set, whether through stronger contextual criteria, a tendency for specific contextual criteria to coincide, or both. We name associative subsets by appending a slash and an

subsets of a larger set *A*. Individual segments can be designated by chronological order within the subset (*A*/*a*1, *A*/*a*2) or relative to the larger set, with subset affiliation attached (*A*1/*a*, *A*2/*a*). To avoid confusion I use only the first notation in this book.

combinational diversity. See *range of variation*.

common set (CS): Set of sonic, contextual, and perhaps also structural criteria that support the segments of an associative set. A *sonic common set* (S/CS) lists the criteria that delineate sonic boundaries for segments in the set. A *contextual common set* (C/CS) identifies contributing criteria in the contextual domain. A *weighted common set* is a multiset that lists criteria and tallies their frequency of occurrence.

core common set (CRS): A common set that lists the contextual, sonic, and perhaps also coincident structural criteria *most characteristic of*—not just most frequently found among—a set's segments. The *core sonic common set* of a set *A*, S/CRS(*A*), lists the sonic criteria most responsible for delineating boundaries of segments in *A*. The *core contextual common set* of *A*, C/CRS(*A*), represents an analyst's interpretation of its most characteristic contextual criteria.

distribution of variation (distribution): The array of frequencies with which individual elements or contextual criteria occur among the genotypes of a set's segments.

element diversity. See *range of variation*.

independent segment: A phenoseg that does not contribute to any associative set under consideration. Independent segments tend to form primarily in the sonic domain, with little or no contextual support. They are named by numerals in square brackets that reflect chronological order, e.g., [1], [2], [3].

instance. See *motive*.

motive. A fairly small set of contextual criteria (*relational* properties) that are highly characteristic of an associative set *A*, in a musical context where segments of *A* are prominent or numerous and have special analytic significance. The *core contextual common set* (C/CRS(*A*)) provides a formal model. An *instance* (of a motive) is a segment that instantiates all or most of the contextual criteria in the motive's C/CRS. Instances can be *structural* (when one or more of the set's characteristic C criteria participates in a linked TC criterion) or *pure* (if no TC criterion is involved and all C and T criteria remain functionally independent). We name motives with mnemonics, set in italicized capital letters (e.g., *TURN*); for instances we append an subscript arabic numeral to reflect chronological order (*TURN*$_1$).

population: A set of segments delimited by temporal adjacency or sonic properties such as register or timbre, with *or without* the integrating action of contextual criteria that is essential to an associative set. Populations are usually named with a letter followed by a numeral, both set in bold italics (to distinguish the population from a segment in an associative set); e.g., *P1* and *P2* indicate two populations (*P*1, *P*2 represent two segments of an associative set *P*).

properties, global properties (of an *associative set* or *population*): These include *size*, *range*, *distribution*, and *strength*.

range of variation (range): An indication of the diversity or richness of an *associative set (population)*. Range has two components. *Element diversity* refers to the vari-

tallies the number of elements that serve as relational properties in each. *Combinational diversity* concerns the degree of linkage or independence among elements from different dimensions (or domains) within genotypes of the set's segments.

size: The number of segments in an *associative set (population).*

strength: The (subjective) perceptual prominence of an *associative set* in a given musical context. A set derives its strength from that of its participating segments, in conjunction with the segments' temporal disposition in the music.

Associative Configurations and Association Graphs

association digraph (DAG): Association graph in which one or more edges is replaced by an arrow (single or double-headed) that indicates an order of precedence for a pair of nodes. *DAGs* can represent score chronology (chronological order in the music) or associative chronology (associative derivation, or order of recognition and entry into the set). These need not coincide.

association graph (AG): A set of nodes and edges that provides a visual representation of an *associative configuration.* The nodes of an *AG*, $N(AG)$, are occupied by segments; edges, $E(AG)$, indicate associative adjacencies by contextual criteria.

association matrix (AMX): Adjacency matrix for an association graph. The $AMX(A)$ for a set A compares each segment in A to every other and lists the contextual criteria that associate each pair of segments.

association subgraph (SAG): A subgraph of an *association graph.*

associative adjacency: In an *AG*, two segments connected directly by an edge.

associative configuration: The associative topology (adjacency and nonadjacency) or geometry (also relative associative proximity and distance) of segments in an associative set.

associative degree: In an *AG*, a refinement of *node degree* that tallies the number of associations a node has to other nodes in the set by individual contextual criteria. To find a node's associative degree, sum the number of contextual criteria attached to each of its incident edges. Before surveying the associative degree of various nodes in a graph, one must carefully prune contextual criteria implied by literal inclusion or logical implication.

associative path (path): A total or partial ordering of nodes traced on an *association digraph* that follows a series of arrows from tail to head. Paths can be represented with angled brackets (< >) for ordered sets, braces ({ }) for unordered sets, and nestings of these for partial orderings.

contextual focus (CF, focus): In an associative set, the segment with the most and strongest connections to its consociates and most prototypical of the set as a whole. The *relations multiset* for the focus will balance greatest cardinality with strongest contextual criteria.

edge-distinct path (ED-path): Path in which every edge in the path is unique.

evolution (EVOL): The evolution of an association graph $EVOL(AG)$ is an ordered set of association subgraphs $<SAG_m, \ldots SAG_n>$ where n is the number of nodes in $N(AG)$, m is a number of nodes from 1 to $n-1$, and each *SAG* in the

node and some number of edges.

node degree: The number of segments reached by edges incident to a node.

node-distinct path (ND-path): A path in which no node is repeated.

relations multiset (RM): In an *AG*, a succinct account of the associative affiliations for a segment via its individual contextual criteria. Given segment *An* in set *A*, the *RM(An)* is a multiset of contextual criteria that records the number of segments in *A* referenced by each of its contextual criteria.

Associative Landscapes

association map (map): A visual representation of one or more plots in an *associative landscape*. A map provides a synoptic view of segments' or sets' temporal disposition or distribution in a passage, as well as general properties of landscape composition. Maps can be small scale (short passages) or large scale (long passages), comprehensive or highly selective. In this book I use three basic kinds of maps. In *cutaway score format*, segments are notated as score excerpts, horizontal alignment conveys set affiliation, and vertical alignment indicates temporal simultaneity. In *running text format*, columns indicate set affiliation; time proceeds left to right, then top to bottom. *Schematic maps* include simple schematics (which represent segments by name rather than in musical notation), schematics of associative rhythm (standard note values represent the onset and duration of individual segments and sets) and bar graph schematics (horizontal bars aligned with measure numbers indicate a set's presence or absence in the texture).

associative conflux (conflux): A point of *contact* between two or more sets in *associative polyphony* (literally or conceptually) at some scale of analysis. When the polyphony is literal, such that sets unfold in the same time span, the conflux is *concrete*; else, it is *conceptual*.

associative discontinuity: Place in the landscape where materials with different associative affiliations are juxtaposed rather than integrated. There are two kinds of discontinuity. A *set dissociation* is a shift from one associative set to another that is largely unmediated by elision or the workings of contextual criteria. A *local anticontextuality* is a segment that does not contribute to any associative set in the vicinity and has no, few, or only very weak associations with segments nearby.

associative elision (elision): A type of *contact* that consists of a brief temporal overlap between two associative sets (subsets) that are otherwise in monophonic succession with respect to one another.

associative heterophony: An *external disposition* in which an associative set and one of its subsets, or two subsets of the same associative set, unfold within the same temporal span, to present two or more versions of the same basic material. A special case of associative polyphony. Contrast with textural heterophony.

associative landscape: A level of organization and analysis concerned with the actual temporal (registral, timbral) disposition of associative sets and segments in a passage or composition. Dispositions are of two kinds, *internal* and *external*.

most or all of its duration. Contrast with textural monophony.

associative polyphony: An *external disposition* in which two or more sets unfold within the same temporal span, distinguished by contextual criteria and usually also by S_2 criteria that effect perceptual stream segregation. Contrast with textural polyphony.

associative rhythm: Rhythm by which associated segments, or sets of associated segments, form or change on the musical surface. Associative rhythm has two components: *segment rhythm* is the rhythm of durations given by individual segments in an associative set or subset; *set rhythm*, that of activity and change from one associative set or subset to another.

clumped: See *internal disposition.*

compositional homogeneity (heterogeneity): Stability or change in the arrangement of associative sets within the landscape.

contact: A place in the associative landscape where two associative sets, or two temporally distant patches of a single associative set, meet. There are three types of contacts: the *associative elision, associative conflux,* and *(associative) flash.*

cutaway score format: See *association map.*

dispersed: See *internal disposition.*

external disposition: Arrangement of segments from one or more sets in an associative landscape. There are three basic external dispositions: *associative monophony, associative polyphony,* and *associative heterophony.* These are reminiscent of, but distinct from, their traditional counterparts, textural monophony, polyphony, and heterophony, which involve the number of distinct parts or functional voices in a texture.

flash (associative flash): A type of *contact,* a flash is a psychological phenomenon tied to a point in the landscape in which two temporally distant segments or patches of a single associative set embedded in distinct musical contexts are suddenly related, interrupting the sense of local continuity.

high-profile associative organization: Surface design in which clear segments are organized into one or more associative sets with strong contextual criteria, core contextual common sets, and crisp boundaries. Temporal and sonic adjacency tend to enhance set unity, while sonic disjunctions articulate associative discontinuities.

internal disposition: Distribution of segments within *one* associative set with respect to time (possibly register or timbre). There are two basic internal dispositions. In a *clumped disposition* segments tend to be temporally adjacent, overlapping, or proximate. Clumped dispositions often set up an *associative rhythm.* In a *dispersed disposition* segments are active over a temporal span that greatly exceeds their combined duration.

landscape study: A comparative analysis of musical design, or changes in design, across two or more plots.

local anticontextuality: See *associative discontinuity.*

low-profile associative organization: Surface design in which (1) segments are supported by weak or uncertain contextual criteria; (2) associative set boundaries are fuzzy or obscured by aspects of sonic organization; or (3) the internal organization of associative sets is weak.

textual criteria active in a landscape and the range of variation they convey.

patch (relative to a background matrix): One or more segments of an associative set that appear in fairly close temporal (registral, timbral) proximity in a musical landscape. A *minimal patch* is a single segment. A *simple patch* is composed entirely of minimal patches that are temporally adjacent. A *compound patch* comprises two or more *component patches* of the same associative set, each of which can be minimal, simple, or compound.

plot: Temporal span in a piece of music, often (but not necessarily) delimited by significant sonic disjunctions or changes in associative sets or associative organization.

running text format: See *association map*.

schematic map: See *association map*.

set dissociation: See *associative discontinuity*.

Schematics and Traversals

schematic (of the theory): A graph (collection of nodes and edges) that represents the topology of concepts defined by the general theory (see ex. 1.1). An *interpreted schematic* is a schematic in which the content of at least some variable nodes is specified (e.g., individual criteria, specific segments), often in reference to a particular analysis (see ex. 10.5).

traversal: A path on a *schematic* that represents an ordering of concepts within the general theory. A traversal can visit any nodes in any order, visit the same node more than once, and define a total or partial ordering of nodes. Traversals can be used to model chronology and motivation in music analysis or in other musical processes such as composition, improvisation, or pedagogy of analysis.

Bibliography

Agawu, Kofi. *Music As Discourse.* New York: Oxford University Press, 2009.

Aldwell, Edward, and Carl Schachter. *Harmony and Voice Leading.* 4th ed. New York: Thomson/Schirmer, 2011.

Alegant, Brian. "Cross-Partitions as Harmony and Voice Leading in Twelve-Tone Music." *Music Theory Spectrum* 23, no. 1 (2001): 1–40.

Alegant, Brian, and Donald McLean. "On the Nature of Enlargement." *Journal of Music Theory* 45, no. 1 (2001): 31–71.

Babbitt, Milton. *The Collected Essays of Milton Babbitt.* Edited by Stephen Peles, Stephen Dembski, Andrew Mead, and Joseph N. Straus. Princeton: Princeton University Press, 2003.

———. "The Composer as Specialist." In *The Collected Essays of Milton Babbitt,* 48–51.

———. "Contemporary Music Composition and Music Theory as Contemporary Intellectual History." In *Perspectives in Musicology,* edited by Barry S. Brook. 151–84. New York: Norton, 1972.

———. *Milton Babbitt: Words about Music.* Edited by Stephen Dembski and Joseph N. Straus. Madison: University of Wisconsin Press, 1987.

———. "Past and Present Concepts of the Nature and Limits of Music." In *The Collected Essays of Milton Babbitt,* 78–85.

———. "Set Structure as a Compositional Determinant." *Journal of Music Theory* 5, no. 2 (1961): 72–94.

———. "Since Schoenberg." *Perspectives of New Music* 12, no. 1 (1974): 3–27.

———. "Some Aspects of Twelve-Tone Composition." *Score and IMA Magazine* 12 (1955): 53–61.

———. "The Structure and Function of Musical Theory." In *The Collected Essays of Milton Babbitt,* 191–201.

———. "Twelve-Tone Invariants as Compositional Determinants." *Musical Quarterly* 46 (1960): 245–59.

———. "Twelve-Tone Rhythmic Structure and the Electronic Medium." In *The Collected Essays of Milton Babbitt,* 109–40.

Barsalou, Lawrence W. "The Instability of Graded Structure: Implications for the Nature of Concepts." In *Concepts and Conceptual Development: Ecological and Intellectual Factors in Categorization,* edited by Ulric Neisser. 101–40. New York: Cambridge University Press, 1989.

Beach, David W. "The Analytic Process: A Practical Demonstration—The Opening Theme from Beethoven's Opus 26." *Journal of Music Theory Pedagogy* 3, no. 1 (1989): 25–46.

———. "Schubert's Experiments with Sonata Form: Formal-Tonal Design Versus Underlying Structure." *Music Theory Spectrum* 15, no. 1 (1993): 1–18.

ronmental Issues. 2nd ed. New York: Oxford University Press, 2004.

Beethoven, Ludwig van. *The 35 Piano Sonatas*, vol. 1, edited by Barry Cooper, with fingering by David Ward. London: The Associated Board of the Royal Schools of Music, 2007.

Beran, Jan. *Statistics in Musicology*. Interdisciplinary Statistics. New York: Chapman & Hall, 2004.

Berg, Alban. "Why Is Schönberg's Music So Difficult to Understand?" 1924. In *Alban Berg*, by Willi Reich, translated by Cornelius Cardew, 189–204. New York: Harcourt, Brace, & World, 1965.

Bergandi, Donato. "'Reductionist Holism': An Oxymoron or a Philosophical Chimera of Eugene Odum's Systems Ecology?" In *The Philosophy of Ecology: From Science to Synthesis*, edited by David R. Keller and Frank B. Golley. 204–17. Athens: University of Georgia Press, 2000.

Bernard, Jonathan. "Voice Leading as a Spatial Function in the Music of Ligeti." *Music Analysis* 13, nos. 2–3 (1994): 227–53.

Blasius, Leslie David. "Late Feldman and the Remnants of Virtuosity." *Perspectives of New Music* 42, no. 1 (2004): 32–83.

Bod, Rens. "Memory-Based Models of Melodic Analysis: Challenging the Gestalt Principles." *Journal of New Music Research* 31, no. 1 (2002): 27–36.

Boretz, Benjamin. "Experiences with No Names." In *Being About Music*. Vol. 2, *Textworks*, 338–52. Red Hook, NY: Open Space, 2003.

———. "Language ,as a Music," *Perspectives of New Music* 1, no. 2 (1979): 131–95.

———. *MetaVariations: Studies in the Foundations of Musical Thought*. 1970. Vol. 1 of *MetaVariations/Compose Yourself*, by Benjamin Boretz and J. K. Randall. Red Hook, NY: Open Space, 1995. (Previously published serially in *Perspectives of New Music*, 1969–73.)

Bregman, Albert S. "Auditory Scene Analysis in Complex Environments." In *Thinking in Sound: The Cognitive Psychology of Human Audition*, edited by Stephen McAdams and Emmanuel Bigand, 10–36. Oxford: Clarendon Press, 1993.

———. *Auditory Scene Analysis: The Perceptual Organization of Sound*. Cambridge, MA: MIT Press, 1990.

Brody, Martin. "'Down to Earth': Bob Morris's Restaging of the Sublime." *Open Space* 8/9 (2007): 74–81.

Broome, Peter, and Graham Chesters. *The Appreciation of Modern French Poetry 1850–1950*. New York: Cambridge University Press, 1976.

Brown, Matthew. *Explaining Tonality*. Rochester, NY: University of Rochester Press, 2006.

———. "A Rational Reconstruction of Schenkerian Theory." PhD diss., Cornell University, 1989.

Brown, Matthew, and Douglas Dempster. "The Scientific Image of Music Theory." *Journal of Music Theory* 33, no. 1 (1989): 65–106.

Burel, Françoise, and Jacques Baudry. *Landscape Ecology: Concepts, Methods, and Applications*. Enfield, NH: Science Publishers, 2003.

Buteau, Chantal, and Guerino Mazzola. "Motivic Analysis According to Rudolph Reti: Formalization by a Topological Model." *Journal of Mathematics and Music* 2, no. 3 (2008): 117–34.

ground Levels in Selected Late Piano Pieces of Johannes Brahms." *Music Analysis* 7, no. 1 (1988): 59–92.

———. "Prolegomena to a General Description of Motivic Relationships in Tonal Music." *Intégral* 2 (1988): 1–35.

Cadwallader, Allen, and David Gagné. *Analysis of Tonal Music: A Schenkerian Approach.* New York: Oxford University Press, 1998.

Cambouropoulos, Emilios. "Melodic Cue Abstraction, Similarity, and Category Formation: A Formal Model." *Music Perception* 18, no. 3 (2001): 347–70.

———. "Musical Parallelism and Musical Segmentation: A Computational Approach." *Music Perception* 23, no. 3 (2006): 249–67.

———. Review of *Conceptualizing Music: Cognitive Structure, Theory, and Analysis,* by Lawrence M. Zbikowski. *Music Perception* 21, no. 1 (2003): 135–53.

———. "The Role of Similarity in Categorization: Music as a Case Study." In *Third Triennial ESCOM Conference: Proceedings,* edited by Alf Gabrielsson, 533–38. Uppsala, Sweden: European Society for the Cognitive Sciences of Music, 1997.

Campbell, Donald T. "'Downward Causation' in Hierarchically Organized Biological Systems." In *Studies in the Philosophy of Biology: Reduction and Related Problems,* edited by Francisco José Ayala and Theodosius Dobzhansky, 179–86. Los Angeles: University of California Press, 1974.

Campbell, Donald T., and Richard Bickhard. "Physicalism, Emergence, and Downward Causation." *Axiomathes* 21 (2011): 33–56. Manuscript accessed online at: http://www.lehigh.edu/~mhb0/physicalemergence.pdf.

Caplin, William. *Classical Form: A Theory of Formal Functions for the Instrumental Music of Haydn, Mozart, and Beethoven.* New York: Oxford University Press, 1998.

Carl, Robert. *Terry Riley's "In C."* New York: Oxford University Press, 2009.

Carlsen, Philip. *The Player-Piano Music of Conlon Nancarrow: An Analysis of Selected Studies.* Brooklyn: Institute for Studies in American Music, 1988.

Carr, Maureen. *Multiple Masks: Neoclassicism in Stravinsky's Works on Greek Subjects.* Lincoln: University of Nebraska Press, 2002.

Chesters, Graham. *Baudelaire and the Poetics of Craft.* New York: Cambridge University Press, 1988.

Clarke, Eric F. "Mind the Gap: Formal Structures and Psychological Processes in Music." In "Music, Mind, and Structure," special issue, *Contemporary Music Review* 3, no. 1 (1989): 1–14.

———. *Ways of Listening: An Ecological Approach to the Perception of Musical Meaning.* New York: Oxford University Press, 2005.

Clendinning, Jane Piper. "Structural Factors in the Microcanonic Compositions of György Ligeti." In *Concert Music, Rock, and Jazz Since 1945,* edited by Elizabeth West Marvin and Richard Hermann, 229–57. Rochester, NY: University of Rochester Press, 1995.

Cogan, Robert. *Music Seen, Music Heard: A Picture Book of Musical Design.* Cambridge, MA: Publication Contract International, 1998.

———. *New Images of Musical Sound.* Cambridge, MA: Harvard University Press, 1984.

Cogan, Robert, and Pozzi Escot. *Sonic Design: The Nature of Sound and Music.* Englewood Cliffs, NJ: Prentice-Hall, 1976.

Music." *Music Theory Spectrum* 14, no. 2 (1992): 150–70.

———. "Complex Hemiolas, Ski-Hill Graphs and Metric Spaces." *Music Analysis* 20, no. 3 (2001): 295–326.

Cohn, Richard, and Douglas Dempster. "Hierarchical Unity, Plural Unities: Toward a Reconciliation." In *Disciplining Music*, edited by Philip Bohlman and Katherine Bergeron, 156–81. Chicago: University of Chicago Press, 1992.

Cone, Edward T. "Stravinsky: Progress of a Method." *Perspectives of New Music* 1, no. 1 (1962): 18–27.

Cross, Ian. "Music Analysis and Music Perception." *Music Analysis* 17, no. 1 (1998): 3–19.

———. "Pitch Schemata." In *Perception and Cognition of Music*, edited by Irène Deliège and John Sloboda, 375–90. Hove, East Sussex: Psychology Press, 1997.

Dannenberg, Roger B., and Ning Hu. "Discovering Musical Structure in Audio Recordings." In *Music and Artificial Intelligence*, edited by Christina Anagnostopoulou, Miguel Ferrand, and Alan Smaill, 43–57. New York: Springer, 2002.

Deliège, Irène. "Grouping Conditions in Listening to Music: An Approach to Lerdahl and Jackendoff's Grouping Preference Rules." *Music Perception* 4, no. 4 (1987): 325–60.

———. "Introduction: Similarity Perception ↔ Categorization ↔ Cue Abstraction." *Music Perception* 18, no. 3 (2001): 233–43.

———. "Prototype Effects in Music Listening: An Empirical Approach to the Notion of Imprint." *Music Perception* 18, no. 3 (2001): 371–407.

Douthett, Jack, and Peter Steinbach. "Parsimonious Graphs: A Study in Parsimony, Contextual Transformations, and Modes of Limited Transposition." *Journal of Music Theory* 42, no. 2 (1998): 241–64.

Drabkin, William. "Figure (ii)," *Grove Music Online*, http://www.grovemusic.com.

Drott, Eric. "Conlon Nancarrow and the Technological Sublime." *American Music* 22, no. 4 (2004): 533–63.

Dubiel, Joseph. "Composer, Theorist, Composer/Theorist." In *Rethinking Music*, edited by Nicholas Cook and Mark Everist, 262–86. Oxford: Oxford University Press, 1999.

———. "Looser, Less Technical, More Uncertain: Music Theory and Pragmatic Values." Paper presented at the University of Maryland School of Music, April 11, 2003.

———. "Motives for Motives (or: I've Got Connections)." Paper presented at the University of Michigan School of Music, March 21, 1997.

———. "Three Essays on Milton Babbitt: Part One, Introduction, Thick Array/of Depth Immeasurable." *Perspectives of New Music* 28, no. 2 (1990): 216–61.

———. "Three Essays on Milton Babbitt: Part Two, For Making This Occasion Necessary." *Perspectives of New Music* 29, no. 1 (1991): 90–123.

———. "Three Essays on Milton Babbitt: Part Three, The Animation of Lists." *Perspectives of New Music* 30, no. 1 (1992): 82–131.

———. "What's the Use of the Twelve-Tone System?" *Perspectives of New Music* 35, no. 1 (1997): 33–51.

———. "When You Are a Beethoven: Kinds of Rules in Schenker's *Counterpoint*." *Journal of Music Theory* 34, no. 2 (1990): 291–340.

rie Anderson, and Five Generations of Experimental American Composers. New York: Schirmer, 1995.

Eriksson, Tore. "The IC Max Point Structure, MM Vectors and Regions." *Journal of Music Theory* 30, no. 1 (1986): 95–112.

Estes, William K. *Classification and Cognition.* Oxford Psychology Series 22. New York: Oxford University Press, Clarendon, 1994.

Evans, Gareth. "Molyneux's Question." In *Collected Papers.* Oxford: Clarendon Press, 1985.

Fahrig, Leonore. "When Is a Landscape Perspective Important?" In *Issues and Perspectives in Landscape Ecology*, edited by John A. Wiens and Michael R. Moss. New York: Cambridge University Press, 2005.

Forman, Richard T., and Michel Godron. *Landscape Ecology.* New York: John Wiley & Sons, 1986.

Forte, Allen. "The Magical Kaleidoscope: Schoenberg's First Atonal Masterwork, Opus 11, Number 1." *Journal of the Arnold Schoenberg Institute* 5, no. 2 (1981): 127–68.

———. *The Structure of Atonal Music.* New Haven: Yale University Press, 1973.

———. "A Theory of Set-Complexes for Music." *Journal of Music Theory* 8, no. 2 (1964): 136–83.

Friedmann, Michael L. "A Methodology for the Discussion of Contour: Its Application to Schoenberg's Music." *Journal of Music Theory* 29, no. 2 (1985): 223–48.

Gann, Kyle. *The Music of Conlon Nancarrow.* New York: Cambridge University Press, 1995.

Ghiselin, Michael T. "A Radical Solution to the Species Problem." *Systematic Zoology* 23 (1974): 536–44.

———. "Species Concepts, Individuality, and Objectivity." *Biology and Philosophy* 2 (1987): 127–43.

Gollin, Edward. "Representations of Space and Concepts of Distance in Transformational Music Theories." PhD diss., Harvard University, 2000.

Goodman, Nelson. "Seven Strictures on Similarity." In *Problems and Projects*, 437–48. New York: Bobbs-Merrill, 1972.

———. *The Structure of Appearance.* Indianapolis: Bobbs-Merrill, 1966.

Hahn, Ulrike, and Michael Ramscar. *Similarity and Categorization.* New York: Oxford University Press, 2001.

Haimo, Ethan. "Isomorphic Partitioning and Schoenberg's Fourth String Quartet." *Journal of Music Theory* 28, no. 1 (1984): 47–72.

———. *Schoenberg's Serial Odyssey: The Evolution of His Twelve-Tone Method, 1914–1928.* Oxford: Clarendon Press, 1990.

Hall, Tom. "Notational Image, Transformation and the Grid in the Late Music of Morton Feldman." *Current Issues in Music* 1 (2007): 7–24.

Hanninen, Dora. "Association and the Emergence of Form in Two Works by Stefan Wolpe." *Open Space* 6 (2004): 174–203.

———. "Associative Sets, Categories, and Music Analysis." *Journal of Music Theory* 48, no. 2 (2004): 147–218.

———. "Contour as a Medium for Musical Association." Paper presented at the 17th annual meeting of the Society for Music Theory, Tallahassee, Florida, 1994.

225–51.

———. "A General Theory for Context-Sensitive Music Analysis: Applications to Four Works for Piano by Contemporary American Composers." PhD diss., University of Rochester, 1996.

———. "On Association, Realization, and Form in Richard Swift's *Things of August.*" *Perspectives of New Music* 35, no. 1 (1997): 61–114.

———. "Orientations, Criteria, Segments: A General Theory of Musical Segmentation." *Journal of Music Theory* 45, no. 2 (2001): 345–433.

———. "Species Concepts in Biology and Perspectives on Association in Music Analysis." *Perspectives of New Music* 47, no. 1 (2009): 5–68.

———. "A Theory of Recontextualization in Music: Analyzing Phenomenal Transformations of Repetition." *Music Theory Spectrum* 25, no. 1 (2003): 59–97.

———. "Understanding Stefan Wolpe's Musical *Forms.*" *Perspectives of New Music* 40, no. 2 (2002): 8–66.

———. "'What Is about, Is Also of, Also Is': Words, Musical Organization, and Boretz's *Language ,as a Music* Part I, 'Thesis.'" *Perspectives of New Music* 44, no. 2 (2006): 14–64.

Hanski, Ilkka. *Metapopulation Ecology.* New York: Oxford University Press, 1999.

Hasty, Christopher. "Broken Sequences: Fragmentation, Abundance, Beauty." *Perspectives of New Music* 40, no. 2 (2002): 155–73.

———. *Meter as Rhythm.* New York: Oxford University Press, 1997.

———. "Segmentation and Process in Post-Tonal Music." *Music Theory Spectrum* 3 (1981): 54–73.

———. "A Theory of Segmentation Developed from Late Works of Stefan Wolpe." PhD diss., Yale University, 1978.

Hempel, Carl G. and Paul Oppenheim. "Studies in the Logic of Explanation." *Philosophy of Science* 15 (1948): 135–75.

Hepokoski, James, and Warren Darcy. *Elements of Sonata Theory.* New York: Oxford University Press, 2006.

Hirata, Catherine. "Analyzing the Music of Morton Feldman." PhD diss., Columbia University, 2003.

———. "The Sounds of the Sounds Themselves: Analyzing the Early Music of Morton Feldman." *Perspectives of New Music* 34, no. 1 (1996): 6–27.

Hull, David L. "Are Species Really Individuals?" *Systematic Zoology* 25 (1976): 174–91.

———. "The Ideal Species Concept—and Why We Can't Get It." In *Species: The Units of Biodiversity,* edited by M. F. Claridge, H. A. Dawah, and M. R. Wilson, 357–80. New York: Chapman and Hall, 1997.

———. "A Matter of Individuality." *Philosophy of Science* 45 (1978): 335–60.

Hyde, Martha. "Musical Form and the Development of Schoenberg's Twelve-Tone Method." *Journal of Music Theory* 29, no. 1 (1985): 85–143.

Isaacson, Eric. "Neural Network Models for the Study of Post-Tonal Music." In *Music, Gestalt, and Computing: Studies in Cognitive and Systematic Musicology,* edited by Marc Leman. 237–50. New York: Springer, 1997.

Jackendoff, Ray. "Musical Parsing and Musical Affect." *Music Perception* 9, no. 2 (1991): 199–230.

ings, edited by Giles Gunn. New York: Penguin Books, 2000.

Johnson, Mark. *The Meaning of the Body: Aesthetics of Human Understanding*. Chicago: University of Chicago Press, 2007.

Jones, Richard H. *Reductionism: Analysis and the Fullness of Reality*. Lewisburg: Bucknell University Press, 2000.

Joseph, Charles M. *Stravinsky and Balanchine: A Journey of Invention*. New Haven: Yale University Press, 2002.

Kassler, Michael. "A Sketch of the Use of Formalized Languages for the Assertion of Music." *Perspectives of New Music* 1, no. 2 (1963): 83–94.

———. "A Trinity of Essays." PhD diss., Princeton University, 1968.

Kielian-Gilbert, Marianne. "The Rhythms of Form: Correspondences and Analogy in Stravinsky's Designs." *Music Theory Spectrum* 9 (1987): 42–66.

Kim, Jaegwon. "Making Sense of Emergence." *Philosophical Studies* 95 (1999): 3–36.

———. "Supervenience as a Philosophical Concept." In *Laws of Nature, Causation, and Supervenience*, edited by Michael Tooley, 25–51. New York: Taylor & Francis, 1999.

Korsyn, Kevin. "Beyond Privileged Contexts: Intertextuality, Influence, and Dialogue." In *Rethinking Music*, edited by Nicholas Cook and Mark Everist, 55–72. New York: Oxford University Press, 1999.

———. *Decentering Music: A Critique of Contemporary Music Research*. New York: Oxford University Press, 2003.

Kramer, Jonathan. "Beyond Unity: Toward an Understanding of Musical Postmodernism." In *Concert Music, Rock, and Jazz Since 1945*, edited by Elizabeth West Marvin and Richard Hermann, 11–33. Rochester, NY: University of Rochester Press, 1995.

———. "The Concept of Disunity and Musical Analysis." *Music Analysis* 23, nos. 2–3 (2004): 361–72.

———. "Moment Form in Twentieth-Century Music." *The Musical Quarterly* 64, no. 2 (1978): 177–95.

———. "New Temporalities in Music." *Critical Inquiry* 8, no. 3 (1981): 539–56.

———. *The Time of Music*. New York: Schirmer Books, 1988.

Laitz, Steven G. *Complete Musician*. New York: Oxford University Press, 2003.

Lakoff, George. *Women, Fire, and Dangerous Things: What Categories Reveal about the Mind*. Chicago: University of Chicago Press, 1987.

Lartillot, Olivier. "An Adaptive Multi-Parametric and Redundancy-Filtering Approach for Motivic Pattern Discovery." Paper presented at the Sound and Music Computing Conference, Paris, 2004.

———. "Automating Motivic Analysis through the Application of Perceptual Rules." *Computing in Musicology* 13. Cambridge, MA: MIT Press; and Stanford: CCARH, Stanford University, 2005.

———. "A Musical Pattern Discovery System Founded on a Modeling of Listening Strategies. *Computer Music Journal* 28, no. 3 (2004): 53–67.

Lefkowitz, David, and Kristin Taavola. "Segmentation in Music: Generalizing a Piece-Sensitive Approach." *Journal of Music Theory* 44, no. 1 (2000): 171–230.

Lerdahl, Fred. *Tonal Pitch Space*. New York: Oxford University Press, 2001.

Lerdahl, Fred, and Ray Jackendoff. *A Generative Theory of Tonal Music*. Cambridge, MA: MIT Press, 1983.

(1992): 1943–67.

Levins, Richard, and Richard C. Lewontin. "Dialectics and Reductionism in Ecology." *Synthese* 43 (1980): 47–78. Revised version included in *Philosophy of Ecology: From Science to Synthesis*, edited by David R. Keller and Frank B. Golley, 218–25. Athens: University of Georgia Press, 2000.

Lewin, David. *Generalized Musical Intervals and Transformations*. New Haven: Yale University Press, 1987.

———. "Music Theory, Phenomenology, and Modes of Perception." *Music Perception* 3, no. 4 (1986): 327–92.

———. *Musical Form and Transformation: Four Analytic Essays*. New Haven: Yale University Press, 1993.

———. "On Partial Ordering." *Perspectives of New Music* 14, no. 2 / 15 no. 1 (1976): 252–59.

———. *Studies in Music with Text*. New York: Oxford University Press, 2006.

———. "Transformational Considerations in Schoenberg's Opus 23, Number 3." In *Music Theory and Mathematics: Chords, Collections, and Transformations*, edited by Jack Douthett, Martha M. Hyde, and Charles J. Smith, 197–221. Rochester, NY: University of Rochester Press, 2008.

Lewontin, Richard C. "The Corpse in the Elevator." *New York Review of Books* (January 20, 1983): 34–37.

Lidov, David. *Is Language a Music? Writings on Musical Form and Signification*. Bloomington: Indiana University Press, 2005.

———. "Musical Structure and Musical Significance." Part I. Working paper. Toronto: Toronto Semiotic Circle Monographs, Working Papers, and Prepublications, 1980.

Lipschutz, Seymour. *Discrete Mathematics*. Schaum's Outline Series. New York: McGraw Hill, 1976.

Lloyd, Rosemary. *The Cambridge Companion to Baudelaire*. New York: Cambridge University Press, 2005.

Loehle, Craig, and Joseph H. K. Pechmann. "Evolution: The Missing Ingredient in Systems Ecology." In *The Philosophy of Ecology: From Science to Synthesis*, edited by David R. Keller and Frank B. Golley, 304–19. Athens: University of Georgia Press, 2000.

London, Justin. *Hearing in Time: Psychological Aspects of Musical Meter*. New York: Oxford University Press, 2004.

Mackenzie, Aulay, Andy S. Ball, and Sonia R. Virdee. *Ecology*. 2nd ed. Instant Notes. Oxford: BIOS Scientific Publishers, 2001.

Mailman, Joshua. "Temporal Dynamic Form in Music: Atonal, Tonal, and Other." PhD diss., University of Rochester, 2010.

Margolis, Eric, and Stephen Laurence. "Concepts and Cognitive Science." In *Concepts: Core Readings*, edited by Eric Margolis and Stephen Laurence, 3–82. Cambridge, MA: MIT Press, 1999.

Martino, Donald. "The Source Set and Its Aggregate Formations." *Journal of Music Theory* 5, no. 2 (1961): 224–73.

Marvin, Elizabeth West. "Generalization of Contour Theory to Diverse Musical Spaces: Analytical Applications to the Music of Dallapiccola and Stockhausen."

Richard Hermann, 135–71. Rochester, NY: University of Rochester Press, 1995.

———. "The Perception of Rhythm in Non-Tonal Music: Rhythmic Contours in the Music of Edgard Varèse." *Music Theory Spectrum* 13, no. 1 (1991): 61–78.

Marvin, Elizabeth West, and Paul A. Laprade. "Relating Musical Contours: Extensions of a Theory for Contour," *Journal of Music Theory* 31, no. 2 (1987): 225–67.

Maus, Fred Everett. "Concepts of Musical Unity." In *Rethinking Music*, edited by Nicholas Cook and Mark Everist, 171–92. Oxford: Oxford University Press, 1999.

Mayr, Ernst. *The Growth of Biological Thought*. Cambridge, MA: Harvard University Press, 1982.

———. *Toward a New Philosophy of Biology: Observations of an Evolutionist*. Cambridge, MA: Harvard University Press, 1988.

———. *What Makes Biology Unique? Considerations on the Autonomy of a Scientific Discipline*. New York: Cambridge University Press, 2004.

McAdams, Stephen, and Daniel Matzkin. "The Roots of Musical Variation in Perceptual Similarity and Invariance." In *The Cognitive Neuroscience of Music*, edited by Isabelle Peretz and Robert Zatorre, 79–94. New York: Oxford University Press, 2003.

McAdams, Stephen, and Emmanuel Bigand. "Introduction to Auditory Cognition." In *Thinking in Sound: The Cognitive Psychology of Human Audition*, edited by Stephen McAdams and Emmanuel Bigand, 1–9. Oxford: Clarendon, 1993.

McCreless, Patrick. "Syntagmatics and Paradigmatics: Some Implications for the Analysis of Chromaticism in Tonal Music." *Music Theory Spectrum* 13, no. 2 (1991): 147–78.

Mead, Andrew. "Detail and the Array in Milton Babbitt's *My Complements to Roger*." *Music Theory Spectrum* 5 (1983): 89–109.

———. *An Introduction to the Music of Milton Babbitt*. Princeton: Princeton University Press, 1994.

———. "Large-Scale Strategy in Arnold Schoenberg's Twelve-Tone Music." *Perspectives of New Music* 24, no. 1 (1985): 89–109.

———. "Some Implications of the Pitch-Class / Order-Number Isomorphism Inherent in the Twelve-Tone System, Part One." *Perspectives of New Music* 26, no. 2 (1988): 96–163.

Medin, Douglas L., and Lawrence W. Barsalou. "Categorization Processes and Categorical Perception." In *Categorical Perception: The Groundwork of Cognition*, edited by Stevan Harnad. Cambridge: Cambridge University Press, 1987.

Meudic, Benoit, and Emmanuel St.-James. "Automatic Extraction of Approximate Repetitions in Polyphonic Midi Files Based on Perceptive Criteria," accessed on September 7, 2012, http://recherche.ircam.fr/equipes/repmus/RMPapers/lncs-meudic.pdf.

Meyer, Leonard B. *Emotion and Meaning in Music*. Chicago: University of Chicago Press, 1956.

———. *Explaining Music*. Berkeley: University of California Press, 1973.

Miller, George A. "The Magical Number Seven, Plus or Minus Two: Some Limits on Our Capacity for Processing Information." *Psychological Review* 63 (1956): 81–97.

and Real Kinds: More Mama, More Milk, and More Mouse." *Behavioral and Brain Sciences* 22, no. 1 (1998): 55–65.

——. *On Clear and Confused Ideas: An Essay about Substance Concepts.* New York: Cambridge University Press, 2000.

Misch, Imke. "On the Serial Shaping of Stockhausen's *Gruppen für drei Orchester.*" *Perspectives of New Music* 36, no. 1 (1998): 143–87.

Moe, Orlin, and William B. Chappell. "Debussy and Baudelaire: Harmonie du soir." *Bonnes feuilles* 4, nos. 1–2 (1975): 122–48.

Monelle, Raymond. *Linguistics and Semiotics in Music.* New York: Harwood Academic Publishers, 1992.

——. "A Semantic Approach to Debussy's Songs." *Music Review* 51, no. 3 (1990): 193–207.

Mörchen, Raoul. "Music as a Musical Process: Morton Feldman's *Palais de Mari.*" *MusikTexte: Zeitschrift fur Neue Musik* 66 (1996): 53–62.

Morris, Robert D. *Advanced Class Notes for Atonal Music Theory.* Hanover, NH: Frog Peak Music, 2001.

——. *Composition with Pitch-Classes: A Theory of Compositional Design.* New Haven: Yale University Press, 1987.

——. "Compositional Spaces and Other Territories." *Perspectives of New Music* 33, nos. 1–2 (1995): 328–59.

——. "Conflict and Anomaly in Bartók and Webern." In *Musical Transformation and Musical Intuition: Eleven Essays in Honor of David Lewin,* edited by Raphael Atlas and Michael Cherlin, 59–79. Roxbury, MA: Ovenbird Press, 1994.

——. "Modes of Coherence and Continuity in Schoenberg's Piano Piece, Opus 23, No. 1." *Theory and Practice: Journal of the Music Theory Society of New York State* 17 (1992): 5–34.

——. "Musical Form, Expectation, Attention, and Quality." *Open Space* 4 (2002): 218–29.

——. "New Directions in the Theory and Analysis of Musical Contour." *Music Theory Spectrum* 15, no. 2 (1993): 205–28.

——. Review of *Musical Form and Transformation: Four Analytic Essays,* by David Lewin. *Journal of Music Theory* 39, no. 2 (1995): 342–83.

——. "Some Things I Learned (Didn't Learn) from Milton Babbitt, or Why I Am (Am Not) A Serial Composer." *Open Space* 3 (2001): 59–127.

——. *The Whistling Blackbird.* Rochester, NY: University of Rochester Press, 2010.

——. "Why Weight: Pitch-Class Duplication in Twelve-Tone Polyphony." Paper presented at the 16th annual meeting of the Society for Music Theory, Montréal, Canada, 1993.

Morris, Robert D., and Brian Alegant. "The Even Partitions in Twelve-Tone Music." *Music Theory Spectrum* 10 (1988): 74–101.

Murphy, G. L. and D. L. Medin. "The Role of Theories in Conceptual Coherence." *Psychological Review* 104 (1985): 266–300.

Nagel, Ernest. "Teleology Revisted." In *Nature's Purposes: Analyses of Function and Design in Biology,* edited by Colin Allen, Marc Bekoff, and George Lauder, 197–240. Cambridge, MA: MIT Press, 1998.

tion-Realization Model. Chicago: University of Chicago Press, 1990.

———. *The Analysis and Cognition of Melodic Complexity: The Implication-Realization Model.* Chicago: University of Chicago Press, 1992.

Nattiez, Jean-Jacques. "Varèse's *Density 21.5*: A Study in Semiological Analysis." *Music Analysis* 1, no. 3 (1982): 243–340.

Nyman, Michael. *Experimental Music.* 2nd ed. New York: Cambridge University Press, 1999.

Ockelford, Adam. *Repetition in Music: Theoretical and Metatheoretical Perspectives.* Royal Musical Association Monographs 13. Burlington, VT: Ashgate, 2005.

O'Neill, Robert V., and Anthony W. King. "Homage to St. Michael; or, Why Are There So Many Books on Scale?" In *Ecological Scale: Theory and Applications,* edited by David L. Peterson and V. Thomas Parker. Complexity in Ecological Systems. 3–16. New York: Columbia University Press, 1998.

O'Sharkey, Eithne. "A Note on Baudelaire's 'Harmonie du soir.'" *French Studies* 33, no. 2 (1979): 155–56.

Palmer, Robert. "Terry Riley: Doctor of Improvised Surgery." *Downbeat,* November 20, 1975.

Pickett, S. T. A., and Kevin H. Rogers. "Patch Dynamics: The Transformation of Landscape Structure and Function." In *Wildlife and Landscape Ecology: Effects of Pattern and Scale,* edited by John A. Bissonette, 101–27. New York: Springer, 1997.

Pople, Anthony. "Analysis, Past, Present, and Future." *Music Analysis* 21 (2002): 17–21.

Potter, Keith. *Four Musical Minimalists: LaMonte Young, Terry Riley, Steve Reich, Philip Glass.* New York: Cambridge University Press, 2000.

Powers, Harold S. "The Structural of Musical Meaning: A View from Banaras." *Perspectives of New Music* 14 no. 2 / 15, no. 1 (1976): 308–34.

Preminger, Alex, and T. V. F. Brogan. *The New Princeton Encyclopedia of Poetry and Poetics.* Princeton: Princeton University Press, 1993.

Quine, W. V. 1953. "Two Dogmas of Empiricism." In *From a Logical Point of View.* Cambridge, MA: Harvard University Press, 1980.

Quinn, Ian. "General Equal-Tempered Harmony (Introduction and Part I). *Perspectives of New Music* 44, no. 2 (2006): 114–59.

———. "Listening to Similarity Relations." *Perspectives of New Music* 39, no. 2 (2001): 108–58.

Rabinowitz, Deborah, Sara Cairns, and Theresa Dillon. "Seven Types of Rarity and Their Frequency in the Flora of the British Isles." In *Conservation Biology: The Science of Scarcity and Diversity,* edited by Michael E. Soulé, 182–204. Sunderland, MA: Sinauer Associates, 1986.

Rahn, John. "Repetition." *Contemporary Music Review* 7 (1993): 49–57.

———. "The Swerve and the Flow: Music's Relationship to Mathematics." *Perspectives of New Music* 42, no. 1 (2004): 130–49.

Read, Ronald C. and Robin J. Wilson. *An Atlas of Graphs.* Oxford Science Publications. New York: Oxford University Press, 1998.

Music, Gestalt, and Computing: Studies in Systematic Musicology, edited by Marc Leman, 57–69. New York: Springer, 1997.

Reynolds, Roger. "Conlon Nancarrow: Interviews in Mexico City and San Francisco." *American Music* 2, no. 2 (1984): 1–24.

Rosch, Eleanor. "On the Internal Structure of Perceptual and Semantic Categories." In *Cognitive Development and the Acquisition of Language*, edited by Timothy E. Moore, 111–14. New York, Academic Press, 1973.

———. "Principles of Categorization." In *Cognition and Categorization*, edited by Eleanor Rosch and Barbara Lloyd, 28–49. Hillsdale, NJ: Lawrence Erlbaum, 1978.

Rosch, Eleanor, and Carolyn Mervis. "Family Resemblances: Studies in the Internal Structure of Categories." *Cognitive Psychology* 7, no. 4 (1975): 573–605.

Ross, Brian H., and Valerie S. Makin. "Prototype versus Exemplar Models in Cognition." In *The Nature of Cognition*, edited by Robert J. Sternberg, 205–45. Cambridge, MA: MIT Press, 1999.

Rothgeb, John. "Design as a Key to Structure in Tonal Music." *Journal of Music Theory* 15, nos. 1–2 (1971): 230–53.

———. "Salient Features." In *Music Theory in Concept and Practice*, edited by James Baker, David Beach, and Jonathan Bernard, 180–96. Rochester, NY: University of Rochester Press, 1997.

———. "Thematic Content: A Schenkerian View." In *Aspects of Schenkerian Theory*, edited by David Beach, 39–60. New Haven: Yale University Press, 1983.

Rothstein, William. "On Implied Tones." *Music Analysis* 10, no. 3 (1991): 289–328.

———. *Phrase Rhythm in Tonal Music*. New York: Schirmer, 1989.

Ruwet, Nicholas. "Methods of Analysis in Musicology." *Music Analysis* 6, nos. 1–2 (1987): 3–36.

Salzer, Felix. *Structural Hearing*. New York: Dover, 1962.

Sani, Frank. "Morton Feldman's *Palais de Mari*: A Pitch Analysis." Accessed February 23, 2009. http://www.cnvill.net/mfsani3/mfsani3.htm.

Schachter, Carl. "Either/Or." In *Schenker Studies*, edited by Hedi Siegel, 165–79. New York: Cambridge University Press, 1990.

———. "Rhythm and Linear Analysis: Durational Reduction." In *Unfoldings*, edited by Joseph N. Straus, 54–78. New York: Norton, 1999.

Schenker, Heinrich. *Five Graphic Analyses*. Edited by Felix Salzer. New York: Dover, 1969.

———. *Free Composition (Der freie Satz)*. 2 vols. Translated and edited by Ernst Oster. New York: Longman, 1979.

Slawson, Wayne. *Sound Color*. Berkeley: University of California Press, 1985.

———. "Sound Structure and Musical Structure: The Role of Sound Color." In *Structure and Perception of Electroacoustic Sound and Music*, edited by S. Nielz and O. Olsson. Amsterdam: Exempla Medica, 1998.

Sloboda, John A. *The Musical Mind: The Cognitive Psychology of Music*. New York: Oxford University Press, 1985.

Smith, Edward E., and Douglas L. Medin. *Categories and Concepts*. Cambridge, MA: Harvard University Press, 1981.

2000.

Sober, Elliott. "Evolution, Population Thinking, and Essentialism." In *Conceptual Issues in Evolutionary Biology*, 2nd ed., edited by Elliott Sober. 161–89. Cambridge, MA: Bradford Books / MIT Press, 1994.

Starr, Daniel V. "Derivation and Polyphony." *Perspectives of New Music* 23, no. 1 (1984): 180–257.

Stein, Deborah, and Robert Spillman. *Poetry into Song.* New York: Oxford University Press, 1996.

Stephan, Achim. "Emergentism, Irreducibility, and Downward Causation." *Grazer Philosophische Studien* 65 (2002): 77–93.

———. "Varieties of Emergentism." *Evolution and Cognition* 5, no. 1 (1999): 49–59.

Sterelny, Kim, and Paul Griffiths. *Sex and Death: An Introduction to Philosophy of Biology.* Chicago: University of Chicago Press, 1999.

Straus, Joseph N. *The Music of Ruth Crawford Seeger.* Cambridge: Cambridge University Press, 1995.

Street, Alan. "Superior Myths, Dogmatic Allegories: The Resistance to Musical Unity." *Music Analysis* 8 (1989): 77–123.

Strickland, Edward. *Minimalism: Origins.* Bloomington: Indiana University Press, 1993.

Sun, Cecilia Jian-Xuan. "Experiments in Musical Performance: Historiography, Politics, and the Post-Cagian Avant-Garde." PhD diss., University of California at Los Angeles, 2004.

Tanguiane, A. S. "A Principle of Correlativity of Perception and Its Application to Music Recognition." *Music Perception* 11, no. 4 (1994): 465–502.

Temperley, David. *The Cognition of Basic Musical Structures.* Cambridge, MA: MIT Press, 2001.

———. "The Question of Purpose in Music Theory: Description, Suggestion, and Explanation." *Current Musicology* 66 (2001): 66–83.

Temperley, David, and Christopher Bartlette. "Parallelism as a Factor in Metrical Analysis." *Music Perception* 20, no. 2 (2002): 117–49.

Tenney, James. Liner notes to *Conlon Nancarrow: Studies for Player Piano.* Wergo 6907–6911, 1999, compact disc.

———. *Meta+Hodos.* 2nd ed. Hanover, NH: Frog Peak Music, 1988.

Tenney, James, and Larry Polansky. "Temporal Gestalt Perception in Music." *Journal of Music Theory* 24, no. 2 (1980): 205–41.

Thomas, Margaret. "Nancarrow's Canons: Projections of Temporal and Formal Structures." *Perspectives of New Music* 38, no. 2 (2000): 106–33.

———. "Nancarrow's 'Temporal Dissonance': Issues of Tempo Proportions, Metric Synchrony, and Rhythmic Strategies." *Intégral* 14–15 (2000–2001): 137–80.

———. Review of *The Music of Conlon Nancarrow*, by Kyle Gann. *Journal of Music Theory* 41, no. 2 (1997): 330–40.

Tooley, Michael, ed. *Laws of Nature, Causation, and Supervenience.* New York: Taylor & Francis, 1999.

Trudeau, Richard J. *Dots and Lines.* Kent, OH: Kent State University Press, 1976.

Tufte, Edward Rolf. *Envisioning Information.* Cheshire, CT: Graphics Press, 1990.

Tversky, Amos. "Features of Similarity." *Psychological Review* 84 (1977): 327–52.

tion, edited by Eleanor Rosch and Barbara Lloyd, 81–98. Hillsdale, NJ: Lawrence Erlbaum, 1978.

Uno, Yayoi, and Roland Hübscher. "*Temporal-Gestalt* Segmentation: Polyphonic Extensions and Applications to Works by Boulez, Cage, Xenakis, Ligeti, and Babbitt." *Computers in Music Research* 5 (1995): 1–38.

van Fraassen, Bas C. *The Scientific Image*. New York: Oxford University Press, 1980.

Vandermeer, John H., and Deborah E. Goldberg. *Population Ecology: First Principles*. Princeton: Princeton University Press, 2003.

Walker, Peter M. B., ed. *Chambers Biology Dictionary*. New York: Chambers/Cambridge University Press, 1989.

Wallis, W. D. *A Beginner's Guide to Graph Theory*. Boston: Birkhäuser, 2000.

Wen, Eric. "Bass-Line Articulations of the *Urlinie*." In *Schenker Studies 2*, edited by Carl Schachter and Hedi Siegel. New York: Cambridge University Press, 1999.

Wenk, Arthur. *Debussy and the Poets*. Berkeley: University of California Press, 1976.

Westergaard, Peter. "Toward a Twelve-Tone Polyphony." *Perspectives of New Music* 4, no. 2 (1966): 90–112.

Williams, Mary B. "Species: Current Usages." In *Keywords in Evolutionary Biology*, edited by Evelyn Fox Keller and Elisabeth A. Lloyd. Cambridge, MA: Harvard University Press, 1992.

Wilson, Robin J. *Introduction to Graph Theory*. 3rd ed. New York: Longman, 1985.

Wimsatt, William C. "Aggregativity: Reductive Heuristics for Finding Emergence." *Philosophy of Science* 64, supplement. Proceedings of the 1996 Biennial Meetings of the Philosophy of Science Association. Part II: Symposia Papers: S372–S384, 1997.

———. "Emergence as Non-Aggregativity and the Biases of Reductionisms." *Foundations of Science* 5 (2001): 269–97.

Wittgenstein, Ludwig. *Philosophical Investigations*. 1953. Translated by G. E. M. Anscombe. London: Blackwell Publishing, 2001.

Wright, Barbara. "Baudelaire's Poetic Journey in *Les Fleurs du Mal*." In *The Cambridge Companion to Baudelaire*, edited by Rosemary Lloyd, 31–50. New York: Cambridge University Press, 2005.

Zbikowski, Lawrence M. *Conceptualizing Music: Cognitive Structure, Theory, and Analysis*. New York: Oxford University Press, 2002.

———. "Large-Scale Rhythm and Systems of Grouping." PhD diss., Yale University, 1991.

———. "Musical Coherence, Motive, and Categorization." *Music Perception* 17, no. 1 (1999): 5–42.

Zohar, Eitan. *Highpoints: A Study of Melodic Peaks*. Philadelphia: University of Pennsylvania Press, 1997.

Index of Names and Subjects

Italicized numerals indicate examples. For analytic applications, also consult the index of works.

bar graph schematic. *See* association maps, bar graph schematics

Baudelaire, Charles, 269–72, 466n3, 466n6, 466n9

Beach, David W., 449n89, 465n11, 465nn13–14, 479n37

Berberian, Cathy, 425

Berg, Alban, 462n115

Behrman, David, 309, 470n8

block (of a pitch-class array), 361

Bod, Rens, 438n4

Boretz, Benjamin
analysis of *Tristan* prelude, 428–29, 479n35
on observational and theoretical terms, 437n20, 445n60, 445n62, 445n65
on primitives, 439n6
on the musical value of theory, 3, 435n3

branch node. *See* node, in a schematic, branch

branching. *See* traversals, branchings in

Bregman, Albert S., 441n29

bridge
and associative reconfiguration, 332
definition of, 120, 155
examples of, 139, 140, 155, 351–52
relation to associative elision and associative conflux, 207

Brown, Matthew, 439n7, 439n10

Buteau, Chantal, 455n30

Cage, John, 20, 178

Cambouropoulos, Emilios, 443n42

Campbell, Donald, 463n126

canons, converging and diverging, 293, 294, 468n8, 468n10

Caplin, William, 462n111, 464nn2–5

Carl, Robert, 310, 469n1, 469–70nn4–5, 470n9, 472n25

Carlsen, Philip, 467n1

Carter, Elliott, 197, 457n65

categories
classical, 12, 98, 452n1

463n125
prototypical, 12, 98, 452n1
See also categorization; prototypicality

categorization, 479n28
as classification, 158, 459n80, 472n2
in music analysis, 435n1, 460n95
as reidentification, 158, 459n87
See also categories

chicken-wire torus, 126

circuit, 120. *See also* path; walk

circuitry, 455n35

Clarke, Eric F., 438n21

classification. *See* categorization, as classification

clear segmentation, 70

clumped disposition
definition of, 163–64
versus dispersed, 197
and scale, 171–72, 174
within specific musical dimension, 172, 173, 174
See also associative rhythm; dispersed disposition; internal dispositions

Cogan, Robert, 20, 416, 437n15, 462n110
theory of oppositions, 441n23

Cohn, Richard, 44, 436n13
association and derivation view of motive, 444n57, 446n71

coincidence, 10–11, *11*, 13, 449n95. *See also* genosegments, coincidence and conflict; genosegments, coincident; phenosegment formation; realization

collective property, 101

combinational diversity
definition of, 102
versus element diversity, 106
relationship to element diversity and distribution of variation, 105, 106, 108

common set (CS), 98, 102, 114–18
definition of, 114
weighted, 114

sound concept, 473n4

spanning tree. *See* tree, spanning

spatial location
    as a sonic criterion, 29, 78, 451n107
    and proximity, 24

species concepts (in biology), 158, 452–53n5, 459nn83–84, 459n87

Starr, Daniel, 444n53, 479n29

Steinbach, Peter, 126

Straus, Joseph N., 74, 75, 450n104

stream segregation, 15, 24, 28, 50, 76, 441n30

structural criteria (T), 43–62
    in a Schenkerian context, 46–47, *48*, 89–91, 448n83
    in a twelve-tone context, 46, *47*, 53–58, 443n48
    definition of, 43
    formal aspects, 44–46
    and genosegments, 63–64
    interactions among, 58–59
    interactions with contextual criteria, 95, 238
    interactions with sonic and contextual criteria, 59–61, 237, 417
    versus look-alike contextual criteria, 45–46, 49, 448n82
    and music perception, 427–29, 448n84
    notation of, 46–47, *47*, *48*
    in poetry, 273, 274
    relative strengths of, 58–59
    subtypes and individual criteria, 46, *47*, *48*
    and theoretic entities (HEs), 54, 438n5
    unrealized, 50
    See also linked types; logical entailment; realization; Schenkerian theory and analysis; terms, observational and theoretical; twelve-tone theory

structural domain, 7–9. *See also* theoretic entities, theoretic framework

structural motive. *See* motive, structural

238, 241, 415, 416, 417

structural segments, interaction with nonstructural segments, 93, 95

structural-contextual criterion (TC). *See* linked types

structural-sonic criterion (TS). *See* linked types

structure and design
    analysis of interactions between, 16, 44, 89, 91
    conflict between, 91–92
    in Schenkerian theory, 449n89, 451n117
    studies of, 262–68
    tripartite division, 62
    in twelve-tone theory, 449n89

style
    analysis of, 422–25
    and improvisation, 10

Subotnick, Morton, 309

Sun, Cecelia, 469n1, 470n7, 470n9, 471n15, 471n19

supervenience, 73, 450n100. *See also* reduction

systematic realization. *See* realization, systematic

Taavola, Kristin, 32, 441n23, 441n25

Temperley, David, 438n21, 441n25, 451n108

Tenney, James
    on Nancarrow's music, 291, 292, 467n1, 469n15
    work on segmentation, 3, 24, 441n23
    work on sonic organization, 20, 415, 416, 437n15, 454n19

Tenney and Polansky algorithm, 31, 415–16, 440n20, 451nn109–10, 478n22

terms, observational and theoretical
    Boretz on, 437n20, 439n6, 445n60, 445n62, 445n65
    and contextual criteria, 33, 45, 46, 443n48
    and neighbor notes, 446n69
    in philosophy of science, 445n61

Index of Works

Italicized numerals indicate examples.